CONSTITUTIONAL RESILIENCE IN SOUTH ASIA

South Asia has had a tumultuous and varied experience with constitutional democracy that predates the recent rise in populism (and its study) in established democracies. And yet, this region has remained largely ignored by constitutional studies and democracy scholars.

This book addresses this gap and presents a contribution to the South Asia-centric literature on the topic of the stability and resilience of constitutional democracies. Chapters deal not only with more extensively covered South Asian countries such as India, Bangladesh, Pakistan and Sri Lanka, but also with countries often ignored by scholars, such as Bhutan, Nepal, Maldives and Afghanistan.

The contributions consider the design and functioning of an array of institutions and actors, including political parties, legislatures, the political executive, the bureaucracy, courts, fourth branch/guarantor institutions, the people and the military, to examine their roles in strengthening or undermining constitutional democracy across South Asia. Each chapter offers a contextual and jurisdictionally-tethered account of the causes behind the erosion of constitutional democracy, with some examining the resilience of constitutional institutions against democratic erosion.

Constitutional Resilience in South Asia

Edited by
Swati Jhaveri
Tarunabh Khaitan
and
Dinesha Samararatne

BLOOMSBURY
NEW DELHI • LONDON • OXFORD • NEW YORK • SYDNEY

BLOOMSBURY INDIA
Bloomsbury Publishing India Pvt. Ltd
Second Floor, LSC Building No. 4, DDA Complex, Pocket C–6&7,
Vasant Kunj, New Delhi 110070

BLOOMSBURY, BLOOMSBURY ACADEMIC INDIA and the Diana logo are trademarks of Bloomsbury Publishing Plc

First published in India 2023
First published in Great Britain 2023

This edition published with permission from Bloomsbury Publishing Plc,
50 Bedford Square, London, WC1B3DP, UK

A catalogue record for this book is available from the British Library.
A catalogue record for this book is available from the Library of Congress.
Library of Congress Control Number: 2023930780

ISBN: 978-93-54351-02-0

Typeset by Compuscript Ltd, Shannon
Printed at Manipal Technologies Limited, Manipal

To find out more about our authors and books
visit www.bloomsbury.com and sign up for our newsletters

To the Peoples of South Asia

FOREWORD

It is an honour to be invited to write the foreword for the newest collection of scholarship on South Asian public law. This is particularly gratifying as the editors – Swati Jhaveri, Dinesha Samararatne and Tarunabh Khaitan – are fellow travellers on the road to increase the visibility of legal scholarship in and about South Asia. I also had the advantage of attending the 2019 conference in Melbourne, where several (though not all) of the chapters in this volume were presented in draft form. That experience allows me to assert that the authors have substantially revised those initial drafts that, while promising much collectively, were very much works-in-progress individually. Much credit is due to the authors for their diligence, and to the editors for steering the process of the polishing of the arguments and analysis that appear in this final form here.

The editors' introduction admirably sets out the contours of the project that led to this volume, their ambitions for the volume and the field it is part of, and a summary of the themes and contents contained within it. If the comprehensive introduction and the individual chapters are akin to a gourmet buffet, the role of this foreword is only to act as an appetiser by highlighting a few of the intellectual delights on offer. Consequently, what I will seek to do here is to emphasise three aspects of this project that I think are valuable and salient. For this purpose, I will reference only some of the chapters here. In doing so, I do not mean to slight those that I have left out – many of which are excellent – due to constraints of space.

The Theme of Constitutional Resilience

As I write, in September 2022, South Asia is beset by a series of natural disasters, human-initiated catastrophes and other crises caused by a combination of the two forces. All of South Asia – like the rest of the world – is struggling to recover from the ravages of the pandemic, the effects of which will extend beyond the short term. Floods in Pakistan that started in June 2022 are estimated to have affected a third of its land mass by August, impacting an estimated 33 million people. In March 2022, Sri Lanka witnessed large-scale protests that led to the fall of the Gotabaya Rajapakse government after a severe economic, political and social crisis. At the time of writing, the recently appointed President and Prime Minister are deploying emergency powers to arrest protesters amidst a tumultuous phase that commentators are describing as unprecedented in the island nation's history. Over in Nepal, in the month that marked the seventh anniversary of the adoption of the landmark 2015 Constitution, the constitutional head of Nepal is at loggerheads with the executive and the judiciary. The crisis involves several issues, including a citizenship bill, ahead of the next general elections scheduled for November 2022. Elsewhere, the political situation in many parts of South Asia remains grim. In the aftermath of the February 2021 coup in Myanmar, the prospects for democracy and basic freedoms continue to be bleak. Similar concerns have arisen in Afghanistan since the takeover by the Taliban in 2021. While the Solih government that was elected in 2019 in the Maldives enjoys popular support, human rights groups report that recent months have witnessed a crackdown on media freedom, rights of accused and rights of LGBTQI individuals. Similar allegations about misuse of power and targeting of opponents of the ruling regime have been levelled against the Awami League government in Bangladesh (in power since 2009) and the Bhartiya Janata Party-led National Democratic Alliance coalition government in India (in power since 2014). Several nations in the region are exhibiting dangerous signs of majoritarian nationalism that are inimical to building robust traditions of constitutionalism.

This summary overview emphasises the constitutional turmoil that seems endemic across the region. Yet, this turmoil is not new, even if we consider the history of South Asia only from the era of decolonisation, that commenced around the middle of the twentieth century. In any decade of the seven that have elapsed since the formal end of colonial rule, a survey of South Asia would throw up similar examples of what a recent work on South Asian public law termed as 'unstable constitutionalism'. Despite such challenges, as several chapters in this volume document, ideas about constitutionalism, often with fairly distinctive local elements, have persisted and remained politically salient and relevant.

It is for this reason that the overall focus of the present volume on constitutional resilience is simultaneously significant while also bearing the potential of providing rich insights. To be clear, this is not a romantic or starry-eyed pursuit: Ebrahim Afsah's excellent analysis of the Afghan civil service's resilience in the face of decades of attempts at reform is a reminder that studying the persistence of deeply entrenched patterns of thought and action that impede the development of constitutional cultures is a vitally important task. Afsah's analysis of problematic constitutional resilience is counter-balanced by Faizan Siddiqi's account of the resilience of affirmative constitutional ideas drawn from his ethnographic study of the Dalit activism of the Gujarati NGO, Navsarjan Trust.

Difference, Not Sameness

For understandable reasons relating to the felt need for justifying the creation of a scholarly field of study, academic work on South Asia dating back to the 1950s has tended to emphasise the similarities that the nations in this vast and populous region share. As the editors' introduction explains in greater detail, this emphasis may have led to a neglect of patterns of differences that are necessary for understanding the constitutional trajectories of individual nations, particularly those that are smaller and less studied. For this reason, several chapters in this volume emphasise particular aspects of individual nations and provide in-depth studies of these characteristics. A good example is the chapter on the weak institutionalisation of the party system and political parties in Pakistan by Muhammad Salman and Marzia Raza. Even as this seems like a common problem across the region, Salman and Raza detail various aspects of this issue that may be unique to Pakistan. Another example is the chapter by Hari Dhungana and Iain Payne, which focuses on the role of the National Human Rights Commission created by the 2015 Constitution of Nepal in empowering local governments to strengthen human rights mechanisms at the grassroots of Nepalese society. Once again, while the ideas and institutions are not new, their working out in Nepal involves very specific dynamics which the authors draw attention towards.

Single Country Studies

This third point is related to the second. The field of comparative constitutional studies has now matured, and it is quite common to find cross-jurisdictional analysis of issues across seven or eight countries in a single article published in its leading journals. As the editors note, this assumes a rich body of work that underlies and provides the bedrock for the higher-level comparisons in such works. However, for regions like South Asia, one stumbling block is that such a foundational base of literature is yet to be commissioned and curated. For this reason, the editors have encouraged authors to de-emphasise comparative aspects while foregrounding the analysis of single jurisdictional factors. In doing so, they emphasise difference (as noted above), while also providing analysis that can become the cornerstone of further scholarly analyses to follow.

This volume includes works that fit both categories identified in the previous paragraph – multi-jurisdiction analyses, as well as single-country studies. Michael Pal's analysis of election commissions in Bangladesh, India, Pakistan and Sri Lanka provides an example of careful cross-jurisdictional analysis that parses issues of constitutional design, history and politics while being mindful of local factors in each of these countries. The chapters by Ahmed Nazeer, on the challenges of securing judicial independence in Maldives, and by Michaela Windischgraetz, on a mixture of 'old powers' and 'new forces' that carry the promise of sustaining the Bhutanese Constitution, are single-country studies that add to the small body of scholarship on the constitutions of the Maldives and Bhutan. Very little is known of these relatively isolated nations, both of which have young constitutions that were adopted in the same year (2008) and seek to balance considerations of continuity and change in deeply religious societies.

I hope I have provided a brief sense of the riches that this volume offers to readers. Even as they detail many narratives of sordid deeds that run counter to basic values of humanity and justice, the chapters focus on aspects that provide hope to those who are committed to the values of the rule of law and constitutionalism.

I conclude by quoting a few lines from the work of the Indian poet, Raahat Indori (1950–2020). Indori wrote and performed in Urdu, and was known for his flamboyant recitations at capacity-crowd *mushairahs*. He could also lay claim to a unique South Asian sensibility, having performed to adoring crowds across the sub-continent in Pakistan, Nepal and Bangladesh besides being a household name in many parts of India.

To my reading, these lines combine an understanding of constitutionalism with a pragmatic tone of optimism, which speak to the state of South Asia today, and to the motivating concerns of this volume:

Jo aaj saahib-e-masnad hain,
Kal nahin honge
Kiraayedaar hain
Zaati makaan thodi hai?

Those who hold power today
Shall not, tomorrow
They are but mere occupants
Residing in houses they do not own[1]

Arun K Thiruvengadam

[1] This is the penultimate stanza in one of the most famous of Raahat Indori's poems, *Agar Khilaaf hain, hone do, Jaan thodi hai*, a work that was most recently recited in multiple venues during the 2019 anti-CAA protests in India. For the full text of the poem, see https://99lyricstore.com/2019/03/agar-khilaaf-hai-hone-do-jaan-thodi-hai.html.

ACKNOWLEDGEMENTS

We express our gratitude to all who have partnered with us in this capacity-building enterprise and walked alongside us in this journey. We first express our thanks to Catherine O'Regan and Farrah Ahmed. They have been integral to the realisation of the vision of this project and volume. They have always been on hand to support the enterprise with a real sense of mission and purpose. They are exemplars of generosity in academia. We would like to thank all our discussants at the 2019 workshop at Melbourne Law School for engaging with such depth with the papers presented and mirrored our aspirations for creating a community of constructive, critical but collegiate feedback: Weitseng Chen, William Partlett, Cheryl Saunders, Tom Daly, Arun Thiruvengadam, Michael Breen, Mayur Suresh, Warwick Gately AM, Scott Stephenson, Zim Nwokora, Michelle Foster, Liora Lazarus, David Bilchitz, Glenn Patmore, Patrick Emerton, Michael Pal, Mario Gomez, Jayani Nadarajalingam, Jeff Redding, Hamza Bin Jehangir and Vanessa MacDonnell.

We thank our institutional partners: the Bonavero Institute of Human Rights at the University of Oxford, the Asian Law Centre, the Centre for Comparative Constitutional Studies and the Legal Theory Workshop at Melbourne Law School, the Indian Law Review, the Centre for Asian Legal Studies at the Faculty of Law at the National University of Hong Kong and Phillip Dann and his colleagues at Verfassung und Recht in Ubersee. These institutions provided the necessary financial, logistical and administrative support. We especially thank Margaret Ang at NUS, Zoe Davis-Heaney at Oxford and Kathryn Taylor at MLS: they provided exceptional and generous administrative support to the organisers before, during and after the workshops. We are grateful for the funding support from the Allen Myers Fund and the Future Fellowship Scheme awarded to one of us (Tarun Khaitan) by the Australian Research Council.

We note with appreciation the generosity of the reviewers of each chapter and thank them for their generosity. We would like to thank Mirza Ahmed and Timothy Lo for their exceptional editorial assistance as we prepared the volume for publication. We would also like to thank Sinead Moloney, Rosemarie Mearns and Kate Whetter at Hart Publishing for supporting us throughout the preparation of this volume.

TABLE OF CONTENTS

PART IV
THE POLITICAL BRANCHES

PART V
THE JUDICIARY

PART VI
FOURTH BRANCH (GUARANTOR) INSTITUTIONS

PART VII
THE MILITARY

PART VIII
THE PEOPLE

PART IX
CONCLUSION

LIST OF CONTRIBUTORS

Ebrahim Afsah is a Professor of Islamic Law at the Faculty of Law of the University of Vienna, an Associate Professor for Public International Law at the Faculty of Law of the University of Copenhagen and a Visiting Professor of International Relations at the University of Brest, France. He has been trained at the Universities of London, Dublin and Harvard, and the Max Planck Institute for International Law in Heidelberg. Prior to his academic posts, he worked for a decade on state-building, legal and administrative reform throughout the Middle East, North Africa and Central Asia, mostly in Afghanistan. In recent years, he has won fellowships to the European University Institute in Florence (Fernand Braudel), the Norwegian Academy of Science (Nordic Civil Wars), Harvard Law School (Islamic Legal Studies Program) and the National University of Singapore (Centre for Asian Legal Studies).

Erika Arban is Senior Research Associate in the Laureate Program in Comparative Constitutional Law at Melbourne Law School. Her research interests include comparative federalism, comparative constitutional law and legal research methodology. Erika is the co-convenor of the IACL research group New Frontiers of Federalism.

Gautam Bhatia is a Delhi-based advocate. He is the author of *Offend, Shock or Disturb: Freedom of Speech under the Indian Constitution* (Oxford University Press, 2016) and *The Transformative Constitution* (Harper Collins, 2019). His work has been cited by the Supreme Court of India, and he has been admitted as amicus curae before the Supreme Court of Kenya in the landmark BBI case.

M Mohsin Alam Bhat is Lecturer (Assistant Professor) in Law at the School of Law, Queen Mary University of London. He works in the area of public law, comparative constitutional law and minority rights, with a focus on political mobilisation, exclusion, violence and citizenship. His most recent publications are on affirmative action, religious freedom, democratic process, and socio-legal and constitutional facets of citizenship.

Devendra Damle works as Senior Manager – Policy at the Open Network for Digital Commerce, India. He was formerly a public policy researcher at the National Institute of Public Finance and Policy (New Delhi, India), where he conducted research on property rights, judicial administration, regulatory governance and parliamentary affairs. He is particularly interested in data-driven studies of institutions of government institutions.

Philipp Dann is Professor at Humboldt University in Berlin, where he holds the Chair in Public and Comparative Law. His research focuses on the role of law in the encounter between South and North – in international and comparative, German and European law, in constitutional theory and legal history. He is the editor-in-chief of the quarterly journal *Verfassung und Recht in Übersee/World Comparative Law*.

Hari Dhungana is Associate Professor of Development Management and Governance at Nepal Open University in Kathmandu, Nepal. Before joining the University, he spent over 20 years working in the development sector, including research and engagements in environmental justice, national and sub-national institutions, and local governance, as well as monitoring and evaluating development interventions. His ongoing teaching and research interests include federal governance, inter-governmental relationships, government accountability and integrity, political economy analysis and governance reform.

Muhammad Omar Faruque is an Assistant Judge/Judicial Magistrate in the Bangladesh Judicial Service. He holds LLM degrees from the Geneva Academy of International Humanitarian Law and Human Rights and the University of Dhaka. His overall works are focused on the efficiency of the institutions and mechanisms in protecting human rights. For this overarching pursuit, he studies different branches of law.

Mario Gomez is the Executive Director at the International Centre for Ethnic Studies, an independent think-tank in Sri Lanka. He has worked in academia, human rights and peace building, and previously taught constitutional law, administrative law and legal theory at the University of Colombo. His previous publications have been in the areas of administrative and constitutional law, transitional justice, socio-economic rights, gender and the law, and the right to information.

Swati Jhaveri has previously taught at the Faculty of Law of the National University of Singapore and the Faculty of Law of the Chinese University of Hong Kong, and is currently an Associate Fellow of the Asian Law Centre at the Melbourne Law School. Swati obtained her Bachelor of Arts in Jurisprudence and Bachelor of Civil Law from the University of Oxford.

Tarunabh Khaitan is the Head of Research at the Bonavero Institute of Human Rights, Faculty of Law, Oxford and the Professor of Public Law & Legal Theory at the University of Oxford. He is also an Honorary Professorial Fellow at Melbourne Law School and the founding General Editor of *Indian Law Review*.

Vikram Aditya Narayan holds a BA, LLB degree from NLIU Bhopal and an LLM degree from University College London. He has worked as a legal practitioner in Delhi for several years. He was a visiting researcher at Humboldt University, Berlin, and has taught constitutional law at NLS Bangalore and NLU Delhi. He is currently a PhD candidate at Humboldt University, Berlin.

Ahmed Nazeer is a Lecturer in Law at Liverpool Hope University. He has previously taught Human Rights and Public Law at the University of Portsmouth, where he obtained his PhD in Constitutional Law. Prior to joining academia, he was a Public Prosecutor in the Maldives.

Zim Nwokora is a comparative political scientist and a Senior Lecturer at Deakin University, Melbourne. His research focuses on constitutions, political parties and political finance.

Jayani Nadarajalingam is a Postdoctoral Fellow with the Laureate Program in Comparative Constitutional Law at the Melbourne Law School. She researches in constitutional law and theory, political philosophy and social theory.

Michael Pal is an Associate Professor in the Faculty of Common Law at the University of Ottawa in Canada. He publishes on comparative constitutional law and the law of democracy.

Iain Payne is a Senior Project Officer at the Institute for Global Development, University of New South Wales. He is also affiliated with the Niti Foundation in Nepal, where he leads a research and policy praxis programme on constitutionalism, building on his work in public policy and legal development in South Asia. Thematically, his work, which is framed within broader analyses of the political economy of the international development aid ecosystem, focuses on constitution-making, federalism and democratic consolidation, decay and renewal.

Marzia Raza is a PhD candidate in Political Science at Universität Heidelberg. She has a Master's degree in Political Science (2021) from the University of Osnabrück in Germany. She has held research and editorial positions at the United Nations and Oxford University Press in the past.

Shubho Roy is a JSD candidate at the University of Chicago. He works in law, economics and public choice theory. Before joining the University of Chicago, Shubho was a researcher at the National Institute of Public Finance and Policy, working on financial regulation, bankruptcy legislation and governance mechanisms. Shubho is trained as an advocate and was a law clerk at the Supreme Court of India.

Muhammad Salman teaches in the Comparative Humanities programme in the School of Arts, Humanities and Social Sciences at Habib University, Karachi. He specialised in party systems in transitioning regimes during his PhD in Political Science (2021) from LUISS Guido Carli, Rome. From 2008 to 2014, he taught International Relations at the University of Karachi. He has also worked on research assignments covering political violence and religious pluralism with the universities of Bielefeld and Erfurt in Germany.

Dinesha Samararatne is Professor at the Department of Public & International Law, Faculty of Law, University of Colombo, Sri Lanka, and a Senior Research Associate of the Laureate Programme in Comparative Constitutional Law, Melbourne Law School. Her research focuses on questions relating to fourth branch institutions, constitutional resilience, women and constitution making, and administrative law in Sri Lanka.

Dian Shah is an Assistant Professor at the Faculty of Law, National University of Singapore. Her research interests span the fields of law and religion, comparative constitutional law and human rights, especially in plural and divided societies. Outside her academic work, she serves as a member of the Malaysia Consultative Council on Foreign Policy, under the Ministry of Foreign Affairs. Dian is the author of *Constitutions, Religion and Politics in Asia: Indonesia, Malaysia and Sri Lanka* (Cambridge University Press, 2017) and a co-editor of *Law and Society in Malaysia: Pluralism, Religion and*

Ethnicity (Routledge, 2018). She is currently working on her second monograph, which analyses democratisation, political change and constitutional commitments in Asia.

Faizan Jawed Siddiqi is a Lecturer at the Department of Urban studies and Planning, Massachusetts Institute of Technology (MIT). He holds a Master's degree and a PhD in Urban Studies and Planning from MIT. He is interested in and has written on a range of topics, including the politics and practice of land governance, law, social movements and democratic deepening, with a geographic focus on India. Prior to academia, Dr Siddiqi worked for several years as a city planning professional in New Delhi.

Farhan Hanif Siddiqi is Associate Professor in the School of Politics and International Relations, Quaid-i-Azam University, Islamabad. His research interests border on ethnicity, conflict analysis and resolution, societal security, democratic consolidation and crisis management in South Asia. He is the author of *The Politics of Ethnicity in Pakistan: The Baloch, Sindhi and Mohajir Ethnic Movements* (Routledge, 2012).

Jahnavi Sindhu holds a BA, LLB degree from NLSIU, Bangalore and an LLM degree from Yale Law School. She has practised in the Delhi High Court and Indian Supreme Court, and has taught constitutional law at NLS Bangalore and NLU Delhi. She is currently a PhD candidate at Humboldt University, Berlin.

Arun Thiruvengadam is a Professor of Law at the National Law School, Bengaluru, India, where he teaches and researches on Indian public law, comparative constitutional studies, law, and development and welfare rights. He is one of three co-editors of *Comparative Constitutionalism in South Asia* (Oxford University Press India, 2013).

Michaela Windischgraetz, Dr habil, is Professor of Law and the Head of the Department of Employment Law and Social Security Law at the Faculty of Law, University of Vienna. She studied law at Vienna University and at the Université Panthéon-Assas Paris II. Additionally, she completed a second diploma in Social Anthropology and Tibetan and Buddhist studies at the University of Vienna. Since 2016, she has been serving as a Visiting Professor at the JSW School of Law in Bhutan.

PART I

Constitutional Resilience Decoded

1

Constitutional Resilience in South Asia: A Primer

SWATI JHAVERI, TARUNABH KHAITAN AND DINESHA SAMARARATNE

I. Introduction

Concerns about the stability of constitutional democracies, even long-standing democracies, have been rising globally.[1] While, at the end of the twentieth century, there were numerous examples of entrenched and generally healthy constitutional democracies, we are seeing a decline in the health of these systems around the world. The problem of decline is compounded by the fact that there are no notable or impactful examples of newly established constitutional democracies, with fewer systems demonstrating a capacity to transition to democratic forms of constitutional government and there being a greater range of competitors to the liberal democratic constitutional tradition.[2] Where there are examples of different systems seemingly adopting institutional tools typically associated with constitutional democracies, there is a concern over the true – ulterior – motives behind the adoption of such features.[3] This concern has prompted

[1] A Huq and T Ginsburg, *How to Lose a Constitutional Democracy* (Chicago, University of Chicago Press, 2018); M Graber, S Levinson and M Tushnet, *Constitutional Democracy in Crisis* (Oxford, Oxford University Press, 2018); Freedom House, 'Freedom in the World 2021: Democracy under Siege' (Washington, DC, March 2021), which downgrades the freedom scores of both the US and India in 2020; L Diamond, 'Facing Up to the Democratic Recession' (2015) 26 *Journal of Democracy* 141.

[2] I Krastev and S Holmes, *The Light that Failed: Why the West Is Losing the Fight for Democracy* (Cambridge, Pegasus, 2020), who argue that the Western liberal democratic model is now in decline, with authoritarianism being an able competitor for capture of the global political landscape. TG Daly further argues that the experiences of the Middle East and North Africa further demonstrate that the predicted 'fourth wave' of democratisation has had a stillbirth: TG Daly, *The Alchemists: Questioning our Faith in Courts as Democracy-Builders* (Cambridge, Cambridge University Press, 2017) 32.

[3] As Dixon and Landau observe, the formal growth in seemingly democratic orders of constitutional governance belie the problematic and abusive borrowing of features of the latter type of system to actually further authoritarian and counter-democratic forms of constitutional governance: R Dixon and D Landau, *Abusive Constitutional Borrowing: Legal Globalisation and the Subervsion of Liberal Democracy* (Oxford, Oxford University Press, 2021) 3. See also W Sadurski, *Poland's Constitutional Breakdown* (Oxford, Oxford University Press, 2019); T Ginsburg and AZ Huq, *How to Save a Constitutional Democracy* (Chicago, University of Chicago Press, 2019); P Norris and R Inglehart, *Cultural Backlash: Trump, Brexit, and Authoritarian Populism* (Cambridge, Cambridge University Press, 2019); OO Varol, 'Stealth Authoritarianism' (2014) 100 *Iowa Law Review* 1673; KL Scheppele, 'Autocratic Legalism' (2018) 85 *University of Chicago Law Review* 545.

a proliferation of academic literature that seeks to decode the problem: the instances and causes of constitutional and democratic decline. However, despite this academic abundance, there remain gaps in the literature, particularly in the geographical coverage of studies. While presenting a wide range of examples of democratic experimentation and decay, and housing a huge portion of humanity,[4] the global South – and South Asia in particular – has remained relatively underexplored by constitutional law and democracy scholars.

This regional gap exposes deficiencies in the existing literature. The preponderance of existing literature rests on the assumption that the threat to constitutional democracy is a relatively recent phenomenon, triggered largely by a rise in populism in politics.[5] Broadening the jurisdictional base of academic studies provides a deeper understanding of the timeline and causality of constitutional decay and decline. As a region, South Asia has had a much longer, tumultuous and varied experience with constitutional democracy that predates the recent rise in populism.[6] Pakistan and Bangladesh have frequently changed regime type, from democracy to autocracy and back. While India has had relatively more consistent constitutional infrastructure, serious concerns are being expressed about the resilience of its democratic institutions. Constitutional instability and insecurity about key institutions like the executive presidency and fourth branch institutions in Sri Lanka are stress testing the broader values and design of constitutional democracy to breaking point. Nepal, the Maldives, Bhutan and Afghanistan, as some of the youngest democracies in the world (and one of them – Afghanistan – already a former democracy), pose another set of questions that focus more on how to start the process of democratic consolidation in an unstable political and social environment.[7] Studying the experience of constitutional democracies in South Asia can thus enrich and broaden the global conversation on the health of democratic governance.

In setting out the subject of study of this volume, this chapter has two major aims. First, it will critically consider the gap in the coverage of South Asia in academic studies on the health of constitutional democracies. Second, it will explain how this volume starts to plug that gap – taking readers through the pre-comparative approach adopted in the volume and the curation and structuring of the volume. It will briefly comment on the chosen lens of 'resilience' for analysing the South Asian experience with constitutional decay and erosion. There have been multiple paradigms within which constitutional democracies have been assessed – for example, 'decay', 'erosion' and 'backsliding'. There have been conceptual disagreements about which term best describes the phenomenon.[8] In electing to discuss the issues from the perspective of

[4] P Chatterjee, *The Politics of the Governed: Reflections on Popular Politics in Most of the World* (New York, Columbia University Press, 2006).

[5] M Tushnet, 'Are Constitutional Democracies Really in Crisis? International Journal of Constitutional Law' (Blog, 10 September 2018); M Tushnet and B Bugaric, *Power to the People: Constitutionalism in the Age of Populism* (Oxford, Oxford University Press, 2022). See also Dixon and Landau (n 3) 12–13 on the dominance of the lens of populism as the main cause for democratic erosion.

[6] M Tushnet and M Khosla (eds), *Unstable Constitutionalism: Law and Politics in South Asia* (Cambridge, Cambridge University Press, 2015).

[7] N Coburn and A Larson, *Derailing Democracy in Afghanistan: Elections in an Unstable Political Landscape* (New York, Columbia University Press, 2013).

[8] Various terms in use include 'decline', 'degradation', 'backsliding' and 'breakdown': for an overview, see R Albert and M Pal, 'The Democratic Resilience of the Canadian Constitution' in Graber et al (n 1) 117.

resilience, the aim is to adopt a forward-looking approach to the topic: while diagnosing the health concerns are important, it may be equally critical to consider the possible solutions to the issues.

II. Pathologies in Comparative Constitutional Studies

The editors of a recent global study on constitutional decay considered the plausibility of the view that constitutional issues in the USA may be fuelling concerns that constitutional democracy is in trouble more generally across the globe – with the constitutional health of the USA being the proverbial canary in the mine.[9] As the editors ultimately concluded, this type of conclusion is symptomatic of an unevenly developing field that is 'modestly comparative'.[10] The field has benefited from a more robust engagement with the Global South in recent times. Studies have confronted existential questions about comparison head on in asking what the field of comparative constitutional law could and should look like when it engages with the Global South.[11] Constitutional studies of European and Latin American jurisdictions, for example, have expanded the traditional Anglo-American focus and have sought to breach the North–South divide.[12]

The field has recently started paying more attention to the question of how to undertake the comparative endeavour. There has been a refreshment of the field in the past decade, with a conscious movement away from the dominance of studies of jurisdictions from the Euro-Anglo-American legal-liberal tradition.[13] This responds to the call to provide 'equal discursive dignity to non-European-American traditions'.[14] The field of comparative constitutional studies is vast, and has grown significantly in the past decade in particular. This might, therefore, be an appropriate time to pause and reflect more deeply on how we conceptualise or approach our organisation of the field depending on our particular purpose at any point in time – pedagogical, scholarly, activist,

[9] Graber et al (n 1).

[10] The editors conclude (at 5) that such perceptions of the causality of the global constitutional crisis reflects nothing more than American parochialism and the exaggerated role the USA plays in comparative constitutionalism. See also DS Law and M Versteeg, 'The Declining Influence of the United States Constitution' (2012) 87 *New York University Law Review* 762; S Roy, 'Privileging (Some Forms of) Interdisciplinarity and Interpretation: Methods in Comparative Law' (2014) 12 *International Journal of Constitutional Law* 786; Tushnet and Khosla (n 6) 3.

[11] P Dann, M Riegner and M Bonnemann, *The Global South and Comparative Constitutional Law* (Oxford, Oxford University Press, 2020) especially the discussion on the 'southern turn'.

[12] P Dann and A Thiruvengandam (eds), *Democratic Constitutionalism in India and European Union: Comparing the Law of Democracy in Continental Polities* (Cheltenham, Edward Elgar, 2021); D Bonilla Maldonado (ed), *Constitutionalism of the Global South: The Activist Tribunals of India, South Africa, and Colombia* (Cambridge, Cambridge University Press, 2013); M Hailbronner, 'Transformative Constitutionalism: Not Only in the Global South' (2017) 65 *American Journal of Comparative Law* 527; C Saunders, 'Towards a Global Constitutional Gene Pool' (2009) 4 *National Taiwan University Law Review* 1.

[13] R Hirschl, *Comparative Matters* (Oxford, Oxford University Press, 2014) 4 and 163.

[14] U Baxi, 'The Colonial Heritage' in P Legrand and R Munday (eds), *Comparative Legal Studies: Traditions and Transitions* (Cambridge, Cambridge University Press, 2003) 50 cited in Hirschl (n 13) 205; S Choudhry, 'Introduction' in S Choudhry (ed), *Constitutional Design for Divided Societies: Integration or Accommodation?* (Oxford, Oxford University Press, 2008) 8–9.

reformist or practical.[15] It is not possible to locate a single 'big bang' moment in comparative constitutional law, but the coverage of Asia, Latin America and Africa is essential, especially studies that seek to breach the North–South divide.[16] However, this has not suspended calls for further intentional broadening of the field. As Ginsburg recently observed, 'the field may be in the midst of an "encyclopaedic turn" … in which the proliferation of scholarship and data drives demand for organization and distillation of knowledge'.[17] This call to broaden the field to make it representative of the true diversity of constitutional systems is also a response to the recent awakening of the field to the enduring problems of colonialism. Some scholars have highlighted how comparative constitutional studies are 'late to the party', with other disciplines having long debated the implications of colonialism and empire on the way their field is structured.[18]

However, many pathologies in constitutional studies await acknowledgement, especially when evaluating the issue of constitutional decay and resilience: South Asia has some of the most complex social and political settings for constitutional government.[19] This section maps out continuing areas of neglect in the comparative endeavour.[20] It focuses on two sets of concerns: first, how far the research agenda and conceptual toolkit for comparative studies is still largely set by the Global North, with the Global South servicing this agenda through the contribution of case studies; and second, issues with existing South Asian studies. On the latter, it looks at issues of intra-regional inequality with existing South Asian comparative work – with certain jurisdictions (especially India) dominating the characterisation of 'South Asia'.

Before considering these issues, we will make an observation about 'South Asia' as a classification. The precise origin of the term 'South Asia' remains contested, as do the reasons for its organisation as a region. Some point to geographical proximity, others emphasise a 'cultural', cognitive or ideational connection within the region.[21] Despite these existential questions relating to the region, a significant advantage to considering this area as a region is that it allows us to think beyond the state as the organising unit in constitutional studies. We recognise, however, that the use of a South Asian lens can occlude other ways of reflecting on regional connections and continuities.

[15] See, eg the models of comparative constitutional studies proposed by DS Law in 'Introduction: Pedagogy and Conceptualization of the Field' in DS Law (ed), *Constitutionalism in Context* (Cambridge, Cambridge University Press, 2022) that are relevant/prevalent in the pedagogical act of teaching.

[16] Some have pushed for the field to move beyond such distinctions and think more carefully about the Global 'North' and 'South' as categories: M De Visser, 'Rethinking the Concept of the Global South, International Journal of Constitutional Law' (*I-CONnect*, 31 March 2022) www.iconnectblog.com/2022/03/rethinking-the-concept-of-the-global-south/, in responding to the arguments in favour of the 'Global South' as a category by Dann et al (n 10).

[17] Law (n 15) 37.

[18] D Samararatne, 'Comparative Constitutional Law, Colonialism and Empire (Part I)' (*IACL-AIDC Blog*, 21 October 2021) https://blog-iacl-aidc.org/2021-posts/2021/10/21/comparative-constitutional-law-colonialism-and-empire-part-i; SS Parmar, 'Academic Imperialism and Universal Academic Accessibility: Echoes from the Global South' *RGNUL Student Research Review* (27 August 2022); Hirschl (n 13) 208.

[19] Tushnet and Khosla (n 6) 3.

[20] See E Orucu, 'Unde Venit, Quo Tendit Comparative Law?' in A Harding and E Orucu (eds), *Comparative Law in the 21st Century* (Kluwer, London, 2002) 1, A Riles, *Rethinking the Masters of Comparative Law* (Oxford, Hart Publishing, 2001) 1–2.

[21] See B Chakma, *South Asian Regionalism: The Limits of Cooperation* (Bristol, Bristol University Press, 2020) especially ch 2 ('The Idea of South Asia as a Region').

The links between constitutions and Buddhism is one example which would open up the prospects for comparison between Sri Lanka, Myanmar, Laos, Thailand and Cambodia, breaching the regional demarcation we have adopted in this volume. The same point can be made about the study of monarchies in constitutional systems in the broader region (comparing the experiences of Nepal, Indonesia, Malaysia and Thailand). We recognise, therefore, that 'South Asia' as a region is only a starting point for pushing the comparative conversations ahead. There is much more work to be done in the broader Asian region: our work on 'South Asia' is a point of departure for reflecting on and learning from under-explored regions and issues.

A. The Hold of the Global North – Dictating the Agenda and Conceptual Toolkit

Who dictates the comparative agenda? There cannot be an assumption that the same questions that ignite interest in other regions will be of interest to South Asia. For example, the *central* concern across the South Asian countries under study in this volume is not, for example, about the most suitable theory of interpreting a constitution's text,[22] nor is it the problem of institutional deadlock under divided government in a scheme of US-style separation of powers;[23] rather, it is questions of optimising and realising sound constitutional design, constitutional negotiation between constitutional actors to address and resolve pressures on the overall system and the domestic risks to which it is exposed.[24] This is not to say there will not be any common ground of interest; however, to be truly enriching, all regions and actors need to be involved in designing comparative studies and setting the agenda for the field. There is support for the argument that there is a stronger need to undertake South Asian studies from within South Asia using phenomena from within those systems rather than ask South Asia to respond to and comment on foreign phenomena.[25] Other commentators go further in arguing that studies should be firmly rooted in the South Asian experience and accordingly should be *for*, *with* and *from* the Global South.[26]

As noted by Dixon and Landau, there is a wide network of transnational and international actors that promote the spread of norms of liberal democratic constitutionalism.

[22] There are no doubt debates about how to interpret a particular constitutional provision: see S Choudry, 'How to Do Comparative Constitutional Law in India: Naz Foundation, Same Sex Rights, and Dialogical Interpretation' in S Khilnani, V Raghavan and AK Thiruvengadam (eds), *Comparative Constitutionalism in South Asia* (Oxford, Oxford University Press, 2012). But the relative merits of originalism, textualism, structuralism, inter-textualism etc are a particularly American obsession inspiring little interest or concern in South Asia.

[23] T Khaitan, 'Executive Aggrandizement in Established Democracies: A Crisis of Liberal Democratic Constitutionalism' (2019) 17 *International Journal of Constitutional Law* 342.

[24] See also Tushnet and Khosla (n 6). On 'Southern' Constitutionalism as an experience of socio-economic transformation; constitutionalism as a site of struggle about political organisation; and constitutionalism as denial of, and access to, justice, see Dann et al, 'The Southern Turn in Comparative Constitutional Law: An Introduction' in Dann et al (n 10). But *cf* Hailbronner (n 12).

[25] Choudry (n 22).

[26] Dann et al (n 10); Z Oklopic, 'The South of Western Constitutionalism: A Map Ahead of a Journey' (2016) 37 *Third World Quarterly* 2080.

However, the allegation is that this network reflects a 'form of Western imperialism', with core members comprising states that have a more powerful geopolitical hold on the narrative and push that version of the narrative via this network.[27] Ultimately, however, they conclude that

> countries such as India, Colombia, and South Africa have become major producers of liberal democratic doctrines and concepts on such issues as socioeconomic rights, the role of constitutional courts, the shape of constitution-making processes, and the unconstitutional constitutional amendment doctrine. Many global south countries have become key participants in the evolving meaning of liberal democratic constitutionalism.[28]

Their book, therefore, proceeds on the assumption that the theory and practice of democratic constitutional governance can have much variance and that the 'ground level' experience is much more varied than the comparative literature presumes. In the same vein, they assert that 'illiberal constitutionalism' – as a competitor for liberal democratic constitutional governance – has become a broad church for absorbing a variety of very different systems, including Russia, Singapore, Turkey and China, and similarly needs disaggregation.[29] What is more, the rise of illiberalism in the Global North has exposed the fragility of even the older, affluent, established democracies in ways that make any attempt to neatly map the North–South divide onto one that is liberal-democratic/illiberal-autocratic no longer tenable.[30] In the same spirit, this volume starts with the assumption that while the nomenclature may be shared, the thicker conceptual meaning behind it is varied and needs to be better ventilated in the literature.

Some have argued that the implications of introducing this heterogeneity into the literature would be the development of homegrown and regionally informed definitions of terminology that the field uses to analyse the practice of constitutionalism in South Asia. This would include the modification of even the most fundamental concepts that we might otherwise readily assume as having a shared meaning: one example is the idea of 'elections' – so, rather than looking at those concepts as defined by the Global North and how they apply in the Global South, the argument is that we need to identify homegrown versions of concepts that better service the interests of the field.[31] For example, a study on Afghanistan concluded that 'democracy' cannot mean the 'political ritual of holding elections ... [the latter] have encouraged violence, stagnation, and the inequitable distribution of resources' in the Afghan context. 'Elections' in the Afghan context, it is argued, cannot be seen as enabling representative governance but instead have come to be a vehicle for competition between different patronage networks (tribal elders, militia, merchants, politicians) etc.[32]

[27] Dixon and Landau (n 3) 10.

[28] ibid 11.

[29] ibid 14.

[30] Khaitan (n 23).

[31] See, eg the work of N Sultany, *Law and Revolution: Legitimacy and Constitutionalism After the Arab Spring* (Oxford, Oxford University Press, 2017) and Z Al-Ali, *Arab Constitutionalism: The Coming Revolution* (Cambridge, Cambridge University Press, 2021), who, in differing ways, attempt to better encapsulate the tumultuous systems of 'constitutional' governance and revolution in the Arab context (that accurately captures the experience of Tunisia, Egypt, Yemen, Libya, Jordan, Morocco and Sudan).

[32] Coburn and Larson (n 7) 1.

So we need to start, it is argued, with a localised understanding of a concept, which we populate with the appropriate cultural content needed to have a meaningful and critical discussion of that concept in that context. We do not take the argument in favour of heterogeneity in theoretical and conceptual discussions so far as to suggest that concepts can be entirely homegrown. There are risks associated with the assumption that concepts lack a minimal or core objective – for example, this assumption can be misused by those prone to 'abusive constitutional borrowing', with anti-constitutional activities being rationalised as constitutional in some way under the pretext that this is just an autochtonisation of ideas and concepts. Rather, we are sympathetic to starting with the assumption that any concept or theory needs to be contextualised to local facts and that theoretical frameworks developed in a different factual context would need to be approached with a healthy curiosity. As Dann has recently argued, there is no reason why a concept like 'liberal constitutionalism' cannot be 'open source' and meaningfully used in non-Global North contexts, but we need to stop short of devising precise concepts and instead approach conceptual conversations with an understanding of 'context and distinction'.[33]

The unitisation of the concept of constitutional democracy as embodying a semi-fixed set of concepts is apparent in much of the existing academic literature. As observed by Dixon and Landau,

> the grammar of liberal democratic constitutionalism – various forms of rights, now normally including both second generation socioeconomic rights and third generation rights such as environmental rights, the architecture of the separation of powers, judicial review, and increasingly other 'independent accountability institutions' such as ombudspersons and anti corruption commissions as well – is now dominant and expected in most contexts where new constitutions are being written.[34]

Some critics argue that accepted definitions of 'constitutional democracy' that are based on a narrow dataset of jurisdictions highlight the need to decolonise the comparative literature. Tully, for example, argues how the key features of modern constitutional democracy are distinctly 'Western' in character and comprise legal and political institutions that have 'imperial' roots. They have been used as tools for dispossessing others of their resources, labour and markets. They have been globally spread through colonialism or skewed free trade. Tully welcomes attempts to 'de-imperialize the imperial dimensions of modern constitutional democracy'.[35] The tools suggested for de-imperialism include, especially pertinently for the purposes of the present discussion, open contestation, criticism, negotiation and modification of the institutions of constitutional democracy that might have been inherited by the South from the North.[36]

[33] P Dann, 'Liberal Constitutionalism and Postcolonialism in the South and Beyond: On Liberalism as an Open Source and the Insights of Decolonial Critiques' (2022) 20 *International Journal of Constitutional Law* 1.

[34] Dixon and Landau (n 3) 10.

[35] J Tully, 'Modern Constitutional Democracy and Imperialism' (2008) 46 *Osgoode Hall Law Review* 461, 464. See also G Frankenberg, *Comparative Law as Critique* (Cheltenham, Edward Elgar, 2019) 13; S Munshi, 'Comparative Law and Decolonizing Critique' (2017) 65 *American Journal of Comparative Law* 207.

[36] O Táíwò, *Against Decolonization* (London, Hurst Publishing, 2022): Táíwò suggests that the decolonisation project is misused by elites within a polity to dominate the 'new' decolonised discourse at the expense of marginalised groups within that polity. Decolonisation comes at the expense of pluralism of viewpoint.

This requires turning our attention to jurisdictions that do not tend to dominate the agenda. As Dann et al observe, the Global South represents a distinctive constitutional experience which is shaped by, inter alia, the history of colonialism and geopolitical marginalisation of the South. They put forward three distinctive elements of constitutionalism in the Global South: it is transformative in socio-economic terms, it is a site of political struggle and contestation, and it has profound implications for access to justice. Dann et al focus broadly on the Global South; our study seeks to zoom in on South Asia further from within this broad category. We turn now to look at previous attempts focusing on South Asia.

B. Indian Hegemony within Existing South Asian Studies

One of our major objectives has been to push back on intra-regional dominance of certain jurisdictions in existing South Asian studies. A quick survey of comparative studies shows the dominance of India in the conversation. This is not surprising, on the basis that the academic infrastructure in India is relatively better resourced and the broader geopolitical dominance of India in the region. There is no reason, however, that either of these reasons should dictate the diversity of contributions from across the region. Existing South Asian studies have attempted to expand the countries that currently engage in scholarly conversations on South Asia. For example, a study by Khosla and Tushnet sought to expand the countries that currently constitute the field in South Asia, going beyond the usual focus on India, Pakistan, Bangladesh and Sri Lanka to include Nepal.[37] In curating this volume, we recognise the need to develop an even deeper and diverse empirical base in South Asia to include the Maldives, Afghanistan, Bhutan and Myanmar. Broadening the empirical base across the region would also lead to a diversification in the topics that are discussed. The literature coming out of India, for example, tends to have as its focus the work of the Supreme Court – with constitutional decisions of the apex court being the easiest product for comparison.[38] Broadening the jurisdictional coverage within South Asia opens up the analysis beyond the usual topics (public interest litigation, social rights, basic structure doctrine etc) that tend to dominate the agenda.

One issue we encountered in curating the chapters for the volume relates to the question of capacity in the region. Academics working at institutions in the region face a chronic shortage of funds and resources for research. This includes insufficient access to legal databases and the lack of funds for travel both within their jurisdiction or region and outside to facilitate a scholarly engagement with others. In addition, there is a reported absence of an incentive structure that promotes the investment of time by scholars in research (in addition to relatively demanding administrative and teaching duties). What was common to all jurisdictions in the region is how academics are

[37] Tushnet and Khosla (n 6); see also S Hossain, S Malik and B Musa (eds), *Public Interest Litigation in South Asia: Rights in Search of Remedies* (Dhaka, University Press, 1997) and Khilnani et al (n 10), who also try to push back on intra-regional imbalance in coverage in studies.

[38] Hirschl (n 13) 153.

now also being stretched into the public domain to actually be part of the counter-manoeuvres against constitutional decline: this places additional calls on the time of academics. Finally, there is an absence of homegrown fora for publication and workshopping ideas and research, with papers from the region needing to compete for airtime in global and international fora. In recognition of this issue, many have worked on developing regional and local fora for publication and workshopping ideas.[39] Within the region there are disparities on all of these metrics, with some jurisdictions lagging behind others in availability of resources, time and infrastructure. This made it challenging to curate chapters from some South Asian jurisdictions. However, there has been a tremendous amount research activity and energy put into reaching broader areas of the region in the past few years and our work now builds on that.[40]

In curating these chapters, we were forced to confront a common problem: who can write about a jurisdiction? Do we need to restrict scholarship about Bhutan to a scholar who is working *in* Bhutan? Or, even more parochially, do you need to be Bhutanese to write about Bhutan? What kind of scholar can provide an authentic rendering of a particular jurisdiction? The idea of 'authenticity' in coverage of a jurisdiction is a common issue raised by scholars. However, as Samararatne points out, authenticity may be problematic in this regard.[41] De Visser points out that there are no clear criteria (language, residency, familiarity through fieldwork, personal connections and network) to help us answer this question. We believe that all perspectives and positionalities – whether internal, external or hybrid – can examine any issue in enlightening ways, and each may be susceptible to certain blind spots. In curating our chapters for this volume, therefore, we avoided being distracted by issues of identity and positionality of authors, focusing instead on ensuring adequate coverage of the region beyond the usual jurisdictions and ensuring that chapters were subject to demanding peer review by colleagues familiar with the relevant jurisdiction. We discuss this in further detail in section III below.

C. Dynamism on the Ground

A final observation to make relates to the dynamic nature of the political climate of the region that we sought to capture and analyse in this volume. Since we commenced the process of curating chapters for this volume, several jurisdictions went through significant constitutional developments. The COVID-19 pandemic brought into sharp focus existing vulnerabilities of constitutional systems across the world. In addition to the governance crisis brought on by the pandemic, South Asian jurisdictions continued to undergo other constitutional changes. Of these, the most unexpected developments took place in Sri Lanka: within two years of electing him to power, Sri Lankans engaged

[39] For example, the *Junior Faculty Forum for South Asian Law Teachers* (https://twitter.com/JFF_ILT) and the *Indian Law Review* (published by Taylor and Francis).

[40] Tushnet and Khosla (n 6); see also Hossain et al (n 37); Khilnani et al (n 10); K Tan and R Hoque, *Constitutional Foundings in South Asia* (Oxford, Hart Publishing, 2021).

[41] Samararatne (n 18).

in protests of unprecedented scale to demand the resignation of President Gotabaya Rajapakse. The political crisis in Pakistan in 2022 and the subsequent removal of Prime Minister Imran Khan was another significant development in the region. In the context of such dynamic constitutional changes, publishing scholarly work is challenging, to say the least. In addition, scholars who are writing about these developments from within the jurisdictions are often spread thin, alternating between responding to rapidly evolving constitutional developments and finding the resources and intellectual space to develop their scholarly work. In crisis-ridden contexts, such as Afghanistan in 2021, Pakistan and Sri Lanka in 2022, scholars located in such jurisdictions have also had to deal with the crises on the personal level, handling the challenges of day-to-day living in difficult circumstances. While it is difficult to capture a moving and dynamic constitutional tableau, the significant insights, claims and conclusions made by our authors remain relevant and hold their currency. In fact, subsequent constitutional developments have validated the cautionary insights offered by them. Tarun Khaitain's claim about executive aggrandisement in India and Jahnavi Sindhu and Vikram Aditya Narayan's claims about the people as constitutional actors are but two examples. These experiences suggest to us that any scholarly efforts on dynamic regions or jurisdictions such as South Asia would require resilience and adaptation to rapidly changing ground realities. These experiences are a reminder that scholars are required to be cautious and modest in their interpretation of constitutional developments. Hurried or partially thought through claims are most likely to be proven wrong, quite quickly.

III. A Proto-comparative Approach

This volume seeks to lay the groundwork for addressing the pathologies in the South Asian comparative endeavour. It brings together chapters that will: (i) examine the reasons why constitutional democracies in the region are under threat, providing a more calibrated account of causes behind constitutional erosion than currently informs global debates; and (ii) evaluate the resilience of democratic institutions to combat those threats. The chapters in this volume consider the design and functioning of institutions such as political parties, legislatures, the political executive, the bureaucracy, courts, fourth branch/guarantor institutions (such as electoral commissions) and the military to understand their role in strengthening or undermining constitutional democracy in the region. It goes beyond the typical focus in constitutional *law* studies (namely courts and, once in a while, legislatures).

Section IVA below provides an insight into our thinking behind the structuring of the volume. The various chapters could have been organised in any number of ways. In choosing to scaffold the volume along institutional fault lines, we were guided by the discussions at the 2019 workshop and thereafter. We intentionally avoided geographical and jurisdictional fault lines, given our specific objective of pushing back against intra-regional imperialism in scholarship in this field – hence the thematic focus on institutions. Because the volume does not include broad intra-South Asian comparison on each of the institutions discussed, there may be an impression of disparateness. This is, however, inevitable, given the field of South Asia-specific comparative constitutional studies is at a relatively early stage of development. Our modest ambition behind the workshop that informed this volume, as well as the subsequent publication effort, has been to nurture this nascent area of scholarship in one of the most populous, violent and diverse, yet remarkably resilient regions in the world.

The genesis of this volume was a workshop co-organised in December 2019 by the Asian Law Centre at the Melbourne Law School, the Bonavero Institute of Human Rights at the University of Oxford and the Centre for Asian Legal Studies at the Faculty of Law of the National University of Singapore. It was the third in a series of workshops organised by a combination of these institutions[42] with two objectives in mind: first, departing from the India focus of the first two workshops, the third iteration sought the mainstreaming of South Asia as a region of study in comparative public law; and secondly, the building of research capacity in the region and, in particular, mentoring and nurturing early career scholars in the region.[43]

The third workshop was focused on an issue that has captured the attention of comparative public law scholars in recent years: the issue of the erosion and resilience of constitutional democracy. The aim of the workshop was, and of this volume is, to address four particular issues within the existing literature. First, we aim to respond to the blind spot that South Asia occupies in existing comparative studies on the theme of the contemporary wave of democratic deconsolidation and constitutional decline. Second, within South Asian studies, we aspire to bring in greater diversity of coverage from the region beyond the 'usual suspects' that are covered in the literature as representative of the South Asian experience. Third, we seek to broaden the conversation to constitutional actors other than the courts, which have dominated the existing literature. Fourth, in a field that is preoccupied with a focus on constitutional decline, we aim to focus on the institutional dynamics of resilience and vulnerability.

With a view to achieving these four objectives, especially the second one, we have supplemented chapters presented at the workshop with a few additional ones. The aim was to spread the coverage of the volume across the breadth of the South Asian region while also ensuring covering of a broad range of institutions and constitutional actors beyond the courts. In addition, we were mindful that the diversity of the region is severely under-represented in the comparative literature on constitutional decay and decline. Therefore, we were intentional in our aim to demonstrate the richness of the data set that South Asia offers to the field. The region is prone to being viewed in unitary terms in the literature and our aim was to explain its diversity in manifesting the problem of constitutional decline. One of the largest studies on the topic of decline, carried out in 2018, had this to say about the region:

> Constitutional democracies and constitutional democracy appear in trouble throughout the world. The United States, Israel, Turkey, South Africa, Hungary, Poland, and Venezuela seem particular problem children, but the Catalonian secession in Spain, Brexit in the United

[42] The first being 'Contemporary Issues in Indian Public Law', organised by the National Law University, Delhi, the University of Oxford and the University of Melbourne in April 2015; and the second – supported by the Jindal Global Law School, the University of Oxford, the National University of Singapore and the University of Melbourne in April 2018 – titled 'Comparative Perspectives on Administrative Law in India'.

[43] And is one of a number of major initiatives for building research capacity and community in the region – partnering with the *Junior Faculty Forum for South Asian Law Teachers* (https://twitter.com/JFF_ILT) and the *Indian Law Review*.

> Kingdom, *the rise of authoritarian constitutionalism in South Asia*, the overthrow of the Morsi government in Egypt, and the continued weakness of constitutional democracy throughout Africa and Latin American [*sic*] suggest that no earthly haven is immune. (emphasis added)[44]

The unitisation of South Asia stands in stark contrast to the particularised treatment of other regions in the above observation, with Europe – broadly drawn – being represented by five examples and South Asia (comprising India, but also Afghanistan, Bangladesh, Bhutan, the Maldives, Myanmar, Nepal, Pakistan, Sri Lanka) being represented as a single case study data point. Our volume aims at broadening this conversation, although, despite our best efforts, Myanmar remains a blind spot for this volume.

The first question we asked ourselves is what should be the objective of a volume focused on 'South Asia'? There are three possible objectives: first, to reveal and promote a new model of 'constitutionalism' to compete with the Anglo-American, legal-liberal paradigms that tend to occupy the terrain; second, to engage in intra-regional comparison and create more opportunities for conversation within the region; and finally, to study a broader range of jurisdictions – individually on their own terms – within the region to upload new data points from a group of jurisdictions in an understudied region. The majority of the volume consists of single jurisdiction studies and intra-South Asian comparisons. However, this aligns with the objectives of the volume. At this stage of the field's development, it is ambitious and premature to generate pan-/intra-South Asian coverage. The latter will be possible once we have developed more jurisdictional studies on South Asia across a range of themes. There is a greater need for systemic single-state studies before robust intra-South Asian comparison can take place.

We acknowledge the incredible efforts of colleagues in the field seeking to undertake the first two tasks. For example, a recent volume embarked on comparative experimentation by studying across two regions that have not really been seen as natural comparative candidates: India and the European Union.[45] The objective of comparative experimentation was to expand the field – perhaps exponentially and not incrementally. It was innovative in comparing 'unusual' comparative partners; breaching the North–South divide, but also comparing a single jurisdiction (India) with a regional network of jurisdictions (the EU). It sought to – interestingly, from our perspective – engage in what they called 'slow' comparison: seeing comparison as an incremental accretion of contextualised awareness of a jurisdiction rather than seeking to reach a place of omniscience instantly.[46] In the spirit of a 'slow' approach to comparison, we retreat one step backwards and focus on laying the foundation for comparison. This involves creating jurisdictional data points: hence the focus on single jurisdiction studies in the volume.

How do we resolve tensions in the demands being placed on comparative studies on South Asian jurisdictions? There is a demand to produce a 'South Asian' counterpoint to the other regional, systemic models out there. On the other hand, there is a further need – one that is pre-comparative in nature – to develop a deeper understanding of the individual jurisdictions in the region in order to be able to create a 'South Asian' model.

[44] Graber et al (n 1).
[45] Dann and Thiruvengandam (n 12).
[46] Building on the initial field work done on the 'law of democracy' in R Pildes, S Issacharoff and PS Karlan, *Law of Democracy: Legal Structure of the Political Process*, 5th edn (Foundation Press, 2016).

Our response to this is to seek to create more opportunity for interaction between different jurisdictional studies within South Asia to greater appreciate their variance and diversity. Stronger methodological attention also needs to be paid to this intra-South Asian endeavour. Comparativist methodologists comment on the need for stronger attention to discerning similarities and differences; understanding local 'culture' (legal, rights, constitutional, social and political culture); and having a disciplined attitude towards being embedded in one's own jurisdiction and the comparator.[47] The demand for intra-South Asian comparison competes with the need for systemic country studies in their own right.[48] Commentators have argued that there is a need for stronger groundwork before comparison is possible: there is a need for *systemic* constitutional analysis of individual jurisdictions that looks at and critiques the constitutional system as a whole.

A review of the chapters in this volume demonstrates the diversity in the constitutional history, make-up and variance within the region. The jurisdictions comprise densely and diversely populated countries presenting unique challenges not found in other populations. The book acknowledges this variance and difference, and does not propose to explain 'South Asian' constitutional resilience but rather constitutional resilience *in South Asia*.[49] Earlier studies have observed that,

> despite their divergent recent histories and political experiences, South Asian countries in fact display a remarkable degree of constitutional and legal kinship. There are several common elements among the region's constitutions, political structures, and legal systems. These elements are drawn from the region's colonial past and from its many diverse indigenous legal traditions.[50]

However, we proceed on the basis that there is much difference that needs to be explored first in individual jurisdictions before we can elevate that to considering the possibility of convergence or even systematising the difference within the region. The differences that inform our approach include the different degrees of constitutional and democratic consolidation across the region (just compare India, Pakistan and Bangladesh – which have been in the process of consolidation since the 1940s–1970s – with Bhutan and Nepal, which have only recently reformed as constitutional republics). In the case of Bhutan and Nepal, it can be argued that what is happening is not so much a reversal or restoration of constitutional democracy as a de nova building of strong institutions to support a new constitutional democracy (departing from a monarchy in both cases)

[47] L Lazarus, *Contrasting Prisoners' Rights: A Comparative Examination of England and German* (Oxford, Oxford University Press, 2004) 4–7.

[48] KL Scheppele, 'The Case for Systemic Constitutional Analysis' (*Law and Other Things*, 30 January 2021); see also J Boswell, J Corbett and RAW Rhodes, *The Art and Craft of Comparison* (Cambridge, Cambridge University Press, 2019) 1: 'Comparison … runs the risk of sacrificing rich, nuanced and context-bound insights on the altar of parsimony, generalisability and theoretical elegance.'

[49] *cf* Saunders (n 12); D Bonilla Maldonado, 'Toward a Constitutionalism of the Global South' in Bonilla Maldonado (n 12). On 'Southern' constitutionalism as an experience of socio-economic transformation; constitutionalism as a site of struggle about political organisation; and constitutionalism as denial of, and access to, justice, see Dann et al, 'The Southern Turn in Comparative Constitutional Law: An Introduction' in Dann et al (n 10).

[50] Khilnani et al (n 10) 2; Frankenberg (n 35).

for the first time. Thus, the deconsolidation phenomenon is not universally present in South Asia, even though the challenges facing constitutionalism and democracy are.[51] A further important difference across the region relates to the particular type of constitutional system: there are examples of federal and unitary states; parliamentary, semi-presidential and presidential systems; and secular versus consciously religious constitutions (as well as those – like Sri Lanka and Bangladesh – somewhere in between). A further difference worth noting is the variety of challenges to constitutional democracy in the region, with challenges posed by plural populations, the involvement of the military, the resurgence of nationalism/populism and instability in constitutional consolidation. We proceed on the basis of difference and diversity and do not, at this stage of the process, attempt to uncover commonality within the region. We turn now to consider the diversity of experience with constitutional resilience in South Asia that this volume seeks to capture.

IV. Diagnosing Constitutional Decay in South Asia – Mapping the Terrain

This section considers the issue of constitutional resilience and decay in the South Asian jurisdictions under discussion. Why are constitutional democracies under siege? There have been many attempts at diagnosing the problem.[52] More recently, Dixon and Landau have observed:

> since the halcyon days of the 1990s, the model of liberal democracy has come under considerable stress. Much of this stress stems from doubts about its performance. In developing and developed countries alike, political and academic critics have argued that liberal democratic constitutionalism has failed to address, or has even worsened, key flaws in market- based economies – including a persistent decline in work, wages, and benefits for many ordinary citizens; problems of increasing economic inequality and corporate power; and large-scale environmental challenges, such as climate change. Newer aspects of constitutional design intended to address these issues, such as socioeconomic rights, often do not seem to be up to the task. Another critique, which goes back at least to Schmitt, argues that liberal democracy unwisely fragments and restrains democratic popular will, by empowering unelected domestic institutions such as courts, as well as international bodies like the EU and the ECHR.[53]

[51] I Payne and G Varughese, 'Dissecting Narratives of Democracy in Nepal' (*The Record*, 26 November 2020): 'contemporary commentaries on Nepali democracy can be situated within three broad narratives of incremental democratic consolidation notwithstanding occasional setbacks; of democratic backsliding and creeping authoritarianism; and of unchanged and enduring patters of kleptocratic patrimonialism … the narratives lead to divergent diagnoses of the fundamental direction that democracy in Nepal is moving in – whether democracy continues to consolidate (moving forwards), whether it is in decline (moving backwards), or whether movement in either direction is more significantly shaped by opportunistic groups of elites serving narrow self-interest (moving sideways)'.

[52] For a robust systemic study of the variables that contribute to decay/resilience outside of the region, see A Huq and T Ginsburg, 'How to Lose a Constitutional Democracy' (2018) 65 *UCLA Law Review* 78; T Ginsburg and AZ Huq, *How to Save a Constitutional Democracy* (Chicago, University of Chicago Press, 2019).

[53] Dixon and Landau (n 3) 12.

The universe of causal factors that can explain this 'siege' and factors that are specific to South Asia is vast. Some are considered in this volume, but it would be impossible for a single volume to capture the complexity of the constitutional politics in the region. We briefly set out here the universe of factors that can explain the corrosion of constitutional democracy. In common with the experience of other regions, there are four categories of causal factors that can explain constitutional decline in the region: (i) changes in the broader socio-economic climate; (ii) latent and/or patent defects in the design of the constitutional and electoral system; (iii) the corruption or capture of constitutional institutions that are usually or have the potential to be a ballast against constitutional decay; and (iv) shifts in the political actors that dominate the constitutional scene. The movement towards populist rhetoric and dominance in electoral politics is a driver behind all four of these categories, but the discussions in this volume sophisticate this populist critique – the causes are much more varied and diverse in the region.[54]

The volume focuses on political actors and constitutional institutions when approaching the issues of constitutional decay and resilience. The dual purpose of the volume – broadening the jurisdictional and institutional focus of the conversations in South Asia – provided us with a range of options for the structuring of the volume. Our aim was to focus on the institutional and design features rather than the geography of the region as the scaffolding for the volume. At a first glance, the volume might appear to be a disparate collection of essays, given the two axes along which the chapters are organised – the jurisdictional and institutional. However, the aim was to go for depth versus breadth of coverage. For this reason, the volume is organised through the institutions and actors that are represented in the region to explain the diversity of forces at play when it comes to the issue of constitutional decay and revival. For example, in the section on the military, the coverage is focused on Pakistan, where the military have been a particularly prominent player in politics.[55] Similarly, the section on federalism has a dominant Sri Lankan presence, given the particular live issues that this raises.[56]

Our ambition at this early stage of development of pan-South Asian comparative public law studies was to take a snapshot of and spotlight the live questions in the region in individual jurisdictions: questions that have captured the imagination of scholars working on the different jurisdictions in the region. Bearing in mind this objective for this stage of development in the field, we structured the volume by the institutions and actors covered. The chapters – with a few exceptions – do not attempt intra-region comparisons, but focus on the issues applicable in the individual jurisdiction under study. We covered our reasons for this in section III above. Our volume can therefore be described as 'proto-comparative', in that the chapters have been written and developed in conversation with each other, and seek to pave the way for more genuinely comparative works in the future. The ambition for any future work should be to develop

[54] PD Kenny, *Populism in South Asia* (Cambridge, Cambridge University Press, 2018) 1–8.

[55] Despite best efforts, we were unable to source a chapter on Myanmar for this section – which would have been an interesting comparative counterpoint in the region. This just highlights the need for broader capacity building within academia.

[56] The discourse on federalism in regional studies has focused on India: see, eg S Krishnaswamy, 'Constitutional Federalism in the Indian Supreme Court' in Tushnet and Khosla (n 6) 355–80. The same volume ventured to also explore Nepal and Sri Lanka: see R Edrisinha, 'Debating Federalism in Sri Lanka and Nepal' in Tushnet and Khosla (n 6) 291–319.

broader comparative studies for each of these and other institutions and constitutional actors, and to have a broad coverage of all of these institutions within different jurisdictions in the region[57] – something akin to the omnibus handbooks that are prominent in scholarship.[58] For the purpose of this project, however, we focus on the issue of decline and resilience by focusing on 'debilitation or elimination of any of the political institutions that sustain an existing democracy' and how that might be reversed.[59]

A. A Word on Resilience

There have been a number of definitional and adjectival terms used to describe the phenomenon of constitutional decay. This includes: 'democracy in retreat';[60] 'democratic recession';[61] 'democratic backsliding';[62] 'constitutional retrogression';[63] 'constitutional failure';[64] and 'constitutional rot'.[65] Conscious of the need for clarity on the paradigm or concepts that are utilised to assess constitutional health, we settled on using 'resilience' as our framing device, as we explain further below.[66] We were intentional in our choice, recognising that the choice of the wrong paradigm or conceptual framework could be counterproductive. For example, the 'backsliding' paradigm can be criticised for reducing instances of decay to movement along a linear spectrum between progress and regression and losing much of the depth of analysis that would otherwise be possible.[67]

So why 'resilience'? Conversations on constitutional health have focused largely on the status of decline: are constitutional democracies around the world experiencing a global crisis or is the apparent weakening of many constitutional democracies simply part of the normal ebb and flow of constitutional democracy that has been ongoing since the rise of constitutional democracy after WWII?[68] There are many who hold this view in the South Asian context, observing that while the success of constitutional democracies has been mixed with significant challenges, systems have managed to

[57] For example, the courts in Pakistan are clearly another site of contestation of constitutional power and the volume does not have this coverage. See instead Y Kureshi, *Seeking Supremacy: The Pursuit of Judicial Power in Pakistan* (Cambridge, Cambridge University Press, 2022); M Cheema, *Courting Constitutionalism: The Politics of Public Law and Judicial Review in Pakistan* (Cambridge, Cambridge University Press, 2022).

[58] See the growth in regional, jurisdictionally focused handbooks in, for example, the handbook series by Oxford University Press (eg *The Oxford Handbook of the Canadian Constitution*, *The Oxford Handbook of Caribbean Constitutions*, *The Oxford Handbook of Constitutional Law in Latin America*).

[59] N Bermeo, 'On Democratic Backsliding' (2016) 27 *Journal Democracy* 5.

[60] J Kurlantzick, *Democracy in Retreat: The Revolt of the Middle Class and the Worldwide Decline of Representative Government* (New Haven, Yale University Press, 2014).

[61] Diamond (n 1) 141.

[62] Bermeo (n 59).

[63] Huq and Ginsburg, 'How to Lose' (n 52) 83.

[64] SA Barber, *Constitutional Failure* (Lawrence, University Press of Kansas, 2014); E Kennedy, *Constitutional Failure: Carl Schmitt in Weimar* (Durham, NC, Duke University Press, 2004).

[65] JM Balkin, 'Constitutional Crisis and Constitutional Riot' in Graber et al (n 1).

[66] L Cianetti and S Hanley, 'The End of the Backsliding Paradigm' (2021) 32(1) *Journal of Democracy* 66.

[67] I Ding and D Slater, 'Democratic Decoupling' [2020] *Democratization* 1; TG Daly, 'Understanding Multi-directional Democratic Decay: Lessons from the Rise of Bolsonaro in Brazil' (2020) 14 *Law & Ethics of Human Rights* 199.

[68] See, eg Graber et al (n 1).

achieve democratic consolidation in the midst of these challenging circumstances.[69] Namely, while being burdened with low literacy, extraordinary ethnolinguistic diversity, highly uneven levels of economic development, widespread poverty and serious external threats to their territorial integrity, constitutional democracies in South Asia have made significant ground in consolidating their systems of government.[70] In this volume, we have sought to extract and isolate those areas of constitutional democracy that are likely to be the source of consolidation and revival.[71]

As Arban recognises in her contribution to this volume, there can be at least three connotations of resilience: (i) resilience as a synonym for elasticity or flexibility, referring to the capacity to adapt and respond to changing circumstances; (ii) resilience as the capacity to recover from difficult circumstances; and (iii) resilience as a coping mechanism under taxing conditions. However, as the project evolved, we saw how there was a need to add an additional axis or category – examples of 'negative resilience', being the endurance and survival of institutions, actors and practices that exert a huge braking force on the healthy evolution of constitutional democracy. As the discussion of the structure of the volume demonstrates, 'resilience' can be good or bad.[72] Some institutions – for example, the executive presidency in Sri Lanka and the bureaucracy in Afghanistan – persist to the detriment of constitutional democracy.

B. Structure of the Volume

The volume looks at six different institutions and actors across the region. We set out here our approach to the structuring of this volume, describing the seven substantive sections that comprise it.

(i) Constitutional Design

The first substantive part, on 'constitutional design', examines the ways in which the design of a constitutional democracy can either hinder or encourage the health of that system. The chapter by Shah and Gomez focuses on the damaging endurance and resilience of the executive presidency – an institution and office that has undermined the realisation of constitutional democracy in Sri Lanka. Shah and Gomez conclude that the resilience of the presidency is attributable to the presence of a political culture that is sympathetic to autocratic or authoritarian norms and that does not place an emphasis on restraint on such power. Therefore, even in the face of changes in the dynastic hold

[69] See S Ganguly, 'India's Unlikely Democracy: Six Decades of Independence' (2007) 18(2) *Journal of Democracy* 30, 31.

[70] For a more charged critique of the 'success' of democracy in India, see A Jalal, *Democracy and Authoritarianism in South Asia: A Historical and Comparative Perspective* (Cambridge, Cambridge University Press, 1995).

[71] For similar endeavours, see S Gardbaum, 'The Counter-Playbook: Resisting the Populist Assault on Separation of Powers' (2020) 59(1) *Columbia Journal of Transnational Law* 1–64.

[72] As some of the chapters in this volume recognise: see, eg ch 2, by D Shah and M Gomez; and ch 9, by E Afsah.

on the office of the executive presidency with the removal of the Rajapaksa family and constitutional amendments that seek to counteract the autocratic hold that the office has on the practice of constitutional democracy in Sri Lanka (including the re-emergence of a fourth branch institution in the form of the Constitutional Council), the prevailing political culture inhibits the ability of such amendments to bear the necessary fruit. The chapter looks at how constitutional amendments and the judiciary have, on occasion, pushed back against the power of the prevailing political culture and what this indicates about the interaction between constitutional law and politics in countries undergoing democratic transitions, and the extent to which the former can truly exert some limit on the, in this case, detrimental impact of the latter.

The second chapter in this part – on Bhutan – looks at the same question of constitutional design and transition, and the relevance of the broader culture in which the constitution is embedded. However, it does so in the context of a much newer constitutional democracy. This is not the only point of departure between the two chapters in this part. The Bhutanese Constitution was adopted just 14 years ago – prior to which Bhutan self-identified as an absolute monarchy. Compared to Sri Lanka's executive presidency, which sought to appropriate power, the monarch – who had significant powers – himself initiated the constitutionalisation and democratisation process in Bhutan which would, as a matter of constitutional law and design, divest the monarch's powers. As an interesting counterpoint to the chapter on Sri Lanka, Windischgraetz's chapter, therefore, looks at how the long-standing institution of the monarchy will be crucial to the stability and growth of constitutional democracy in Bhutan – compared to the executive presidency, whose durability is a major hindrance to such democratisation in Sri Lanka. Windischgraetz's chapter indicates how 'newer' aspects of the constitution – which are actually emblematic of constitutional and electoral democracy – will in fact hinder the stability of constitutional governance – in this case, a system of political parties that has no fertile soil in which to plant itself. The institution of a party system in Bhutan risks creating religious and ethnic cleavages which were hitherto managed by the monarchy and other institutions.

What both chapters share is their focus on the durability of institutions, and both demonstrate how the question of durability is either a hinderance or a facilitator of democracy, depending on the broader political culture and climate. In addition, the interaction between law and politics creates paradoxes in both systems on the question of resilience of their constitutional system. In Sri Lanka, the paradox takes the form of 'resilience', which is normally viewed as a positive attribute, of the executive presidency as a major barrier to broader/thicker democratic values. In the Bhutanese context, it is the non-democratic institutions (the monarchy and judiciary) that are more likely sources of durability for constitutional democracy than democratic features, like political parties.[73] The executive presidency in the Sri Lankan context – though an elected office – is bad news, as it reflects a broader political culture that favours autocratic rule

[73] See, eg T Khaitan, 'Political Parties in Constitutional Theory' (2020) 73 *Current Legal Problems* 89; KL Scheppele, 'The Party's Over' in M Graber, S Levinson and MV Tushnet (eds), *Constitutional Democracy in Crisis?* (Oxford, Oxford University Press, 2018) 513; A Sethia, 'Where's the Party?: Towards a Constitutional Biography of Political Parties' (2019) 3 *Indian Law Review* 1.

and the absence of political checks and balances. By contrast, the monarchy reflects a political culture of benign self-disempowerment. Therefore, its durability will be critical to the safe transition of Bhutan's constitutional democracy. Both chapters are important case studies on the issue of constitutional design versus constitutional practice – and the influence of political culture on the operation of both.

(ii) Federalism

Part 3 tackles a major issue of design facing a large part of the region – the question of federalism. While we amalgamate South Asia into a unitary region, it is marked out by the diverse ethnic–language–religious communities that exist across and within jurisdictions. This ethnic diversity is a major driver for the conversations on the forms of federalism that exist in the region. The jurisdictional focus of the part is Sri Lanka and Nepal as systems that have yet to design and implement federal features. Nadarajalingam and Nwokora, taking the seeming impossibility of federalism in Sri Lanka as their starting point, propose a way forward. Their proposal is modest on two accounts. First, it is a 'functional' federalism that is not reflected in the formal amendment or reordering of extant constitutional arrangements but, rather, is an organic arrangement on the ground reflected in an institutional set-up. Their motivation for a de jure unitary state and a de facto or functional federal state is rooted in the complexity of the identity claims of the different ethnic groups and, in particular, the Sinhala Buddhist majority to whom the lands of Sri Lanka wholly and indivisibly belong. This 'political fact' complicates the federalism project; moving to a full-fledged federal state would not only be unlikely, but also susceptible to creating broader political instability, at the risk of the broader constitutional consolidation process. Nadarajalingam and Nwokora propose that this political fact creates a path dependency that determines the journey of federalism in Sri Lanka. Secondly, related to the first and pending broader change to the political cultural change on the position and identity of the Sinhala Buddhist majority, they propose a gradual and incremental institutional change that creates a path dependency resulting in a functional federalism. On the latter, they propose, in particular, that powerful political actors located with Sri Lanka's bureaucracy can introduce federal practices in Sri Lanka. Their chapter's engagement with the logistics of realising normative change makes it a rare, and valuable, contribution to comparative constitutional studies more generally.

Arban's chapter also focuses on the question of federal design: proposing an alternative model for the practice of federalism in Sri Lanka, again in recognition of the complexities that prevent the formation of a 'typical' federal state that devolves and disperses fiscal and governance powers. Because the current political climate does not favour fully fledged federalism, Arban recommends a strengthening of the devolution of powers through solidarity-based mechanisms as an interim and more neutral compromise. Conceptualising 'solidarity' as the idea of loyalty and fraternity between different units in the quasi-federal structure, Arban contends that this is less ideologically and politically divisive than federalism, but can have a role in integrating diversity and social cohesion in a deeply divided social and political context. Arban, in contradistinction to Nadarajalingam and Nwokora, envisages the need for a constitutional amendment to foster the feeling of federal loyalty between central and provincial councils, including provisions that explicate the need for support and cooperation, mutual consideration and restraint. What is common to both chapters is their sense of the impossibility of a 'typical' constitutional federation and the need to moderate the federal aspirations in Sri Lanka.

The climate for federation is, to state the obvious, different in Nepal, which has been a de jure federal democratic republic since 2008. The chapter by Dhungana and Payne on Nepal therefore focuses on the implementation of the federal structure and, in particular, the fate of human rights protection – the latter being a major focus of the latest and major constitutionalisation exercise in 2015, with the introduction of a whole slate of civil, political, economic, social and cultural rights into the Constitution. As observed in their chapter, despite the explicit constitutional commitment to human rights and the establishment of the National Human Rights Commission in Nepal, the local units of the federation are seen to have different or conflicting priorities and capacities. Accordingly, as the federation evolves and consolidates, the protection of human rights at the provincial level will be a key item for scrutiny.

The chapters in this part are an interesting analysis of either side of a federal partnership: the chapters on Sri Lanka look at the hold that the centre/majority has on the possibility of federal governance of a polity, whereas the chapter on Nepal focuses on the role of the provinces/local government in achieving a major federal objective (the protection of human rights).

(iii) The Executive

From this analysis of questions of constitutional design in Parts 2 and 3, the volume turns to look at the different institutions that make-up constitutional democracies in the region in the remaining parts. Part 4 starts with a look at the political executive. In common with much of the literature on constitutional decay, the political executive is considered a major threat to the health of the institutions that make up constitutional democracies.[74] Khaitan's chapter seeks to sophisticate this critique of the political executive, drawing a distinction between the *systemic* and intentional dismantling of executive accountability mechanisms that form the lifeblood of liberal constitutional democratic orders and discrete ad hoc executive actions that we may disagree with ideologically but, nonetheless, do not undermine the democratic order. As Khaitan demonstrates, the Modi government has incrementally, but intentionally, strategically and systematically, undermined three categories of executive accountability mechanisms: vertical (electoral accountability to the people); horizontal (accountability to other state institutions, political opposition, guarantor institutions); and diagonal (accountability to the media, academy and civil society).

While Khaitan's chapter provides a landscaped view of the systemic dismantling of constitutional democracy in India, Damle and Roy zero in on a particular instantiation of this dismantling in their chapter. They focus on executive interference in the management of legislative business in the lower house of Parliament in India. In common with

[74] GJ Postema, 'Constitutional Norms – Erosion, Sabotage and Response' (2022) 35 *Ratio Juris* 99; P Cane, 'Executive Primacy, Populism and Public Law' (2019) 28 *Washington International Law Journal* 527.

other Westminster parliamentary systems, the executive occupies positions of power that have a significant influence on the way in which the agenda for legislative business is settled. In the Indian context, the power of the executive is supposedly mediated by the Business Advisory Committee, which typically has a multi-partisan membership. However, as Damle and Roy demonstrate in their chapter, the Speaker of the lower house of Parliament is elected to the position by a majority of the members of the house, thus inflecting the office of the supposedly neutral Speaker with partisanship on behalf of the ruling party. As Damle and Roy demonstrate, this has influenced the capacity of Parliament to have meaningful and constructive debates on policy matters. Specifically, they focus on the fact that the manner in which the agenda is set and the powers of the Speaker in this regard have compromised the amount of time allocated for debate on major policy matters and also the amount of advance notice given to members of the house of parliamentary business for any particular sitting.

Both Khaitan and Damle and Roy demonstrate through their chapters the infiltration of state institutions by the incumbent party, making the institutions open to manipulation by the executive leads to the fusion of the party and the state: a particularly problematic version of constitutional decay.

Looking at the bureaucracy, Afsah analyses a different form of manipulation – in this case, by the civil service personnel, who have consistently obstructed international state-building efforts in Afghanistan. The desperation to survive any externally imposed reform out of a concern that it would lead to their ousting or reform of the modalities of governance for which they were not skilled has led to the civil service entrenching themselves through rent-seeking efforts. Ultimately, the inability to renovate governance in Afghanistan contributed to the overall state failure and takeover by the Taliban insurgency. In contrast, in other constitutional democracies, the survival of the civil service and the continuity of a modicum of functionality in the governance of a polity has been a sign of stability amidst transition.[75] However, the stickiness of the civil service has been obstructive to democratisation in the Afghan context.

(iv) The Judiciary

This theme of the executive's capture of major state institutions continues in Part 5, which focuses on the judiciary as one such captured institution. The two chapters in the part present different visions of what judicial capture or compromise might look like. Nazeer's chapter on the Maldives looks at compromises in the process of appointing and removing judges, whereas Bhatia's chapter on India looks at the judiciary's de facto empowerment of the executive through its mismanagement in scheduling the hearing of constitutional cases and flawed decision-making. Nazeer's chapter on the Maldives provides a layered account of the many ways in which the judiciary can be captured by the political branches and can then become a tool for inter-branch vying for power and control over the constitutional system. In common with other systems, the Judicial Service Commission (JSC) in the Maldives, which is responsible for the appointment

[75] L Sossin, 'Speaking Truth to Power? The Search for Bureaucratic Independence in Canada' (2005) 55 *University of Toronto Law Journal* 1–59.

of judges, acts in a partisan manner; it is open to control by either Parliament or the President, depending on how the majority is formed in Parliament. It has, therefore, been a site for inter-branch (and, therefore, partisan) politics and conflict. Presidential and/or parliamentary control of the JSC becomes a high stakes political issue, with both branches seeking to control the judiciary and mobilise its appointees to emasculate the other branch under divided government when the two branches are controlled by different parties. Nazeer's chapter provides multiple examples of this inter-branch manipulation of the JSC and judicial appointees in constitutional cases.

In the context of constitutional disputes relating to the division of powers between the federal government and state-based government, Bhatia sets up three devices by which the courts have inadvertently (or perhaps consciously) empowered the executive. First, judicial evasion – forestalling the hearing of crucial constitutional disputes, which leads to the maintenance of a constitutionally questionable status quo by the incumbent federal government. Secondly, judicial vagueness – when it does rule, the Supreme Court's judgment is couched in vague language that, in effect, imposes no real restraint or limit on the incumbent federal government. Finally, judicial revisionism – which involves the Supreme Court ignoring, reinterpreting or misinterpreting its own precedent.

Both chapters elaborate on our understanding of the modalities by which executive capture and empowerment of the judiciary can take place and the nefarious real impact this has on constitutional politics and the broader decay of constitutional democracy within a polity.

(v) Fourth Branch or Guarantor Institutions

Given the concerns that exist with respect to courts and their incapacity to protect against constitutional erosion, the literature has started to relocate the trusteeship of this endeavour. Part 6 of the volume focuses on the supposedly 'fourth branch' of government – a group of institutions that have captured academic attention as an important counterfoil to the forces that have been responsible for constitutional erosion.[76] Discussions of fourth branch (or guarantor) institutions and the decline of constitutional democracies tend to coalesce around the view that healthy and independent fourth branch institutions are a necessary indicator of the degree of resilience exhibited by a constitutional order.[77] Samararatne's chapter sets the tone for the section, exploring the mixed successes of building a fourth branch – or guarantor branch – in Sri Lanka. Samararatne argues that – pending broader constitutional reform on major issues like the executive presidency and federalism – constitutional resilience and revival will take the form of more modest constitutional reform through the establishment and consolidation of the guarantor branch in Sri Lanka. However, barriers to this reform exist in the form of

[76] See B Ackerman, 'The New Separation of Powers' (2000) 113 *Harvard Law Review* 633; M Tushnet, *The New Fourth Branch* (Cambridge, Cambridge University Press, 2021); T Khaitan, 'Guarantor Institutions' (2022) 16(S1) *Asian Journal of Comparative Law* S40; T Khaitan, 'Guarantor (or "Fourth Branch") Institutions' in J King and R Bellamy (eds), *Cambridge Handbook of Constitutional Theory* (Cambridge, Cambridge University Press, forthcoming).

[77] See, eg Bermeo (n 5); Huq and Ginsburg, 'How to Lose' (n 52); Huq and Ginsburg, *How to Save* (n 52).

obstacles from other constitutional actors, including hostile political parties, an agnostic judiciary and a self-sabotaging guarantor branch that has sometimes acted without the requisite transparency to acquire political and constitutional credibility. In such a situation, the guarantor branch is left to consolidate and evolve by 'stealth'. This involves co-opting support from civil society when the branch comes under threat, mobilising public opinion in their favour and making political action against the branch difficult. The political branch is forced to comply with public opinion in order to galvanise support at elections. Samararatne's chapter also shows that the characterisation of the guarantor branch as an attempt to depoliticise constitutionalism may be misplaced:[78] with a clearly political appointment system and continuing political oversight, it seems that what countries like Sri Lanka are attempting is a de-*partisanisation* of certain constitutional actors, rather than their depoliticisation. In other words, the effort is to secure a cross-partisan political supervision of these institutions, quite distinct from the design of the higher judiciary.

The existential question about guarantor institutions is also taken up by Pal in looking at electoral commissions across South Asia. The next three chapters in this part focus on electoral commissions in the region. This focus is unsurprising, given their location at the coalface of protecting the function and health of elections – the basic process by which democratic turnover is possible. As Ackerman writes, the 'democracy branch', in the form of electoral commissions, have become major constitutional actors responsible for ensuring the depolicitisation of the process by which elections are conducted.[79] Pal's chapter sets the stage for the discussion on this institution, focusing on the more existential question regarding electoral commissions: is there indeed a departure from the traditional tripartite conception of the separation of powers in South Asia and are electoral commissions part of this fourth branch? Answering this in the affirmative, Pal argues that there is a distinct South Asian model of election commissions. The South Asian model of election commissions share a number of characteristics, including, for example: the fact that they are creatures of constitutional design and not just ordinary statute – but with variance in the precise mode by which they are constituted and their relationship with other branches within the constitutional separation of powers framework; they tend to be composed of technocrats/experts rather than civil servants or members of political parties; and they are bolstered – in theory, at least – by the imposition of a constitutional duty on other branches of government to assist the electoral commission in the discharge of its functions. As the scholarship on guarantor institutions evolves, it will have to contend with the issue of what makes a 'branch' of a state a 'branch', and when – if ever – these institutions qualify as such.

Pal's chapter then takes a critical turn from these observations in conversation with the chapters by Faruque and Bhat. While Pal and Faruque look at the issue of political capture of the electoral commission in India and Bangladesh, respectively, Bhat takes on the question of how to check the checker, ie how to ensure the legal accountability of the electoral commission. The latter question becomes crucial when the commission is at risk of political capture: it is precisely in such a situation where its powers

[78] See, eg ch 20 in this volume, by P Dann.

[79] B Ackerman, 'The New Separation of Powers' (2000) 113 *Harvard Law Review* 633.

are being exercised instrumentally for the consolidation of a particular party or bloc's powers that we need to be able to check the checker. The political climate and context of India – reinforced in Pal's analysis – informs the analysis by Bhat. Bhat focuses on the role of the Supreme Court in holding the electoral commission to account.

(vi) The Military

The theme of dysfunctional institutions that asphyxiate constitutional democracy continues in Part 7. This part looks at an institution that is under-discussed in comparative constitutional studies that do not sufficiently represent regions like South Asia: the military. Both chapters in this part are focused on Pakistan, given the prominence of the military in the country's politics: the military are seen as instrumental to the survival of any elected government, they control the country's defence budget and are also seen as the face of foreign relations in Pakistan. This focus on Pakistan is not an indication that the military or paramilitary forces are not critical elsewhere in the region; indeed, the absence of a chapter on Myanmar (which the editors were unable to source for the volume) is an obvious omission from this part. What the two chapters on Pakistan do provide is insight into how polarising academic studies on the role of the military are: the chapters present drastically different views on the latter and the implications for Pakistan's transition to a functioning constitutional democracy.

Siddiqi argues – contrary to mainstream analysis – that the role of the military has been inflated and does not adequately account for the real challenge posed by civilian political elites. Siddiqi focuses less on the outcome of elections and military coups in the country and more on what he terms the 'dynamics of contestation' between civilian political parties and the military. Siddiqi pushes back against the familiar narrative of Pakistan's constitutional democracy as one characterised by the military's supremacy, a weak electoral process, dynastic politics, and inefficient and corrupt governance. Instead, the chapter highlights the hope presented by more recent civilian political elites. The stepping up of these elites has started to force the military to understand that they can no longer rely on the might of a coup to attain political power but need to participate in the political process. The military, it is argued, are now sensitive to the need to appeal to the public and improve the legitimacy deficit they suffer. The latter in itself is problematic – how far should the military participate in democratically elected government (especially in a situation where it has such significant control over defence and security and also foreign relations)?

The chapter by Salman and Raza cannot take a more different view, observing at the outset that one of the factors standing in the way of constitutional and democratic consolidation in Pakistan is the country's weak system of party politics, which enables the powerful military establishment to control politics. The chapter treats political parties as the basic institutions of democracy. Therefore, Salman and Raza focus on parties as their unit of analysis to comment on the health of Pakistan's democracy. They argue that the weak institutionalisation and rootedness of Pakistan's political parties makes them seek out the beneficence of tutelary institutions, such as the military, in times of crisis. This dependence on the goodwill of the military casts a shadow on the incumbents, who accumulate much reputational damage by opponents while they are in power, but it also creates uncertainty about the survival of their terms, feeding into the cycle of political instability in Pakistan. While, ideally, this should prompt transformations in the behaviour of parties, Salman and Raza demonstrate, through an analysis of recent events, that the political parties are more willing to work alongside the military as a political partner than to address deficiencies of their structures to consolidate democracy. However, what the chapters are in agreement on is that the focus on the military is disproportionate to the range of issues that impact constitutional consolidation: hence, Siddiqi focuses on the system of political parties as the source of hope and Salman and Raza focus on the source of the problems.

(vii) The People

The volume thus far has focused on normative and functional institutions – the constitution, judiciary, fourth branch institutions, the political executive and the federal government. The final part of the volume looks at a major human actor – the people. As a number of chapters in the earlier parts indicate, vertical accountability between the elected government and the people is a key driver for constitutional health and resilience. Awareness of public sentiment and the possibility of changing fortunes in elections has been a potential source of constitutional rejuvenation. The two chapters in this part focus on the different roles that people play as constitutional actors, beyond their role as a voter.

Siddiqi astutely observes in his chapter that the institutional focus of constitutional studies (on the major institutional actors) can project constitutional performance in a particularly negative light, given the dysfunction that exists within the institutions (as many of the earlier chapters suggest). Siddiqi suggests that ignoring 'ordinary citizens' and their unique mode of interpreting and using constitutional law can provide an alternative, equally important narrative of constitutional performance. The chapter focuses, in particular, on the role of constitutional law as a discursive tool for achieving social justice by marginalised communities – in the case of Siddiqi's chapter, the Dalit community in India. Using field research in Gujarat, Siddiqi demonstrates the Indian Constitution's role as an authoritative text on the question of equality: this has an empowering effect, giving the marginalised Dalit community a sense of political agency in the social and economic sphere.

The role that the Constitution plays in the life of citizens is also the focus of Sindhu and Narayan's chapter. While Siddiqi looks at the role of the Constitution in empowering citizens, Sindhu and Narayan look at people as empowered to protect and guard the Constitution and constitutionalism. Using the frame of 'constitutional patriotism', they propose seeing citizens not just as litigants and voters, but as advocates for constitutionalism. Using the examples of recent popular movements that pushed back against the rise of Hindu nationalism in India, they sought to hold institutions accountable to constitutional values as examples of such patriotism.

V. Furthering the Field of Study

The aim of this chapter has been to locate our volume in the literature. In this project, we have sought to break down pathologies in comparative constitutional studies generally and in existing South Asian studies in particular. We do this by broadening the jurisdictional coverage from the region. This is a modest first step. As we have explained in section III, most of the chapters in this volume do not attempt comparison, but are proto-comparative. We set out here (with a few exceptions) a group of single-jurisdiction studies on a range of institutions, developed in conversation with other chapters of the volume covering the region. It is an essential first step towards making comparison possible. What should be next for studies in the region? We envisage the need for more thematic or topical single-jurisdiction studies before we can extrapolate from that a broader comparative endeavour that attempts two things: first, being seriously comparative within the region; and secondly, exploring the possibilities that there is something 'South Asian' that can be unearthed. On the latter, we maintain an agnosticism. It is only after we have done sufficient concept-building and thick description in thematic single-jurisdictional studies that can we explore the possibilities that exist for understanding 'South Asian' constitutional patterns.

PART II

Constitutional Design

2

Institutional Resilience and Political Transitions in Sri Lanka and Beyond

DIAN AH SHAH AND MARIO GOMEZ[1]

I. Introduction

Since the fall of President Mahinda Rajapaksa in the January 2015 presidential elections, Sri Lanka's experience with political and constitutional change has garnered scholarly attention.[2] Rajapaksa's defeat – unexpected as it may have been – sparked interest and hopes for building a constitutional democracy in the country, after enduring a decade of seemingly durable autocratic rule. Although the country's formal political and institutional structures reflected the trappings of a constitutional democracy – for instance, elections are regularly held, and the Constitution contains a bill of rights and diffuses power between the legislature, the executive and the judiciary – the powerful executive presidency left power virtually concentrated in the hands of Rajapaksa. As Ginsburg and Huq argue, Sri Lanka has gradually reverted to authoritarianism since 1981 – a reversion marked by the existence of tainted elections, political violence and repressive constitutional amendments.[3] In 2010, Rajapaksa augmented his powers by engineering the Eighteenth Amendment, leaving commentators concerned that enough power had been amassed to ensure the endurance and resilience of the Rajapaksa regime, even against popular will.[4] The Amendment was significant in two main respects.

[1] We would like to thank the co-editors of the volume (T Khaitan, D Samararatne and S Jhaveri) for their insights and guidance on an earlier draft of this chapter. We are also grateful for the institutional support provided by the Centre for Asian Legal Studies (CALS) at the National University of Singapore, and the constructive comments from William Partlett, Arun Thiruvengadam and participants of the 'Constitutional Resilience in South Asia Workshop' at the University of Melbourne in December 2019. This chapter was first written in 2019 based on the events that prevailed in 2015–19. It was subsequently revised in 2020, but due to the rapidly evolving situation in Sri Lanka and limitations in this volume as a whole, we do not attempt to comprehensively deal with the slew of events after the Rajapaksa family returned to power in 2019 or the events leading up to the resignation of President Gotabaya Rajapaksa in July 2022.

[2] See, eg T Ginsburg and A Huq, 'How to Lose Your Constitutional Democracy' (2018) 65 *UCLA Law Review* 78; N DeVotta, 'A Win for Democracy in Sri Lanka' (2016) 27(1) *Journal of Democracy* 152; G Gunatilleke, 'The Constitutional Practice of Ethno-religious Violence in Sri Lanka' (2018) 13 *Asian Journal of Comparative Law* 359; A Welikala, 'Sri Lanka's Long Constitutional Moment' (2015) 104 *The Round Table* 551.

[3] Ginsburg and Huq (n 2) 104.

[4] N DeVotta, 'Sri Lanka: From Turmoil to Dynasty' (2011) 22(2) *Journal of Democracy* 130.

First, it removed the two-term limit on the presidential office, which paved the way for Rajapaksa to create a political dynasty by allowing him to run for office for a third term. Second, it abolished the Constitutional Council, which had introduced a layer of institutional check against the president's discretionary powers to appoint members of the judiciary and key independent commissions.[5]

These structural changes, enacted under the pretext of spurring development in post-war Sri Lanka,[6] became the source of abuse of powers, declining rule of law and democratic backsliding in the country. In this regard, Sri Lanka appeared to be re-living its past experience: during the administration of President JR Jayewardene (1978–89), similar justifications were made for instituting a strong executive presidency.[7] Yet, the development that was said to justify the need for a strong executive was not forthcoming; instead, economic development and redistribution of wealth remained problematic as the Rajapaksa family controlled over 70 per cent of the economy.[8] In addition, the country experienced grave human rights violations; independent commissions that are supposed to provide mechanisms for accountability were severely crippled; and the judiciary became susceptible to executive interference. The impeachment of Chief Justice Shirani Bandaranayake in 2013 was one of the key highlights of the decay in Sri Lanka's political and constitutional infrastructure.

Despite the obvious flaws and shortcomings, this chapter confronts the following overarching question: how resilient are these institutional structures in Sri Lanka? More specifically, how resilient are such institutions in the face of political transitions and constitutional change? What we mean by 'resilience' in the context of this chapter is the ability of institutions to react against and survive challenges against them. In answering these questions, we will consider the developments in Sri Lanka's constitutional order following the political transition in 2015 and illustrate the paradox of institutional resilience in the country. This chapter stresses the significance of political culture and changing political dynamics in understanding institutional resilience (for better or for worse). In discussing 'political culture', what we mean are the beliefs, expectations and attitudes towards the political system and how they are practised by political actors, citizens and state officials alike.[9]

To some extent, the focus on political culture and dynamics speaks to a line of scholarship that analyses the relationship between the operation and stability of political systems with political culture,[10] and when political actors internalise and abide by

[5] The commissions include the Public Service Commission, the Election Commission, the National Police Commission, and the Human Rights Commission.

[6] See R Venugopal, 'Democracy, Development and the Executive Presidency in Sri Lanka' (2015) 36 *Third World Quarterly* 670; P Saravannamuttu, 'The 18th Amendment: Political Culture and Consequences' in R Edrisinha and A Jayakody (eds), *The Eighteenth Amendment to the Constitution: Substance and Process* (Centre for Policy Alternatives, 2011) 19, www.cpalanka.org/wp-content/uploads/2015/01/The-Eighteenth-Amendment-to-the-Constitution-Substance-and-Process.pdf.

[7] Edrisinha and Jayakody (n 6) 9. See also AJ Wilson, *The Gaullist System in Asia: The Constitution of Sri Lanka* (London, Macmillan, 1978).

[8] 'A War Strange as Fiction' *The Economist* (7 June 2007).

[9] See generally G Almond and S Verba, *The Civic Culture: Political Attitudes and Democracy in Five Nations* (Princeton, Princeton University Press, 1963).

[10] See, eg SM Lipset, 'Presidents vs Parliaments: The Centrality of Political Culture' (1990) 1(4) *Journal of Democracy* 80.

the norms and rules that guide their office. For example, Schauer suggests that judges apply rules that they have internalised.[11] Aziz Huq also posits that both law and politics work as 'interlocking complements' in constraining executive exercises of power.[12] However, in our account of Sri Lanka (and in our reference to similar case studies in Southeast Asia), we show that politics not only constrains executive discretion; rather, it also empowers or provides opportunities for political actors to act in certain ways. More specifically, the presence of a political culture that is sympathetic to or embraces autocratic or authoritarian norms and resists limits on power may explain the resilience of a powerful executive presidency in Sri Lanka.

Thus, even as a new constitutional commitment to curtail executive authority (in the form of the Nineteenth Amendment, as we will discuss below) was instituted, we illustrate that 'old habits' – shaped by the prevailing political culture – die hard, so-to-speak. Indeed, these habits triggered challenges against the Nineteenth Amendment during the 2018 constitutional crisis and subsequently through the recent Twentieth Amendment, which reversed the limits imposed by the Nineteenth Amendment. The political culture account we pursue is, of course, not the only explanation for institutional resilience in Sri Lanka. Legal rules and legal institutions – such as the judiciary – are not always feeble forces in delineating executive power and attempts to undermine the Constitution. This points towards another facet of resilience – the resilience of law.[13] In short, while we emphasise – in the limited domain that this chapter allows – the significance of political culture, we do not discount the role of law and we leave this to be examined in greater detail in subsequent research.

In thinking about institutional resilience in Sri Lanka, we are presented with a paradox. On the one hand, the powerful executive presidency has displayed a continuing measure of resilience and durability through different phases of political transitions. From its inception under President JR Jayewardene in 1978 to its re-emergence under both Rajapaksa presidencies in 2005 and 2019, the hyper-presidential system – a system where the formal trappings of separation of powers are maintained, but with limited effective checks on presidential power[14] – has managed to resist reforms that sought to improve horizontal accountability mechanisms. For example, even as the Nineteenth Amendment sought, among others, to reduce the presidential term, (re)impose term limits and (re)establish the Constitutional Council, the impulses to unravel those commitments and return the powers of the president illustrate a degree of 'resilience' in the institution.

On the other hand, there is another story of resilience – short-lived though it may be – illustrated through the events in 2018, when President Sirisena attempted to remove the Prime Minister and prorogue and dissolve Parliament. We will describe

[11] F Schauer, 'Judicial Self-understanding and the Internalization of Constitutional Rules' (1990) 61 *University of Colorado Law Review* 749.

[12] AZ Huq, 'Binding the Executive (by Law or by Politics)' (2012) 79 *University of Chicago Law Review* 777, 783.

[13] ibid 789.

[14] S Rose-Ackerman et al, 'Hyper-Presidentialism: Separation of Powers without Checks and Balances in Argentina and the Philippines' (2011) 29 *Berkeley Journal of International Law* 246, 247; E Bulmer, 'Presidential Legislative Powers' (2017) 15 *International IDEA Constitution-Building Primer* 3.

in greater detail below how this constitutional crisis unfolded and how it was subsequently resolved. However, at this point, suffice it to say that the Supreme Court stepped in to nullify the President's appointment of Mahinda Rajapaksa as Prime Minister and the dissolution of Parliament. This turn of events demonstrates the judiciary's resilience in the face of changing political dynamics, and this is especially significant considering the history of executive attacks on judicial independence in Sri Lanka.[15] In addition, we argue that the Supreme Court's determination in these two cases and the subsequent adherence to the decisions by the relevant political actors illustrate some measure of 'resilience' in the constitutional commitments embedded in the Nineteenth Amendment.

At this juncture, it is worth noting that Sri Lanka has not been alone in navigating questions around institutional resilience, political culture and changing political dynamics. In fact, the Sri Lankan story is comparable to the experiences of other countries in the region that have undergone (or are undergoing) political transitions that carried with them aspirations for a stronger constitutional democracy. For example, the fall of Indonesia's second president, Suharto, in 1998 was unanticipated and, as in Sri Lanka, the autocratic and personalistic (in the sense that the ruler maintained an extensive patron–client network as the basis of his political support)[16] New Order regime seemed set to remain in power. Although Sri Lanka had a more formidable opposition (unlike Indonesia's weak, divided and virtually incapacitated opposition) and a more established practice of electoral democracy (since independence, Indonesia had only experienced one free national election), it shared with Indonesia the problems of endemic corruption and nepotism, imbalance in political power due to the concentration of authority in the executive, a poorly functioning legal system, gross human rights abuses and ethnic conflict. Some of these conditions also accompanied – and indeed triggered – the unexpected fall of Malaysia's Barisan Nasional (BN) coalition (which had ruled the country since independence), led by former Prime Minister Najib Razak, in May 2018.

In all these instances, political change was accompanied by promises of democratic reforms, and those reforms were – to some extent – fulfilled by legal and constitutional changes to renovate problematic institutions and facilitate political transformation. In Malaysia, for example, the newly elected government's manifesto contained key institutional and political reforms that it sought to achieve within five years. This included the proposal to introduce a two-term limit for the offices of Prime Minister (at federal level) and Chief Minister (at state level), to set up parliamentary select committees for important appointments to independent commissions such as the Elections Commission and the Judicial Appointments Commission, and to enhance the autonomy of Parliament in the law-making process. Sri Lanka, like Indonesia (through its four-year constitutional reforms exercise), did not disappoint in this respect. The Nineteenth Amendment sought to remedy the problems with governance and the balance of power within government. The Sri Lankan government's 100-day programme of reforms spoke to the

[15] M Gomez, 'The Courts Respond to Executive Tyranny in Sri Lanka' (*International Journal of Constitutional Law Blog*, 24 January 2019) www.iconnectblog.com/2019/01/the-courts-respond-to-executive-tyranny-in-sri-lanka.

[16] DL Horowitz, *Constitutional Change and Democracy in Indonesia* (Cambridge, Cambridge University Press, 2012) 8.

key problems underpinning the Rajapaksa presidency. By raising these additional case studies, we seek to demonstrate similar dynamics in the relationship between institutional resilience and political culture and in the paradoxes of institutional resilience. To put it in more concrete terms, we show that in Sri Lanka and in other Asian countries that have undergone political change within the past two decades, reforms, renovation and resilience are shaped by the political culture and dynamics. Therefore, at a broader level, our analysis in this chapter attempts to shed light on the interaction between constitutional law and politics in countries undergoing democratic transitions.

This chapter is organised into three main parts. In section I, we explain the key legal and constitutional reforms since the political change in Sri Lanka in January 2015. This includes the passing of the Nineteenth Amendment and the Right to Information Act, as well as the re-emergence of the Constitutional Council. These reforms reflected a commitment to constitutional democracy, with the hope that they would remedy the institutional decay from a long period of unaccountable executive power and improve transparency and fundamental rights protection. Section II focuses on institutional resilience. Here, we evaluate the evolution and implications of the structural reforms by highlighting key events that have tested the durability of the new (and old) legal and political structures. In particular, we will highlight the role of the judiciary in pushing back against various attempts to defy the Nineteenth Amendment in Sri Lanka. By studying these events in Sri Lanka and highlighting similar issues elsewhere, we highlight the paradox of resilience that we have alluded to above. In section III, we then interrogate the political factors and conditions shaping the challenges against, and resilience of, constitutional institutions in Sri Lanka. As we explore the significance of political culture and dynamics, we draw attention to the salience of ethnicity and religion in Sri Lanka's social and political landscape. Finally, we conclude by considering the presidential elections in November 2019, which saw the re-emergence of the Rajapaksa family in the government after the election of President Gotabaya Rajapaksa and the appointment of Mahinda Rajapaksa as Prime Minister, and the recently enacted Twentieth Amendment. Given these developments, we suggest that understanding the influence of political culture and dynamics in assessing institutional resilience becomes all the more necessary, especially in countries undergoing political transitions.

II. Political Change and Institutional Reforms

A. Initial Conditions: Contextualising Reforms and Resilience

The 2015 political change in Sri Lanka marked the beginning of efforts to build a constitutional democracy. The change was highly unlikely to begin with, set as it was within a legal and political system that facilitated and perpetuated abuses of power, government impunity and autocratic rule. Several other, wider contextual factors made the change seem even more unlikely. First, Sri Lanka was in the aftermath of a near-three-decade civil war, which ended in 2009. Second, President Mahinda Rajapaksa took enormous credit for the victory against the LTTE (Liberation Tigers of Tamil Eelam) and the end of the war, which earned him high levels of popular support. In the January 2010 presidential elections, Rajapaksa defeated General Sarath Fonseka – also a key figure in the war against the LTTE – with an approximately 17 per cent vote margin. Third, riding on the wave of popular support among the Sinhalese (the dominant ethnic group), the Rajapaksa administration concentrated power within and around the presidency and the Rajapaksa family, thus effectively bolstering constitutional autocracy in the country.

The Constitution underwent its 18th amendment shortly after Rajapaksa's victory in 2010. At the heart of the Eighteenth Amendment was the desire to restrict – if not to completely remove – any checks and balances on the executive presidency. And this took place swiftly: at the end of August 2010, the Rajapaksa government announced its proposal to introduce the Eighteenth Amendment; the President and the cabinet of ministers endorsed the proposal as an 'urgent bill' on 30 August, and it was quickly sent to the Supreme Court for review on 31 August. The Supreme Court rejected objections that the bill violated entrenched provisions of the Constitution and required a referendum *in addition* to a two-thirds majority vote in Parliament.[17] A week later, on 8 September, the Parliament passed the Eighteenth Amendment with the requisite two-thirds majority.

Apart from removing the two-term limit on the executive presidency and restoring the President's unfettered power of appointments to key public institutions,[18] the Eighteenth Amendment repealed the Seventeenth Amendment to the Constitution, which had been passed unanimously by Parliament in October 2001. To strengthen checks and balances on executive power, the Seventeenth Amendment had established a Constitutional Council comprising the Prime Minister, the speaker of Parliament, the leader of the opposition and seven unelected members, nominated by the President (one member), by the Prime Minister and the leader of the opposition (five members), and by parties in Parliament not already represented in the Council (one member). The Council's diffused composition (through multi-party representation) was to strengthen its independence, ensuring that it was not dominated by a single political party. The Constitutional Council was responsible for approving or recommending appointments to the independent commissions, such as the Elections Commission, the National Police Commission, the Public Service Commission and an Administrative Appeals Tribunal,[19] as well as the Supreme Court, the Court of Appeal and the Attorney-General. Under the Eighteenth Amendment's scheme, however, a Parliamentary Council set up to replace the Constitutional Council could not bind the President's discretionary powers of appointment. The President 'shall seek' the observations of the Parliamentary Council, but he could make appointments at his sole discretion if the Council failed to provide its observations to the President within a week.[20]

[17] See Arts 120–24 of the Constitution of Sri Lanka (1978). In an opinion communicated to the Speaker of Parliament, the Supreme Court held that the amendments did not require a referendum and could be passed with a two thirds majority.

[18] M Gomez, 'Keeping Rights Alive: Reform and Reconciliation in Post-War Sri Lanka' (2011) 17 *Asian Yearbook of International Law* 117.

[19] Seventeenth Amendment to the Constitution of the Democratic Socialist Republic of Sri Lanka, certified on 3 October 2001.

[20] Unlike the Constitutional Council, which had a larger composition, the Parliamentary Council comprised five members: the Prime Minister, the Speaker of Parliament, the Leader of the Opposition and two Members of Parliament nominated by the Prime Minister and Leader of the Opposition.

To be sure, the seeds for autocracy had been sown long before Rajapaksa ascended to power. In 1972, the country adopted a new constitution which concentrated power in Parliament, but in 1978, the second republican constitution created a Gaullist system which built the centre of power in and around the executive presidency. The 1978 Constitution established a powerful executive presidency with few accountability mechanisms[21] – the President is the Head of State, chief of the executive and government, and Commander-in-Chief of the Armed Forces.[22] This was the most significant change to Sri Lanka's political structure since independence.[23] The Constitution also created a system of direct elections for the presidency, with a fixed term of six years.[24] This eliminated parliamentary accountability mechanisms, as the president's authority is not dependent on parliamentary confidence, nor is he answerable to the Parliament. The President may also declare an emergency and to govern by way of emergency regulations with little judicial oversight.[25] The Constitution also enabled the President to assume any ministerial portfolio, including that of Minister of Finance, and appoint members to the cabinet with no obligation to consult the Prime Minister or the legislature on these appointments.[26] The President possessed immunity from judicial review while in office and held the power to dissolve a democratically elected legislature without giving reasons – there were instances where the legislature was dissolved before its term would normally have ended.[27] A slew of constitutional amendments imbued the executive presidency with more authority and weakened checks and balances against the institution. For instance, apart from the Eighteenth Amendment, the Third Amendment empowered the President to call for an election after four years, at his or her discretion.[28]

As we mentioned at the beginning of this chapter, there was (and perhaps still is) a belief that rapid economic development and social and political stability objectives necessitated a strong executive presidency. However, aside from the paternalistic approach to governance, it is worth noting several dynamics in the creation and functioning of the political institutions in Sri Lanka. First, there are arguments suggesting that these structures were established to facilitate executive convenience[29] or fulfil the political interests of the President. For instance, the Third Amendment is said to have been motivated by the desire to undermine parliamentary processes and to accord

[21] See, generally Wilson (n 7); A Welikala (ed), *Reforming Sri Lankan Presidentialism: Provenance, Problems and Prospects* (Centre for Policy Alternatives, 2015); K Senaratne, 'The Executive and the Constitutional Reforms Process in Sri Lanka' [2019] *The Round Table*, https://doi.org/10.1080/00358533.2019.1688500.

[22] Constitution of the Democratic Socialist Republic of Sri Lanka (31 August 1978, Art 30(1).

[23] Venugopal (n 5) 670.

[24] Constitution, Art 30(2).

[25] See Art 154(J)(2) of the Constitution, according to which a proclamation of emergency by the President under the Public Security Ordinance (PSO) cannot be challenged in a court of law. Emergency Regulations issued under the PSO, however, cannot violate the constitution. See D Udagama, 'An Eager Embrace: Emergency Rule and Authoritarianism in Republican Sri Lanka' in Welikala, *Reforming Sri Lankan Presidentialism* (n 21) 285–332.

[26] See Arts 44, 45 and 46 of the Constitution (prior to the 19th Amendment).

[27] Constitution (prior to the 19th Amendment), Art 70.

[28] Third Amendment to the Constitution (1982).

[29] A Welikala, 'The Rajapaksa Regime and the Constitutionalisation of Populist Authoritarianism in Sri Lanka' (*The Constitution Unit Blog*, 2 February 2015) https://constitution-unit.com/2015/02/02/the-rajapaksa-regime-and-the-constitutionalisation-of-populist-authoritarianism-in-sri-lanka/.

President Jayewardene a tactical advantage to remain in power.[30] Second, motives aside, such structures could also be said to facilitate abuses of power and the culture of impunity amongst political actors. In 2003, for example, the then-President, Chandrika Kumaratunga, took over three important ministries, dissolved the Parliament without providing any reasons nor consulting the Speaker of Parliament, and called for elections in April 2004. The vast powers reposed in the presidency had also enabled the office holder to influence many of the independent institutions that were part of a scheme for promoting balanced constitutional government. For example, soon after the April 2010 parliamentary election, the Attorney-General was brought directly under the purview of the President. There was also a time when the Presidential Secretariat controlled funding allocations for the Human Rights Commission.

Finally, there is the simple fact that even as limitations were introduced on presidential powers, they might not be adhered to or enforced. This was evident in the case of the Constitutional Council and in independent commissions established under the Seventeenth Amendment – their roles had become compromised even before Rajapaksa engineered the Eighteenth Amendment. For instance, when the terms of six Constitutional Council members expired in 2005, parties in Parliament were in a deadlock for two years in deciding new nominees, thereby rendering the Constitutional Council virtually defunct.[31] And when this was resolved in January 2008, President Rajapaksa refused to make the appointments and constitute the Constitutional Council. Instead, he continued to exercise his discretion in appointments to key public positions, including the courts and the independent commissions, in violation of explicit constitutional provisions requiring those appointments to be recommended or approved by the Constitutional Council.[32]

In thinking about institutional resilience, therefore, it is pertinent to bear in mind these broader dynamics, especially in terms of how they might preserve, shape or challenge the status quo (in Sri Lanka's case, a powerful executive presidency and weak institutional checks and balances) and reforms in the future. There has been some evidence of these dynamics in countries like Malaysia and Indonesia too, even though these countries operate under a parliamentary system and presidential system, respectively. For example, in Indonesia, the original 1945 Constitution established at independence government powers broadly divided among the three branches (executive, legislature and the judiciary). However, certain structures in the Constitution facilitated, justified and even preserved, for more than five decades, authoritarian governance and flagrant abuses of power. In particular, the 1945 Constitution accorded the President

[30] WA Wiswa Warnapala, 'Parliamentary Government or One Party Dictatorship? The Case of Sri Lanka' (1982) 38 *India Quarterly* 267, 284; H Ranjith and AGTS Somarathna, 'Sri Lanka's Executive Presidency: A Critical Analysis of Its Powers and Functions Under the Constitutions of 1978 and Subsequent Constitutional Amendments' (2013) 1 *Social Sciences and Humanities Review* 75, 89.

[31] For a more detailed discussion of these developments, see Transparency International, 'The Forgotten Constitutional Council: An Analysis of the Consequences of the Non-Implementation of the 17th Amendment' (28 August 2008) www.tisrilanka.org; C Siriwardhana, 'Public Institutions and De-politicisation: Rise and Fall of the 17th Amendment' in E Nissan (ed), *Sri Lanka: State of Human Rights 2007* (Colombo, Law & Society Trust, 2008) 237–61.

[32] See Transparency International, 'The Forgotten Constitutional Council' (n 31).

(the executive) enormous powers but limited constitutional controls.[33] In addition, the Constitution also appeared to have 'constitutionalised' – in its general elucidation – a kind of political culture that emphasised the 'political goodwill' of the government and political leaders and the (paternalistic) notion of an 'integralistic state'.[34] As we will illustrate later, against these backdrop elements, one of the key challenges in Indonesia's democratic transition following the fall of the Suharto regime was to dismantle these structures and norms of impunity.

B. Reforming Troubled Institutions: Restraints on the Executive Presidency

Set against the backdrop of corruption, nepotism and abuse of power under the Rajapaksa government, the new government led by President Maithripala Sirisena pledged to enhance good governance and the rule of law. This began with reforms to the institution that was at the core of the slew of problems that Sri Lanka had endured: the executive presidency. As DeVotta noted, the system allowed Rajapaksa to arrogate so much power that Sri Lanka rapidly slid into an 'authoritarian morass'.[35] Still, there were deep divisions on what those reforms should look like. In particular, while pro-Rajapaksa loyalists were bent on retaining the hyper-presidential system, there were others who sought to abolish the executive presidency altogether.[36] What emerged, in the end, was a compromise[37] – a middle-ground, centrist solution that retained an executive presidency but with substantially trimmed powers.

Packaged as the Nineteenth Amendment to the Constitution, the key changes to the presidency involved several aspects. The first concerns the terms of office: the Amendment reduced the presidential and parliamentary terms from six to five years; restored the two-term limit on the presidential office; and restricted the eligibility criteria for presidential candidates (namely, that candidates shall not hold dual citizenship and be under 35 years old). The latter was likely introduced to stem the development of the Rajapaksa political dynasty, as Mahinda Rajapaksa's son, Namal, and his brother, Gotabaya, who holds a US dual citizenship, seemed probable alternatives for the presidential office. In addition, one might recall from the preceding discussions that Rajapaksa had abolished the two-term limit in 2010 in order to facilitate his running for a third term in office. Second, the Amendment sought to improve the balance of power

[33] D Indrayana, *Indonesian Constitutional Reform 1999–2002: An Evaluation of Constitution-Making in Transition* (Jakarta, Kompas, 2008) 125.

[34] ibid 131–32. This idea was expounded by the chief architect of the 1945 Constitution, Soepomo, who argued that an integralistic state is one where the government and the governed are one and the same; where there are no conflicts of interest between the two; and where the government is assumed to be good and wise and ever-protective of the people's interests. See also DAH Shah, *Constitutions, Religion, and Politics in Asia: Indonesia, Malaysia, and Sri Lanka* (Cambridge, Cambridge University Press, 2017) 30.

[35] DeVotta, 'A Win for Democracy' (n 2) 163.

[36] ibid 160.

[37] A Welikala, 'Sri Lanka: The Nineteenth Amendment to the Constitution – from Start to Finish' (*Constitutionnet*, 26 May 2015) http://constitutionnet.org/news/sri-lanka-nineteenth-amendment-constitution-start-finish.

between the executive and the legislature, and to limit presidential discretion vis-à-vis the legislature. Under the Amendment, the President could not dissolve Parliament before four and a half years of its term and is required to appoint a Prime Minister who can command the confidence of the majority of the Members of Parliament. The 1978 Constitution originally stated that the Prime Minister may be removed from office 'by writing under the hand of the President'. This, too, was repealed by the Nineteenth Amendment. Instead, the Prime Minister and the cabinet of ministers would cease to hold office by operation of law if Parliament: (i) rejects the Statement of Government Policy; (ii) rejects the Appropriation Bill; or (iii) passes a vote of no confidence in the government.[38] It would thus appear that, once appointed, the Prime Minister may not be removed from office by the President at will.

Finally, aside from addressing executive–legislative dynamics, the Nineteenth Amendment also sought to curtail potential abuses of power, for example, by limiting presidential immunity from suit. More specifically, the President's official acts became subject to the Supreme Court's fundamental rights jurisdiction. Previously, the President possessed blanket immunity: no proceedings could be instituted against the President so long as he or she remained in office. In addition, the Amendment precluded the President from holding cabinet portfolios, and the size of the cabinet was restricted to 30.[39] This sought to remedy the long-standing problems of patronage appointments and vote-bloc clientelism, which have been entrenched in Sri Lankan political culture.[40] Under the Rajapaksa government, these practices were especially obvious: Rajapaksa himself held key ministerial positions, such as the Minister of Law and Order, the Minister of Finance and Planning, and the Minister of Highways, Ports and Shipping, and there were at least 60 cabinet ministers. This practice of rewarding support and allies with ministerial posts not only resulted in a bloated cabinet; it also allowed Rajapaksa extensive control over government decision-making, so much so that most ministers dared not make important decisions on their own accord.[41]

C. Strengthening Institutional Checks and Balances

A crucial checks-and-balances mechanism reintroduced by the Nineteenth Amendment was the Constitutional Council. As we explained earlier, the Constitutional Council was initially established in 2001 by the Kumaratunga government, but it was then rendered defunct, and subsequently abolished, by President Rajapaksa. In the Nineteenth Amendment's original formulation, the Constitutional Council was to have a majority

[38] In addition, the PM and cabinet would cease to hold office by way of death, resignation and ceasing to be an MP altogether. A motion of no-confidence in the government is moved by the Leader of the Opposition and is different from a motion of no-confidence in the Prime Minister, which, in parliamentary practice, is a Private Member's Bill of low priority.

[39] An exception to this limitation on size is where a national government is formed comprising the largest and second largest parties in Parliament. In such circumstances, the cabinet size could be expanded by an Act of Parliament.

[40] Welikala, 'Sri Lanka: The Nineteenth Amendment' (n 37).

[41] DeVotta, 'A Win for Democracy' (n 2) 156.

of non-political persons as its members. This changed during parliamentary debates, and in the end, the Nineteenth Amendment provided that the Council shall comprise 10 members, including three civil society members who are not Members of Parliament, and it shall be chaired by the Speaker of Parliament. In light of past experiences, especially where the President effectively sidestepped and ignored the recommendations of the Constitutional Council, the Nineteenth Amendment conferred significant powers on the Council. Specifically, the Constitutional Council had the authority to recommend the appointment of members of independent commissions to the President.[42] If the President did not act pursuant to its recommendations, the appointments would be effective by operation of law after 14 days. The Constitutional Council was also constitutionally mandated to approve the President's nominees to the higher courts and other key offices such as the Attorney-General, the Inspector-General of Police and the Auditor-General.[43]

Another important milestone in the reforms that took place in 2015 through the Nineteenth Amendment was the constitutionalisation of the right to access information in the Bill of Rights.[44] This was followed by the Right to Information Act, which was passed in 2016 in an attempt to improve government transparency and accountability, as well as address the 'opaque processes of public decision-making'.[45] Aside from buttressing rights guarantees in Sri Lanka, this development is significant in light of the country's legal and political contexts, where the lack of government transparency, the absence of ex-post constitutional review of legislation, patronage politics and the culture of authority prevailed. Over the years, these factors – combined with the emergence of an authoritarian regime – have stunted meaningful participatory democracy and impaired the functioning of democratic institutions in Sri Lanka.

The right to information (RTI) law had actually been in the pipeline for over a decade.[46] Although the new government pledged to implement RTI law within the first 100 days of taking office, the law was only passed in Parliament in August 2016 and it became operational in February 2017.[47] The RTI law establishes a Right to Information Commission to supervise the implementation of the law and hear appeals where requests for disclosure of information are refused by government bodies. The Commission consists of five members, who are appointed by the President on the recommendation of the Constitutional Council. The Bar Association, media groups and civil society are also entitled to nominate one Commissioner each.[48]

In a short span of two years since its inception, the RTI Commission has heard appeals on a broad range of subjects. Among other things, it has ordered the disclosure

[42] These include the National Police Commission, the Elections Commission, the Human Rights Commission, the Public Service Commission and the Judicial Service Commission. Constitution, Art 41B.

[43] Constitution, Art 41C(1).

[44] Constitution, Art 14A.

[45] M Gomez, 'The Right to Information and Transformative Development Outcomes', 12(3) Law and Development Review (2019) 837, 840.

[46] ibid 850–52; M Gomez, 'Lifting the Veil of Secrecy: Right to Information Regimes in Emerging and Existing Democracies' (unpublished paper on file with the author).

[47] Right to Information Act, No 12 of 2016. See also K Pinto-Jayawardena (ed), 'Reflections on Sri Lanka's RTI Act and RTI Regime' (Right to Information Commission of Sri Lanka, 2019) 82, www.rticommission.lk/web/images/pdf/books/reflections-on-sri-lankas-rti-act-06032019.pdf.

[48] Right to Information Act 2016, s 12.

of information pertaining to the rehabilitation of former LTTE combatants and the commercial activities of the armed forces; the release of a draft law on the rights of persons with disabilities and the proposed Truth and Reconciliation Commission; the disclosure of expenses incurred by politicians on overseas travel; and the release of reports by commissions of inquiry.[49] As of 31 December 2018, the RTI Commission had considered over 1000 appeals, 654 of which had been concluded.[50] In several cases, the Commission issued interim orders ordering release of the information sought by the applicants. At the same time, the RTI Commission's orders have also been challenged at the Court of Appeal.[51] What has been especially promising about the work of the RTI Commission is the high level of compliance with the RTI Commission's orders, signifying the possible emergence of a more open and transparent political culture and perhaps even the gradual strengthening of the rule of law since 2015. This compliance is facilitated by the Commission's processes in hearing appeals for disclosure. The Commission has sought to provide reasons for its orders, to justify its conclusions and to adhere to the rules of natural justice and principles of fair hearing. All this has allowed the Commission to develop a degree of institutional credibility and legitimacy.[52]

D. Navigating Reforms and Institutional Resilience: Sri Lanka in Comparative Perspective

The proposals for reform via Nineteenth Amendment was spearheaded by the Sirisena–Wickremesinghe ruling coalition, which had no clear majority in the 225-member Parliament at that time. At least at the outset, there appeared to be some hesitancy amongst existing MPs to support Sirisena's agenda for reform, particularly in relation to the pledge to abolish the executive presidency and empower the Prime Minister relative to the President.[53] These aspects were later abandoned in favour of the compromise embodied in the Nineteenth Amendment, and in the end, 215 of the Members of Parliament voted for the Nineteenth Amendment, one voted against, while the remaining MPs either abstained or were absent.[54]

The fractious and contentious nature of drafting and passage of the Nineteenth Amendment illustrates that consensus on the nature and character of the executive presidency was hard to come by. This was evinced by the fact that certain concessions had to be made eventually, and there were multiple committee-stage amendments before the Amendment was finally certified as law on 15 May 2015.[55] We will delve more

[49] See Right to Information Commission of Sri Lanka, 'Selected Orders of the Right to Information Commission of Sri Lanka 2017–2018' (2019) www.rticommission.lk/web/images/pdf/books/selected-orders-of-the-rtic-06032019.pdf.

[50] See Gomez, 'The Right to Information' (n 45) 856.

[51] ibid.

[52] ibid.

[53] DeVotta, 'A Win for Democracy' (n 2) 160.

[54] The Sirisena–Wickremesinghe coalition subsequently obtained a parliamentary majority in the 17 August 2015 parliamentary election.

[55] Welikala, 'Sri Lanka: The Nineteenth Amendment' (n 37).

into the political dynamics underpinning the Nineteenth Amendment in section III below, but at this juncture, we highlight instead the paradox of institutional resilience in Sri Lanka. Here, despite the political change and Sirisena's electoral pledge to change or abolish the executive presidency (a pledge that had arguably received popular support and mandate),[56] this institutional structure has remained largely resilient.

One way to understand this is to consider that a complete breakaway from established institutions might have been too costly, particularly for those who have reaped the political, economic and social benefits from such institutions. As we mentioned earlier, pro-Rajapaksa loyalists were particularly averse to abolishing a hyper-presidential state, as the existing system was seen as favourable to maintaining the unitary character of the state and fending off calls for devolution of power to the Tamil minority.[57] In other words, abolishing hyper-presidentialism could come at the expense of Sinhala-Buddhist dominance. In addition, the prospect of a parliamentary system that empowered the Prime Minister by rendering the President's actions subject to prime ministerial advice struck some raw nerves, especially as this meant that Ranil Wickremesinghe of the UNP (a minority political party ideologically opposite to the dominant SLFP) would have been in charge of the running of the government.

Yet, setting aside – for the moment – the political pressures that eventually rolled back the extensive, planned changes to the presidency, it is worth noting Sirisena's commitment to reducing the powers of the office that he was occupying. Perhaps one might see this simply as the fulfilment of an electoral pledge. However, the phenomenon of elites engaging in (and permitting) transformation and hence challenging the preservation of existing institutions in form, substance or both, even if it meant curtailing their own powers, has been observed elsewhere. For example, in Indonesia, the original 1945 Constitution granted the MPR (Majelis Permusyawaratan Rakyat, or People's Consultative Assembly)[58] 'sovereignty', while 'government power' was granted to the president.[59] The MPR previously possessed significant powers, including the appointment and impeachment of the President, judicial review of laws for constitutionality and enactment of the Broad Outlines of State Policy. In fact, while the constitution amendment processes were ongoing, the MPR removed President Abdurrahman Wahid from office in July 2001.

In evaluating the costs of transforming (or retaining, as the case might be) institutions, a variety of considerations could be at play. In Indonesia's case, the MPR – which was more politically diverse than it was during the Suharto era – was determined to keep its role of overseeing the executive.[60] This role did not materialise in practice during Suharto's regime because the MPR mainly comprised Suharto's loyalists and

[56] The Sinhala version of Sirisena's manifesto has used the word 'change', while the English version referred to abolition.

[57] DeVotta, 'A Win for Democracy' (n 2) 160.

[58] The MPR is a super-legislative assembly. It comprises members of the DPR (Dewan Perwakilan Rakyat, or People's Legislative Council) and the DPD (Dewan Perwakilan Daerah, or Regional Representative Council), both of which are elected houses. Before the constitutional amendments, the MPR comprised elected members, appointed members, and representatives from both the military and the police.

[59] See Horowitz (n 16) 92.

[60] ibid 93.

appointees. On the other hand, the most dominant party in the MPR at the time of the reforms process (PDI-P) was initially bent on retaining the status quo, in part out of the belief (driven by past practices) that the current arrangements would create a strong presidency, which could serve the PDI-P Chairperson's presidential aspirations in the future.[61] The removal of President Wahid, however, served as a warning of what a powerful MPR could be capable of. In the end, the Third Amendment passed by the MPR in August 2001 reduced its own powers – it is now left with powers only to amend the Constitution and substantially reduced powers to remove the President or Vice President, as a new process of impeachment required a referral to the Constitutional Court.[62] In addition, the First Amendment in 1999 clipped the wings of the presidency by implementing a two-term limit and curtailing the power of the President to make legislation.[63]

In any case, it is apparent at this point that in thinking about the extent to which existing institutions can be retained (thus demonstrating some degree of resilience) and reformed, the issue of costliness is intricately tied to the preservation of elite interests. The interaction between these elements can be seen in the Malaysian experience. Unlike Sri Lanka, when the Pakatan Harapan (PH) government assumed power in May 2018, wide-ranging constitutional reform – either through incremental amendments or through the making of a new constitution – was not explicitly on the PH government's agenda. While recognising the importance of institutional reforms, the government had in mind piecemeal reforms in specific areas, and they pledged instead to work within the framework of the existing constitution. A key site of reform was in improving the federal–state balance of power, particularly with regard to the East Malaysian states of Sabah and Sarawak. In this regard, as in Sri Lanka, the political transition opened the opportunity to raise the issues of recalibrating the division of power between the central government and the states (or provinces, in the case of Sri Lanka).

Substantively, the promise to 'restore' Sabah and Sarawak's status as equal partners in the Federation of Malaysia would entail restoring the spirit of the 1963 Malaysia Agreement (an international treaty that established the Federation of Malaysia), which spells out a list of autonomous powers and rights enjoyed exclusively by the two states in matters such as religion, language, immigration and fiscal management.[64] In the broader scheme of things, this pledge was also about remedying the abuses of power under the previous BN government, which was facilitated by its political dominance at both federal and state level.[65] However, it was not clear from the amendment engineered

[61] ibid 112. There was also the fear that any significant amendments might open a Pandora's box that would eventually alter the character and identity of the Constitution. ibid 93.

[62] ibid 115.

[63] This is important in Indonesia's political context because the MPR had always been dominated by the Golkar party (Suharto's party), and this secured Suharto's position for over three decades. Golkar was virtually the only party that operated in Indonesia's political scene during Suharto's New Order regime.

[64] For instance, under the 1963 Malaysia Agreement, English (as opposed to the Malay language) would remain the official language for Sabah and Sarawak; the two states would retain control over immigration (thus allowing them to control entry by Malaysians from other states); and although Islam is constitutionally enshrined as the 'religion of the Federation', this would not apply to Sabah and Sarawak.

[65] See W Tay, 'Restoring the Constitutional Status of Sabah and Sarawak: First Step in a Long Journey of Redemption' (*Constitutionnet*, 29 March 2019) http://constitutionnet.org/news/restoring-constitutional-status-sabah-and-sarawak-first-step-long-journey-redemption.

by the PH government that these substantive aspects were part of the package. The amendment eventually failed during the voting process in Parliament as the PH coalition fell short of 10 votes to garner the requisite two-thirds majority. Fifty-nine MPs, who comprised opposition politicians as well as some representatives from Sarawak and Sabah, abstained from voting.[66] On the surface, this outcome was odd, as Sarawak and Sabah (and their political elites) arguably stood to gain from the amendment's equal partner status. However, as we mentioned, it emerged that various quarters from both states felt aggrieved by the lack of concrete, substantive changes with regard to the federal government obligations vis-à-vis the rights and interests of the two states.[67] From this perspective, the amendment was to serve only as window-dressing; it was unclear to what extent the federal government – which for many decades has controlled, among other things, the proceeds of vast natural resources from the states and matters implicating religion – would concede its long-held political and economic interests in Sabah and Sarawak. In short, the vagueness and unresolved questions surrounding the amendment, which were tethered to the preservation or loss of interests, ultimately led to the retention (or, one could say, resilience) of existing federal–state arrangements implicating Sabah and Sarawak.

III. Evolution and Implications of Reforms

A. The First Challenge to a Renovated Institution

In democratising countries, where deep rooted practices and political culture have yet to evolve, the durability of new or reformed institutions is bound to be challenged. Consider, again, the case of Indonesia. The Constitutional Court was established in 2003, along with many other institutional innovations and renovations to facilitate democratisation. Through its constitutional review and electoral dispute resolution functions, the Court has – especially in the first decade of its establishment – augmented democratic practice in Indonesia and even stymied impulses towards authoritarian reversion or democratic regression.[68] It has earned considerable public trust, and a reputation for integrity and independence. However, the arrest and conviction of two of its justices in 2013 and 2017 for corruption sent a stern reminder that Indonesia's justice system continues to be vulnerable to the problems it faced in the past.[69] In a similar vein, the democratic momentum and transformation proved to be fragile in Malaysia. Even though there was enthusiasm and early steps to improve government accountability and the rule of law by reforming key institutions (such as the judiciary and independent

[66] M Vanar, 'Golden Opportunity Lost for Sabah and Sarawak to Regain Status, Says Liew' *The Star* (10 April 2019) www.thestar.com.my/news/nation/2019/04/10/golden-opportunity-lost-for-sabah-and-sarawak-to-regain-status-says-liew.

[67] Hansard of the Parliament of Malaysia, 14th Parliament, 2nd Term, 1st Meeting (9 April 2019) 55–70.

[68] S Butt, *The Constitutional Court and Democracy in Indonesia* (Leiden, Brill, 2016) 2–3.

[69] See, in general, S Pompe, *The Indonesian Supreme Court: A Study of Institutional Collapse* (Ithaca, NY, Cornell University Press, 2008).

commissions), attention soon turned towards repelling ethnic and religious nationalist rhetoric drummed up by the political opposition.[70] The rhetoric was constructed around the idea that the Malay Muslims (the dominant ethnic group) were on their way to 'losing' their homeland and interests, as the government was dictated by a Chinese-dominant party. This not only led to the government retracting its pledge to ratify the Rome Statute and the International Convention on the Elimination of Racial Discrimination, it also deepened the cracks within the ruling coalition – cracks that eventually led to the coalition's downfall in February 2020. Here, the politicisation of race and religion, together with political machinations to secure power, triumphed over democratic reforms.

The foregoing examples from Indonesia and Malaysia shed light on the other facet of the resilience story – the resilience of reforms or renovated institutions. Sri Lanka has not been spared such tests. Consider, as a starting point, one of the major reforms under the Nineteenth Amendment: the introduction of a five-year term limit on the presidential office. It took President Sirisena – who was by then losing interest in the constitutional change project – less than three years to challenge the commitments behind the Nineteenth Amendment that he had supported pursuant to his pledge to improve good governance. In a bid to extend his term by another year, he sought the opinion of the Supreme Court in January 2018 on the applicability of the term limit to his presidency. From Sirisena's perspective, his term in office would be governed by the pre-Nineteenth Amendment six-year term and this would also be in line with his electoral mandate. The Attorney-General argued that President Sirisena assumed office before the passage of the Nineteenth Amendment and he was therefore entitled to serve a six-year term. He also contended that reducing his term to five years would be an infringement of the sovereignty of the people and universal franchise.

Although Sirisena's arguments against the retrospective application of the Nineteenth Amendment appeared logical, there was a more fundamental issue at stake. In particular, a six-year term would have allowed Sirisena to remain as President until January 2021 (which was beyond the life of the former Parliament), and since the Constitution permitted the President to dissolve Parliament after four and a half years, Sirisena would have been able to do so after February 2020. With his incumbency advantage, he would have had the opportunity to influence the composition of the next parliament to his benefit. Sirisena's arguments, however, did not appeal to the Supreme Court as it unanimously held that the current President was subject to the provisions of the Nineteenth Amendment.[71] Sirisena's underlying motivation for insisting on a six-year term remained unclear, but it was possible that he had his sights set on another term in office, and perhaps, this time, without the coalition that backed his presidential

[70] DAH Shah and A Harding, 'Constitutional Quantum Mechanics and a Change in Government in Malaysia' (*International Journal of Constitutional Law Blog*, 8 April 2020) www.iconnectblog.com/2020/04/constitutional-quantum-mechanics-and-a-change-in-government-in-malaysia/.

[71] See D Bastians, 'After SC Rules Five Years, President Still under Fire for Asking the Question' (*Daily FT*, 18 January 2018) www.ft.lk/top-story/After-SC-rules-five-years-President-still-under-fire-for-asking-the-question/26-647370; M Srinivasan, 'Presidential Term Is Only Five Years, Sri Lankan SC' *The Hindu* (15 January 2018) www.thehindu.com/news/international/presidential-term-is-only-five-years-sri-lankan-sc/article22444477.ece.

bid in 2015. There was, however, a larger political context behind this that is worth mentioning. Since 2017, the President and the Prime Minister found themselves in a series of conflicts and disagreements, and the fractures in the government culminated in the coalition government's defeat in the local council elections in February 2018 and the subsequent departure of several MPs (including cabinet ministers) from Sirisena's United People's Freedom Alliance party from the government in April 2018. This political crisis set the foundations for the constitutional crisis in 2018.

B. The Constitutional Crisis of 2018

The political transition of 2015 saw the emergence of a more dynamic and open political culture, growing judicial independence and robust independent institutions. However, the palpable sense that the country was returning to a rule-of-law-based constitutional government was shattered three years later by the constitutional chaos in October and November 2018.

In October 2018, President Sirisena's party withdrew from the coalition government with Prime Minister Wickremesinghe's United National Front. The President contended that the collapse of the coalition government meant that the cabinet was now effectively dissolved, and he could legitimately appoint a new Prime Minister. This then led to Wickremesinghe's unceremonious removal on 26 October 2018 and his replacement by former president Mahinda Rajapaksa, whom Sirisena had previously defeated in the January 2015 presidential election. Sirisena's political move – ostensibly driven by his irreparable friction with Wickremesinghe – threw the country into constitutional crisis. While Wickremesinghe remained defiant and declared that he will continue to carry out his duties as Prime Minister, Rajapaksa was promptly sworn into office. This left the country with two competing suitors to the prime ministerial office. However, under Article 43(3) of the Constitution, the President 'shall appoint as Prime Minister the Member of Parliament who in his opinion is most likely to command the confidence of Parliament'. At the point of Rajapaksa's appointment, it was unclear what evidence Sirisena relied on to conclude that Rajapaksa had commanded such confidence. One could presume that he relied on Rajapaksa's representations or assurances, or worse, that he had no evidence at all. Of course, under Westminster constitutional conventions, the determination of confidence is done on the floor of parliament. To facilitate this, Sirisena swiftly prorogued Parliament for two weeks, which was thought to allow Rajapaksa enough time to cobble the support he needed from the Members of Parliament. Wickremesinghe's ouster was also prompted by the support that a Member of Parliament, who was also a senior member of the United National Party (UNP), had offered Sirisena. He had indicated that he was ready to cross the floor with 20 other Members of Parliament and that would enable Sirisena's prime ministerial nominee to obtain a parliamentary majority.[72]

[72] See D Bastians, 'The Siege: Inside 52 Days of Constitutional Crisis in Sri Lanka' in A Welikala (ed), *Constitutional Reform and Crisis in Sri Lanka* (Centre for Policy Alternatives, 2019) 30.

When it became clear that Rajapaksa was struggling to find a parliamentary majority to support him (which tells us that Sirisena had no basis to appoint Rajapaksa and thus could be said to have acted unconstitutionally), Sirisena purported to dissolve Parliament and fix parliamentary elections for January 2019. This decision, ie to dissolve Parliament and call a fresh election, defied the constitutional provision that empowers the President to dissolve Parliament only after four and a half years. A parallel to this scenario occurred in 1982, when then-President JR Jayewardene postponed a parliamentary election and held a referendum instead in an attempt to prolong his five-sixths parliamentary majority. On that occasion, the Supreme Court, by a narrow majority, ratified his decision and permitted him to proceed with the referendum in lieu of a parliamentary election.

Sirisena's political machination was immediately challenged before the Supreme Court, which subsequently issued a decision against him in December 2018.[73] The Court held that the President could not dissolve Parliament until the lapse of four and half years, and in doing so, the Court drew on key constitutional principles. First, the Court emphasised the principle of separation of powers and co-equality, stressing that all three branches of government must be able to maintain effective checks and balances on each other. Second, in reiterating the idea that constitutional interpretation ought to advance the rule of law, the Court rejected the exercise of unfettered discretion. It asserted that all public authorities, including the President, must function according to the law and the Constitution. Third, this weight accorded to the constitutional limits of government power was linked to the emphasis on the principle of constitutional supremacy. In this regard, although Sri Lanka's Constitution does not permit ex post judicial review of legislation (and thus the Supreme Court does not have the jurisdiction to strike down legislative action as unconstitutional), it can still declare executive action to be unconstitutional. More crucially, the Court held that the right to equality and equal protection of the law contained in Article 12(1) provides protection against arbitrary and the mala fide exercise of power while guaranteeing natural justice and legitimate expectations. All this reflects principles that have become part of the Sri Lankan jurisprudence on public law. For example, the Supreme Court has, in a long chain of judicial decisions, held that public power is held in trust and must be exercised reasonably, fairly and for the public's benefit.[74]

The judiciary's intervention continued in another case concerning a writ of *quo warranto* filed by 122 MPs to prevent Rajapaksa and his cabinet from performing governmental functions until a final determination was made on the merits of this case.[75] In their application, the 122 MPs argued that there were two no-confidence motions passed in Parliament, on 14 and 16 November 2018, against the Rajapaksa-led government and therefore he and his government had no right to continue in office. The Court noted that over half of the members of Parliament had established that the Prime Minister did not command the confidence of a majority of its members. For the Court,

[73] *Sampanthan v Attorney General*, SC Minutes (13 December 2018).

[74] See M Gomez, 'Blending Rights with Writs: Sri Lankan Public Law's New Brew' (2006) *Acta Juridica* suppl; M Gomez, 'The Modern Benchmarks of Sri Lankan Public Law' (2001) 118 *South African Law Journal* 581.

[75] Court of Appeal (Writ) Application 363/2018, CA Minutes of 3 December 2018.

the damage that could have ensued by temporarily restraining a lawful cabinet of ministers from functioning was outweighed by the damage that could be caused by allowing a set of persons who are not entitled in law to do so to function as the Prime Minister and the cabinet of ministers. In other words, the magnitude of the latter damage was serious and potentially irreparable. In these circumstances, the Court of Appeal issued an interim order restraining Rajapaksa and his cabinet from functioning until a final determination was made on the merits.[76] Rajapaksa appealed against this order to the Supreme Court, but the Supreme Court refused to vacate the interim order and instead ordered that the matter be taken up in the Supreme Court later, in January 2019. As a result of these decisions, Rajapaksa resigned as Prime Minister and Wickremesinghe was reappointed to the post.

IV. Political Culture and Lessons on Institutional Resilience

The Nineteenth Amendment survived the 2018 constitutional crisis in Sri Lanka, as well as earlier attempts to undermine commitments relating to the presidential term. In both instances, a key element that helped maintain the resilience of the arrangements and renovated institutions under the Nineteenth Amendment was the judiciary. As we showed in the previous section, in both cases the courts enforced limits on executive power by relying on the notions of constitutional supremacy and constitutionalism. These decisions are all the more significant for two reasons. First, the judiciary would have still been left reeling from the blatant executive interference with judicial independence when Shirani Bandaranyake was unceremoniously impeached in 2013. In this regard, the Malaysian experience provides yet another lesson on how executive interference with the judiciary undermines judicial independence and shapes the judicial psyche for years to come. In 1988, Prime Minister Mahathir Mohamad engineered the removal of the Chief Justice and two other Supreme Court judges, following a series of cases and decisions that were seen as prejudicial to the interests of the ruling government. It took decades before the judiciary slowly recovered its independence and integrity. Perhaps what was different between Malaysia and Sri Lanka was that the judiciary in Sri Lanka was operating in a far more open political culture (a point to which we will return shortly), while authoritarian tendencies remained pervasive in Malaysia throughout the 1990s and during the turn of the century. Second, that the judiciary managed to secure compliance with its decisions is also remarkable, given the evolving political dynamics at the time and the history of the fragile rule of law in Sri Lanka. In this respect, one could also say that the judiciary has demonstrated a degree of resilience, particularly in navigating politically charged issues such as the formation of government and executive–legislative dynamics.

In any case, the Sri Lankan experience illustrates that the reform, operation and resilience of constitutional arrangements and (revitalised) democratic institutions may hinge on the contexts they find themselves in. To begin with, the compromise and

[76] Ibid 11–12.

consensus underpinning the Nineteenth Amendment was crucial to its subsequent two-thirds approval in Parliament, and this tells us that reforms often necessitate a balancing exercise between achieving the ideal and settling for what is politically possible under the prevailing circumstances. In this regard, returning to our earlier comparison with the Indonesian experience, proceeding consensually[77] – particularly on fundamental issues such as a directly elected president, religion, the role of the military in politics and maintaining the Constitution's preamble – allowed different political factions to iron out their differences and achieve significant institutional reforms for Indonesia's democratisation.

In addition, to some extent, a strong constitutional and legal framework is crucial in shaping a democratic political culture. In a similar vein, as rational choice theorists would argue, political institutions could structure the opportunities available to politicians, and that might explain how political actors act and react. Sri Lanka's experience has shown that the concentration of power in the executive – undoubtedly enabled by the 1978 Constitution – allowed authoritarianism to flourish and generated a constitutional and political culture that enabled impunity. We have seen that even as checks and balances were later introduced (for instance, the establishment of the Constitutional Council via the Seventeenth Amendment), these could not reverse the entrenched practices surrounding what became an authoritarian presidency that functioned with minimal accountability.

There is yet another contextual factor that has been highly salient in shaping political culture in Sri Lanka, particularly where there is intense competition for positions of power: the politicisation of religion and ethnicity. In this regard, one ought to consider the ways in which the executive presidency has also acquired an ethno-religious significance beyond what is plain in the constitutional text. Scholars have highlighted the ways in which a powerful president is projected as a contemporary Sinhala-Buddhist monarch – as guardians of the country's Sinhala-Buddhist interests and heritage.[78] For example, when the state defeated the LTTE in May 2009, President Rajapaksa, who was in power at the time, likened himself to the ancient Sinhala king, Dutugemunu, who was said to have defeated the Tamil King Elara. It is an encounter that is steeped in myth, and is celebrated in historical works, novels and some contemporary artwork. Ancient rituals, including agricultural and religious rituals, have also been relied on by holders of the office to add additional layers of social and political legitimacy.

The powers of pardon vested in the President have also been used to build popular support among a Sinhala-Buddhist constituency. Two recent examples relate to the release of a hardline Buddhist monk and the release of an army officer convicted of multiple murders during the country's ethnic war. Venerable Galagoda Aththe

[77] Horowitz (n 16) 74.

[78] DeVotta, 'A Win for Democracy' (n 2) 160. For scholarship that discusses the connection between Sinhala-Buddhism, heritage and the presidency, see the following five articles in Welikala, *Reforming Sri Lankan Presidentialism* (n 21): A Welikala, 'Nation, State, Sovereignty and Kingship: The Pre-Modern Antecedents of the Presidential State', 498–546; R de Silva Wijeyeratne, 'Cosmology, Presidentialism, and JR Jayewardene's Constitutional Imaginary', 547–68; A Abeysekera, 'The "Line" between Religion and Politics', 569–603; K Senaratne, 'Jathika Chintanaya and the Executive Presidency', 604–41; and M Roberts, 'Mahinda Rajapakse as Modern *Mahavasala* and Font of Clemency? The Roots of Populist Authoritarianism' 642–55.

Gnanasara Thero, who leads the hardline Sinhala-Buddhist organisation the Bodu Bala Sena, was convicted for contempt of court under Article 105 of the Constitution when he interrupted an inquiry into the disappearance of a journalist and hurled abuse at the presiding magistrate.[79] His conviction was subsequently confirmed by the Supreme Court. Gnanasara Thero had earlier been convicted for criminal intimidation and harassment in relation to the same incident. In May 2019, former President Maithripala Sirisena, without consultation with the Minister of Justice or the Attorney-General, exercising his power of pardon, released Gnanasara Thero, an act that is currently being challenged by way of a fundamental rights application before the Supreme Court.[80] At the end of March 2020, during the operation of a curfew and in the midst of the COVID-19 pandemic, the current President, exercising his constitutional powers of pardon, released an army officer who was convicted for multiple murders during the civil war with the LTTE. The officer had previously lost his appeal against his conviction in the Supreme Court. It was one of the rare convictions for crimes committed during the war which ended in 2009.[81]

In any case, it is worth noting that under the Nineteenth Amendment, Sri Lanka began to transition from a strong presidential system to a more balanced scheme of semi-presidentialism by instituting limits to presidential power. The rebirth of the Constitutional Council, as well as the introduction of the RTI law and the operation of the RTI Commission and the independent Human Rights Commission, signified small but significant steps forward in cultivating a political and constitutional culture underpinned by checks and balances and the rule of law. Unlike previous occasions where independent commissions were hamstrung by government interference and where the Constitutional Council was virtually redundant, the fact that there is a high degree of compliance with the RTI Commission's orders, along with Sirisena's respect for the Constitutional Council's role, suggested that there was at least some basis for optimism in Sri Lanka's democratic consolidation. Political actors who have been accustomed to defying or manipulating constitutional commitments found themselves having to commit to the 'rules of the game'.

Yet, the converse could also be true. The Sri Lankan story – particularly as evident in the events in 2018 and the subsequent unravelling of the Nineteenth Amendment after the Rajapaksa family returned to power – also cautions us about the fragility of democratisation. Changing political dynamics and political practices that revolve around entrenching power and preserving self-interests may continue to pose a challenge to democratisation. In other words, the interaction between politics and constitutional law and practice is highly dynamic, and it is capable of producing ironic and unforeseen consequences. In the 2018 constitutional crisis, a President who no longer wished to be bound by the rules relating to his office and, more crucially, whose political ambitions and survival were at stake resorted to turning against the Constitution. Here, it appears

[79] *In re Galagoda Aththe Gnanasara* (Court of Appeal Minutes, 8 August 2018).

[80] M Gomez, 'Prosecuting Religious Violence in Sri Lanka' in L Thio and JL Neo (eds), *Religious Offences in Common Law Asia Colonial Legacies, Constitutional Rights and Contemporary Practice* (Oxford, Hart Publishing, 2021) 245–80.

[81] *Hate Speech in Sri Lanka During the Pandemic* (National Christian Evangelical Alliance of Sri Lanka, 2020); see NCEASL – Hate Speech_final (E).pdf (minormatters.org).

that no matter what reforms are instituted, the lack of appreciation and internalisation of the norms of democratic governance is a continuing challenge that Sri Lanka will have to face in its constitutional journey. Several months before the 2018 constitutional crisis, there were already potent signs of a political crisis. The resignation of cabinet members and MPs, which we mentioned earlier, was in fact preceded by a no-confidence vote launched by the opposition against Prime Minister Wickremesinghe to hold him accountable for an alleged bond market scam and the anti-Muslim riots in March 2018.

Although the Prime Minister survived the no-confidence vote, this episode could also be viewed with a more positive lens: not only did it reflect the emergence of an improved mechanism of parliamentary checks and balances on the government of the day; it also illustrates the development of a more progressive political and constitutional culture – one that is not overwhelmingly dictated by autocratic personalities who are able to act with clear disregard of the constitutional limits on their power. Put differently, in spite of the political manoeuvrings and tussles for political power, the political actors – at least in this instance – attempted to conduct themselves according to the (formal) terms of the Constitution. And, despite Sirisena's antics, this changing political culture also appears to have shaped the outcome of the crisis in October, as the manoeuvre to oust Wickremesinghe fell through. There were Members of Parliament who declined to cross the floor even though they were offered large sums of money to do so, and opposition parties such as the Tamil National Alliance and the Janatha Vimukhti Peramuna took a principled stance against the President's decision to prorogue Parliament in order to pave way for Rajapaksa to take office.[82] Thus, the outcome of the constitutional crisis of 2018 arguably reaffirmed some faith in the emerging culture of democratic politics (short-lived though it might be, as we illustrate in the next section).

Through all this, the role of the courts in Sri Lanka has been crucial, particularly in supporting constitutional and institutional resilience. The principled decisions of the Supreme Court and Court of Appeal in November and December 2018 illustrate the willingness and ability of courts to enforce constitutional limits on executive power.[83] That the political elites accepted those decisions of the courts was significant in light of the prevailing culture at that time and paved the way for a solution that lay within the Constitution and the law. In this regard, another crucial piece of the constitutional law and politics puzzle in Sri Lanka – one that is also key in building a political culture conducive for institutional resilience – is public opinion. In the Sri Lankan case, the mobilisation of the middle and professional classes was important in sustaining renovated democratic institutions in moments of crisis. In 2018, public outrage, at least on the part of some sections of the public at the sacking of the Prime Minister and the subsequent purported dissolution of Parliament, had an impact on the decisions of the courts that reversed those political decisions.[84]

[82] See generally the contributions in Welikala, *Constitutional Reform* (n 72); M Gomez, 'Constitutional Change and Institutional Resilience in Si Lanka' in H Glaser (ed), *Shifting to a New Constitutionalism: Changing Political Orders in Asia* (Baden-Baden, Nomos, 2022).

[83] The conviction of a Buddhist monk for contempt of court in August 2018 is another example illustrating that courts are increasingly ready to suppress impunity, particularly in politically sensitive cases. See *In re Gallagodaaththe Gnanasara*, CA (CC) Application No 4 of 2016, CA Minutes of 8 August 2018.

[84] See Bastians (n 60); S Hattotuwa, 'Framing a Putsch: Twitter and Facebook in Sri Lanka's Constitutional Crisis' in Welikala, *Constitutional Reform* (n 72) 179–239 and the rest of the chapters in that volume.

V. Conclusion: The Twentieth Amendment, Constitutional Realities and the Road Ahead

At this juncture, what appears to be obvious, recurring forces in our discussion of Sri Lankan constitutional politics and institutional resilience are the salience of ethno-religious politics (and loyalties) and the entrenchment of political self-interest. These are significant issues that shape the country's political culture and practices, and they will continue to play an important role in testing the durability of the Constitution and democratic institutions in the country. Sri Lanka (much like democratising countries like Malaysia and Indonesia) remains a deeply divided society where identity-based markers (such as ethnicity and religion) and hostilities are used as tools for political mobilisation. This could well render the constitution-building project hostage to rapidly changing political exigencies, as there are deep divisions over the direction and substance of constitutional, political and institutional reforms. These implicate crucial questions such as responses to the legacy of past violence and abuses of power and the ways in which root causes of societal conflict and exclusion are addressed. In addition, the search for durable constitutional and political arrangements requires both the need to moderate majority anxieties over their political and economic security and to enforce minority protection and limits on government power.

Most recently, following the victory of the Rajapaksas in the presidential and parliamentary elections in 2019 and 2020, the constellation of these forces provided the backdrop for the return of hyper-presidentialism in Sri Lanka. Before delving into this point, it is first important to note that, prior to the passing of the Twentieth Amendment in October 2020, the country functioned in an ambiguous constitutional reality. While there were no overt attacks on the Nineteenth Amendment, the series of events we highlighted in the foregoing sections did not reflect the core spirit of the Amendment. In addition, the popular mandate obtained by the President in November 2019 enabled him to appoint his brother Mahinda Rajapaksa as the Prime Minister. The Prime Minister's popularity was not subject to a floor test in Parliament as the opposition decided to respect the electoral mandate of November 2019 and not challenge the appointment. While the Nineteenth Amendment trimmed the powers of the executive president substantially, those powers had re-emerged as a matter of constitutional practice *before* the Twentieth Amendment was passed. The relationship between the two Rajapaksa brothers enabled the President to exercise power he may otherwise not have been able to do if the Prime Minister were less pliant. For example, while the Constitution after 2015 prohibited the President from holding any subject ministries, the President refrained from appointing a Minister of Defence, and instead appointed a Secretary of Defence and a State Minister of Defence. This enabled the President to function as *de facto* Defence Minister and oversee this portfolio in practice. In short, despite the Nineteenth Amendment, it proved hard to limit – as a matter of practice – the powers concentrated in this historically resilient and much-debated institution.

The President dissolved Parliament in March 2020 on the completion of four and a half years, as he was legally entitled to do. However, elections could not be conducted within the stipulated period due to the COVID-19 pandemic. The country was thus in a legal vacuum for three months until parliamentary elections were held in August 2020. Here, again, we see how the Sri Lankan electorate produced supermajorities that facilitated constitutional manipulation and the centralisation of state power, as it did in the legislative elections of 1972 and in the executive elections of 1978 and 2010, thus triggering a lapse into hyper-presidentialism. These events illustrate not only the resilience of an institution that many have strived to reform or eliminate, but also the fragility of the commitments to constitutional democracy. Rifts between the former President Sirisena and Prime Minister Wickremesinghe, a shaky political coalition and a serious lapse in security (which followed from the rift between the President and the Prime Minister) that contributed to the Easter Sunday bombings of April 2019 provided the perfect storm for hyper-presidentialism to re-emerge. Gotabaya Rajapaksa threw his hat into the ring within a week of the Easter bombings, stating that he could provide the stability and security that the country needs. He won convincingly in the 2019 November presidential election, in part by rallying the Sinhala-Buddhist majority against the 'threats' posed by minorities and by promising the protection of the unitary Buddhist state.

The Twentieth Amendment to the Constitution was placed on the order paper of Parliament within a month of the sweeping win of Rajapaksa's party in the August 2020 parliamentary election. The objective of that amendment was to reverse the changes of the Nineteenth Amendment and revert to a system where the executive President operates with minimal checks on his power. However, the contents of the draft amendment were challenged before the Supreme Court, and in its determination, the Court ruled that several provisions required a two-thirds majority *and* a referendum, two of which are particularly significant in our discussion of the 'resilience' of hyper-presidentialism. The first was a provision that sought to provide blanket immunity to the President's official acts; the second was the President's power to dissolve the Parliament after one year. The Bill was subsequently amended and passed by a two-thirds majority.

Many of the changes introduced by the Nineteenth Amendment were reversed, although a few remain. For example, the five-year term limits for both the President and Parliament and the right to information included in the Bill of Rights in 2015 remain. There was a proposal to reintroduce urgent bills, which could hamper the role of the Supreme Court in exercising its checking function as it would provide limited time for the Supreme Court to review the constitutionality of such bills. This now applies only in relation to bills on national security and disaster management. However, other important powers the President exercised before the Nineteenth Amendment have been restored. The President may remove the Prime Minister at will and hold any cabinet portfolio and assign ministerial portfolios, and there is no limitation on the size of the cabinet. The President may also dissolve Parliament after two and a half years without giving a reason, and a last-minute change at the Committee stage of the Amendment Bill increased the sizes of the Court of Appeal and Supreme Court. Crucially, the Constitutional Council that acted as a restraint on the President's power to make key appointments has been replaced by a Parliamentary Council, whose authority and power are significantly diminished compared to that of the Constitutional Council. In particular, the recommendations of the Parliamentary Council in key appointments (including to the superior courts and independent commissions) do not bind the President. Aside from politicising accountability institutions, these measures dilute, if not eliminate, any institutional checks on the presidency. For now, the hyper-presidency seems to have prevailed and has proven to be resilient through cycles of political change in Sri Lanka.

3

Old Powers and New Forces in the Bhutanese Constitution – Anticipating the Resilience of a Young Constitution

MICHAELA WINDISCHGRAETZ

I. Introduction

This chapter assesses some crucial issues relating to the young constitutional democracy of Bhutan and explores questions that have significant implications for how it will stabilise over time. It questions which constitutional powers could enhance stability in moments of crisis and which elements appear too weak to play a major role. Since the adoption of the Bhutanese Constitution 14 years ago, the Bhutanese state has not faced any major constitutional crisis. I proceed from the hypothesis that it will be those factors that have been growing over a longer period, providing stability and continuity, that will ensure the resilience of Bhutanese constitutional democracy in a potential future crisis.

Bhutan is a small, landlocked country in the Himalayas, located between India and China, with a total land area of about 38,000 km^2. It is divided into 20 Dzongkhags – or administrative districts. The current population is 748,931 according to the Bhutanese National Statistics Bureau.[1] The population consists of numerous ethnic groups: the politically and culturally dominant Ngalop in the north and west, the Sharchop in the east and the Lhotsampa in the south being the biggest of them. While most of the northern and eastern Bhutanese follow Buddhism, the Lhotsampa in the south are of Nepali origin, and to a large extent follow Hinduism.

Compared to most of the other states in South Asia, Bhutan is characterised by several peculiarities. Firstly, it has never been colonised. Thus, unlike many other Global South countries, the Bhutanese legal order is not shaped by legal pluralism caused by the imposition of a colonial legal order. Secondly, Bhutan's constitutional history is only about 14 years old. Its Constitution was adopted on 18 July 2008 and has not been amended so far. Thirdly, the transformation of an absolute monarchy into a democratic constitutional monarchy was not triggered by internal problems or external pressure,

[1] National Statistical Bureau, *Statistical Yearbook 2020*, V.

but by the initiative of the monarch himself. Thus, Bhutan's democratisation process has been described as 'one of the most astonishing and unique transitions to democracy witnessed by scholars so far'.[2]

To understand the principles of the Bhutanese Constitution, which emphasises tradition and continuity of the Bhutanese state throughout the centuries and builds on institutional foundations established in the last decades of the twentieth century, I will first provide an overview of the historical development of the country. Founded in 1625 by Zhabdrung Ngawang Namgyal – a Buddhist Lama – the country saw nearly 300 years of theocratic rule by the Buddhist Drukpa Kagyu order (1625–1907), which was replaced by a hereditary absolute monarchy in 1907. This relatively new order eventually evolved into a democratic constitutional monarchy in 2008. Major legal and institutional changes initiated by the third king – Dorji Wangchuck (r 1952–72) – and even more by the fourth king – Jigme Singye Wangchuck (r 1972–2006) – must be understood as important preparatory actions for Bhutan's smooth transition to democratic rule and stable constitutional governance.

In the second section, I will outline the design and drafting of the Constitution, as well as its central features. I seek to capture the constitutional vision of its designers, which is built on the idea of a nation united around ethnicity and a common heritage shared by all citizens.[3] Stressing the unity of the people and banning actions that could divide them along ethnic, religious or regional lines, the Constitution aims to secure the stability and credibility of Bhutan as a nation-state, particularly in its vulnerable position between powerful neighbours.

The third section of the chapter will focus on constitutional institutions that could become crucial factors in the event of a constitutional crisis in the country. 'Old powers' like the monarch but also the well-established institution of the judiciary seem to guarantee the stability of Bhutan's constitutional system. On the other hand, 'new forces' like the establishment of a system of political parties in 2008, due to the original unfamiliarity to the people and because of various legal and institutional restrictions, seem a rather weak player in ensuring the stability of constitutional governance.

A. Historical Background

In 1616, the seventeenth hierarch of the Ralung Drukpa Kagyu order Zhabdrung Ngawang Namgyal (1594–1651) left the Tsang kingdom of Central Tibet for exile in the southern region Lhomonkhazhi, which eventually became known as Bhutan.[4] In about 1625, the Zhabdrung established a theocratic state based on a vision that closely reflected the governing institutions of his home monastery, Ralung.[5] The Zhabdrung

[2] M Gallenkamp, 'Democracy in Bhutan: An Analysis of Constitutional Change in a Buddhist Monarchy' [2010] *Institute of Peace and Conflict Studies* 2.

[3] For the outdatedness of ethno-nationalism as a source of national unity in many nations today, see M Tushnet, *Advanced Introduction to Comparative Constitutional Law* (Cheltenham, Edward Elgar, 2014) 116.

[4] The name 'Bhutan' was shaped by the British, *cf* K Phuntsho, *The History of Bhutan* (London, Random House India, 2016) 5, 11.

[5] J Ardussi, 'The Traditional Institutions of Governance in Bhutan before 1907 and their Modification with the Coming of the Monarchy' [2015] *The Druk Journal*, www.drukjournal.bt/the-traditioonal-institutions-of-governance-in-bhutan-before-1907-and-their-modification-with-the-coming-of-the-monarchy/.

implemented what was known in Tibetan-Buddhist political theory as 'dual government' (*chos srid gnis*) – a spiritual and temporal rule.[6]

At the end of the nineteenth century, various circumstances led to a power vacuum in Bhutan, which paved the way for the election of Ugyen Wangchuck as a hereditary monarch in 1907.[7] The pinnacle of the crowning ceremony was the endorsement of a document, called the *genja* (treaty), containing the contract for the new monarchical system. The document bore 50 seals of various state officials, religious persons and peoples' representatives, and, on top, it included the seal of Zhabdrung Ngawang Namgyal.[8] The involvement of the people of Bhutan in the election of the first king is still an important element in the current discourse of a long-standing democratic rule in Bhutan, which goes back far before the time of the current constitution.[9] The *genja* is perceived as a 'social contract' in the sense of both Rousseau and the Buddhist myth of Mahasammata.[10]

While the first and second kings did not substantially alter the medieval administrative and legal system, the major social, institutional and legal reforms of the third king, Jigme Dorji Wangchuck (r 1952–72), are perceived as 'the creation of a modern Bhutanese state'.[11] In 1953, King Jigme Dorji Wangchuck abolished serfdom and carried out a major land reform, which led to the break-up of the aristocratic estates and the reallocation of land to the former serfs.[12] In the same year, he established the first National Assembly (NA) as an assembly of representatives of the people and government.[13] While the NA was initially conceived as an advisory body,[14] its decisions eventually became final and binding, and the NA transformed into a sovereign body.[15] During the process of drafting the Constitution of 2008, King Jigme Dorji Wangchuck began a discussion which saw much controversy. The king expressed his desire for, and eventually introduced, a system of no-confidence votes by the NA against the king, as it opined that a king should rule for only as long as he enjoyed popular support.[16]

Another major initiative launched by the third king was the enactment of the first comprehensive law book of Bhutan, the Thrimzhung Chenmo (Supreme Law),[17] which

[6] *cf* R Whitecross, 'Buddhism and Constitutions in Bhutan' in R Redwood French and MA Nathan (eds), *Buddhism and Law. An Introduction* (Cambridge, Cambridge University Press, 2014) 356.

[7] ibid 357; Phuntsho (n 4) 514ff.

[8] Instructive on the *genja*: S Kinga, 'The Genja of 1907' (*RIGGS Podcast*) episode 5, https://rigss.bt/podcast/5.

[9] See, eg S Tobgye, *The Constitution of Bhutan: Principles and Philosophies* (Thimphu, Bhutan National Legal Institute, 2015) 13.

[10] *cf* Agganjja Sutta of the Pali Canon. Mahasammata means 'The Great Elect' and implies a theory of kingship according to which the people elected the most able person to govern them in exchange for a share of their crops.

[11] S Kinga, *Polity, Kingship and Democracy. A Biography of the Bhutanese State* (Thimphu, Ministry of Education, 2009) 217.

[12] ibid 223; Whitecross, 'Buddhism and Constitutions' (n 6) 357.

[13] Kinga, *Polity* (n 11) 228.

[14] ibid 229.

[15] For this development, see ibid 229, 232.

[16] ibid 233. See also K Ura, *The Hero with a Thousand Eyes. A Historical Novel* (Thimphu, Center for Bhutan Studies, 1995) 277.

[17] Thorough research on the sources of the Thrimzhung Chenmo is long overdue. On the one hand, traditional concepts of the king as the lawmaker and the character of the Thrimzhung Chenmo as based on the customary laws of the country are emphasised. On the other hand, informants assume at least some of the roots of the Thrimzhung Chenmo in Indian Law: *cf* R Whitecross, 'The Thrimzhung Chenmo and

comprised both criminal and civil laws, in 1959.[18] The implementation of the new law required a modern justice system. In 1960, the king appointed the first *thrimpon* (judges) to several district courts, and, in 1967, he established the High Court, with the intention of separating the judiciary from the executive.

When the fourth king, Jigme Singye Wangchuck, ascended the throne in 1972 at the age of 16, he continued the modernisation of Bhutan's society, economy and politics. Before commanding the drafting of the Constitution in 2001, King Jigme Singye Wangchuck undertook two major steps towards democracy. The first was the decentralisation of institutional power and the second was the devolution of personal power.[19] This was done by introducing government at the local level. In 1981, the Dzongkhag Yargay Tshogdu (DYT) was established as a new representative institution at the district level, and, in 1991, the Gewog Yargay Tshogdu (GYT) was established at the village level, with the *gup* (headman) as the chairman of the GYT. One of the most important facts regarding these steps towards decentralisation was the transfer of some fiscal power and responsibility to the GYT and DYT.[20] Additionally, the Bhutanese people were, for the first time, confronted with individual secret ballots in the nationwide *gup* elections held in 2002.[21] In 1998, the king issued an edict appointing a cabinet to which he devolved full executive power, declaring that he would remain only as head of state, and no longer as head of government.[22]

B. The Making of the Constitution

The drafting of a Constitution for Bhutan was the pinnacle of the political and legal reforms, introduced by the fourth king of Bhutan, Jigme Singye Wangchuck, on 4 December 2001. Many were curious about the king's motives. In any case, the decision to lead the country towards democracy must not be seen as a spontaneous one. Rather, it was a continuous development in the political and legal sector initiated by the third king and continued by the fourth king. This development saw a continuous reduction of absolute power, an increasing participation of the population in political decisions and a development of a modern body of laws.

King Jigme Singye Wangchuck held the strong conviction that democracy, despite its imperfections, was the best form of government for any outward-looking country that was seeking to survive in the modern world.[23] Besides these personal political convictions of the king, observers identified external factors that might have driven the king

the Emergence of the Contemporary Bhutanese Legal System' in K Ura and S Kinga (eds), *The Spider and the Piglet: Collected Papers on Bhutanese Society. Proceedings of the First Seminar on Bhutan Studies* (Thimphu, Centre for Bhutan Studies, 2004) 355–78, 357.

[18] Kinga, *Polity* (n 11) 235.

[19] Kinga, *Polity* (n 11) 276.

[20] ibid 280.

[21] ibid 282.

[22] ibid 283.

[23] V Iyer, 'Constitution-Making in Bhutan: A Complex and Sui Generis Experience' [2019] *Chinese Journal of Comparative Law* 359; see also: Tobgye, *Constitution* (n 9) 22.

to push Bhutan towards democracy. One of them was the aggravating tensions between the Lhotsampa minority and the Drukpa majority in Bhutan in the 1990s.[24] Another trigger for the king's constitutional reform might have been the historical events in Bhutan's neighbouring states.[25]

Thus, on 4 December 2001, King Jigme Singye Wangchuck commissioned a committee consisting of 39 representatives from various sections of society to draft a Constitution. Chief Justice Lyonpo Sonam Tobgye served as the head of the committee. The other members were two monks nominated by the Je Khenpo (chief abbot), three judges nominated by the Chief Justice, 20 elected members for each Dzongkhag of Bhutan and 13 persons from other organisations nominated by the king.[26] The committee discussed their visions for the Constitution, looked into Bhutan's traditional laws and royal decrees, went through the literature as well as international human rights conventions and scrutinised about 100 constitutions from around the world.[27] Eventually, a draft was sent to the Government of India, on whose recommendation the Indian jurist KK Vengugopal advised the drafting committee during the constitution-making process. After the king's suggested amendments, the draft was distributed to every household in Bhutan and made available on the internet.[28]

The drafters were aware of the concept of constituent power as the basis for explaining the normative basis for a constitution's claim to authority.[29] Though the Preamble of the Constitution makes it clear that the constituent power lies with the people of Bhutan ('We, the people of Bhutan'), many see the Constitution as a 'gift from the King'.[30] The chairman of the Drafting Committee reported popular caution towards the Constitution when it was made known to the population.[31] Many were wary of the prospect of democracy and wanted instead to reserve powers to the king, especially residual powers in case the government failed.[32] Thus, the fourth king and the then crown prince (the current fifth king), accompanied by members of the Drafting Committee, toured the country to explain and discuss the Constitution. The fact that the whole population of Bhutan was thus involved in the constitution making process explains the vesting of constituent power in the people and forms the basis for the legitimacy of the Constitution's authority within the new democratic system. Moreover, from a sociological point of view, the involvement of the whole population could be viewed as having united all layers of

[24] Iyer (n 23) 367; SD Muni, 'Bhutan: Marching towards Democracy' (Singapore, National University of Singapore, Institute of South Asian Studies, 2008) ISAS Brief No 63, 1.

[25] Tibet had lost its independence to China in 1959 and Sikkim to India in 1975, thus leaving Bhutan as the last Buddhist Himalayan Kingdom, and the Nepali king and his family were assassinated in 2001. This instability and volatility may have motivated the constitutional movement.

[26] S Tobgye, 'Interview with Rohan Mukherjee' (Governance Traps 20 November 2009) 4, www.successfulsocieties.princeton.edu/interviews/sonam-tobgye.

[27] ibid 5.

[28] *cf* ibid 7. There were more than 300 national and more than 300 international comments via internet posts.

[29] *cf* Tushnet, *Advanced Introduction* 15.

[30] Tobgye, *Constitution* (n 9) 5; S Kinga, 'The Constitution: The King's Gift: Difiling [sic] and Sanctifying a Sacred Gift' (11–14 October 2009) *Conference on Beyond the Ballot Box: Deepening and Sustaining Democracy in Asia* 5, www.bhutanstudies.org.bt/publicationFiles/Conference Proceedings/DemocracyConference2009/05; Muni (n 24) 1.

[31] Tobgye, *Constitution* (n 9) 20.

[32] Tobgye, 'Interview' (n 26) 8.

society, thus helping to stabilise governance. After these public consultations, the final draft was submitted to the first democratically elected Parliament. On 18 July 2008, the Constitution was adopted and signed by the king and Parliament.

II. The Vision of the Constitution

In this section, I elaborate on the vision of the Bhutanese Constitution, which, according to the chairman of the Drafting Committee, encapsulates the people's aspiration to preserve the sovereignty and identity of Bhutan, the monarchy's adherence to the concept of grassroots level democracy and the decision of His Majesty Jigme Singye Wangchuck, the Fourth Druk Gyalpo, to effectively transfer power to the people.[33] The Preamble of the Constitution, which in all its brevity addresses key issues, serves as a starting point.

A. A Unified Nation Rooted in Tradition and Buddhism

The Preamble, by stating 'we, the people of Bhutan, hereby ordain and adopt this Constitution', refers to the people of Bhutan as a national entity that serves as the constituent power-holders of the Constitution as well as the sovereign of Bhutan.[34] According to the Preamble, the objectives of the Constitution are to strengthen the sovereignty of Bhutan and to ensure liberty, justice and tranquility, as well as the unity, happiness and well-being of the people.

Considering the geopolitical situation of Bhutan, with its powerful neighbours China and India – and its status as the last independent Buddhist Himalayan kingdom – the Bhutanese Constitution engineers the sovereignty and stability of the country around a uniform national identity to prevent any instability arising from conflict within Bhutan. The fourth king had already been promoting the idea of 'One Nation, One Country' in the 1970s. He addressed the Lhotsampa of Nepali origin by stating, 'You, the citizens of Southern Bhutan must never regard yourself as aliens, … All of us must remain united as one people and as one nation'.[35] Today, the concept of Bhutan as a nation-state is generally accepted among all the component ethnic groups in the country.[36]

Of the various provisions of the Constitution that sustain this vision of national unity of the people, Article 15 is particularly significant, as it is intended to limit the possibilities of political fragmentation or conflict based on identity lines such as region, gender, religion, culture, class or ethnicity.[37] In this provision, political parties are charged with

[33] Tobgye, *Constitution* (n 9) 5.

[34] See also Art 1, s 1: 'Bhutan is a Sovereign Kingdom and the Sovereign power belongs to the people of Bhutan.'

[35] Tobgye, *Constitution* (n 9) 14.

[36] *cf* Bertelsmann Stiftung, 'BTI 2016, Bhutan Country Report' 6, www.bti-project.org/content/en/downloads/reports/country_report_2016_BTN.pdf.

[37] Tobgye, *Constitution* (n 9) 264.

ensuring that national interests prevail over all other interests. Candidates and political parties shall not resort to regionalism, ethnicity and religion to incite voters for electoral gain. A political party can only be registered by the Election Commission if its membership is not based on region, gender, language, religion or social origin. It has to be broad-based, with cross-national membership and support, and be committed to national cohesion and stability.

To construct a uniform national identity for Bhutan, the Constitution draws heavily on religion and culture. By its special graphical design and its referral to transcendental forces – the Three Jewels of Buddhism[38] and guardian deities – the Preamble imagines the national identity of the people of Bhutan as a Buddhist nation.[39] Moreover, the idea of a Buddhist nation becomes manifest in Article 9 of the Constitution, according to which the state 'shall strive to create conditions that will enable the true and sustainable development of a good and compassionate society rooted in Buddhist ethos and universal human values'.

The Constitution furthermore emphasises a common history of the Bhutanese people. It refers explicitly to *chos srid gnyis* (dual government), an expression with deep historical meaning, as it was Zhabdrung Ngawang Namgyal who implemented this political concept of a spiritual and secular rule in Bhutan. According to Article 2(2), the Druk Gyalpo (king of Bhutan) as a Buddhist shall be the upholder of the *chos srid* and is thus seen as continuing the rule of the Zhabdrung and his successors. By declaring Buddhism as the spiritual heritage of Bhutan (Article 3) and defining several Buddhist sites and objects as part of the cultural heritage of Bhutan (Article 4), the Constitution makes clear that the religious and cultural roots of Bhutan lie in Buddhism.

Although we might expect that this emphasis on Buddhism could provoke antagonism by followers of other religions, this does not seem to be the case in Bhutan. Conflicts are not fought out along religious fault lines. The Constitution provides for security for the followers of other religions: according to Article 7(4), every Bhutanese citizen has the fundamental right to freedom of religion, and, according to Article 3(2) of the Constitution, the king is 'the protector of all religions (*chos lugs*) in Bhutan'.

Nevertheless, the special way of regulating religion within the new constitutional framework had the potential for conflict. Contrary to the past, the drafters of the Constitution intended to separate religion from politics and objected to the establishment of Buddhism as a state religion.[40] Thus, religious institutions and personalities shall remain above politics; in turn, it is their responsibility to promote the spiritual heritage of Bhutan (Article 3(3)). As Bhutan has many religious institutions and religious personalities held in high esteem by the population, the drafters of the Constitution feared that the functioning of the democratic system could be distorted if religious persons and institutions involved themselves in political activities. Hence, the separation of religion from politics is thought to preserve Bhutan's spiritual heritage while eschewing fundamentalism and sectarian policies.[41] In accordance with this principle, section 184 of the

[38] ie the Buddha, the Dharma and the Sangha.

[39] Whitecross, 'Buddhism and Constitutions' (n 6) 362–63 analyses the textual and graphic design of the preamble, which draws on familiar Buddhist iconography.

[40] Tobgye, *Constitution* (n 9) 108.

[41] ibid 111.

Election Act 2008 bars religious persons (especially ordained persons)[42] from participating in the electoral process as a voter for or candidate, member or supporter of a political party.[43]

These regulations shifted the balance of power in Bhutan. Before 2008, the Zhung Dratshang (Central Monastic Order) was an important political force, and most of the Bhutanese people felt deeply embedded in Buddhism, whilst wholly unfamiliar with the concept of secularism.[44] The Central Monastic Body sent 10 representatives to the NA and two representatives to the Royal Advisory Council. This was meant to ensure the continuity of the dual system of governance and permit intersections of the spiritual and political systems.[45] After the transition to democracy in 2008, the monastic contribution to these bodies was dissolved. This reportedly caused tensions between the government and religious organisations.[46] However, there does not appear to be any ongoing damage to the relationship between the state and the religious bodies. The drafters of the Constitution seem to have found a compromise that suits all parties.

B. A Unified Nation Committed to the Rule of Law

Bhutan, like many other modern nation-states in South and South-East Asia, has adopted a constitution that complies with global standards of the rule of law, the separation of powers and the implementation of fundamental rights. The Constitution defines the nature of the polity, the role and position of the monarchy, and citizenship, while providing for fundamental rights and duties, and establishing the principles of state policy.[47] Further provisions deal with aspects of the rule of law and separation of powers in the system of elections and Parliament, local and central government, and the executive and the judiciary.[48] The king stressed in his audiences the central ideas of justice and good governance,[49] which is also a major component of the development programmes negotiated with international development partners.[50]

[42] In detail, *cf* Election Commission of Bhutan, Guidelines for Interpretation of Section 184 of the Election Act of the Kingdom of Bhutan, 2008 concerning Religion and Elections, www.ecb.bt/legislation/guidelines/GuidelinesforReligionAbovePolitics.pdf.

[43] This has the same logic as it is used in Thailand and Myanmar to limit the franchise of Buddhist monks. On this, *cf* T Larsson, 'Keeping Monks in Their Place?' [2016] *Asian Journal of Law and Society* 17; T Larsson, 'Monkish Politics in Southeast Asia: Religious Disenfranchisement in Comparative and Theoretical Perspective' [2015] *Modern Asian Studies* 40.

[44] Whitecross makes an important point in emphasising that many of the Constitution's elite draftspersons had been educated in India and might have been aware of the debates of secularism there: Whitecross, 'Buddhism and Constitutions' (n 6) 364.

[45] G Dorji, 'Zhung Dratshang: The Central Monk Body of Bhutan' (2015) *The Druk Journal*, winter edition, www.drukjournal.bt/zhung-dratshang-the-central-monk-body-of-bhutan/.

[46] ibid.

[47] For these principles, see Art 9 of the Constitution.

[48] Reasoning on the rule of law in Bhutan: K Wangmo, 'Rule of Law – A Comparative Analysis of Rule of Law in Australia and Bhutan' (2018) Bhutan Law Network/JSW Law Research Paper Series No 18-6, www.ssrn.com/abstract=3271777.

[49] Cited in Tobgye, *Constitution* (n 9) 25.

[50] eg Austria supports the Kingdom of Bhutan in consolidating its young rule of law regime, www.entwicklung.at/en/ada/news/detail-en/justice-for-all. For an extremely critical approach towards the engagement of international bodies in constitution-making, see V Sripati, *Constitution-Making under UN Auspices: Fostering Dependency in Sovereign Lands* (New Delhi, Oxford University Press, 2020).

Unlike other countries, the Preamble of the Constitution does not refer to individual equality, rights and freedoms, but stresses collective values like tranquillity, happiness and the well-being of the people. Nevertheless, the Bhutanese Constitution contains a catalogue of fundamental rights as well as a list of fundamental duties. Article 7 distinguishes between human rights and citizens' rights. While all persons are equal before the law and have the right to life, liberty and security of the person, only Bhutanese citizens enjoy political rights, such as the right to freedom of speech, opinion and expression and the right to freedom of peaceful assembly and freedom of association, other than membership to associations that are harmful to the peace and unity of the country. Furthermore, only Bhutanese citizens have the right to freedom of thought, conscience and religion. All the rights and freedoms may be subjected to reasonable restrictions by law when it concerns the interests of the sovereignty, security, unity and integrity of Bhutan and the interests of peace, stability and well-being of the nation.[51] This again gives the state wide powers to restrict actions of separatist or 'anti-national' character that could be seen as undermining the unity, and thus stability, of the country.

C. A Unified Nation Striving for Happiness

In the Preamble to the Constitution, the people of Bhutan pledge to 'enhance [the] happiness and well-being of the people'. Happiness as the paramount objective of the legal order in Bhutan is not new. According to the 'Golden Yoke' (*gser gyi nya' shing*) – an inscription attributed to the founder of the Bhutanese state, Zhabdrung Ngawang Namgyal – the ultimate objective of the Drukpa rule and the introduction of the law in Bhutan is to bring benefit and happiness to all beings of the country.[52] Further, the legal code (*bka' khrims*) of 1729 states that 'if there is no law, happiness for the beings does not arise; if the beings are not happy, there is no sense that the Dharma masters of Drukpa uphold the twofold teachings'.[53] Similarly, the Bhutanese Constitution emphasises the historical tradition of the Bhutanese state system and its legal order, and the objectives of the Constitution converge with those found in the earliest legal sources of Bhutan.[54]

Article 9(2) of the Constitution obliges the state to strive to promote those conditions that will enable the pursuit of 'Gross National Happiness' (GNH). Bhutanese authors emphasise the idea that in a developing country like Bhutan, both social welfare and economic development goals need to be secured by the Constitution to achieve the goal of GNH.[55] The term GNH was coined by the fourth king as early as 1972.[56] The first occasion on which this declaration was recorded and reported publicly was at

[51] See Tobgye, *Constitution* (n 9) 147.

[52] M Windischgraetz and R Wangdi, *The Black-Slate Edict of Punakha Dzong* (Thimphu, Kuensel, 2019) 14.

[53] bsTan-'dzin chos-rgyal, *Lho'i chos 'byung 'phro mthud 'jam mgon smon mtha'i 'phreng ba* (Thimphu, KMT Publisher, 2004) 261 (trans M Windischgraetz).

[54] Which are themselves based on early legal-historical sources of the Tibetan imperial period: *cf* Windischgraetz and Wangdi (n 52) 15.

[55] L Dubgyur, '70th Constitution Day of India and Its Reflection on Democratic Transition in Bhutan' (Kunsel, 1 December 2019).

[56] eg K Ura, S Alkire and T Zangmo, *The Gross National Happiness Index of Bhutan – Method and Illustrative Results* (Thimphu, Center for Bhutan Studies, 2011) www.gnhcentrebhutan.org/what-is-gnh/history-of-gnh/.

the Bombay (Mumbai) airport in 1979, when an Indian journalist had posed a question about Bhutan being an underdeveloped nation. The fourth king responded that 'Gross National Happiness was more important than Gross National Product',[57] questioning the prevailing measurement system, gross domestic product (GDP). GNH became the central philosophy guiding all state authorities in Bhutan to promote sustainable development that gives equal importance to non-economic aspects of well-being. Progress should be viewed not only through the lens of economics, but also from spiritual, social, cultural and ecological perspectives. The concept of GNH has been directing the country for more than four decades, and exists both as a guiding principle in the minds of the Bhutanese and as the overarching objective in almost all official documents of the country.[58]

The Gross National Happiness Commission (GNHC) is charged with implementing GNH in Bhutan. It is the central government body for coordinating and spearheading policy formulation to ensure cohesion between sectoral policies and alignment with the national development objectives and GNH. The GNHC has to guide and direct the formulation of long-term perspective plans to provide guidance for future development policies and to provide guidance and direction for the formulation of the five-year development plans. The practical basis for developing these policies is the GNH survey, which is conducted by the Centre for Bhutan & GNH Studies (CBS) every five years, questioning people throughout the country on the nine dimensions of GNH: psychological well-being, health, education, cultural diversity and resilience, time use, good governance, community vitality, living standard, and ecological diversity and resilience.[59]

III. Old Powers and New Forces

As shown above, Bhutan's Constitution builds upon several continuities. The most significant of these is the pattern of the introduction of an advisory representative body of the people which eventually becomes a law-giving institution. This occurred with the National Assembly from the 1950s onward, and likewise with the cabinet of ministers to whom the king ceded successively more and more of his powers. The development of these institutions seems to have led to uncontested stability, which forms the basis of their continued effectiveness. As we saw above, a major force that lost political power by the adoption of the Constitution was the Central Monastic Body, but they seem to have found their new constitutional role by raising their voice against political decisions which pose a threat to Buddhist values, as happened in the debate over the establishment of slaughterhouses in Bhutan.[60] In the following, I want to address three forces that are of great importance to the stability of constitutional governance in Bhutan: first,

[57] J Locke, 'Buddhist Modernism Underway in Bhutan: Gross National Happiness and Buddhist Political Theory' [2020] *Religions* 297, fn 4.

[58] K Ura, S Alkire, T Zangmo and K Wangdi, *An Extensive Analysis of GNH Index* (Thimphu, Center for Bhutan Studies, 2012) 7.

[59] For detailed information about the GNH Index see ibid.

[60] D Gyelmo, 'Dratshang Petitions against Meat Processing Project' (Kuensel, 2015) www.kuenselonline.com/dratshang-petitions-against-meat-processing-project/.

political parties, which are fundamental to the functioning of any liberal democracy,[61] though their impact in Bhutan is still low; second, the judiciary, the development of which began with the establishment of the district courts and the High Court in the 1960s; third, the king, the oldest and most widely accepted force in shaping the country's destiny, a fact which – at least for the time being – makes his interventions highly effective in crises.

A. Political Parties

Any democratisation process relies on the factors of 'ideology' and 'social mobilisation'.[62] For both factors, the prerequisites in Bhutan were weak. With regard to the political consciousness of the average Bhutanese populace, Mathou points out that it has always been very low. The politicisation process that had a significant impact on large sections of the population in other South Asian countries had not mobilised Bhutanese crowds, except for Nepalese Bhutanese in the southern districts of Bhutan.[63] Up to the beginning of the constitutional era, the existence of a largely unchallenged ruling elite, and their willingness to hold on to leadership, had prevented the emergence of organised factional politics.[64]

In addition to this issue of civic unfamiliarity with political associations, the Constitution imposes several restrictions on the formation of parties and the eligibility of representatives for the NA, which hinder the creation of a larger and more diverse political field. According to Article 15(1) of the Constitution, political parties shall ensure that national interests prevail over all other interests. As shown above, candidates and political parties shall not resort to regionalism, ethnicity or religion to incite voters (Article 15(2)). Further restrictions in Article 3(3) require members of monastic communities and other religious persons to remain apolitical (see above). They are neither allowed to vote nor be elected. Furthermore, the election laws lay down that no one can contest parliamentary elections without having a formal university degree, thus striving for a body of educated decision-makers for the country.[65] Regulations on party funding are an additional factor in the weak institutionalisation of political parties and their lack of a strong grassroots presence. Parties have small memberships, and they can only raise funds from the small amount given by the Election Commission to each candidate and from members' contributions, which have a ceiling. This means that parties have very limited funds and are of the purely electoral type, springing to life close to elections but dormant or operating with limited staff between elections.[66]

The Election Commission of Bhutan (ECB) has been taking these restrictions seriously. Thus, before the first elections to the National Council, candidates were

[61] See generally T Khaitan, 'Political Parties in Constitutional Theory' [2020] *Current Legal Problems* 89.

[62] T Mathou, *How to Reform a Traditional Buddhist Monarchy. The Political Achievements of His Majesty Jigme Singye Wangchuck, the Fourth King of Bhutan (1972–2006)* (Thimphu, Center for Bhutan Studies, 2008) 5.

[63] ibid 4.

[64] ibid 4.

[65] Election Act of the Kingdom of Bhutan 2008, Arts 176 and 177.

[66] Bertelsmann (n 36) 14.

disqualified because they lacked a formal university degree.[67] The ECB also disqualified a political party (BPUP[68]) because it could not fulfil the national aspirations, visions and goals in terms of its ability to run the government and have candidates who could be members of the cabinet and the Parliament.[69] The ECB also disqualified a candidate of the Peoples' Democratic Party (PDP) who tried to bring to the fore the problem of Bhutanese of Nepali origin. This was done to send a firm message that there was no room in Bhutan for communal and sectarian politics.[70]

As far as ideology is concerned, there is little diversity. Since Bhutan's opening up to the outside world in the 1960s, official rhetoric has tended to be modernist in content, particularly due to the influence of India, and focused on the imperative of development.[71] As the ideological principle of Bhutan's modernisation process, GNH has contributed heavily to the population's political maturation. Mass media and education have both helped to convince the Bhutanese population that progress has to be seen in the context of genuine sustainable human development, rather than just income growth.[72] Due to the paramount place of GNH within the state ideology of Bhutan and the restrictions on the formation of political parties, the existing parties have all declared their commitment to implementing and realising the goals of GNH.[73]

Nevertheless, facing the third elections in 2018, the parties improved and diversified their manifestos. The PDP (the reigning party from 2013 to 2018) manifesto highlighted five 'economic jewels', which, if harnessed efficiently, should help Bhutan realise its economic potential in the region. These economic jewels were: hydropower and energy, mining, agriculture, tourism and cottage (small and medium-sized) enterprises. The DPT (the opposition party from 2013 to 2018; the reigning party from 2008 to 2013) manifesto traditionally advocated the maintenance of GDP for bringing about peace and prosperity in Bhutan. The winning DNT manifesto in 2018 was titled 'Narrowing the Gap', and revolved around ensuring inclusive economic development and reducing the widening gap between the rich and the poor.[74]

Analysing the outcomes of the first and second elections, in 2008 and 2013, the latter represented a process of democratic consolidation, with more parties and candidates participating. The results showed that the Bhutanese electorate could oust incumbent parties and members if it so desired.[75] The third election, in 2018, in turn, saw a higher voter turnout (71.61 per cent, roughly 5.5 per cent more than in the 2013 election) and resulted in a new party (DNT) winning. Additionally, the 2018 election saw the highest number of women elected to the NA in Bhutan's short electoral history. In conclusion, it may be observed that the Bhutanese are undergoing a period of increased political

[67] Kinga, *Polity* (n 11) 209.
[68] Bhutan People United Party.
[69] Kuensel, 28 November 2007, cited in Kinga, *Polity* (n 11) 307.
[70] Muni (n 24) 2.
[71] Mathou (n 62) 5.
[72] ibid 6.
[73] For the two parties that contended for the first elections of the country, see Kinga, *Polity* (n 11) 313; Bertelsmann (n 36).
[74] Summarising, NR Nihar, 'Bhutan National Assembly Elections 2018: A Mandate for Change?' (Manohar Parrikar Institute for Defence Studies and Analyses, 12 November 2018) IDSA Issue Briefs, www.idsa.in/issuebrief/bhutan-elections-2018_nnayak-rsingh-akbehuria-121118#footnoteref6_gr7ed9p.
[75] Bertelsmann (n 36) 9.

awareness and consciousness on the political application of their democratic rights and particularly to express their desire for change.

B. The Judiciary

Under Article 21(1) of the Constitution, the Bhutanese Judiciary is independent and charged with upholding the rule of law. The Supreme Court is at the apex of the judicial authority, is the highest appellate authority to entertain appeals against the judgments, orders or decisions of the High Court in all matters and has the power to review its judgments and orders. According to Article 1(11), the Supreme Court is the guardian of the Constitution and the final authority on its interpretation. The Supreme Court has – together with the High Court – the authority for constitutional review and may, on its own motion or on an application made by the Attorney General or by a party to a case, withdraw any case pending before the High Court involving a substantial question of law of general importance relating to the interpretation of the Constitution and dispose of the case itself (Article 21(9)). Additionally, according to Article 21(11), the king may refer a question of law or fact to the Supreme Court for its consideration if it is of such a nature and such public importance that it is expedient to obtain the opinion of the Supreme Court.

The Supreme Court has so far managed to act as the guardian and interpreter of the Constitution, and has developed credibility both domestically and internationally. Its independence was first tested in 2010, when the leader of the opposition party in the NA challenged the government before the High Court on the introduction of a tax rise by an administrative measure rather than through legislation. On appeal, the ruling of the High Court, deeming the government's actions unconstitutional, was upheld by the Supreme Court.[76]

Furthermore, all levels of the judiciary demonstrated independence in 2013 when finding the Speaker of the NA and a cabinet minister guilty of improper land allocation. The district court's initial ruling was upheld by the High Court and then by the Supreme Court.[77] A long-standing dispute regarding the ownership of a taxi parking area in Thimphu is another pertinent example, as the lawsuit was first filed with the courts before the adoption of the Constitution on 18 July 2008. Thimphu City Corporation had appealed to the High Court in 2007, after the district court's verdict in favour of Tashi Commercial. The High Court upheld the district court's verdict. In August 2008, Thimphu City Corporation appealed to the king against the judgment of the High Court, although the new Constitution no longer provided for such a remedy. The king redirected the case to be reviewed by the current justices of the High Court since the appeal was 'post constitutional'.[78]

[76] See www.judiciary.gov.bt/judg/2016/Supreme%20Court/englishj.pdf.

[77] Bertelsmann (n 36) 11.

[78] 'Thimphu Thromde to Approach Supreme Court on High Court's Taxi Parking Verdict' *The Bhutanese* (12 July 2012) www.thebhutanese.bt/thimphu-thromde-to-approach-supreme-court-on-high-courts-taxi-parking-verdict/.

C. The Monarch

Whereas political parties were new to the people of Bhutan, the monarchy provided continuity and a smooth transition from the old system to the new. The king remains of paramount importance in the functioning of the state from both legal and more informal political perspectives.

The Druk Gyalpo (king of Bhutan) is the head of the state and is formally above the law. He is not answerable in a court of law (Article 2(15) of the Constitution) and acts through several royal prerogatives. According to Article 2(16), he may grant titles as well as amnesty, pardon and reduce sentences; he may grant citizenship, land *kidu* and other *kidu*.[79] Probably the most important royal prerogative is the residual or reserved powers of the king under Article 2(16e), according to which the king exercises powers relating to matters which are not provided for by the Constitution or by other laws.

According to Article 10 of the Constitution, the Druk Gyalpo is part of Parliament and summons the first sitting of Parliament after each general election. He may address or sit in the proceedings of either House or joint sittings of Parliament, and he may address either House or both with messages that have to be answered with opinions by the addressed House. According to Article 2(16), the king may command Bills and other measures to be introduced in Parliament. Furthermore, he has the power of assent for Bills in Parliament. Further, the monarch may return Bills with recommendations for amendments; however, he must abide by the final decision of both Houses (Article 13(10) and (11)). As for the composition of the National Council, the king nominates five eminent persons besides the 20 other members elected by the Dzongkhags.

The king and the institution of the monarchy are held in high esteem in Bhutan, and the two Houses of Parliament are perceived to be unlikely to make proposals with which the king would strongly disagree. There is thus an anticipatory element to policy making in Bhutan.[80] Some reports suggest that the king could be a potential veto player.[81] However, the king has shown a serious commitment to protecting the sanctity of the Constitution. Sonam Kinga reports several conflicts that took place shortly after the first elections to the NA when the various stakeholders had not yet become accustomed to the authority of the Constitution. When the government wanted to hold the *gup* (village headmen) elections in 2008 on the basis of two Acts that had already been repealed in 2007, as no new laws had yet come into force, the king issued a *kasho* (royal decree) to the ECB suggesting that the incumbent heads be allowed to continue until relevant laws were reviewed to harmonise them with the Constitution.[82]

The Constitution contains regulations regarding the end of the monarch's reign that are exceptional by international standards. According to Article 2(6), the Druk Gyalpo has to step down when reaching the age of 65. Article 2(20)–(25) contains provisions for the abdication of the monarch. The Druk Gyalpo shall abdicate the throne in favour

[79] Benefits granted by the king; *cf* the glossary annexed to the English translation of the Constitution of Bhutan.

[80] Bertelsmann (n 36) 9.

[81] ibid 9.

[82] Kinga, *Polity* (n 11) 156.

of his heir in case of permanent mental disability or wilful violation of the Constitution. This requires a motion submitted by no less than two-thirds of the total Members of Parliament to be passed in a joint sitting of Parliament. If no less than three-quarters of the total number of Members of Parliament pass the motion, a national referendum has to be held, by which the people of Bhutan decide with a simple majority.

The idea of the devolution of power and abdication is not a new one. As discussed earlier, the third king had already introduced the idea of motions of no confidence by the NA against the king. Although the population of Bhutan has always been hesitant about such provisions, they were included in the Constitution under the direction of the king. The king desired that all future kings of Bhutan shall be physically and mentally fit to serve the country.[83]

IV. Conclusion

Bhutan has not yet faced a major crisis in which the mechanisms of the Constitution of 2008 have been significantly tested. However, by examining the reactions of Bhutan's stakeholders during the COVID-19 pandemic, we can get a sense of what crisis management looks like – and might look like in future crises – in Bhutan.

Under the direction of the fifth king, the National Resilience Fund (NRF) was set up in April 2020 to provide economic relief to those people who suffered most due to the COVID-19 pandemic. While the government deliberated on the next tranche of NRF financing in April 2021, the NRF task force submitted several options for funding, including transfers from the government budget, borrowing from the domestic market and concessional loans from multilateral development banks. However, the king directed that efforts to replenish the NRF should neither disrupt the economy nor affect the development plans and projects of the government. Instead, the king issued a royal command that the next tranche of the NRF will be financed in its entirety from the Monarch's Kidu Fund and the Sungchop Fund. The Royal Kidu Fund has been used to grant *kidu* to Bhutanese people to alleviate hardship and to provide the ultimate social safety net. The Sungchop Fund was established by the kings as a security fund for the country during times of need.[84] Thus, the king of Bhutan plays an active and creative role in steering the country, and, at least for the time being, we can expect the same for any crisis to come. Starting from the hypothesis that the institutions with the greatest continuity would likely be the most effective in a crisis case, this chapter has highlighted political and institutional continuities and innovations throughout the 400 years of Bhutan's history that have resulted in the creation of a cohesive, independent state. The reforms of the third and the fourth kings from the 1950s onwards in particular initiated the change from an absolute to a democratic constitutional monarchy. Gradually, the people of Bhutan are becoming accustomed to representation in Parliament, governance

[83] Tobgye, *Constitution* (n 9) 85.

[84] Prime Minister's Office press release (22 April 2021) www.royalkidu.bt/wp-content/uploads/2021/04/Press-Release-22-April-2021.pdf.

by a cabinet of ministers to whom the king has delegated his executive powers, electing representatives at the local level and solving their legal conflicts in the courts.[85] Thus, when the Constitution was adopted, it built upon strong existing institutions. One of the most powerful institutions remains the king, who, besides his constitutional powers, has a significant de facto social and political power and influence on the population of Bhutan, actively steering and shaping the country's agenda. The judiciary is a younger but well-established institution, which for several decades has established its capacity and willingness to perform its constitutional function. In contrast, political parties, widely seen as a salient factor of any liberal democratic system, still remain weak due to various legal restrictions, but primarily because the Bhutanese have not yet fully become accustomed to this new socio-political formation.

Concluding this assessment of constitutional governance in Bhutan and trying to place Bhutan's constitutionalism within the array of other constitutions in South Asia, we must reckon with Bhutan's unique position. When the editors of this volume aptly state that, while the twentieth century saw a broad acceptance of democracy, the twenty-first century sees its decline, Bhutan shows the opposite. Being an absolute monarchy until 2008, it has just embarked on the adventure of democracy. It is too early to anticipate possible fractures. The strength of the Constitution and constitutional governance in Bhutan can be seen in the continuity of old institutions like the monarchy. Much will depend on the king's person. The fact that the king himself initiated the transition from monarchy to democracy, guiding the process of designing a constitution that corresponds both to international standards and to Bhutanese particularities, allows the prognosis that this still-young democracy will develop healthily.

[85] Though it must be said that mediation out of court plays a huge role in Bhutan, even today.

PART III

Federalism

4

Territorial Dynamics in Sri Lanka: Federalism, Unitarism and Path Dependence

JAYANI NADARAJALINGAM AND ZIM NWOKORA[1]

I. Introduction

Sri Lanka is characterised by rich pluralism along many axes, including linguistic, ethnic and religious divisions.[2] But, as Asanga Welikala notes:

> While all aspects of this societal pluralism have cultural and political salience for constitutional debates, it is the schism between the Sinhalese [majority] and the Tamil [minority] that has defined the deep divide at the heart of Sri Lanka's constitutional unsettlement.[3]

Sinhalese communities make up approximately three-quarters of the country's population (as reported in the 2012 census), while the Tamil minority accounts for about 11 per cent.[4] As is well known, the long-running conflict between the Sri Lankan state and the Tamil secessionist movements came to an end in 2009 with the military defeat of the latter by the former. The 2019 presidential election, some 10 years later, revealed a country that remains deeply divided. President Gotabaya Rajapaksa won

[1] The authors would like to thank Erika Arban, Ros Dixon, Rohan Edrisinha, Mario Gomez, Swati Jhaveri, Tarun Khaitan, Kate O'Regan, Dinesha Samararatne, Cheryl Saunders and the participants of the 2019 Workshop on Constitutional Resilience in South Asia for helpful discussions in relation to the ideas and arguments in this chapter. Special thanks to Michael Breen for his excellent commentary at the 2019 Workshop and to Patrick Emerton, Dinesha Samararatne and an anonymous referee for their feedback on earlier drafts. Pedram Gholipour-Shahraki and John Sebastian provided outstanding research assistance during the final stages. We would also like to acknowledge the generous support of the University of Melbourne's Statelessness Hallmark Research Initiative.

[2] Please see D Shah and M Gomez, ch 2 and D Samararatne, ch 12 in this volume for introductions to the Sri Lankan constitutional context.

[3] A Welikala, 'Constitutional Migrations in the Commonwealth: The *Quebec Secession Reference* and Sri Lankan Constitutional Discourse' in G Delledonne and G Martinico (eds), *The Canadian Contribution to a Comparative Law of Secession* (London, Palgrave Macmillan, 2019) 139.

[4] Sri Lankan Muslims and Indian Tamils make up 9.3% and 4.12% of the Sri Lankan population, respectively. 'Census of Population and Housing of Sri Lanka 2012' (Department of Census and Statistics, 30 July 2015) www.statistics.gov.lk/Population/StaticalInformation/CPH2011/CensusPopulationHousing2012-FinalReport.

over 52 per cent of the votes in the first round of elections in the country's preferential voting system. In the North and East, however, where the Sinhalese are a small minority, Gotabaya was strongly rejected. He received, for instance, just over 6 per cent of the vote in the Jaffna Peninsula, where Tamils constitute the overwhelming majority.[5]

It is in this historical and political context that the case for federalism has generally been made, by both political actors[6] and scholars.[7] The path by which this goal might be fully realised, however, remains long and difficult at best, and may currently be non-existent. In this chapter, we engage and contribute to this debate by exploring the implications raised by theories of institutional path dependence for our understanding of territorial arrangements in present-day Sri Lanka. The study of institutional path dependence is well established in political science and sociology, and a major recent innovation to this research agenda has been the acknowledgement of the possibility, and often vital importance, of incremental or gradual institutional change in the context of stable institutions.[8] Building on and extending this theoretical lens, our analysis identifies a novel, gradualist pathway by which Sri Lanka may be able to transition in practice, and to a considerable degree, from unitarism to federalism.

We take for granted that federalism is a desirable goal in the Sri Lankan context. While the merits and limitations of federalism in general continue to be debated,[9] at least in the Sri Lankan case there seems to be a reasonable consensus among constitutional experts that federalism would provide a better arrangement for the country than the existing form of unitarism, given the country's social cleavage structures.[10] We also take as given the stability of the unitary state as set out in Article 2 of Sri Lanka's second republican Constitution. Article 2 states that 'The Republic of Sri Lanka is a Unitary State'. This premise follows from the widespread acknowledgement that formal

[5] '2020 Sri Lankan Parliamentary Elections' (Election Commission of Sri Lanka, 6 August 2020) results. elections.gov.lk/. The last official census (2012) reported that the Jaffna district had a 98.9% population of Sri Lankan Tamils. See Department of Census & Statistics, *Census of Population and Housing 2012* (Ministry of Policy Planning and Economic Affairs, Government of Sri Lanka) 145, www.statistics.gov.lk/Population/StaticalInformation/CPH2011/CensusPopulationHousing2012-FinalReport.

[6] The political actors include, most notably, members of the Ilankai Thamil Arasu Katchi (ITAK, the Federal Party). It is important to note that the Tamils were not the first to advocate for federalism in the Sri Lankan context. As Edrisinha notes, 'in the late 1920s … representatives of the highland Kandyan Sinhalese, who had always viewed themselves as separate from the coastal Sinhalese, demanded a federal Ceylon with three provinces including a province for the northeast': R Edrisinha, 'Multination Federalism and Minority Rights in Sri Lanka' in W Kymlicka and B He (eds), *Multiculturalism in Asia* (Oxford, Oxford University Press, 2005) 247.

[7] Most notable among the scholars is R Edrisinha. See, eg ibid; R Edrisinha, 'Debating Federalism in Sri Lanka and Nepal' in M Tushnet and M Khosla (eds), *Unstable Constitutionalism: Law and Politics in South Asia* (Cambridge, Cambridge University Press, 2015) 291–319. See also M Breen, *The Road to Federalism in Nepal, Myanmar and Sri Lanka: Finding the Middle Ground* (London, Routledge, 2018); Welikala, 'Constitutional Migrations' (n 3). Welikala ultimately argues for a pluri-national solution in the Sri Lankan context. Such a solution, he argues, moves away from the unitarism v federalism dichotomy. See generally A Welikala, 'Constitutional Form and Reform in Postwar Sri Lanka' in Tushnet and Khosla (ibid).

[8] See, eg J Mahoney and K Thelen, 'A Theory of Gradual Institutional Change' in J Mahoney and K Thelen (eds), *Explaining Institutional Change: Ambiguity, Agency, and Power* (Cambridge, Cambridge University Press, 2009).

[9] For a helpful and recent summary, see C Saunders, 'Federalism and Constitutionalism: Challenges Presented by Dominant Conceptions of the Unitary State' in J Kincaid (ed), *A Research Agenda for Federalism Studies* (Cheltenham, Edward Elgar, 2019) 40.

[10] See, eg Edrisinha, 'Multination Federalism' (n 6); Breen (n 7).

constitutional change – that is, replacement of the text of Article 2 – though the most obvious and direct path to federalism, is not a realistic possibility in the current political context. The events of 2022 have certainly increased political uncertainty in Sri Lanka, and thus institutional reforms that only recently were thought to be infeasible – including dissolution of the country's imperial presidency – have become eminently possible. Yet, even in these more uncertain times, there is little to suggest that the stability of the unitary state as set out in Article 2 is up for grabs, given that there is little support for such a reform within the majority Sinhalese communities.

A 'functional federalism', however, can be encouraged without formal change to the text of the Constitution. In other words, the unitary state depicted in the Constitution would remain. The key to unlocking this potential, as we will see, is the 2017 Supreme Court case of *Chandrasoma v Senathiraja*.[11] The functional federalism that may emerge incrementally through this new pathway is likely to be a limited arrangement, especially early on. In other words, it will be less effective at enabling minority self-rule and decentralising authority than formal federalism combined with 'a genuinely federal culture'.[12] Yet it represents a major step in the right direction and one which may open up pathways to more radical change in the future.

The remainder of the chapter proceeds as follows. Section II details the core ideas of institutional path dependence, which we draw on to analyse territorial dynamics in Sri Lanka. We propose a revision of the standard account of path dependence to make it more relevant and useful for the case we study, and potentially for other countries in the Global South. In particular, we observe that traditional accounts often neglect the role of social and political identity as a constraint on institutional change.[13] Furthermore, we identify tools for the analysis of gradual institutional change, which we apply to our case study. In section III, we explain the stability of the unitary state in Sri Lanka as the result of an 'inner logic' deeply rooted in the identity claims of the Sinhala-Buddhist majority. Section IV identifies a feasible path to functional federalism despite this logic, which involves gradual change, and more specifically conversion, through opportunities created by *Chandrasoma*. We end the chapter with a brief discussion of the limitations associated with this pathway.

II. Path Dependence of Institutions

Central to the vast literature on institutional path dependence is the idea that 'history matters' for understanding how institutions operate and develop over time.[14] This research aims to go beyond the general proposition that 'history matters', however, and attempts to causally link historical events with present-day structures and practices

[11] *Chandrasoma v Senathiraja and Thurairasasingham* [2017] (27 March 2014, unreported) SC SPL.

[12] Saunders (n 9) 42. See also Edrisinha, 'Multination Federalism' (n 6) 257–58.

[13] One exception is Capoccia. See G Capoccia, 'Critical Junctures and Institutional Change' in J Mahoney and K Thelen (eds), *Advances in Comparative Historical Analysis* (Cambridge, Cambridge University Press, 2015) 148.

[14] See, eg P Pierson, *Politics in Time* (Princeton, Princeton University Press, 2004); Mahoney and Thelen, 'Theory of Gradual Institutional Change' (n 8); Capoccia (n 13).

and an institution's possible futures. Like any other social science explanation, path-dependence theories are grounded in a causal mechanism. The specific mechanism in these theories is self-reinforcement or positive feedback, meaning that past events and choices (whether intended or not) within and beyond an institution shape its development into the future, by closing off or constraining some potential pathways while opening up or enabling others. In Paul Pierson's influential account, self-reinforcement is theorised specifically as 'increasing returns'.[15] Taken from economics, this concept suggests that institutions will tend to generate higher payoffs for users as they continue to be used. Thus, institutional change becomes costlier and more difficult with time.

The moments in which institutions are created, and when significant changes to existing ones becomes possible, are often referred to as 'critical junctures'.[16] The constraints that lead to self-reinforcement relax at such times, typically as a result of a shock. Paradigmatic examples of shocks include wars, natural disasters, economic depression and technological disruption. Shocks are typically characterised as either exogenous or endogenous. Shocks are exogenous if they are considered external to the institution in question, whereas they are endogenous if they are internal to the institution in question.[17] Endogenous shocks can also be deliberately brought about by actors internal to the institution in question.[18] Capoccia notes that 'it is possible that a critical juncture in the development of a given institution is generated endogenously by power holders that may disrupt existing institutional equilibria to achieve political objectives'.[19] The current economic crisis in Sri Lanka certainly has the characteristics of a shock. Preliminary analysis seems to point towards the shock being best characterised as an endogenous one as its underlying causes seem largely (although by no means exclusively) internal to the Sri Lankan political system.[20] Although critical junctures feature prominently in path-dependent accounts of institutional change, there has been growing recognition of the potential for institutional transformation, or more accurately evolution, to occur even when a critical juncture has not arisen. We develop this point below, in our discussion of gradual institutional change, but note here, echoing Pierson, that 'not only "big" events have big consequences; little ones that happen at the right time can have major consequences as well'.[21]

[15] P Pierson, 'Increasing Returns, Path Dependence, and the Study of Politics' (2000) 94 *American Political Science Review* 251. See also Pierson, *Politics in Time* (n 14).

[16] On critical junctures, see generally Capoccia (n 13).

[17] In certain instances, whether something counts as an exogenous or endogenous shock is, to some extent, open for interpretation: this is primarily because what counts as external or internal to the institution in question can be up for debate. This point is by no means an abstract one. It has salience, for instance, in deeply divided societies in which political conflict – particularly in the form of revolution or secession – exists. During the Sri Lankan civil war, the Tamil secessionist non-state actors were arguably viewed as an endogenous shock from the perspective of the Sri Lankan state, whereas the non-state actors are likely to conceive of themselves as an exogenous shock (given their aspiration to form their own independent polity). It is not necessary, for the purposes of this chapter, to settle this question, but it is important to keep in mind that the identification of what counts as endogenous or exogenous – particularly in the context of deeply divided societies such as Sri Lanka – is itself not a straightforward question.

[18] Exogenous shocks can also be deliberately brought about, but by actors external to the institution in question.

[19] Capoccia (n 13) 151.

[20] See, the analysis of N DeVotta, 'Behind the Crisis in Sri Lanka – How Political and Economic Mismanagement Combined to Plunge Nation into Turmoil' *The Conversation* (19 July 2022) https://theconversation.com/behind-the-crisis-in-sri-lanka-how-political-and-economic-mismanagement-combined-to-plunge-nation-into-turmoil-187137.

[21] Pierson, 'Increasing Returns' (n 15) 263.

At a critical juncture, well-placed actors have greater – though not unconstrained – agency over several historically available options. So, their capacity to redirect policy and shift the terms of a debate, or even reconfigure the institution, expands during this time. As these actors face a broader than the typical range of feasible options,[22] their choices at this moment will matter more than they did immediately prior to the juncture and more than they will once it passes. Due to this heightened agency, the resulting outcomes should be regarded as contingent; they were neither necessary nor inevitable, given the alternatives on the table during the critical juncture.[23] It is important to point out that determining what new (previously unavailable) choices are on the table as a result of a critical juncture is a complex task that requires careful historical analysis. These choices are ones that were (actually) historically available to the relevant political actors and not simply choices that were hypothetically possible.[24] Thus, when engaging in critical juncture analyses, close attention must be paid to 'how close [key] actors came to selecting an alternative option, and what likely consequences the choice of an alternative option would have had for the institutional outcome of interest'.[25] Importantly, as Capoccia observes, 'different kind of … shocks may affect some decision-making arenas and not others … [E]ven when political systems as a whole face "unsettled times," many institutions within the system may remain unaffected'.[26]

As we suggested earlier, the economic and political crisis of 2022 has resulted in 'unsettled times' for the Sri Lankan political system as a whole, but the unitary state has not been affected and, we conjecture, that is unlikely to change. Indeed, even though the crisis has triggered reflection about constitutional structures, the nature of federalism has not been prominent in these debates, which instead have focused on other things, especially the future of the executive (and whether presidentialism remains the best model for the country) and the strengthening of fourth branch institutions.[27] Indeed, despite the demands of Tamil leaders, as Samararatne observes, 'To date, [the protest] has fallen short of bringing within its discourses the question of self-determination of Sri Lankan Tamils'.[28] The institutions emerging out of the critical juncture are reproduced through self-reinforcing processes that generate efficiencies for actors but also, it should be stressed, identities. The longer an institution has been in this reproduction or inertia phase, the harder it becomes for a reversal 'up the path', or some other change, to occur.

[22] Capoccia (n 13) 151.

[23] Contingency here is not to be equated with randomness, however. As Pierson notes, 'although sometimes junctures are treated as highly contingent or random, generally analysts seek to generate convincing explanations for why one path rather than another was chosen': Pierson, *Politics in Time* (n 14) 51. See also Capoccia (n 13).

[24] Capoccia (n 13) 159.

[25] ibid 159.

[26] ibid 167, quoting W Streeck and K Thelen, 'Introduction: Institutional Change in Advanced Political Economics' in W Streeck and K Thelen (eds), *Beyond Continuity: Institutional Change in Advanced Political Economies* (Oxford, Oxford University Press, 2005) 1–39.

[27] See the text of the Twenty First Amendment Bill, www.parliament.lk/files/pdf/constitution/amendment-proposals/2022/sjb-proposal-en.pdf.

[28] D Samararatne, 'The People in the Palace' (*Verfassungsblog*, 15 July 2022) https://verfassungsblog.de/the-people-in-the-palace/.

A. Identity and Institutional Change

Perhaps due to its origins in economic theory, most accounts of path dependence understand lock-in during the path-dependent phase in terms of efficiency (or welfare). But, particularly in politics, it is crucial to also pay attention to what institutional change means for people's institutional roles and identities. This type of 'cost' receives less attention than efficiency costs, but may be more important in many settings, including, we argue, in the politics of federalism in Sri Lanka. With the emergence of new institutions comes new institutional roles that can have a significant impact on identity formation.[29] It follows that the effects of (particularly drastic) institutional change are likely to include the loss of meaning and connection for some, which cannot be readily captured in terms of efficiency. Indeed, it is probably best to interpret the relationship between identity and efficiency as one of incommensurability since the loss of a deeply entrenched identity to the community (and individuals) concerned cannot be straightforwardly measured, or compensated, in terms of some other good.

As an example, consider the rationalisation of farming following the emergence of industrial capitalism. This economic transformation created new institutional roles and identities, including the wage labourer and capitalist, but also abolished old roles and identities, such as the peasant farmer. An important consequence in this case, as documented by Anthony Giddens, was that

> by the early period of the sixteenth century … there exists in England the beginnings of a proletariat – a stratum of dispossessed peasants who are a 'floating' mobile group, separated from their means of production [which determined their old identity] and thrown onto the market as 'free' wage-labourers [a newly emerging identity].[30]

The longer the path-dependent institution of the independent peasantry had existed (to a point of equilibrium), the greater the cost of the abolition of the identity of the peasant farmer. Of course, in many instances, there may be good reasons to advocate for the abolition of certain institutional identities. But the identity loss that often accompanies wholesale abolition needs to be taken into consideration when thinking about institutional change.

To clarify this point, consider the classic case of the path dependence of left- or right-handed driving, which can be well explained in terms of efficiency and welfare. During the critical juncture phase, one side of the road, either left or right, is selected by key actors and that choice becomes locked in over time. The increasing difficulty of

[29] For a contrast between 'sociological institutionalism' and 'historical institutionalism', see, eg PA Hall and RC Taylor, 'Political Science and the Three New Institutionalisms' (1996) *44 Political Studies* 936. As they argue, the former school of thought takes seriously the relationship between institutions and identity formation, whereas path dependence theorising is, intellectually speaking, firmly located in the latter school of thought. The authors argue for greater 'interchange' between the three institutionalisms (the third being 'rational choice'): our analysis in this section could pave the way for one possible way in which this interchange between sociological and historical institutionalisms could be further developed. See also PA Hall, 'Historical Institutionalism in Rationalist and Sociological Perspective' in Mahoney and Thelen, *Explaining Institutional Change* (n 8). See also Capoccia (n 13) 147–48.

[30] A Giddens, *Capitalism and Modern Social Theory: An Analysis of the Writings of Marx, Durkheim and Max Weber* (Cambridge, Cambridge University Press, 1973) 32–33.

change can be explained in terms of increased welfare costs associated with switching to the other side once a society has settled on this choice. One does not need to take into account any serious loss of identity – for example, that of a driver who was 'forced', at a critical juncture, to drive on the left side of the road instead of the right. In a clear demonstration of the welfare calculus involved in this case, Samoa, in 2009, was able to overcome the path dependence of driving on the right-hand side of the road and switch to driving on the left when it became apparent that the practical costs of not changing began to exceed the costs of changing.[31] Although such a change is by no means an easy feat – indeed, Samoa is one of only a few countries that has attempted this change – it did not have any impact on institutional roles and identities.

B. Gradual Institutional Change

As we noted above, opportunities for institutional change – especially the wholesale creation or replacement of an institution – arise at a critical juncture. But institutional change, including a change that turns out to be quite radical, may also be possible in the absence of a critical juncture, during the path-dependent stage of an institution. This has been termed 'bounded' or 'evolutionary' change. One such mechanism, conversion, is particularly relevant in the Sri Lankan context, as we explain later.[32]

Conversion occurs when political agents succeed in authoritatively redirecting, reinterpreting or reappropriating institutions towards goals that go beyond their original intent or purpose, often in ways that respond to changing political and social contexts.[33] As Hacker et al observe, 'conversion … combines elements of constancy in institutional *form* with changes in institutional *impact*' (emphasis added) and, as a result, 'allows reformers to pursue important substantive changes even in the face of formidable obstacles to more direct forms of institutional reengineering'.[34] As an institution persists, strategies of change through conversion will tend to become 'both more attractive and more difficult to reverse'.[35] We identify the possibility of conversion in Sri Lanka's territorial arrangements while the country's unitary state endures. The result of this process will, over time, be the accommodation within the existing Constitution of a functional form of federalism.

Elaborating on conversion, Hacker et al give the example of the redeployment, by the Labour government that came to power in Britain in 1945, of wartime economic institutions to promote economic growth and redistribution following the end of World War II.[36] While the conversion process, in this case, involved the system's power holders,

[31] For a brief analysis of the costs of changing versus not changing, see, eg M Dobie, 'Samoa Drivers Brace for Left Turn' *BBC News* (6 September 2009) news.bbc.co.uk/2/hi/asia-pacific/8236773.stm.

[32] Other mechanisms of gradual institutional change include layering ('the introduction of new rules on top of or alongside existing ones') and drift ('the changed impact of existing rules due to shifts in the environment'). Mahoney and Thelen, 'A Theory of Gradual Institutional Change' (n 8) 15–16.

[33] ibid 17–18; JS Hacker, P Pierson and K Thelen, 'Drift and Conversion: Hidden Faces of Institutional Change' in Mahoney and Thelen, *Advances in Comparative Historical Analysis* (n 13).

[34] Hacker et al (n 33) 185.

[35] ibid 189.

[36] ibid 186.

this mechanism can also potentially be exploited by less powerful actors. As Mahoney and Thelen note,

> those who are disadvantaged by an institution can get traction out of conversion strategies. Lacking the capacity to destroy an institution, institutional challengers may be able to exploit its inherent ambiguities in ways that allow them to direct it towards more favourable functions and effects.[37]

As we explain, the Supreme Court's judgment in *Chandrasoma* turns on the inherent ambiguity of Article 2 of the Constitution. It thus provides an authoritative reinterpretation of the constitutional text, making it compatible with a functional form of federalism.

C. Path Dependence and Institutional Change in the Global South

We end this toolkit component of our chapter by establishing the relevance of path dependence in the context of the Global South. The most obvious way of doing so is by pointing to the many studies that use this concept to explore institutional dynamics in Global South countries. For example, Kohli discusses how Indira Gandhi deliberately disrupted the path dependence of the institutions that constituted the Indian federal state to realise her political goals.[38]

A deeper way of establishing the relevance of path dependence in the Global South is by engaging the arguments that are critical of it. Notable in this regard are Levitsky and Murillo, who contend that the politics of 'institutional weakness', rather than path dependence, is the dominant pattern in many parts of the Global South.[39] Likewise, Brinks, Levitsky and Murillo observe that

> the dynamics of institutional change can be quite different in a weak institutional environment. Rather than being characterized by 'stickiness', [ie path dependence] institutional change tends to be rapid and thoroughgoing, often following a pattern of serial replacement, in which rules and procedures are replaced wholesale – without ever settling into a stable equilibrium.[40]

Brinks et al are conscious of the fact that their diagnosis of institutional weakness – what we might also describe as 'institutional fragility') – seems to relate especially to the institutions of the modern state. This may draw our attention to the fact that, in many parts of the Global South, the state is not the only – or even the main – political actor.[41]

[37] Mahoney and Thelen, 'A Theory of Gradual Institutional Change' (n 8) 18.

[38] A Kohli, 'Can Democracies Accommodate Ethnic Nationalism? The Rise and Decline of Self-Determination Movements in India' (1997) 56 *Journal of Asian Studies* 325. See also Capoccia (n 13) 151. Capoccia characterises Gandhi's actions as an instance of an endogenously motivated shock. In the context of Sri Lanka, a notable recent contribution is the recent monograph by Breen (n 7).

[39] DM Brinks, S Levitsky and MV Murillo, *Understanding Institutional Weakness: Power and Design in Latin American Institutions* (Cambridge, Cambridge University Press, 2019).

[40] Brinks et al (n 39) 5. The authors seem to suggest that the mechanism of conversion may also be relevant in contexts of institutional weakness.

[41] JS Migdal, *Strong Societies and Weak States: State-Society Relations and State Capabilities in the Third World* (Princeton, Princeton University Press, 1989). See also Saunders (n 9) 49.

In these countries, there are often also important non-state institutions, located in the society and grounded, for instance, in clan and familial lineages, that are deeply path-dependent in the sense suggested by mainstream theories of path dependence.[42] Thus, if we consider the interplay between state and non-state institutions in a specific Global South context, it may be that state institutions are weak precisely because competing non-state institutions are path-dependent. Furthermore, the transition for a country historically ordered by these non-state institutions to a state-based one is likely to be a fraught process, characterised by the irretrievable destruction of institutional roles and identities, along the lines discussed earlier, in section IA.[43]

Consider, for instance, the roles of *bigman* and *kin group member* in parts of the Pacific and their potential transformation, and indeed abolition and replacement, by *state politician* and *citizen*. As Boege et al note:

> The discord between the bigman approach of local political leadership in Melanesian societies and the requirements of representative democracy provides an example that demonstrates the dilemma of conflating or blending introduced formal, and indigenous informal, logics of authority. A bigman has to affirm his customary status by means of distributing gifts to his kin, while a politician is obliged to act in the interest of the common good, not pursuing the interest of kin group members, but of citizens. A bigman who is at the same time a politician will have problems reconciling these two roles. For example, situations can evolve in which bigmen must become politicians, as only then will they get access to state coffers which make it possible to distribute gifts to their kin, and politicians must first be bigmen, as only then can they rely on the support of a loyal and powerful kinbased constituency.[44]

Understanding path dependence in a way that goes beyond welfare costs to take account of identity, while considering the interplay between state and non-state institutions, may place us in a better position to appreciate how and why path dependence matters in Global South contexts. Brinks et al ultimately argue that institutional weakness 'has not been adequately conceptualized or theorized', leaving us poorly positioned to 'identify, measure and compare different forms of institutional weakness'.[45] Along similar lines, we argue that it is crucial to unpack the various combinations of institutional weakness and path dependence that shape politics in Global South countries.

Against this backdrop, Sri Lanka stands out as an interesting case study. Its unitary state structure, as we discuss in the next section, is path-dependent, and not weak in Brinks et al's sense of the term. The Sri Lankan state therefore goes against the dominant pattern in the Global South, as described by Brinks et al. Furthermore, we are not talking about a path-dependent non-state institution, but rather a modern state institution. Later, after discussing the path dependence of the Sri Lankan unitary state, we suggest a possible reason why it goes against the dominant pattern described by Brinks et al.

[42] Migdal, *Strong Societies and Weak States* (n 41).

[43] And history, of course, reveals that this transition was often violently imposed in the Global South in the broader context of colonisation.

[44] V Boege, A Brown, K Clements and A Nolan, 'Building Peace and Political Community in Hybrid Political Orders' (2009) 16 *International Peacekeeping* 599, 603.

[45] Brinks et al (n 39) 2.

III. Unitarism in Sri Lanka: Why it is Stable

In this section, we explain why unitarism in Sri Lanka is 'stable', in the sense suggested by path dependence theory. In doing so, we build upon existing analyses of the unitary nature of the Sri Lankan state by Edrisinha and Welikala, leading scholars of the Sri Lankan Constitution, arguing that their analyses can be reconstructed as accounts of a unitary and path-dependent state form.

As Edrisinha notes, it was 'the First Republic Constitution of 1972 … that inserted [via Article 2] the claim that Sri Lanka … was a "unitary" state'.[46] This Constitution also gave Buddhism 'the foremost place' and confirmed Sinhala as being the only official language.[47] The Second Republican Constitution of 1978 changed the status of Article 2 to that of an entrenched provision, which could be amended only by achieving a special two-thirds majority vote in Parliament in addition to approval by the people through a referendum. Despite an attempt, in 1987, to introduce devolution – in the form of the Thirteenth Amendment ––the unitarism of the Sri Lankan state has become firmly entrenched.[48]

We agree with Edrisinha that 'one could argue that the ideal of a "unitary state" is relatively recent within Sinhalese political culture'.[49] Yet the state form envisaged by Article 2 mediates what should be regarded as the long-standing Sinhala Buddhist self-understanding (or collective identity) that the lands of Sri Lanka belong, wholly and indivisibly, to the Sinhala Buddhist majority. Recall in the previous section we argued that the path dependence of some institutions cannot be explained in relation to increasing welfare costs alone. The unitary state structure has, since 1972, become a new institutional means of giving effect to the self-understanding – prevalent in the Sinhala Buddhist communities – that Sri Lanka in its 'indivisible' form belongs to them.

Welikala captures in the following passage the institutional mediation – by Article 2 – of this long-standing Sinhala-Buddhist identity:

> In the Sinhala-Buddhist nationalist worldview, the island is the only homeland of the Sinhalese people, who are, moreover, the inheritors of a sacred duty to preserve and protect Theravada Buddhism. This is the heritage of race and religion that the Sinhala-Buddhists have defended with much sacrifice and resilience from time immemorial. These central elements of Sinhala-Buddhist nationalism are elaborated and reproduced in a powerful tradition of historiography, which continues to inform contemporary political and cultural discourse, in particular in relation to a specific view of the form and foundation of the Sri Lankan state. The three major elements of post-colonial Sinhala-Buddhist nationalism's constitutional agenda – the recognition of a special place for Buddhism and the Sinhala language, and a centralized unitary state – were constitutionally entrenched when the country became a republic in 1972. *In this view, there is no distinction between the collective identity of the ethnic majority and the Sri Lankan nation state.* (emphasis added)[50]

[46] Edrisinha, 'Multination Federalism' (n 6) 249.

[47] The First Republic Constitution, Art 6 adds that 'it shall be the duty of the State to protect and foster Buddhism while assuring to all religions the rights granted [by section 18(1)(d) of the Constitution]'.

[48] See generally Edrisinha, 'Multination Federalism' (n 6); K Guruparan, 'The Irrelevancy of the 13th Amendment in Finding a Solution to the National Question: A Critical Note on Sri Lanka's Post-War Constitutional Discourse' [2013] *Junior Bar Law Review* 3.

[49] Edrisinha, 'Multination Federalism' (n 6) 245.

[50] Welikala, 'Constitutional Migrations' (n 3) 140 (citations omitted).

In short, the unitarism of the Sri Lankan state mediates the collective identity of the Sinhala majority. We describe this fact as the 'inner logic' of the (unitary) state in Sri Lanka. Thus, in working out how to disrupt, or work around, entrenched path-dependent unitarism, more than welfare cost needs to be taken into account. The nature of the reinforcement mechanism in this case – namely, the stability of the country's ethnoreligious identities and relations – explains why we do not view the possibility of a formal constitutional change to Article 2 any time soon to be a realistic possibility.

This inner logic of unitarism also explains why Edrisinha suggests that transition to federalism first requires cultural change – the Sinhalese majority must become more accepting of the idea of federalism – before any attempt is made to change the constitutional text.[51] In doing so, Edrisinha makes the case for consciousness-raising to bring about cultural change. This would involve, among other things, drawing attention to 'historical roots … within both the Sinhalese and Tamil communities … for ideas of multination federalism'.[52] Edrisinha argues that, over time, such consciousness-raising may change the societal culture, paving the way for amendment of Article 2. As we noted at the beginning of this chapter, we agree that federalism, if it is to be fully realised in a stable and enduring manner, requires mutually reinforcing constitutional text and societal transformation. Although efforts in this direction are certainly worthwhile and perhaps particularly fruitful in the current context of widespread protests, the proposal we develop in the remainder of the chapter accepts as given the stability of the unitary state which we believe still accurately reflects the political reality in Sri Lanka today.

An important reason, in our view, why the Sri Lankan unitary state is path-dependent (and hence not weak in Brinks et al's sense) and thus goes against the dominant pattern of institutions in the Global South is because of its grounding in a pre-existing path-dependent (namely, ethnoreligious) institution. It does this, as established earlier in this section, by providing a new means by which an existing – and firmly entrenched – dominant collective ethnoreligious identity is mediated. The unitary state can withstand the strength of existing (non-state) institutions by incorporating them, establishing itself firmly in society and securing its position as a result. Of course, it would be good for governance in Sri Lanka if this path dependence could be disrupted. More generally, by studying this case, we may be able to learn more about how the institutions of states and societies, characterised by weakness or path dependence (and various combinations thereof), operate in the Global South.

IV. The Possibility of Federalism: A Viable Pathway

In our view, the conversion mechanism offers the most realistic path to a more federal political arrangement in Sri Lanka. We flesh out this path below. It should be noted, though, that the 'federalism' that results would be of a functional kind, lacking the formal prescriptions that are normally cited as the definitional requirement of a federation.[53]

[51] This is arguably also true in relation to the Tamils. See generally Edrisinha, 'Multination Federalism' (n 6).
[52] Edrisinha, 'Multination Federalism' (n 6) 256.
[53] See, eg Saunders (n 9).

Nonetheless, the development we map would probably help to improve the country's complex social divisions and perhaps also accelerate the process of cultural change, followed by formal constitutional change, as Edrisinha recommends.

It is unlikely that a critical juncture will open up any time soon during which the unitary state might be replaced, via a constitutional amendment, by a federal structure. The reason is due to the inner logic of the unitary state, detailed earlier. Arguably, if such a juncture ever existed in the contemporary Sri Lankan context, it was in 2002, during the third session of peace talks between the Sri Lankan government and the Liberation Tigers of Tamil Ealam (LTTE), an important Tamil secessionist non-state actor. In their official statement, the Norwegian government, which brokered the 2001 Ceasefire Agreement, stated that, during the talks,

> [in] respon[se] to a proposal by the leadership of the LTTE, the parties agreed to explore a solution founded on the principle of internal self-determination in areas of historical habitation of the Tamil-Speaking people, based on a federal structure within a united Sri Lanka. The parties acknowledged that the solution had to be acceptable to all communities … Guided by this objective, the parties agreed to initiate discussions on substantive political issues such as, but not limited to: Power-sharing between the centre and the region, as well as within the centre …[54]

Edrisinha et al observe that:

> Notwithstanding the parties', and especially the LTTE's subsequent ambivalence with regard to the precise implications of the language and concepts used in the Oslo Communique, it was undeniable that this formulation of framework principles was of major significance … The Oslo formulation rejected the anomalous unitary state … The future Sri Lankan state would be federal in nature … Understood this way, the ideas represented in the Oslo Communique were historic and remarkable.[55]

We leave as an open question whether the Oslo Communiqué – and the peace talks more generally – is best characterised as an endogenous or exogenous shock (arguably the former). Regardless, it was a time when some previous constraints relaxed and at least one previously unavailable option – namely, a constitutionally enshrined federal state – was on the table. Edrisinha et al argue that the goal of transforming the unitary state into a federal one 'was and is [in 2008]' possible.[56] They note that:

> [In 2002], mismanagement of the [peace] process as well as a seeming absence of the critical 'ripe moment' prevented any further progress to be made from this significant breakthrough. Nevertheless, it is undeniable that those ideas retain enduring relevance to a negotiated constitutional settlement to Sri Lanka's conflict in the future.[57]

[54] R Edrisinha, M Gomez, VT Thamilmaran and A Welikala (eds), *Power Sharing in Sri Lanka: Political and Constitutional Documents 1926–2008* (Colombo, Centre for Policy Alternatives, 2009) 642. Similar to our position, the Centre for Policy Alternatives (CPA) has argued that 'formalistic classifications between 'unitary' and 'federal' are best avoided'. For their reform proposal in response to the 2020 Expert Committee appointed to draft a new Constitution, see Centre for Policy Alternatives, 'Submission by the Centre for Policy Alternatives (CPA) to the Ministry of Justice Experts Committee to Draft a New Constitution' (27 November 2020) www.cpalanka.org/wp-content/uploads/2020/12/CPA-Submission-to-Experts-Committee-FINAL-27.11.2020.pdf.

[55] Edrisinha et al, *Power sharing* (n 54) 645.

[56] ibid 645.

[57] ibid 645.

This was the case in 2008 and remains so today. With that in mind, we now turn to the path we argue for. The recent Supreme Court case of *Chandrasoma* provides a possible route to a functional form of federalism, without the need to abolish Article 2. As Welikala notes:

> The … case was triggered by a petitioner in March 2014 by applying to the Supreme Court for a declaration that the Federal Party had secession as one of its aims, and for the consequent application of a proscription on it as required by the Sixth Amendment.[58]

Importantly for our purposes, the court found that Article 2 could be interpreted in a way that is compatible with a functional form of federalism. This sets the stage for the mechanism of conversion to get off the ground. Recall that conversion requires the active reinterpretation of existing formal rules to (re)direct them towards new ends.[59] Given the reinterpretation of Article 2 by the Supreme Court, the functional form of federalism could be set up by actors with significant political power (recall, for instance, the example of British economic institutions after World War II). As mentioned earlier, actors who occupy less powerful positions can also access this mechanism. Thus, Article 2 challengers could still exploit its inherent ambiguities – and arguably the ambiguities of the Sri Lankan Constitution more generally – in ways that allow them to direct it towards more favourable functions and effects, ie the realisation of federalism in practice.

But where, in the text of Article 2, is the ambiguity needed for this conversion mechanism to be activated? The Chief Justice of the Supreme Court, with whom the other judges agree, identifies the ambiguity in Article 2 as follows:

> The labelling of states as unitary and federal sometimes may be misleading. There could be unitary states with features or attributes of a federal state and vice versa. In a unitary state if more powers are given to the units it could be considered as a federal state. Similarly in a federal state if the centre is powerful and the power is concentrated in the centre it could be considered as a unitary state. Therefore sharing of sovereignty, devolution of power and decentralization will pave the way for a federal form of government within a unitary state …[60]

In short, the court is suggesting that a federal state can be established in practice without abolishing Article 2.[61] At this point, the Thirteenth Amendment, and particularly the Thirteenth Amendment case, must be addressed. After the signing of the Indo-Lanka Accord in 1987, the Sri Lankan government introduced a weak – and arguably non-existent – system of devolution within the unitary state.[62] In the Thirteenth Amendment case,[63] the court considered whether the devolution introduced by the Thirteenth

[58] Welikala, 'Constitutional Migrations' (n 3) 148.

[59] See generally Hacker et al (n 33).

[60] *Chandrasoma* (n 11) 17.

[61] For further examples of unitary state structures gradually evolving into federal state structures and a discussion on how such evolutions take place, see, eg J Broschek, 'Between Path Dependence and Gradual Change: Historical Institutionalism and the Study of Federal Dynamics' in A Benz and J Broschek (eds), *Federal Dynamics* (Oxford, Oxford University Press, 2013) 102–13.

[62] For critical analysis of the system of devolution established by the Thirteenth Amendment, see, eg Edrisinha, 'Multination Federalism' (n 6); Guruparan (n 48).

[63] *Re the Thirteenth Amendment to the Constitution and the Provincial Councils Bill* [1987] 2 SLR 312.

Amendment was constitutional, especially in terms of its consistency with Article 2. The majority stated:

> The term 'unitary' in Article 2 is used in contradistinction to the term 'Federal' … The two essential qualities of a Unitary State are (1) the supremacy of the central Parliament and (2) the absence of subsidiary law-making bodies. It does not mean the absence of subsidiary law-making bodies, but it does mean that, they may exist and can be abolished at the discretion of the central authority …[64]

Welikala argues that:

> In reconciling the devolution of power with the existing structure of a centralized unitary state as envisaged by the 1978 Constitution, the interpretational choices available to the majority in the Supreme Court [in the Thirteenth Amendment case] were perhaps limited, in the presence of Articles 2 and 3 in the constitutional text … The majority were impelled to stress that ultimate power and supremacy continued to be vested with the central Parliament and the President … this meant that Provincial Councils came to be regarded from the outset as subordinate bodies to central institutions. This had implications for the way in which devolution was implemented, with administrative practices and subsequently enacted central legislation clearly being based on a notion of central supremacy and superiority …[65]

In *Chandrasoma*, however, the court seems to be suggesting that the text of Article 2 only imposes, at most, a weak limitation concerning the functional form of federalism. Nowhere in the judgment does the court in *Chandrasoma* suggest that Article 2 dictates that ultimate power and supremacy must continue to be vested with the central Parliament and the President. Instead, the court seems to be suggesting that rather than analysing the terms 'unitary' and 'federal' in the abstract, one must pay close attention to the phenomena they refer to in the real world.[66] And, at least in some contexts, the term 'unitary state' in a country's constitution refers to what seems to be a state with federal dimensions in practice and, at times, the term 'federal state' refers to what seems to be a state with unitary dimensions in practice.[67] Welikala ultimately concludes that:

> [The court in *Chandrasoma*] was not seeking to alter settled law or reinterpret doctrines established in prior cases such as the *Thirteenth Amendment Case* … However, it cannot also be doubted that … the court was giving judicial approval to normative perspectives [on claims to peoplehood and internal self-determination] … that are fundamentally at odds with the tenor of its previous approaches to such questions …[68]

But what we are ultimately interested in – and what underlies the possibility of conversion – is not any normative perspectives put forward by the court; rather, it is the interpretative methodology used by the court in authoritatively identifying the inherent ambiguities in the text of Article 2. By engaging with complex political and social phenomena in the real world, rather than simply exploring the meaning of concepts in the abstract, the court *is* putting forward an alternative interpretation of Article 2 to the

[64] ibid 319.
[65] Welikala, 'Constitutional Migrations' (n 3) 147.
[66] See generally Welikala, 'Constitutional Migrations' (n 3).
[67] The Constitution of India (1950), Art 1 describes India as a 'Union of States' rather than a federation. Nevertheless, federalism operates in practice in India. We thank Tarun Khaitan for suggesting this example.
[68] Welikala, 'Constitutional Migrations' (n 3) 153–54.

one articulated in the Thirteenth Amendment case.[69] And this change of interpretation could pave the way for the conversion of territorial arrangements in the country to a functional form of federalism.

Welikala ultimately concludes that:

> Any attempt to use … [the *Chandrasoma* decision] … as a cue for a rejuvenation of *constitutional reform* in a pluralistic direction is thus likely to meet with a stiff ethnocratic backlash from Sinhala-Buddhist nationalists. It would seem, therefore, that a quiet burial in the dusty annals of the Supreme Court's case law is the most likely fate of this otherwise praiseworthy judgment. (emphasis added)[70]

We share Welikala's pessimism, or perhaps realism, regarding the possibility of relying on *Chandrasoma* for constitutional reform. What Welikala seems to overlook, however, is that the interpretative methodology put forward by the court in *Chandrasoma* does not require any formal constitutional reform in that it does not require any existing institution to be constitutionally amended or abolished and a new one established in its place. What it does require, though, is the willingness of strategically placed actors – including those who are not in official positions of power – to take advantage of the opportunities afforded by this decision to gradually introduce federal practices, and thereby convert the state's unitary structure. Such actors are likely to be located within the Sri Lankan bureaucracy. There is no guarantee that this will happen, of course. But we assess the chances of this pathway being taken to be much greater than the obvious alternatives, involving formal constitutional change or cultural change (or some combination thereof).

V. The Limits of Functional Federalism in Sri Lanka

The crux of our argument has been that a functional form of federalism in Sri Lanka is possible through a process of conversion via the recent *Chandrasoma* decision. The resulting governance arrangement would, in all likelihood, have important limitations as compared to fully fledged federalism textually entrenched in the Constitution and widely accepted by the polity. Indeed, we would readily admit that, as an instrument to achieve certain social goals, a functional form of federalism will be inferior to formal federalism, let alone one in which textual guarantee is accompanied by the requisite culture. But the functional federalism we identify may well be the best territorial arrangement for the country within the set of currently feasible possibilities. Further, and importantly, we are not arguing that functional federalism should be construed as the end goal. Instead, we think there are sensible reasons why its operation may eventually open up opportunities for more radical change in the future; thus, it is suggested that functional federalism – in the sense that this chapter is using the term and in the contemporary Sri Lankan context – is a potential *means* to the end goal of fully fledged federalism in Saunders's sense.[71] There is some evidence that even well-entrenched

[69] ibid.
[70] ibid 156.
[71] Saunders (n 9).

identities can change over time, though such change tends to occur slowly and perhaps even, at times, indirectly.[72] One possibility, then, is that the successful operation of functional federalism may foster cultural change, tantamount to identity change, in the Sinhalese and Tamil communities. As federal practices become more widespread, these communities may become more familiar with the implications of federalism and, in particular, the fact that federalism implies the sharing of powers and not necessarily a zero-sum transfer of powers from one group to another, and that it does not imply a slippery-slope-style breakdown of the country's sovereign integrity through secession. Indeed, a working federation has been identified as a way to hold together a country that might otherwise be torn apart by its social divisions.[73] In the Sri Lankan case, then, gradual change through processes such as conversion to overcome strong yet undesirable institutions may be an important sign of societal resilience.

[72] See, eg A Grief and DD Laitin, 'A Theory of Endogenous Institutional Change' (2004) 98 *American Political Science Review* 633.

[73] See, eg Breen (n 7).

5

Proposing a Solidarity-Based (Federal) Solution for Sri Lanka

ERIKA ARBAN[1]

I. Introduction

Investigating the resilience of a constitution requires an examination not only of how it fosters peace and stability, but also of the aspirational value of solidarity – whether between individuals, collectives or institutions – as a means of reconciling diversity and ensuring social cohesion. As a widely used, cross-disciplinary term, resilience acquires different meanings across contexts. There are at least three connotations of resilience that could be employed: (i) resilience as a synonym for elasticity or flexibility, referring to the capacity to adapt and respond to changing circumstances; (ii) resilience as the capacity to recover from difficult circumstances; and (iii) resilience as a coping mechanism under taxing conditions. In this chapter, resilience will be construed as blending these three definitions, relating to a constitution's responsiveness to the social and political context in which it operates. This is particularly relevant for countries characterised by histories of enduring ethnocultural and political conflict like Sri Lanka.

A central question that emerges in Sri Lanka (as in other South Asian countries) is how to reconcile diversity while trying to keep the country together, and whether constitutional design can offer some practical solutions.[2] Although there are no easy answers, this chapter contributes to the debate by proposing one possible mechanism for tempering tensions in Sri Lanka.

Sri Lanka hosts a multi-ethnic and multi-religious society. Consequently, it has struggled to find the right balance in accommodating pluralism, especially after reaching independence.[3] Its ethnolinguistic richness is due to its unique geographical position

[1] Senior Research Associate, Centre for Comparative Constitutional Studies, Melbourne Law School. This research was fully funded by the Australian Government through the Australian Research Council (ARC) Laureate Program 'Balancing Diversity and Social Cohesion in Democratic Constitutions'.

[2] D Udagama, 'The Democratic State and Religious Pluralism. Comparative Constitutionalism and Constitutional Experiences of Sri Lanka' in S Khilnani, V Raghavan and A Thiruvengadam (eds), *Comparative Constitutionalism in South Asia* (Oxford, Oxford University Press, 2013) 145.

[3] ibid 146.

as an island close to major sea routes.[4] Furthermore, Sri Lanka has been subject to three different colonial rulers: the Portuguese from 1505, the Dutch from 1668 and the British from 1796.[5] The main cleavage runs along the ethnolinguistic-religious divide between the Sinhalese majority (mainly Buddhist) and the Tamil minority (mainly Hindu),[6] a schism which culminated in a secessionist war beginning in 1983 and lasting more than 25 years.[7]

Against this backdrop of ethnocultural-linguistic and religious diversity, the resilience of the Sri Lankan Constitution can be measured by the extent to which it has been capable – through institutional mechanisms of the division of powers such as federalism – of responding to the social and political context in which it operates. Yet, as observed by Welikala, among others, all Sri Lankan Constitutions – in their various instantiations – have never properly reflected, nor have they been adequately responsive to, the rich pluralism of the country.[8] Rather, the Sri Lankan constitutional architecture has remained anchored to the idea of a strong, unitary and centralised state that does not offer meaningful space (particularly in the form of political power) to the Tamil people or to other minorities. Article 2 of the Sri Lankan Constitution boldly affirms that 'the Republic of Sri Lanka is a unitary state'. This reflects a Sinhala conceptualisation of the nation linked to the idea that the land belongs to the Sinhalese majority, which fits neatly with the colonial legacy of a modern, centralised state.[9] As a result, the Sinhala resent the dispersion of powers (and, ultimately, federalism) as a way to reconcile unity and diversity because of the fear of division of a country that they consider indivisible.[10] Although Article 27(4) mandates that the state 'shall strengthen and broaden the democratic structure of government and the democratic rights of the People by decentralising the administration and by affording all possible opportunities to the People to participate at every level in national life and in government' and the Thirteenth Amendment to the 1978 Constitution has introduced a mild form of devolution of powers, most, if not all, political authority is still retained at the centre by the Sinhala majority.

It may be argued that Article 2 represents a limit to peace and social harmony in the country, something that could be overcome by resorting to fully fledged federalism or by strengthening the current devolution of powers ingrained in the Thirteenth Amendment. Building on this, the chapter contends that the dispersion of powers and authority typical of federal and devolved systems might not be enough to pursue peace and social cohesion. It proposes that the principle of solidarity must be taken into

[4] ibid 157.

[5] ibid 157.

[6] I acknowledge that reducing the Sri Lankan ethnic conflict to one that is uniquely between Sinhala and Tamils might be too simplistic, as other, often overlapping minorities (eg Sri Lankan Muslims) have also been impacted by the political cleavage. I also acknowledge that not all Tamils have been affected by the ethnocultural-linguistic conflict in the same way.

[7] Udagama (n 2) 157.

[8] A Welikala, 'Constitutional Form and Reform in Postwar Sri Lanka. Towards a Plurinational Understanding' in M Tushnet and M Khlosa (eds), *Unstable Constitutionalism: Law and Politics in South Asia* (Cambridge, Cambridge University Press, 2015) 328.

[9] N Tiruchelvam, 'The Politics of Federalism and Diversity in Sri Lanka' in Y Ghai (ed), *Autonomy and Ethnicity* (Cambridge, Cambridge University Press, 2000) 199.

[10] J Uyangoda, 'The State and the Process of Devolution in Sri Lanka' in S Bastian (ed), *Devolution and Development in Sri Lanka* (Colombo, ICES, 1994) 109.

account, and uses it in the context of the debate on the distribution of powers. The focus on solidarity stems from the fact that its aspirational value helps reconcile diversity and social cohesion. Fostering solidarity can strengthen resilience and thus responsiveness to a deeply divided social and political context. The argument thus advanced here is that federalism in Sri Lanka should remain the objective to pursue. However, because the current political climate does not favour federalism (which continues to be resented by the majority), strengthening the devolution of powers through solidarity-based mechanisms could represent an interim, more neutral compromise. Solidarity could thus become the key to resilience, and to the reconciliation of diversity and social cohesion.

Sections II and III of this chapter briefly paint the current constitutional context, while section IV sketches the multifarious nature of the principle of solidarity in theoretical but also comparative terms. Finally, section V argues that rediscovering solidarity could be key to bridging the existing ideological gap and thus promoting diversity while trying to keep the country united.

II. The Current Constitutional Context in Sri Lanka

This section sketches the current constitutional context in Sri Lanka as a unitary but devolved state, and briefly elucidates the debate on the creation of a fully-fledged federation.[11] This will help to show why solidarity could become a key mode of reconciling diversity and social cohesion and could thus stimulate constitutional resilience and responsiveness to social and political realities.

As anticipated, the three constitutions that have governed Sri Lanka since independence have always favoured a unitary state rather than a federal form of government.[12] The first post-independence Constitution, the Soulbury Constitution of 1948, envisaged Sri Lanka as a unitary and centralised state, with legislative powers vested in the national Parliament,[13] characterised by territorial unity, with no political or administrative decentralisation, and generally reflecting the interests of Sinhala people rather than those of other minorities.[14] Federalism was not yet advocated by Tamil leaders; at that stage, they simply favoured other forms of legislative representation and power-sharing at the centre, as long as their concerns could be properly addressed.[15] The aspiration

[11] This account starts from the post-colonial period, although arguments in favour of a federal solution had been made even in the 1920s, well before Ceylon (as it was then called) reached independence. The reader interested in the federalism debates in colonial Ceylon can look at Uyangoda (n 10) 96 and Tiruchelvam (n 9) 197. Furthermore, it is not the purpose of this contribution to retrace in great detail the history and facts of the debate on a unitary versus federal state in Sri Lanka, including the devolution reform, as an exhaustive literature already exists on the subject: among many, see eg Uyangoda (n 10) 83ff; Tiruchelvam (n 9) 197ff.

[12] A Welikala, 'Constitutional Migrations in the Commonwealth: The *Quebec Secession Reference* and Sri Lankan Constitutional Discourse' in G Delledonne and G Martinico (eds), *The Canadian Contribution to a Comparative Law of Secession* (Cham, Palgrave MacMillan, 2019) 141.

[13] Uyangoda (n 10) 91. It should be noted, however, that s 29(2) of the Soulbury Constitution imposed a restriction on legislative power, as it prohibited discriminatory legislation. This section was interpreted as the 'solemn balance of rights' according to which Ceylonese accepted the Soulbury Constitution (see *Bribery Commissioner v Ranasinghe*, Privy Council).

[14] Uyangoda (n 10) 95; Tiruchelvam (n 9) 199.

[15] R Edrisinha, 'Debating Federalism in Sri Lanka and Nepal' in Tushnet and Khosla (n 8) 292ff; Uyangoda (n 10) 92.

for decentralisation, autonomy and federalism found a place in the Tamil political agenda only when this approach failed,[16] once the centralised state and its 'majority rule' enacted 'discriminatory legislative measures'[17] and 'assumed a considerable degree of social, ethnic and cultural homogenisation of society'.[18]

With the government repeatedly failing to address Tamil demands for autonomy and accommodation, discontent and frustration emerged over time among many Tamils,[19] who then started to advocate a federal solution premised on the idea that Tamils were a different nation within Sri Lanka because of a separate historical past, a different language and a different territory of traditional habitation.[20] The Tamil narrative contended that they were a 'historic national community' claiming constitutional accommodation based on their being a 'distinct nation' whose homeland is in the North East, and as such entitled to self-determination and self-government.[21] Such claims challenged the concept of a unitary state favoured by the Sinhalese majority.[22]

In 1957 and 1965, the two Prime Ministers then in power tried to accommodate the demands for decentralisation made by the Tamil Federal Party by proposing regional councils.[23] Such a scheme was eventually rejected by the Sinhala majority, who believed that the accommodation of such decentralisation requests would conduce to the disintegration of the state.[24] Many Sinhala people resented federalism because they feared that it would divide a country they considered otherwise indivisible,[25] an idea deeply embedded in the majority's national consciousness and posited in the concept of *Eksath Lankava* ('united Sri Lanka') as necessary for political order.[26] They also believed that Sri Lanka should be 'an exclusively Sinhalese entity'.[27]

In the early 1970s, a process of constitutional reform began with the purpose of replacing the 1948 Constitution. The first step was the enactment of the 1972 Constitution, which, however, marked the 'formal constitutionalization of Sinhalese majoritarianism'.[28] It embedded majoritarianism and abolished important minority protections: for example, it gave Buddhism a prominent place (thus undermining the secular character of the state), and Sinhalese (the language of the majority) was constitutionally recognised as the only official language.[29] At this stage, the Tamil Federal Party proposed the establishment of a federal state to promote peace, diversity and social

[16] ibid 293.
[17] Tiruchelvam (n 9) 198.
[18] Uyangoda (n 10) 93.
[19] Edrisinha, 'Debating Federalism' (n 15) 293.
[20] Uyangoda (n 10) 101.
[21] Welikala, 'Constitutional Migrations' (n 12) 140.
[22] Uyangoda (n 10) 103.
[23] ibid 103.
[24] ibid 103.
[25] ibid 109.
[26] ibid 110.
[27] ibid 110.
[28] GJ Jacobsohn and A Shankar, 'Constitutional Borrowing in South Asia. India, Sri Lanka, and Secular Constitutional Identity' in Khilnani et al (n 2) 193, quoting Welikala.
[29] Edrisinha, 'Debating Federalism' (n 15) 294. It should be pointed out, however, that Sinhala was declared as the only official language by way of legislation in 1956.

cohesion,[30] but this proposal was rejected by the Constituent Assembly. The repudiation of Tamil's federal aspirations was a driving force in transforming Tamil nationalism from mere agitation to 'armed secessionism'.[31] Facing further alienation, the Tamil leadership started to mobilise.[32] The 1978 Constitution that ensued, and which is still in force, did not bring much change (but see below for a discussion on the Thirteenth Amendment and devolution), as it reinforced the idea of a strong and centralised government, and introduced a strong executive by implementing a presidential system.[33]

In its current constitutional framework, Sri Lanka is thus a unitary state, as boldly spelt out in Article 2. However, references to the unity of the state can also be found in chapter VI of the Constitution, on Directive Principles of State Policy and Fundamental Duties: specifically, Article 27(3) mandates that the state 'shall safeguard the independence, sovereignty, unity and the territorial integrity of Sri Lanka', whilst Article 28(b) spells out a duty for every person to 'foster national unity'.

III. The Thirteenth Amendment and Devolution

Article 2 is an entrenched article, since it is part of a series of provisions whose amendment requires not only a two-thirds affirmative vote in Parliament, but also a popular referendum.[34] However, a timid attempt to pursue devolution was nonetheless introduced with the implementation of the Thirteenth Amendment.[35] This Amendment emerged out of a 'decentralization agreement negotiated under Indian auspices in the Indo-Sri Lankan accord of 1987' that followed the conflict between the Sri Lanka government and a guerrilla group referred to as the Liberation Tigers of Tamil Eelam (LTTE).[36] India participated in the conflict to 'disarm the Tamil rebels in return for the commitment of the government of Sri Lanka to devolve power to newly created Provincial Councils, including a Tamil-majority Council in the Northern and Eastern Provinces'.[37] The Accord declared that Sri Lanka was 'a multi-ethnic and multi-lingual plural society' consisting primarily of four ethnic groups: Sinhalese, Tamils, Muslims and Burghers. It further recognised that the northern and eastern provinces 'had been areas of historical habitation of the Tamil speaking population'.[38]

The Thirteenth Amendment tried to address the demands for equal language rights and increased autonomy advanced by the Tamils.[39] The first request was achieved with the amendment of Article 18, which now includes Tamil as the official language along

[30] Edrisinha, 'Debating Federalism' (n 15) 293; Welikala, 'Constitutional Migrations' (n 12) 141; Tiruchelvam (n 9) 198.

[31] Welikala, 'Constitutional Migrations' (n 12) 142.

[32] Edrisinha, 'Debating Federalism' (n 15) 293.

[33] ibid 294.

[34] ibid 295.

[35] ibid 295; Jacobsohn and Shankar (n 28) 196.

[36] Jacobsohn and Shankar (n 28) 196.

[37] Welikala, 'Constitutional Migrations' (n 12) 142.

[38] Tiruchelvam (n 9) 202.

[39] Jacobsohn and Shankar (n 28) 196.

with Sinhala (English being the link language).[40] The request for greater autonomy was realised with the introduction of a Provincial Council Bill that created a system of devolution – or provincial councils – within the unitary state.[41] The eight provincial councils so created are elected based on proportional representation – with their own legislative and executive powers.[42]

Devolved powers are listed in the 9th schedule of the Constitution,[43] along with a list of concurrent powers between central and provincial governments, while residual powers are vested in the centre.[44] With regard to concurrent powers, Article 154G provides that any law passed by Parliament on a subject matter listed therein shall prevail over any contrary provision contained in a provincial statute on the same subject matter, meaning that legislative powers of provincial councils on concurrent matters are subordinate to the central Parliament.[45] The central government retains the exclusive powers enumerated on the 'Reserve List'.[46] Article 155(3A) further mandates that, during a state of emergency, the President can enact emergency regulations on any matter enumerated in the provincial council list or the concurrent list, thus suspending or overriding a provincial statute.[47]

The executive power is held by a chief minister, a board of ministers, and a governor who is appointed by the President, holds office at the will of the latter and acts per the will of the board of ministers.[48] Provincial councils would be financed through direct grants coming from the centre, but also via revenue-sharing arrangements and limited forms of taxation.[49] However, overall the Tamil population did not accept this devolution package, with some Tamil political forces such as the LTTE rejecting this deal. The latter began military action against the Indian Peace Keeping Forces first, and then against the Sri Lankan military, thus prompting a bloody civil war that lasted until 2009.[50]

The Thirteenth Amendment has been criticised by academics. For instance, Edrisinha contends that it 'failed to introduce substantial and secure devolution of power. It provided for a veneer of devolution while retaining vast powers with the centre.'[51] Furthermore, it failed to 'grant complete control over any subject to a

[40] ibid 196. More specifically, the 1978 Constitution introduced Tamil as a national language, which became the official language of Sri Lanka in 1987. As scholars have noted, however, doubts and problems remain regarding the effective implementation of bilingualism: see Tiruchelvam (n 9) 200.

[41] Edrisinha, 'Debating Federalism' (n 15) 295.

[42] Tiruchelvam (n 9) 200.

[43] They include police and public order, provincial planning, local government, provincial housing and construction, agriculture and agrarian services, rural development, health, indigenous medicine, cooperatives and irrigation: see Tiruchelvam (n 9) 201.

[44] ibid 201.

[45] ibid 203.

[46] These reserved powers include important subjects such as defence and national security, foreign affairs, post and telecommunications, broadcasting, television, justice, foreign trade and commerce, ports and harbours, aviation, national transports, minerals and mines, and elections: see ibid 201.

[47] ibid 204.

[48] ibid 200.

[49] ibid 201.

[50] Uyangoda (n 10) 87–88; Welikala, 'Constitutional Migrations' (n 12) 142.

[51] R Edrisinha, 'Sri Lanka: Constitutions without Constitutionalism. A Tale of Three and a Half Constitutions' in R Edrisinha and A Welikala (eds), *Essays on Federalism in Sri Lanka* (Colombo, Centre for Policy Alternatives, 2008) 39.

Provincial Council', making it easier for the centre 'to retake powers'.[52] It also failed to establish a clear 'division of powers between the central government and the Provincial Councils',[53] and vested most powers to the central government, thus leaving provincial councils almost powerless.[54] The reform also fell short of other typical federal traits, such as a second or upper chamber representing the interests of provincial councils at the centre.[55]

While it was still a Bill, the proposed amendment was challenged before the Supreme Court as breaching Article 2 (Sri Lanka as a unitary state), Article 3 (inalienable sovereignty of the people) and Article 9 (Buddhism clause) of the Constitution. The majority of judges concluded that the Bill did not change the unitary nature of the country or the pre-eminent position of Buddhism, and interpreted this devolutionary scheme as part of a unitary structure.[56]

Federalism came back on the agenda during the peace process (2001–06), particularly in the so-called Oslo Communiqué of 2003, facilitated by Norway between Sri Lanka and the LTTE.[57] Amongst other things, the Communiqué invited parties to explore and agree upon a commonly acceptable solution premised on the principle of self-determination and a federal structure within a united Sri Lanka.[58] However, these negotiations eventually fell through.

As noted, the demand for federal solutions was fuelled by a desire for recognition due to a perception of discrimination and lack of equality among the minority groups, especially the Tamils.[59] Yet, federalism has been strongly resisted by the Sinhala majority, for the reasons sketched above. But federal solutions have also triggered the so-called 'minorities within minorities' critique, whereby the Muslim minority (the third-largest group in Sri Lanka) feared that an accommodation in federal terms of the Tamil requests would be 'detrimental to their interests'.[60]

In any event, the limited devolution implemented through the Thirteenth Amendment still represents the only 'attempt at constitutional accommodation' in Sri Lanka,[61] although very few take it seriously and it remains largely unimplemented.

[52] ibid 39.

[53] ibid 39.

[54] Edrisinha, 'Debating Federalism' (n 15) 295; see also Jacobsohn and Shankar (n 28) 195–96; Tiruchelvam (n 9) 204.

[55] Edrisinha, 'Debating Federalism' (n 15) 295.

[56] *In Re Thirteenth Amendment to the Constitution and the Provincial Councils Bill* (1987) 2 Sri LR 312. A good analysis of this decision, as well as a general comment on devolution, can be found in A Welikala, 'Devolution under the Thirteenth Amendment: Extent, Limits, and Avenues for Reform' (2016) CPA Working Papers on Constitutional Reform No 10. See also Jacobsohn and Shankar (n 28) 196; Tiruchelvam (n 9) 203.

[57] The third session of peace talks between the Government of Sri Lanka (GOSL) and the Liberation Tigers of Tamil Eelam (LTTE) (Oslo Communiqué) www.peaceagreements.org/wview/1160/The%20third%20sesson%20of%20peace%20talks%20between%20the%20Government%20of%20Sri%20Lanka%20(GOSL)%20and%20the%20Liberation%20Tigers%20of%20Tamil%20Eelam%20(LTTE)%20(Oslo%20Communique); see also Welikala, 'Constitutional Migrations' (n 12) 136.

[58] ibid.

[59] Edrisinha, 'Debating Federalism' (n 15) 299.

[60] ibid 299. According to Rajasingham, Muslims 'now advance claims for a separate administrative district in the east' and their relations with Sinhala have worsened: S Rajasingham, 'Federal or Unitary? The Power-sharing Debate in Sri Lanka' (2019) 108 *The Commonwealth Journal of International Affairs* 653, 655.

[61] Welikala, 'Constitutional Migrations' (n 12) 135.

However, fully fledged federalism to reconcile unity and diversity is unlikely at this stage.[62] One means of potentially overcoming this political and institutional impasse could be to strengthen the current devolution of powers by rediscovering the principle of solidarity, which pursues similar aims to federalism. Devolution could be construed as a form of quasi-federalism, but firmly grounded on a principle – solidarity – that brings together diversity and social cohesion without resorting to a contested idea such as federalism. Section IV sketches the meaning of solidarity and offers some comparative insights.

IV. The Meaning of Solidarity

As observed above, Sri Lanka has for a long time been torn by this deep, internal conflict triggered by ethnic division. In this context, the principle of solidarity might be helpful to curb the conflict, at least partially. This observation stems from the perception that solidarity has never been seriously discussed in the Sri Lankan context and it has never featured prominently in the constitutional and political debate, which has mainly revolved around the idea of power-sharing, societal pluralism and multi-ethnicity, thus emphasising differences rather than solidarity. This chapter thus proposes to take solidarity seriously to promote diversity and social cohesion within the current framework of devolution of powers as a form of quasi-federalism. Eventually, solidarity might become the building block on which a fully-fledged federal system might rest when the political climate favours such a transition.

First, it shall be pointed out that solidarity is a multifarious concept. As such, it may appear elusive and difficult to frame. Intuitively, solidarity in common parlance suggests sentiments such as friendship, reciprocal help, support or compassion.[63] In this sense, it also incorporates a spiritual or moral hue, and it is preached by many faiths. Solidarity, however, also features in many constitutions, sometimes as an aspirational value, at other times as an expression of other principles. Occasionally, it is entrenched explicitly – where the Constitution contains the term 'solidarity' – while in other cases it features implicitly, for example by embedding some other solidarity-based value.[64] This chapter focuses particularly on two meanings of solidarity that could be particularly useful in the current constitutional and political debate in Sri Lanka: (i) solidarity as *Bundestreue*; and (ii) solidarity as brotherhood and fraternity. To this end, I will analyse the principle comparatively. A third meaning of solidarity, one that directly relates to fiscal federalism, will also be briefly sketched but not further elaborated upon.

[62] In a 2014 decision before the Supreme Court (www.supremecourt.lk/images/documents/sc_spl_03_2014.pdf), a petitioner challenged the manifesto of a registered Tamil political party as it violated the constitutional prohibition on advocating for separatism contained in the 6th Amendment. The Supreme Court dismissed the petition and in doing so elaborated on concepts of power sharing, the nature of the Sri Lankan state, etc. For further discussion, see Nadarajalingam and Nwokora, ch 4 in this volume.

[63] J Ottmann, 'The Concept of Solidarity in National and European Law: The Welfare State and the European Social Model' (2008) 2 *Vienna Online Journal on International and Constitutional Law* 36, 38; E Arban, 'Exploring the Principle of (Federal) Solidarity' (2017) 22 *Review of Constitutional Studies* 241, 242.

[64] Arban (n 63) 242.

A. Solidarity as *Bundestreue*

An important manifestation of the principle of solidarity is *Bundestreue*. This doctrine has emerged mainly in the context of German constitutionalism, and it infuses the current architecture of the German federal system. Although it has not been crystallised as such in the 1949 German *Grundgesetz*, solidarity as *Bundestrue* has been recognised judicially by the German *Bundesverfassungsgericht* in its case law.[65] Literally speaking, *Bundestreue* means fidelity, loyalty or faith (*Treue*) in the federal structure (*Bund*). In this sense, it is also referred to as *federal loyalty*. As such, it invites the various levels of government and organs of the state to collaborate with each other while at the same time refraining from hindering each other's responsibilities and tasks.

Besides Germany, *Bundestreue* features in several constitutions of federal and quasi-federal systems. For example, Article 143(1) of the Belgian Constitution mandates that 'In the exercise of their respective responsibilities, the federal State, the Communities, the Regions and the Joint Community Commission act with respect for federal loyalty, in order to prevent conflicts of interest'.

Likewise, Article 44 of the Swiss Constitution mandates that

1. The Confederation and the Cantons shall support each other in the fulfilment of their duties and shall generally cooperate with each other.
2. They owe each other a duty of consideration and support. They shall provide each other with administrative assistance and mutual judicial assistance.
3. Disputes between Cantons or between Cantons and the Confederation shall wherever possible be resolved by negotiation or mediation.

Turning to the South Asia region, Article 51 of the Nepali Constitution provides that the state shall pursue the promotion of 'national unity by developing relations of mutual cooperation between federal units'.

Building on the German doctrine of *Bundestreue*, Article 41 of the South African Constitution spells out what is perhaps the most complete illustration of federal loyalty in the following terms:[66]

1. All spheres of government and all organs of state within each sphere must-

a. preserve the peace, national unity and the indivisibility of the Republic;
b. secure the well-being of the people of the Republic;
c. provide effective, transparent, accountable and coherent government for the Republic as a whole;
d. be loyal to the Constitution, the Republic and its people;
e. respect the constitutional status, institutions, powers and functions of government in the other spheres;

[65] ibid 247–48. In a 1958 decision, the Bundesverfassungsgericht explained that 'In a federal state the federal government and the Lander have the common duty to preserve and maintain constitutional order throughout the entire union. Where the federal government does not have the power in its own right to maintain constitutional order, but is dependent on the co-operation of the Lander, such Lander are obliged to act. This follows from the unwritten rule of the duty of Bundestreue': cited in B De Villiers, 'Federations: Shared Rule and Self-Rule in the Search for Stable Governance' (2012) 39 *Politikon* 391, 396; see also Arban (n 63) 248.

[66] D Brand, 'The South African Constitution: Three Crucial Issues for Future Development' (1998) 9 *Stellenbosch Law Review* 182, 186.

f. not assume any power or function except those conferred on them in terms of the Constitution;
g. exercise their powers and perform their functions in a manner that does not encroach on the geographical, functional or institutional integrity of government in another sphere; and
h. co-operate with one another in mutual trust and good faith by-
    i. fostering friendly relations;
    ii. assisting and supporting one another;
    iii. informing one another of, and consulting one another on, matters of common interest;
    iv. co-ordinating their actions and legislation with one another;
    v. adhering to agreed procedures; and
    vi. avoiding legal proceedings against one another.

As these examples illustrate, solidarity as *Bundestreue*, or federal loyalty, basically refers to a broad concept of trust among institutions and levels of government in a composite state, and respect for their reciprocal tasks and powers as enshrined in the constitution. It also refers to a duty of loyalty and respect for the principles embedded in the constitution, as well as for the constitutional structure in place. It means collaboration and support, and amicable resolution of disputes, to avoid legal proceedings among different branches of government. This understanding of solidarity builds on the idea that in a multilevel system of government – federal or quasi-federal – there are multiple institutions of power which should not be seen as competing against each other, but as working together towards the same objective, which is the reconciliation of unity and diversity.

Incidentally, *Bundestreue* should not be confused with cooperative federalism, although the two do share some common features, and the latter could be seen as an expression of the former. Cooperative federalism refers to those mechanisms of interaction and collaboration in policy-making between different levels of government – usually at the executive level.[67] These mechanisms can be formalised or have a more informal nature. While cooperative federalism also rests on this idea of collaboration and interaction, solidarity as *Bundestreue* takes on a more expansive meaning, as it encompasses a broader spirit of mutual respect, support, trust and loyalty.

Likewise, *Bundestreue* is not the same as shared rule, which is a distinctive feature of federalism, since it fosters the participation of the federated entities in decision-making at the centre.[68] Usually, this occurs with the presence of a federal senate, or by participating in the constitutional amendment process. Shared rule fosters collaboration, of

[67] Scholarship on cooperative federalism (and the twin concept of intergovernmental relations) is particularly developed in the ambit of Canadian federalism and the EU multilevel governance. Readers interested in the topic can resort to the following as a preliminary reading: JF Gaudreault-DesBiens and J Poirier, 'From Dualism to Cooperative Federalism and Back? Evolving and Competing Conceptions of Canadian Federalism' in P Oliver, P Macklem and N DesRosiers (eds), *The Oxford Handbook of the Canadian Constitution* (Oxford, Oxford University Press, 2017); J Poirier, C Saunders and J Kinkaid (eds), *Intergovernmental Relations in Federal Systems: Comparative Structures and Dynamics* (Oxford, Oxford University Press, 2015); R Schütze, *From Dual to Cooperative Federalism. The Changing Structure of European Law* (Oxford, Oxford University Press, 2009).

[68] D Elazar, *Exploring Federalism* (Tuscaloosa, University of Alabama Press, 1987) 5.

course, and in that it expresses federal loyalty. However, like cooperative federalism, federal loyalty goes beyond such institutional mechanisms to refer to a broader spirit of mutual trust and respect.

Solidarity as *Bundestreue* operates vertically, mediating the relationships between central and peripheral institutions, which are required to respect their reciprocal duties and responsibilities without interfering with each other's authority.[69] However, this form of solidarity can also run horizontally, among peripheral institutions.[70] For example, Article 48(3) of the Swiss Constitution, in allowing cantons to enter into intercantonal agreements, mandates that 'Agreements between Cantons must not be contrary to the law, to the interests of the Confederation or to the rights of other Cantons. The Confederation must be notified of such agreements.'

Although the text does not say it explicitly, the requirement to comply with the rights of the other cantons – and not just with those of the confederation as a whole – is evocative of a duty of horizontal loyalty.

In any event, solidarity as *Bundestreue*, horizontal or vertical, tends to run among institutional bodies, not among private individuals. What binds individuals or the collectivity is rather the spirit of solidarity as fraternity, as the next sub-section illustrates.

B. Solidarity as Fraternity or Brotherhood

In this second sense, solidarity loses its institutional character to refer to a sense of unity, harmony and trust among people of various communities, or between citizens and institutions. As such, solidarity can be contrasted with sentiments such as selfishness, discordance, hatred, antagonism or separation.[71] So conceived, solidarity bears a close resemblance to notions such as fraternity or brotherhood.

In this understanding, solidarity has perhaps a more moral, spiritual or aspirational meaning, but it is still a common feature of constitutional texts, where it is found both in the preambular section and in the actual body of constitutions. For instance, the preamble of the Indian Constitution mandates that the people of India commit to promoting among them 'fraternity assuring the dignity of the individual and the unity and integrity of the Nation'. Likewise, the preamble of the Constitution of Pakistan mandates that the people of Pakistan 'resolve to protect our national and political unity and solidarity by creating an egalitarian society'.

Outside the region, other examples of solidarity as fraternity come from several European countries, such as Spain, where the principle is embedded in Article 2 in the following terms:

> The Constitution is based on the indissoluble unity of the Spanish Nation, the common and indivisible homeland of all Spaniards; it recognises and guarantees the right to self-government of the nationalities and regions of which it is composed and the solidarity among them all.

[69] Arban (n 63) 252.
[70] ibid 254.
[71] ibid 242.

The Swiss Constitution also features solidarity as fraternity where it provides that 'The Swiss People and the Cantons … resolved to renew their alliance so as to strengthen liberty, democracy, independence and peace in a spirit of solidarity and openness towards the world'.

In South Africa, the desire to overcome the horrors of apartheid led to the inclusion in Article 41 of the requirement discussed above that all spheres of government and organs of the state shall foster the national unity and indivisibility of the country, an idea also crystallised in the preamble.[72] In Nigeria, the principle of 'federal character' has been introduced in the Constitution to promote a representative bureaucratic apparatus and public service that does not reflect just one ethnic group.[73] According to Article 318(1), the purpose of the federal character provision is to promote a sense of national unity and loyalty, and to instil a sense of national belonging to all Nigerian citizens that cuts across tribal and group divisions and thus fosters intra-communal solidarity.

Although other examples of solidarity as fraternity can be drawn from many other constitutional texts, the examples outlined here are sufficient to explicate this idea of solidarity as an element of inter-communal cohesion, to preserve the unity and harmony among the diverse populations despite their differences. Implicit illustrations of solidarity in this sense can be found also in all those constitutional references to principles such as unity, equality, mutual help, fairness, democracy and respect for one another.

In multinational countries like Sri Lanka, this kind of solidarity as fraternity among individuals may also refer to the unity and harmony among the various nations that compose the communal fabric. As such, solidarity as fraternity can refer to a broader idea of solidarity as the balance between the unity of the country and the desire for more autonomy on the part of the various national groups, between centripetal and centrifugal forces, or between local and national interests.[74]

[72] Y Fessha, *Ethnic Diversity and Federalism: Constitution Making in South Africa and Ethiopia* (Farnham, Ashgate, 2010) 98.

[73] The federal character principle is enshrined in Art 14(3) of the Nigerian Constitution. It mandates that 'The composition of the Government of the Federation or any of its agencies and the conduct of its affairs shall be carried out in such a manner as to reflect the federal character of Nigeria and the need to promote national unity, and also to command national loyalty, thereby ensuring that there shall be no predominance of persons from a few states or from a few ethnic or other sectional groups in that Government or in any of its agencies'. The reader interested in the federal character principle can read, *ex multis*, L Adamolekun, J Erero and B Oshionebo, '"Federal Character" and Management of the Federal Civil Service and the Military' (1991) 21 *Publius* 75, 75; AHM Kirk-Greene, 'Ethnic Engineering and the "Federal Character" of Nigeria: Boon of Contentment or Bone of Contention?' (1983) 6 *Ethnic and Racial Studies* 457, 460.

[74] It is beyond the scope of this chapter to discuss the nature of multinational states, as an abundant literature already exists. Here, multinational states are construed as states composed of two or more nations, with the term 'nation' defining people who 'share the same culture, where culture … means a system of ideas and signs and associations and ways of behaving and communicating', and who 'recognise each other as belonging to the same nation'; nations see themselves as distinct societies and demand various forms of autonomy or self-government to ensure their survival as distinct societies: see J Pinder, 'Multinational Federations' in M Burgess and J Pinder (eds), *Multinational Federations* (London, Routledge, 2007) 3–4, quoting Gellner. For other, yet similar definitions of nation see, *ex multis*, S Tierney, *Constitutional Law and National Pluralism* (Oxford, Oxford University Press, 2004) 13; W Kymlycka, *Multicultural Citizenship. A Liberal Theory of Minority Rights* (Oxford, Clarendon Press, 1995) 11. According to Welikala, Sri Lanka should be characterised as a plurinational state, meaning that in Sri Lanka there are at least two historic nations that make up part of the state, in addition to other communities: Welikala, 'Constitutional Form' (n 8) 340.

Similar to *Bundestreue*, solidarity as fraternity works as a glue to promote the unity and integrity of the nation, but it is not incompatible with a decentralised state: the examples from Switzerland, Spain, Pakistan, India and Nepal just illustrated are all taken from countries that are federal, quasi-federal or have discussed decentralisation at some point. Consequently, the desire for unity, fraternity or solidarity is a universal value that transcends the federal or quasi-federal character of the state but pursues the similar objective of reconciling diversity and social cohesion.

C. Solidarity in Fiscal Federalism

For purposes of completeness, the realm with which the principle of solidarity is most traditionally associated is perhaps fiscal federalism. Federal and quasi-federal constitutions often contain constitutional provisions entrenching equalisation mechanisms intended to grant the transfer of funds from the central government to the regions and territories that have lesser fiscal capacity and sometimes also between wealthier and poorer sub-entities. Such equalisation mechanisms are typically grounded on solidarity because they allow – at least ideally – to level deep economic differences among territories. However, fiscal federalism will not be further discussed here.[75]

To conclude, solidarity as *Bundestreue* and solidarity as fraternity echo the idea of reciprocity as elaborated by Welikala, wherein he asserts that sub-state nations owe some obligations to the host state, for example, to

> reciprocally recognise the 'national status' of other entities within the state, to work 'in good faith to consolidate the state as a common polity' and to respect the rights and interests of all citizens arising out of the common citizenship of the state as a whole.[76]

It is on this double understanding of solidarity that I propose to rediscover this principle within the Sri Lankan political and constitutional discourse, as section V will illustrate.

V. Entrenching Solidarity in the Sri Lankan Constitutional Discourse

I observed above how federalism has recurrently been invoked in Sri Lanka as a mechanism to reconcile unity and diversity, and tame the existing ethnocultural and linguistic conflict, despite strong resistance from the Sinhala majority. The Thirteenth Amendment of 1987 has not fulfilled the aspirations for more autonomy voiced by the Tamil minority, although it devolves some legislative powers to provincial councils. As a result, Sri Lanka continues to work basically as a unitary and centralised state despite the devolution measures in the Constitution. Although federalism represents an ideal

[75] The literature on fiscal federalism is extensive. As a starting point, the reader interested in this subject can consult A Shah and J Kinkaid (eds), *The Practice of Fiscal Federalism: Comparative Perspectives* (Montreal, McGill-Queen's University Press, 2007).

[76] Welikala, 'Constitutional Form' (n 8) 353, quoting Tierney.

way to reconcile unity and diversity, in the current political climate a constitutional reform in federal terms seems extremely unlikely. But while it should stay on the political agenda as the most desirable objective, federalism remains a highly charged idea that might potentially fuel – rather than placate – internal conflicts.

One possible way out of this deadlock might be the rediscovery of the principle of solidarity – both as federal loyalty and as fraternity – as sketched in section IV. Solidarity is less ideologically laden – and thus less objectionable – than federalism, but it aspires towards the same objective, that of integrating diversity and social cohesion and thus responding to a deeply divided social and political context. Solidarity is perfectly compatible with the current devolved system of government as enshrined in the Thirteenth Amendment: by construing it as a solidarity-based, quasi-federal scheme, devolution might help the transition to a future fully fledged federal model, to be implemented when the political context is more favourable.

In this final section, I suggest that the devolution of powers currently in place can be seen as a form of hybrid or quasi-federal system in which the value of solidarity could be ingrained.

A. Federalism as a Broad Umbrella Term Encompassing Federations and Quasi-federal Systems

Federalism is often advocated as an ideal institutional and constitutional mechanism to reconcile unity and diversity by combining 'self-rule' and 'shared-rule'.[77] However, scholars are aware of the difficulties that exist in offering a universal definition of federalism or federal systems. The first theorisations of federalism defined this mode of governance using the US model as the archetype, as the 1787 US Constitution is regarded as the first federal constitution. Consequently, the main features that defined the US system have been incorporated into a checklist for measuring whether a system is federal or not. Despite some differences due to the unique local context, the Swiss, Canadian, Australian, German and Austrian federal systems can also be traced back to the broad federal model formulated in the US Constitution according to the following indicators:[78] (i) a federal constitution construed as a covenant between the federal government and the constituent units; (ii) a federal constitution that entrenches a division of legislative powers between two or more levels of government; (iii) a federal senate, representing the interests of the sub-units at the central level; (iv) a federal umpire to settle disputes of attribution between two or more levels of government; (v) fiscal federal arrangements, whereby both levels of government enjoy autonomy of revenues and expenses; (vi) a constitution that is written, supreme and amendable only with the direct or indirect participation of the various levels of government; and (vii) constituent power for the sub-units, so that they can introduce their own constitutions as an expression of their autonomy.

However, the dividing line between unitary and federal systems based on these indicators became more blurred especially after WWII, when several countries developed

[77] Elazar (n 68) 5.

[78] R Watts, *Comparing Federal Systems* (Montreal, Institute of Intergovernmental Relations, 2008) 9.

systems that were not fully federal, nor entirely unitary. Furthermore, some states, particularly in Africa and Asia, resorted to federally inspired solutions as a way to curb internal ethnolinguistic and cultural-religious divisions. In addition, there was a change from a broader trend of 'coming together' federalism, with previously independent units surrendering part of their sovereignty and uniting under a common, federal constitution, towards 'holding together' federalism, with previously unitary systems progressively decentralising to avoid secessionist movements and accommodate the requests for more autonomy coming from certain regions.[79] Regional states like Spain and Italy, devolved systems like the UK, the European Union as a supranational model combining federal and confederal elements, and ethnic federalism in countries such as Ethiopia and Nigeria have all come to enrich the theory of federalism so that federalism has now become an umbrella term that incorporates vastly different experiences. Such models – suspended between federalism and unitarism – have been defined in many ways, including hybrid or quasi-federal systems. The fact is that all these models present some federal elements, but other aspects still work as if they were unitary. One reason for this new category of models is the fact that some countries are not entirely at ease with federalism, as they believe it heralds separation, division and secession. At the same time, internal differences of various types suggest that a purely unitary state does not allow the accommodation of these cleavages. However, although these quasi-federal systems can be defined as 'incomplete' federations, they still showcase some federal elements and, therefore, I would consider them to belong to the family of 'federalism'.

Consequently, although in Sri Lanka many believe that federalism is the only solution to tame the country's internal conflicts, the devolution system that is in place at the moment can be seen as a quasi-federal model, a compromise between a unitary state (advocated by the Sinhala majority) and a federal state (invoked by the Tamil minority). Furthermore, Article 27(4) of the Constitution mandates that

> [t]he State shall strengthen and broaden the democratic structure of government and the democratic rights of the People by decentralising the administration and by affording all possible opportunities to the People to participate at every level in national life and in government.

This provision can be seen as an expression of the principle of subsidiarity, which is often present in many federal and quasi-federal systems.[80] Therefore, the solidarity-based proposals that will be sketched out in the remainder of the section can be applied to the devolved system of government in place in Sri Lanka, and fall under the broad umbrella of federalism.

[79] F Palermo and K Kössler, *Comparative Federalism* (Oxford, Hart Publishing, 2017) 9.

[80] It is beyond the scope of this chapter to discuss in detail subsidiarity, which remains a concept still lacking a universally accepted meaning. However, the principle is commonly understood (at least in its vertical dimension) as implying that legislative or administrative action should be taken, whenever possible, at the lowest appropriate level of government at which a given objective can be achieved, with the central authority merely playing a subsidiary role and thus performing only tasks that cannot be better completed at local level. By inviting the state to decentralise administration, Art 27(4) of the Sri Lankan Constitution can be seen as an expression of vertical solidarity. However, subsidiarity also presents a horizontal component, in that it should promote the autonomous initiatives of citizens, both as individuals and as members of associations, relating to activities of general interest. In Art 27(4), the Constitution asks the state to afford opportunities to private citizens to participate in national life and governance, thus promoting horizontal subsidiarity.

B. Solidarity in the Sri Lankan Context

With its emphasis on power-sharing, self-rule and shared rule, greater accountability and participation, and thus democracy, federalism is increasingly embraced by countries torn along ethnolinguistic lines as a positive principle that promotes unity and diversity. However, in some specific contexts, federalism can also be perceived as a negative, destructive force, one that would disrupt unity rather than promote territorial and socio-economic cohesion. When that is the case, federalism is resisted and becomes anathema to its own stated goals. And even when some form of decentralisation is implemented, it is usually referred to by another name to avoid the use of the term 'federalism'.[81]

Sri Lanka should certainly continue to pursue the path towards full federalisation. However, considering the political climate that resists such transition and the current absence of a 'federal' spirit – a necessary component of any successful federal model – strengthening the idea of solidarity both as *Bundestreue* and fraternity under the devolved scheme could continue the reconciliation of unity and diversity under a less charged and more neutral name. Solidarity could further the idea that a composite state can also promote unity if the emphasis is placed on collaboration, mutual help and harmony. In other words, strengthening solidarity under the current devolved constitutional scheme might help pave the way for more explicitly federal reform. Solidarity emphasises positive values like collaboration, trust and help, rather than focusing on the division of powers and responsibilities, as is the case with federalism.

In section IV, we saw that the idea behind solidarity as *Bundestreue* is that the various organs in a composite state cooperate in mutual trust, respect and reciprocity with each other and facilitate – rather than impede or constrain – intergovernmental relations. Considering the pervasive mistrust, fear and suspicion that characterise institutional relations in Sri Lanka between the various groups and political leaders of opposing factions,[82] the explicit grounding of devolution in federal loyalty could contribute to develop a form of trust among central and provincial institutions. It seems that central institutions do not leave much room for provincial councils, even in the limited areas that the Constitution grants to them. The reason behind this might be the consequence of a lack of federal culture among institutions, caused by the generally negative perception of power diffusion among institutional elites and by a long tradition of unitary governance. The entrenchment of specific provisions explicitly requiring support and cooperation among central government and provincial councils, mutual consideration and restraint from encroaching on others' responsibilities, thus avoiding conflicts of interest, should be encouraged. In this regard, Article 41 of the South African Constitution could be an interesting model to follow.

One problem with this would be enforceability: how can we ensure that constitutional provisions fostering reciprocal loyalty and cooperation are complied with? If solidarity-inspired doctrine and principles remain merely aspirational, they would not be enforceable and thus justiciable in a court of law. A justiciable principle of

[81] For example, 'devolution' in Sri Lanka, 'state of autonomies' in Spain, 'regional state' in Italy, etc.
[82] Rajasingham (n 60) 654.

federal loyalty would facilitate the promotion of this attitude of mutual respect and consideration.

As for solidarity as fraternity, this value is fostered at the collective or interpersonal level to promote mutual respect and reciprocity among individuals but also among the various nations that compose a multinational state such as Sri Lanka. This is usually done by entrenching such values in directive principles or preambles, and the comparative study presented above illuminates possible ways in which this could be effectively done. In this regard, however, it should be pointed out that solidarity in the sense of fraternity somehow already features in the Sri Lankan constitutional text: without mentioning solidarity as such, the spirit of this principle is present in Article 27(5) of the Constitution, in the part where it says that

> [t]he State shall strengthen national unity by promoting co-operation and mutual confidence among all sections of the People of Sri Lanka, including the racial, religious, linguistic and other groups and shall take effective steps in the fields of teaching, education and information in order to eliminate discrimination and prejudice.

Furthermore, Article 27(6) mandates that 'The State shall ensure equality of opportunity to citizens, so that no citizen shall suffer any disability on the ground of race, religion, language, caste, sex, political opinion or occupation'.

The problem with these provisions is that they have rarely, if ever, been used. Furthermore, according to Article 29, they are not enforceable in any court or tribunal, and 'no questions of inconsistency with such provisions shall be raised in any court or tribunal'.[83] More so than federal loyalty, solidarity as fraternity might be very difficult to implement considering its aspirational nature. However, it could materialise in other ways. As Khaitan posits, although not directly enforceable or justiciable, directive principles can nonetheless have some legal effects, including constructing a country's constitutional identity or using them as interpretative aids (as was the case in India).[84] Some countries equally divided along ethnolinguistic and cultural-religious lines have tried to foster this sense of inter-communal solidarity by introducing clauses such as the 'federal character' principle of the Nigerian Constitution briefly discussed above, whereby the composition of all public organs should reflect the diverse ethnic composition of the country, thus preventing central institutions from domination by the majority.

Asymmetrical solutions could also be seen as measures fostering solidarity. Asymmetry can be accomplished in many ways, by the devolution of asymmetrical powers to the different provincial councils or the creation of special powers to certain cities (in addition to provincial councils), for example. This type of institutional diversification could be seen to promote solidarity among the different communities, as it takes into account the different context in which each level of government operates.

[83] It should be noted, however, that, at least in relation to education and the protection of the environment, the Supreme Court has relied on directive principles of state policy. In fact, although the education and the environment are not expressly recognised as fundamental rights in the Constitution, courts have enforced those rights by relying on directive principles. See www.supremecourt.lk/images/documents/sc_fr_141_2015.pdf (p 50 in particular).

[84] T Khaitan, 'Constitutional Directives: Morally-Committed Political Constitutionalism' (2019) 82 *MLR* 603, 629–30.

VI. Conclusion

I started this chapter by arguing that finding a balance between diversity and social cohesion is a constant challenge for many constitutional systems, especially in the Global South, where ethnolinguistic and cultural-religious cleavages are particularly intense. Sri Lanka is an especially good illustration of a country where tensions between the two main ethnic groups have never been fully resolved. It could thus be argued that the various Sri Lankan constitutions implemented since independence have not been resilient enough, in the sense that they have not been able to adequately respond to the social and political context in which they have operated. Federalism has repeatedly been invoked – especially by Tamil advocates – as the only possible way to tame these tensions, but it has been continually rejected by the Sinhalese leaders. The incomplete devolution of powers instituted by the Thirteenth Amendment to the Sri Lankan Constitution represents the largest step towards distribution and division of powers between the centre and the periphery, while any further constitutional reform towards federalism seems out of the question in the current political climate, especially after the 2019 presidential elections and the recent change in government following public protest.[85] As a result, Sri Lanka continues to be characterised by a culture of centralism and unitarism, and federalism remains an ideologically controversial concept.

The objective of this chapter has been to contribute to the debate on how to reconcile diversity and social cohesion in a deeply torn country like Sri Lanka, where federalism is off the agenda. The argument presented was to take the principle of solidarity more seriously as an alternative way to promote unity in diversity under the current constitutional framework. By drawing on comparative examples both from the region and elsewhere, it has presented the two main frameworks through which solidarity can be understood: solidarity as *Bundestreue* and solidarity as fraternity, with the latter having more of an aspirational value. Further, it suggested that solidarity could become the building block on which a future (federal) system should be grounded. In the absence of appetite for constitutional reform, solidarity could find a more prominent space within the present scheme of devolution of powers to overcome reciprocal distrust and progressively build a more 'federal' mentality that would prepare Sri Lanka for future transition to federalism. Fostering the idea of trust, respect, faith and reciprocity, both between institutions (solidarity as *Bundestreue*) and among communities, peoples and nations (solidarity as fraternity), could provide a fertile ground on which to build better relationships in the future. In other words, by fostering collaboration, dialogue, mutual assistance, negotiation and mediation at the institutional level, solidarity might soften the divisive perception of federalism by the Sinhala people. It would thus make federalism less objectionable by shifting the focus on the positive and constructive forces promoted by solidarity.

Of course, merely acknowledging that solidarity is perceived to be a more neutral principle than federalism, and one that pursues the same goals, does not solve all

[85] For an overview of recent events in the country, see, eg A Wijayalath, 'Sri Lanka in a Constituent Moment' (IACL-AIDC Blog, 26 July 2022) https://blog-iacl-aidc.org/new-blog-3/2022/7/7/sri-lanka-in-a-constituent-moment; D Samararatne, 'The People in the Palace' (*VerfBlog*, 15 July 2022) https://verfassungsblog.de/the-people-in-the-palace/.

problems. In section V, I have indicated that one obstacle to the full implementation of solidarity is its justiciability. In the specific Sri Lankan context, it could also be pointed out that the country's party politics itself pose a threat to building solidarity. Parties representing ethnoreligious minorities – TNA and the SLMC, for instance – can prevent the development of solidarity in the political culture. Similarly, the two main political parties are understood to be Sinhala-Buddhist. These blocks to political solidarity have a direct impact on constitutional implementation and reform.[86] A more thorough discussion on political obstacles to solidarity shall be done in another chapter. However, in a country like Sri Lanka, where federalism continues to fuel disagreement, rediscovering the principle of solidarity could be helpful: solidarity is more neutral, it would be compatible with the system of provincial councils currently in place and it might help the transition to a fully fledged federal system when the opportunity arises.

[86] I am indebted to D Samararatne for raising these political obstacles to solidarity.

6

The Constitutional Resilience of Human Rights in New Federal States: Local Government and the National Human Rights Commission in Nepal

HARI P DHUNGANA AND IAIN PAYNE[1]

I. Introduction

Respect for human rights constitutes a core and fundamental commitment of modern democracies. Increasingly, states entrust this commitment to national human rights institutions (NHRIs) that posit themselves at the intersection of state and society. NHRIs are considered a standard feature of the modern democratic state,[2] and according to the Paris Principles are expected to have a clearly defined mandate, independence and institutional capacity required to protect and promote human rights.[3] Having proliferated worldwide, mostly during the post-1990 'wave' of democratisation, these relatively new institutions are seen as vanguards for human rights norms, including both those norms established in international conventions as well as those which are established within domestic law. However, while NHRIs seek to fulfil their role, they encounter not only the actors involved in organised violence and a multitude of human rights abuses, but also a landscape of contestation and struggle between and across society and state, between different branches of government, and among different governments in federal states. Accordingly, the promotion and protection of human rights in a state depends not only upon the commitment and capacity of the

[1] Author correspondence: h.dhungana@gmail.com; iain.payne@gmail.com. We are grateful to the editors and Mirza Rizwaan Ahmad, as well as Binendri Perera and the participants of the workshop on 'The Fourth Branch in South Asia', hosted by Niti Foundation, for their comments on previous drafts of this chapter. This chapter contributes to a broader research programme undertaken by Niti Foundation on fourth-branch institutions in Nepal, funded by the National Endowment for Democracy.

[2] A Wolman, 'National Human Rights Institutions and their Sub-National Counterparts: The Question of Decentralization' (2017) 6 *International Human Rights Law Review* 1.

[3] United Nations, *Principles Relating to the Status of National Institutions (The Paris Principles)*, adopted by the General Assembly, 48/134 of 20 December 1993, www.un.org/ruleoflaw/files/PRINCI~5.PDF.

NHRI, but also on the ways in which the NHRI engages the actors within the state structure and civil society. Constructive engagement by NHRIs with these actors is essential to developing a culture of human rights and ensuring their institutionalisation within state and societal institutions.

This chapter explores this theme by looking at the possibility of achieving the constitutional resilience of human rights in newly federated states. Once established, new federations evolve dynamically and through a continual process of conflict.[4] In addition to broad-ranging confrontation in the political arena between political parties and other groups and actors, new federations tend to have significant potential for institutionalised tussles within the constitutional framework itself, as federalised institutions pursue autonomy as well as cooperation at the same time.[5] Even with an overarching constitutional commitment to human rights, different units of the federation may not commit equally to their realisation, as they may have different or conflicting priorities and capacities. As such, the fate of human rights as a constitutional commitment over extended periods, particularly during crises or disasters in which federalism provides an 'additional layer of complexity',[6] depends on how the different units of the federation relate to the human rights agenda. This chapter focuses on the relationship between NHRIs and the state's various federal units, and the bottlenecks and possibilities which affect the realisation of the human rights commitments enshrined in the constitution.

We elaborate on the above themes and arguments through a case study of Nepal. With the promulgation of a new Constitution in 2015, Nepal transformed itself from a centralised unitary state to a federal state. Emerging against the backdrop of the decade-long Maoist 'People's War', which led to the abrogation of the 1990 Constitution, the 2015 Constitution brought wholesale change to the Nepali state, promising to bring about a more equal and inclusive 'Naya' ('New') Nepal. Among the most significant and far-reaching of these reforms is the transformation of the historically highly centralised, unitary state into a three-tiered federation. In addition, the new Constitution enshrines a more expansive package of rights to the people, including an enlarged collection of social, economic and cultural rights. These twin reforms – federalism and the constitutionalisation of human rights – are central to, but not the only components of, the 'progressive restructuring' of the state, which guided the post-conflict constitutional moment and is conceived as the basis for the realisation of full and inclusive democracy in Nepal.[7] Both human rights and federalism are therefore important for the ongoing credibility and resilience of the 2015 Constitution and thus the maintenance of sustainable peace.[8] Under this new constitutional dispensation, federalism

[4] M Burgess, *Comparative Federalism: Theory and Practice* (London, Routledge, 2006).

[5] C Colino, 'Understanding Federal Change: Types of Federalism and Institutional Evolution in the Spanish and German Federal Systems' in J Erk and W Swenden (eds), *New Directions in Federalism Studies* (London, Routledge, 2010).

[6] Forum of Federations, *Emergency Management in Federal Countries. Proceedings of the Workshop on Emergency Management in Federal Countries* (2014) www.forumfed.org/wp-content/uploads/2016/02/EmergencyManagement_in_Federal_Countries.pdf.

[7] See, eg Interim Constitution of Nepal 2007, preamble; B Karki, 'State Restructuring and Federalism Discourse in Nepal' in B Karki and R Edrisinha (eds), *The Federalism Debate in Nepal*, vol 2 (Kathmandu, United Nations Development Programme, Support to Participatory Constitution Building in Nepal, 2014).

[8] On this latter point, see L Nathan, 'The Real Deal? The Post-Conflict Constitution as a Peace Agreement' (2020) 41 *Third World Quarterly* 1556.

and human rights will interact with each other to shape governance outcomes. Indeed, the nascent federal system will, over time, evolve in a manner to give rise to a plurality of policy, legal, administrative or programmatic priorities or approaches across the three tiers, as each tier will have its own specific needs and priorities, and will have to respond to particular political dynamics in their jurisdictions. The transition to a federal system has significant implications for the enjoyment and protection of rights and freedoms.

The National Human Rights Commission of Nepal (the NHRC, or the Commission), was established by the 2015 Constitution as an independent 'constitutional body', upgrading its legal status from its original founding in 2000. Despite the federalisation of the country, the NHRC has maintained a unitary structure – that is, the NHRC's mandate encompasses all three tiers of the federation; the Constitution has not created additional subnational NHRIs at the provincial or local levels. The NHRC is expected to ensure that Nepal's human rights laws are complied with and international commitments are fulfilled, and it bears the burden of ensuring the respect, protection, promotion and effective enforcement of human rights throughout the entire state, across all three tiers of the federation. However, as we discuss, as a centralised, unitary entity headquartered in Kathmandu, the NHRC has yet to adapt to the country's federal structure. The emerging context of policy plurality on the side of the federation's political institutions and the imperative for standardisation of human rights commitments on the part of the NHRC presents a unique challenge for Nepal's constitutionalism, enforcing uniform human rights commitments while nurturing democracy in a plural society organised under the new federal structure. In this chapter, we emphasise the salience of local governments in contributing to the resilience of human rights and the need for the NHRC to engage deeply at the local level.

The chapter is divided into six parts. Following this introduction, section II highlights the role of NHRIs as fourth branch institutions within federal countries. Section III discusses why strengthening human rights in post-conflict Nepal is both necessary and prioritised by the 2015 Constitution. The chapter then turns its attention to the local level. Section IV emphasises the importance of local government as a key human rights actor in Nepal's federal system, but in section V attention is drawn to the accountability and capacity challenges for rights protection at the local level. Then, looking at the NHRC, section VI identifies the role that the Commission can play in lessening these concerns and supporting local rights protection, but describes the challenges preventing it from doing so. Section VII concludes.

II. The Fourth Branch and Federal States

Constitutional authorisation for an independent, constitutional body protecting human rights places an expectation on such an institution to serve as the custodian for rights and freedoms. The constitutional resilience of human rights, accordingly, depends upon the competence of these institutions in their engagement with state institutions. This is shaped by their design, status and capacity. Scholarly literature has begun to examine the way in which federations confront the question of how to disperse the authority of independent or fourth branch institutions across multiple orders of government.[9] For example, Michael Pal identifies two design approaches for election management bodies (EMBs) in federations. In the 'unitary model', a central EMB administers both national and sub-unit elections, while in the 'division of powers model', separate central and sub-unit EMBs administer elections within their respective jurisdictions.[10] A unitary design that incorporates sub-national representation, as is the case for the Independent National Electoral Commission in Nigeria, where two members of a 12-member body are drawn from each of the country's six geopolitical zones,[11] presents a third possible model. This general schematic can be applied to other fourth branch institutions (anti-corruption agencies, human rights institutions, audit institutions, etc).[12]

Focusing on the issue of partisan capture – a primary concern of the fourth branch literature – Pal highlights how both the unitary and division of powers models offer advantages but also pose particular dilemmas for democratic resilience. The 'unitary model of election administration empowers a national, independent institution as a check on abuses by local political majorities', which scholarship has generally understood to be a greater risk to democracy in federations, 'By pooling authority over federal and state/provincial elections into the hands of a single central institution'. However, this pooling of authority may make the possibility of institutional capture easier. As Pal notes, 'Centralization creates fewer pressure points in the system, but increases the possible harm caused by capture of the institution of election administration'.[13] Building on Pal's insight, our discussion of Nepal's NHRC demonstrates that under the unitary model, which the NHRC adopts, the structural links established with the federation-level political branches and actors encourage fourth branch institutions to be more responsive to central concerns. Rather than acting as a force for greater decentralisation, in the long term, we expect that the unitary model institutional design of the NHRC will tend towards supporting centripetal forces within the Nepali federation.

Andrew Wolman has explored the arguments for and against the establishment of sub-national human rights institutions in federal systems – that is, the value of adopting

[9] See C Murray, 'The Human Rights Commission et al: What Is the Role of South Africa's Chapter 9 Institutions?' (2009) 9 *Potchefstroom Electronic Law Journal/Potchefstroomse Elektroniese Regsblad* 122; T Khaitan, 'Guarantor Institutions' (2021) 16(S1) *Asian Journal of Comparative Law* S40; M Tushnet, 'Institutions Protecting Democracy: A Preliminary Inquiry' (2018) 12 *The Law & Ethics of Human Rights* 181; M Tushnet, 'Institutions Supporting Constitutional Democracy: Some Thoughts about Anti-Corruption (and Other) Agencies' [2019] *Singapore Journal of Legal Studies* 440; M Tushnet, 'Institutions Protecting Constitutional Democracy: Some Conceptual and Methodological Preliminaries' (2020) 70 *University of Toronto Law Journal* 95.

[10] M Pal, 'Constitutional Design of Electoral Governance in Federal States' (2021) 16(S1) *Asian Journal of Comparative Law* S23.

[11] See O Akinduro, 'Nigeria: Independent National Electoral Commission' in H Catt et al (eds), *Electoral Management Design*, revised edition (Stockholm, International Institute for Democracy and Electoral Assistance, 2014) 131, http://aceproject.org/ace-en/topics/em/annex/electoral-management-case-studies/nigeria-a-need-for-modernization. A similar kind of design is also adopted in Bosnia and Herzegovina and Pakistan, see I Payne, 'Federalism and the Fourth Branch: An Introductory Survey' Unpublished Manuscript.

[12] As Khaitan (n 9) notes, exactly what constitutes the fourth branch is dependent on constitutional context.

[13] Pal (n 10) S39.

what Pal has described as the 'division of powers model'.[14] The establishment of sub-national human rights institutions, Wolman highlights, can make the institutions more proximate and accessible, which in turn will help them to provide better services and be more culturally nuanced. The creation of sub-national human rights institutions can also more robustly influence sub-national government policy and promote local innovation in human rights. On the other hand, he highlights that sub-national human rights institutions can be more financially costly for the state. They can also be less efficient and less effective if economies of scale lead to deficiencies in human, financial or technical resources. Furthermore, the creation of multiple institutions can lead to undesirable fragmentation across the units of the federation – either normatively as regards the content of rights or practically as to their implementation – resulting in undesirable inequality or disparities among citizens across the country in their enjoyment of rights. In light of these considerations, Wolman concludes that the establishment of sub-national human rights institutions is more desirable where a national institution lacks authority or legitimacy, where sub-national jurisdictions are territorially large (requiring large distances to be covered) and transport is inefficient, and where there are culturally diverse populations that are territorially concentrated. In addition to these considerations, we argue that the Nepal case study highlights the relevance of a country's basic federal dynamics, orientations and goals when making this assessment. As opposed to the well-established federations – such as the USA, Canada and Australia – which are characterised by a 'coming together' of distinct polities into a union, federalism in Nepal was introduced with the overt aim of devolving power away from a highly concentrated and centralised state. It is in this context in Nepal that the potential for the unitary model to support centripetal tendencies in the federation must be evaluated.

In addition to the structural character of fourth branch institutions, it is equally important to pay attention to how structures on paper come to life in practice, and how their capacity to act shapes the constitutional resilience of human rights. We emphasise that this requires an exploration of the NHRC's engagement and commitment at the local level, where the fruit of human rights protection is experienced by citizens. This is especially important in Nepal, where local government is a constitutionally entrenched third tier in an 'hourglass' federation and assumes a significant role in the management of public services and the protection of rights. The 2015 Constitution bestows on local governments significant human rights responsibilities, and local government performance has a substantial bearing on the enjoyment of rights by citizens within the new constitutional dispensation. However, as we highlight, accountability and capacity concerns persist that threaten to undermine local government's ability to be a strong rights promoter and protector. We discuss how the NHRC has unfortunately been unable to provide external accountability. Institutionally, from the NHRC's perspective, this is principally an issue of constrained resources. However, we also identify this shortcoming as partly a function of the NHRC's unitary design. This organisational structure means that the NHRC is more dependent on federal political office holders and is thus more sensitive to concerns of the federal political class than the sub-national priorities and needs of, in particular, local governments and local constituencies.

[14] Wolman (n 2).

III. Human Rights in Post-conflict Nepal

In Nepal's political or public discourse, 'human rights' entered with a big bang in the early 1990s, and with the beginning of the Maoist 'People's War' in 1996 the human rights agenda became more salient and grew in significance. With the resolution of the insurgency as part of the peace settlement of 2006, ensuring that the state better protects and promotes fundamental human rights is a central burden borne by Nepal's 2015 Constitution. The Constitution commits itself to civil liberties and human rights,[15] and guarantees 31 fundamental rights and duties of citizens,[16] far more than the 20 rights enumerated in the 2007 Interim Constitution[17] and the 12 rights contained in the 1990 Constitution.[18] In the 2015 Constitution, there is an emphasis on economic, social and cultural rights, which are essential components of the Constitution's commitment to:

> Protecting and promoting social and cultural solidarity, tolerance and harmony, and unity in diversity … resolving to build an egalitarian society … [ensuring] economic equality, prosperity and social justice, by eliminating discrimination based on class, caste, region, language, religion and gender and all forms of caste-based untouchability …[19]

Two legacies are important in shaping the new Constitution's enlarged concern for these rights. The first is the Nepali state's long history of social, political, cultural and economic exclusion, which is recognised as a root cause of conflict, particularly the decade-long Maoist insurgency.[20] Inequalities in Nepal are structured along ethnic, caste, linguistic and gender lines, with corresponding regional dimensions, and have been reinforced by the state and other institutions. Different ethnic and linguistic groups have also experienced highly divergent developmental outcomes, with large disparities in access to land, food, healthcare, education and other basic needs. Thus, the Human Development Index is far higher for upper-caste Hindus (Brahmins and Chettris), at 0.538, than for Janajatis (Indigenous) (0.482), Madhesis (0.454) and Dalits (0.434).[21] Consequently, many groups continue to deplore the denial of equality and dignity to their person and community. Responding to these entrenched inequalities, the Maoist insurgency was a violent expression of dissatisfaction with the state's failure to ensure the equal enjoyment of core economic, social and cultural rights for its citizens. The incorporation of several of the insurgents' demands in the Comprehensive Peace Accord, the peace settlement signed between the government and the Maoist combatants in 2006, and subsequently in the new Constitution of 2015, helped to bring an end to the conflict.

[15] Constitution of Nepal 2015, preamble.

[16] See ibid pt 3.

[17] See Interim Constitution of Nepal 2007, pt 3.

[18] See Constitution of the Kingdom of Nepal 1990, Arts 11–22. On the historical development of constitutionalised human rights in Nepal, see B Adhikari, 'Constitutional Recognition of Human Rights: A Reflection on The Constituent Assembly Discourse in Nepal' in B Karki and R Edrisinha (eds), *Participatory Constitution Making in Nepal: Issues of Process and Substance*, vol 2 (Kathmandu, United Nations Development Programme, Support to Participatory Constitution Building in Nepal, 2014).

[19] Constitution of Nepal 2015, preamble.

[20] See, eg K Macours, 'Increasing Inequality and Civil Conflict in Nepal' (2011) 63 *Oxford Economic Papers* 1.

[21] P Sharma, B Guha-Khasnobis and DR Khanal, *Nepal Human Development Report 2014: Beyond Geography, Unlocking Human Potential* (Kathmandu, Government of Nepal, National Planning Commission and United Nations Development Programme, 2014).

Indeed, addressing the economic and social disparities central to the conflict has been central to the political agenda of the post-conflict democratic transition. In addition to agreeing to the 'progressive restructuring of the state by ending … [its] current centralized and unitary form' (the precursor language to the adoption of federalism),[22] the Comprehensive Peace Accord committed both parties 'to creat[ing] an atmosphere for the Nepali people to enjoy their civil, political, economic, social and cultural rights and … to creating an atmosphere where such rights are not violated in the future under any condition'.[23] The parties further committed themselves 'to adopt[ing] a policy of establishing the rights of all citizens to education, health, housing, employment and food security'.[24] While the constitutionalisation of these rights in the 2015 Constitution is an important step, the realisation of these rights requires resources and capacity on the part of the state agencies and a credible commitment to deliver them.

The human rights violations perpetrated – by the insurgents and the state's security forces – during the Maoist insurgency is a second legacy issue that makes the goal of enhanced human rights protection under the 2015 Constitution additionally important. The atrocities committed by both sides of the conflict have been well documented. A report from the UN Office of the High Commissioner for Human Rights, for instance, catalogues the various forms of rights violations that took place.[25] In several districts across the country, survivors, as well as the relatives of the victims of these atrocities, continue to await justice. In Madi Municipality, Chitwan District, for example, the victims of the Badarmude bus bombing incident have not received justice for the past 16 years.[26] More broadly, as a result of the conflict, more than 17,000 people were killed, an estimated 100,000–150,000 people were internally displaced and today 1300 'disappeared' persons remain unaccounted for. People's property was seized or destroyed. Targeted gender and sexual violence were common, and were often perpetrated by state actors; more than 2500 alleged cases of torture have been recorded, though most incidents have gone undocumented.[27] Moreover, the guerrilla nature of the insurgency resulted in highly localised dynamics, shaped by local power relations and disputes. Violence, from both sides, was generally calculated and targeted, exacerbating divisions within communities.

By the end of the conflict in 2006, addressing human rights issues assumed a central place in the national discourse on peace and constitution-building. This was primarily focused on highlighting the limitations of political rights, and favoured including all other economic, social and cultural rights in the constitutional framework. Indeed,

[22] Comprehensive Peace Accord, Government of Nepal – Communist Party of Nepal (Maoist), signed on 22 November 2006, Art 3.5. It is unclear why federalism was not explicitly mentioned in the Accord. However, as Karki notes, 'there is no prize for guessing that federalism was at the back of their minds'. See Karki (n 7) 8.

[23] Comprehensive Peace Accord, Art 7.1.2.

[24] ibid Art 3.9.

[25] United Nations Office of the High Commissioner for Human Rights, 'Nepal Conflict Report' (Geneva, UNOHCHR, 2012) 14–23.

[26] See RK Paudel, 'Thirteen Years On, Victims of the Badarmude Incident Await Compensation' *The Kathmandu Post* (6 June 2019) https://kathmandupost.com/national/2019/06/06/thirteen-years-on-victims-of-the-badarmude-incident-await-compensation.

[27] MV Ariño, 'Nepal: A Gender View of the Armed Conflict and the Peace Process' (Barcelona, School for a Culture of Peace, Autonomous University of Barcelona, 2008) Peacebuilding Papers 4.

social movements and activism, especially from the marginalised communities of Janajatis, Madhesis, Dalits and women, have focused on lobbying constitution-makers to enshrine the rights of marginalised communities in the 2015 Constitution.[28] Now that the formalisation of those rights into the Constitution has been achieved, the challenge lies in how state agencies – particularly the three tiers of government – work together with the NHRC to deliver them in practice.[29]

IV. Local Government: An Important All-Weather Rights Actor

In addition to the heightened emphasis on human rights, federal restructuring in Nepal has also emerged as a tool for ending discrimination, mitigating conflict, ensuring balanced development across all regions of the country and increasing participation – especially of members of historically marginalised groups – in governance.[30] There is a synergistic relationship between the project of human rights and federalism in Nepal and, if well-calibrated, the two can work in tandem towards a more equal and inclusive state.

Indeed, in the new federated Nepal, it is an obligation for all 761 governments – 753 local units, seven provinces and the centre – to ensure that the rights contained within the Constitution are realised and do not become mere empty promises.[31] Given its dominant revenue and spending capacity, and the primacy given to it in the vertical division of powers, the federal government has a principal role in this respect. Under this responsibility, the federal Parliament has enacted 16 distinct pieces of legislation specifically designed to give effect to the Constitution's fundamental rights provisions.[32] The federal Right to Food and Food Sovereignty Act 2018, for example, provides a concrete legal framework to implement constitutional rights relating to food sovereignty, freedom from hunger and access to clean drinking water.[33] The provinces too, through the

[28] See Niti Foundation, *Why Nepal's 'Other' Commissions Matter for Justice and Inclusion* (2022) https://nitifoundation.org/why-nepals-other-commissions-matter-for-justice-and-inclusion/.

[29] Indeed, there is still yet to be adequate accountability for many of these atrocities, and the provisions of non-impunity in both the Comprehensive Peace Accord and the new Constitution have been criticised as merely a façade to avoid international condemnation. See R Jeffery, 'Nepal: From Tacit Acceptance to Noncompliance' in *Negotiating Peace: Amnesties, Justice and Human Rights* (Cambridge, Cambridge University Press, 2021) 149.

[30] Karki (n 7).

[31] Constitution of Nepal 2015, Art 52.

[32] These are the Social Security Act 2018, the Consumer Protection Act 2018, the Public Health Services Act 2018, the Right to Housing Act 2018, the Right to Food and Food Sovereignty Act 2018, the Individual Privacy Act 2018, the Land (Seventh Amendment) Act 2018, the Compulsory and Free Education Act 2018, the Right to Employment Act 2018, the Caste-Based Discrimination and Untouchability (Offence and Punishment) (First Amendment) Act 2018, the Rights of Persons with Disabilities (Amendment) Act 2018, the Environment Protection (Amendment) Act 2018, the Crime Victims Protection Act 2018, the Children Act 2018, the Public Security (Third Amendment) Act 2018 and the Right to Safe Maternal and Reproductive Health Act 2018.

[33] Constitution of Nepal 2015, Arts 35(4) and 36. On the Right to Food and Food Sovereignty Act 2018, see Amnesty International, *Right to Food in Nepal: Analysis of the Right to Food and Food Sovereignty Act 2018* (Kathmandu, Amnesty International, 2019) www.amnesty.org/download/Documents/ASA3101302019ENGLISH.pdf.

exercise of their legislative and executive powers given to them by the Constitution, are required to act.[34]

Local governments must also assume a central role in ensuring that citizens experience constitutionally assured rights and freedoms. The Constitution's 'hourglass' federal system elevates local government to the role of key actors in the management of public services and the protection of rights.[35] Under the new federal division of power, local units can autonomously raise revenue and have greatly enhanced expenditure power. They have executive and legislative authority, which is exercised by a directly elected executive that is integrated into the local legislature.[36] Schedule 8 of the 2015 Constitution catalogues 22 functions that form the exclusive jurisdiction of local units, including basic and secondary education, basic health and sanitation, the management of local services such as vitals registration (births, deaths, marriage and migration), local development projects and programmes, local economic development, and the protection and development of languages and cultures. In addition, through Schedule 9, they share with the centre and provinces legislative and executive responsibility for 15 matters. Overall, local governments are responsible for around one-quarter of state expenditure, compared to around only 10 per cent for the provinces.[37] Local governments are thus empowered with significant powers to carry out their constitutionally mandated role of promoting economic, social and cultural rights.[38]

Moreover, as the unit of government that is closest to the people, local government is particularly salient in the lives of citizens. During the 2017 election campaign, candidates from all parties regularly employed the popular slogan 'singha durbarko adhikar gaun-gaunma' ('the power of Singha Durbar [the central administrative block in Kathmandu] in every village'), a slogan which emphasised that, under the new federal structure, government services would reach closer to the people, by forcing government from Kathmandu to the villages. High hopes have been placed on local representatives to deliver significant change.[39] For most Nepalis, local government is the 'front door' when engaging with the state, providing an immediate and accessible space for citizens to seek the fulfilment of their needs, regardless of which state agency or level of government within the federation is formally or actually responsible. Indeed, beyond its formal roles, local government represents the vast social capital of local elected members, which constituents draw on to access a whole array of government services.[40] It is thus unsurprising that an overwhelming majority of respondents in the *Survey of the Nepali People*

[34] Provincial powers are outlined in Schedules 6, 7 and 9 of the 2015 Constitution.

[35] I Payne and MG Breen, 'Hourglass Federalism in Nepal: The Role of Local Government in Post-Conflict Constitutions' (unpublished manuscript).

[36] See Constitution of Nepal 2015, pts 17 and 18. The constitutional framework is further elaborated in the Local Government Operations Act 2017.

[37] See, eg the figures for the 2019–20 financial year in Financial Comptroller General Office, *Government of Nepal Consolidated Financial Statement: Fiscal Year 2019/20* (Kathmandu, FCGO, 2021) 7, www.fcgo.gov.np/storage/uploads/reportpublication/2021-05-17/20210517185110_CFS_2019_20%20final.pdf.

[38] Constitution of Nepal 2015, Art 52.

[39] The Asia Foundation, 'Diagnostic Study of Local Governance in Federal Nepal 2017' (2018) 3.

[40] See, eg the discussion of earthquake relief grants discussed in B Bhusal et al, 'Does Revolution Work? Evidence from Nepal's People's War' (Center for Effective Global Action, University of California 2020) Working Paper Series No 116.

in 2020 identified local government as the arm of the state that is principally responsible for education, healthcare and the maintenance of infrastructure.[41]

Through its constitutionally entrenched powers and proximity to citizens, local governments have the capacity to substantially influence the enjoyment of rights. For example, across the country, local governments have been focused on making laws and implementing programmes on issues including child marriage, women's rights, education and gender-based violence.[42] However, the scope of local law-making is restricted to the powers enumerated in Schedules 8 and 9 of the Constitution. Further, several violations manifest locally but exist outside of local government jurisdiction.

One key example is the contravention of customary rights over natural resources, such as access to national parks or usufruct rights, as acknowledged in international human rights instruments such as the International Labour Organization Convention 169 on the Rights of Indigenous and Tribal Peoples. For instance, in Bagmati Province's Madi Municipality, local people have been denied their customary rights of access to areas inside the Chitwan National Park, and have been subject to constant harassment and beatings by the park personnel.[43] Local Indigenous people in the area have been reportedly stopped from fishing, as well as restricted from collecting wild fruits, vegetables and grass. Some of the local Indigenous community's houses have been demolished by the army without due process, while others have been chased away through the deployment of elephants. In such situations, local government representatives must navigate a tension between supporting local and Indigenous peoples' demands or conforming to federal laws which impinge on the rights of the people in their constituencies. In Madi, the mayor and other elected representatives worked with the Indigenous communities to oppose the decision and helped to elevate the issue to the national media and civil society organisations. While these efforts by local officials are positive in terms of the increased representation of local concerns in the public sphere, human rights abuses by federal park authorities remain widespread across the country. More formal and legal measures are required to address the disjuncture between the top-down agenda of ecological and park conservation and Indigenous concerns about livelihoods and access to resources.

Another category of systemic human rights violations is the ill-treatment of women, particularly those accused of witchcraft, and the ill-treatment of Dalits in many different forms.[44] Conventionally, in Nepal, these have been left outside the ambit of 'human rights', which have been seen as only concerned with direct actions of the state itself. However, these forms of discrimination and oppression are endemic in society, often normalised to the extent that they are rendered invisible. For instance, while the Mayor of Beni Municipality in Gandaki Province insists that while local law-making does not

[41] D Giri, U Pyakurel and CL Pandey, *A Survey of the Nepali People in 2020* (Kathmandu University, Interdisciplinary Analysts and The Asia Foundation 2020) 121, 131 and 137.

[42] Ministry of Federal Affairs and General Administration, *Report on the Comparative Study of Laws Issued by the Local Level* (Kathamdnu, MOFAGA, 2021).

[43] Based on consultations held with local leaders, 2021.

[44] Dalits constitute the lowest social strata in Hindu communities in South Asia, and for centuries have been denied equal access to resources, dignity and representation in public roles as well as in the socio-cultural milieu.

consciously promote caste discrimination, the Municipality has so far been unable to effectively address this problem. Reports abound of women alleged to be witches – most often by their family members or close relatives – and, as a result, they are beaten to death, harassed or subjected to other forms of mistreatment. Criminal cases have been registered by the police in such matters; however, this has failed to effectively reduce such instances on a national scale. These cases are complex problems, pertaining to entrenched societal practices which are reproduced despite a general commitment by state actors to address them. It is most clear in these cases that local governments can take the lead in generating public discourse on the importance of securing human rights according to the vision of the 2015 Constitution.

In many other cases, it is the local governments that are the perpetrators of rights abuses. For example, most local governments have focused on bringing *bikas* (development, but often narrowly construed as road building) to their communities, with little focus on other pressing issues.[45] While, from 2002 onwards, there was provision for local governments to earmark funds for specific marginalised groups – women, Dalits, Janajatis or Madhesis – from their budget, this provision has been discontinued since federalisation.[46] Now it has been noted that local elected leaders negotiate fund allocations in a mostly wholesale manner, resulting in relatively equal budgets for mostly infrastructural work for each of the wards within the municipality. This conception of development as infrastructure-only sidelines significant social, economic and cultural issues which require immediate action in local government jurisdictions.

The prioritisation of infrastructure by local governments also often leads to significant rights violations. Widespread reports suggest that local development work, especially road construction, frequently results in encroachment on private property without adequate compensation as required by Article 25(3) of the Constitution. The powerful discourse on infrastructure has limited understanding of human rights and has silenced voices against such injustices. Sometimes, people's homes or land are appropriated. In other cases, while private property is not trampled upon in the strict sense, construction has led to significant collateral negative effects on the welfare and security of vulnerable households and communities. In the case of Dalit households in the Badimalika Municipality in Sudurpaschim Province, for instance, a new road jeopardised an entire Dalit settlement when its construction severely increased the community's vulnerability to landslides.

Moreover, many local governments have been alleged to support the persistence of caste-based discrimination. For example, despite a constitutional guarantee in Article 24(1) that 'No person shall be subjected to any form of untouchability or discrimination in any private and public place on grounds of his or her origin, caste, tribe, community, profession, occupation or physical condition', several local governments have deployed public funds to build segregated public water taps – traditional caste-based purity practices prohibit Dalits from physically accessing water from

[45] J Rai, 'Status and Process of Law-Making in Local Governments: Reflections from Two Provinces' (Kathmandu, International Alert and Saferworld, 2020) 14–15.

[46] The provision for allocating public funds to marginalized groups was originally outlined in the country's Tenth Plan or 'Poverty Reduction Strategy Paper' in 2002 and subsequently included in the government guidelines on local budget formulation.

sources used by higher castes. Local Dalit communities very much see this as state-sponsored caste discrimination.[47]

Other examples could also be presented. In our interviews with elected representatives and civil society organisations in local governments across the country, we heard about cases where local government extraction of riverine materials had made nearby settlements more vulnerable to landslides, floods and other risks. Such extraction generally most severely affects Dalits and other marginalised groups who live in more disaster-prone areas. Some local human rights defenders accused government officials of hiding information about the extraction, and their support of unfair settlements with those affected. Furthermore, some local leaders have allegedly been involved in the extra-judicial settlement of rape cases, without proper recourse to justice. Local leaders have also lobbied against the registration of cases against those accused of inhuman treatment of alleged 'witch' women.

In summary, local governments have real human rights responsibilities, and their action (or inaction) will have a substantial bearing on the extent to which citizens can enjoy these rights under the new constitutional dispensation. This is not unique to Nepal's new federal context. Indeed, the importance of the connection between local government and human rights has been increasingly emphasised in the wider literature. Recently, for example, the UN Human Rights Advisory Committee has written that while central governments have the primary responsibility for the promotion and protection of human rights, 'local government has a complementary role to play' because in many instances it is local government that can actually 'translate national human rights strategies and policies into practical application'.[48] Indeed, 'Local authorities are close to citizens' everyday needs and they deal with human right issues on an everyday basis' and thus 'the real effect of human rights is experienced locally'.[49]

What is new for Nepal in the federal context, however, is the extent to which federal devolution amplifies the opportunity for local governments to pursue divergent policy priorities and agendas according to local needs and the varying dispositions of their elected governments. This, indeed, is the core logic of establishing a federation in the first place and is the natural outcome of 'self-rule'. Different policy agendas will have different and even conflicting consequences for rights and freedoms, positive or negative. José Woehrling shows that the governmental power in federalism may work to further the protection of rights and freedoms by providing an additional check on state power and by increasing citizen participation in political affairs.[50] However, Woehrling

[47] See, eg S Prakash, 'One Source, Different Taps: Caste-Based Discrimination Still Prevalent' *The Himalayan Times* (24 April 2019) https://thehimalayantimes.com/nepal/one-source-different-taps-caste-based-discrimination-still-prevalent; 'Untouchability Thriving in Rural Bajura' *The Himalayan Times* (25 April 2019) https://thehimalayantimes.com/nepal/untouchability-thriving-in-rural-bajura; A Shrestha, D Joshi and D Roth, 'The Hydro-Social Dynamics of Exclusion and Water Insecurity of Dalits in Peri-Urban Kathmandu Valley, Nepal: Fluid yet Unchanging' (2020) 28 *Contemporary South Asia* 320.

[48] Human Rights Council Advisory Committee, 'Role of Local Government in the Promotion and Protection of Human Rights: Final Report of the Human Rights Advisory Committee' (United Nations General Assembly, 2015) 6.

[49] ibid 7–8.

[50] J Woehrling, 'Federalism and the Protection of Rights and Freedoms: Affinities and Antagonism' in A-G Gagnon and JM Sauca (eds), *Negotiating Diversity: Identity, Pluralism and Democracy* (Brussels, PIE Peter Lang, 2014) 106–14.

highlights how 'the localisation of a substantial amount of political power can also bring negative consequences, such as a greater likelihood of sectoral tyranny through the creation of localised minorities, and the increased burden created by complex multi-level legal systems'.[51] Moreover, he argues that the connection of federalism with legal constitutionalism also exacerbates the legalisation of politics and that the universalistic nature of human rights can lead those who seek to protect rights and freedoms to distrust the diversity and flexibility that federalism embraces.[52] As Woehrling frames it, federalism and human rights are in constant tension. The challenge is to find a path that ensures respect for human rights but not at the expense of respect for the federal principle.[53]

Thus, as a linchpin of Nepal's federation, local governments are critical for constitutional resilience with respect to human rights. This role will manifest both through their own policies and priorities and in their collaboration with other institutions of the state, provincial and federal, as well as independent institutions like the NHRC. However, as we will discuss, current NHRC engagement has failed to capitalise on the full potential of the structuring of local government under federalism. This chapter contends that, in order to achieve resilience of human rights, the NHRC must engage local governments in a meaningful and structured manner. For this engagement, the NHRC needs a strategy and institutional arrangement for communication, monitoring, awareness-raising and capacity building with local governments, civil society, political leaders and social activists at the local level. This is an essential requisite for promoting a culture of human rights and enhancing capacity and demands for human rights 'from below' in Nepal.

V. Challenges to Human Rights Implementation at the Local Level: Accountability and Capacity

While Nepal's local governments possess significant human rights responsibilities, and much expectation has been placed on them to deliver, two issues have the potential to undermine their ability to emerge as rights-promoting institutions. The first of these issues is related to the design of local government itself, which raises concerns about ensuring governmental accountability in the protection of rights. Local accountability takes place, first and foremost, politically through the electoral process. After federalisation, local legislatures and executives were elected first in 2017, and subsequently in 2022, each to serve a five-year term.[54] Under the 2015 Constitution, local governments cannot be disbanded or have their responsibilities assumed by the federation's

[51] ibid 107.

[52] AL Parrish has written, for example, that the 'universalistic outlook [of human rights] is in tension with the idea of states as laboratories, each developing its own novel version of human rights'. See AL Parrish, 'State Court International Human Rights Litigation: A Concerning Trend?' (2013) 3 *UC Irvine Law Review* 25, 42.

[53] Woehrling (n 50) 117.

[54] Constitution of Nepal, Art 225. On the 2017 local elections, see Democracy Resource Centre, 'Nepal's Local Elections 2017: Final Observation Report' (2017), www.democracyresource.org/reports/nepals-local-elections-2017-final-observation-report/.

higher-order governments.[55] The second issue with the new local governance system, which introduces a directly elected executive that sits within the local legislative chamber, is that there is no mechanism to remove local executives via a vote of no confidence or motion of impeachment. Opposition parties do sit within the legislature (and, due to their direct election, in many cases also have leadership positions within the executive) and can provide at least a modicum of discursive accountability. However, it is not uncommon for local governments to be dominated by a single political party, and in some localities there is only one party represented in the entire elected assembly.[56]

The basic design of local government thus presents a model that muddles the separation of powers and the role of the political opposition – both of which have the potential to undermine accountability for rights implementation. First and foremost, the Constitution and the Local Government Operation Act of 2017 do not conceive of an opposition party in the local government, primarily because most members of the executive are elected directly by the people. Representatives from different political parties can become part of the same executive, even without having been in any electoral alliance or forming any coalition for local government. The Constitution envisions local government as being driven by a more consensual decision-making process, with little partisanship. Secondly, some institutional structures have been established to provide a degree of accountability over executive action. These include primarily the 'monitoring committee', led by a deputy mayor, and public accounts and good governance committees. Depending upon local political set-ups and partisan representation structures, the effectiveness of these institutions is highly variable on a case-by-case basis. Thirdly, even while some oppositional structures may develop, it is likely that, due to quotidian relationships between different local leaders, the notions of 'separation of powers' and 'checks and balances' will not be as effective in the local context. Accordingly, the virtues of the separation of power, checks and balances, and the politics of opposition or dissent – which are considered key institutional hallmarks of modern democracies – need to be tested against the way the members of the local executive and legislature play their roles in representing citizens' concerns and raising their voice about policies and the use of executive power. Thus, local governments need to be tested partly on the side of politics, involving the processes of deliberation and debate on citizens' concerns and the policies to respond to them, and partly on the structural or institutional set-up that sets out the roles and authorities of different actors and the relations between them.

The Local Government Operations Act 2017 is the federal umbrella legislation that expands upon the Constitution to fill out the legal framework for the local units.[57] The

[55] Compare the situation for provincial governments and assemblies, which may be suspended or dissolved and brought under temporary federal rule through a presidential order, made on the ratification of two-thirds of the federal Parliament. See Constitution of Nepal 2015, Art 232.

[56] This is the case, for example, in Bhaktapur Metropolitan City. See The Asia Foundation (n 39) 22.

[57] Although, it should be pointed out that there are some notable inconsistencies between the Act and the constitutional provisions on local government. See, eg B Paudel and KP Sapkota, *Local Levels in Federalism: Constitutional Provisions and the State of Implementation* (Kathmandu, Swatantra Nagarik Sanjal Nepal, 2018) 17–21, https://asiafoundation.org/publication/local-levels-in-federalism-constitutional-provisions-and-the-state-of-implementation/.

Act, together with the Constitution, envisages a legislature, an executive and a judicial committee in local government's overall structure. It requires local legislatures to establish at least three assembly committees: an audit committee, a legislative committee and a good governance committee.[58] The audit committees monitor the local government's financial accounts, while the legislative committees draft or review proposed legislation. The good governance committees are designed to promote good governance, transparency and accountability within local governments by, for example, measuring and publishing social and economic progress for constituents.[59] Establishing other special rights-specific accountability mechanisms, such as the creation of specialised human rights committees, is also possible under the Act;[60] however, to our knowledge, no local units have taken this path to date. Further, in many instances, even these mandatory committees are inactive or are not functioning adequately, especially in the smaller rural municipalities,[61] resulting in 'a severe lack of legislative oversight bodies in local governments'.[62]

This institutional lack of legislative oversight of local level executive power is owing to a normative assumption in the Constitution itself. It envisages consensual decision-making and far less partisanship in local government decision-making. Many of the mayors that we have consulted point out that the only effective institution to hold the executive to account was the audit committee; the others were less effective in practice. One part of the problem pertains to the capacity of the judicial committees that are mainly entrusted to mediate local-level civil cases, such as land disputes or matrimonial issues. Both their scope of jurisdiction and their members' capacity to raise human rights issues are limited. Local elected representatives who serve on the local judicial committee mediate disputes with recourse to local customs and social practicalities. These representatives neither possess the juridical sophistication expected of judges or human rights lawyers nor do they necessarily follow due process in their work. Accordingly, there will be less local judicial restraint on the local executive power.

This brings us to a second issue that threatens to undermine local government's emergence as rights-protecting institutions: capacity. The shift to federalism – especially of the three-tiered nature adopted by Nepal – is an enormous and challenging task. While significant strides have been made since 2015, there remains much to be done. In particular, administrative capacity continues to be an issue that undermines the ability of local governments to fulfil their constitutional mandates. Many local governments still do not have a full corps of administrative staff appointed, including in key positions such as legal drafting. This has proved to be one of the principal reasons preventing local governments from enacting legislation. Moreover, only a handful of Nepal's more

[58] Local Government Operations Act 2017, Art 22.

[59] Ministry of Federal Affairs and Local Development, *Good Governance Promotion Strategy and Action Plan: Sample (Draft)* (Kathmandu, MOFALD, 2017) https://mofald.gov.np/sites/default/files/News_Notices/Sushasan.PDF.

[60] Local Government Operations Act 2017, Art 22.

[61] Speaking of the legislative committees, Janak Rai, for example, observes that 'many of the committee members are unaware of and are not involved in the law-making process. In practice, only a few male elected members participate in the drafting of legislation'. See Rai (n 45) 5.

[62] B Bhurtel, 'Fiscal Federalism: An Analysis of Its Initial Implementation in Nepal' (International Alert and Saferworld, 2020) No 6, 18.

than 35,000 local elected representatives have any experience in government. On top of this, very few of the elected officials have had previous experience engaging in human rights-related work or advocacy. Thus, the awareness of the need for rights compliance within local government remains very low. A common refrain among local civil society leaders is that local governments are insufficiently aware of their human rights responsibilities and, where there is a general understanding of the need to protect rights, knowledge of how to do so is limited. This sentiment is also generally echoed by local elected representatives, who concede that they require more training and accompaniment through capacity development as they seek to govern and make decisions. Furthermore, an even more glaring gap is the limited understanding of the decisions on 'development work' and local human rights concerns, as the local government leaders consulted for this study interpreted their mandate and preference for (infrastructure) development without consideration of rights concerns. Similarly, there exists a high degree of confusion and lack of understanding around how federal laws and institutions can impact the rights of local and Indigenous populations, especially as local leaders find themselves required to navigate between more conservative federal laws on the one hand and the rights and interests of their constituencies on the other.

VI. The National Human Rights Commission: Guaranteeing Rights Across All Levels of the Federation

Ensuring there is accountability for the implementation of human rights by local government is not solely in the hands of local actors. Indeed, the constitutional resilience of human rights hinges upon productive links between the NHRC and all units of the federation, as well as with the wider civil society. Despite local government's entrenched political autonomy through the federal system, its accountability for the protection and promotion of rights extends beyond mechanisms housed at the local level and includes provincial and federal institutions, as well as the judiciary and the independent national constitutional bodies. Of particular interest here is the NHRC, which is the constitutional body that is mandated to ensure the respect, protection, promotion and effective enforcement of human rights throughout the entire state. Due to its national mandate – the Commission's jurisdiction is not confined merely to federal jurisdiction – the NHRC ought to have an important role to play to protect rights at the local level.

The NHRC was established in 2000, under the National Human Rights Commission Act 1997 (later replaced by the National Human Rights Commission Act 2012). It was elevated to constitutional status in the 2007 Interim Constitution,[63] and this was continued in the 2015 Constitution.[64] The Commission's mandate is the protection, promotion and respect of human rights.[65] It does this through investigating rights abuses and making recommendations to the government for redressal. In addition, it can, of its

[63] Interim Constitution of Nepal 2007, pt 15.
[64] Constitution of Nepal 2015, pt 25.
[65] ibid Art 249.

own accord, initiate judicial proceedings against rights violators. It also has a monitoring function, reviewing laws for their human rights compatibility and consulting with the executive.[66]

There are several ways that the NHRC can support the protection of rights in local government. For one, there is an obvious need for local governments to receive external support to build their capacity to protect rights. As mentioned above, this is something that is welcomed by local elected representatives. However, local governments are – perhaps rightfully – suspicious of assistance given by the higher-order governments, particularly the centre, whose assistance is viewed as undermining their political independence and promoting a recentralising political agenda. Local government leaders complain that the federal government's bureaucrats issue directives in a manner they used to do during the pre-2015 pre-federal period.[67] They consider these top-down communications as violations of their autonomy. They think that, rather than helping the capacity of local government, the federal government is intent on encroaching on their political-administrative autonomy. Local representatives have thus resisted the continued development of model laws for local government by the Ministry of Federal Affairs and General Administration. As a body with national reach but with independence from the central executive, the NHRC can assist and support local governments through the process of institution-building and the enactment and implementation of local legislative instruments. Given the above difficulties, the NHRC requires a more nuanced political approach to aiding local governments.

A second way that the NHRC can support rights at the local level is by helping to close the accountability gap. As discussed above, significant accountability concerns persist in local government. Interviews with local stakeholders reveal a desire for the NHRC to assume a monitoring role at the local level. As one mayor suggested to us:

> We have a committee [at local government] to formulate laws. But the committee does not have subject matter expertise, as local representatives are not legal experts, and hence we cannot prepare laws according to the need of our times. Thus, the National Human Rights Commission can support us in making such committees competent and help the development of people- and human rights-friendly laws.

For promoting human rights at the local level, most advocacy in Nepal is undertaken by local civil society organisations (CSOs). However, they have neither the scale nor the institutional legitimacy that the NHRC enjoys as a constitutional body. There is an acknowledgement from both the NHRC and governments of the important role of civil society and human rights defenders. The ways in which human rights institutions can provide accountability are well discussed in the scholarly literature. Christina Murray, for example, discusses in the South African context how the country's independent institutions can provide a check on government power 'by providing a legitimate and authoritative account of government's record, which can be used by citizens and Parliament in scrutinising government's performance'.[68] Drawing on Linda

[66] ibid.
[67] Consultation with Municipal Association of Nepal, 2021.
[68] Murray (n 9) 131.

Reif's framework, Murray argues that these institutions provide accountability through 'answerability' (demanding information and reasons) rather than 'enforceability' (punishing negative behaviours) and promote governmental compliance through 'cooperative control' – that is, being 'facilitative and proactive, using advice and persuasion, wherein the actors confer and dialogue to try to obtain the desired result and change behaviour'.[69] But again, human rights CSOs also face their own capacity constraints, unless they are supported by donors, the government or the NHRC. Sustaining a vibrant civil society to champion human rights remains a challenge, especially in a highly donor-dependent context. Through the collection, publication and deployment of robust evidence, the NHRC can provide discursive accountability to local governments.

While external, independent accountability and support for local government are necessary, to date, the NHRC has been unable to provide this. Indeed, aside from a few very limited interactions and discussion programmes, the NHRC has had virtually no substantive engagement at the local level.[70] The Commission normally visits localities in response to the complaints they receive, or as part of a *suo moto* case. They are known to occasionally visit local governments, as for some years the NHRC has been engaged in efforts to support human rights-friendly local governance, but these efforts are episodic and event-oriented. This lack of sustained systemic engagement has many, compounding reasons. The NHRC's lack of physical presence in local areas is the biggest hindrance. While, for the monitoring of violations, NHRC staff from the regional offices do liaise with and consult government officials and other local actors, the latter primarily assume the role of 'informants' rather than key stakeholders. In the consultations held for this study, local representatives also indicated that NHRC engagement was very limited in their local government units. Their visits to these sites are not regular, and they tend to only visit for larger, high-profile issues that receive national media or public attention and work their way into the national political-legal discourse. In many local units, especially in remote areas, years pass between NHRC visits. And this is not only the case for those areas that are distant from NHRC offices. In Bajura and Myagdi Districts, in Sudurpaschim Province and Gandaki Province, where we consulted, local government leaders mentioned that the last visit happened two years ago. In the Khotang District in Province One, the staff at the NHRC's 'outreach office' in Diktel (one of only two such offices in the country) noted that it has been over five years since an NHRC commissioner last visited the office.

Accordingly, the NHRC's local engagement is usually reactive, and highly dependent on victims lodging complaints. While complaints can be lodged electronically or by phone, or through mobile applications, local civil societies highlight that this often does not generate a response. Thus, victims often feel compelled to travel to the nearest NHRC office to lodge an in-person petition, which is seen as a much more reliable way to ensure that the NHRC commences an investigation. This was the case recently in Navrajpur Rural Municipality in Madhesh Province, where the husband of a woman accused of witchcraft (and subsequently abused by groups within the community) was

[69] ibid 131–32.

[70] See, eg National Human Rights Commission of Nepal, *Annual Report: 2020* (Lalitpur, NHRC, 2021) www.nhrcnepal.org/nhrc_new/doc/newsletter/Annual%20Report%20FY%202019-20_compressed.pdf.

compelled to travel to the NHRC office in Janakpur (at least a whole day round trip) to ensure that the case elicited a response. Compared to many other local units, Navrajpur is relatively proximate to an NHRC office. More broadly, due to the 'normalisation' of rights violations in several localities, many victims or survivors do not know that it is the NHRC that is charged with helping to address their concerns. Given this, public education about the existence and role of the NHRC is essential.

The NHRC's limited local engagement is quite clearly, in part, a result of the physical structure of the Commission, which remains Kathmandu-centric. After the founding of its central office in Lalitpur in the Kathmandu Valley in 2000, beginning in late 2004, the NHRC began establishing regional offices, of which there are now eight in total across the country. The decision to build an office was initially based on the severity of the Maoist insurgency in the early 2000s, with areas which experienced a greater intensity of armed conflict receiving priority in NHRC office establishment. This was due to the desired goal of making the registration of complaints by victims easier, and monitoring and investigation more effective and efficient. Later, additional offices were established so that there was one in each of the five Development Regions. In 2018, the NHRC began the process of restructuring to align its administrative structure with the new federal configuration – essentially aligning its current regional offices with the seven new provinces.[71] However, approval from the Ministry of Finance, which is required before the restructuring can proceed, has yet to be given.[72]

Another factor is the limitation of the NHRC's constrained financial and human resources. While the NHRC enjoys considerably more resources than the newly established identity-based, 'Other' commissions, which also have a rights-promoting function,[73] overall, it has a very meagre budget. This is particularly the case when compared to the budgets of the other constitutional bodies. The NHRC's budget is around one-third that of the Public Service Commissions and the Auditor General, and is around one-sixth of that enjoyed by the Commission for the Investigation of Abuse of Authority.[74] A more important point about the resources, however, is that the NHRC requires authorisation from the federal Finance Ministry if it is to expand offices or incur any significant expenditure. Accordingly, while it is autonomous constitutionally, its operations or its engagements with civil society or local governments may be constrained due to a lack of support from the Ministry, and by other legislation, including those related to public procurement.[75]

However, these are not the only issues at play. Another important concern is that the NHRC is much more sensitive to federal concerns than to those at the sub-national level. As already noted, the Commission's engagement in local and sub-national issues is heavily shaped by the extent to which these become salient in national political-legal

[71] The Ministry of Finance has yet to give its required approval, refusing to provide the Commission with the additional finances required to expand its office presence, and thus the current structural configuration of the NHRC remains in limbo.

[72] National Human Rights Commission Act 2012, Art 32.

[73] On these, see Niti Foundation (n 28).

[74] See, eg Financial Comptroller General Office (n 37).

[75] Public procurement law is attracted if NHRC engages an NGO or other actors to provide services. The law is considered cumbersome and inflexible, and is in the process of review as of late 2021.

discourse. This is a natural product of the NHRC's centralised place within Nepal's governance imagination. For one, the struggles for human rights from which the Commission emerged – the fight against the increasingly authoritarian Shah monarchy and the Maoist insurgency – were of national concern. While the Maoist conflict triggered the initial decentralisation of the NHRC, compelling it to establish regional offices to investigate conflict rights violations, the work of these offices was designed to collect information that would feed into what was a national political issue. As such, decentralisation was not instituted primarily to deal with the diversity of issues present at the local and regional levels.

However, once the Maoist conflict came to a close following the Comprehensive Peace Accord in 2006, the NHRC's momentum slowed. It faced hurdles in convincing the Ministry of Finance to garner more resources, especially as government officials view the Commission as a body opposed to and critical of the government. This attitude reflects an insufficient appreciation on the part of government officials for the rationale of having the NHRC as a protector, guarantor and promoter of human rights, entrenched within the Constitution. For them, 'human rights' are principally an international agenda to which some degree of compliance is anticipated to satisfy donor countries that provide official development assistance. The human rights governance agenda is more oriented towards UN agencies than to rights that are relevant and experienced by 'ordinary' people, and thus the rights discourse tends to make more reference to international commitments than to how these translate to improve people's lives and livelihoods.

Moreover, as already noted, the Commission's physical location – in the Kathmandu Valley – has meant that its chief decision-makers (the five appointed commissioners and the senior bureaucrats) are influenced by the experiences and concerns of a Kathmandu-centric political discourse. Natural and institutional links exist between its commissioners, civil servants, federal politicians and bureaucrats, as they all inhabit a shared Kathmandu-centric political culture. More than this, through the appointment, financing and accountability process, structural links exist between federation institutions and the Commission. The commissioners are appointed by the President upon the recommendation of the Constitutional Council, a multi-partisan and inter-institutional body, all the members of which are drawn from federation-level institutions.[76] The NHRC submits its annual report to the President, who then passes it on to the federal Parliament for deliberation.[77] Like the other constitutional bodies, it is reliant on the executive branch (via the Ministry of Finance) to approve its yearly budget, as well as for any major organisational changes (eg opening of new offices),[78] and the enactment of its delegated legislation.[79] The three-year delay, as of 2022, to the approval of the NHRC's revised organisational structure is illustrative of the dependence on the central

[76] Constitution of Nepal 2015, Art 248. On the Constitutional Council and the appointments process generally, see Niti Foundation, *Evaluating Constitutional Body Appointments: The Constitutional Council* (forthcoming).

[77] Constitution of Nepal 2015, Art 294.

[78] National Human Rights Commission Act 2012, Art 26.

[79] ibid Art 32.

executive for its basic functioning. The restructuring of the NHRC entails costs such as for staff and infrastructure, and hence it requires the federal government's approval via the Ministry of Finance. In contrast, there is no structural link between the NHRC and provincial or local governments. Thus, it should not be surprising that the NHRC is more responsive to federal concerns, and while the NHRC is intended to be a national body that services all three levels of the federation, in actuality it serves much more like a federal/central body.

VII. Conclusion and Recommendations

In this chapter, we examined the constitutional resilience of human rights in newly established federations. With a focus on Nepal's National Human Rights Commission, we have presented empirical material as well as arguments about how a fourth branch human rights institution can forge links with different units in a federation, in particular local government, and wider civil society for protecting and promoting rights.

Nepal's Constitution makes a clear commitment to respect, protect, promote and effectively enforce human rights in their expansive form, including political, economic, social and cultural aspects. We have highlighted that the twin reforms of federalism and the elevation of human rights are central to the 'progressive restructuring' of the Nepalese state, which guided the post-conflict constitutional moment, and which is intended to be the basis for the realisation of full and inclusive democracy. Both federalism and human rights are therefore important for the ongoing credibility and resilience of the 2015 Constitution and thus the maintenance of sustainable peace. Furthermore, we have discussed the importance of the newly entrenched local governments as human rights actors, not least because it is through local government that Nepalis principally engage with the state. However, we have highlighted the persistence of accountability and capacity challenges, which may undermine local government's ability to be strong rights-upholding institutions.

As the constitutional body mandated to guarantee the respect, protection, promotion and effective enforcement of human rights, we have emphasised the supportive role that the NHRC can play to support the protection of rights in local government. Indeed, the NHRC's mandate is national, extending across all tiers of the new federation. However, we have discussed that, to date, the NHRC has been unable to provide the independent accountability and supportive accompaniment required at the local level. While the NHRC has begun to restructure itself to calibrate to the new federal context, it has not yet adapted to engage differently and independently with the three tiers of the state. Institutionally, from the NHRC's perspective, this is principally an issue of constrained resources. However, we have further argued that this is also linked to the NHRC's unitary design. The unitary nature of the NHRC's organisation creates structural and relational linkages with the federal political branches, which means that it is more sensitive to federal tier concerns than sub-national ones. Over the long term, this unitary design is expected to tend towards supporting centripetal forces within the federation, potentially acting as an additional obstacle to the Constitution's federal devolutionary intent. This is a consideration that ought to be considered when assessing the value of the unitary design of the NHRC in Nepal and assessing its ongoing performance in supporting human rights. It is insufficient for the Commission's vision to be limited to federal/central affairs; it is critical that it reaches down and is also an effective guarantor at the provincial and local levels of government.

Overall, we have argued that the structure of local government, as envisaged under Nepal's new federal Constitution, presents a unique opportunity to strengthen human rights, serving as institutions to connect human rights discourse and standards to the local social-cultural milieu and the processes of decision-making. Harnessing this potential will necessarily be a long process that will require sustained engagement between local leaders, human rights defenders and the NHRC, which necessitates the NHRC prioritising the development of institutional mechanisms to engage with local governments as autonomous actors.

PART IV

The Political Branches

7

Killing a Constitution with a Thousand Cuts: Executive Aggrandisement and Party–State Fusion in India

TARUNABH KHAITAN[1]

'[W]e must … observe the caution which John Stuart Mill has given to all who are interested in the maintenance of democracy, namely, not 'to lay their liberties at the feet of even a great man, or to trust him with powers which enable him to subvert their institutions'.

JS Mill,[2] quoted by BR Ambedkar on 25 November 1949,[3] requoted by the sitting Chief Justice of India on Constitution Day (26 November 2018).[4]

I. Introduction

As established democracies, such as Poland, Hungary, Turkey, Brazil, South Africa and Israel, have witnessed democratic deconsolidation,[5] the world's largest democracy has sadly not been an exception. To be sure, there are no tanks on the streets of Delhi, nor is there an official declaration of a national emergency. Rights have not, formally, been suspended and elections will take place on time. The mode of democratic decline in India, inasmuch as it is incremental and systemic, also seems to be following the global trends of the early twenty-first century.[6] There are key differences too, for India's

[1] This chapter was first published in *Law & Ethics of Human Rights* in 2020. I am grateful to Ken Kiat for help with formatting references.

[2] JS Mill, *Considerations on Representative Government* (Longmans, Green & Co, 1872) 3.

[3] Constituent Assembly Debates, Vol 11 (25 November 1945), Speech by Bhimrao Ramji Ambedkar, [324], http://cadindia.clpr.org.in/constitution_assembly_debates/volume/11/1949-11-25?.

[4] A Sanyal, '"Don't Lay Your Liberties at the Feet of Even a Great Man": Chief Justice' *NDTV* (27 November 2017) www.ndtv.com/india-news/constitution-day-2018-ranjan-gogoi-chief-justice-of-india-supreme-court-dont-lay-your-liberties-at-f-1953713.

[5] MA Graber, S Levinson and M Tushnet (eds), *Constitutional Democracy in Crisis?* (Oxford, Oxford University Press, 2018).

[6] T Khaitan, 'Executive Aggrandizement in Established Democracies: A Crisis of Liberal Democratic Constitutionalism' (2019) 17 *International Journal of Constitutional Law* 342.

experience with democratic deconsolidation has been different from Hungary's or Poland's. India's longer history with democracy and the relative strength of its institutions has meant that one term in office (between 2014 and 2019) was insufficient for the ruling party to establish its stranglehold on power. And yet, sufficient groundwork was laid for the successor Bharatiya Janata Party (BJP) administration to secure its oft-repeated public hope of an 'India free of the Congress Party' (the BJP's main political rival) and of ruling the country for the next 50 years.[7]

While there has been much discussion of executive aggrandisement and the decay of democratic controls in Indian political discourse, this chapter fills a scholarly gap by offering a thick description of the events during the first term of Mr Narendra Modi as the Prime Minister of India as evidence of the phenomenon in India. In doing so, the chapter takes pains to avoid castigating any permissible political agenda a right-wing party in power may seek to pursue and focuses only on the actions that, taken as a whole, imperilled the continuing operation of liberal democratic constitutionalism. The focus is not on everything that ails Indian democracy, but only on those actions of the BJP government that threatened it.

This chapter will show how the first Modi government in power in India between May 2014 and May 2019 consistently sought to erase the distinction between the party and the state by incrementally, but systemically, seeking to undermine or capture mechanisms that seek executive accountability. Section II will outline three key ways in which liberal democratic constitutions make the executive accountable: vertically, by demanding electoral accountability to the people; horizontally, by subjecting it to accountability demands of other state institutions like the political opposition, the judiciary and fourth branch institutions; and diagonally, by requiring discursive accountability to the media, the academy and other civil society institutions. These institutional mechanisms are *undermined* when their power relative to the political executive is diminished ('executive aggrandisement'); they are *captured* when party loyalists take over the functioning of these institutions and make them pliant to the executive ('party–state fusion').

Sections III–VI will map how the government headed by Mr Modi incrementally and systemically undermined these three forms of accountability in its first five years in office, either by executive aggrandisement or by reducing the separation between the ruling political party and the state. These sections tend towards the descriptive, painstakingly documenting detailed evidence; however, this is essential in order to sustain the systemicity claim made in this chapter.

This incremental fusion of the party and the state and the erosion of mechanisms seeking executive accountability were rationalised through a discourse of hyper-nationalism (which equated political opposition to the party with treason), a managerial discourse that promised probity, decisiveness and efficiency (and painted political opponents, as well as checking institutions as corrupt, indecisive or inefficient)[8] and a

[7] Express Web Desk, 'Assam in Kitty, Amit Shah Sets Eyes on Congress-Mukt 2019' *Indian Express* (19 May 2016) https://indianexpress.com/article/india/india-news-india/assam-result-amit-shah-bjp-agp-assembly-poll-result-congress-mukt-bharat/.

[8] A Basu, 'Narendra Modi and India's Populist Democracy' (2018) 1 *Indian Politics and Policy* 83.

welfarist-developmental-populist discourse that characterised procedural requirements as hurdles that got in the way of delivering development to the people.

A brief, if unavoidably simplistic, overview of the political context leading up to Narendra Modi's spectacular victory in 2014 might be helpful to readers who are less familiar with the Indian context. India became independent of British colonial rule in 1947, and in 1950 adopted a largely liberal, democratic, secular and egalitarian Constitution. It included entrenched, judicially enforceable, fundamental rights; a parliamentary system of government with an indirectly elected and largely ceremonial presidency; a quasi-federal division of state power with a centralist bias; and a separation of powers, with a powerful and independent judiciary. Minorities of various stripes were given multiple forms of accommodation, including limited expressive accommodation of illiberal ideological groups such as Hindu nationalists.[9] Until the late 1980s, India more or less functioned as a dominant party system, at least at the federal level. The Congress Party governed the country for most of this period, barring its disastrous, but brief, electoral punishment for the Emergency imposed by Prime Minister Indira Gandhi in the mid-1970s.

The BJP, a Hindu-nationalist majoritarian party, won only two seats in the Lower House of the federal Parliament in the 1984 general elections. In the 1990s, however, it rode a remarkable wave of popularity on the back of a demand for the construction of a Hindu temple on a site occupied by a mosque – the Babri Masjid – which was destroyed in late 1992, allegedly with the support and complicity of several prominent BJP leaders. It first came to power in 1998 and governed in a coalition with smaller parties until 2004, under the premiership of its relatively centrist leader Mr Atal Bihari Vajpayee. The Congress Party unexpectedly returned to power in 2004 and ruled as a coalition government under Prime Minister Manmohan Singh until 2014. During its last years, its government was mired in numerous corruption allegations, and Mr Modi rode a powerful anti-incumbency wave to form a coalition government in 2014.

Two clarifications are necessary before we begin. First, the article suggests that something distinctive happened during the first five Modi years. The systemicity of its assaults on all accountability-seeking mechanisms made it different from previous governments, which had all been constitutionally naughty every now and then; the subtlety and incrementalism of its assaults distinguished it from more direct assaults on constitutionalism during the Emergency years under Indira Gandhi,[10] the three-and-a-half decades-long Communist Party rule in the state of West Bengal[11] and, possibly, even the second Modi administration, elected with a full parliamentary majority for the BJP in 2019. These comparisons make clear that assaults on democracy can, and have, come from the political left as well as the political right.

[9] T Khaitan, 'Directive Principles and the Expressive Accommodation of Ideological Dissenters' (2018) 16 *International Journal of Constitutional Law* 389.

[10] PN Dhar, *Indira Gandhi, the 'Emergency', and Indian Democracy* (Oxford, Oxford University Press, 2000). Most of the constitutional excesses of the Emergency were reversed by the Constitution (Forty-fourth Amendment) Act 1978, enacted by the Janata Party government that came to power after defeating Indira Gandhi in the 1977 general elections.

[11] S Mukherjee, 'The Use and Abuse of Democracy in West Bengal' (2007) 42 *Economic and Political Weekly* 101, 101–08; PS Banerjee, 'Party, Power and Political Violence in West Bengal' (2011) 46 *Economic and Political Weekly* 16, 16–18.

Second, by documenting these assaults on existing constitutional mechanisms, I do not intend to suggest that the existing system was perfect. Far from it; in many cases, its weaknesses facilitated these attacks or helped justify them. It is, in fact, a key feature of incremental authoritarianism that – like pretextual discrimination – it always rationalises its assaults on constitutional governance on broadly accepted justifications (such as probity or efficiency). Myriad strands need attention in order to arrive at an all-things-considered judgement on the merits of each move, making it impossible for a thickly descriptive chapter of this sort to decide in each case whether the purported rationales were wholly pretextual, partly so or largely legitimate. Sections III–VI, therefore, document an act or attempt if one of its probable effects was executive aggrandisement or party–state fusion. Even if some of them turn out, on a fuller analysis, to be largely legitimate (despite their democratic costs), the systemicity and incrementalism of the techniques used would nonetheless be apparent. One only needs to look at Figure 7.1, based on data from the extremely reputable Varieties of Democracies Index,[12] depicting India's performance on various democratic criteria from the inauguration of its Constitution in 1950 until 2019, the last year for which the data was available at the time of writing.

Figure 7.1 India's Year-wise V-Dem Scores between 1950 and 2019

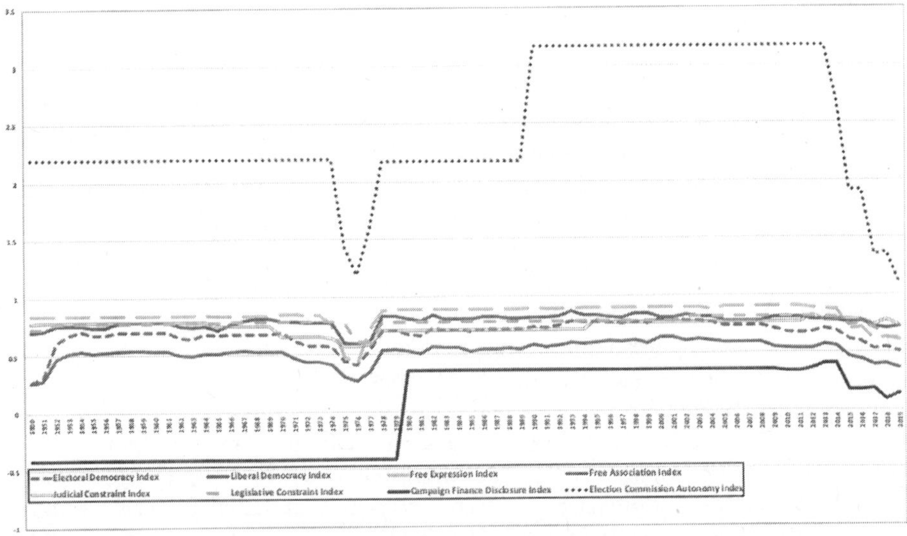

The two vertical lines in the figure mark the lead up to two periods of consistent decline across most markers of the health of democracy in India: Gandhi's Emergency in 1975

[12] M Coppedge et al, 'V-Dem Dataset Version 10', V-Dem: Varieties of Democracy (2020) https://doi.org/10.23696/vdemds20; D Pemstein et al, 'The V-Dem Measurement Model: Latent Variable Analysis for Cross-National and Cross-Temporal Expert-Coded Data' (2018) V-Dem Working Paper No 21, https://papers.ssrn.com/sol3/papers.cfm?abstract_id=3167764. See generally SY Quarishi, 'Slipping on Democracy' *Indian Express* (26 February 2019) https://indianexpress.com/article/opinion/columns/democracy-index-economist-intelligence-unit-slipping-on-democracy-5600569/.

and Modi's premiership in 2014. During the Emergency, democratic decline in India was evident, and stark, across all the indicators depicted. In the Modi years, as I plan to argue, the decline has generally been less spectacular (barring the rapid decline in the independence of the Election Commission and campaign finance transparency), and evidences his incremental, but systemic, undermining of India's democracy. Thus, the social science evidence for the argument in this chapter is strong, despite the caveats above. What I now propose to do is to defend the arguments with more specific evidence, organised in a clear analytic framework.

II. Mechanisms for Executive Accountability[13]

In this section, I provide an analytic framework of the ways in which liberal democratic constitutions seek executive accountability. Przeworski famously described democracy as a system in which parties lose elections.[14] As such, democracies – at least of the representative variety – are inherently unstable systems of organising political power in one respect: every victorious democrat has an incentive to undermine its continued operation so that she does not lose her hard-won power in the next round of elections. Alongside the military and corporate wealth, the ruling political party is one of the biggest potential sources of threat to any democracy.[15] Contrast this with other regime types. An autocracy is stable in the sense that those with the most power – the autocrats – have an interest in maintaining their power. The same is true of wealth-based oligarchies or inheritance based monarchies. It may be that these other regimes face a greater degree of external threats (external to the regime, that is, not to society at large). However, they are self-enforcing to the extent that they grant plenary political power to the individuals and groups who are most interested in maintaining the stability of that particular regime type. The threat to a democratic regime comes from within.

The very idea of democracy requires that every group must have a genuine hope of acquiring some level of state power – at least some of the time.[16] If this condition is breached, and a group in the polity is locked out of power semi-permanently, the regime is no longer a democracy. Furthermore, the stability of such a regime becomes vulnerable to external threats – those locked out of power have no reason not to try and upend it. Thus, democracies trade off internal instability for external stability, whereas other – more exclusionary – regime types are internally more stable and externally more vulnerable.

Democracies seek to protect themselves from this internal threat by creating mechanisms to ensure that those who currently enjoy political power do not foreclose the possibility of others acquiring it in their stead in the future. Although, in theory, all

[13] This section draws heavily from Khaitan, 'Executive Aggrandizement' (n 6).

[14] A Przeworski, *Democracy and the Market: Political and Economic Reforms in Eastern Europe and Latin America* (Cambridge, Cambridge University Press, 1991) 10.

[15] See generally T Khaitan, 'Political Insurance for the (Relative) Poor: Why Liberal Constitutionalism Should Resist Plutocracy' (2019) 8 *Global Constitutionalism* 536 (discussing wealth's threat to democracy).

[16] See S Issacharoff and RH Pildes, 'Politics as Markets: Partisan Lockups of the Democratic Process' (1998) 50 *Stanford Law Review* 643.

state power needs to be checked, it is the political executive, wielding the power of the sword, that is usually the most dangerous branch that internally threatens a democracy. Thus, the political executive is the main target of the accountability mechanisms liberal democratic constitutions put in place.

The purpose of this framework is to assure democracy over time, as it seeks to guarantee democratic governance not only to the people today, but to all future peoples of that country. While each elected government has the mandate to implement its policies over a wide range of issues, seeking to reduce the effectiveness of these modes of accountability is best understood as an effort to entrench the ruling party's stranglehold on power in ways that are inimical to the continued operation of democracy. A democracy's accountability demands can be organised around three axes.

In the first of these axes, democracy seeks *electoral* – also called *vertical* – accountability from the political executive.[17] The executive is required (either directly, as in presidential systems, or indirectly, as in parliamentary systems) to periodically seek the endorsement of the people through free and fair elections. In parliamentary systems, vertical accountability can be undermined in several ways: the political executive may extend the interval between elections, remove Parliament's power to vote down a government and seek new elections or do away with the requirement that ministers must be elected representatives. Vertical accountability mechanisms can be captured by reducing the separation between the ruling party and the state through measures such as gerrymandering, electorate manipulation, vote-rigging, voter disenfranchisement, biased campaign finance and other electoral laws that give the ruling party an unfair electoral advantage over the opposition.

The threat of losing the next election often stops the executive from overreaching in ways that may not go down well with the electorate. On the other hand, this also encourages it to overreach in ways that will. In particular, electorates can sometimes be tempted to compromise their interest (and the interest of future generations) in democratic governance over the long term for (often illusory) short-term promises. A prejudiced majority can persecute a hated minority too, often by seeking to permanently exclude it from political power. Furthermore, even for the electorate to express its will, a free and fair electoral contest is necessary – this at least needs a neutral referee and is not something one of the contestants can be trusted with. This is why most liberal constitutions tend not to be satisfied with electoral accountability alone.

The second axis of accountability for the executive is therefore *institutional* or *horizontal*. To secure this, a constitution subjects the actions of the executive to the scrutiny of several other state institutions, including a legislature, a judiciary and various 'fourth branch' institutions that include an auditor-general, an electoral commission, a human rights watchdog, an anti-corruption ombudsoffice, a chief public prosecutor and so on.[18] These institutions are variously constituted. Some of them are themselves

[17] On vertical and horizontal accountability, see G O'Donnell, 'Horizontal Accountability in New Democracies' in MF Plattner, A Schedler and L Diamond (eds), *The Self-Restraining State: Power and Accountability in New Democracies* (Boulder, CO, Lynne Rienner Publishers, 1999) 29.

[18] On the fourth branch, see B Ackerman, 'The New Separation of Powers' (2000) 113 *Harvard Law Review* 633; C Fombad, 'The Diffusion of South-African Style Institutions? A Study in Comparative

elected, primarily the legislature, and are therefore most likely to be controlled or influenced by the political executive (in parliamentary systems). Usually, it is only the political opposition within the legislature that performs any checking function.[19] Other institutions, such as the judiciary and other high constitutional offices, are constituted through *appointments*. The appointment mechanism, especially the balance between the respective roles of the political executive and the political opposition in appointments, along with their functional autonomy, is key to the independence of these appointed institutions. Finally, some of these institutions, especially the lower-ranked offices in the bureaucracy and the judiciary, are *selected* – often through competitive exams.

The political opposition and independent, unelected state institutions are best able to keep the ruling party and the political executive in check – so long as they remain independent and powerful enough to do their job. This ability also makes them extremely attractive targets for executive subordination or party capture.

The third dimension of executive accountability is *discursive*: to continue with the spatial metaphor, we could call this *diagonal* accountability.[20] This is the requirement for the executive (along with other state institutions) to justify its actions through a public discourse with what is called 'civil society'. Particular civil society institutions, which play a key role in ensuring this discursive accountability, include the media, universities, campaign groups, non-governmental organisations, trade unions, religious organisations and charities.

A pressure on the discursive axis often takes the form of a direct violation of the liberal guarantees of free speech and association (including press freedom and academic freedom). The goal is often to silence or buy out criticism of and encourage praise for the executive and/or the ruling political party.[21] The most extreme method of securing this is by shutting down civil society organisations seen as hostile to the ruling party or capturing them through a takeover by party loyalists. Frequently, lower-level threats, violence and ill-motivated regulation suffice. These pressures undermine not only liberty but also democracy, because electoral accountability needs discursive accountability to operate effectively. Citizens cannot exercise their function of electorally holding governments to account unless they are properly informed by discursive civil society institutions.

Constitutionalism' in R Dixon and T Roux (eds), *Constitutional Triumphs, Constitutional Disappointments: A Critical Assessment of the 1996 South African Constitution's Local and International Influence* (Cambridge, Cambridge University Press, 2018) 359; AJ Brown, 'The Integrity Branch: A "System", an "Industry", or a Sensible Emerging Fourth Arm of Government?' in M Groves (ed), *Modern Administrative Law in Australia: Concepts and Context* (Cambridge, Cambridge University Press, 2014) 301; R Albert and M Pal, 'The Democratic Resilience of the Canadian Constitution' in Graber et al (n 5).

[19] This is especially true of India, where individual representatives risk losing their seats if they defy a party whip: see generally Constitution of India, sch 10.

[20] AJ Brown calls it the 'social dimension': see AJ Brown, 'The Fourth, Integrity Branch of Government: Resolving a Contested Idea' (24 July 2018) 11 (transcript on file with author).

[21] For a successful use of a buying-out strategy in Hungary, see P Kingsley and B Novak, 'The Website That Shows How a Free Press Can Die' *NY Times* (24 November 2018) www.nytimes.com/2018/11/24/world/europe/hungary-viktor-orban-media.html.

III. Attacks on Electoral Accountability

Since it came to power in 2014, the BJP has tried to give itself a partisan advantage in future electoral contests by seeking to change the rules of the game. At least some of these efforts succeeded in the first Modi term, while the others are being vigorously pursued in the second term, which began in 2019. At the macro level, this is especially apparent in the nose-diving V-Dem indices concerning campaign finance transparency and the Election Commission's autonomy.[22]

A. Demographic Change

The BJP has a long-standing policy of seeking demographic change by increasing the proportion of Hindus in relation to Muslims. While its main motivation is ideological, such demographic change is likely to benefit the party electorally: although not all Hindus vote for the BJP, very few Muslims do, given that the party's main political plank is unrelenting hostility towards Muslims. The Rashtriya Swayamsevak Sangh (RSS), the BJP's ideological mentor, has long advised Hindu couples to produce more children.[23] Despite constitutional guarantees of religious freedom, several BJP-ruled states have passed anti-conversion laws over the years, which make it harder for a person to change their religion (in a Hindu-majority country, the target of these laws are clearly minority religions).[24]

Accusing Muslim men of romancing Hindu girls through a 'love jihad', the BJP launched a campaign to encourage Hindu men to marry Muslim women while discouraging Muslim men from marrying Hindu women (based, no doubt, on the patriarchal assumption that a woman adopts her husband's religion upon marriage).[25] The BJP government tabled an amendment to India's citizenship laws – hitherto based on *jus soli* principles – that was designed primarily to extend citizenship to non-Muslim undocumented migrants in the state of Assam, while permitting the deportation of millions of Muslims who failed to prove their residence in India before 1971.[26] A senior BJP leader and a minister in the Assam government bragged publicly that the Bill was designed to make Assam a 'fort' for India's 'indigenous people' – a code for non-Muslims for a party

[22] Only the former is discussed in this section. Issues concerning electoral administration are dealt with in a later section on horizontal mechanisms.

[23] M Ali, 'Produce More Children, RSS Tells Hindu Couples' *The Hindu* (22 August 2016) www.thehindu.com/news/national/other-states/Produce-more-children-RSS-tells-Hindu-couples/article14582028.ece; on the RSS generally, see WK Andersen and SD Damle, *The RSS: A View to the Inside* (Harmondsworth, Penguin, 2018).

[24] T Ahmad, 'State Anti-Conversion Laws in India' (Library of Congress, 2018) www.loc.gov/law/help/anti-conversion-laws/india.php.

[25] 'Hindu Outfit Plans "beti bachao, bahu lao" Campaign to Counter Love Jihad' *Hindustan Times* (1 December 2017) www.hindustantimes.com/lucknow/hindu-outfit-plans-beti-bachao-bahu-lao-campaign-to-counter-love-jihad/story-HVxTzT8Vn8bAYmYNYVZysI.html. See also *Shafin Jahan v Asokan KM* (2018) 16 SCC 368 (India).

[26] M Poddar, 'The Citizenship (Amendment) Bill, 2016: International Law on Religion-Based Discrimination and Naturalisation Law' (2018) 2 *Indian Law Review* 108, 108–18.

that has long associated Islam in India with foreign invaders.[27] The virulent form of exclusive nationalism practised under the Modi regime would have been bad enough for India's democracy;[28] pursuing demographic changes as part of this ideological agenda challenged even minimalist conceptions of democracy. The government was unable to get the Bill enacted in its first term because of stiff opposition in the Upper House of the federal Parliament (Rajya Sabha, or Council of States), but succeeded in doing so in the first year of its second term. Even though the actual demographic dividends did not accrue directly to the BJP in the 2019 general elections, it allowed the party to run a sharply polarised anti-Muslim campaign that is likely to have benefited it electorally.

B. Campaign Finance

In 2014, two major national parties – the BJP and the Congress – were held liable for illegally accepting foreign contributions.[29] In response, the BJP government retrospectively amended the Foreign Contribution (Regulation) Act 2010 to narrow the definition of a foreign company and thereby remove the illegality.[30] This was done surreptitiously, not through a stand-alone Bill amending the 2010 Act, but via clauses slipped into the Finance Act 2016 (which granted retrospective immunity for receiving illegal foreign donations after 2010)[31] and another amendment through the Finance Act 2018 (which extended the immunity to all donations received since 1976).[32] The amendments not only legalised foreign funding of political parties, but also created a new funding vehicle called 'electoral bonds' that ensured full anonymity of the donor.[33] Finance Bills have hundreds of clauses containing many big-ticket items that are in the public domain for a very limited period, so the possibility of proper legislative scrutiny is limited. Furthermore, the Rajya Sabha cannot veto 'money Bills'.[34] The partisan

[27] 'Citizenship Bill, Assam Accord, ST Status Will Make Assam a Fort for Indigenous People, Says Himanta Biswa Sarma' *News18* (24 January 2019) www.news18.com/news/politics/citizenship-bill-assam-accord-st-status-will-make-assam-a-fort-for-indigenous-people-says-himanta-biswa-sarma-2012611.html.

[28] M Tudor, 'India's Nationalism in Historical Perspective: The Democratic Dangers of Ascendant Nativism' (2018) 1 *Indian Politics and Policy* 107.

[29] *Association of Democratic Reforms v Union of India* (2014) 209 DLT 609.

[30] A Srivas, 'Finance Bill Amends FCRA Again to Condone Illegal Donations to BJP, Congress from Foreign Companies' (*The Wire*, 1 February 2018) https://thewire.in/business/finance-bill-seeks-amend-fcra-condone-illegal-donations-bjp-congress-received-foreign-companies.

[31] Finance Act, No 28 of 2016, India Code, s 236.

[32] Finance Act, No 13 of 2018, India Code, s 220.

[33] G Bhatia, 'The Electoral Bonds Scheme is a Threat to Democracy' *Hindustan Times* (18 March 2019) www.hindustantimes.com/analysis/the-electoral-bonds-scheme-is-a-threat-to-democracy/story-PpSiDdUjIw5WNBUzDsSzxI.html?fbclid=IwAR3SrL9-N741ftcthrZBQ_XQBrHHbtzMsrZ7_C58FlQnbHwBJZzjJGpHO1k; A Rashid, 'Electoral Bonds Have Legalised Crony Capitalism: Ex-Chief Election Commissioner SY Quraishi' *Outlook India* (7 April 2019) www.outlookindia.com/website/story/india-news-electoral-bonds-have-legalised-crony-capitalism-ex-chief-election-commissioner-sy-quraishi/328299. See also G Bhatia, 'An Ineffectual Angel' *The Hindu* (29 April 2019) www.thehindu.com/opinion/lead/an-ineffectual-angel/article26974278.ece; G Bhatia, 'Judicial Evasion and the Electoral Bonds Case', *Indian Constitutional Law and Philosophy* (13 April 2019) https://indconlawphil.wordpress.com/2019/04/13/judicial-evasion-and-the-electoral-bonds-case/.

[34] See generally S Parthasarathy, 'Trickeries of the Money Bill' *The Hindu* (11 April 2019) www.thehindu.com/opinion/lead/trickeries-of-the-money-bill/article26799226.ece.

character of the new electoral bonds – the only legal way in which a party may secure foreign funding – is evident from these figures: in the 2017–18 financial year (the first year during which the scheme operated), the BJP received anonymous donations through electoral bonds amounting to Rs 210 crores (or 2.1 billion rupees – amounting to about 20.4 per cent of the BJP's total declared earnings), the Congress received Rs 5 crores (or 50 million rupees) and the regional parties received nothing.[35] In other words, the BJP garnered 97.7 per cent of the funds that were legitimised by the surreptitious changes to the campaign finance laws! This resulted in the costliest Lok Sabha (lower chamber of Indian Parliament, or House of the People) elections in history, with the BJP accounting for an estimated 45 per cent of the total expenditure.[36] While the precise role of this financial advantage in the electoral outcome is hard to pin down, its sheer scale makes it difficult to dismiss it as irrelevant to the party's spectacular victory.

C. Electoral Schedule

One of the major changes in the Indian electoral system that Prime Minister Modi personally advocated for time and again during his tenure was to hold simultaneous elections for the lower chamber of the Indian Parliament and state-level legislative assemblies. Each of these Houses has a five-year term. The national and state-level elections had been automatically synchronised until 1967.[37] Since then, elections have taken place in a staggered manner because of the early dissolution of some legislatures. Today, at least one election takes place each year.[38] Those in favour of a move to a 'one country, one poll' system argue that back-to-back electoral campaigns cause a distraction from effective governance.[39] They further argue that making elections a once-in-five-years affair will reduce the costs of conducting and contesting elections.[40] Offering such managerial justifications (like efficiency and rationalisation) for a reform that would deliver a partisan bonus was a key characteristic of this government's rhetoric.

In addition to the political opposition, only one state institution resisted the move in public debates: the outgoing Election Commissioner of India.[41] Disagreeing with the efficiency rationale for simultaneous polls, OP Rawat claimed that, given the logistical

[35] Association for Democratic Reforms, 'Analysis of Sources of Funding of National Parties: FY 2017–18' (2019) 5, https://adrindia.org/download/file/fid/6364.

[36] 'At an Estimated Rs. 60,000 Crore, Lok Sabha Elections Costliest Ever; BJP Spent 45% of It, Shows Study' *News18* (4 June 2019) www.news18.com/news/politics/with-about-rs-100-cr-spent-in-each-ls-constituency-we-just-witnessed-the-most-expensive-election-ever-2171789.html?ref=hp_top_pos_7.

[37] In some cases, the central government dismissed the state governments using its power of imposing 'President's Rule' under Art 356. See Law Commission of India, 'Draft Report: Simultaneous Elections 2–3' (30 August 2018) www.lawcommissionofindia.nic.in/reports/Simultaneous_Elections.pdf.

[38] ibid 3.

[39] L Mathew, 'Simultaneous Elections for Lok Sabha and Assembly: How Idea Came, What Implementation Will Mean' *Indian Express* (31 January 2018) https://indianexpress.com/article/explained/holding-lok-sabha-and-assembly-polls-together-how-idea-came-what-implementation-will-mean-5045403/.

[40] ibid.

[41] 'Chief Election Commissioner on Holding Simultaneous Polls: No Chance at All' *Indian Express* (23 August 2018) https://indianexpress.com/article/india/no-chance-at-all-chief-election-commissioner-o-p-rawat-on-holding-simultaneous-polls-5321447/.

difficulties of holding simultaneous polls in a country of India's size, 'instead of savings, there may be losses and the costs could get higher'.[42] The proposal was shelved in the face of the opposition, but has been revived by the second Modi administration. Furthermore, very serious allegations were made about the schedule of the 2019 general elections campaign, which, critics pointed out, was designed to benefit the BJP.[43]

A system of simultaneous polls every five years across India would probably lead to executive aggrandisement because it is likely to take away the legislature's power to dismiss an administration that no longer enjoys its confidence (at least in cases where there is no alternative administration that can command its confidence either). BJP President Amit Shah did not even disguise the fact that the move was designed to secure fixed tenures for the political executive in his letter to the Law Commission recommending it.[44] A key tenet of parliamentary democracy is the ability of the legislature and the political executive to fire one another. Essentially, a simultaneous polls system, as currently proposed, would take away the legislature's power to fire the political executive, thereby shifting the regime towards the BJP's long-sought-after ideological goal of a presidential system – or as close as you can get to it while still pretending to be abiding by parliamentary democracy. Since parliamentary democracy is part of the unamendable basic structure of India's Constitution; an informal constitutional change is being attempted.[45]

Simultaneous polls are also likely to give an electoral advantage to the BJP, at least in the short term, thereby reducing the distance between the ruling party and the state. When multiple elections take place simultaneously, big-ticket elections (usually the federal elections) tend to influence down-ballot races at the state level – even if, technically, a voter is free to choose candidates from different parties in the two races.[46] Given the party system in India, this is likely to benefit national parties at the cost of state-based regional parties.[47] Furthermore, fully aware of the populist appeal of Prime Minister Modi and the absence of a similarly populist leader in its main rival – the Congress Party – a nationwide simultaneous poll in the prevailing political climate could have significantly cemented the BJP's electoral advantage across the country.

[42] Express News Service, 'OP Rawat: "Note Ban Had Absolutely No Impact on Black Money. During Polls We Seized a Record Amount"' *Indian Express* (2 December 2018) https://indianexpress.com/article/india/op-rawat-cec-note-ban-black-money-polls-assembly-elections-mizoram-5474369/.

[43] R Tewari, 'Why 2019 Lok Sabha Election Schedule Could Advantage BJP' *The Print* (11 March 2019) https://theprint.in/politics/why-2019-lok-sabha-election-schedule-could-mean-advantage-bjp/204210/.

[44] 'Opposition to Simultaneous Polls Is "Politically Motivated": Amit Shah to Law Commission' (*The Wire*, 14 August 2018) https://thewire.in/politics/amit-shah-law-commission-bjp-simultaneous-elections.

[45] See generally O Doyle, 'Informal Constitutional Change' (2017) 65 *Buffalo Law Review* 1021.

[46] JS Chhokar, 'Simultaneous Elections: Striking at the Roots of Parliamentary Democracy 22' (2018) Hindu Centre for Politic and Public Policy, Issue Brief No 8, 22, www.thehinducentre.com/publications/article23669303.ece/BINARY/Issue%20Brief%20No8.pdf; G Abbas, 'A Poll Wind: How General Elections Influence Simultaneously Held State Elections in India' *News18* (11 March 2019) www.news18.com/news/politics/a-poll-wind-how-general-elections-influence-simultaneously-held-state-elections-in-india-2062149.html.

[47] S Palshikar, 'Polls Apart' *Indian Express* (24 November 2017) https://indianexpress.com/article/opinion/columns/election-commission-simultaneous-elections-in-india-lok-sabha-assembly-elections-4951569/; Vivek Dahejia, 'Simultaneous Elections Are a Bad Idea' *Livemint* (10 July 2018) www.livemint.com/Opinion/MgitLxJasfNAbKDhnCQgUJ/Simultaneous-elections-are-a-bad-idea.html.

The last two changes – the proposal for simultaneous elections and the changes to foreign political donations laws – were designed to target smaller, regional parties, which often force the national parties into coalition governments and are a key check on the political executive. In state government, regional parties tend to act more independently of the will of the federal government and are a constant source of irritation to the national parties. The BJP government is therefore trying to nudge India's electoral system towards a two-party system by stifling the space occupied by the smaller parties. Combined with its efforts to decimate the national political rival, the Congress Party, and to accrue electoral advantages by disenfranchising Muslims, it aspires to achieve an effectively one-party state.

IV. Erosion of Institutional Accountability I: Containing the Opposition

Not only did the BJP government seek to undermine electoral accountability to the citizens, it also systematically assaulted institutions that seek horizontal accountability from the political executive.[48] These political institutions provided a voice to the opposition and therefore invited frequent 'constitutional hardball' tactics from the government.[49]

A. Weakening the Political Opposition: Non-appointment of the Leader of the Opposition

Levitsky and Ziblatt argue that denying the legitimacy of political opponents by describing them as subversives posing an existential threat is a key feature of authoritarian behaviour.[50] A BJP General Secretary's accusation of treason against the political opposition when it formed an anti-BJP alliance in Kashmir is typical of the BJP's characterisation of the Congress Party and very much meets Ziblatt and Levitsky's criterion.[51]

In the 2014 general elections, the BJP secured a comfortable majority in Lok Sabha. In India, the Leader of the Opposition is (at least textually) not a constitutional office.[52] According to a 1977 legislation that governs the position, the leader of the largest opposition party *and* recognised by the Speaker as such is the Leader of the Opposition.[53]

[48] L Mathew, 'Country Higher than Any Institution, Don't Weaken Elected, Says Arun Jaitley' *Indian Express* (28 October 2018) https://indianexpress.com/article/india/country-higher-than-any-institution-dont-weaken-elected-says-arun-jaitley-5421730/.

[49] On 'constitutional hardball', see MV Tushnet, 'Constitutional Hardball' (2004) 37 *John Marshall Law Review* 523.

[50] S Levitsky and D Ziblatt, *How Democracies Die: What History Reveals About Our Future* (Harmondsworth, Penguin, 2018) 23.

[51] S Daniyal, 'The Daily Fix: By Accusing Opposition Parties of Treason, BJP is Subverting Indian Democracy' *Scroll.in* (23 November 2018) https://scroll.in/article/903159/the-daily-fix-by-accusing-opposition-parties-of-treason-bjp-is-subverting-indian-democracy.

[52] See generally SC Kashyap, 'Qualifying for Leader of the Opposition' *The Hindu* (17 June 2019) www.thehindu.com/opinion/op-ed/qualifying-for-leader-of-the-opposition/article27957618.ece.

[53] Salary and Allowances of Leaders of Opposition in Parliament Act, No 33 of 1977, India Code, s 2.

However, the BJP-appointed Attorney General opined that no law obliges the Speaker to recognise a Leader of the Opposition if no opposition party's numerical strength is at least equal to the quorum of the House (ie one-tenth of its membership, or 55 seats).[54] The BJP-appointed Lok Sabha Speaker refused to recognise a Leader of the Opposition on the ground that the Congress Party had garnered only 44 out of 543 seats.[55] Although several commentators doubted the legality of this decision,[56] India's overburdened courts failed to rule on the legality of the Speaker's decision even as the 16th Lok Sabha completed its five-year tenure in 2019.[57]

Before 2014, the office of the Leader of the Opposition had not been vacant since 1989.[58] The absence of a designated Leader of the Opposition mattered because it denied certain perks of office – like a salary and secretarial staff – to the opposition. Further, since 1989, Parliament had reformed or established several independent fourth branch institutions, whose appointment mechanisms require the participation of the Leader of the Opposition.[59] The orchestrated vacancy in this office was used by the government as an excuse to stall certain appointments to these fourth branch institutions.[60] The Supreme Court intervened to allow these appointments despite the vacancy in the office,[61] which gave the government a free hand in such appointments.[62] The 17th Lok Sabha, elected in 2019, does not have an opposition leader either.

B. Undermining Bicameralism: Overriding the Rajya Sabha's Veto

In many parliamentary systems, bicameralism is a serious check on the power of the political executive, which normally controls the lower legislative chamber.[63] Generally, both Houses of the bicameral Parliament must approve a Bill to enact it into law.

[54] M Rohatgi, 'Recognition of Leader of the Opposition in Sixteenth Lok Sabha', Off. Attorney General of India, [5] (23 July 2014) https://barandbench.com/wp-content/uploads/2016/11/lokpal.pdf; K Kausik, 'Inside Man: The Convenient Opinions of Attorney General Goolam Vahanvati' *Caravan Magazine* (1 May 2013) https://caravanmagazine.in/reportage/inside-man.

[55] S Prabhu, 'Declined: Speaker Rejects Congress Claim for Leader of the Opposition' *NDTV* (19 August 2014) www.ndtv.com/india-news/declined-speaker-rejects-congress-claim-for-leader-of-opposition-650355.

[56] PDT Achary, 'The LoP Excuse' *Indian Express* (3 May 2017) https://indianexpress.com/article/opinion/columns/the-lop-excuse-4637880/.

[57] The Delhi High Court refused to entertain a public interest petition challenging this decision of the Speaker: *Imran Ali v Union of India* (2015) SCC OnLine Del 6707. See generally T Khaitan, 'The Indian Supreme Court's Identity Crisis: A Constitutional Court or a Court of Appeals?' (2020) 4 *Indian Law Review* 1, empirically demonstrating the Supreme Court's disproportionate disregard of its constitutional docket.

[58] See generally Rohatgi (n 54).

[59] See, eg The Right to Information Act, No 22 of 2005, ss 12 and 15; The Lokpal and Lokayuktas Act, No 1 of 2014, s 4.

[60] *Common Cause v Union of India* (2017) 7 SCC 158.

[61] ibid.

[62] See '"Special Invitee" Mallikarjun Kharge Refuses to Attend Lokpal Meet' *NDTV* (19 September 2018) www.ndtv.com/india-news/special-invitee-mallikarjun-kharge-refuses-to-attend-lokpal-meet-1919092, quoting Senior Congress leader Mallikarjun Kharge stating that 'An invitation as a special invitee without the right of participation, recording of opinion and voting in the procedure is an eyewash'.

[63] See generally J Waldron, 'Bicameralism and the Separation of Powers' (2012) 65 *Current Legal Problems* 31, 43–51 (discussing the importance of bicameralism in ensuring executive and judicial independence in Westminster-style governments).

However, in India, certain bills regulating financial matters enlisted under Article 110 of the Constitution can be enacted as 'money Bills'. Once a Bill is certified as a money Bill by the Speaker of the Lower House, the Bill does not require the assent of the Upper House to be enacted as law.[64] In order to circumvent scrutiny by Rajya Sabha, where the BJP did not enjoy a majority, a partisan Lok Sabha Speaker characterised the Aadhaar Bill 2016 – validating the national biometric identity programme (*Aadhaar*) – as a money Bill.[65] The provisions of the Bill traversed far beyond the grounds for which the money Bill process is normally allowed.[66] However, the Supreme Court, in a split verdict, upheld the constitutionality of the process.[67] The dissenting judge went on to call the use of the money Bill route to pass the Aadhaar Act a 'fraud on the Constitution'.[68]

While the Aadhaar Act attracted the most attention, the BJP government used the money Bill route with unprecedented frequency, sidestepping the scrutiny by the Upper House on some of the most controversial issues.[69] As already noted, two of these uses were to amend campaign finance laws to retrospectively validate foreign donations to the BJP that had already been declared illegal by the Delhi High Court. The Finance Act 2017 also amended the Representation of the People Act 1951 and the Reserve Bank of India Act 1934 to permit unlimited and anonymous corporate donations to political parties through the newly issued electoral bonds.[70] With the Supreme Court's endorsement of the Speaker's extremely expansive understanding of a money Bill, the Upper House – often the sole repository of opposition power – was politically enervated.

C. Unfair Legislative Process: Ignoring the Opposition

In 2018, to avoid a parliamentary debate on crucial financial issues, the government passed the Finance Bill and the Appropriation Bill under an extraordinary parliamentary procedure known as the 'guillotine', despite several suggested amendments and strong protest by the opposition.[71] This procedure allows the Speaker of the House to put a Bill to vote without any discussion.[72] The use of this procedure was especially

[64] Constitution of India, Art 110. See, eg P Datta, S Malhotra and S Tyagi, 'Judicial Review and Money Bills' (2017) 10 *NUJS Law Review* 75.

[65] R Narayan and A Gupta, 'The Money Bill Cloud Persists over the Aadhaar Act' *LiveLaw* (13 October 2018) www.livelaw.in/the-money-bill-cloud-persists-over-the-aadhaar-act/.

[66] S Parthasarathy, 'Aadhaar Act as a Money Bill: It Can Lead to a Great Deal of Public Harm' *Hindustan Times* (28 September 2018) www.hindustantimes.com/columns/aadhaar-act-as-money-bill-it-can-lead-to-a-great-deal-of-public-harm/story-Xu3TtHMSXyrrydO4VcBZgM.html.

[67] *Justice KS Puttaswamy v Union of India* (2019) 1 SCC 1, [368] (Dipak Misra CJ, Sikri and Khanwillkar JJ).

[68] ibid [1143] (Chandrachud J).

[69] D Chhetri, 'As Justice Chandrachud Calls Aadhaar Law "Unconstitutional", Government Increases Use of Controversial Short Cut' *Bloomberg Quint* (3 October 2018) www.bloombergquint.com/law-and-policy/as-justice-chandrachud-calls-aadhaar-law-unconstitutional-government-increases-use-of-controversial-short-cut.

[70] Representation of the People Act, No 43 of 1951, ss 29C and 31; Reserve Bank of India Act, No 2 of 1934, India Code, s 13–A; Income Tax Act, No 43 of 1961, India Code, as respectively amended by the Finance Act, No 14 of 1971, India Code, ss 11, 135 and 137.

[71] S Meghnad, 'How to Get Away with Murder: Parliament Edition' *Newslaundry* (14 March 2018) www.newslaundry.com/2018/03/14/finance-bill-2018-appropriation-bill-parliament-speaker-fm-arun-jaitley.

[72] Special Correspondent, 'Guillotine on Budget Debate' *The Telegraph* (15 March 2018) www.telegraphindia.com/india/guillotine-on-budget-debate/cid/1338698.

disingenuous, given that there were still three weeks left in the session of the House, so time was not of the essence.[73] In 2019, with elections due within a couple of months, a lame-duck government used the interim budget procedure to present a full, populist budget – the sixth annual budget from a government with a five-year term. Yashwant Sinha, the Finance Minister of India in a former BJP government, described it as a 'mockery of the Constitution'.[74]

In 2018, when several opposition parties came together to move a no-confidence motion against the government, the Speaker delayed the motion for over a month.[75] This delay on the part of the Speaker in accepting the no-confidence motion was unprecedented. Even though the government had the numbers, no-confidence motions serve an important function in seeking political accountability from the government, and therefore typically receive priority from the Speaker of the day.[76] While the government comfortably won the no-confidence motion when it was eventually brought up, it managed to avoid a publicly televised parliamentary debate on its performance before a crucial state election in Karnataka.[77]

D. Attacking Federalism: Abuse of the Offices of Governors and Lieutenant Governors[78]

By no means the first government to do so, the BJP government continued India's long and unfortunate tradition of abusing a constitutional design flaw – the centrally appointed office of a governor in every state in the country, who holds office at the President's pleasure (manifested on the advice of the Prime Minister).[79] Although a largely ceremonial head, the governor performs certain key political functions. Most importantly, in case of a hung assembly where no party has a clear majority, the governor appoints the leader of the party she believes is most likely to secure the confidence of the House as Chief Minister. The advantage of political office is so immense that even the few days within which a new Chief Minister must prove her majority in the assembly are usually sufficient to coax, cajole, buy or coerce the support of smaller parties,

[73] ET Bureau, 'Lok Sabha Passes Budget without Debate; Both Houses Adjourn Amid Din' *Economic Times* (15 March 2018) https://economictimes.indiatimes.com/news/politics-and-nation/finance-bill-to-be-taken-up-in-lok-sabha-at-noon/articleshow/63296956.cms.

[74] Y Sinha, 'With Sixth Budget, Government Has Made a Mockery of Constitution' *NDTV* (2 February 2019) www.ndtv.com/opinion/with-sixth-budget-government-has-made-a-mockery-of-constitution-1987434.

[75] PDT Achary, 'The Speaker Is Wrong to Not Allow No-Confidence Move to Be Tabled' (*The Wire*, 26 March 2018) https://thewire.in/government/the-speaker-is-wrong-to-not-allow-no-confidence-move-to-be-tabled.

[76] MR Madhavan, 'Confidence in the House' *The Hindu* (5 April 2018) www.thehindu.com/opinion/op-ed/confidence-in-the-house/article23437310.ece.

[77] HS Bal, 'India's Embattled Democracy' *NY Times* (30 May 2018) www.nytimes.com/2018/05/30/opinion/india-democracy.html.

[78] On the Modi government's impact on political federalism, see generally CK Sharma and W Swenden, 'Modi-fying Indian Federalism? Center–State Relations under Modi's Tenure as Prime Minister' (2018) 1 *Indian Politics and Policy* 51. For a possible impact of the Modi governments tax policy on fiscal federalism, see S Parthasarathy, 'Taxing Times for the States' *The Hindu* (25 July 2017) www.thehindu.com/opinion/lead/taxing-times-for-the-states/article19346974.ece.

[79] *BP Singhal v Union of India* (2010) 6 SCC 331.

independents and even factions within the main political rivals. Like its predecessors, the BJP government dismissed nine governors appointed by the previous government soon after assuming power in 2014.[80] BJP-appointed governors have typically obliged their political masters.

In 2016, obliging governors of the states of Uttarakhand and Arunachal Pradesh – which were ruled by parties that were in opposition at the centre – reported that the constitutional machinery in these states had broken down, leading to the federal government dismissing the state governments and assuming direct rule.[81] In both cases, the Supreme Court intervened to restore the dismissed governments.[82]

In 2017, when the Goa assembly returned with a hung verdict, the governor invited the alliance led by the BJP, which had superior numbers to the single-largest party (the Congress Party) to form a government. However, in 2018, the Karnataka governor decided to invite the single-largest party lacking a majority (the BJP) rather than a coalition with a clear majority (including the Congress Party) to form a government.[83] It is clear that the decisions were motivated not by the likelihood of confidence, but by partisan considerations. The Supreme Court made an uncharacteristically timely intervention by ordering an immediate floor test in Karnataka,[84] which the BJP failed.[85] Consequently, its nominee stepped down as the Chief Minister, and the coalition formed the government.[86]

In November 2018, when the non-BJP parties formed a coalition with a clear majority to form a government in the state of Jammu and Kashmir, the governor simply dissolved the House and called for fresh elections, characterising the alliance as 'unholy'.[87] The governor later hinted that by dissolving the assembly, he chose the lesser of two evils and resisted pressure from the federal government to install a minority BJP government in the state instead.[88]

[80] Sharma and Swenden (n 78) 59.

[81] R Tripathi, 'President's Rule Imposed in Uttarakhand After Governor's Report' *Economic Times* (28 March 2016) https://economictimes.indiatimes.com/news/politics-and-nation/presidents-rule-imposed-in-uttarakhand-after-governors-report/articleshow/51570914.cms; 'Nabam Tuki Blames RSS and BJP For Dismissal of His Government in Arunachal' *NDTV* (20 February 2016) www.ndtv.com/india-news/nabam-tuki-blames-rss-and-bjp-for-dismissal-of-his-government-in-arunachal-1279499.

[82] U Anand, 'Lessons from Uttarakhand and Arunachal: What Court Orders on Central Rule Say' *Indian Express* (15 July 2016) https://indianexpress.com/article/explained/arunachal-pradesh-verdict-nabam-tuki-harish-rawat-uttarakhand-president-rule-supreme-court-modi-government-2914435/.

[83] K Rajagopal, 'Legal Experts Divided Over Karnataka Governor's Invitation to Yeddyurappa to Form Government' *The Hindu* (16 May 2018) www.thehindu.com/elections/karnataka-2018/let-karnataka-governor-explore-all-alternatives/article23905846.ece.

[84] B Sinha and V Gopal, 'Supreme Court Orders BJP's Yedurappa to Face Floor Test in 24 Hours' *Hindustan Times* (18 May 2018) www.hindustantimes.com/india-news/supreme-court-asks-yeddyurappa-to-prove-majority-tomorrow-does-not-get-into-legality-of-governor-s-decision/story-St4IAbhb1ZwusGnHuzOtDP.html.

[85] 'Karnataka Governor Invites Congress-JDS Alliance to Form Government' *Hindustan Times* (19 May 2018) www.hindustantimes.com/india-news/karnataka-governor-invites-congress-jds-alliance-to-form-government-15-days-to-prove-majority/story-yh89AgZdEqjex2SjmgT0ZP.html.

[86] ibid.

[87] M Ehsan, 'Jammu and Kashmir's Political Thriller Ends in Anti-Climax, Assembly Dissolved' *Hindustan Times* (22 November 2018) www.hindustantimes.com/india-news/j-k-s-political-thriller-ends-in-anti-climax-house-dissolved/story-Cp8VZPABYgZtrEqAScAsoI.html.

[88] N Masoodi and D Ghosh, 'J&K Governor Talks 'Threat of Transfer' after Controversy Over Remarks' *NDTV* (28 November 2018) www.ndtv.com/india-news/jammu-and-kashmir-governor-satya-pal-malik-talks-threat-of-transfer-after-controversy-over-remarks-1954488.

While the occasion for abusing the governors' offices arises only rarely, BJP-appointed lieutenant governors (LGs) – with a wider range of powers – have been unrelenting in the abuse of their office in the union territories of Delhi and Puducherry. In 2015, a new party – the Aam Aadmi Party – arising out of an anti-corruption movement, formed a government in the National Capital Territory (NCT) of Delhi.[89] Soon after the Delhi election, the federal government, acting through the LG, not only made key appointments contrary to the wishes of the Delhi cabinet but also obstructed major policies and legislative initiatives of the elected government of Delhi.[90] In part, these controversies are down to Delhi's peculiar status in the Indian constitutional scheme. While it does have an elected parliamentary government, the powers of Delhi's elected executive are somewhat less than those of fully fledged states.[91]

When the matter concerning the extent of the LG's powers reached the Supreme Court, the Court interpreted the LG's powers narrowly,[92] holding that he cannot override a decision of the elected government of Delhi unless an 'executive act of the government of the NCT is likely to impede or prejudice the exercise of the executive power of the Union government'.[93] While the judicial caveat left enough ambiguity for the LG to continue with some meddling,[94] even this limited relief came after the elected Delhi government had already completed almost three and a half of its five years in office. While LGs, like governors, are political appointees of the federal government, this level of interference by an LG is unprecedented.[95] Furthermore, in Puducherry, another territory with a peculiar constitutional status comparable to Delhi, its LG – also appointed by the federal government – continued to interfere in policy decisions and day-to-day administration by the elected government until the intervention of the Madras High Court.[96]

[89] Election Commission of India, 'Statistical Report on General Election, 2015 to the Legislative Assembly of NCT of Delhi', https://eci.gov.in/files/file/3878-delhi-2015/.

[90] R Saikumar, 'More Constitutional than Political' *The Hindu* (23 May 2015) www.thehindu.com/opinion/lead/more-constitutional-than-political/article7236281.ece; 'Delhi LG Anil Baijal Blocking Scheme for Education Loan to Poor, Alleges Manish Sisodia' *Indian Express* (22 September 2017) https://indianexpress.com/article/india/delhi-lg-anil-baijal-blocking-scheme-for-education-loan-to-poor-alleges-manish-sisodia-4856617/.

[91] Constitution of India, Art 239AA(4), amended by The Constitution (Sixty-ninth Amendment) Act, 1991 ('in the case of difference of opinion between the Lieutenant Governor and his Ministers on any matter, the Lieutenant Governor shall refer it to the President for decision and act according to the decision given thereon by the President').

[92] *State (NCT of Delhi) v Union of India* (2018) 8 SCC 501, [284.18] (Misra J).

[93] ibid [474] (Chandrachud J).

[94] HV Nair, 'Delhi CM vs L-G: Round 2 Begins in SC Tomorrow' *India Today* (16 July 2018) www.indiatoday.in/mail-today/story/delhi-cm-vs-l-g-round-2-begins-in-sc-tomorrow-1286575-2018-07-16; 'Delhi Govt vs LG: "Govt Paralyzed, Can't Appoint/Transfer Officers", Submits Delhi Govt but SC Defers Hearing of Pending Issues' *Livelaw* (26 July 2018) www.livelaw.in/kejriwal-vs-lg-govt-paralyzed-cant-appoint-transfer-officers-submits-delhi-govt-but-sc-defers-hearing-of-pending-issues-to-july-26/.

[95] A Ghosal, 'Delhi Deadlock: How It Was under Sheila Dikshit and What Changed after Arvind Kejriwal Came to Power' *News18* (14 February 2019) www.news18.com/news/india/delhi-deadlock-how-it-was-under-sheila-dikshit-and-what-changed-after-arvind-kejriwal-came-to-power-2035781.html.

[96] *K Lakshminarayanan v Union of India*, WP 28890 of 2017 (2019) http://164.100.79.153/judis/chennai/index.php/casestatus/viewpdf/462147. See also M Kaveri, 'Win for Puducherry CM, Madras HC Rules LG Cannot Interfere in Govt's Daily Affairs' *News Minute* (30 April 2019) www.thenewsminute.com/article/win-puducherry-cm-madras-hc-rules-lg-cannot-interfere-govt-s-daily-affairs-100943; 'CM vs LG: Puducherry Power Struggle May Now Become a Legal Tussle' *News Minute* (2 July 2017) www.thenewsminute.com/article/cm-vs-lg-puducherry-power-struggle-may-now-become-legal-tussle-64536;

Conventions surrounding centre–state relations have also been breached. One opposition-ruled state that has earned the particular ire of the federal government is Bengal, whose chief minister has been an outspoken critic of Prime Minister Modi. In 2016, the government deployed the army throughout the state without the prior consent of the state government, and with no obvious threat to national security.[97] In 2019, the centre-controlled Central Bureau of Investigation (CBI) moved to arrest the chief of the state police (who function under the supervision of the state government), again without the consent of the state government.[98]

E. Sidelining the Cabinet and Rivals within the Party

The leadership tried to sideline not only the political opposition, but also allies and cabinet ministers from the BJP. Unlike a presidential system of government, in a parliamentary system, the Prime Minister is technically the first among equals. No doubt, the actual power and influence of a Prime Minister depends on her personality and charisma, and the support she enjoys within the parliamentary party. Even so, members of the cabinet have usually exercised some restraint on her powers. Given the opaqueness around internal cabinet politics and the principle of collective responsibility, it is usually hard to know for certain whether and to what extent the cabinet has acted as a check on a Prime Minister. But the resignation letter of a minister from Modi's cabinet does offer some clues:

> You have systemically dismantled the functioning of the cabinet of the government that is mandated in our constitution. The Union Cabinet has been reduced to a mere rubber stamp, simply endorsing your decision without any deliberation. Ministers and officers posted in ministries have become figureheads as virtually all decisions are taken by you, your office and the BJP President. (Which is anti-constitutional)
>
> …
>
> It is unfortunate that priority of the government is not to work for the poor and the oppressed but to fix political opponents by hook or by crook. Investigating agencies are being remote controlled by your office and the BJP President with the sole purpose of harassing leaders with contrarian views. Constitutional offices are being undermined and virtually every institution in the government has been subjected to political appropriation.[99]

R Nair, 'SC Verdict Relevant to Puducherry Too, Chief Minister Narayanasamy' *The Hindu* (4 July 2018) www.thehindu.com/news/cities/puducherry/sc-ruling-on-l-gs-powers-applies-to-puducherry-too-says-narayanasamy/article24330112.ece; 'Puducherry Power Tussle: Here's L-G Kiran Bedi's Counter to CM Narayanasamy's Contempt Threat' *Financial Express* (5 July 2018) www.financialexpress.com/india-news/puducherry-power-tussle-heres-l-g-kiran-bedis-counter-to-cm-narayanasamys-contempt-threat/1232354/.

[97] A Ghosal, 'Mamata Banerjee Compares Situation in Bengal to "Military Coup"' *Indian Express* (2 December 2016) https://indianexpress.com/article/india/mamata-banerjee-army-deployment-nh-2-in-west-bengal-military-coup-4405871/.

[98] PS Jha, 'We Are Witnessing the Death of the CBI. Will Indian Democracy Follow?' (*The* Wire, 6 February 2019) https://thewire.in/politics/cbi-mamata-banerjee-narendra-modi; A Ghosal, '"There Was a Plan": How Mamata's Offensive Escalated to Catch Modi Govt Off Guard' *News18* (4 February 2019) www.news18.com/news/india/there-was-a-plan-how-mamatas-offensive-escalated-to-catch-modi-govt-off-guard-2024455.html.

[99] 'Upendra Kushwaha's Strongly Worded Resignation Letter: Full Text' *DNA India* (10 December 2018) www.dnaindia.com/india/report-upendra-kushwaha-s-strongly-worded-resignation-letter-full-text-2694312 (parenthesis in the original).

Of course, the words of a disgruntled ally, spoken when the relationship is breaking down, need to be taken with a pinch of salt. However, complaints of autocratic behaviour have not just come from disgruntled allies, but from within the BJP itself. Soon after assuming power, the BJP President Amit Shah effectively purged the party of its veteran leaders by consigning them to a powerless advisory council (Margdarshak Mandal).[100] These forcibly retired party insiders felt compelled to issue a public statement complaining that 'the party is forced to kow-tow to a handful and … its consensual character has been destroyed'.[101]

V. Erosion of Institutional Accountability II: Capturing or Undermining the Judiciary and Fourth Branch Institutions

The Modi government undermined mechanisms that allow appointed institutions to seek accountability from the executive. These institutions are constituted not by elections, but by various appointment processes, and typically include high constitutional offices. The higher judiciary is a key component. So are a variety of fourth branch institutions that do not neatly fit into the traditional tripartite division between the executive, the legislature and the judiciary, and include the Reserve Bank of India, the Auditor General, the anti-corruption watchdog, the Information Commission, the Election Commission, the Human Rights Commissions and various equality commissions. Although often appointed by the executive in India, these fourth branch institutions are usually meant to function independently and are typically not required to report to any governmental ministry.

A. Interference with Judicial Independence and Appointments

The Indian Constitution envisages a wide jurisdiction for the Supreme Court.[102] It is an eccentric court that some commentators have described as 'the most powerful court of the world'.[103] It has significant influence over other judiciaries in the Global South.[104]

[100] A Bhardwaj and A Sinha, 'Margdarshak Mandal: Resentment Boils Over, Was Simmering for Long' *Indian Express* (11 November 2015) https://indianexpress.com/article/india/india-news-india/margdarshak-mandal-resentment-boils-over-was-simmering-for-long/; DK Jha, 'BJP meet: Party Agog with Talk that Veteran Will Propose that Margdarshak Mandal Be Scrapped' *Scroll.in* (8 September 2016) https://scroll.in/article/815940/bjp-meet-party-veteran-said-to-be-set-to-propose-that-the-margdarshak-mandal-be-scrapped.

[101] D Acharya, 'After Advani, It's Yashwant Sinha's Turn: What's Going on in BJP Party Ranks Is Hardly Unexpected' *FirstPost* (1 February 2016) www.firstpost.com/politics/after-advani-its-yashwant-sinhas-turn-whats-going-on-in-bjp-party-ranks-is-hardly-unexpected-2606360.html.

[102] AK Thiruvengadam, 'The Crisis in Context' *Frontline* (16 February 2018) www.frontline.in/cover-story/the-crisis-in-context/article10055190.ece. The very wide appellate jurisdiction of the Court has, in fact, become an impediment to its ability to satisfactorily perform its constitutional defence function: see generally T Khaitan, 'The Supreme Court as a Constitutional Watchdog' (2019) 721 *Seminar* 22.

[103] ibid.

[104] See generally A Thiruvengadam, 'Global Dialogue among Courts: Social Rights Jurisprudence of the Supreme Court of India from a Comparative Perspective' in CR Kumar and K Chockalingam (eds), *Human Rights, Justice, and Constitutional Empowerment*, 2nd edn (Oxford, Oxford University Press, 2007) 264;

Unsurprisingly, the power over the appointment of its judges has been a cause of the fraught relationship between the executive and the judiciary for almost the entire life of the Constitution.[105] Partly in response to Indira Gandhi's quest for a pliant judiciary in the 1970s, the Supreme Court established the 'collegium', a body comprising the five senior-most judges, in 1993.[106] On a strained interpretation of the Constitution, the collegium was primarily tasked with appointments to the higher judiciary and subsequently came to be regarded as a bulwark for judicial independence.[107] Although fiercely independent in its appointments process, Supreme Court judges retire at the relatively young age of 65 (for High Court judges, the retirement age is even lower, at 62). Most of these former judges are appointed to various tribunals and fourth branch institutions upon retirement from the judicial office, appointments which are made by the political executive, allowing it significant systemic influence over the career of a judge.

In 2014, the Modi government, with the support of the opposition, passed a constitutional amendment to overhaul the process of appointments to the higher judiciary.[108] The amendment took away judicial primacy in judicial appointments and gave the executive the upper hand. In 2015, the Supreme Court struck down the amendment on the grounds of erosion of judicial independence, which is part of the basic structure of the Constitution.[109] While the amendment itself had broad political support, the executive's retaliation after it was struck down has been conspicuous.[110] The government has since then selectively resisted the elevation of nominees who were seen as unfavourable for partisan or ideological reasons.[111] At the time of writing, a petition concerning these delays in judicial appointments was pending before the overburdened Supreme Court.[112] Its appointment of a retired Chief Justice as the governor of a state – a political appointment – was only the second time a Supreme Court judge was thus appointed, a move heavily criticised for its implications for judicial independence.[113]

There were some serious allegations against the government for meddling with judicial function behind the scenes. In January 2018, four of the five senior-most judges of the Indian Supreme Court, who constituted its collegium, held an unprecedented joint

A Thiruvengadam, 'Revisiting the Role of the Judiciary in Plural Societies (1987): A Quarter-Century Retrospective on Public Interest Litigation in India and the Global South' in S Khilnani, V Raghavan and A Thiruvengadam (eds), *Comparative Constitutionalism in South Asia* (Oxford, Oxford University Press, 2012).

[105] https://www.nomos-elibrary.de/10.5771/0506-7286-2018-3-273/from-executive-appointment-to-the-collegium-system-the-impact-on-diversity-in-the-indian-supreme-court-jahrgang-51-2018-heft-3?page=1.

[106] *Supreme Court Advocates-on-Record Association v Union of India* (1993) 4 SCC 441.

[107] R De and T Khaitan, 'In Defence of Constitutionalism' (*I-CONnect*, 19 January 2018) www.iconnectblog.com/2018/01/in-defence-of-constitutionalism/.

[108] Constitution of India, amended by The Constitution (Ninety-ninth Amendment) Act, 2014.

[109] See *Supreme Court Advocates-on-Record Association v Union of India* (2016) 5 SCC 1.

[110] '"Indian Democracy Cannot Be a Tyranny of the Unelected": A Jaitley's "Alternative View" on NJAC Verdict' *Firstpost* (19 October 2015) www.firstpost.com/politics/indian-democracy-cannot-be-a-tyranny-of-the-unelected-arun-jaitleys-alternative-view-on-the-njac-verdict-2473218.html.

[111] K Parameshwar, AP Kumar and T Khaitan, 'Was the Centre Right in Resisting Justice Joseph's Elevation?' *The Hindu* (4 May 2018) www.thehindu.com/opinion/op-ed/was-the-centre-right-in-resisting-justice-josephs-elevation/article23764213.ece.

[112] 'SC to Hear Plea on Govt Delays over Appointment of Judges in Higher Judiciary after 8 Weeks' *Times of India* (2 November 2018) https://timesofindia.indiatimes.com/india/sc-to-hear-plea-on-govt-delays-over-appointment-of-judges-in-higher-judiciary-after-8-weeks/articleshow/66480494.cms.

[113] V Venkatesan, 'Justice as Governor' *Frontline* (3 October 2014) https://frontline.thehindu.com/the-nation/justice-as-governor/article6412702.ece.

press conference. They released an open letter to the fifth member of the collegium, the then Chief Justice of India (CJI), and complained that long-standing conventions governing the CJI's role as the 'master of the roster' were being ignored.[114] The Indian Supreme Court sits on benches of varying sizes. While ordinarily the composition of different benches and allocation of cases between them is decided through an automated system, the CJI, as the master of the roster, retains the residual power to assign benches.[115] This time, the suggestion was that the CJI may have used his powers to benefit the ruling party and its leaders in certain politically sensitive cases.[116] In particular, there was high drama around the assignment of a case concerning the alleged murder of a trial court judge who was investigating a murder case that implicated the BJP President Amit Shah.[117] The irregular assignment of this case to a bench headed by the then-CJI, which decided that there was no need for further investigation into the case, was one of the primary motivations for the press conference by the four other members of the collegium.[118] One of the four senior judges who held the press conference publicly confirmed after his retirement that they did indeed believe that the CJI was acting under 'external influence' and that bench allocations were tainted by 'political bias'.[119] Another wrote in a letter to the CJI that:

> We, the judges of the Supreme Court of India, are being accused of ceding our independence and our institutional integrity to the Executive's incremental encroachment. The Executive is always impatient, and brooks no disobedience even of the judiciary if it can. Attempts were always made to treat the Chief Justices as the Departmental Heads in the Secretariat. So much for our 'independence and preeminence' as a distinct State organ.[120]

After the press conference, given the seriousness of the charges, a few members of the parliamentary opposition filed an impeachment motion against the CJI.[121] However, India's Vice President – a former president of the BJP – refused to allow the motion to proceed without even ordering a preliminary investigation into the allegations.[122]

While the BJP's hand in the above-mentioned episode is shrouded in mystery, its role in calling for open defiance of a judicial order is very public. In a 2018 decision, the

[114] 'Full Text of the Letter Four Supreme Court Judges Wrote to India's Chief Justice' *Quartz* (12 January 2018) https://qz.com/1178370/full-text-of-the-letter-four-supreme-court-judges-write-to-the-chief-justice-of-india/.

[115] *Asok Pande v Supreme Court of India* (2018) 5 SCC 341.

[116] S Ray, 'India's Top Judges Accuse Chief Justice of Undue Influence in Hearings' *Telegraph* (14 January 2018) www.telegraph.co.uk/news/2018/01/14/indias-top-judges-accuse-chief-justice-undue-influence-hearings/.

[117] D Dave, 'Death of a Judge: There is Much More Than Meets the Eye' *Bar & Bench* (19 January 2018) https://barandbench.com/judge-loya-death-dushyant-dave/.

[118] 'Loya Case the Tipping Point, Four SC Judges Say Democracy Is in Danger' (*The Wire*, 12 January 2018) https://thewire.in/law/sc-justices-hold-historic-press-conference-triggered-judge-loya-case.

[119] 'We Thought Ex-CJI Dipak Misra Was under "External Influences": Kurian Joseph' (*The Wire*, 3 December 2018) https://thewire.in/law/dipak-misra-kurian-joseph-supreme-court.

[120] AK Aditya, 'Bonhomie between Judiciary and Government Sounds the Death Knell to Democracy; Chelameswar J in Letter to CJI' *Bar and Bench* (29 March 2018) https://barandbench.com/bonhomie-between-judiciary-and-government-sounds-the-death-knell-to-democracy-chelameswar-j-in-letter-to-cji/.

[121] A Kazmin, 'India's Opposition Moves to Impeach Supreme Court Chief Justice' *Financial Times* (21 April 2018) www.ft.com/content/90ca99ba-4486-11e8-803a-295c97e6fd0b.

[122] Shri M Venkaiah Naidu, Order by the Vice President (23 April 2018) https://rajyasabha.nic.in/rsnew/HC_orders_mothion.pdf; A Kazmin, 'Congress Party Motion to Impeach India's Top Judge Rejected' *Financial Times* (24 April 2018) www.ft.com/content/ffadea5e-46f6-11e8-8ae9-4b5ddcca99b3.

Supreme Court ordered that women should be allowed to worship in a Hindu temple in Southern India, where women of certain ages were previously prohibited from entering.[123] While the Communist Party government in the state where the temple is located hailed the verdict, BJP President Amit Shah threatened to uproot the state government if it continued to enforce the order by arresting people protesting (and frustrating) the implementation of the Supreme Court's order (by physically blocking access to the temple by female activists).[124] The BJP also led protests against its enforcement,[125] resulting in several violent incidents.[126]

B. Disabling or Capturing the Fourth Branch

Contemporary constitutions subject the executive to the scrutiny not only of the political opposition and the judiciary, but also various fourth branch institutions that typically include an auditor-general, an electoral commission, a human rights watchdog, an anti-corruption ombudsoffice, a chief public prosecutor and so on.[127] In India, some of these institutions, like the Election Commission, are created by the Constitution itself. Others, like the Human Rights Commission, established by statutes, have quasi-constitutional status. The Modi government has worked systematically to either cripple these institutions to prevent them from performing their accountability-seeking function (often by simply refusing to fill vacancies) or to pack them with party ideologues to ensure their institutional capture. The fact that the political executive has an exclusive (or, at least, dominant) say in appointments to most of these institutions has aided the project of ideological capture of these institutions, which are increasingly being staffed by affiliates of the BJP's parent organisation and ideological mentor: the RSS.

(i) Lokpal

After a long-drawn-out anti-corruption movement, the outgoing government, headed by the Congress Party, enacted the Lokpal and Lokayuktas Act in 2013. This Act aimed to establish an independent anti-graft ombudsoffice (the Lokpal). Despite the BJP's prominent role (then as an opposition party) in demanding the legislation, and repeated reprimands by the Supreme Court, the Modi government failed to appoint a Lokpal for

[123] *Indian Young Lawyers Association v The State of Kerala* (2018) SCC OnLine SC 1690.

[124] G Mukherjee and M Prasad, 'By Threatening Kerala's Government for Enforcing Sabarimala Order, Amit Shah Breached His Oath as MP' *Scroll.in* (18 November 2018) https://scroll.in/article/902308/by-threatening-keralas-government-for-enforcing-sabarimala-order-amit-shah-breached-his-oath-as-mp?fbclid=IwAR1fuAjAzfhIomEK8VRzcmZ4tsnpYS40nhQJ8oqetPaUIf_xNa52UsWVXUU.

[125] S Philip, 'Amit Shah Asks on Sabarimala: Why Issue Orders that Can't be Enforced?' *Indian Express* (28 October 2018) https://indianexpress.com/article/india/amit-shah-asks-on-sabarimala-why-issue-orders-that-cant-be-enforced-5421715/.

[126] K Schultz, 'Clashes Blocking Women from Temple in India Bring Over 2,000 Arrests' *NY Times* (26 October 2018) www.nytimes.com/2018/10/26/world/asia/india-hindu-temple-arrests.html.

[127] Albert and Pal (n 18).

most of its tenure of five years.[128] The government took more than four years to even establish a search committee,[129] based on which an appointment was made in the dying days of the first Modi government. In the absence of an official opposition leader, the opposition was sought to be represented on the selection committee by a special invitee who could attend but not vote; the invitee understandably turned down the insulting invitation.[130]

(ii) Central Bureau of Investigation

The CBI is the premier investigative agency in the country.[131] Despite its crucial role, the Bureau does not stand on firm constitutional ground.[132] It is a federal body with police powers in a constitutional scheme where such powers ordinarily reside with state governments.[133] The complicated legal status not only raises questions about the constitutionality of the Bureau,[134] but also compromises its independence and accountability.[135] The Director of the CBI – selected by a committee comprising the Prime Minister, the Leader of the Opposition and the Chief Justice of India – enjoys a fixed tenure of two years.[136] However, there is little independence, as the Bureau's administrative control vests with the government.

Allegations of the politicisation of the CBI are not new. Previous governments frequently used the CBI to selectively investigate their political adversaries, which led the Chief Justice of India to describe the body as 'a caged parrot speaking in its master's voice'.[137] Even against the backdrop of this fraught history, the crisis under the Modi government was unprecedented.[138] The top two officers of the agency made allegations

[128] *Common Cause v Union of India* (2017) 7 SCC 158; K Rajagopal, 'Govt Stand on Lokpal Appointment is "Wholly Unsatisfactory", Says Supreme Court' *The Hindu* (24 July 2018) www.thehindu.com/news/national/govt-stand-on-lokpal-apointment-is-wholly-unsatisfactory-says-supreme-court/article24502495.ece.

[129] B Jain, 'Centre Announces 8-Member Search Committee for Lokpal' *Times of India* (27 September 2018) https://timesofindia.indiatimes.com/india/centre-announces-8-member-search-committee-for-lokpal/articleshow/65985596.cms.

[130] M Langa, 'Justice P.C. Ghose Appointed First Lokpal' *The Hindu* (19 March 2019) www.thehindu.com/news/national/justice-pc-ghose-appointed-first-lokpal/article26582874.ece; Anjali Bhardwaj, 'How Not to Appoint a Lokpal' (*The* Wire, 20 March 2019) https://thewire.in/government/how-not-to-appoint-a-lokpal.

[131] AG Noorani, 'A Charter for the CBI' *The Hindu* (21 August 2013) www.thehindu.com/opinion/lead/a-charter-for-the-cbi/article5042518.ece.

[132] See generally M Idiculla, 'CBI Does Not Need to Be Saved from Narendra Modi. It Needs to Be Dismantled' *Scroll.in* (13 February 2019) https://scroll.in/article/912652/cbi-does-not-need-to-be-saved-from-narendra-modi-it-needs-to-be-dismantled.

[133] A Chowdhry, 'Independence of CBI: Myth and Reality' *Rediff* (15 May 2013) www.rediff.com/news/column/independence-of-cbi-myth-and-reality/20130515.htm.

[134] 'SC Stays Gauhati High Court Order Declaring CBI Unconstitutional' *Indian Express* (18 February 2018) https://indianexpress.com/article/india/india-others/sc-stays-gauhati-high-court-order-declaring-cbi-unconstitutional/. See *Navendra Kumar v The Union of India* (2013) SCC OnLine Gau 305, [179] (in which the court declared the establishment of the CBI to be ultra vires of the Indian Constitution).

[135] M Tewari, 'Is CBI a Legal Entity?' *Deccan Chronicle* (28 October 2018) https://deccanchronicle.com/opinion/columnists/281018/is-cbi-a-legal-entity.html.

[136] Delhi Special Police Establishment Act, No 25 of 1946, India Code, s 4B.

[137] R Colvin and S Bhattacharjya, 'A "Caged Parrot": Supreme Court Describes CBI' *Reuters* (10 May 2013) https://in.reuters.com/article/cbi-supreme-court-parrot-coal/a-caged-parrot-supreme-court-describes-cbi-idINDEE94901W20130510.

[138] R Sarin, 'A Lower Low' *Indian Express* (26 October 2018) https://indianexpress.com/article/opinion/a-lower-low-5418861/.

of bribery against each other.[139] After the Director of the Bureau filed a case against the Deputy Director, the latter complained to the government about the former.[140] The government reacted to this by sending both top officials on indefinite leave despite the legally guaranteed fixed tenure of the CBI Director.[141] The government's justification was that since the two were at loggerheads, sending them on forced leave was essential to conduct an impartial inquiry into the charges levelled against them.[142] The CBI Director approached the Supreme Court, challenging the government's decision, and also claimed that the government was exercising its influence to interfere with the CBI's functioning.[143] Opposition parties alleged that the suspension of the CBI Director was an orchestrated attempt to thwart an investigation into recent corruption allegations against the government.[144] Less than 48 hours after the Supreme Court invalidated his suspension,[145] the committee empowered to appoint the director unceremoniously removed him from office by a two-to-one vote.[146] The Supreme Court judge who added his vote to the Prime Minister's to achieve the majority had been offered an attractive post-retirement job by the government,[147] an offer he rejected after media reports connected the two developments.[148] Such was the level of distrust that two states forbade the CBI from conducting any investigations within their jurisdiction without their express permission.[149]

(iii) The Central Information Commission

In 2005, India passed the Right to Information Act after a long-drawn-out social campaign led by civil society activists.[150] The Act, aimed at increasing transparency and

[139] 'The Corruption Scandal Marring India's CBI' *BBC* (26 October 2018) www.bbc.com/news/world-asia-india-45988193.

[140] ibid.

[141] ibid.

[142] ibid.

[143] M Sebastian, 'CBI Director Cannot Be Divested of Powers without Approval of High Powered Committee, Contends Alok Verma in SC' *LiveLaw* (24 October 2018) www.livelaw.in/cbi-director-cannot-be-divested-of-powers-without-approval-of-high-powered-committee-contends-alok-verma-in-sc-read-petition/.

[144] 'CBI Power Shift: Opposition Slams "Illegal Removal" of CBI Chief Alok Verma' *Indian Express* (25 October 2018) https://indianexpress.com/article/india/cbi-power-shift-opposition-slams-illegal-removal-of-cbi-chief-alok-verma/.

[145] S Choudhury and D Ghosh, 'Alok Verma Back as CBI Boss without Powers as Court Scraps Centre's Order' *NDTV* (8 January 2019) www.ndtv.com/india-news/alok-verma-reinstated-as-cbi-chief-by-supreme-court-he-was-sent-on-forced-leave-in-october-1974272.

[146] S Prabhu and D Chatterjee, '"Very, Very Hasty Decision" on Alok Verma: Ex-Judge Who Monitored Probe' *NDTV* (12 January 2018) www.ndtv.com/india-news/justice-ak-patnaik-ex-supreme-court-judge-says-no-evidence-of-corruption-against-alok-verma-1976618?pfrom=home-topscroll.

[147] M Chhibber, 'Justice Sikri, Whose Vote Decided Alok Verma's Fate, Gets Modi Govt Mod for Plum Posting' *The Print* (28 January 2019) https://theprint.in/governance/justice-sikri-whose-vote-decided-alok-vermas-fate-gets-modi-govt-nod-for-plum-posting/177191/.

[148] K Rajagopal, 'Justice Sikri Refuses Offer from Government to Nominate Him to Commonwealth Tribunal' *The Hindu* (13 January 2019) www.thehindu.com/news/national/justice-sikri-withdraws-consent-to-govt-offer-to-nominate-him-to-csat/article25986368.ece.

[149] 'After Andhra Pradesh, West Bengal Withdraws "General Consent" to CBI' *Times of India* (16 November 2018) https://timesofindia.indiatimes.com/india/after-andhra-pradesh-west-bengal-withdraws-general-consent-to-cbi/articleshow/66657701.cms.

[150] A Roy, 'Excerpt: The RTI Story: Power to the People' *Hindustan Times* (13 April 2018) www.hindustantimes.com/books/excerpt-the-rti-story-power-to-the-people-by-aruna-roy-with-the-mkss-collective/story-V5AWqGRa84dCxyoVsR2o4L.html.

accountability, requires a timely response to citizen inquiries from 'public authorities'.[151] In order to oversee compliance and resolve disputes pertaining to information requests, the Act also establishes the office of Information Commissioner at both federal and state levels. The Commissioners have the powers of a civil court and can direct a public authority to disclose any information it is legally required to disclose.[152] To maintain their independence from the government, the Commissioners' 'salaries, allowances, and other terms and conditions' are protected by the Act.[153]

In 2014, after assuming office, the government entrusted the Commission's financial powers to a governmental department, but they were restored to the Commission within a year following protests by activists and opposition parties.[154] Later, in 2018, the government introduced an amendment Bill to give itself significant discretion to determine the salaries, perks and tenures of the Commissioners.[155] The Commission continued to work seriously understaffed because of numerous unfilled vacancies.[156] In its judgment in early 2019,[157] the Supreme Court castigated both the amendment and the failure to fill vacancies in order to frustrate the purposes of the Act, stating that: 'By not filling up vacancies in information commissions in a timely manner, the Central and State Governments are frustrating the very purpose of the RTI Act as receiving information in a time-bound manner is the essence of the law'.[158]

Notwithstanding this judicial reproach, the Modi government saw the enactment of the Right to Information (Amendment) Act 2019 within a few months of the start of its second, more confident and less cautious, tenure. The Transparency Commission has been effectively downgraded from an autonomous fourth branch quasi-constitutional body to a department of a governmental ministry.

(iv) Senior Bureaucracy

A non-partisan bureaucracy which can provide frank and fearless advice to the political executive is crucial for the impartial implementation of laws and policies. The top bureaucracy in India is filled by senior officers initially selected by competitive

[151] Right to Information Act, No 22 of 2005, s 4.

[152] ibid s 18.

[153] ibid ss 13 and 16.

[154] A Tikku, 'CIC's Financial Powers Restored by Government' *Hindustan Times* (1 August 2015) www.hindustantimes.com/india/cic-s-financial-powers-restored-by-government/story-oBSX52JwNbR44qG4JvZqiN.html.

[155] V Lalwani, '"Serious Attack": Activists Say Centre's Proposed Amendments Will Weaken RTI Act', *Scroll.in* (18 July 2018) https://scroll.in/article/886927/serious-attack-activists-say-centres-proposed-amendments-will-weaken-rti-act; N Dey, B Yadav and B Julka, 'Has the Right to Information Act Been Weakened?' *The Hindu* (27 July 2018) www.thehindu.com/opinion/op-ed/has-the-right-to-information-act-been-weakened/article24523104.ece.

[156] M Sridhar, 'Apex Court Opposes Amendment to RTI' *Hans India* (26 February 2019) www.thehansindia.com/posts/index/Editorial/2019-02-25/Apex-court-opposes-amendment-to-RTI/502185.

[157] *Bharadwaj v Union of India* (2019) SCC Online SC 205.

[158] ibid [3] (Sikri J).

examinations at the entry level, conducted by an independent constitutional body called the Union Public Service Commission.[159] This system of appointments has, to some degree, protected civil services from political influence – although appointments to senior bureaucracy are indeed political, the pool from which candidates may be chosen has hitherto been limited and professional.[160] However, the Modi government introduced a direct lateral-entry system, calling upon 'talented and motivated Indian nationals' from various professional backgrounds to apply for high-ranking positions in the federal government bureaucracy.[161] Despite a specialised constitutional body for public services, the government retained the power of appointment for this parallel system for itself. Several commentators criticised this move as a return of the 'spoils system, in which civil service positions may be awarded to party supporters by bypassing the constitutionally mandated mechanism'.[162] Yet again, a move designed to facilitate the partisan capture of a state institution was justified in terms of managerial rationales such as efficiency and diversity of talent.

(v) National Statistical Commission

The National Statistical Commission saw two of its members resign in protest after the government disallowed the publication of its report on unemployment.[163] This left the Commission with only two remaining members, one of whom was an ex officio member. The leaked report allegedly reported skyrocketing unemployment figures under the Modi government.[164]

[159] KAV Shetty, 'Lateral Entry into Senior Bureaucracy: A Flawed Approach' Hindu Centre for Politics and Public Policy (11 July 2018) www.thehinducentre.com/the-arena/current-issues/article24386653.ece.

[160] ibid.

[161] 'Government Opens Doors to Lateral Entry' *The Hindu* (10 June 2018) www.thehindu.com/news/national/government-opens-doors-to-lateral-entry/article24130060.ece; U Bhaskar, 'Nine from Outside the IAS Set to Become Joint Secretaries in Government' *Livemint* (13 April 2019) www.livemint.com/politics/policy/nine-from-outside-the-ias-set-to-become-joint-secretaries-in-government-1555133560315.html.

[162] KAV Shetty, 'Are We Ushering in the Spoils System in Senior Bureaucracy?' *The Hindu* (19 June 2018) www.thehindu.com/thread/politics-and-policy/lateral-entry-into-senior-bureaucracy-opening-the-floodgates-for-a-spoils-system/article24201356.ece.

[163] 'All Members of National Statistical Commission Resign after Centre Failed to Publish Jobs Report' *Scroll.in* (29 January 2019) https://scroll.in/latest/911289/no-members-on-national-statistical-commission-after-resignations-over-centre-burying-jobs-report; N Menon, 'A Short History of Data' *The Hindu* (21 March 2019) www.thehindu.com/opinion/lead/a-short-history-of-data/article26593687.ece?fbclid=IwAR2ynm-91DC7BoX2kAgw5MkvN_Vl11O08Rsfl0h8hZz67rETmErDM6Ov2Uo.

[164] J Gettleman and H Kumar, 'India's Leader Is Accused of Hiding Unemployment Data before Vote' *NY Times* (31 January 2019) www.nytimes.com/2019/01/31/world/asia/india-unemployment-rate.html. See generally Press Trust of India, '108 Economists from Around the World Object to "Political Interference" in Statistics in India, Cite GDP and Job Data' *News18* (14 March 2019) www.news18.com/news/business/108-economists-from-around-the-world-object-to-political-interference-in-statistics-in-india-cite-gdp-and-job-data-2066997.html?ref=hp_top_pos_9. See also 'Raghuram Rajan Raises Questions about India's Growth Rate, Calls for Impartial Body to Clean Up Data' *Scroll.in* (26 March 2019) https://scroll.in/latest/917963/raghuram-rajan-raises-questions-about-indias-growth-rate-calls-for-impartial-body-to-clean-up-data.

(vi) Reserve Bank of India

The importance of the independence of the central bank to democracy is especially noted by Lijphart in his classic work *Patterns of Democracy*.[165] He notes that 'independent banks are widely considered to be better at controlling inflation and maintaining price stability than banks that are dependent on the executive'.[166] The Reserve Bank of India (RBI), India's central bank, is in charge of the country's monetary policy. While previous governments have had disagreements with the bank, they have usually managed to reach compromises through negotiations behind closed doors.[167] During Modi's tenure, the relationship between the government and the Bank was fraught, with several public stand-offs, which soared after the government's demonetisation policy (invalidating 86 per cent of currency notes) was implemented without prior approval from the Bank.[168] Other policy disagreements concerned interest rates, the bad debt crisis of Indian public sector banks, setting up a separate regulator for payment wallets and, most importantly, cutting the RBI reserves.[169] In 2016, the then independent-minded RBI Governor Raghuram Rajan resigned after it was made clear to him that he did not have the government's confidence.[170] The government continued to clash on the issue of central bank reserves with his successor, Urjit Patel, whom the bank itself had appointed.

The level of governmental interference can be gauged by the highly unusual move of the Deputy Governor of the Bank making a strong case for the independence of the central bank in a public speech in 2018.[171] According to some commentators, the government's attack on the RBI's reserve was motivated by its political need to increase public spending on populist policies before the 2019 general elections.[172] The government

[165] A Lijphart, 'Central Banks: Independence versus Dependence' in A Lijphart (ed), *Patterns of Democracy: Government Forms and Performance in Thirty-Six Countries*, 2nd edn (New Haven, Yale University Press, 2010) 226.

[166] ibid 20. See also P Tucker, *Unelected Power: The Quest for Legitimacy in Central Banking and the Regulatory State* (Princeton, Princeton University Press, 2018).

[167] V Iyer, 'Urjit Patel: RBI Governor and His Governance' *Indian Express* (4 November 2018) https://indianexpress.com/article/india/governor-his-governance-rbi-urjit-patel-5433021/.

[168] A Srivas, 'Explained: The Widening Rift between the RBI and the Modi Government' (*The Wire*, 10 December 2018) https://thewire.in/economy/explained-the-widening-rift-between-the-rbi-and-the-modi-government; Express Web Desk, 'PM Modi Went Ahead with Demonetisation Before RBI's Formal Approval: RTI' *Indian Express* (11 March 2019) https://indianexpress.com/article/business/economy/demonetisation-pm-modi-rbi-board-urjit-patel-black-money-rti-5620929/.

[169] S Biswas, 'RBI: What Is the Indian Central Bank's Conflict with the Government?' *BBC News* (1 November 2018) www.bbc.com/news/world-asia-india-46054042.

[170] E Barry, 'Raghuram Rajan Says He'll Step Down as Head of India's Central Bank' *NY Times* (18 June 2016) www.nytimes.com/2016/06/19/business/head-of-indias-central-bank-says-he-will-step-down.html. See generally Press Trust of India, 'Centralisation of Power One of India's Main Problems: Raghuram Rajan' *NDTV* (10 November 2018) www.ndtv.com/india-news/raghuram-rajan-centralisation-of-power-one-of-indias-main-problems-1945426.

[171] VAcharya, Deputy Governor, Reserve Bank of India, 'On the Importance of Independent Regulatory Institutions – The Case of the Central Bank', AD Shroff Memorial Lecture, Mumbai (26 October 2018) https://rbidocs.rbi.org.in/rdocs/Speeches/PDFs/ADSML51EEB918B7194BC6AA8B764B05006B15.PDF.

[172] MS Sharma, 'Why RBI Is Suddenly Standing Up to Modi: and What's at Stake' *NDTV* (31 October 2018) www.ndtv.com/opinion/what-modi-vs-rbi-is-all-about-its-an-election-year-stupid-1940419?pfrom=home-opinion.

threatened to invoke its never-before-used statutory power to issue a binding directive to the RBI.[173] The threat of the directive, and pressure from the government's allies packed onto the Bank's board to corner the governor,[174] forced a compromise of sorts whereby the government mostly got its way.[175] Ultimately, Governor Patel also resigned.[176] His successor, Shaktikanta Das, was a career bureaucrat, unlike his two economist predecessors.[177] With a pliant governor finally in place, the RBI relented to fund the government's election-season projects.[178]

VI. Silencing Discursive Accountability Mechanisms

While the independence of fourth branch institutions has some legal protection in India, the media, universities and non-governmental organisations that are critical to seeking diagonal accountability from the executive have been extremely vulnerable. The Indian judiciary has a mixed record of defending press freedom and academic freedom, and its free speech jurisprudence has been rather flexible.[179] While every previous government has sought to control and influence these civil society institutions, the scale of the countrywide attacks – including violent attacks – on discursive institutions between 2014 and 2019 was unprecedented, excepting only the Emergency years under Indira Gandhi.

The BJP, its cultural-ideological mentor the RSS and numerous sister organisations that help with political mobilisation and supply politically expedient violence with arm's-length deniability together constitute the Sangh Parivaar (the 'family of the Sangh [RSS]'). The Sangh Parivaar has a long history of hostility to freedom of expression. Acting as a self-appointed censor, it has used legal, extra-legal and illegal means to target artists, academics, journalists and activists that it seea (through its expansive lens) as denigrating Hinduism or Indian culture. Even before the BJP's electoral victory in 2014,

[173] 'What is Section 7 of the RBI Act and Why This Extreme Step May See Urjit Patel Call It Quits' *News18* (31 October 2018) www.news18.com/news/business/what-is-section-7-of-the-rbi-act-and-why-this-extreme-step-may-see-urjit-patel-call-it-quits-1925835.html.

[174] M Kumar and S Choudhury, 'Narendra Modi Stacks RBI Board with Allies to Turn Heat up on Governor' (*The Wire*, 18 November 2018) https://thewire.in/government/narendra-modi-stacks-rbi-board-with-allies-to-turn-heat-up-on-governor.

[175] M Shetty and S Gupta, 'Government Mostly Gets Its Way, but RBI Has a Deal It Can Live With' *Times of India* (20 November 2018) https://timesofindia.indiatimes.com/business/india-business/government-mostly-gets-its-way-but-rbi-has-a-deal-it-can-live-with/articleshow/66700156.cms.

[176] 'Urjit Patel Resigns as RBI Governor amid Rift with Govt, PM Modi Says He'll Be Missed "Immensely"' *News18* (10 December 2018) www.news18.com/news/business/urjit-patel-steps-down-as-rbi-governor-citing-personal-reasons-1967787.html; 'Urjit Patel's Exit Is Another Sign of Modi's Limited Faith in Institutional Guidance' (*The Wire*, 12 December 2018) https://thewire.in/economy/urjit-patels-exit-is-another-sign-of-modis-limited-faith-in-institutional-guidance.

[177] 'Shaktikanta Das Appointed as the New RBI Governor' *Economic Times* (13 December 2018) https://economictimes.indiatimes.com/industry/banking/finance/banking/shaktikanta-das-appointed-as-the-new-rbi-governor/articleshow/67045353.cms.

[178] A Nag and V Beniwal, 'RBI Gives Rs. 28,000 Crore Interim Dividend to Government before Elections' *NDTV* (18 February 2019) www.ndtv.com/business/pm-modi-gets-rs-28-000-crore-cash-from-central-bank-before-polls-1995406?pfrom=home-livetv.

[179] See generally R Dhavan, *Only the Good News: On the Law of the Press in India* (New Delhi, Manohar Publications, 1987); G Bhatia, *Offend, Shock, or Disturb: Free Speech under the Indian Constitution* (Oxford, Oxford University Press, 2016).

for example, Sangh Parivaar outfits managed to bully Penguin into recalling and pulping a book titled *On Hinduism*, authored by Wendy Doniger, a professor of religion at the University of Chicago.[180]

What changed with power in 2014 was that the targets of its censorship came to include not only cultural and ideological enemies, but also political opponents. And the weapons became more potent. An academic, an activist and a journalist were, for example, booked for sedition after protesting against a divisive Bill seeking to amend India's citizenship law.[181]

A. Attacks on Universities and Academic Freedom

The University Grants Commission (UGC) is a statutory body set up to set standards, promote and monitor higher education, and allocate grants to universities for the purposes of research, teaching and infrastructure.[182] Although not completely independent, the UGC enjoys a limited degree of autonomy. For instance, its chairperson has a fixed tenure,[183] and it does not normally need any authorisation by the federal government regarding the exercising of its powers.[184]

In June 2018, the government released a draft of new legislation that would have overhauled the entire regulatory scheme for higher education.[185] Under the draft Bill, the new regulator would enjoy limited institutional autonomy.[186] While this draft was shelved after protests, in the same year, the government issued a directive to public universities to implement Central Civil Services Rules for their employees. This meant that, like civil servants, academics employed by public universities would not be allowed to criticise the government or its policies.[187] Amid severe protests that such a measure would undermine academic freedom, the government declared that the directive was recommendatory, not mandatory.[188] Similarly, the Union Ministry of Human Resource

[180] S Biswas, 'Why Did Penguin Recall a Book on Hindus?' *BBC* (12 February 2014) www.bbc.co.uk/news/world-asia-india-26148875; R Lakshmi, 'The "Ban Man": India's Self-Appointed Book Censor Wields Real Clout' *Washington Post* (23 June 2014) www.washingtonpost.com/world/asia_pacific/the-ban-man-indias-self-appointed-book-censor-wields-real-clout/2014/06/23/6f71eca2-b73f-4102-96e0-21d5a52e59a7_story.html?utm_term=.79b8123123d0.

[181] A Saha, 'Protest against Citizenship Bill: Assam Academic Hiren Gohain, Two Others Booked for Sedition' *Indian Express* (11 January 2019) https://indianexpress.com/article/north-east-india/assam/assam-intellectuals-hiren-gohain-akhil-gogoi-manjit-mahanta-booked-for-sedition-for-remarks-on-citizenship-amendment-bill-5531915/.

[182] University Grants Commission Act, No 3 of 1956, s 12.

[183] ibid s 6.

[184] ibid s 20.

[185] The Higher Education Commission of India Bill, 2018 (Repeal of University Grants Commission Act, No 3 of 1956).

[186] A Sengupta, 'The Higher Education Commission of India Bill: A Failure of Imagination' 5 (Observer Research Foundation, Issue Brief No 252, 2018) www.orfonline.org/research/43521-the-higher-education-commission-of-india-bill-a-failure-of-imagination/.

[187] S Niazi, 'Ministry Backpedals on "Gagging" Rules for Academics' *University World News* (26 October 2018) www.universityworldnews.com/article.php?story=20181026124012244.

[188] ibid.

Development briefed vice-chancellors of central universities to 'discourage research in irrelevant areas' and focus PhD research on 'national priorities' instead, prompting the Central University of Kerala to draft an approved list of PhD topics.[189] Using its executive powers, the government also withheld special funding from key universities, allegedly for blatantly partisan reasons – basically, private universities whose patrons were seen as anti-Modi had their funding withdrawn.[190]

The government was also extremely enthusiastic about bringing sedition charges against students and academics for mere speeches.[191] The Jawaharlal Nehru University in Delhi, a prestigious public university that has often been regarded as the bastion of left-wing ideology, especially drew the government's ire. A new university administration was put in place in 2016 to disrupt its internal functions and, some claim, compromise academic freedom.[192] Five of its students were charged with sedition for protesting the execution of a Kashmiri separatist (and allegedly shouting 'anti-India' slogans during the protest). The university itself was labelled 'anti-national'.[193] This was despite a magistrate's report confirming that no such slogans were shouted; and even if they were, the law on sedition is contravened only if the impugned speech has the tendency to incite violence.[194] A well-known politics professor at the university, Nivedita Menon, faced prolonged vilification in the pro-government media for being 'anti-national' after she publicly supported the students.[195] Another university that was singled out was the Aligarh Muslim University. Fourteen of its students were booked for sedition after clashing with journalists from the pro-government television network Republic TV.[196]

As in other spheres, the government took many small steps towards institutional capture in the education field. Some invited vociferous protests or judicial intervention, and had to be rolled back; others managed to stick.

[189] 'HRD Says PhDs Only on "National Priority" Topics, Kerala Prof Quits Central Univ Board' *Indian Express* (24 March 2019) https://indianexpress.com/article/education/hrd-says-phds-only-on-national-priority-topics-kerala-prof-quits-central-univ-board-5639915/?fbclid=IwAR0tcmztNPZZhyVc4mHSbLxL0PFkQryk0phGAeOQeSjfkO9lfOPSSvWMBlo.

[190] N Pandey, 'Intelligence Bureau Red-Flags PVT Universities Seeking Eminence Tag for Anti-Modi Patrons' *The Print* (28 January 2019) https://theprint.in/governance/intelligence-bureau-red-flags-pvt-universities-seeking-eminence-tag-for-anti-modi-patrons/184151/?fbclid=IwAR1Hl19OSK0dET_ZgcLh8AfcYyU6soC-IWbQ_AIpW2UKDvXuLGnfzza2l_4.

[191] See generally N Sundar, 'Academic Freedom and Indian Universities' (2018) 53 *Economic and Political Weekly* 16; P Chatterjee, 'Freedom of Speech in University' (2016) 51 *Economic and Political Weekly* 35, 35–37.

[192] G Arunima, 'The Battle for JNU's Soul' (*The Wire*, 25 December 2018) https://thewire.in/education/the-battle-for-jnu-soul.

[193] H Kausar and S Chettri, 'JNU Row a Year Later: Kanhaiya to Khalid, How Lives of 5 Students Changed' *Hindustan Times* (2 March 2017) www.hindustantimes.com/delhi-news/jnu-protests-a-year-on-how-the-feb-9-anti-national-event-changed-five-lives/story-4jbNO1ByQtC9B8XbOMFFUK.html.

[194] 'Despite SC's Stance on Sedition, Charge Slapped on JNU's Kanhaiya Kumar, Others' (*The Wire*, 15 January 2019) https://thewire.in/rights/despite-scs-stance-on-sedition-charge-slapped-on-jnus-kanhaiya-kumar-others.

[195] J Sen, '"Vilification" of JNU Professor Nivedita Menon as "Anti-National" Labelling Continues' (*The Wire*, 5 March 2016) https://thewire.in/politics/vilification-of-jnu-professor-nivedita-menon-as-anti-national-labelling-continues.

[196] '14 Aligarh Muslim University Students Booked for Sedition after Fracas with Republic TV Crew' (*Scroll.in*, 13 February 2019) https://scroll.in/latest/913063/14-aligarh-muslim-university-students-booked-for-sedition-after-fracas-with-republic-tv-crew.

B. Silencing Independent Media

The use of an imperfect guarantee of free speech by governments and political parties to harass journalists is not a new phenomenon in India. What changed under the Modi regime was the scale, severity and systemicity of these responses.[197] The BJP maintains a comprehensive list of individual Indian journalists and classifies them as pro- or anti-BJP.[198] Instead of using the much-abused law against criminal defamation to silence journalists, even more diabolical colonial-era laws, such as the one criminalising sedition, were deployed.[199] In a system where the criminal process can take several years before a final verdict is arrived at, safeguards built into the substantive law lose much of their value: the process becomes the punishment. The *Milli Gazette* was harassed through the criminal process so much after it exposed an official policy of anti-Muslim discrimination in a government department that it felt compelled to end its print run.[200] Media houses were pressurised, sometimes successfully, to let go of unbending editors.[201] Some uncompromising editors, like Gauri Lankesh, were murdered by goons belonging to sister organisations affiliated with the Sangh Parivaar.[202] Self-censorship also grew – two large newspapers published and then removed stories on a report by Reporters Without Borders which had claimed that the Indian press had become less free under Prime Minister Modi.[203]

The CBI (an investigative agency that is, as we have already seen, tightly controlled by the government) conducted four simultaneous raids in the offices and residences connected to the news corporation NDTV. While the CBI stated loan defaults as the ostensible reason for such raids, several senior media personalities, highlighting NDTV's anti-government stance, argued that the raids amounted to political harassment and that the government has not been so enthusiastic with its raids on other loan defaulters.[204]

[197] A Gowen, 'In Modi's India, Journalists Face Bullying, Criminal Cases and Worse' *Washington Post* (15 February 2018) www.washingtonpost.com/world/asia_pacific/in-modis-india-journalists-face-bullying-criminal-cases-and-worse/2018/02/13/e8176b72-8695-42ab-abd5-d26aab830d3e_story.html?noredirect=on&utm_term=.83936cfbc268.

[198] I Mishra, 'Pro-BJP or Anti-BJP: Inside the Modi-Shah Media Tracking "War Rooms"' (*The* Wire, 11 August 2018) https://thewire.in/politics/narendra-modi-amit-shah-bjp-india-media.

[199] See generally N Banerjee, 'Centre "Trying to Silence Media" Unconstitutionally: Chandrababu Naidu' *NDTV* (7 March 2019) www.ndtv.com/india-news/centre-trying-to-silence-media-unconstitutionally-chandrababu-naidu-2004199.

[200] G Sarkar, 'The Curious Case of "The Milli Gazette"' *Newslaundry* (14 February 2019) www.newslaundry.com/2019/02/14/the-curious-case-of-the-milli-gazette.

[201] R Gopalakrishnan, 'Indian Journalists Say They Are Intimidated, Ostracised if They Criticise Modi and the BJP' *Reuters* (26 April 2018) https://uk.reuters.com/article/uk-india-politics-media-analysis-idUKKBN1HX1EO.

[202] 'Gauri Lankesh: Indian Journalist Shot Dead in Bangalore' *BBC News* (6 September 2017) www.bbc.com/news/world-asia-india-41169817; J Gettleman and H Kumar, 'In India, Another Government Critic is Silenced by Bullets' *NY Times* (6 September 2017) www.nytimes.com/2017/09/06/world/asia/gauri-lankesh-india-dead.html?module=inline; R Romig, 'Railing against India's Right-Wing Nationalism Was a Calling. It Was also a Death Sentence' *NY Times* (14 March 2019) www.nytimes.com/2019/03/14/magazine/gauri-lankesh-murder-journalist.html?fbclid=IwAR2U1GRen4WjkOB2_Sm3Gwsdlb80sL5wZWYfpWkffMjk_Ug5EnaqXq3Rc9g.

[203] The Hoot, 'The India Freedom Report: Media Freedom and Freedom of Expression in 2017' (2001) 17, http://asu.thehoot.org/public/uploads/filemanager/media/THE-INDIA-FREEDOM-REPORT-.pdf. See generally '2019 World Press Freedom Index, Reporters without Borders' (2019) https://rsf.org/en/ranking.

[204] E Barry, 'Raids in India Target Founders of News Outlet Critical of Government' *NY Times* (5 June 2017) www.nytimes.com/2017/06/05/world/asia/india-ndtv-raids-narendra-modi-prannoy-roy.html.

The violence against the media was also expressive. A minister in Modi's cabinet characterised journalists as 'presstitutes'.[205] A major BBC report on fake news in India concluded that 'On the network analysis map produced during this research, we see that many more of the Twitter handles that have published fake news sit in the pro-BJP cluster, than in the anti-BJP cluster'.[206]

All this is just what is in the public domain and may well be the tip of the iceberg. Behind-the-scenes attempts to capture or silence media organisations – especially those that function outside the Delhi-centric national discourse – are very difficult to document, but are likely afoot. Discursive freedoms – never robust in India to begin with – suffered badly under the Modi regime. Conscious of the climate of hatred and violence being created, the former President Pranab Mukherjee, before and since his retirement in 2017, made repeated public calls for greater tolerance in political discourse.[207]

C. Confronting NGOs and Other Civil Society Actors

The Modi government vehemently repressed certain civil society organisations. It cancelled foreign contribution licences of more than 20,000 non-governmental organisations (NGOs),[208] making them ineligible to receive foreign funding.[209] Some NGOs were in genuine violation of the law – for instance, by failing to submit their accounts.[210] However, many of these licences were cancelled under a vaguely worded provision that empowers the government to do so if 'necessary in the public interest'.[211] Many organisations against which this provision was used were engaged in human rights advocacy, frequently targeting the government for its human rights breaches.[212] NGOs were raided, harassed or worse, including reputed international ones like Amnesty and Greenpeace.[213] While the government was harsh on civil society organisations, without

[205] 'VK Singh in New Row, Calls Media "Presstitutes"' *Times of India* (8 April 2015) https://timesofindia.indiatimes.com/india/VK-Singh-in-new-row-calls-media-presstitutes/articleshow/46844032.cms.

[206] S Chakrabarti, L Stengel and S Solanki, 'Duty, Identity and Credibility: "Fake News" and the Ordinary Citizen in India' (2018) 10, https://downloads.bbc.co.uk/mediacentre/duty-identity-credibility.pdf.

[207] 'President Pranab Mukherjee Stresses on the Need for Tolerance in Speech: Full Text' *Firstpost* (26 May 2017) www.firstpost.com/india/president-pranab-mukherjee-stresses-on-the-need-for-tolerance-heres-the-full-text-of-his-speech-3482493.html.

[208] D Bhattacharya, 'FCRA Licences of 20,000 NGOs Cancelled: Act Being Used as Weapon to Silence Organisations' *Firstpost* (26 October 2018) www.firstpost.com/india/fcra-licences-of-20000-ngos-cancelled-act-being-used-as-weapon-to-silence-organisations-3181560.html.

[209] Foreign Contributions Regulation Act, No 42 of 2010, s 14.

[210] T Shastri, 'NGOs, Foreign Funds and a Trust Deficit' *The Hindu* (29 June 2015) www.thehindu.com/opinion/op-ed/ngos-foreign-funds-and-a-trust-deficit/article7364282.ece.

[211] Foreign Contributions Regulation Act, No 42 of 2010, s 14(1)(c).

[212] A Khullar, 'FCRA and NGOs: What Lies behind the Government's Crackdown?' (*The Wire*, 30 December 2016) https://thewire.in/rights/fcra-ngos-lies-behind-governments-crackdown; Amnesty International, 'Suspension of Human Rights NGO's Foreign Funding License Must Be Revoked' (Amnesty International India, 3 June 2016) https://amnesty.org.in/news-update/suspension-human-rights-ngos-foreign-funding-license-must-revoked/.

[213] 'ED Raids Amnesty India over FEMA Irregularities: A Brief History of Centre's Crackdown on NGOs' *Firstpost* (26 October 2018) www.firstpost.com/india/ed-raids-amnesty-india-over-fema-irregularities-a-brief-history-of-centres-crackdown-on-ngos-5450341.html; A Ojha, 'Raid at Greenpeace Office, ED Claims Evidence of

a trace of irony it enthusiastically allowed foreign contributions to political parties, a move that mainly benefited the BJP.

When Bollywood actor Aamir Khan raised concerns about the growing climate of intolerance in the country,[214] the backlash that followed was vicious.[215] A minister in the Modi government pretty much owned and justified this backlash, saying that 'if anyone speaks like this, he has to be taught a lesson of his life'.[216] Activist Anand Teltumbde was arrested despite a Supreme Court order forbidding the state from doing so – he was released only after a lower court intervened to characterise the arrest as contempt of court.[217]

BJP-controlled state governments, which retain control of police powers, repeatedly used their powers of search and seizure against several other human rights and media organisations, which had taken a stand against its policies and actions.[218] Going beyond search and seizure, the BJP-ruled state governments also used their police powers to arrest several human rights lawyers and activists, describing them as 'urban Maoists'.[219] The BJP government in Assam brought 245 sedition cases in less than two years in power.[220] Leaders of anti-religious 'rationalist' movements were murdered by Sangh Parivaar affiliates.[221] Muslim citizens were lynched for allegedly possessing or consuming beef,[222] which inspired over 50 filmmakers, writers and others to return

Corruption' *India Today* (11 October 2018) www.indiatoday.in/india/story/raid-at-greenpeace-office-ed-claims-evidence-of-corruption-1360468-2018-10-11; 'ED "Crackdown" Will Not Stop Our Fight against Climate Change: Greenpeace India' *Times of India* (2 February 2019) https://timesofindia.indiatimes.com/india/ed-crackdown-will-not-stop-our-fight-against-climate-change-greenpeace-india/articleshow/67810498.cms?UTM_Source=Google_Newsstand&UTM_Campaign=RSS_Feed&UTM_Medium=Referral.

[214] 'Aamir Khan on Intolerance: I am Alarmed, My Wife Suggested Moving Out of India' *ETimes* (24 November 2015). See www.bbc.co.uk/news/world-asia-india-34918428.

[215] S Biswas, 'What the Backlash against Bollywood's Aamir Khan Tells Us about India' *BBC* (25 November 2015) www.bbc.co.uk/news/world-asia-india-34918431.

[216] PS Biswas, 'Parrikar Takes Swipe at Actor (Aamir): Those Who Speak Like This Must Be Taught Lesson' *Indian Express* (31 July 2016) https://indianexpress.com/article/india/india-news-india/parrikar-takes-swipe-at-actor-aamir-khan-intolerance-remark-those-who-speak-like-this-must-be-taught-lesson-2945440/.

[217] N Brahme and S Shantha, 'Court Rules Anand Teltumbde's Arrest Illegal, Orders Immediate Release' (*The Wire*, 2 February 2019) https://thewire.in/rights/court-orders-anand-teltumbdes-arrest-illegal.

[218] 'Income Tax Officials Leave the Quint's Office in Noida after 22 Hours' *Scroll.in* (11 October 2018) https://scroll.in/latest/897830/income-tax-officials-visit-the-quints-office-in-noida-and-founder-raghav-bahls-home; KN Das, 'Amnesty India Says Raid, Frozen Accounts Aimed at Silencing Government' *NY Times* (26 October 2018) www.nytimes.com/reuters/2018/10/26/world/asia/26reuters-india-amnesty.html.

[219] M Alam and N Mehrotra, 'There Is No Disputing the "Emergency-Like" Situation in the Country' (*The Wire*, 29 July 2018) https://thewire.in/government/there-should-be-no-debate-about-the-countrys-emergency-like-situation.

[220] A Saha, '245 Sedition Cases in Assam under New Govt' *Indian Express* (5 February 2019) https://indianexpress.com/article/north-east-india/assam/245-sedition-cases-in-assam-under-new-govt-5569142/.

[221] S Biswas, 'Who Killed Dr Malleshappa Kalburgi?' *BBC News* (31 August 2015) www.bbc.com/news/world-asia-india-34105187.

[222] S Biswas, 'Is India Descending into Mob Rule?' *BBC News* (26 June 2017) www.bbc.com/news/world-asia-india-40402021; H Regan and S Gupta, 'Indian Authorities Failed to Stop "Cow Vigilante" Violence: Report' *CNN* (21 February 2019) https://edition.cnn.com/2019/02/20/asia/india-cow-vigilante-hrw-report-intl/index.html. On the rise of majoritarian violence under Modi, see M Mate, 'Constitutional Erosion and the Challenge to Secular Democracy in India' in Graber et al (n 5) ch 22.

their national awards in protest.[223] Despite several allegations against Hindu nationalist groups, the federal and state governments were unable or unwilling to check, punish, credibly investigate or even condemn vigilante violence.[224] In fact, many BJP lawmakers publicly expressed support for some of these groups.[225]

It is the extensive use of violence and criminality against discursive actors that especially distinguishes democratic deconsolidation in India from similar efforts elsewhere, chiefly Hungary and Poland.

VII. Conclusion

The BJP government incrementally but systemically attacked nearly all existing mechanisms that are in place to hold the political executive to account, either by ensuring that these mechanisms became subservient to the political executive or were captured by party loyalists. Almost all the techniques of what Sadurski calls the twenty-first-century authoritarian's 'playbook' were deployed.[226] Section III shows that the electoral field was skewed to give the ruling party an advantage. In section IV, we see that the political opposition was constrained, especially by targeting the offices and institutions in which it still held sway (such as the Upper Chamber in the federal Parliament, state governments it controlled and the office of the Leader of the Opposition). Section V outlines the government's attack on (ideally) non-partisan accountability-seeking institutions, such as the judiciary and fourth branch bodies. Section VI details its silencing of discursive bodies, such as the media, universities and NGOs. The combined reading of all these efforts makes it very difficult to deny a systemic blueprint to comprehensively secure executive aggrandisement and party–state fusion in India. With multiple small steps, the state is being identified with the party, and patriotism with the BJP's narrowly defined majoritarian nationalism.[227] Opponents of the party are being labelled anti-national or traitors,[228] and independent institutions are billed as ineffective, corrupt and inefficient. An ostensible developmental agenda was used to justify the defanging of institutions that allegedly got in the way of delivering welfare to the people.

The tools for inflicting the thousand cuts were various. Measures that sought to undermine electoral accountability chiefly sought legislative or constitutional change.

[223] A Gudavarth, *India After Modi: Populism and the Right* (London, Bloomsbury, 2018) 22; 'Remove BJP, "Protect Democracy", Say 100 Filmmakers in a Joint Statement' *NDTV* (29 March 2019) www.ndtv.com/india-news/remove-bjp-protect-democracy-over-100-filmmakers-in-a-joint-statement-2014866?pfrom=home-topstories.

[224] Human Rights Watch, 'India: Unchecked Attacks on Religious Minorities, Human Rights Watch World Report' (18 January 2018) www.hrw.org/news/2018/01/18/india-unchecked-attacks-religious-minorities.

[225] ibid.

[226] W Sadurski, *Poland's Constitutional Breakdown* (Oxford, Oxford University Press, 2019) 269–70. For a documentation of some of the early moves in this direction by the first Modi regime, see A Thiruvengadam, *The Constitution of India: A Contextual Analysis* (Oxford, Hart Publishing, 2017) 235–40.

[227] See generally S Widmalm, 'Under Modi Govt, a Two-Pronged Attack on India's Democracy' (*The Wire*, 7 April 2019) https://thewire.in/politics/india-democracy-modi-government.

[228] M Kumar, 'Those Who Skip PM Rally Are Traitors, Said Giriraj Singh. Then He Bunked' *NDTV* (4 March 2019) www.ndtv.com/india-news/bjp-leader-giriraj-singh-calls-those-who-miss-pms-rally-traitors-he-also-bunks-2002513?pfrom=home-topstories.

On the other hand, while some assaults on the institutional accountability mechanisms were indeed sought through legal and constitutional change, many of them pushed against established precedents, practices and ways of doing things that were not necessarily illegal, but were certainly a breach of constitutional civility or comity.[229] Many of these acts were not so much *un*constitutional (although some clearly were) as constitutionally shameless. By claiming to be the sole repository of legitimate state power, the political executive refused to respect any autonomous zone of operation for other state institutions. Attacks on discursive institutions were either plainly violent and illegal or used the protracted and often draconian criminal law process itself as punishment. While the constitutional and legislative changes that succeeded are likely to bemore tenacious, other actions of the government also created precedents for future administrations to cite in legitimising their own excesses – just as this government cited the excesses of its predecessors even as it scaled them up to new levels of abuse.

The Constitution was being killed with a thousand cuts. This became possible in part because of some original design flaws in the Constitution (such as the centrally appointed office of governor and the inadequate protection of opposition rights), the failure of key institutional watchdogs to do their duty and the political failure of the opposition to launch a united resistance. Responding to these multiple, small-scale, incremental assaults is very difficult for checking institutions. Seen in isolation, each assault is relatively unthreatening to the constitutional scheme taken as a whole, especially when many of these abuses have been inflicted on the Constitution by previous governments as well. What set them apart was their systemicity – that so many of them were launched against constitutional institutions simultaneously and in an evidently choreographed fashion.[230]

None of this is to deny the resistance that the government faced, from state institutions as well as from the political opposition and discursive organisations. Many of its attempts on the Constitution failed precisely because of this resistance.[231] But there is need to take stock of the political and institutional weaknesses in the Indian constitutional scheme that allowed or facilitated a lot of this to happen. Indira Gandhi's excesses in the 1970s were undone politically because she lost the general elections in 1977 to a united opposition, allowing the short-lived Janata Party government to reverse her authoritarian moves by the Constitution (Forty-fourth Amendment) Act 1978. Narendra Modi, on the other hand, not only won, but increased his majority, in the 2019 general elections. In the early days of his second regime, it appears that his government has given up on the incremental techniques for constitutional evisceration that were a hallmark of his first term in office. Not only has the government moved swiftly to enact and concretise some of its proposals from its first term, it has also thrown caution to the wind by downgrading Kashmir's constitutionally guaranteed autonomous status

[229] Tushnet (n 49); T Endicott, 'Comity among Authorities' (2015) 68 *Current Legal Problems* 1.

[230] See generally 'Why Modi Must Go' *National Herald India* (16 March 2019) www.nationalheraldindia.com/opinion/why-modi-must-go-2?fbclid=IwAR0zrg_Utv91ePUjYrGuRtOG6k19attdV20RCfZlgaYHzBj02GHtdFE21Ws.

[231] See generally M Yadav, 'Even under Attack, India's Democratic Institutions Are Pushing Back' (*The Wire*, 11 March 2019) https://thewire.in/government/modi-government-pushback-democratic-institutions.

following a preposterous procedure, effectively amending the Constitution through executive action.[232]

Ultimately, the three modes of seeking executive accountability ensure that today's political losers can be tomorrow's winners. They provide political insurance to the losing side, giving them hope of future victories and thereby securing their consent to play by the rules of the democratic game and resolve disputes politically rather than violently.[233] Undermining democratic checks ultimately risks authoritarianism, and is therefore inefficient as well as unpatriotic. The people of India publicly and communally reciting the Preamble to their Constitution in continuing protests that have erupted across the country since December 2019 appear to understand this, even as India's dithering institutions either fail to grasp the enormity of the stakes or are unable or unwilling to do very much about it.

[232] B Nair, 'Abrogation of Article 370: Can the President Act without the Recommendation of the Constituent Assembly?' (2019) 3 *Indian Law Review* 254.

[233] R Dixon and T Ginsburg, 'The Forms and Limits of Constitutions as Political Insurance' (2017) 15 *International Journal of Constitutional Law* 988.

8

Dysfunction and Ad Hocism in Agenda Setting: Compromising of the Lok Sabha in India

DEVENDRA DAMLE AND SHUBHO ROY

I. Introduction

Amendments to the constitution of a country should be instituted through a cautious, deliberative process. However, India's 124th Constitutional Amendment was passed by the Lok Sabha (the Lower House of the Indian Parliament, also known as the House of the People) on the same day it was announced and introduced. The next day, the last day of that parliamentary session, the Rajya Sabha (the Upper House, also known as the Council of States) voted in favour of the Bill and the 124th Constitutional Amendment became law.[1] The controversial amendment made provisions for reservations (affirmative action quotas) for economically deprived upper caste persons in government jobs and educational institutions. It was the fastest amendment to the Indian Constitution, passed after a debate of less than eight hours.[2] How was the incumbent government able to enact such an important piece of legislation with so little advance notice and so little deliberation?

In the Westminster system, which the Indian Parliament follows, the executive is usually in charge of setting the agenda of the legislature.[3] In the early years of its independence, the Indian legislature was relatively well-functioning – a rare case among post-colonial states.[4] However, in the recent past, the Indian Parliament has often been

[1] For the legislative history of the Bill, see PRS Legislative Research, 'The Constitution (One Hundred and Twenty Fourth Amendment) Bill 2019', Briefing Note, https://prsindia.org/billtrack/the-constitution-one-hundred-and-twenty-fourth-amendment-bill-2019.

[2] For a similar example from the Rajya Sabha, see M Verma, 'Diminishing the Role of Parliament: The Case of the Jammu and Kashmir Reorganisation Bill' (2019) 54(45) *Economics and Political Weekly*, www.epw.in/engage/article/diminishing-role-parliament-case-jammu-and-kashmir.

[3] See generally S Kalitowski, 'Rubber Stamp or Cockpit? The Impact of Parliament on Government Legislation' (2008) 61 *Parliamentary Affairs* 694, https://doi.org/10.1093/pa/gsn030; R Rogers and R Walters, *How Parliament Works*, 6th edn (London, Pearson Longman, 2006).

[4] JS Wallack, 'India's Parliament as a Representative Institution' (2008) 7(2) *India Review* 91.

criticised as dysfunctional.[5] One of the reasons for this dysfunction is that parliamentary rules, as they currently stand, make it difficult to ensure constructive debate.[6] There are two commonly cited problems with the rules. One is that the opposition has little say on setting the agenda of Parliament.[7] The other is that the Speaker has sweeping discretionary powers in running the business of the House and these powers are frequently invoked in ways that deny the political opposition the right to seek to influence legislation.[8]

For Parliament to have a constructive debate on any issue, a minimum of three conditions must be fulfilled. First, Parliament should function without disruptions. Second, adequate time should be allotted for discussions. Third, Members of Parliament (MPs) should have a reasonable opportunity to prepare for parliamentary business.

While there is some literature examining the first two points, there is little to none on the third point.[9] While anecdotal accounts of the lack of adequate time for preparation exist, the magnitude of the issue has not yet been systematically quantified. In particular, the impact of the agenda-setting function and process on the efficacy of Parliament's deliberative function is underexplored in the existing literature. However, an examination of the conduct of parliamentary business and, in particular, how the agenda for each sitting of Parliament is determined is crucial to understanding the efficacy of the legislature as a check on the executive. Supposedly simple procedural aspects – such as the amount of notice given to MPs on the business of the House – impact the ability of individual members to exercise their checking function on the executive.

In this chapter, we investigate the agenda-setting record of the Lok Sabha and provide some evidence on its effect on the quality of deliberations and participation by legislators.

[5] M Guruswamy, 'Governance Failing as Houses Dysfunctional' *Deccan Chronicle* (21 December 2017) www.deccanchronicle.com/opinion/columnists/211217/governance-failing-as-houses-dysfunctional.html.

[6] J Seddon, 'The Limits of Control in Parliament' *Live Mint* (17 December 2015) www.livemint.com/Opinion/pBckM1YyJAYtsDyxabhbNP/The-limits-of-control-in-Parliament.html.

[7] MR Madhavan, Parliament Can Take Certain Steps to Reduce Disruptions' *Economic Times* (13 February 2014) https://economictimes.indiatimes.com/news/politics-and-nation/parliament-can-take-certain-steps-to-reduce-disruptions/articleshow/30363580.cms?from=mdr.

[8] A Mohammed, 'Parliament Logjam Part 3: Core Problem Cannot Be Fixed Till We Introduce Checks on Speaker's Discretionary Powers' *Firstpost* (25 April 2018) www.firstpost.com/politics/parliament-logjam-part-3-core-problem-cannot-be-fixed-till-we-introduce-checks-on-speakers-discretionary-powers-4445007.html.

[9] See Madhavan (n 7); C Roy, 'Parliamentary Disruption Has Become the Norm, This Lok Sabha Mirrors the Decline' *Indian Express* (10 January 2019) https://indianexpress.com/article/opinion/columns/a-house-in-disorder-lok-sabha-parliament-session-proceedings-5530948/; A Banare, 'Parliament Logjam Part 4: Strengthening Committee System Can Improve Quality of Drafted Laws, Fast-Track Implementation' (PRS Legislative Research, 30 April 2018) https://prsindia.org/articles-by-prs-team/parliament-logjam-part-4-strengthening-committee-system-can-improve-quality-of-drafted-laws-fast-track-implementation; PS Bajwa, 'Minimum Working Days for MPs, MLAs Needed' *Tribune India* (15 December 2018) www.tribuneindia.com/news/archive/comment/minimum-working-days-for-mps-mlas-needed-698436; RD Hedlund and PK Freeman, 'A Strategy for Measuring the Performance of Legislatures in Processing Decisions' [1981] *Legislative Studies Quarterly* 87, www.jstor.org/stable/439715.

II. Agenda Setting in the Lok Sabha

The agenda-setting power usually resides with the incumbent government and executive branch in parliamentary systems, and with the legislature in presidential systems.[10] The Indian legislature, on paper, has adopted a rare middle path for setting the legislative agenda. Though India has inherited a Westminster-style parliamentary system of government, unlike the UK, the executive has limits imposed on its powers to decide the legislative agenda. Both Houses of Parliament have inherited a system developed by India's Constituent Assembly when drafting the Indian Constitution.[11] Each House of Parliament, the Lok Sabha and the Rajya Sabha, has its own Business Advisory Committee (BAC). The BAC is composed of members from the relevant House of Parliament nominated by the Speaker of the House.[12] While the rules give the Speaker the power to nominate anyone, by convention, the Speaker ensures that most parties in Parliament have a representative on the BAC.[13] This section focuses on the role of the BAC in the Lok Sabha.[14]

The BAC, as its name suggests, is an advisory committee. Its primary function is to produce reports, which are then laid before the House for approval. The Speaker of the Lok Sabha has significant powers relating to agenda setting.[15] However, as a matter of convention, the BAC's recommendations are generally considered binding on the Speaker and the House at large.[16]

In addition to the powers of the BAC and the Speaker, the legislative agenda is also constrained by the Rules of Procedure governing the House. These rules do not control the subject matter of motions but prescribe aspects of procedure relating to those motions, including, for example, the notice period for any motion that needs to be given to members of the House. Any sitting of the House is governed by a List of Business (LoB), which is circulated in advance to each member of the House.[17] Different categories of motions have different notice requirements. For example, a motion to refer a Bill to a select committee requires two days' notice.[18] In such cases, the LoB must be published early enough to provide the requisite notice.[19] Once the LoB has been published, the rules state that it should not be changed.[20]

[10] G Tsebelis, *Veto Players: How Political Institutions Work* (Princeton, Princeton University Press, 2011) 127.

[11] For a discussion about the origins of the Business Advisory Committee, see generally BB Jena, *Parliamentary Committees in India* (Scientific Book Agency 1966).

[12] Lok Sabha Secretariat, *Rules of Procedure and Conduct of Business in Lok Sabha*, 16th edn (2019) Rule 287 (hereinafter referred to as the Rules of Procedure); Rajya Sabha Secretariat, *Rules of Procedure and Conduct of Business in the Council of States*, 6th edn (2016) Rule 30. We use the term 'Speaker' to refer to the Speaker of the Lok Sabha and the Vice-Chairman of the Rajya Sabha. Both officials perform the same functions in their respective Houses of Parliament.

[13] As evidenced by a survey of the affiliations of members of past BACs.

[14] References to 'the House' refer to the Lok Sabha.

[15] See, eg Rules 187, 190 and 194 of the Rules of Procedure.

[16] Speaker's observations on the debate on Allocation of Time Order in *Parliamentary Debates: Lok Sabha. 28 July, 1955*, C 8695–8713.

[17] Rule 31 of the Rules of Procedure.

[18] Rule 75 read with Rule 74 of the Rules of Procedure.

[19] Rule 31(3) of the Rules of Procedure.

[20] Rule 31(2) of the Rules of Procedure.

In addition, the Bill-sponsoring department of the government must circulate copies of any Bills it wants to debate to each member of the House at least two days before any motion.[21]

The combination of the BAC and the Rules of Procedure governing the minimum notice period required for the introduction of any motion in the House should result in a process that: (i) reflects a broad consensus about the work to be done by the legislature, given the inter-party membership of the BAC; and (ii) ensures adequate notice is given to all members of the House to give them sufficient time to prepare for debating any motions in advance of the actual proceedings of the House. However, there are aspects of the Rules of Procedure themselves that inhibit the achievement of these aims. The most significant of these issues is that almost every Rule of Procedure in the Lok Sabha governing agenda setting may be suspended by the Speaker.[22] The rules indicate that the Speaker should use this power only when conditions exist which require such deviation.[23] For example, the rule preventing the change in the order of business for the day states: 'Provided that such order of business shall not be varied on the day that business is set down for disposal unless the Speaker is satisfied that there is sufficient ground for such variation.'[24]

The executive branch of the government (typically a cabinet minister) may seek the Speaker's permission to take up business not listed in the LoB or to waive the requisite advance notice period for a particular item of business. This change in the business for a day is typically effected by publishing a Revised List of Business (RLoB) and/or a Supplementary List of Business (SLoB), depending on when the Speaker permits the change to be made. The RloB and SloB are not explicitly mentioned in the Rules of Procedure, and consequently there are no rules specifically governing these agenda-setting documents. They are issued under the powers granted to the Speaker to allow business not listed in the LoB and the power to allow business without the normally required advance notice.[25] As such, there are no explicit rules governing when these documents are to be published. As will be demonstrated, in practice, RLoBs are typically published before the commencement of a day of sitting, while SLoBs may be published any time, including after the day of sitting has commenced.

Taken together, these four agenda documents – the BAC Reports, the LoBs, RLoBs and SLoBs – form the universe of agenda-setting documents that are used to conduct parliamentary business in the House.[26]

This chapter provides an analysis of these documents in order to shed light on the imbalances present in the processes of parliamentary business. The discussion will show that these processes are politically charged, at worst, and procedurally dysfunctional, at best. This state of affairs compromises the quality of democratic deliberation, but also

[21] Rule 74 of the Rules of Procedure.

[22] All the rules governing agenda and business-scheduling have provisions which allow the speaker to waive the rule, except the rule that before a Bill is considered for a motion, it must be circulated amongst the members.

[23] Verma (n 2).

[24] Proviso to Rule 25 of the Rules of Procedure.

[25] See Rules 31, 74 and 77 of the Rules of Procedure.

[26] Conversations with experts confirmed the fact that there are no other agenda documents.

significantly weakens the Lok Sabha's institutional role as a check on the power of the executive. As such, these shortcomings have a severe effect on the smooth and effective functioning of the parliamentary system of India.

III. Analysing Agenda Setting in Practice: Methodology

To analyse the ground-level balance of power in the process of agenda setting in the Lok Sabha, we analysed different facets of agenda-setting documents of the period from 1 June 2009 to 13 February 2019. This time frame covers two different terms of the Lok Sabha: the fifteenth and sixteenth Lok Sabhas. During these terms, the House sat for a total of 31 sessions (15 sessions for the fifteenth House and 16 sessions for the sixteenth House).[27] For these sittings, there were a total of 116 BAC Reports, 551 LoBs, 510 RLoBs and 86 SLoBs, representing a total of 694 days of sitting (Table 8.1).

Table 8.1 Number of agenda-setting documents

Document	Fifteenth Lok Sabha	Sixteenth Lok Sabha
Advisory Committee reports	55	61
Lists of Business	217	334
Revised Lists of Business	271	239
Supplementary Lists of Business	27	59

The data set covers the fifteenth and sixteenth Lok Sabhas. The fifteenth Lok Sabha held 15 sessions, with the first session beginning on 1 June 2009 and the last session concluding on 21 February 2014. The sixteenth Lok Sabha held 16 sessions, with the first session beginning on 4 June 2014 and the last session concluding on 13 February 2019.

The metadata of the files downloaded from the House's website yielded information about the possible creation date, and thus time frame for the circulation of agenda documents.

Eight LoBs and 12 RLoBs had a time stamp later than the commencement time of the sitting for the day to which it corresponds. These time stamps indicate that these lists may have been created after that day's sitting of the House had already commenced. Of these, one document has a time stamp over a year after the day of sitting, another has a time stamp over 50 days after the date of sitting and one has a time stamp over 28 days after the date of sitting. These time stamps are obviously erroneous. Other documents with time stamps listed after the commencement of the corresponding sitting may also be considered erroneous. Therefore, a total of 31 documents were excluded from our data set. Similarly, four LoBs and three RLoBs have time stamps bearing a date of more than a year before the day of the sitting of the House. The time stamps on these seven

[27] We are unable to extend our analysis before this period as the documents are not computerised and available online in the same systematised way as they are from 2009 onwards.

documents were also classified as erroneous and the documents were therefore also excluded from the data set.[28]

To ensure that all the relevant agenda-setting documents were captured in our study, the documents were tallied against the records published by the House for a statistically significant two per cent of the dates for which the agenda documents were available. This manual check did not reveal any notable discrepancies. We further confirmed – informally, through conversations with experts and members of the House – that there were indeed no other agenda-setting documents not already captured online.

While the Lok Sabha has multiple functions, such as debating non-legislative motions, creating government reports and posing questions to the incumbent government, our focus here is solely on the legislative business of the House. The nature of some of the House's non-legislative activities is such that advance notice, or the lack thereof, is less likely to affect a member's ability to participate meaningfully in a debate on those matters. For example, the government provides no advance notice on the questions it will answer on a particular day. This, however, does not significantly affect an MP's ability to prepare for the day's business. The MP who asks a question will be prepared with supplementary questions in case the government answers it, and other MPs can always ask related questions separately. For legislative business, on the other hand, advance notice is critical. The passing of a new law relates to the coercive power a state has over its people. Thus, the issue of notice is most significant when debating a legislative Bill, as these are sizeable policy matters that require sufficient preparation in advance of the debate.

For MPs to be able to take part in deliberative functions of the House, it is necessary for the final agenda for a day of sitting to have a measure of predictability and largely follow what was decided in advance by the BAC. MPs should also be provided with adequate time to prepare for motions and debates on Bills. This study measures the ease of participation by assessing the agenda setting of the Lok Sabha with reference to two indicators: the predictability of the legislative agenda and the impact this has on the quality of deliberation in the House.

A. Predictability of the Legislative Agenda

To measure the predictability of the legislative agenda, we considered a few key questions:

- How many of the Bills recommended by the BAC made it to the LoB or RLoB?
- How many Bills were put on the RLoB without first being considered by the BAC or without being included in a LoB?
- How many Bills were put on the agenda through a SLoB without first being mentioned in any BAC Report or LoB?
- What was the duration of the notice period for the final agenda for a particular day of a parliamentary sitting (whether reflected in a LOB, RLoB or SLoB)?

[28] As per the Rules of Procedure, there should have been 694 LoBs (one for each day of each sitting); however, this discrepancy does not seem to be because of missing documents on the website. Rather, where there was no LoB, there was an RLoB. Therefore, there was always some form of agenda-setting document – either an LoB or an RLoB – for each day of each sitting of the House.

To carry out this analysis, we used a text-mining program to extract all Bills mentioned in the four sets of documents set out in Table 8.1.[29] Since there were slight variations in the names of the Bills, the Bill name data was manually cleaned up after extraction. A sample of Bills was randomly checked to ensure that our data set was comprehensive. This exercise yielded references to 637 unique Bills for the study period (2009–19).[30] For each of these Bills, we documented their inclusion in BAC Reports, LoBs, RLoBs or SLoBs. In addition, the dates of the BAC Reports, as well as the dates of the sittings for which the other three documents were intended, were collected from the Lok Sabha website. We were thus able to measure how many Bills considered by the BAC made it to the final agenda.

According to the Rules of Procedure of the Lok Sabha, for any Bill to be put on the final agenda, it must first be recommended for placement on the agenda by the BAC in its report for a relevant sitting. The government should then list the Bill in the relevant sitting's LoB and then finally in any RLoB (as the final agenda for any given day of sitting). To gauge the predictability of the legislative agenda, we analysed how often the government followed this procedure for the 637 Bills in the data set.

The LoB is intended to be the formal agenda for any given day of a sitting, as set out in the Rules of Procedure. However, the LoB has in practice generally been superseded by the RLoB, which is not currently even mentioned in the Rules of Procedure.[31] To measure the time available to an MP for preparation for a given day of a sitting, it is necessary to examine the earliest time at which these two documents may have been published. The metadata of the respective PDF files yielded the date and time of the creation of each LoB and RLoB.[32] The difference between this time stamp and the commencement time of the relevant sitting of the House, which is typically 11 am on the designated day, is likely the extent of the advance notice.[33] To illustrate the point, consider a situation where the day of sitting is 2 February and the time stamp on the LoB for that day is 3:00 pm on the day prior. The duration of advance notice is the difference, in hours, between 3:00 pm on 1 February to 11:00 am on 2 February, ie 20 hours.

There are also instances where the government issues a SLoB to further modify the agenda for any given day. This is not provided for in the Rules of Procedure. While it is not as regular a feature of the agenda-setting practice of the Lok Sabha,[34] a SLoB introduces a significant degree of unpredictability as they are typically issued with no

[29] We used the PDFminer utility for Linux to convert PDF files to text. We then used the Python 3.5 implementation of regular expressions for all text-mining.

[30] The data does not include private members' Bills but focuses on Bills introduced by the incumbent government – it is the debate of these Bills in the Lok Sabha that speaks to the capacity of the House to exercise a check on government policy as manifested in Bills introduced by the government. Further, the number of private members Bills is very large, they are rarely mentioned in the BAC Report or LoB and are almost never taken up for consideration. Thus, including them in this analysis would not have been useful for the present exercise.

[31] See Rule 31, which only provides for an LoB.

[32] We used the *pdfinfo* utility for Linux to extract the metadata.

[33] We confirmed, through informal interviews with recently retired officials of the Lok Sabha Secretariat, that the PDF of the LoB or RLoB circulated among the members and the one posted on the website are the same document. Further, through informal interviews with the staff of MPs, we were able to confirm that since 2009, the MPs themselves use the LoB and RLoB as posted on the Lok Sabha website to plan their business. They find this to be convenient because the LoBs and RLoBs are published there well before the MP's office receives the printed versions in their official communication.

[34] As shown in Table 8.1, there were only 86 SLoBs, compared with 551 LoBs and 510 RLoBs, for the duration of the study period.

advance notice and often after the sitting for a day commences. This is indicative of a disregard for the need for sufficient notice for parliamentary deliberations.[35] Therefore, this analysis also considers the timing of the circulation of any SLoB.

B. Quality of Legislative Deliberation

To examine whether the lack of predictability in the legislative agenda had any bearing on the quality of deliberation, we looked into how much MPs participated in debates on Bills. This study measures the degree of participation using two parameters:

1. *Time spent discussing Bills:*
   How much time did MPs spend debating Bills on the final agenda of the House? Was there a difference in the time spent debating Bills that followed the de jure agenda-setting procedure compared to those which did not?
2. *Amendments tabled for Bills:*
   How many amendments were tabled for Bills on the final agenda of the House after the setting of the final agenda? Was there a difference in the number of amendments tabled for Bills that follow the appropriate agenda-setting procedure compared to those which do not?[36]

To carry out an analysis of the quality of the debate, we again looked at publicly available records from the Lok Sabha. The Lok Sabha's Secretariat publishes a 'Résumé of Work' after every session which identifies all of the Bills passed in the session and records the time that was spent on debating each one. These documents report the date a Bill was introduced and passed, the time spent debating the Bill, and the number of amendments tabled and carried for each Bill. After tabulating this data for each Bill, we further analysed it in relation to the data on the predictability of the legislative agenda for the relevant Bill. The Bills were then classified into two groups, based on whether or not the proper agenda-setting process was followed before listing them in the final agenda. The proper procedure would be indicated by a first listing in an Advisory Committee Report, then in a List of Business and subsequently in a Revised List, if applicable.

Fifteen Résumés of Work are available for the fifteenth Lok Sabha and 17 are available for the sixteenth Lok Sabha. While the sixteenth Lok Sabha held only 16 sessions, one of the sessions was held in two parts – so there are two separate Résumés of Work for the sixteenth session of the sixteenth Lok Sabha. Of the 637 Bills identified from the agenda-setting documents, 511 appeared on the final agenda of the House through either an RLob or SLoB. The Résumés of Work contain information on the time spent debating these Bills and the amendments tabled for 406 of them. Out of these 406 Bills, 84 were appropriations Bills. Appropriations Bills are not debated, and no amendments

[35] Also, while quantitatively there are fewer instances of an SLoB being issued, it would be interesting to note the nature of the Bills or amendments to Bills included on the SLoB and whether significant government policy was transacted under the revised agenda set out in the SLoB.

[36] The amendments tabled for a Bill are also indicative of the predictability of the agenda, since devising and drafting an amendment would require adequate advance notice. However, the fact of tabling an amendment speaks to the engagement of an MP in the deliberative process, and therefore we include it under the indicators of the quality of deliberation.

can be tabled for them.[37] These 84 Bills were, accordingly, excluded from our data set, which focuses on the remaining 322 non-appropriation Bills from the original 511 Bills identified from the agenda-setting documents.

IV. Analysing Agenda Setting in Practice: Unpredictability and Dysfunction in the Agenda-Setting Process

Our analysis shows that the BAC – despite its powers under the Rules of Procedure – does not exercise substantial control over the agenda of the Lok Sabha. There are frequent and substantial changes to the agenda of the House, with MPs typically only getting a few hours' advance notice to prepare for debates on Bills. As such, there is a high degree of unpredictability in relation to the agenda.

The problem of unpredictability appears to be at least partially rooted in the lack of regular BAC meetings to discuss and set the agenda for the House. Figure 8.1 shows the distribution of the duration between consecutive BAC Reports. There is a large variation in the number of days between meetings of the BAC. At times, BAC meetings take place within a span of two days, while at other times there is a gap of more than 120 days between meetings. The average number of days between meetings is 30, with a standard deviation of 38 days. Typically, the gap between two BAC meetings could be anywhere between seven days (25th percentile) and 37 (75th percentile).

Figure 8.1 The duration between consecutive BAC Reports varies greatly

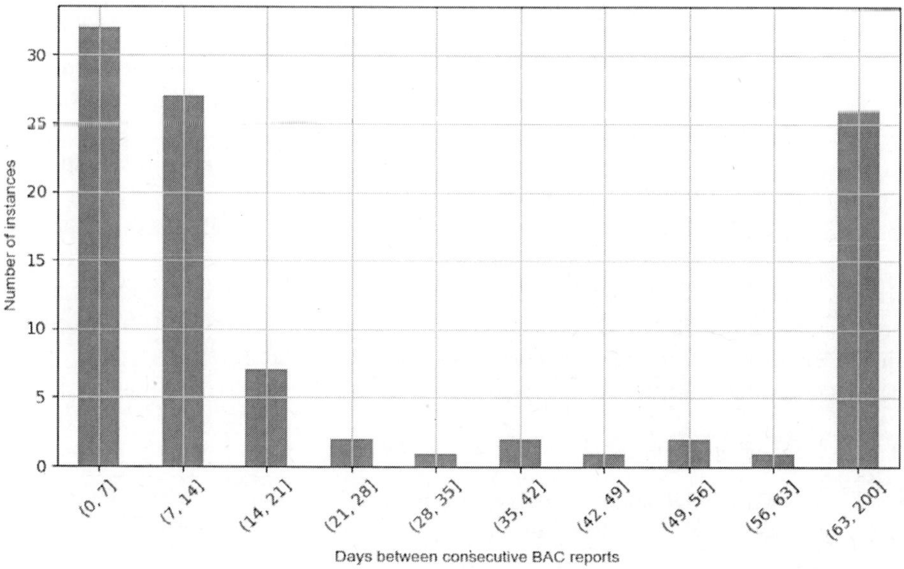

[37] Appropriation Bills merely authorise the drawing of funds from the Consolidated Fund of India in accordance to an already approved money Bill that has been debated and passed by the legislation. Therefore, appropriation Bills are seen as a technical requirement and not a substantive new law. As per convention, they are not debated.

The BAC Reports also rarely allocated a date for the discussion of the Bills they recommended be placed on the agenda, although the Reports did specify the recommended number of hours to be spent debating a particular Bill. The reason for the omission of a recommended date is unclear.

A. Unpredictability of the Legislative Agenda

The irregularity of the BAC meetings, by itself, would not have been a significant issue if the LoBs and RLoBs were followed during a sitting.

In total, 637 unique Bills were brought before the fifteenth and sixteenth Lok Sabhas. If the Lok Sabha Rules of Procedure were correctly adhered to, a Bill would first be discussed in a BAC meeting, then be included in a BAC Report to the Speaker recommending its inclusion in the agenda for the next sitting, then subsequently be included in an LoB and then in an RLoB (if any). In an ideal situation, the recommended LoB or RLoB would be sent out sufficiently in advance of a sitting. On occasion, however, the House would run out of time on a given day and have to postpone some of its business.

When the House runs out of time before the business of the day is finished, there are two approaches to deal with the items of business that are left over: either the Bill is shifted to another day within the same session or it is abandoned for that session and picked up again in a subsequent one. In both circumstances, if MPs receive adequate advance notice, the Rules of Procedure are not undermined. However, if a Bill that is recommended for debate by the BAC is subsequently omitted from the LoB or RLoB, this is a severe contravention of the required procedure.

Bills that are not in the BAC Report or the LoB should ideally not be listed in an RLoB, and especially not an SLoB. Both these documents are artefacts that exist due to the Speaker's discretion to allow business to be conducted without advance notice, as discussed above. As such, these documents are not explicitly provided for in the Rules of Procedure for the Lok Sabha. Bearing in mind the importance of MPs having adequate notice to prepare for and participate in debate, neither of those documents should form the basis for agenda setting, except in exceptional situations.

Listing Bills for debate in an SLoB in particular lowers predictability, because they are typically issued after a sitting has commenced. However, SLoBs have become a regular feature of the agenda-setting process. To mitigate the impact they have on the predictability and quality of debate, they should at least adhere to the recommendations made by the BAC and any earlier LoB – not making significant departures from previously agreed agenda items. Table 8.2 sets out the number of Bills appearing in each document type.

Table 8.2 Listing of Bills in agenda-setting documents

Document	Total number of Bills appearing in the document	Expected number of Bills in the document
BAC Report	348 (54.6 per cent)	637
LoB	391 (61.4 per cent)	637
RLoB	476 (74.7 per cent)	637
SLoB	86 (13.5 per cent)	0

This data demonstrates that 45.4 per cent of the Bills brought before the House were not recommended for debate by the BAC in its report.[38] Similarly, 38.6 per cent of the Bills included in LoBs were never actually debated in the relevant sitting. This indicates that the incumbent government systematically disregarded the proper process for setting the legislative agenda. This is further made clear by an examination of where the Bills typically originated and the parliamentary process through which they were included in the agenda.

(i) Origins of Bills

As a matter of procedure and under Rules 190, 288 and 290A, all 637 Bills should only have been introduced in the Lok Sabha if they were recommended for inclusion by the BAC in its report for a relevant sitting. It should then have been included in an LoB and carried through into an RLoB. However, the data shows that the introduction of most Bills did not follow this process.

Table 8.3 First appearance of Bills by type of agenda-setting document

Origin of Bills	Number	Percentage
Bills originating in an Advisory Committee Report	175	27.5
Bills originating in a List of Business	208	32.7
Bills originating in a Revised List	195	27.5
Bills originating in a Supplementary List	59	9.3
Total	637	100

As Table 8.3 shows, less than one-third of all Bills in our data set were considered and recommended by the BAC. Of the 175 Bills originating from a BAC recommendation, 95 actually ended up on the final agenda of the House, whether in an RLoB or SLoB. A substantial number of Bills originated in the LoB. While there was some degree of advance notice in the case of LOB-originated Bills, these are still instances of the government bypassing the BAC and therefore undermining the consensus-building mechanism that the BAC is supposed to provide.

A large number of Bills are first put on the agenda through RLoBs, meaning many of the Bills were put on the agenda without any significant advance notice, bypassing the BAC. Finally, a significant number of Bills originated in SLoBs. These were almost always issued after the commencement of the House proceedings, thus representing a gross violation of the letter and spirit of the agenda-setting rules.

It is important to note that some Bills that initially bypassed the BAC and were put on the agenda for the first time through an LoB, RLoB or SLoB were then subsequently sent for consideration to the BAC and then only put on the relevant list again after a proper BAC recommendation. However, this corrective action was not followed for all Bills. Table 8.4 summarises such instances.

[38] Numbers total more than 637 because many Bills appear in multiple documents.

Table 8.4 Abandoned Bills and Bills listed without following the proper procedure

Where a Bill was mentioned	No
Bills only mentioned in an Advisory Committee Report	75
Bills only mentioned in a List of Business	40
Bills only mentioned in a Revised List	82
Bills only mentioned in a Supplementary List	30

Table 8.4 shows that 75 of the 348 Bills recommended for inclusion on the agenda by the BAC were never mentioned in any other list of business. These are instances of the government completely ignoring the recommendations of the BAC. The 40 Bills that were listed in an LoB but not in a subsequent RLoB or SLoB are instances of the government indicating a certain agenda in advance but ultimately not following it. Finally, the 112 Bills which only ever appeared in an RLoB or SLoB are instances of more egregious abuse of process by the government. These are Bills that were put on the agenda without any advance notice, and without any attempt at utilising the consensus-based BAC.

(ii) Journey of a Bill

An examination of the journey of the 348 Bills featured in the BAC's recommendations provides an insight into the government's failure to comply with the Rules of Procedure, and thus yields a finer understanding of issue of predictability. Of these 348 Bills, 175 originated in a BAC Report, ie the government gave the House advance notice of its intention to put the Bills on the agenda. However, 173 of the 348 Bills made their first appearance in a document other than a BAC Report, but were subsequently recommended by the BAC.

There are five reasons why this could have happened – ie that a Bill was only subsequently referred to in a BAC Report. First, when a Bill is referred to the Rajya Sabha (the Upper House) but the Rajya Sabha either passes it with some amendments or rejects it, the Lok Sabha has to reconsider the Bill. Second, when the President exercises their power under Article 111 of the Constitution of India to return a Bill to Parliament for reconsideration, both Houses have to consider and pass the Bill again, with or without amendments. Third, when the House votes to refer a Bill to a Parliamentary Committee for scrutiny, the Committee studies the Bill and then tables its report on the Bill, along with any recommended amendments. The House then has to consider the Bill alongside these recommendations. In all three cases, the government may have introduced the Bill on the agenda without sufficient advance notice, but upon subsequent consideration of the same Bill it gave advance notice by procuring a recommendation from the BAC. Fourth, the government may attempt to put a Bill on the agenda without notice but it does not get taken up, either because of disruptions or because of a paucity of time. Fifth, the Bill may be large and complex, necessitating multiple days of deliberation. In such cases, the government may give advance notice by seeking a recommendation from the BAC for any subsequent times it wants to put the Bill on the agenda.

Both types of Bill – BAC-originated ones as well as those subsequently recommended by a BAC Report – are included in the analysis in this section. There are two reasons for this. First, it is not easy to determine which of the aforementioned cases applies to a given

Bill. The information may or may not be mentioned in the BAC Report or the Résumé of Work. Second, this study is attempting to gauge how often the government followed the proper agenda-setting procedure. These instances of corrective action, ie where the government initially attempted to put a Bill on the final agenda without advance notice but subsequently did follow the proper procedure, need to be included. Table 8.5 summarises the journey of the 348 Bills that were recommended (at any point) in BAC Reports.

Table 8.5 Journey of a Bill from the BAC

Chronology of Bills appearing in different lists	**No**
Total Bills appearing in an Advisory Committee Report	348
1. Bills that make it to the final agenda with some advance notice	
1.1 Bills listed in a Advisory Committee Report, followed by a List of Business, followed by a Revised List on a date before the next Advisory Committee Report is issued, but within the same session (ie proper procedure)	112
1.2 Bills listed in an Advisory Committee Report, followed by a List of Business, followed by a Revised List on a date after the next Advisory Committee Report is issued, but within the same session	1
1.3 Bills listed in an Advisory Committee Report, followed by a List of Business, followed by a Revised List in a subsequent session	19
2. Bills that make it to the final agenda without proper advance notice	
2.1 Bills listed in an Advisory Committee Report, followed by a Revised List, skipping the List of Business	60
2.2 Bills listed in an Advisory Committee Report, followed by a Supplementary List, skipping the List of Business and Revised List	24
2.3 Bills listed in an Advisory Committee Report released on the same date as the Revised List	31
2.4 Bills listed first in a Revised List and then listed in an Advisory Committee Report at some later date	10
3. Bills that never make it to the final agenda	
3.1 Bills listed in an Advisory Committee Report, followed by a List of Business but not in a Revised List or Supplementary List (ie not on the final agenda of the House)	16
3.2 Bills listed only in an Advisory Committee Report	75

As Table 8.5 shows, 112 of the 348 Bills recommended by the BAC (ie 32 per cent) were put on the agenda of the House with proper advance notice. This represents 17 per cent of the total Bills in the data set. In other words, less than one-fifth of the legislative agenda of the House was set with the appropriate procedure envisaged in the Lok Sabha Rules of Procedure. Similarly, 36 per cent of the Bills recommended by the BAC (19 per cent of the total) were taken up in the House, but without sufficient advance notice. Finally, 26 per cent of the Bills recommended by the BAC were never taken up by the House. This indicates that the government has set the majority of the legislative business of the House on short notice and without consulting the opposition through the BAC. This is further reflected in the number of Bills that do not originate in a BAC Report, as shown in Table 8.4.

It must be noted that this is a lenient assessment of the agenda-setting process. As already explained, in this analysis, if the government lists a Bill incorrectly in the first instance but then follows the procedure for any later considerations of the same Bill, this has been counted as compliance with the proper procedure. This should not be taken to mean that the government always and consistently takes this corrective action, without any further attempts to bypass the BAC; only in the case of 71 of the 348 Bills (20 per cent) did the government take such action.

The indicators above are just one way of measuring the efficiency of the agenda-setting process. As the next sub-section shows, even when a Bill is listed using the right process, this does not on its own result in the strong predictability of parliamentary business at any particular sitting.

(iii) Regularity of the Listing in Each Agenda-Setting Document

Only 136 of the 637 Bills in the data set were listed using the proper process. However, even in these instances, there is considerable variation in the time between the recommendation by the BAC and its listing in an LoB and subsequently in an RLoB. Table 8.6 summarises the duration between the time that the Bills were listed in each of these documents.

Table 8.6 Duration between listing in different agenda-setting documents

Time (in days)	Median	Max	Min
Time gap between listing in an Advisory Committee Report and a List of Business	6	426	0
Time gap between listing in a List of Business and a Revised List	1	302	0
Time gap between listing in an Advisory Committee Report and a Revised List	8	479	0

As the table demonstrates, even when the government follows the proper sequence for listing a Bill on the agenda, there is little consistency in the duration between the Bill receiving the BAC's recommendation and its listing on the final agenda (ie RLoB). In the most egregious cases, some Bills recommended by the BAC were only listed on the final agenda more than a year after the recommendation, while at the opposite end, some Bills were added to the RLoB on the same day as a recommendation by the BAC.

In summary, the final agenda for a day of sitting cannot be reliably predicted from the preceding BAC Report (or previous LoB in the case of an RLoB). This on its own would not be a problem if the relevant LoB was issued well in advance of the actual day of a sitting. However, that is not the case. The next sub-section examines how much in advance LoBs, RLoBs and SLoBs were issued.

B. Unpredictable Notice Periods

The Rules of Procedure require notice of the agenda to be given at least one day before the sitting for most legislative work. As Table 8.7 shows, on average, LoBs were created

53.2 hours (ie a little over two days) in advance of a sitting. While, on average, members receive approximately two days' notice of the legislative agenda for a sitting, in 63 per cent of the cases, the LoB was created less than two days in advance – in contravention of the rules.

Table 8.7 Hours from publication to commencement of sitting

Indicator	List of Business	Revised List	Supplementary List
Median (typical value)	44.7	15.7	–1.9
Maximum (ie earliest)	160.9	64.6	5.3
Minimum (ie latest)	0.3	0.1	–27.5

For 75 per cent of the sittings, the LoB was superseded by an RLoB. Furthermore, RLoBs were on average published 16.4 hours before the commencement of the relevant sitting. Most members therefore have only nine office hours to prepare for items on the agenda. SLoBs almost always carry a time stamp of creation that is after the sitting of the House commences. In the most egregious case, a backdated list was published the day after a sitting.[39]

The occasions where Bills are put on the agenda through a SLoB are especially problematic. On a total of five occasions, the SLoBs carried a time stamp that was after the conclusion of the sitting of the House. Effectively, in these cases, the government discussed a Bill in the House and published the agenda after the fact. A total of six Bills have been taken up in the Lok Sabha in this manner.

Of all the Bills brought before the House through SLoB, 19 were mentioned in either a report by the BAC or an LoB or RLoB beforehand. Many of the Bills put on the agenda through SLoBs included Bills of the kind that require extensive deliberation. This includes finance Bills, which deal with government expenditure, Bills which introduced significant changes to the tax structure (eg Goods and Services Tax Bills), Bills which introduce new criminal offences (eg the Benami Transactions Prohibition Bill, 2015), Bills which introduce major structural reforms (eg Insolvency and Bankruptcy Code, 2016), major changes to the securities trading laws, Bills for establishing the offices of Lokayukta and Lokpals (offices that are supposed to investigate cases of government corruption), Bills for exercising the eminent domain powers of the government and Bills which redraw the boundaries of states. This leads to the possible conclusion that SLoBs were used to prevent substantial discussion on important Bills.

Some of the problems of the short notice to MPs about the business of the House would be mitigated if MPs were informed about the Bills to be discussed in a session of the House. MPs would not have information about the daily agenda, but the BAC recommendations would give MPs a general idea of the business the House would transact over the session. However, as our analysis shows, the general legislative agenda is rarely decided well in advance. This, combined with the fact that RLoBs are published

[39] This is technically permissible because the notice of the modification to the agenda via an SLoB can be submitted in the House without publishing it or disseminating it among the MPs. The Speaker has the discretion to allow the items in the SLoB so submitted to be put on the agenda of the House.

just hours before the commencement of a day of sitting, leads to extreme unpredictability. The result is that an MP can rarely be adequately prepared for a day of business in the House.

C. Quality of Debate and Participation by MPs

The indicators examined so far – the predictability of the legislative agenda and the notice times – are both indicative of the status of the input side of legislative business. This sub-section explores the consequences of this in relation to the output-side indicators. As has been established, MPs do not have adequate time to prepare for and thus participate in parliamentary proceedings. As a result, it would be expected that for Bills that have been put on the agenda in compliance with the agenda-setting process, participation from MPs would be greater. To examine this, we used two measures as indicators of the degree of participation by MPs: time spent on debating a Bill and the number of amendments tabled.[40] The Bills in the data set have been classified on the basis of whether or not the proper agenda-setting process was followed.

Figure 8.2 shows a box-and-whisker plot of the distribution of the time spent on discussion of each Bill in the House. The top boundary of the box represents the 75th percentile, the bottom boundary represents the 25th percentile and the line in the middle represents the median. The ends of the 'whiskers' represent the maximum and minimum, ie the 100th percentile and 0th percentile, respectively.

Figure 8.2 Following the proper process leads to greater time spent on discussion

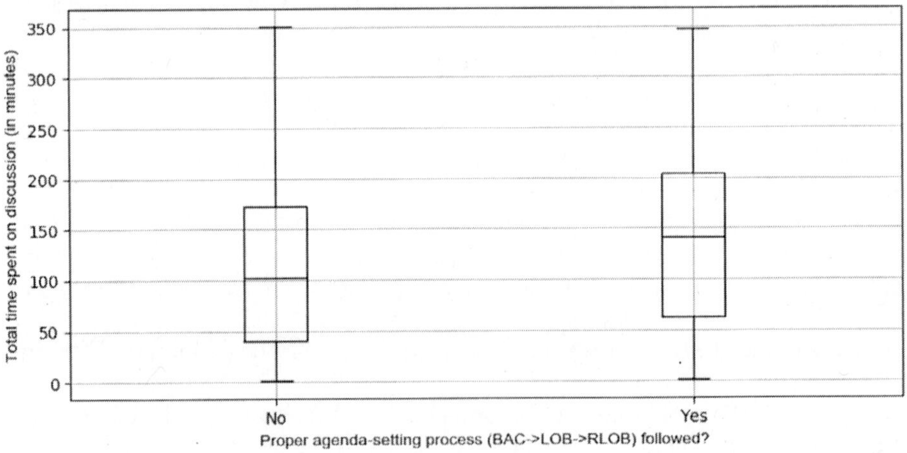

[40] We acknowledge that the duration of debate does not equate to good 'quality' debate – but are using it as one indicator to determine how much preparation might have been possible; preparation being manifested in the extent of the contribution MPs were able to make.

As the figure shows, Bills that were put on the agenda after following the proper agenda-setting process were typically discussed for a longer time than those that were put on the agenda without following the proper process. The median time spent debating Bills that did not follow the proper process was 102 minutes, while the median discussion time for properly processed Bills was 141 minutes. In other words, the duration of discussion was 38 per cent longer for Bills brought to the House following the proper process as compared to the other Bills. This difference in the discussion time is statistically significant.[41] Even though both time spans – 141 and 102 minutes – may seem insufficient for thorough deliberation, the fact that compliance with the agenda-setting process increases the total time spent on discussion is significant.

Figure 8.3 shows a box-and-whisker plot of the distribution of the number of amendments tabled for each Bill in the House.

Figure 8.3 When the proper process is followed more amendments are tabled

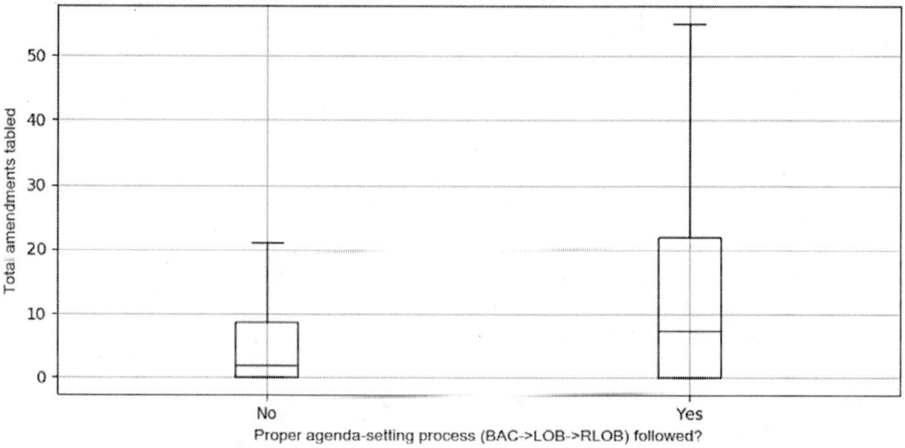

As Figure 8.3 shows, the Bills in which the proper agenda-setting process was followed attracted significantly more amendments from MPs. The median number of amendments tabled for Bills in which the agenda-setting process was not followed was 0, while the median number of amendments tabled for Bills in which the process was faithfully followed was 7.5. In other words, MPs typically tabled amendments on Bills far more frequently when the legislative agenda was predictable as compared to when it was not. One can also estimate the statistical likelihood that no amendments will be tabled for a Bill that was not tabled following the correct procedure, using odds ratios.

[41] A Welch's t-test was used to compare the mean discussion time for Bills in which the proper process was followed and the Bills in which it was not. It gave a p-value of 0.035, which means the difference is significant at the 5% level of significance.

Table 8.8 When the proper procedure is followed there is more participation in legislative work

	Proper process followed?	
At least one amendment tabled?	**Yes**	**No**
Yes	83	117
No	30	92

Using the values shown in Table 8.8, if a Bill follows the consultative process, the odds ratio of an amendment being proposed is 2.175, and the 95 per cent confidence intervals are 3.583 and 1.321.[42] This indicates that when the proper process is followed, the likelihood that at least one amendment will be tabled for a Bill is nearly double that of when the process is not followed; this difference is statistically significant.[43] Both these indicators – the likelihood of amendments being tabled and the duration of debate – demonstrate that the predictability of the legislative agenda has tangible effects on MPs' participation in the House. Greater predictability is correlated with greater participation by MPs. Whilst these indicators do not necessarily equate to a higher quality of deliberation, their relationship with the predictability of the legislative agenda is nonetheless salient.

V. Conclusion

Our study shows that there is a great degree of ad hocism in the Lok Sabha's agenda-setting process. The BAC does not meet regularly, and the duration between meetings varies. Most of the Advisory Committee's recommendations are not included in the formal agenda of the House. Almost half of the Bills recommended by the BAC are never put before the House. Only one-quarter of the Bills brought before the House originate from a BAC Report, with approximately three-quarters of all Bills originating in an LoB, RLoB or SLoB. Legislative business is often added to the agenda without first being approved by the BAC. Furthermore, the final agenda often does not resemble the formal agenda as declared in the LoB. In a few instances, new Bills are put on the agenda after the sitting of the House has already commenced. This further undermines the BAC's consensus-building role. It also creates a great deal of unpredictability in the agenda for any given day. A Bill being recommended by the BAC or being listed in the LoB is not a reliable indicator of whether the Bill will be taken up by the House on the specified day or any day shortly after the day for which the LoB is intended. This indicates that the BAC's role as a consensus-building forum for agenda setting has been systematically undermined by incumbent governments.

[42] The odds ratio for an amendment being tabled if the proper agenda-setting process is followed is calculated as $(83 \times 92)/(117 \times 30) = 2.175$.

[43] An odds ratio greater than 1 indicates that the likelihood of an amendment getting tabled is higher in the case of Bills in which the proper process was followed. The statistical significance of the effect is confirmed by the values of the upper and lower 95% confidence intervals. Since both these values are above 1, there is only a 5% probability that the association we observe between the proper process being followed and amendments being tabled is due to random chance.

There is also a severe lack of time given to MPs for adequate consideration of Bills proposed by the government. The formal agenda set out in the LoB is changed substantially on short notice. The LoB is typically prepared 44 hours (approximately two days) before the day of the sitting of the House, while the RLoB is prepared 16 hours in advance. For approximately one-quarter of all Bills that originate in an RLoB, MPs get a mere 16 hours of advance notice. It is also not uncommon for Bills to be introduced without any advance notice, through SLoB, which is typically issued two hours after the commencement of the sitting. The effect of compliance or non-compliance with the agenda-setting process is reflected in the duration of debates and the number of amendments, both of which offer some indication of the ability of MPs to prepare for deliberations. Inadequate preparation and low-quality input from MPs also impact public confidence in the legislature. Additionally, such lack of notice undermines the rights of the opposition to prepare and debate the government's legislative proposals.[44]

This leads to an important question: is the discretion afforded to the Speaker in deciding the business of the House being misused by the incumbent governments to prevent substantive discussion over Bills? The constitutional function of the Lok Sabha – as a check on the executive – depends on the quality of input members can provide on government policy manifested in legislative Bills. The exact effect size of the unpredictability in business scheduling on the quality of debate is difficult to isolate, given the existence of a multitude of structural issues plaguing the Lok Sabha (and Rajya Sabha). However, even if some of the reforms – such as dedicated opposition days and increased overall number of days of sitting – are implemented, the quality of debate will remain low if parliamentary process continues to be abused. While there are no guaranteed solutions, a greater focus on preventing abuse of process could help to transfer control of House business from the executive to the MPs. In this regard, further empowering the BAC and introducing more stringent checks on the Speaker of the House may help to prevent the abuse of the process by the incumbent government.

Several potential measures may be considered. Firstly, the House could be required to publish a full legislative calendar before the session begins. Similarly, a rule could be introduced requiring a two-thirds majority in the House for any amendments to the legislative calendar. The same mechanism could be instituted for the daily agenda, with the full listing of business published at least two days before the sitting and any changes requiring a House vote. A further intervention worth considering is to institute a mandatory one-week period between the introduction and publication of a Bill, the clause-by-clause consideration and the passing of the Bill. To allow the government to fast-track certain legislation in emergencies, the rules could allow for the one-week interval to be waived if the House votes for it by a two-thirds majority.

The business allocation and scheduling mechanism in the Lok Sabha is broken. There is no doubt the Speaker needs some discretion in setting the agenda. However, as it stands, the system makes it almost impossible for even well-meaning MPs to participate effectively in the Lok Sabha's proceedings. Until this is fixed, MPs cannot reasonably be

[44] See generally E Bulmer, *Opposition and Legislative Minorities: Constitutional Roles, Rights and Recognition* (Stockholm, International Institute for Democracy and Electoral Assistance, 2021).

expected to be able to engage in constructive debate in the Lok Sabha. This chapter has offered a detailed analysis and diagnosis of the procedural shortcomings in the legislative process. Further, the proposals presented here strike a balance between respecting the prerogative of the government to set the agenda of the House and preventing it from abusing its power to negatively affect the deliberative process. This will ensure that the executive seeks compromise with the opposition parties to enact any changes to the pre-decided agenda. While these suggested changes to the rules are merely a small part of a broader range of much-needed reforms, they are a significant step towards strengthening the essential deliberative role of the legislature in India's parliamentary democracy.

9

Dysfunctional Resilience in the Afghan Civil Service

EBRAHIM AFSAH

The concept of resilience is at the centre of current debates in development, climate change adaptation and humanitarian aid. However, it is not clear what resilience is, or how it can or should be promoted during and after crises.[1]

I. Introduction

Resilience describes people's ability to cope with shocks. Innate characteristics, conscious choices and the vicissitudes of the shock itself all affect how well the individual or group can recover from it and return to a stable equilibrium. A useful quality for any individual or group, there has been considerable research on the nature, genesis and development of resilience,[2] defined as 'the process of, capacity for, or outcome of *successful adaptation* despite challenging or threatening circumstances' (emphasis added),[3] Being able to take a hit and bounce back is a much-revered quality, even if it remains unclear why some stumble while others thrive.[4] The attractiveness of this elusive quality has given the term much traction well beyond the disciplines of psychology[5] and ecology,[6] where

[1] S Levine et al, 'The Relevance of "Resilience"?' (September 2012) HPG Policy Brief No 49, 1 www.odi.org/sites/odi.org.uk/files/odi-assets/publications-opinion-files/7818.pdf.

[2] 'Building the resilience of nations communities to disasters' is the explicit aim of the Hyogo Framework for Action (HFA), a 10-year plan endorsed by the UN General Assembly in its Resolution A/RES/60/195 and implemented UN Office for Disaster Risk Reduction (UNISDR). For more information, see www.unisdr.org/we/coordinate/hfa.

[3] AS Masten, KM Best and N Garmezy, 'Resilience and Development: Contributions from the Study of Children who Overcome Adversity' (1990) 2 *Development and Psychopathology* 425, 425.

[4] 'My exploration has taught me much about resilience, although it's a subject none of us will ever understand fully. Indeed, resilience is one of the great puzzles of human nature, like creativity or the religious instinct'. D Coutu, 'How Resilience Works' (2002) 80(5) *Harvard Business Review* 46, 47.

[5] In psychology, the importance of the concept had been recognised for centuries, as noted with reference to Pinel by M Rutter, 'Resilience in the Face of Adversity: Protective Factors and Resistance to Psychiatric Disorder' [1985] *British Journal of Psychiatry* 598.

[6] Perhaps the originator of the term is CS Holling, 'Resilience and Stability of Ecological Systems' [1973] *Annual Review of Ecology and Systematics* 1.

it had originally developed,[7] so that today it is sometimes described as the 'sexiest new buzzword in international development'.[8]

Afghans take great pride in being a hardy people, a quality necessitated by the country's unforgiving geography and endemic conflict. It is undeniable that decades of conflict have exacted a heavy toll on her people and institutions, leaving an exceedingly thin veneer of formal governance. The recent withdrawal of American troops, which ended the presence of international assistance in Afghanistan, was dramatic, but hardly unexpected. The speed of the collapse of the Afghan state might have been surprising, but not its brittleness and the lack of loyalty from its personnel. The failure to create a reasonably coherent state has been apparent for many years and this chapter examines one important but under-studied factor in that failure, namely the ability of the civil service to resist externally imposed administrative reform.

Surprising to the uninitiated but well known to area experts[9] is the relative strength of *informal* institutions persisting despite the prolonged strain of violent conflict.[10] The aim of this chapter is therefore *not* to discuss the theory and practice of what euphemistically is called 'hybrid governance', namely the discharge of essential public functions by a shifting array of private and informal actors.[11] Rather, this chapter argues that the persistence of informal institutions is partly the result of the successful adaptation of *formal* institutions – here, the bureaucracy in Afghanistan – to externally imposed change considered challenging or threatening. In other words, this chapter shows how the very resilience of the Afghan bureaucracy constitutes a major obstacle to the creation of effective statehood and more formal governance.

This is a counter-intuitive finding in the literature on the administrative state. Most comparative public law scholarship takes the extant administrative structure as a given, which is useful for investigating highly institutionalised, stable and prosperous states. The underlying administrative and institutional structure is seen as a major source of long-term stability. Even profound normative change does not affect this solid foundation, reflected in the well-worn adage repeated by generations of German law students that 'constitutional law withers, but administrative law remains'.[12] This reflects the evident continuity of German and Austrian public law, administrative culture and

[7] A good overview of the genesis of the concept can be found in SB Manyena, 'The Concept of Resilience Revisited' [2006] *Disasters* 434.

[8] M Hussain, 'Resilience: Meaningless Jargon or Development Solution?' *The Guardian* (5 March 2013).

[9] PA Calogero and S Schütte, 'Informalität von oben und unten. Stadtentwicklung in Kabul im Kontext von Staatsaufbau und militärisch-humanitärer Intervention' [2018] *Zeitschrift für kritische Stadtforschung* 7; LM Edwards, 'State-Building in Afghanistan: A Case Showing the Limits?' [2010] *International Review of the Red Cross* 967, 987.

[10] The strength of tribal culture and kinship ties is emphasised in all anthropological descriptions of Afghanistan before the war. See, eg L Dupree, *Afghanistan* (Princeton, Princeton University Press, 1980) 248–51; see also F Barth, *Political Leadership among Swat Pathans* (London, Athlone Press, 1959). Much of this informal structure survived the years of war surprisingly intact, see F Barth, *Afghanistan og Taliban* (Oslo, Pax Forlag 2010); BR Rubin, *The Search for Peace in Afghanistan: From Buffer State to Failed State* (New Haven, Yale University Press, 1995).

[11] For a good introduction to this line of thought, correctly stressing path dependency and the importance of local context, see BG Peters and J Pierre, 'Governance without Government? Rethinking Public Administration' [1998] *Journal of Public Administration Research and Theory* 223.

[12] 'Verfassungsrecht vergeht, Verwaltungsrecht besteht', foreword to O Mayer, *Deutsches Verwaltungsrecht*, Band I, 3rd edn (Berlin, Springer, 1969, first published 1924).

organisational structure despite the cataclysmic transformations after 1918 from monarchy to republic to dictatorship and back after 1945.[13] One of the most vivid illustrations of this overarching truth has been the programmatic Directive JCS 1067 of April 1945, which laid out the aims of the Allied occupation of Germany. The directive instructed the Commander-in-Chief of the occupation forces to remove politically suspect individuals, associations and institutions from public life, but also ordered the vast majority of the organs and officials of the defeated state to return to work and operate as before: 'American policy has consistently favoured the strengthening of a democratic Germany by assigning important administrative functions to German governmental units as rapidly as their political reliability was clearly established.'[14]

Occupation – and eventually reconstruction – policy was therefore premised on removing and punishing ideologically suspect elements through de-Nazification, while assuming that the state machinery, including most of the private and public law of the land, would remain in place and continue to operate.[15] The single biggest conceptual failure of the American occupation policy in Iraq has been the application of this framework to the entirely different Iraqi context. As such, it was expected that the authoritarian state could be purged of its ideologically suspect elements, ie so-called 'de-Baathification',[16] while leaving an otherwise operational state apparatus in place.[17] The underlying administrative system turned out to be much weaker and less cohesive, and the ideological element much harder to identify than in the German context, leading to the near-collapse of governance institutions.

Still, the underlying continuity of administrative practices and organisational forms does create strong path dependencies in all political communities, weak and strong. One example has been the remarkable continuity after the 1979 Iranian revolution, where French law and administrative practices remained oddly impervious to ideological changes.[18] The Afghan state likewise offers a notable illustration of continuity amidst pervasive change, despite the endemic weakness of most of its organs. That country's modern history has been characterised by consecutive periods of 'fusion and fission', during which an urban elite built certain aspects of modern statehood and used it to often devastating effect against a recalcitrant rural population, only to be swept away by the inevitable backlash.[19]

[13] See, eg RG Moeller, *War Stories: The Search for a Usable Past in the Federal Republic of Germany* (Berkeley, University of California Press, 2001).

[14] United States Department of State, *Occupation of Germany, Policy and Progress 1945–46* (Washington, DC, US Government Printing Office 1947) 18.

[15] J Dobbins et al, *America's Role in Nation-Building from Germany to Iraq* (Santa Monica, CA, RAND 2003) 3–23.

[16] E Afsah, 'Iraq: From "Troubled Law of Occupation" to Constitutional Order?' in I Schneider and T Hanstein (eds), *Beiträge zum Islamischen Recht 19* (Frankfurt am Main, Peter Lang, 2006) 21.

[17] For an enthusiastic, naively optimistic defence of that approach, see Dobbins et al (n 15) 167–221. More realistic assessments include MR Hover, 'Report on Occupation and Other Forms of Administration of Foreign Territory' [Spring 2012] *International Review of the Red Cross* 339.

[18] S Zubaida, *Law and Power in the Islamic World* (London, IB Tauris, 2005) discusses Egypt at 167–68 and Iran at 197ff.

[19] 'By political fusion and fission, I mean the following pattern of events: A charismatic leader arises in a tribal society and, by military power, intrigue, and judiciously arranged marriages, unites several tribes into a confederation, which spreads as far as its accumulated power permits, creating an empire, not a nation-state.

These elements of formal statehood were invariably derived from foreign models, often unsuited to local conditions and at odds with underlying organisational principles relying on different foreign models and advisers. The change from one government to the next was rarely peaceful, with incumbent governments tending to espouse and impose diametrically opposed ideologies to their predecessors. This resulted in repeated purges of the civil service, which was therefore never seen as an institution comprised of neutral servants working for the public good.

The impact of these purges on staffing, retention and promotion in the public administration is usually discussed from the perspective of corruption and the prevalence of patron–client relationships.[20] In a tribal and ethnically diverse society, kinship plays an inordinate role in the staffing of budding formal state organs.[21] The result has been a state lacking in permanence and strength.[22]

Following the American invasion in the autumn of 2001, the task of building from that legacy a somewhat sustainable structure of governance was formidable. The initial twofold decision was sensible: foundational normative questions were postponed in lieu of a broad-based agreement on timelines and procedures, while the existing legal and institutional legacy was reinstated in its entirety.[23] That basic choice is reflected in the Bonn Agreement, which lists in an Annex an exhaustive list of existing governmental 'departments' to be carried over into the transitional period with no attempt at prioritisation or elimination.[24]

It was acknowledged that these existing structures would require extensive technical assistance, organisational restructuring and retraining; in other words, public administration reform. This difficult and painful process was meant to occur over an extensive period coinciding with the political transitional period and beyond. It was meant to be supported by very considerable financial and technical assistance from the international community (primarily through the World Bank), and centrally coordinated and led by the newly created cabinet-level Independent Administrative Reform and Civil Service Commission.[25]

With (sometimes before) the death of the emperor, fission occurs, and the great empire once again segments into a multiplicity of tribal kingdoms. Later, another charismatic leader arrives and the process is repeated': Dupree (n 10) xix and 344.

[20] S Chayes, 'Afghanistan's Corruption Was Made in America – How Self-Dealing Elites Failed in Both Countries' [3 September 2021] *Foreign Affairs*.

[21] For the early history, see inter alia B Glatzer, 'Political Organisation of Pashtun Nomads and the State' in R Tapper (ed), The Conflict of Tribe and State in Iran and Afghanistan (St Martin's Press, 1983).

[22] O Roy, 'De la stabilité de l'État en Afghanistan' [2004] *Annales Histoire, Sciences Sociales* 1183; BR Rubin, *The Fragmentation of Afghanistan: State Formation and Collapse in the International System* (Yale University Press 2nd ed. 2002).

[23] I have described that process and its underlying rationale at length before. See E Afsah and AH Guhr, 'Afghanistan: Building a State to Keep the Peace' (2005) Max Planck UNYB 373; E Afsah, 'The Challenge of Civil Service Reform: The Elusive Goal of Governance' in H-G Justenhoven and E Afsah (eds), *Das internationale Engagement in Afghanistan in der Sackgasse? Eine friedensethische Auseinandersetzung* (Baden-Baden, Nomos, 2011).

[24] E Afsah, 'Constitutionalism without Governance: International Standards in the Afghan Legal System' in A Nollkaemper, C Ryngaert and E Kristjansdottir (eds), *Importing International Law in Post-Conflict States: The Role of Domestic Courts* (Cambridge, Intersentia, 2012).

[25] See further World Bank, 'Afghanistan: Building an Effective State. Priorities for Public Administration Reform' (2008) http://tinyurl.com/25agjkd.

The reform process was envisioned as technocratic, meritocratic and advantageous to both Afghan society and international donors. However, at no point were effective strategies developed to persuade or neutralise internal spoilers. While the failure to effectively deal with spoilers outside of formal political and administrative structures, especially local warlords and insurgents, has been a much-discussed reason for the failure of the Afghanistan intervention,[26] the internal aspect of the ethos and attitudes of those formally committed to the state has remained under-examined.[27] Much of the resistance of the sitting cadre of Afghan civil servants to the gospel of administrative reform can be explained through principal–agent theory, ie the divergence between the interests and incentives of the civil servant as an agent from that of the amorphous public principal.[28] This is also basically a story about corruption and insider dealing, and it does indeed explain a large part of the problem.[29]

But there is an additional personal level quite disconnected from the opportunistic pursuit of material and personal benefits by civil servants. One needs to recognise the extreme psychological toll endemic conflict extracts from the population, including those manning the wheels of government. Some individuals develop psychopathologies as a response to trauma,[30] while others do not.[31] It is neither analytically nor practically helpful to describe those that develop pathological symptoms in terms of moral failure.[32] Resistance to public administration reform and other seemingly irrational idiosyncrasies in the Afghan civil service have usually been linked to nefarious motives, such as corruption. Such opportunistic dereliction of duty can be morally condemned, but it does not encompass all forms of obstruction.

Likewise, one should guard against immediately passing moral judgement on a society that responds to an external shock in a seemingly irrational, comprehensively dysfunctional manner. In this vein, I seek to explain the failure to create effective Afghan governance by looking at the way its civil service responded to the international reconstruction effort. I argue that one major element of the failure of the effort has been the widespread assumption that reasonably effective state structures had existed prior to the onset of conflict in the 1970s. Administrative structures were then supposedly completely obliterated through decades of conflict, creating a situation in 2001 where there was not only an evident lack of administrative capacity, but also no meaningful administrative structure. These assumptions appear faulty. The administrative output

[26] D Mukhopadhyay, *Warlords, Strongman Governors, and the State in Afghanistan* (Cambridge, Cambridge University Press, 2014); D Filkins, 'Rule of the Gun. With US Aid, Warlord Builds Afghan Empire' *New York Times* (5 June 2010).

[27] Exceptions include T Murray, 'Police-Building in Afghanistan: A Case Study of Civil Security Reform' [February 2007] *International Peacekeeping* 1.

[28] The best description is still M Olson, *The Logic of Collective Action: Public Goods and the Theory of Groups* (Cambridge, MA, Harvard University Press, 1971, first published 1965); TM Moe, 'Political Control and the Power of the Agent' [2006] *Journal of Law, Economics & Organization* 1.

[29] See, eg F Khan, 'Corruption and the Decline of the State in Pakistan' [2007] *Asian Journal of Political Science* 219.

[30] Masten et al (n 3).

[31] The observation of precisely this startling fact lies at the origin of the interest in the concept of resilience. See Rutter (n 5).

[32] D Cicchetti and DJ Cohen (eds), *Developmental Psychopathology, Volume 3, Risk, Disorder, and Adaptation* (New York, John Wiley & Sons, 2006).

of Afghan civil servants, which was highly variable and even at the best of times never particularly impressive, does not adequately describe the social importance attached by the civil servants and society at large to their positions within a structure they deemed meaningful. The civil servants who manned this structure when the international assistance mission began often did not deliver useful services to citizens, but they derived material, emotional and social benefits from their positions. They consequently had a strong interest in defending the existing structure and their role within it against reform efforts seeking greater public accountability or bureaucratic efficiency.

II. Reform and the Reality of Governance

Post-conflict governance involves engaging with complex dysfunctional organisations that are often highly skilled at evading externally imposed reform. It is the failure to recognise the repercussions of such conflict-induced 'adaptive change', an otherwise highly beneficial phenomenon,[33] which accounts for the dismissive descriptions of Afghan (and other post-conflict) bureaucracy as nothing but atavistic, irrational, opportunistic or predatory.[34]

Given the complexity and contradictory nature of the phenomena involved, the search for a simplistic heuristic is an entirely understandable, yet unhelpful, attempt to make sense of the confusion. Calogero laments 'four expected narratives' in the existing literature, which obscure as much as they explain. These dominant perspectives depict Afghanistan as: (i) a source of Islamist terror and a society seeking to return to medieval conditions; (ii) a victimised society, where especially women and children are exposed to violence and poverty; (iii) a source of narcotics; and (iv) having an incompetent, increasingly corrupt government infiltrated by and abetting traffickers.[35]

In his comprehensive study of urban planning in Kabul, Calogero is critical of the dominant narratives, according to which 'developed' and 'developing' are used as synonyms for 'mature' and 'immature', leaving the implication that a least-developed, despondently poor, war-ravaged society like Afghanistan 'needs to be treated like a very immature child'. He laments the resulting condescension and '"infantilization" of Afghans [which] profoundly frames the international aid project',[36] and contrasts it throughout his study with an in-depth account of local civil servants professionally implementing, adapting and refining an urban master plan devised in 1923, revised in the 1960s and carried out despite massive political turmoil and violent conflict. He highlights that urban planning is rarely an entirely rational, deductive process by

[33] CS Holling and LH Gunderson, 'Resilience and Adaptive Change' in CS Holling and LH Gunderson (eds), *Panarchy: Understanding Transformations in Human and Natural Systems* (Washington, DC, Island Press, 2009) 25–62.

[34] International Crisis Group, 'Afghanistan: Elections and the Crisis of Governance' (25 November 2009) Asia Briefing No 96, www.crisisgroup.org/asia/south-asia/afghanistan/afghanistan-elections-and-crisis-governance.

[35] PA Calogero, 'Planning Kabul: The Politics of Urbanization in Afghanistan' (Dissertation, University of California – Berkeley, 2011) 4.

[36] ibid.

'the state', but rather an inherently political process in which 'multiple rationalities' are at play and in competition.[37]

Under such circumstances, civil servants respond to a plethora of countervailing incentives, including corruption and violence, but do so within a structure that predates the conflict and in which they are invested, both personally and professionally. In other words, they operate within an organisational structure that Cohen described in a different context as 'first, fundamentally *political*; and second, fundamentally *institutional*' (emphasis added).[38] What makes Calogero's study so compelling is his explicit recognition that institutions persist despite conflict, and that governmental functions, despite impairment, continue to operate within existing broad parameters. His study thus amounts to a renunciation of the *tabula rasa* metaphor that informs much post-conflict strategic and operational thinking:

> Kabul is generally assumed to be a site of sustained conflict where social and governmental institutions were presumably wiped out. But why do Westerners presume that chronic warfare erases institutions? … perhaps the vivid imagery of these many films 'stands in' for lack of direct familiarity with anything resembling Afghanistan. The idea that property-claims, municipal agencies, and urban plans would persist through the incredible violence of Afghanistan's civil war might feel anticlimactic.[39]

This approach runs counter to conventional wisdom, which describes Afghanistan as a place where the state and most institutions had been 'completely' destroyed by decades of conflict, leaving essentially a blank slate onto which something new could be inscribed,[40] dispensing with the need to understand local context and contingency.[41] This does not, of course, mean that the Afghan government had miraculously emerged from the conflict unscathed, ready to assume responsibility and deliver services, as the convenient legal fiction of an international 'light footprint' postulated.[42] Not only had Afghan state institutions sustained severe damage, they had never been particularly strong to begin with, even during the supposedly halcyon days of Zahir Shah in the 1960s.[43]

This endemically weak state had artificially been kept alive throughout the nineteenth and twentieth centuries by transfer payments from outside powers, creating a rentier logic that persists to this day.[44] Irrespective of the conflict, Afghanistan is thus in

[37] ibid 55–78.

[38] EA Cohen, *Citizens and Soldiers: The Dilemmas of Military Service* (Ithaca, NY, Cornell University Press, 1985) 19.

[39] Calogero (n 35) 5–6.

[40] SF Starr, 'Sovereignty and Legitimacy in Afghan Nation-Building' in F Fukuyama (ed), *Nation-Building beyond Afghanistan and Iraq* (Baltimore, MD, Johns Hopkins University Press, 2006) 111.

[41] Perhaps the starkest example of this hubris was the presumed ability of the US Army to substitute government services in areas it had taken from insurgents through preassembled teams of its own servicemen: 'Recruiting logisticians, strategic planners, program managers, and budget experts from across the DoD may offer a way to rapidly build host nation capacity': SA Mackey, 'Government in a Box' [March 2014] *Small Wars Journal*. See also N Shachtman, 'Marjah's "Government in a Box" Flops as McChrystal Fumes' *Wired* (25 May 2010).

[42] Afsah, 'The Challenge of Civil Service Reform' (n 23) 145–47.

[43] Afsah and Guhr (n 23) 375–78.

[44] '[A]id rentierism limits the possibilities for capacity building altogether … In a rentier state, the bureaucracy will be used to allocate resources to supporters and not for tax collection and productivity enhancement, as intended by "state builders"': W Verkoren and B Kamphuis, 'State Building in a Rentier State: How Development Policies Fail to Promote Democracy in Afghanistan' [2013] *Development and Change* 501, 502.

many ways like any other rentier state, in that its institutions have a weak level of administrative capability and are detached from a society that does not finance its civil service through legitimate fees and taxes, but also receives little in services.[45] Consequently, institutions able to extract revenue directly remained surprisingly intact, while others withered. Part of this corresponds to Tilly's classical notion of the 'state as organised crime',[46] which in Afghanistan can often be taken literally[47] – for instance, the extraction of 'customs duties' at the border and internal checkpoints.[48]

Perhaps more interesting for present purposes, however, are those institutions that can levy and directly collect reasonable fees for their administrative services, permitting them to operate as silos of effectiveness amidst the general dysfunction. Examples of entirely professional, completely non-corrupt, fully transparent administrative operations include the Foreigner Registration Office, which collects photographs and registration data for every single non-national entering the country, paid for by a 10-dollar exit tax payable at the airport. Such silos of competence were sometimes consciously created to respond to particularly pressing functional needs. This was done highly successfully with the Kabul Airport Police, trained (and initially paid for) by Germany, as well as, less successfully, by the British and American governments for the Counter-Narcotics Task Force, which attempted to recreate a parallel justice system replete with prosecution, court, police and prison service.[49]

That this weak state fractured under the impact of sustained conflict is not surprising. It is likewise well known that such state failure became recognised after 9/11 as a problem for the USA[50] and the rest of the world,[51] misgivings about costly overseas military nation-building operations notwithstanding.[52] In principle, this convergence of interests in the international arena facilitated agreement on where to intervene,[53]

[45] U Abulof, '"Can't Buy Me Legitimacy": The Elusive Stability of Mideast Rentier Regimes' [2015] *Journal of International Relations and Development* 1.

[46] C Tilly, 'War Making and State Making as Organized Crime' in PB Evans, D Rueschemeyer and S Theda (eds), *Bringing the State Back In* (Cambridge, Cambridge University Press, 1985) 169–91.

[47] 'In other words, if Pashtuns have often revolted against the Afghan state (whether foreign-backed or purely indigenous), they have often had good reasons to': A Lieven, 'An Afghan Tragedy: The Pashtuns, the Taliban and the State' [June–July 2021] *Survival* 7, 9.

[48] On police corruption and extortion, see A Giustozzi and M Isaqzadeh, *Policing Afghanistan* (London, C Hurst & Co, 2013) 21, 78–96, 153–63.

[49] For details, see E Afsah, 'Terminal Evaluation Report AFG/U10: Fast-track Capacity Building for a Functioning Counter-Narcotics Criminal Justice System' (University of Copenhagen, March 2008).

[50] BR Rubin, 'Peace Building and State-Building in Afghanistan: Constructing Sovereignty for Whose Security?' [2006] *Third World Quarterly* 175.

[51] That something is recognised as a problem does not, however, mean that proper responses exist, irrespective of expansive discourses about the 'right to protect' or the 'right to rebuild'. See Edwards (n 9) 971–72.

[52] These misgivings arose from the experience of her troubled engagements in Somalia, Haiti, Bosnia and Kosovo, discussed, for instance, in Dobbins et al (n 15). See also A Giustozzi and A Kalinovsky, *Missionaries of Modernity: Advisory Missions and the Struggle for Hegemony in Afghanistan and Beyond* (London, C Hurst & Co, 2016).

[53] 'Failed states, as Somalia, Sierra Leone, and Afghanistan have shown, export terror, regional instability, organized crime, uncontrolled immigration flows, and drugs. These new challenges essentially solve the issue of triage that has dogged interventions: why here, why not there, and so on. In a post-11 September environment, intervention is likely to be targeted at those places that present a security or terrorist challenge, and not at those places where the challenge is merely humanitarian': M Ignatieff, 'State Failure and Nation-Building' in JL Holzgrefe and RO Keohane (eds), *Humanitarian Intervention: Ethical, Legal and Political Dilemmas* (Cambridge, Cambridge University Press, 2003) 306.

and the primary means of intervention, namely building state institutions. As Goodson argues. 'bolstered by rare international solidarity, the United States and the United Nations could use the consensus and goodwill to attack the problem with laser-like intensity'.[54] But, as we have learnt, the process of transferring institutions is difficult and requires a degree of psychological sensitivity and contextual knowledge rarely available to external interveners. Solutions have to be locally contingent and not only adapted to unique institutional trajectories, but able to respond to volatile material and psychological needs. Consequently, successful public administration reform can never be firm science, but rather is a dexterous art.[55]

III. Failed States can be Surprisingly Resilient

When the USA belatedly accepted the futility of its engagement in Afghanistan, the withdrawal was hasty and traumatic. The drama and trauma were not the result of any particular tactical miscalculation, but the inevitable denouement of a strategy based on problematic preferences derived from indefensible assumptions. During two decades of failed international reconstruction efforts,[56] strategic decision-making in Afghanistan was dominated by several momentous misperceptions.[57] The country, like others in similar dire straits, is often described as a 'failed state', a description simultaneously accurate and misleading.[58] On the one hand, the 'daunting reality was that every economic and political element in Afghanistan would have to be rebuilt', indeed 'virtually every aspect of Afghan society would need reconstruction'.[59] But on the other hand, this did *not* mean that Afghan institutions, or even just its formal governance structures, had been 'completely wiped out' by decades of conflict. This assumption, however, informed international assistance and donor efforts, and remained remarkably hard to dislodge, as noted by the UN Assistance Mission in an early programme document:

> It is frequently stated that the formal justice system has been 'totally destroyed' by the 23 years of civil unrest and war. This is an imprecise perception/assessment of the situation. It does not consider the *role and functioning of the existing mechanisms and practices*; imprecise because the *formal* legal tradition and mechanisms are *much less consolidated than usually presumed.* (emphasis added)[60]

[54] LP Goodson, 'The Lessons of Nation-Building in Afghanistan' in Fukuyama, *Nation-Building* (n 40) 146.

[55] F Fukuyama, 'Why There Is No Science of Public Administration' [2004] *Journal of International Affairs* 189.

[56] '[T]he United States is propping up a corrupt and weak pauper state': CJ Chivers, 'The Limits of US Strategy in Afghanistan, by the Numbers' *New York Times* (7 February 2020).

[57] For our purposes, the most important 'myth' that Carpenter and Innocent correctly criticise is the belief that 'America Can Build a Modern, Stable Afghanistan': TG Carpenter and M Innocent, 'Escaping the "Graveyard of Empires": A Strategy to Exit Afghanistan' (The Cato Institute, 28 January 2010) 8–9.

[58] P Englebert and DM Tull, 'Postconflict Reconstruction in Africa: Flawed Ideas about Failed States' (2008) 32(4) *International Security* 106.

[59] Goodson, 'Lessons' (n 54) 147.

[60] M Toscano-Rivalta and A Drury, 'Securing Afghanistan's Future – Considerations on Criteria and Actions for Strengthening the Justice System – Proposal for a Long-term Strategic Framework' (8 February 2004) 4.

Excessively weak to start with,[61] formal state organs sustained considerable, perhaps terminal, damage.[62] Still, the human beings who made up these organisations and whose patterns of behaviour constituted these institutions never ceased to feel attached to the idea of belonging to, say, the Ministry of Justice or the Attorney General's Office, as I observed in a decade of 'embedded' work among them.[63]

Likewise, warring factions felt that control over physical buildings and the individuals working in them carried practical relevance.[64] Contrary to what most foreigners continue to assume, no social, political or armed formation in Afghanistan seriously contemplates secession or dismemberment.[65] The cohesion of the national polity remained intact throughout the experience of war, displacement, exile and ethnic fissures. Similarly, the notion of a common Afghan identity and attachment to a unitary state persevered.[66] While the capacity of the state and its organs to deliver services had been erased, its formal structures survived and were considered important by those working within, expecting patronage and prestige from this association and competing for positions.[67]

The emergence of a common Afghan identity corresponding to a broader national-territorial entity larger than the tribe was a long and precarious process, with uncertain implications. What had begun in the 1880s under the 'Iron Amir' Abdur Rahman Khan continued throughout the twentieth century with successive governments backed by foreign assistance, using coercive power to break rural tribal resistance to the demands of the central state, primarily taxation. Whenever the central state enjoyed sufficient external financial and material aid, its coercive institutions allowed it to impose a greater degree of physical and social control, including the inculcation of national identity. Invariably, such efforts floundered against strong traditionalist, tribal resistance. It is important to note that such resistance was not expressed as a preference for a different type of state, for instance, one based on a particularistic ethnic identity or attachment to a neighbouring state sharing a Persian/Tajik, Uzbek, Turkman or Pashto ethnicity. Rural resistance was, in contrast,

[61] Afsah and Guhr (n 23) 375–78.

[62] Accurate accounts of the process of disintegration under the strains of conflict can be found in Rubin, *The Fragmentation of Afghanistan* (n 22); LP Goodson, *Afghanistan's Endless War: State Failure, Regional Politics, and the Rise of the Taliban* (Seattle, University of Washington Press, 2001).

[63] See also A Schwarz, 'Justizreform und Islam in Afghanistan' [2005] *Zeitschrift für ausländisches öffentliches Recht und Völkerrecht* 257.

[64] The Northern Alliance grab of the institutions of government in Kabul in the run-up to the Bonn Agreement is critically described by Starr (n 40) 108–14.

[65] ibid 109.

[66] CJ Schetter, 'Die Territorialisierung nationaler und ethnischer Vorstellungen in Afghanistan' [2003] *Orient* 75.

[67] Chivers (n 56). Very considerable funds have been disbursed through a 'reformed' but dysfunctional state structure, mostly to little positive effect: 'Donors, led by the United States, currently provide some $8.5 billion a year in on-budget grants to the Afghan government and in off-budget spending for reconstruction. These financial inflows account for about 75% of the country's public expenditures for security, education, law enforcement, health, and other development functions. The United States alone provides more than $4 billion a year for reconstruction efforts in Afghanistan – not including the costs of U.S. military operations there': JF Sopko, '46th Quarterly Report to the United States Congress' (30 January 2020) 126, www.sigar.mil/pdf/quarterlyreports/2020-01-30qr.pdf.

aimed against encroachment by the state as such on traditional prerogatives and ways of life:

> The Pashtun tragedy lies in the fact that in practice, this rejection of state interference has usually amounted to a rejection of the modernising state as such, since modernising states need to raise taxes to pay for development, find it very hard to base themselves on tradition, and by definition have to set out to change society.[68]

Paradoxically, it was the experience of exile, displacement and common struggle against the modernising socialist state and its Soviet backers that ultimately achieved what a century of state-led social engineering could not: the emergence of a common identity not supplanting but complementing prior tribal identities. The anti-Soviet struggle became a *national* struggle, reflected, for instance, in the sacralised image of the state's boundary and national flag. Previously largely unknown and meaningless to the vast majority of people living extremely local lives, the country's shape on a map became virtually ubiquitous on political insignia and propaganda, and was represented on carpets and handicrafts,[69] becoming a truly popular expression of common identity.[70]

Consequently, the international reconstruction effort that commenced in 2001 mistakenly referred to nation-building as the chief challenge. Ethnicity had indeed been a major resource during the conflict, acting as a crystallisation point for the various resistance groups.[71] The intense rivalry between these groups and their leaders was *the* major cause for the destructiveness of the civil war.[72] Contrary to expectation, however, in the Afghan context these rivalries did not translate into a desire to create competing polities, but merely reflected the absence of a culture of co-operation in a society devoid of political institutions in which interests could be formulated and negotiated peacefully. In short, what Afghanistan needed and still needs is state-building, because it had already become a nation during the conflict after 1979.[73]

The reconstruction effort that began at the Bonn Conference towards the end of 2001 took the existing structure of the Afghan state as a given. The four groups representing the major competing factions reinstated virtually all previous laws and re-mandated all existing line ministries and several independent agencies. This was a pragmatic decision based on the impossibility for a group of exiled political leaders to ascertain factual conditions on the ground. Rather than artificially create a novel organogram of the Afghan state, it seemed sensible to take the existing one – or, more precisely, the last known one. Similarly, the structure of the administration under Taliban rule had largely but imperfectly followed the traditional distribution of competencies, just as it again took over the existing structure in August 2021. The name and ideological outlook of the state might have changed drastically, but its administrative form much less so.[74]

[68] Lieven (n 47) 8.

[69] B Spooner, 'Afghan Wars, Oriental Carpets and Globalization' [2011] *Expedition* 11.

[70] Schetter, 'Die Territorialisierung' (n 66).

[71] CJ Schetter, *Ethnizität und ethnische Konflikte in Afghanistan* (Berlin, Reimer, 2003).

[72] Described at some length in Rubin, *The Fragmentation of Afghanistan* (n 22).

[73] A Wimmer and C Schetter, 'Putting State-Formation First: Some Recommendations for Reconstruction and Peace-making in Afghanistan' [2003] *Journal of International Development* 525.

[74] CB Lombardi and AF March, 'Afghan Taliban Views on Legitimate Islamic Governance. Certainties, Ambiguities, and Areas for Compromise' (United States Institute of Peace, 28 February 2022) www.usip.org/publications/2022/02/afghan-taliban-views-legitimate-islamic-governance.

The negotiators in Bonn did not seek to reduce the administrative complexity of the Afghan state in order to focus reconstruction efforts on those elements deemed most necessary. To the contrary, ministries and positions were taken as they had been bequeathed by the last recognised government under Rabbani and distributed among the four groups negotiating in Bonn (the Northern Alliance; the Rome Group around the former king; the Cyprus Group, representing the Iranian diaspora; and the Peshawar Group, representing the Pakistani diaspora), with little regard for the administrative competence or functional logic of the distribution.[75] As the Afghan state remains largely incapable of financing its expenses – a pattern now continued by the Taliban – virtually the entire administration remained heavily dependent on external financial and technical support. This support was distributed by national donors, international agencies and trust funds in a highly uneven fashion, reflecting donor preferences and the vicissitudes of project management, that is, according to the internal logic of the international development industry.[76]

Certain local leaders were far more adept at securing 'cargo' from the donor community than others. In some cases, this was due to personal connections made while in exile, such as Attorney General Aloko or Foreign Minister Dadfar Spanta's close relationship with Germany. Historical links, such as Germany's role in police training since the 1960s, or French, German and Russian high and vocational schools, led to resumed resource flows to these institutions. Certain other agencies coincided with political desires in donor nations, and thus received vastly disproportionate funding well beyond their absorption capacities, such as the newly created Ministry of Women's Affairs and the Independent Afghan Human Rights Commission.

Based on a decade of 'embedded' collaboration, mainly as a technical advisor with the Independent Administrative Reform and Civil Service Commission working in the justice sector,[77] I argue that the overall failure of bureaucratic reform is also the result of a perverse kind of ingenuity. The Afghan civil service successfully resisted externally imposed change by using the same qualities and strategies otherwise exhorted as 'resilience'. Because the reform effort mistook dysfunctional service delivery and opaque, seemingly arbitrary organisational forms as evidence of an essentially non-existent civil service, it proposed a variety of entirely new models based on alien, locally incomprehensible concepts. These reform ideas were usually oblivious to what had come before, including reform efforts driven by previous foreign advisers, and were therefore unnecessarily complex and often incompatible with existing patterns.

As a result of ignorance, if not outright disregard, of individual biographies, organisational trajectories and corporate cultures, the reform project was perceived by civil servants as yet another external shock in a long line of violent transformations and

[75] Afsah and Guhr (n 23) 408.

[76] See generally W Easterly, 'The Cartel of Good Intentions: Bureaucracy versus Markets in Foreign Aid' (New York University, 2002) Center for Global Development Working Paper No 4/2002, www.nyu.edu/fas/institute/dri/Easterly/File/carteljan2003.pdf.

[77] The Commission has been the major conduit for technical assistance and played a critical part in disbursing the considerable trust funds made available by the international community. For more information, see https://iarcsc.gov.af/en/.

purges following previous regime changes.[78] The administration thus mobilised well-honed individual and organisational strategies of 'adaptive change' that sought to neutralise the external threat and restore institutional equilibrium serving bureaucratic rather than societal interests. Evident corruption and opportunism notwithstanding, these strategies are not necessarily moral failings but traits that, under different circumstances, could have been harnessed towards constructive ends.

IV. Troubled Memories

For present purposes, it is not necessary to decide whether the term 'resilience' is merely 'meaningless jargon' or indeed a 'development solution'.[79] Instead, I simply posit resilience as a coping mechanism that permits individuals and organisations to withstand exceptional stress. Like other coping strategies, an initially useful adaptation can outlive the circumstances which gave rise to it and come to worsen the pathological condition it was meant to address.[80] Very few people could avoid substantial trauma when subjected to protracted conflict of the kind that has afflicted Afghanistan.

Anyone working with rank-and-file bureaucrats in a post-conflict setting will become aware of the aftermath of trauma, even in the most mundane, technical of settings. The position of an individual within a valued social setting, in this case his professional environment, should not be dismissed as merely an opportunistic avenue for graft or social advancement. Instead, it needs to be recognised as a crucial part of the 'characteristic triad of active, task-oriented coping strategies, strong sociability, and internal locus of control' found in those who manage to cope with extraordinary events, lessening post-traumatic stress disorders.[81]

The people manning the lower wheels of government are those whose relative lack of resources did not allow them to escape and thus often had to endure repeated purges, restructurings and physical violence. They emerged from this only to find themselves in an exposed, highly volatile situation dominated by returning exiles and foreign advisors. Those who bear responsibility for the past resumed positions of power in the 'new' government,[82] precluding any possibility for a serious reckoning and lowering incentives towards constructive change.[83] It might appear counter-intuitive to describe a supposedly technocratic phenomenon like administrative reform in the language of psychopathology. Nonetheless, to understand the difficulties involved, it is imperative

[78] The strategy was laid out by World Bank as the lead agency in a number of programmatic documents. See World Bank, 'Afghanistan: Building an Effective State' (n 25); World Bank, 'Afghanistan: State Building, Sustaining Growth, and Reducing Poverty' (2005). The depressing lack of progress is evident despite the careful diplomatic language in World Bank, 'Afghanistan – Systematic Country Diagnostic' (1 February 2016).

[79] M Hussain, 'Resilience: Meaningless Jargon or Development Solution?' *The Guardian* (5 March 2013).

[80] See J Lewis Herman, *Trauma and Recovery*, revised edn (New York, Basic Books, 1997) 57–61.

[81] ibid 59.

[82] Mukhopadhyay (n 26); M Kimberly, 'Warlordism in Comparative Perspective' (2006) 31(3) *International Security* 41.

[83] K Menkhaus, 'Governance without Government in Somalia: Spoilers, State Building, and the Politics of Coping' (2006) 31(3) *International Security* 74.

to recognise that human beings constitute the administration, that these human beings and their organisations have histories that predate the reform effort, and that individual and organisational memories are conflicted and contradictory.[84]

The foreign administrative professionals tasked with helping to re-establish functioning government structures in an overwhelmingly complex, dangerous and culturally alien environment characterised by large operational challenges might be forgiven for not being particularly attentive to the psychopathology of trauma survivors. After all, such a professional is placed in an environment where there are strong incentives to forget and move on; to essentially 'take the side of the perpetrator [because a]ll the perpetrator asks is that the bystander do nothing'.[85] The perpetrator wants to escape accountability for his crimes and thus promotes forgetting and discourages remembrance. In a situation like Afghanistan, where the chief culprits of past crimes have taken over the government and entered into lucrative arrangements with the new foreign military masters,[86] there was little official interest in acknowledging, let alone addressing, the nefarious role of warlords and armed criminal entrepreneurs.[87] This creates a perverse conflict of interest, 'on one side the victims who perhaps wish to forget but cannot, and on the other all those with strong, often unconscious motives who very intensely both wish to forget and succeed in doing so'.[88]

Official commitment to administrative reform, with its underlying implications of meritocracy in personnel selection and promotion, accountability in budgeting and delivery, and predictability of mandate and execution, must ring hollow to staff members working under strongmen-turned-governors. External interveners claim to engage in meritocratic state-building inimical to the interests of those who had captured ministries, while simultaneously waging counterinsurgency warfare necessitating the military support of these very same warlords. This has left meaningful administrative reform in a precarious position.[89] The misalignment of interests between civil servants wishing to retain sinecures and society at large requiring effective and accountable service delivery has further confounded the situation.

Administrative reform is a political process that will create winners and losers within the existing administrative machinery, thus requiring a strategy for dealing with potential spoilers, ideally co-opting them to the overall process by realigning individual and corporate interests to those of taxpayers and citizens.[90] It also needs to address the above-outlined psychological need of the individual to maintain a professional community that also functions as his or her support group.

[84] Herman (n 80) 1.

[85] ibid 7.

[86] Filkins (n 26).

[87] T Schweich, 'Is Afghanistan a Narco-State?' *New York Times* (27 July 2008).

[88] L Eitinger, 'The Concentration Camp Syndrome and Its Late Sequelae' in EJ Dimsdale (ed), *Survivors, Victims and Perpetrators* (London, Hemisphere, 1980); quoted in Herman (n 80) 8.

[89] V Felbab-Brown, 'Afghanistan: When Counternarcotics undermines Counterterrorism' [Autumn 2005] *Washington Quarterly* 55.

[90] T Trefon, 'Administrative Obstacles to Reform in the Democratic Republic of Congo' [2010] *International Review of Administrative Sciences* 702; C Spanou and DA Sotiropoulos, 'The Odyssey of Administrative Reforms in Greece, 1981–2009: A Tale of Two Reform Paths' [2011] *Public Administration* 723.

Such realignment of interests and incentives is a demanding process, intellectually, operationally and morally, requiring painful trade-offs to be made. Before even attempting to balance such costs and benefits, however, it is necessary to recognise that the object of the reform, namely the dysfunctional administration of a failed state, actually exists. The situation is therefore decidedly not a blank slate, but one in which actual human beings inhabit formal structures that they value, however dysfunctional these may be in terms of service delivery.

Public administration reform in Afghanistan, as elsewhere, proceeded under the seemingly simple, commonsensical premise that a higher quality civil service would be in everyone's interest. Given extremely low legacy salaries, the promise of higher salaries (financed by foreign donors, often through trust fund arrangements)[91] was viewed as providing ample incentive to undergo the necessary organisational restructuring and individual retraining. The need to remove excess capacity was deemed to be negligible, as legacy salaries were so low that people could simply stay in their jobs until natural attrition would resolve the issue.

This approach to reform failed due to: (i) the lack of political commitment by higher management, both legacy and newly hired, who were interested in keeping and extending opportunities for patronage; (ii) the inability of technical advisors to impose structural changes in the face of internal obstruction; and, most importantly, (iii) the ability of ordinary civil servants to neutralise change they reasonably perceived as threatening their personal and group interests. Such obstruction took many forms, the most important of which was simply the ability to 'wait out' external advisors usually working under fairly rigid project time frames and attendant reporting and delivery obligations. As the reform process was financed, managed and desired almost exclusively by foreigners yet dependent on local 'ownership', perverse incentive structures developed. These were characterised by 'marriages of convenience' between local power holders, their tribal clients and civil servants wishing to maximise opportunities for embezzlement and patronage while minimising disruption to existing organisational arrangements.

Quite apart from the lack of political buy-in at a ministerial level comprised of people with questionable pasts and interests,[92] ordinary civil servants often had legitimate fears about an externally imposed reform effort likely to unravel their personal careers, organisational cultures and cherished identities. As such, state-building in post-conflict settings involves all the usual difficulties of organisational restructuring requiring persuasion, intimidation, interest alignment, etc.[93] But these general challenges are compounded by the existence of trauma, unaddressed personal and institutional memories, a deeply insecure future and well-founded distrust in optimistic promises about the benefits of change.

[91] World Bank, 'Afghanistan: Building an Effective State' (n 25).

[92] '[T]he state is run by a political elite whose objectives seem diametrically opposed to those of the international community – a dynamic similar to one identified in Somalia': Edwards (n 9) 967–68. See also JF Kerry, *Afghanistan's Narco War: Breaking the Link Between Drug Traffickers and Insurgents: A Report to the Committee on Foreign Relations, US Senate* (Darby, PA, Diane Publishing, 2010); Schweich (n 87).

[93] For a classic account of the benefits and challenges of organisation change, see DC North, *Institutions, Institutional Change and Economic Performance* (Cambridge, Cambridge University Press, 1990).

V. Cherished Continuities and Reasonable Resistance

The administrative reorganisation initiated at the Bonn Conference in 2001 began with the explicit recognition that the law of the land and the existing institutional structure would remain in place.[94] Annex IV of the *Provisional Arrangements* assigned ministerial posts for 29 'departments', corresponding to the previously existing ministries.[95] This distribution arguably doomed the state-building effort before it had even begun, for it 'tacitly ratified the fait accompli of Northern Alliance rule and domination of the new administration, while vigorously denying that it had done so'.[96]

How the ethnically predominantly Tajik and Uzbek Northern Alliance established its dominance in the capital's formal structures of government and the manner in which Pashto factions were subsequently co-opted is not germane to the present discussion. What characterised the subsequent administrative reform process was the fact that tens of thousands of ordinary civil servants maintained allegiance to their posts throughout the conflict and returned to duty in the fall of 2001. This created multilayered structures of overstaffed, ill-defined public bodies almost completely divorced from wider society. Many of these civil servants had never stopped working in their posts, despite unspeakably difficult working conditions under successive regimes. Many returned for duty after having previously been purged by one or several successive antagonistic regimes. They brought with them vastly different educational and personal outlooks, again often reflecting the peculiar circumstances prevailing at the time of their training and/or hiring.

In the justice sector, with which I am most familiar, the three major institutions were the Attorney General's Office, the Ministry of Justice and the Supreme Court, with its lower courts. The first had been set up in the 1950s on the model of the Soviet *prokuratura*, the Ministry followed several Western models, while the Court adhered to traditional Islamic notions of jurisprudence. Not surprisingly, the Attorney General thrived under the Communist regime, with many of its cadres having received training in the Soviet Union, while for that very reason it suffered particularly harshly during the Mujahideen civil war and subsequent Taliban rule.

The Ministry had its heyday under the monarchy, having been the recipient of significant American and other Western countries' largesse. During the Communist era, the Ministry personnel faced great disruption, retraining, purges and reorganisation. By contrast, the civil war and Taliban eras upended these reforms and brought very considerable personnel change, but fewer organisational and legislative ones. The Supreme Court and the lower courts entered the transitional period after 2001 with comparably little disruption, as its historical Islamic ethos and structure had isolated it better against Mujahideen and Taliban interference. Chief Justice Shinwari, who had been appointed by the Taliban, remained in office throughout the transitional period well into President Karzai's first term.

[94] The process and the substantive outcome of the negotiations are discussed in Afsah and Guhr (n 23) 406ff.

[95] 'Agreement on Provisional Arrangements in Afghanistan Pending the Re-establishment of Permanent Government Institutions (Bonn Agreement)' (5 December 2001) S/2001/1154, www.un.org/News/dh/latest/afghan/afghan-agree.htm.

[96] Starr (n 40) 112.

The courts in principle were better placed than the rest of the justice sector to capitalise on the existing needs of Afghan society, given the ubiquity of weapons and an 'obsession with honour and prestige'.[97] This made dispute resolution a relevant service, while the other two institutions were not seen as offering something society needed. Unfortunately, the endemic weakness and corruption of formal state structures, especially law enforcement, made access to the courts both difficult and often ineffective.[98] This was a void the insurrection seized upon, drawing on its previous track record and reputation for harsh but effective justice, for 'the role of dispute resolution in Pashtun society cannot be emphasised enough … In post-2001 Kandahar, the Taliban's judicial services became one of the key advantages that the movement had over the state'.[99]

In the non-justice context, institutions continued very distinct organisational cultures after 2001, often immediately recognisable in the manner of dress, modes of interaction and bureaucratic communication stemming from the peculiar genesis of their respective organisational unit. The administrative output of these structures, both old and newly created, was highly variable. For example, some function surprisingly well and were reasonably service-minded, like Kabul Municipality or the Ministry of Public Health, while others were exclusively occupied with themselves, meeting no conceivable public need, like the Academy of Sciences or the Afghanistan Atomic Energy High Commission.[100]

In the four line agencies comprising the justice sector, these differences remained palpable throughout the decade of my engagement with public administration reform. The Attorney General's Office retained its distinctly Soviet Central Asian ethos, down to the preferred suits worn by the men and women; the Ministry of Justice self-consciously tried to return to its reformist, Weberian ethos inspired by Western advisers in the 1960s; while the Supreme Court for a long time retained a remarkable personnel and ideological continuity from the Taliban era,[101] with a heavily Pashto-dominated workforce dressed invariably in *shalwar-kameez* and tribal wear and a management culture inspired by traditional *qadis* and the Egyptian religious institutions some of their key personnel had attended. The prison service, which had been reassigned to the Ministry of the Interior from the Ministry of Justice, exhibited many of the same peculiarities observed in the general police force.[102]

[97] Lieven (n 47) 8.

[98] K Barker, 'At the Supreme Court, an Unlikely New Hero. Afghanistan's Chief Justice Has Launched a Quiet Revolution, Targeting Corrupt Judges and Demanding Accountability in the Country's Long-Inept Judiciary' *Chicago Tribune* (21 January 2007).

[99] A Gopal, 'The Taliban in Kandahar' in PL Bergen (ed), *Talibanistan: Negotiating the Borders between Terror, Politics and Religion* (Oxford, Oxford University Press, 2013) 23–24.

[100] Perhaps more than any other, this agency illustrates the complete lack of prioritisation in terms of the service needs of the population, which further compromised the problematic strategic logic of reform. The Commission enjoyed considerable financial and technical assistance, employed some 138 people and was started at the impetus of a retired staff member of the International Atomic Energy Commission in Vienna, who happened to be a personal friend of then-President Karzai. It has since produced many polished strategy papers and draft laws, but, needless to say, there is absolutely no prospect of the country ever developing nuclear power. For more information, see https://aaehc.gov.af/en.

[101] Barker (n 98).

[102] T Murray, 'Police-Building in Afghanistan: A Case Study of Civil Security Reform' (2007) 14(1) *International Peacekeeping* 1081.

Throughout, there was a remarkable continuity of personnel, corporate culture and considerable personal attachment to professional positions, quite unrelated to the abysmal salary or opportunities for graft. Equally apparent was the enormous, and in hindsight entirely justified, scepticism by the rank and file towards the gospel of reform propagated by a duplicitous Afghan political elite and its foreign advisers. The response of the administration was not open defiance, but hunkering down, treating the enormous and often incomprehensible changes that befell them after 2001 as yet another iteration of countless previously endured disruptions, prompting similar responses.

This administrative resistance was hardly a coordinated, conscious effort at sabotage. Rather, it appears to have been a mixture of incomprehension of the jargon spewed by the sudden influx of foreign advisors and the Afghan exiles accompanying them, but also a well-grounded scepticism about both the risk of displacement by younger, English-speaking returnees and of future retribution, when (not if) the present form of government would inevitably fall. Compounding both aspects was the overarching desire to minimise personal and organisational risk by withholding information of any kind, reticence to take even the most mundane decisions at the working level and avoiding the perception of collaboration with the outsiders.

Infuriating as such behaviour certainly was for the technical adviser, it was a logical and legitimate response to lessons learnt in successive previous reforms and purges, which the rank and file had, quite literally, survived. Even obtaining something as simple as an organisational chart of the Ministry of Justice or the names and locations of provincial judges was a task that defied several international missions and required very patient personal persuasions conducted in Persian before I was permitted to take photographs of these documents, treated like state secrets.

The English term resilience is derived from the Latin verb *resilire*. The *Pons* Latin-German dictionary offers three translations, all of which are indicative of the way the Afghan civil service has dealt with extraordinary change and adversity in the past. The first two meanings are those usually associated with the term, accounting for the positive connotation described at the outset, namely (1) to bounce back or (2) to bounce off.[103] It is this ability to shrug off and recover from a negative external stimulus that we associate with the term resilience. It has given the term central currency in fields as diverse as psychology, ecology and disaster management.[104]

But there is a third meaning, more ambivalent and very relevant to the story of the Afghan bureaucracy's successful resistance against the externally imposed 'shock' of administrative reform. The word *resilire* also means (3) to shrivel, to make oneself small.[105] It is this coping strategy countless Afghan civil servants have used to survive repeated purges by successive regimes, essentially waiting out and passively obstructing reform. Amidst the violence and insecurity that many were forced to endure for

[103] R Hau et al, *Pons Globalwörterbuch Lateinisch-Deutsch* (Stuttgart, Ernst Klett Verlag, 1986) 899.

[104] 'Resilience has become a central concept in government policy understandings over the last decade. In our complex, global and interconnected world, resilience appears to be the policy "buzzword" of choice, alleged to be the solution to a wide and ever-growing range of policy issues': D Chandler, *Resilience: The Governance of Complexity* (London, Routledge, 2014) i.

[105] '1. zurückspringen; 2. zurück-, abprallen; 3. sich zusammenziehen, zusammenschrumpfen, sich verkleinern': Hau et al (n 103) 899, usage examples omitted.

decades, 'survival' has taken on a literal meaning. This led to a deeply ingrained scepticism about the promises of reform, resulting in a strategy of 'invisibility' and passivity. Such passive obstruction might be frustrating for the reformer, but it is an entirely rational defence of countervailing interests and must therefore inform our analysis of post-conflict state-building.

VI. Conclusion

The ignominious American withdrawal in 2021 finally unmasked the futility of a faulty international state-building effort. Despite unprecedented financial and manpower resources, a reasonably effective state could not be established. Political and military organs of the state proved unwilling and unable to defend the existing order, leading to a cascading collapse and takeover by the Taliban insurgency. It is unlikely that the Taliban will be more successful in establishing effective, let alone inclusive, governance, not least because they will be hampered by much of the same passive administrative resistance described above. The most likely scenario is the descent into a renewed cycle of intense civil war, something that has been apparent for several years already.[106]

From the outset of the international mission, the establishment of effective state structures had been viewed as indispensable. Coercive institutions in particular were deemed to be a precondition for the establishment of local and thus international security.[107] The failure to achieve this aim has doomed the international effort, irrespective of polite diplomatic formulas meant to obfuscate the reality of a humiliating defeat. Why have efforts at administrative reform been so catastrophically ineffective, despite the almost complete financial dependence of the Afghan state on external financing and donors' awareness of the necessity to improve the performance and legitimacy of the civil service?

A large part of the answer is the singular ability of successive Afghan governments to extract rents from competing external powers, who remained confused about which strategy to pursue. The results have been devastating for the Afghan population, international security and Western taxpayers, to say nothing of the thousands of civilians and security personnel killed and maimed. Understanding this spectacular failure – coming after similarly poor experiences in virtually all Western interventions in recent decades, from Somalia to Kosovo, Iraq, Libya and beyond – requires us to look beyond graft, ineptitude and venality, and to recognise the peculiar, often perverse incentives that exist for ordinary members of the civil service in a post-conflict setting. Part of the difficulty of understanding and countering these ordinary civil servants' reluctance to embrace constructive reform has to do with the rational basis for much of their resistance. While the overall result has been disastrous for society, we must recognise that civil servants, in their largely successful resistance to externally imposed reform, exhibited many of the same characteristics usually applauded as 'resilience'.

[106] T Gibbons-Neff, R Najim and H Jim, 'Back to Militias, the Chaotic Afghan Way of War' *New York Times* (17 July 2021) A4.

[107] See the section 'Political Society' in Afsah and Guhr (n 23) 396–97.

PART V

The Judiciary

10

The Maldives: A Parable of Judicial Crisis, Institutional Corrosion and Democratic Demise

AHMED NAZEER

I. Introduction

The Maldives is an island nation in the Indian Ocean located south-southwest of Sri Lanka and India. The country is spread over 26 coral atolls comprising 1190 islands, of which only about 200 are inhabited. The islands sit on the Chagos–Laccadive Ridge, a submarine mountain range in the Indian Ocean. The atolls are composed of live coral reefs and sand bars, surrounded by deep lagoons. With an area of 298 km^2 and a population of almost 500,000, the Maldives is one of the smallest countries in Asia, in terms of both land area and population. The average ground-level elevation in the country is 1.5 metres above sea level, making it one of the flattest and lowest countries in the world.[1] The Maldives sits atop crucial sea lines of communication in the Indian Ocean, including the East–West oil transportation routes.[2] The strategic location of the Maldives makes it important for international trade and regional security.

The history of the Maldives dates back to antiquity, when trading vessels from Arabia, India and China visited its shores. For most of its history, the Maldives was a monarchy ruled by kings, or sultans (the terms are used interchangeably in the Maldives). The first sultanate was established in 1153, and a succession of kings ruled the country until 1558, when the Portuguese took over the country. The Portuguese were eventually driven out, but it was colonised again in 1887 by the British Empire. The British government was in charge of international relations and defence during this period.[3] While still subject to British suzerainty, the political elites of the Maldives adopted the

[1] S Brown, 'Land Raising as a Solution to Sea-Level Rise: An Analysis of Coastal Flooding on an Artificial island in the Maldives' (2020) 13(suppl 1) *Journal of Flood Risk Management*, www.onlinelibrary.wiley.com/doi/epdf/10.1111/jfr3.12567.

[2] J Chowdhury, 'Maldives: Helping China Counter American Design' (Mantraya, 30 November 2015) Mantraya Analysis No 07, www.mantraya.org/maldives-helping-china-counter-american-design.

[3] N Mohamed, 'Note on the Early History of the Maldives' (2005) 70 *Archipel* 7, www.persee.fr/doc/arch_0044-8613_2005_num_70_1_3970.

country's first Constitution in 1932. This was done under the instruction of the British rulers.[4]

The British Governor of Ceylon, Sir Bernard Henry Bourdillon, directed the king to design a Constitution to resolve persistent political problems within the royal family.[5] The general population had little say in the creation of the Constitution. The Constitution did not last long, and the Maldivians went on to adopt multiple Constitutions.[6] The major goal of these Constitutions has been to keep the ruling elite politically stable.[7] However, the most recent Constitution, enacted in 2008, attempted to end decades of human rights violations and begin the country's transition to a constitutional democracy from a dictatorship.[8]

More than a decade has passed since the adoption of the 2008 Constitution. Nonetheless, the Maldives has struggled to reap its benefits.[9] The rights enshrined in the Constitution have frequently been construed more narrowly than its provisions allow, political parties have captured the judiciary and there has not been any progress towards democratic consolidation.[10] The Constitution of the Republic of Maldives 2008 was heralded as a major step forward for the country, offering new assurances of democratic freedoms. It is no surprise that hopes were high for the new democracy to take root in the archipelago nation. Yet, since its implementation, the Maldives has witnessed a gradual decline in the health of its constitutional democracy.[11]

One fundamental factor that hinders the effective implementation of the 2008 Constitution is the lack of judicial independence.[12] A strong judiciary can be an antidote to democratic backsliding.[13] However, the judiciary, like other institutions of the state, is vulnerable to being targeted by political actors for their own ends.[14] If political

[4] S Falaah, 'Towards a Maldivian Nation-State: The Constitutions of 1932 and 1968' in KYL Tan and R Hoque (eds), *Constitutional Foundings in South Asia* (Oxford, Hart Publishing, 2021).

[5] AHH Manik, 'Mohamed Shamsuddeen Radhunge Dhigu Raskamuge Hithaamaveri Nimun (The End of the Long Reign of King Mohamed Shamsuddeen)' (unpublished manuscript) http://saruna.mnu.edu.mv/jspui/handle/123456789/983.

[6] The Maldives adopted different Constitutions throughout 1932 to 2008. However, the texts of most Constitutions did not see major changes and are similar to the process of 'cycling'. Scholars have defined cycling as occurring when a country is 'caught in the grip of two competing and irreconcilable groups' that 'bounce back and forth between Constitutions according to which group is in power'. See Z Elkins, T Ginsburg, and J Melton, *The Endurance of National Constitutions* (Cambridge, Cambridge University Press, 2009).

[7] AA Rasheed, 'Historical Institutionalism in the Maldives: A Case of Governance Failure' (2014) 2 *The Maldives National Journal of Research*.

[8] See section II below for details of the pre-2008 era. See also F La Rue, 'Report of the Special Rapporteur on the Right to Freedom of Opinion and Expression' (United Nations Human Rights Council, 2009) www.ohchr.org/Documents/Issues/Opinion/A.HRC.11.4.Add.3.pdf.

[9] The Maldives have remained a partly free country since 2009 without making significant improvements. See S Repucci and A Slipowitz, 'Freedom in the World: Democracy under Siege' (Freedom House, 2021) www.freedomhouse.org/sites/default/files/2021-02/FIW2021_World_02252021_FINAL-web-upload.pdf.

[10] ibid.

[11] Democracies do not always suffer sudden deaths. It can also be a slow process. See C de la Torre and A Ortiz Lemos, 'Populist Polarization and the Slow Death of Democracy in Ecuador' (2016) 23 *Democratization* 221 www.doi.org/10.1080/13510347.2015.1058784; See also Repucci and Slipowitz (n 9).

[12] See G Knaul, 'Report of the Special Rapporteur on the Independence of Judges and Lawyers' *UN Human Rights Council* (2013) www.digitallibrary.un.org/record/757845?ln=en#record-files-collapse-header.

[13] T Ginsburg and A Huq, *How to Save a Constitutional Democracy* (Chicago, University of Chicago Press, 2018).

[14] See KL Scheppele, 'Autocratic Legalism' (2018) 85 *University of Chicago Law Review* 545.

leaders manipulate, capture and politicise the judiciary, the courts can become a tool for facilitating constitutional breakdown.[15] The judiciary then becomes an instrument to validate the executive's agenda, imprison political opponents, eliminate political competition, restrict the media and the freedoms of speech, assembly and association, and facilitate the manipulation of elections.

The Maldives has seen political actors attack the constitutional order and unravel constitutional democracy with the help of the Supreme Court. This chapter analyses the Supreme Court's role in degrading constitutional democracy in the Maldives. The chapter's main argument is that the Maldives Constitution 2008 has institutional design flaws that facilitate the political capture of the Supreme Court. As a result, the Supreme Court has aligned with partisan political actors and acted as an accomplice in the democratic breakdown of the Maldives. To demonstrate this, the chapter focuses on two facets of the Maldivian judiciary: first, how the Constitution facilitates political capture of the Supreme Court; and second, how the Supreme Court sided with the government of the day and undermined the independence and operation of other constitutional institutions, such as the Parliament and fourth branch institutions.

This first section of the chapter introduces the democratic and constitutional system of the Maldives. Section II details the general constitutional design in the 2008 Constitution and examines the institutional design flaws that enable politicians to manipulate the Supreme Court. This includes the composition of the Judicial Service Commission (JSC) and the appointment and dismissal procedures of Supreme Court judges. Section III explores the politicisation of the Supreme Court by analysing how the Court has misinterpreted the Constitution to tamper with elections and interfere with the operations of 'fourth branch institutions' (or guarantor institutions)[16] and Parliament.[17] Section IV concludes the chapter with a consideration of the options for reforming the judiciary into an independent institution capable of playing its constitutional role. These reforms, whilst arising out of the Maldivian experience,

[15] Newer democracies have armed the courts with strong judicial review powers and made the courts a powerful institution to protect democracy. See generally M Elliott, *The Constitutional Foundations of Judicial Review* (Oxford, Hart Publishing, 2001); T Ginsburg, *Judicial Review in New Democracies: Constitutional Courts in Asian Cases* (New York, Cambridge University Press, 2003). See also G Helmke and F Rosenbluth, 'Regimes and the Rule of Law: Judicial Independence in Comparative Perspective' (2009) 12 *Annual Review of Political Science* 345.

[16] The place of these institutions within the state is not clear. They are not part of any of three branches of the state under the Constitution of Maldives 2008. The Constitution has a chapter for each branch of the state. Offices and institutions under each branch are clearly identified in the Constitution. However, these are listed as 'Independent Commissions and Independent Positions' in ch 7 of the Constitution. Nonetheless, more research is needed to further evaluate their place in the modern state. For a discussion of these new institutions and their role as guarantor institutions, see T Khaitan, 'Guarantor Institutions' (2021) 16 *Asian Journal of Comparative Law* 40.

[17] For the role of fourth-branch institutions in a democracy, see F Vibert, *The Rise of the Unelected: Democracy and the New Separation of Powers* (New York, Cambridge University Press, 2007); B Ackerman, 'The New Separation of Powers' (2000) 111 *Harvard Law Review* 633; Mahomed, 'The Fourth Branch: Challenges and Opportunities for a Robust and Meaningful Role for South Africa's State Institutions Supporting Democracy' in D Bilchitz and D Landau (eds), *The Evolution of the Separation of Powers: Between the Global North and the Global South* (Cheltenham, Edward Elgar, 2018); M Tushnet, *The New Fourth Branch: Institutions for Protecting Constitutional Democracy* (New York, Cambridge University Press, 2021); G O'Donnell, 'Horizontal Accountability in New Democracies' (1998) *Journal of Democracy* 9, 112, www.muse.jhu.edu/article/16904; T Khaitan, 'Killing a Constitution with a Thousand Cuts: Executive Aggrandizement and Party-State Fusion in India' (2020) 14 *Law and Ethics of Human Rights* 49.

may be of broader relevance for other polities struggling with the issue of judicial independence.

II. Impact of Constitutional Design on Democratic Decay and Breakdown

A. The Pre- and Post-2008 Constitutional System

The implementation of the 2008 Constitution was a pivotal moment in the constitutional history of the Maldives. It replaced the 1998 Constitution drafted under the administration of Maumoon Abdul Gayoom – ruler of the country for three decades.[18] Under the 1998 Constitution, the President effectively headed the judiciary, Parliament and the executive whilst also acting as Commander-in-Chief of the security forces.[19] As Head of the Judiciary, the President had the power to appoint and dismiss the Chief Justice and Justices of the High Court.[20] The President also decided which cases the High Court could hear on appeal.[21]

There was, accordingly, no separation of powers. Therefore, the President was able to rule the country with impunity. The security forces routinely arrested and tortured journalists and political activists.[22] Political parties were prohibited.[23] Criticising the government or politicians could result in criminal prosecution. Therefore, most Maldivians did not get involved in politics.[24] However, there was a small but active group of political activists campaigning against Gayoom's regime led by the Maldivian Democratic Party (MDP).[25]

Despite being imprisoned several times for 'anti-government' activities, they persisted in their struggle.[26] The MDP gained greater prominence when a mass movement against Gayoom erupted in 2003 after the military shot and killed prisoners in Maafushi Prison.[27] The protests and campaigning emerging out of the 2003

[18] N Langton, 'In Maldives: First Democratically-Elected President Sworn In' (The Asia Foundation, 2008) www.asiafoundation.org/2008/11/12/in-maldives-democracy-begins.

[19] See Arts 4 and 33 of the Constitution of Maldives 1998.

[20] The High Court of the Maldives was at the time the Apex Court of the Maldives. See Art 117 of the Constitution of Maldives 1998. For presidential powers over the High Court, see Art 39 of the Constitution of Maldives 1998.

[21] Constitution of Maldives 1998, Art 115.

[22] Amnesty International, 'Amnesty International Report 2004 – Maldives' (2004) www.refworld.org/docid/40b5a1fbc.html.

[23] Until 2005, political parties were not allowed in the Maldives. See A Bansal, 'Onset of Multiparty Democracy in Maldives' (Manohar Parrikar Institute for Defence Studies and Analyses, 2005) www.idsa.in/idsastrategiccomments/OnsetofMultipartyDemocracyinMaldives%20_ABansal_030905.

[24] MR Einfeld, 'Strengthening the Maldiviam Judicial System' (Mv Law, 2005) www.mvlaw.gov.mv/pdf/publications/9.pdf.

[25] At the time, the MDP was not registered as a political party because political parties were not allowed in the Maldives.

[26] Freedom House, 'Freedom in the World 2006 – Maldives' (2005) www.refworld.org/docid/473c55745.html.

[27] R Harding and N Morgan, 'Strengthening Custodial Services in the Maldives' (Mv Law, 2004) www.mvlaw.gov.mv/pdf/publications/2.pdf.

Prison Incident ended a long period of relative political quietism on the part of most Maldivians. The movement formed in 2003 and continued protesting despite government efforts to stop them, ultimately forcing the government to agree to a reform agenda in 2004.[28] The government's roadmap for reform included introducing multi-party democracy, strengthening judicial independence and adopting a new Constitution.[29] After announcing the reform agenda, Gayoom convened a Constitutional Assembly to draft a new Constitution.[30]

The Constitution of 2008 separated the three branches of the state.[31] The institutional design of the 2008 Constitution is based on a presidential system.[32] However, the cabinet ministers require parliamentary approval once appointed[33] and are subject to parliamentary confidence.[34] Likewise, a two-thirds majority of Parliament can impeach the President and Vice President from office for one of the causes stipulated in the Constitution.[35]

The 2008 Constitution, for the first time, established the judiciary as a separate branch of the state and incorporated a comprehensive catalogue of fundamental human rights.[36] The Constitution also established fourth branch institutions, such as the Human Rights Commission of the Maldives (HRCM) and the Elections Commission (EC). It formally separated them from the three traditional branches of the state.[37]

[28] European Parliament, 'Note on the Maldives' (2006) www.europarl.europa.eu/meetdocs/2004_2009/documents/fd/200/200605/2006052_maldivesen.pdf.

[29] See n 8 above; La Rue (n 8).

[30] Commonwealth Secretariat, 'Maldives Parliamentary Elections 22 January 2005: Report of the Commonwealth Expert Team' (2005) www.aceproject.org/ero-en/regions/asia/MV/maldives-final-report-parliamentary-elections-1/at_download/file.

[31] For a discussion on the crucial role separation of powers play in a democracy, see generally A Huq and JD Michaels, 'The Cycles of Separation-of-Powers Jurisprudence' (2016) 346 *Yale Law Journal* 262; MS Flaherty, 'More Real than Apparent: Separation of Power, the Rule of Law, and Comparative Executive Creativity in Hamdan v Rumsfeld' (2005–06) 51 *Cato Supreme Court Review* 51; MS Flaherty, 'The Most Dangerous Branch' (1996) 105 *Yale Law Journal* 1725; NW Barber, 'Prelude to the Separation of Powers' (2001) 60 *CLJ* 59; PL Strauss, 'Separation of Powers in Comparative Perspective: How Much Protection for the Rule of Law' in P Cane (eds), *The Oxford Handbook of Comparative Administrative Law* (Oxford, Oxford University Press, 2021); T Persson, 'Gerard Roland, and Guido Tabellini, Separation of Powers and Political Accountability' (1997) 112 *Quarterly Journal of Economics* 1163; R Albert, 'Presidential Values in Parliamentary Democracies' (2010) 8 *International Journal of Constitutional Law* 207; RL Brown 'Separated Powers and Ordered Liberty' (1991) 139 *University of Pennsylvania Law Review* 1513; DJ Levinson and RH Pildes, 'Separation of Parties, Not Powers' (2006) 119 *Harvard Law Review* 2312; ME Magill, 'Beyond Powers and Branches in Separation of Powers Law' (2001) 150 *University of Pennsylvania Law Review* 603.

[32] S Abbott, 'Voters Choose Presidential System in Maldives Referendum' *The Guardian* (2007) www.theguardian.com/world/2007/aug/22/uk.stephenabbott.

[33] The Constitution of Maldives 2008, Art 129(c) states that 'the President must receive the approval of the People's Majlis for all appointments to the Cabinet'.

[34] The Constitution of Maldives 2008, Art 101 states that Parliament can remove cabinet ministers by a no confidence vote that can be passed by a majority of the total membership of Parliament. The Maldives Supreme Court in *Ali Waheed and Jumhoory Party vs Attorney-General* (2010/SC-C/25)(2010/SC-C/26) ruled that the Maldives was not a pure presidential system since the Parliament had the authority to dismiss members of the cabinet.

[35] The Constitution of Maldives 2008, Art 100 states that Parliament can pass a resolution to remove the President or the Vice President on the grounds of violation of Islam of the Constitution, serious misconduct, and inability to perform the responsibilities of office.

[36] See Arts 141 and 142 of the Constitution of Maldives 2008. See ch 2 of the Constitution of Maldives 2008 for a list of constitutional rights the Constitution guarantees.

[37] See ch 7 of the Constitution of Maldives 2008.

However, despite these changes, the constitutional design contains flaws enabling the influence of political actors in the judiciary and fourth branch institutions.[38]

Under the current legal system, the Maldives' judiciary has a three-tier system: Magistrate Courts, Superior Courts and Appellate Courts. Both Magistrate Courts and Superior Courts are first instance courts – collectively referred to as the 'lower courts'.[39] There are five superior courts in the Maldives: the Criminal Court, Civil Court, Family Court, Juvenile Court and Drug Court.[40] Cases concluded in the lower courts can be appealed to the High Court and then the Supreme Court.[41]

Prior to 2008, judges did not need to have any specific academic qualifications.[42] This allowed the President to appoint anyone as a judge – most notably, political allies and loyalists.[43] Therefore, immediately after the 2008 Constitution was introduced, the judges in place were people Gayoom had hand-picked during his presidency.[44] The Constitution required the JSC to set eligibility requirements for judges and remove judges that did not meet the new standards within two years.[45] It was hoped that the new eligibility requirements would reform the judiciary by removing unqualified judges.

However, the judicial reform envisaged by the Constitution could not be achieved. In the years after 2008, the JSC became heavily politicised (on partisan grounds), as it was composed of Members of Parliament and the executive. At the time the JSC was formed, the president did not possess a parliamentary majority, and the opposition MPs and the executive members in the JSC did not cooperate in formulating an independent judiciary. Representatives from both sides fought to capture the JSC and the judiciary. When the 2008 Constitution came into effect, Gayoom's party won a majority in Parliament even though his long-term rival Mohamed Nasheed was elected President.[46] This led to a JSC comprised of long-standing political enemies from the executive and Parliament. It accordingly became a site of political contestation, with both Parliament and the executive jostling to capture the judiciary.

The executive-appointed JSC members wanted to overhaul the judiciary, while parliamentarians in the JSC wanted to keep the existing judges.[47] The parliamentarians were from Gayoom's party, and the existing judges were appointed by Gayoom when he was President. The new President wanted to overhaul the judiciary and the Supreme Court so that he could appoint his own loyalists. However, because of the way the

[38] See below for details.

[39] Judicature Act 2010, s 2.

[40] See s 53 of the Judicature Act 2010 for a list of Superior Courts. The Drug Court was established under the Drug Act 2011. For the details of the functions of these courts, see the Judicature Act 2010 and the Drug Act 2011.

[41] Constitution of Maldives 2008, Art 143(c).

[42] See L Despouy, 'Report of the Special Rapporteur on the Independence of Judges and Lawyers' (UN Human Rights Council, 2007) www.digitallibrary.un.org/record/600685?ln=en.

[43] See, eg the relationship between the Chief Justice and President Gayoom as described by Justice Marcus R Einfeld's report. See n 24 above.

[44] A Velezinee, 'The Failed Silent Coup: In Defeat, They Reached for the Gun' (Dhivehi Sitee, 2012) www.dhivehisitee.com/wp-content/uploads/2012/The%20Failed%20Silent%20Coup.pdf.

[45] See Art 285 of the Constitution of Maldives 2008.

[46] To see the number of seats opposition won, see M Omidi, 'Political Parties Scramble for Independents' *Minivan News* (2009) www.minivannewsarchive.com/politics/political-parties-scramble-for-independents-1500.

[47] See n 44 above.

JSC is organised, Parliament has greater authority over the JSC than the government, hence whoever has a majority in Parliament can also control the Commission.[48] After a prolonged period of disagreement, the JSC decided that the constitutional provisions on judicial qualifications were not mandatory and that existing judges could remain on the bench.[49] This revealed how Parliament could control the judiciary through the JSC. As a result, the Supreme Court became strongly politicised, serving the interests of the executive if the President controlled the legislature, and the legislature if the President failed to gain a parliamentary majority.

The political conflict between the representatives of the two branches of the state at the JSC demonstrates a key issue facing Maldivian democratic politics: the lack of a culture of cooperation between political parties. As a result, the JSC became a site of contestation between the two branches.

B. Constitutional Compromise of Judicial Independence

The appointment and dismissal procedures of judicial members and the composition of the JSC are particularly problematic aspects of the 2008 Constitution.[50] The Constitution divided the powers relating to the appointment and removal of justices between three institutions: the JSC, the President and Parliament. The JSC is in charge of starting the appointment process by inviting interested candidates to apply for Supreme Court vacancies and evaluating potential candidates.[51] After this initial evaluation, the JSC forwards a shortlist of candidates to the President,[52] who then decides which candidates he will nominate to Parliament for approval.[53] Parliament can approve nominees to the Supreme Court with a simple majority of the members present and voting.[54]

As the JSC occupies a central role in this process, this institution must remain an independent body that can ensure that judicial appointments are merit-based and free from political influence. However, its membership consists of MPs, a minister, a presidential appointee, one representative of the legal profession, a member of the public nominated by Parliament, the Head of the Civil Service Commission (CSC) and three judges.[55] Thus, while the JSC is theoretically autonomous – as an organisation that is not

[48] This is because the parliamentarians in the JSC and the members in the JSC that are appointed by Parliament, such as the President of the Civil Service Commission, outweigh the number of executive-appointed members.

[49] JJ Robinson, 'A Justice System in Crisis: UN Special Rapporteur's Report' *Minivan News* (2013) www.minivannewsarchive.com/politics/a-justice-system-in-crisis-un-special-rapporteurs-report-58541.

[50] This will be further elaborated below.

[51] Judges Act 2010, s 17(b).

[52] ibid s 17(c).

[53] ibid s 17(d).

[54] ibid s 17(e).

[55] The Constitution of Maldives 2008, Art 158 states that the Judicial Service Commission shall consist of: (a) the Speaker of the People's Majlis; (b) a judge of the Supreme Court other than the Chief Justice, elected by the judges of the Supreme Court; (c) a judge of the High Court, elected by the judges of the High Court; (d) a judge of the Trial Courts, elected by the judges of the Trial Court; (e) a member of the People's Majlis appointed by it; (f) a member of the general public appointed by the People's Majlis; (g) the Chair of the Civil Service Commission; (h) a person appointed by the President; (i) the Attorney-General; and (j) a lawyer elected from among the lawyers licensed to practise in the Maldives by themselves.

nominally part of or embedded in the other branches of the state – its functioning is in fact highly influenced by its members' political backgrounds.

Furthermore, the inclusion of judges on the JSC has been equally problematic. The trial courts, the High Court and the Supreme Court have very few judges.[56] There is concern that the tight-knit professional and social network of Maldivian judges may lead to a strong incentive for individual and group preservation.[57] Supreme Court Justice Husnu Suood remarked in his suggestion for JSC reform that judges on the JSC may hesitate when faced with the duty of taking action against their colleagues to prevent disputes with them.[58]

The Head of the CSC is seemingly an independent figure, since the CSC does not belong to any branch of the state.[59] However, the Head's neutrality and independence are limited by a key structural issue: the CSC's membership is controlled by Parliament.[60] The CSC's membership is subservient to the legislature due to its composition. The fact that incumbent CSCs have been replaced with more loyal members when the parliamentary majority moves from one political party to another demonstrates its subjugation.[61] As a result, despite the constitutional promise that the CSC is an impartial institution, its members are compelled to serve the interests of the majority party in order to remain in office.[62]

This is made abundantly clear in the appointment process; Transparency Maldives – a national chapter of Transparency International – found that Parliament disregarded CSC nominees' qualifications and interview scores.[63] The study found that 'political loyalty' was the main factor Parliament considered when appointing members to the CSC.[64]

Apart from the judges and the CSC Head, the remaining members of the JSC are the Speaker of Parliament, one MP, one member from the public that Parliament appoints, a presidential nominee and the Attorney-General.[65] These are all influential political

[56] H Suood, 'A Proposal for Reforming JSC' www.academia.edu/36781201/Proposal_for_reforming_JSC.

[57] ibid.

[58] ibid.

[59] The Constitution of Maldives 2008, Art 179(b) states that 'The Civil Service Commission is an independent and impartial institution. It shall perform its duties and responsibilities in accordance with the Constitution and any laws enacted by the People's Majlis.' The Civil Service Commission is listed under independent institutions in the Constitution.

[60] A detailed analysis of the political capture of the Commission is not possible here. However, it is sufficient here to mention that Art 180(b) of the Constitution of Maldives 2008 stipulates that members of the Commission should be appointed by the Parliament and the President. This process has politicised the CSC appointments. See also s 13 of the Civil Service Act 2007.

[61] See, eg how the current Parliament dismissed the Civil Service Commission members, accusing them of being politically motivated in carrying out their work. F Shaahunaz, 'Parliament Committee Launches Probe into "Political" CSC' *The Edition* (31 October 2019) www.edition.mv/civil_service_commission/13251.

[62] The Constitution of Maldives 2008, Art 179(b) reads: 'The Civil Service Commission is an independent and impartial institution. It shall perform its duties and responsibilities in accordance with the Constitution and any laws enacted by the People's Majlis. The Civil Service Commission shall strive to achieve and maintain an effective and efficient civil service with high standards of professional ethics.' See s 13 of the Civil Service Act 2007 (Second Amendment). See also M Malsa, 'Parliament Dismisses All CSC Members Except Amira' *The Edition* (29 June 2020) www.edition.mv/civil_service_commission/17549.

[63] Transparency Maldives, 'Review of Appointment and Dismissal of Members of Selected Independent Institutions of Maldives 2008–2016' (2017) www.transparency.mv/v16/wp-content/uploads/2017/04/Review_Report_Web.pdf.

[64] ibid.

[65] The current Speaker is Former President and Leader of MDP, Mohamed Nasheed. Z Zalif, 'Speaker Nasheed Appointed as JSC Member' *Raajje MV* (2019) www.raajje.mv/57020.

representatives from the executive and Parliament, except for the member from the public. Generally, the MPs on the JSC are allied to the majority party in Parliament. For example, the current MP nominated by Parliament, and the JSC's current president, is Hisaan Hussain.[66] Hussain is the personal lawyer of former President Mohamed Nasheed.[67] In addition, influential MPs such as Faris Maumoon, Afrasheem Ali and Ibrahim Riza have previously sat on the JSC.[68] Their presence on the Committee has led to its control by political actors, resulting in the appointment of judges based on political loyalty. This form of internal capture has also permitted judges with strong political ties to avoid punishment for judicial misconduct and criminal offences.[69]

Furthermore, the President's power to disregard the JSC's recommendations and the requirement for a simple majority of MPs to approve Supreme Court justices have also been problematic.[70] Since the President has the authority to discard JSC-recommended candidates, prospective candidates with a political connection with the president or his political party are arguably at an advantage.[71] In addition, since a simple majority is sufficient to approve Supreme Court justices, the political party that forms the majority in Parliament can approve their preferred candidate and vote down other candidates.[72]

The Maldives is a country that has experienced a democratic decline over the past years. This decline has resulted in a lack of faith among the people in their judiciary. Several political issues facing the country have contributed to this problem, but they all have one common cause: the failure to create and maintain credible institutions. For example, according to a study by Transparency Maldives in 2015, 51 per cent of

[66] 'MP Hisaan Appointed as President of JSC' *Sun* (2019) www.en.sun.mv/56561.

[67] Prior to winning the Parliamentary Elections, Hisaan was Nasheed's lawyer and close friend. See 'Nasheed: Attempts to Smear the Name of My Attorney are Cowardly – She Has My Full Confidence' *One Online* (2019) www.oneonline.mv/en/7248.

[68] MP Faris Maumoon is the son of former President Gayoom. See Z Zalif, 'President Solih Appoints Members to the Judicial Service Commission' *Raajje MV* (2018) www.raajje.mv/45028. MP Afrasheem Ali was a close aide to former President Gayoom. MP Ibrahim Riza is a close aide to former President Yameen.

[69] See, eg Z Rasheed, 'Supreme Court Judge Ali Hameed Cleared of Misconduct in Sex Tape Scandal' *Minivan News* (2014) www.minivannewsarchive.com/politics/supreme-court-judge-ali-hameed-cleared-of-misconduct-in-sex-tape-scandal-87684.

[70] The Judges Act 2010, s 17(d) states that the President can nominate to the Parliament any candidate from the shortlisted candidates.

[71] The Supreme Court bench currently consists of Chief Justice Muthasim Adnan, Justice Dr Azmiralda Didi, Justice Aisha Shujoon, Justice Mahaz Ali Zahir, Justice Husnu Suood, Justice Ali Rasheed Hussain and Justice Dr Mohamed Ibrahim. A brief evaluation of their background shows some of them have political affiliations, and political loyalty may have been a key factor in their selection. For example, Husnu Suood was a cabinet member under Nasheed's government. He was also involved in the MDP Presidential Campaign of 2018. See 'Leadership Change a Necessity this Election: Suood' *The Edition* (2018) www.edition.mv/news/6267. Until 2013, he was a member of the MDP. See Sun, 'Suood Leaves MDP' *Sun* (2013) www.en.sun.mv/17265. Zahir and Shujoon were nominated to the Supreme Court by the President. See 'President Nominates Azmiralda and Shujoon as Judges for Supreme Court' *Corporate Maldives* (2019) www.corporatemaldives.com/president-nominates-azmiralda-and-shujoon-as-judges-for-supreme-court/; 'JSC Accepts Shujune and Azmiralda for Supreme Court' *One Online* (2019) www.oneonline.mv/en/14207. Furthermore, Zahir is the daughter of Ahmed Zahir, the Speaker of Parliament during Gayoom's presidency, who had also served in Gayoom's cabinet as Justice Minister. However, both Gayoom and Zahir became critics of former President Abdulla Yameen during his presidency. When Yameen's term came to an end, Zahir was appointed as a Supreme Court Justice. See 'Elder Statesman Rails Against Authoritarian Reversals' *Maldives Independent* (2016) www.maldives independent.com/politics/elder-statesman-rails-against-authoritarian-reversals-124100.

[72] Judges Act 2010, s 17(e).

Maldivians said they had no confidence in the judiciary.[73] The design flaws with the JSC and the judicial appointment process have hindered the struggle for judicial independence in the Maldives and have resulted in the loss of public confidence in the independence of the judiciary.

C. Dismissal Procedures

The 2008 Constitution and the Judicature Act 2010 ostensibly protect the security of tenure of the judicial branch. The 2008 Constitution stipulates that judges shall not be removed from office 'during good behaviour and compliance with judicial ethics … [but] only if the [JSC] finds that the person is grossly incompetent … guilty of gross misconduct'.[74] However, 'good behaviour' and 'judicial ethics' are undefined in the Constitution.

To remove a judge, the JSC must submit a resolution to Parliament, which must be supported by two-thirds of those present and voting.[75] Although two-thirds of the total membership is a high threshold, two-thirds of the members present at the meeting could be a low absolute number. This raises the possibility of manipulation of parliamentary procedure to control who makes up the quorum when voting on a removal motion.[76]

A more significant issue is the possibility of bypassing the constitutional procedure for removing judges. There are two bypass mechanisms. The first requires amending the Judicature Act 2010 to reduce the number of Supreme Court justices. The Constitution does not stipulate the number of judges in the Supreme Court. Primary legislation – such as the Judicature Act 2010 – can be amended by a simple majority.[77] The three administrations that have come to power since 2008 – President Nasheed, his successor Abdulla Yameen and the current President – have all altered the composition of the Supreme Court bench in this way. The five justices on the bench when Nasheed came to power in 2008 were Gayoom-era justices.[78] Nasheed increased the Supreme Court bench from five to seven during his administration in 2010 by adding two perceived 'loyalists'.[79]

[73] 'Transparency Maldives 2015 Maldives Democracy Survey Points to a Troubled Future for Democracy in the Maldives' *Transparency Maldives* (2015) www.transparency.mv/files/media/8b9ed87e579a58703e0bcd09181b0064.pdf.

[74] Constitution of Maldives 2008, Art 154(a).

[75] The Constitution of Maldives 2008, Art 154(b) stipulates that 'a Judge may be removed from office only if the Judicial Service Commission finds that the person is grossly incompetent, or that the Judge is guilty of gross misconduct, and submits to the People's Majlis a resolution supporting the removal of the Judge, which is passed by a two thirds majority of the members of the People's Majlis present and voting'.

[76] See, eg 'Speaker Accused of Subverting Parliamentary Rules' *Maldives Independent* (2016) www.maldivesindependent.com/politics/speaker-accused-of-subverting-parliamentary-rules-127840.

[77] This Act has been amended several times to reduce and increase the Supreme Court bench, eg by the First Amendment to Judicature Act 2010 (Amendment Number 40/2014) and the Third Amendment to Judicature Act (Amendment Number 6/2019).

[78] See Human Rights Watch, 'An All-Out Assault on Democracy' (2018) www.hrw.org/report/2018/08/16/all-out-assault-democracy/crushing-dissent-maldives#_ftn151.

[79] This change was made when the interim Supreme Court transitioned to a permanent court. Senior members of Nasheed's party alleged that the Supreme Court bench was selected by making secret deals

Similarly, Yameen amended the law in 2014 to remove the two judges added by Nasheed.[80] The removal of the two judges was widely condemned as an arbitrary decision by members of the international community, attracting global criticism.[81] Following the removal of the two Nasheed-appointed judges, there was a striking absence of dissenting opinions in the Court's more controversial cases.[82] After Yameen's defeat to the MDP (Nasheed and the current President Solih's party) in 2018, the judges appointed by Yameen were, in turn, removed and replaced.[83]

The second constitutional bypass mechanism for removing judges is more unconventional: the executive has used the security forces to arrest justices of the Supreme Court and senior judges, opening the door for their replacement. There have been two notable instances of this: once in 2012, during the administration of President Nasheed, and a second time in 2018, under President Yameen.

During his tenure, Nasheed dealt with several issues, including domestic terrorism, growing extremism and the tutelary elements of the previous dictatorial regime. He also made enemies with his strong rhetoric against radical Islamists. Though he came to power with the support of many political parties, those parties left his government soon after the election. Nasheed was politically weak as the political parties, religious extremists, Gayoom-appointed judicial members and MPs united against him. The only way for Nasheed to remain in power was to arrest the opposition leaders and suppress the growing opposition movements against him. However, the courts frequently released political leaders arrested on various charges, ranging from treason to bribery.

Frustrated by the release of the opposition leaders, Nasheed's government claimed that the Criminal Court Chief Judge Abdulla Mohamed was impeding the police's efforts to investigate high-profile corruption cases against political leaders and ordered the military to detain him. Before his arrest, Judge Mohamed had been at the centre of many controversies.[84] Despite all the accusations, the Parliament-controlled JSC

between Nasheed's party and the opposition at the time. JJ Robinson, 'Constitutional Disaster Averted as Parliament Approves Supreme Court' *Minivan News* (2010) www.minivannewsarchive.com/politics/constitutional-disaster-averted-as-parliament-approves-supreme-court-10233.

[80] International Commission of Jurists, 'Maldives: Removal of Supreme Court Judges an Assault on Independence of the Judiciary' (2014) www.icj.org/maldives-removal-of-supreme-court-judges-an-assault-on-independence-of-the-judiciary/.

[81] See the joint statement by the Commonwealth Lawyers Association, the Commonwealth Legal Education Association, the Commonwealth Magistrates' and Judges' Association www.cmja.org/downloads/news/CLA%20CLEA%20CMJA%20Statement%20December%202014.pdf; see also United Nations Human Rights Office for the High Commissioner, 'Maldives: Arbitrary Removal of Supreme Court Judges Deeply Concerning, UN Expert Warns' (2014) www.ohchr.org/EN/NewsEvents/Pages/DisplayNews.aspx?NewsID=15446&LangID=E.

[82] An example of their dissention before their removal is the electoral case submitted in 2013 by Jumhoory Party, Supreme Court Case Number 2013/SC-C/42. The majority of the Supreme Court ruled that the Presidential Election 2013 was not legitimate and ordered a rerun. However, the judges who were Nasheed's loyalists dissented and ruled that the election was legitimate. The cases that came between 2014 and 2018 after their removal had no dissenting opinion and every case ended in favour of the government.

[83] 'Maldives Lawmakers Dismiss Chief Justice and Senior Judge' *Euronews* (2019) www.euronews.com/2019/11/18/maldives-lawmakers-dismiss-chief-justice-and-senior-judge.

[84] For details of the complains against Abdulla Mohamed, see JJ Robinson and A Naish, 'Chief Judge "Took Entire Criminal Justice System in His Fist": Afeef' *Minivan News* (2012) www.minivannewsarchive.com/politics/chief-judge-took-entire-criminal-justicesystem-in-his-fist-afeef-30926.

refused to act against him.[85] This is because, as already explained, the JSC is a politically controlled body, and judges with connections to influential politicians have not been held accountable.[86] Gayoom appointed Judge Mohamed, and Gayoom's party had strong parliamentary support. Thus, Judge Mohamed remained loyal to Gayoom even after he lost power and was therefore protected.

A day before his arrest, Judge Mohamed had ordered the police to release Dr Ahmed Jameel, an opposition leader detained for 'making fabricated statements' against the government, which was an offence at the time under the (now repealed) Penal Code.[87] The military continued the judge's detention in defiance of High Court and Supreme Court orders.[88] The Supreme Court, the High Court, the Prosecutor General and the HRCM all called for his immediate release.[89] The opposition political parties also launched a series of protests demanding the judge's release. Eventually, one night, the military and police officers abandoned their duties, joined the protesters and demanded the government's resignation.[90] A few hours later, Nasheed's government resigned after a series of failed negotiations with the mutinying officers. Nasheed's Vice President remained in office and formed a new government for the remainder of the term.[91] Judge Mohamed was released soon after Nasheed resigned.

In a similar move, in 2018, Abdulla Yameen's government ordered the military and police forces to arrest the Chief Justice and another justice of the Supreme Court.[92] The arrest came following a ruling of the Supreme Court ordering the release of senior opposition figures arrested on various charges since Yameen came to power in 2013.[93] The Supreme Court order stated that the charges against the opposition leaders were politically motivated and that the court rulings against them were issued due to the influence exerted on the judiciary and law enforcement agencies.[94] Yameen refused to execute the court order and accused the Supreme Court of planning to overthrow the executive.[95] Initially, there was confusion among the state institutions, particularly

[85] The Parliament at the time was controlled by the opposition parties led by former President Gayoom. See n 44 above.

[86] For example, in this case, Judge Abdulla Mohamed was appointed by Gayoom. He was known to be someone who had close connections to Gayoom.

[87] For details of the charges, see A Naish, 'Police Interrogate, Briefly Detain DQP Leaders over "Slanderous" Allegations' *Minivan News* (2012) www.minivannewsarchive.com/politics/police-interrogate-briefly-detain-dqp-leaders-over-slanderous-allegations-30693.

[88] Supreme Court Order Number 2012/SC-SJ/01 and High Court Order Number 95-CR/2012/2. This reflects the lack of objective control of the military. The Maldivian governments have always had subjective control of the military. However, this discussion is not relevant to this chapter. For objective and subjective control of the military, see S Huntington, *The Soldier and the State: The Theory and Politics of Civil-Military Relations* (Cambridge, MA, Belknap Press, 1967).

[89] International Commission of Jurists, 'Justice Adrift: Rule of Law and Political Crisis in the Maldives' (2015) www.refworld.org/docid/57ee7b6e4.html.

[90] JJ Robinson, 'The Maldives: What Went Wrong with the Democracy Experiment?' (2016) 105 *The Round Table* 223.

[91] Nasheed's Vice President was from a different political party and formed a government with Nasheed's opposition parties.

[92] 'Maldives: Supreme Court Judges Arrested Amid Political Crisis' *BBC News* (2018) www.bbc.co.uk/news/world-asia-42955132.

[93] 'Maldives Supreme Court Orders Release of All Opposition Leaders, President Yameen Defiant' (*The Wire*, 2018) www.thewire.in/external-affairs/maldives-supreme-court-orders-release-of-all-opposition-leaders-president-yameen-defiant.

[94] 2018/SC-SJ/01.

[95] 'Will Not Comply with Any Top Court Order to Impeach President' *The Edition* (2018) www.edition.mv/news/5117.

within the Prosecutor General, an independent body that does not belong to any branch of the state, as to which branch it should follow when conflicting directives were issued. Therefore, the Prosecutor General did not act on the Supreme Court orders.

A few days later, the President declared a statement of emergency, and the military and police publicly announced that they would follow the government's advice over the orders of the Supreme Court. Soon after their announcement, the military and police forces stormed the Supreme Court chambers and arrested both the Chief Justice and Justice Ali Hameed. The two judges were charged with terrorism, obstruction of justice, influencing official conduct and conspiring to overthrow the government.[96] The pair were found guilty of some of these charges and removed from the Supreme Court. The remaining members of the Supreme Court quickly issued an order nullifying its previous order.[97]

As demonstrated in this section, every administration elected post-2008 has used one or both of these constitutional bypass mechanisms to remove judges that were seen as obstructive to the incumbent party's hold on political power.

III. Effects of Politicisation of the Judiciary: Judicial Overreach and Disruption of Constitutional Institutions

Where the Supreme Court has been politically captured and compromised, this has manifested in judgments of the Supreme Court on constitutionally important issues. The Supreme Court has been utilised to interfere with presidential elections and the functions of fourth branch institutions – such as the EC and the HRCM. This section details examples of judicial interference in elections, fourth branch institutions and Parliament.

A. Interference with Elections

Before the 2013 presidential elections, the MDP members and their leader – Nasheed – had on several occasions criticised the judiciary and promised that the party would reform it.[98] This had been a campaign pledge of the MDP in almost every election since 2008.[99] It should be noted, however, that the MDP members and Nasheed's refusal to make constitutional changes to remove barriers to judicial independence demonstrated

[96] 'Teary-Eyed Judge Declares Innocence in Terror Trial' *Maldives Independent* (2018) www.maldivesindependent.com/crime-2/teary-eyed-judge-declares-innocence-in-terror-trial-137950.

[97] Supreme Court Order 2018/SC-SJ/03.

[98] M Naahee, 'Supreme Court Majority Judges "Do Not Know What They Are Doing": Nasheed' *Minivan News* (2013) www.minivannewsarchive.com/politics/supreme-court-majority-judges-do-not-know-what-they-are-doing-nasheed-68452; A Naish, 'MDP Will Reform the Judiciary, Pledges Nasheed' *Minivan News* (2014) www.minivannewsarchive.com/politics/mdp-will-reform-the-judiciary-pledges-nasheed-77906.

[99] See 'JSC Must be Reconstituted During the Last Stages of Judicial Reform' *Avas* (31 December 2019) https://avas.mv/en/75715#:~:text=%27JSC%20must%20be%20reconstituted%20during%20the%20last%20stages,step%20for%20the%20last%20stage%20of%20judicial%20reform.; FA Hassan, 'Nasheed: JSC's Composition Will Be Revised, It's Not Getting Delayed' *Sun* (2020) www.en.sun.mv/64052; 'Democracy Hijacked: JSC Edition' *Maldives Financial Review* (2021) www.mfr.mv/governance/democracy-hijacked-jsc-edition.

that they did not intend true judicial reform. In 2019, the MDP won a super-majority in Parliament. Instead of using these powers to reform the JSC and free the judicial appointment and dismissal procedures from political influence, the party appointed their loyalists to the JSC and as justices of the Supreme Court.

Before going into the details of how the Supreme Court interfered in elections, a cursory look at the political context behind elections might be helpful. As already mentioned, Nasheed's government fell in 2012 after mutinying police and military officers joined the opposition and demanded his resignation following the arrest of Criminal Court Chief Judge Abdulla Mohamed.[100] However, Nasheed stood for the presidential election in 2013. If Nasheed came into power again, the judiciary – including Gayoom-sympathetic judges – was aware he would attempt to replace them.[101] Therefore, the Supreme Court justices had a stake in the outcome of the 2013 election.

The President of the Maldives is elected by a majority vote in a single national constituency. To be elected in the first round, a candidate must receive more than half the votes cast. If no candidate meets this requirement, the two leading candidates compete in a run-off election. In the run-off, the candidate who receives the most votes wins. During elections in the Maldives, three major political parties compete: the MDP, the Progressive Party of Maldives (PPM) and the Jumhoory Party (JP).[102] The MDP and the PPM are the two largest political parties in terms of membership. Nonetheless, no political party in the Maldives has enough support to win more than 50 per cent of the votes. In the three presidential elections held since the adoption of the 2008 Constitution, no political party has won an election without the support of other political parties. This makes the JP a key player in the Maldivian elections.

The MDP and PPM are long-time rivals and have never worked together. The prospects of them working together are low. In this context, the tie-breaker has always been the JP.[103] Whichever party the JP sides with can win the election.[104] In the first round of the 2013 elections, the three political parties contested without a coalition, and Nasheed – from the MDP – secured 45 per cent of the votes, while Abdulla Yameen from the PPM secured 25 per cent. The JP candidate received 24 per cent of the votes.[105]

Nasheed was close to winning, and due to the disparity of votes between Nasheed and his opponents, he could win by encouraging more supporters to vote and by appealing to JP voters who do not like the idea of the JP working with the PPM. Before the run-off election took place, the remaining candidates accused the MDP and the EC of electoral fraud and tampering with the electoral roll, and filed a case with the Supreme Court to annul the results. In *Jumhoory Party, Attorney-General, and Progressive Party of Maldives v Elections Commission (2013)*, the claimants argued that because the EC had

[100] For details of the events that led to Nasheed's resignation, see J Yardley, 'Amid Outcry, President of Maldives Steps Down' *New York Times* (2012) www.nytimes.com/2012/02/08/world/asia/maldives-president-quits-amid-protests.html.

[101] M Naahee, 'Former President Nasheed Promises to Reform Judicial Service Commission Within 68 Days' *Minivan News* (2013) www.minivannewsarchive.com/politics/former-president-nasheedpromises-to-reform-judicial-service-commission-within-68-days-60589.

[102] Political parties were allowed in the Maldives in 2005 under the Reform Agenda of President Gayoom.

[103] This was the case in the 2008 election and the 2013 election.

[104] The JP has shifted from the MDP to the PPM and vice versa several times. In 2008, the JP sided with the MDP. In 2013, the party sided with the PPM. In 2018, it sided with the MDP again.

[105] See www.elections.gov.mv/megadownloads/Presidential-Election-2013/Results/7th_Sept_Results.pdf.

tampered with the electoral roll, many had lost their right to vote.[106] The Supreme Court annulled the first round of the 2013 presidential election.[107] This led to a new election, which gave Abdulla Yameen a subsequent victory.[108]

There are three issues with the Supreme Court's judgment in *Jumhoory Party (2013)*: the question of the Court's jurisdiction; evidential issues; and a potential breach of the separation of powers by the Court.[109] In assuming jurisdiction in the case, the Supreme Court sidestepped a jurisdictional point of confusion. There are legal provisions that stipulate that electoral petitions must be heard at the High Court in the first instance. Article 172 of the Constitution and section 64 of the Elections Act 2008 stipulate that the High Court can hear electoral cases at the first instance.[110] Conversely, Article 113 of the 2008 Constitution provides that the Supreme Court has the sole and final jurisdiction to determine disputes concerning qualification or disqualification, the election, the status of a presidential candidate or running mate, or the removal of the President by the Parliament.[111] Furthermore, sections 11(a)(1) and (3) of the Judicature Act 2010 provide that the Supreme Court has inherent jurisdiction to adjudicate constitutional issues, which may lead the country into a constitutional void, and constitutional issues concerning public interest.[112] In relying on these latter provisions, the Court characterised the case as a 'constitutional' issue within its jurisdiction, as opposed to an 'electoral dispute' within the High Court's jurisdiction.

The primary evidence the Court used to adjudicate the case was a confidential police forensic report. The report was not shown to the Commission's lawyers or the members of the Commission, and the Commission's lawyers could not cross-examine the evidence. However, the report was leaked, and it was discovered that it contained erroneous information. For example, the document contained a list of dead people who should not be on the electoral roll. Nonetheless, the records showed that they had voted. Later, it was revealed that the people listed as dead in the document were actually alive.[113]

[106] *Jumhoory Party, Attorney-General, and Progressive Party of Maldives vs Elections Commission* (2013/SC-C/42).

[107] ibid.

[108] 2013/SC-C/42.

[109] ibid.

[110] The Constitution of Maldives 2008, Art 172(a) states that 'a person may challenge a decision of the Elections Commission concerning an election or a public referendum, or may challenge the results of an election, or contest the legality of any other matter related to an election, by means of an election petition presented to the High Court'. The Elections Act 2008, s 64(a) stipulates that 'where any person does an act in contravention of this Act or regulations made hereunder, or the specific law pertaining to an election or regulations made thereunder, or a person is dissatisfied with a decision of the Elections Commission pursuant to a complaint raised under section 62 of this Act, or is dissatisfied with the results of the election, the dissatisfied person can file a petition with the High court'.

[111] The Constitution of Maldives 2008, Art 113 states that 'the Supreme Court, sitting together in session, shall have sole and final jurisdiction to determine all disputes concerning the qualification or disqualification, election, status, of a presidential candidate or running mate or removal of the President by the People's Majlis'.

[112] The Judicature Act 2010, s 11(a) states that 'a) The Supreme Court has the jurisdiction to adjudicate on constitutional issues with the following characteristics as matters within the inherent jurisdiction of the Supreme Court. 1. An issue with legal reasons which may send the country into a constitutional void or remove it from the constitutional framework; or 2. A dispute between two powers or institutions of the State regarding the interpretation of the Constitution; or 3. A constitutional issue concerning public interest of the nation'.

[113] For details of the report and the inaccuracies, see The Commonwealth, 'Report of the Commonwealth Observer Group: Maldives Presidential Election 7 September 2013 and Re-Run of Maldives Presidential

Therefore, there were concerns about the fairness of the proceedings. The defendants were denied access to the evidence against them, and the Supreme Court's decision was based on an incorrect report.

Furthermore, as part of its judgment, the Court issued detailed directives that the EC must follow when conducting elections.[114] These included requirements to obtain the candidates' signatures on the electoral roll before voting begins – giving political candidates the power to refuse to sign the electoral roll and delay the elections.[115] Following the Supreme Court's intervention in the elections, the international community, including the UN Office of the High Commissioner of Human Rights, accused the Court of subverting the democratic process and influencing the EC.[116] The Supreme Court did not justify its authority to issue a guideline dictating the work of the EC. Neither the Constitution nor the laws gave the Supreme Court the powers to do so. Thus, the Court arguably overstepped its role as a watchdog institution.

The significance of the requirement for candidates' signatures is that it allowed candidates to delay the elections. As mentioned earlier, no political party has been able to secure enough votes to win on its own, but Nasheed's MDP almost reached the 50 per cent mark in the first round. Therefore, if more people came out to vote in the second round, there was a chance that MDP could reach the 50 per cent+1 threshold.[117] On the other hand, if Yameen could get more time, he could try to make a deal with the JP, and the two parties combined would defeat Nasheed. Thus, it was favourable for Nasheed to hold the elections as soon as possible, whereas Yameen wanted to delay the elections to negotiate with the JP to form a coalition.[118]

B. Interference with Fourth Branch Institutions

Following its judgment in *Jumhoory Party (2013)*, the Supreme Court issued a regulation giving itself the power to conduct *suo moto* proceedings.[119] It argued that the Court could conduct such cases based on Articles 141, 144 and 156 of the Constitution and sections 9(e), 11(a)(3) and 22 of the Judicature Act 2010 – despite none of these provisions expressly granting these powers to the Court.[120] After interpreting the

Election 9 November 2013 and Maldives Presidential Run-Off Election 16 November 2013' (2013). See also Z Rasheed, 'Pronounced Dead: "Deceased" Voters Found to Be Alive' *Minivan News* (2013) www.minivannewsarchive.com/politics/pronounced-dead-deceased-voters-found-to-be-alive-70355; A Naseem, 'Translation: Election Annulment's Confidential Police Report' *Minivan News* (2013) www.minivannewsarchive.com/politics/translation-election-annulments-confidential-police-report-70519.

[114] 'Translation: Supreme Court Verdict on Jumhooree Party vs Elections Commission' *Minivan News* (2013) www.minivannewsarchive.com/politics/translation-supreme-court-verdict-on-jumhooree-party-vs-elections-commission-68169.

[115] ibid.

[116] See UNHR Office of the High Commissioner, 'Maldives Supreme Court is Subverting the Democratic Process – Pillay' (2013) www.newsarchive.ohchr.org/EN/NewsEvents/Pages/DisplayNews.aspx?NewsID=13917&LangID=E.

[117] The Maldives generally has a high voter turnout. In the last presidential election held in 2018, there were 262,135 eligible voters, of whom 233,889 voted.

[118] 'Maldives Election: Abdulla Yameen Wins Run-off Vote' *BBC News* (2013) www.bbc.co.uk/news/world-asia-24974019.

[119] Supreme Court Regulation of 6 February 2014.

[120] The Constitution of Maldives 2008, Art 141 states that '(a) The judicial power is vested in the Supreme Court, the High Court, and such Trial Courts as established by law. (b) The Supreme Court shall be the highest

aforementioned provisions to include *suo moto* powers, the Supreme Court charged the entire EC with contempt of court for criticising its judgment in *Jumhoory Party (2013)*.[121] After a hasty trial in 2014, the president of the Commission was sentenced to six months' imprisonment under section 88 of the Penal Code, and the president and vice president of the Commission were removed from office.[122]

The basis for these charges was the EC's statements to Parliament and the media about the discrepancies and factual inaccuracies in the forensic report adduced as the main evidence in *Jumhoory Party (2013)*. Furthermore, the Commission was charged with ignoring a Supreme Court judgment in its decision to dissolve political parties that had failed to gain 3000 members, the minimum number of supporters required under the Political Parties Act 2013 to register a political party. The SC had declared that provisions of the Act that specified the 3000 members rule were unconstitutional on the grounds that they violated constitutional rights.[123] After a speedy trial, the Supreme Court sentenced the president of the EC to six months in prison and stripped the president and the vice president of the Commission of their membership.[124]

authority for the administration of justice in the Maldives. The Chief Justice shall be the highest authority on the Supreme Court. All matters adjudicated before the Supreme Court shall be decided upon by a majority of the judges sitting together in session. (c) No officials performing public functions, or any other persons, shall interfere with and influence the functions of the courts. (d) Persons or bodies performing public functions, through legislative and other measures, must assist and protect the courts to ensure the independence, eminence, dignity, impartiality, accessibility and effectiveness of the courts'; Art 144 states that 'when deciding a constitutional matter within its jurisdiction, a court: (a) may declare that any statute, regulation or part thereof, order, decision or action of any person or body performing a public function that is inconsistent with the Constitution is invalid to the extent of the inconsistency; and (b) may in connection with a declaration pursuant to article (b) make any order that is just and equitable, including: 1. an order providing just compensation for any damage sustained by any person or group of persons due to any statute, regulation or action that is inconsistent with the Constitution; or 2. an order suspending the declaration of invalidity (of a statute, regulation or action due to inconsistency with the Constitution) for any period and on any conditions, to allow the competent authority to correct the defect: (c) may make an order limiting the retrospective effect of a declaration of invalidity of a statute, regulation or part thereof, order, decision or action of any person or body performing a public function that is inconsistent with the Constitution'; and Art 156 stipulates that 'the courts have the inherent power to protect and regulate their own process, in accordance with law and the interests of justice'. The Judicature Act 2010, s 9(e) states that 'the power to adjudicate on the following is held by the Supreme Court (e) matters submitted to the Supreme Court under Art 143 (a) of the Constitution'; s 11(a)(3) states 'the Supreme Court has the jurisdiction to adjudicate on constitutional issues with the following characteristics as matters within the inherent jurisdiction of the Supreme Court … constitutional issue concerning public interest of the nation'; and s 22 states that 'in addition to the powers conferred on the Supreme Court by the Constitution and the jurisdiction of the court laid out under various Articles of this Act, the Supreme Court has the jurisdiction to do the following. a) The power to give all orders under this Act and the Supreme Court Regulation, relating to a matter or a case submitted to the court, and to administer justice with regard to such matters or cases, and to take necessary actions to prevent the misuse of the judicial system and to uphold the confidence in the judicial system. b) In its own initiative or at the behest of a concerned party, in order to administer justice and to prevent the exploitation of the judicial system the power to issue various orders in accordance with the law, if any party is found to have violated this law or any principles of the Supreme Court regulation. c) In accordance with the law and regulation, the power to summon people in relation to a case or matter submitted to the Supreme Court. d) In relation to a case or matter submitted to the Supreme Court and for the purpose of finding the truth or any facts surrounding the case, the power to pose any question to any witness or party to the case at any time or in any manner. e) The power to issue an order requesting for the submission of any document required by the court in relation to a case or matter submitted to the Supreme Court'.

[121] Supreme Court Case Number 2014/SC-SM/15.

[122] At s 88, the Penal Code states that disobeying a lawful order is a criminal offence. Note that the sentence was suspended.

[123] Supreme Court Judgment 2013/SC-C/11.

[124] 2014/SC-SM/15.

There are a number of problems with the Supreme Court ruling. First, the Supreme Court does not have the power to conduct *suo moto* cases. Second, the authority to commence criminal proceedings lies with the Prosecutor General. Third, only the Parliament is given the power to remove and appoint members of fourth branch institutions like the EC.[125] The most prominent of these problems is the unconstitutional removal of the two members. According to the Constitution, the EC is an institution independent from the other branches of the state. They can be removed only on the grounds of misconduct, incapacity or incompetence, and only by the Parliament.[126] The Supreme Court's dismissal of the heads of the EC and the sentencing of the Commission's president attracted global criticism.[127]

The Supreme Court has further used its *suo moto* jurisdiction to charge the HRCM in relation to the report it submitted to the United Nations Universal Periodic Review (UPR).[128] In its report, the Commission noted that the Maldives judiciary is questionable on the grounds of independence, transparency, interference, influence, competency, consistency and accessibility.[129] The report also highlighted that the Supreme Court interfered with the work of the lower courts.[130] In the Supreme Court's case against the HRCM, the Court ruled that the UPR submission was unlawful and ordered the Commission to abide by a set of guidelines attached to the ruling.[131] The ruling restricted the Commission's work and prohibited it from communicating directly with international organisations.[132]

C. Supreme Court's Usurpation of Parliamentary Powers

The Court, through political instrumentalisation, has also been used to interfere in the jurisdiction of Parliament over matters such as the dismissal of MPs and no-confidence votes. The Court was first moved to act when Yameen's government lost its parliamentary majority after a group of influential pro-government MPs crossed the floor to join

[125] Constitution of Maldives 2008, Art 223.

[126] The Constitution of Maldives 2008, Art 177 states that Election Commission members 'shall be removed from office only for the reasons specified in article (a), and in the manner specified in article (b): (a) on the ground of misconduct, incapacity or incompetence; and (b) a finding to that effect by a committee of the People's Majlis pursuant to article (a), and upon the approval of such finding by the People's Majlis by a majority of those present and voting, calling for the member's removal from office, such member shall be deemed removed from office'.

[127] See Commonwealth Human Rights Initiative, 'Searching for a Lost Democracy: A Fact Finding Mission Report on the Maldives' (2016) www.humanrightsinitiative.org/download/Maldives%20CHRI%20Fact%20Finding%20Mission%202016.pdf.

[128] Supreme Court Case Number 2014/SC-SM/42.

[129] Human Rights Commission of the Maldives, 'Human Rights Commission of the Maldives – UPR submission 2014' (2014) www.hrcm.org.mv/en/publications/hrcmsubmission-to-the-universal-periodic-review of-the-maldives-april-may-2015-22nd-session.

[130] This was in reference to the Supreme Court's decision to take control of the management of the lower Courts by issuing a judgment abolishing ch 8 of the Judicature Act 2010.

[131] See UNHR Office of the High Commissioner, 'Supreme Court Judgement Gravely Undermines Maldives Human Rights Commission – Zeid' (2015) www.ohchr.org/en/NewsEvents/Pages/DisplayNews.aspx?NewsID=16106&LangID=E.

[132] ibid.

the opposition[133] and sought to remove the Speaker of Parliament, the President and influential cabinet members from office.[134]

Amid this political tension, the Attorney-General filed two cases with the Supreme Court seeking to bar MPs from floor-crossing, preventing Parliament from dismissing cabinet members and the president.[135] In the first case, *Attorney-General* (2017/SC-C/11), the government sought a ruling that would require the Supreme Court's approval for all future no-confidence votes.[136] In the second case, *Attorney-General* (2017/SC-C/17),[137] the Attorney-General asked the Court to rule that MPs who switch political parties or face dismissal from their political party would automatically lose their parliamentary seat.[138] The Supreme Court accepted these two cases as constitutional cases.

In both cases, the Supreme Court granted the orders sought by the Attorney-General. In the first case, concerning the legality of no-confidence votes, the Supreme Court ruled that such votes should be considered as 'impeachment', and the results should be forwarded to the Supreme Court to decide on the legality of the votes. The Court argued that this is because 'the checks and balance system adopted in the Maldives is based on a presidential system, and Parliament has to follow "due process" when dealing with no-confidence motions'.[139]

The Supreme Court held that parliamentary no-confidence votes would not have an effect unless and until the Court itself decides that the vote is valid.[140] The Supreme Court positioned itself as the custodian of the Constitution on the basis of Articles 144 and 145(c) of the 2008 Constitution.[141] Article 144 provides that the Supreme Court has the authority to rule on whether actions by any institution performing a public function are consistent with the Constitution.[142] Article 145(c) positions the Supreme Court as the final authority on constitutional interpretation. Neither of these provisions naturally led to the conclusion the Supreme Court reached on its powers to adjudicate the 'constitutionality' of no-confidence motions. Thus, the Supreme Court read into the Constitution powers not explicitly given to it and broadened its jurisdiction.

Commentators have argued that the Court's judgment in 2017/SC-C/11 amounted to a de facto amendment of the Constitution.[143] However, the most significant issue

[133] It is common practice in the Maldives for MPs to switch from one party to another.

[134] The Constitution of Maldives 2008, Art 100 allows the Parliament to remove the President from office with a two-thirds majority.

[135] Attorney General (2017/SC-C/11) and Attorney-General (2017/SC-C/17).

[136] The Constitution of Maldives 2008 does not require Supreme Court's approval for no-confidence motions. However, a court ruling requiring the court's approval would mean that even if the opposition MPs were able to pass no-confidence motions, the Supreme Court will have the final say before it can have legal effect, thus preventing the Parliament from removing ministers of the President. For the background story, see 'Supreme Court Asked to Restrict Parliament's Powers to Sack Ministers' *Maldives Independent* (2017) www.maldives-independent.com/politics/supreme-court-asked-to-restrict-parliaments-powers-to-sack-ministers-130581.

[137] This case was filed as a constitutional case.

[138] There are no constitutional provisions or laws that address the issue of floor-crossing in the Maldives.

[139] 2017/SC-C/11.

[140] ibid.

[141] The Constitution of Maldives 2008, Art 145(c) states that 'the Supreme Court shall be the final authority on the interpretation of the Constitution, the law, or any other matter dealt with by a court of law'.

[142] Constitution of Maldives 2008, Art 144(a).

[143] '"A Dark Day": Lawyers and Legal Experts React to Supreme Court Judgment' *Maldives Independent* (2017) www.maldivesindependent.com/politics/a-dark-day-lawyers-and-legal-experts-react-to-supreme-court-judgment-130751.

arising out of the ruling is the conflicting nature of the Supreme Court's newly established jurisdiction to act as the final authority on all no-confidence votes and the constitutional immunity given to Parliament. Any power that the Supreme Court may read into Articles 144 and 145(c) needs to be balanced against Article 88(b) of the Constitution. Article 88 provides that a court cannot question the validity of parliamentary proceedings.[144] The Supreme Court not only expanded its influence into the legislative branch, but also gave itself powers that conflict with the constitutionally protected immunity of parliamentary powers.

In the second case, 2017/SC-C/17, the Attorney-General argued that Articles 26(c), 30(a), 74 and 75 of the Constitution prohibited MPs from leaving the political party they were registered with at the time of their election. Articles 26(c) and 30(a) provide citizens with the right to take part in public affairs and the right to participate in political activities, while Article 74 concerns the Court's jurisdiction to adjudicate on questions related to qualification, removal or vacancy of Members of Parliament.[145] Additionally, Article 75 stipulates that MPs should act in the national interest and represent their constituencies and the country as a whole.[146] No constitutional or legal provision explicitly regulates floor-crossing.[147]

In adjudicating the case, the Supreme Court first established its jurisdiction to do so. It held that the questions raised are 'constitutional matters', which Article 274 of the Constitution defines as any proceeding where the courts are required to interpret an Article of the Constitution in order to determine the constitutionality of acts and decisions of public officials, laws, regulations and orders issued by state authorities.[148]

The Court also, again, referred to section 11(a)(3) of the Judicature Act 2010, which sets out its inherent jurisdiction – including the jurisdiction to hear constitutional issues that concern the public interest of the nation.[149] Following this assumption

[144] The Constitution of Maldives 2008, Art 88(b) states that 'unless otherwise specified in this Constitution, the validity of any proceedings in the Parliament shall not be questioned in any court of law'. See also *Fahmy Hassan vs Parliament* (2012/SC-C/35).

[145] The Constitution of Maldives 2008, Art 26(c) states that 'unless otherwise provided in this Constitution, every citizen of the Maldives eighteen years of age or older has the right to take part in the conduct of public affairs, directly or through freely chosen representatives'; Art 30(a) states that 'every citizen has the right to establish and to participate in the activities of political parties'; and Art 74 states that 'questions concerning the qualifications or removal, or vacating of seats, of a member of the Parliament shall be determined by the Supreme Court'.

[146] The Constitution of Maldives 2008, Art 75 stipulates that 'members of the People's Majlis should be guided in their actions by considerations of national interest and public welfare foremost, and should not exploit their official positions in any way for their own benefit or for the benefit of those with whom they have special relations. They shall represent not only their constituencies but the country as a whole.'

[147] The ballot papers have the names of all the people that are standing in the parliamentary elections – Candidate A, Candidate B, Candidate C, etc – and the voters are required to tick the name of the single candidate they choose.

[148] The Constitution of Maldives 2008, Art 274 stipulates 'constitutional matter' means proceedings where the determination of the meaning of an Article of the Constitution or any part thereof is required or proceedings requiring a determination of whether a law or any part thereof, a regulation or any part thereof, an order issued by a state authority, or an act committed or a decision taken by an official of that authority contravenes the Constitution.

[149] The Judicature Act 2010, s 11(a) states that 'the Supreme Court has the jurisdiction to adjudicate on constitutional issues with the following characteristics as matters within the inherent jurisdiction of the Supreme Court'.

of jurisdiction, the Court ruled in favour of the Attorney-General and ordered that Parliament and the EC take the necessary steps to remove MPs that crossed the floor.

The Court, in effect, read into the Constitution an anti-floor-crossing rule which, in this case, prevented pro-government MPs from leaving the ruling party to join the opposition. Without these MPs, the opposition did not have enough votes to remove the Speaker or cabinet ministers. The significant political implications of the Court's judgment amplify concerns about the political capture of the judiciary. Following the Court's decision, the ruling party dismissed the relevant MPs from the political party on disciplinary grounds and ordered the military to prevent them from entering Parliament.[150]

IV. The Road to Resilience: A Proposal for the Constitutional Reform of the Judiciary

The political capture of the Court and the consequent impact on judicial independence has serious implications for the constitutional health of the Maldives. The constitutional framework needs to be strengthened to create a firewall around the judiciary to protect it from politicisation.

As demonstrated in the previous sections of this chapter, multiple factors contribute to the failure of the 2008 Constitution to secure judicial independence in the Maldives. In short, these are the inclusion of political actors in the JSC, appointment and dismissal procedures of Supreme Court judges, and the lack of genuine politicians willing to commit to democratic norms and establish an independent judiciary. Below, I propose solutions to the first two problems. The final problem is related to the Maldivian culture of repression. As Lipset famously observed, cultural influences carried down through history are extremely difficult to modify, while political institutions and constitutional frameworks can be rewritten.[151] Therefore, this section will concentrate on what adjustments can be made to the legal framework and the Constitution to increase the judiciary's independence.

Firstly, recent history has made it abundantly clear that the current composition of the JSC is an obstacle to the development of an independent judiciary.[152] Due to political domination, the JSC has failed to appoint independent judges and take action against judges who are connected to influential politicians.[153] There is no perfect model for the composition of the JSC.[154] However, reducing the number of politicians and replacing

[150] 'Disqualification of Three MPs "Egregiously Partisan Move"' *Maldives Independent* (2017) www.maldivesindependent.com/politics/disqualification-of-three-mps-egregiously-partisan-move-133897.

[151] SM Lipset, 'Presidents vs Parliaments: The Centrality of Political Culture' (1990) 1 *Journal of Democracy* 80.

[152] As demonstrated above, the JSC has been internally and externally captured. For a discussion of how internal and external capture occurs, see JA Colquit, 'Rethinking Judicial Nominating Commissions: Independence, Accountability, and Public Support' (2007) 34 *Fordham Urban Law Journal* 73, www.ir.lawnet.fordham.edu/ulj.

[153] See, eg the case of Judge Abdulla Mohamed discussed above. See also the case of Supreme Court Justice Ali Hameedh's sex tape scandal. Rasheed, 'Supreme Court Judge Ali Hameed' (n 69).

[154] For a comparative study of Judicial Councils, see N Garoupa and T Ginsburg, 'Guarding the Guardians: Judicial Councils and Judicial Independent' (2009) 57 *American Journal of Comparative Law* 103. See also PD Webster, 'Selection and Retention of Judges: Is There One "Best" Method?' (1995) 23 *Florida State University Law Review* 1, www.ir.law.fsu.edu/lr.

them with independent members could help to strengthen the JSC's judicial oversight function. For any political appointees, Parliament should vote on their membership on the JSC not based on a simple majority of the members present, but through a more consensual decision-making model that includes cross-party selection mechanisms.

The process for approving judges should be based on a similar decision-making model. A parliamentary committee for approving judicial appointments could be a progressive move in this regard. This committee would have an equal number of MPs from each party, regardless of which party is in the majority. This is similar to the concept of 'weighted multipartisanship',[155] but with some differences, because the Maldives has very few political parties that are represented in Parliament, and the ones that are often work together as a single (coalition) party. Therefore, the weighted multipartisanship approach with a few modifications might work better for the Maldives.

Under this model, parliamentary committees concerning any independent institution must have MPs from each legislative party regardless of the size of the party. Furthermore, the committee must make decisions based on a consensus model and should not arrive at decisions based on a majoritarian model. Additionally, when members are selected for such a committee, political parties should be divided based on how they operate rather than on their legal status as separate political parties. For example, three political parties that have a coalition agreement and are working together cannot have MPs from each party on the committee. Instead, they will be counted as a single party and their committee members will be chosen on that basis.

The Supreme Court nominees would have to receive unanimous support from the committee members under this arrangement before their names could be brought to the Parliament floor for voting. This means that whomever the committee nominates will have the support of all political parties in Parliament. This ensures that judicial selections have no political affiliations to either the opposition or the ruling parties. The ruling party representative on the committee could reject anyone with links to the opposition, and the opposition representatives could reject any prospective judges with links to the ruling party. This model also has a low risk of causing political deadlock because rejection of a nominee by one political party on the committee would mean that there is no general consensus that the nominee is qualified on the basis of independence or any other grounds. This is because, as previously mentioned, a nominee will need to gain the vote of all the political parties on the committee. Nonetheless, as an additional guarantee to reduce deadlock and prevent MPs from stalling the process, the committee should have a constitutionally specified period of time in which to either approve or reject a nominee. Failure to meet the deadline could have political repercussions.

In addition, the Constitution should be amended to remove the President's powers to prioritise Supreme Court nominees. Under the current system, prospective candidates apply to the JSC, and the JSC interviews and nominates candidates to the President. The President then prioritises the candidates in the order he favours and forwards the list to Parliament. If Parliament is under the control of his political party, the parliamentarians know which candidates the president favours and who are likely to serve government

[155] For the concept of weighted multipartisanship, see T Khaitan, 'Balancing Accountability and Effectiveness: A Case for Moderated Parliamentarism' (2021) 7 *Canadian Journal of Comparative & Contemporary Law* 81.

interests. This procedure results in the appointment of politically connected judges rather than the most qualified candidates for the position.

Therefore, in order to avoid politicisation, prospective judges should apply to the JSC, which would review the applications and nominate everyone that meets all the requirements. These requirements should be clear and basic so that anyone can understand how points are given to those who apply. The JSC-vetted applications should be forwarded immediately to the parliamentary committee mentioned above, which would then ensure that all political parties in Parliament support the JSC's nominees.

Maldivian politicians have also taken advantage of the Constitution's silence on the required number of justices on the Supreme Court bench. As aforementioned, the Constitution only requires the Supreme Court to have an odd number of justices.[156] The number of justices on the Supreme Court's bench is determined by primary legislation, which can be amended by a simple majority in Parliament. Therefore, to avoid politicisation, the Constitution should be amended to stipulate the number of justices on the Supreme Court bench. However, even this safeguard is insufficient to prevent abuse of the system, as a political party may be able to secure enough votes to amend the Constitution itself. (Both former President Yameen and current President Solih were able to secure enough parliamentary support to do this.) This raises the broader problem of discouraging constitutional amendments.[157]

Putting in place procedural impediments, such as needing a greater quorum to commence amendments or demanding confirmation of the amendment through referendums or successive legislatures, may be beneficial. For example, the Constitution could specify that the number of Supreme Court judges should be five and erect procedural hurdles to amending the clause. This would prohibit political parties with strong parliamentary support from decreasing or increasing the number of judges in order to select loyalists in place of incumbent judges who may resist them; it would not preclude Parliament or the JSC from removing judges for reasons permitted by the Constitution.

Finally, the absence of genuinely democratic political actors willing to commit to democratic norms is a major challenge to judicial independence and democratic progress in the Maldives. One of the most popular promises made in the Maldives during elections is the establishment of an independent judiciary devoid of political interference and manipulation. However, the truth is rather different. The judicial system has been systematically undermined to ensure that it remains subservient to politicians. There is no political will to remove the tools of political capture of the Constitution and the judiciary. In the absence of a broader shift in the culture of politics in the Maldives, these vulnerabilities will continue to plague the process of democratic consolidation in the country.

[156] The Constitution of Maldives 2008, Art 145(a) states that 'the Supreme Court shall consist of the Chief Justice and such number of Judges as provided by law. The Supreme Court shall consist of an uneven number of Judges.'

[157] Eternity clauses can sometimes be risky for new democracies. For eternity clauses and the risk they pose to new democracies, see A Friedman, 'Dead Hand Constitutionalism: Honduras and the Danger of Eternity Clauses in New Democracies' (2011) 4 *Mexican Law Review* 77. For multilayered procedural safeguards, see J Elster, *Ulysses Unbound: Studies in Rationality, Precommitment, and Constrains* (Cambridge, Cambridge University Press, 2000). For a comparative study of different procedural requirements for formal amendments across jurisdictions, see R Albert, 'The Structure of Constitutional Amendment Rules' (2014) 49 *Wake Forest Law Review* 913.

11

Judicial Evasion, Judicial Vagueness and Judicial Revisionism: A Study of the *NCT of Delhi v Union of India* Judgment(s)

GAUTAM BHATIA[1]

I. Introduction

This chapter considers contemporary constitutional resilience in India from the lens of the relationship between the political executive and the Supreme Court. There is an extensive body of literature on the structure and functioning of the Indian Supreme Court, a brief reiteration of which follows. The Supreme Court is India's highest judicial forum, exercising both appellate and original jurisdiction. It has the power of judicial review, ie that of striking down legislative and executive action for incompatibility with the Indian Constitution. A peculiar feature of the Indian Supreme Court is its strength (32 judges at the time of writing), especially in proportion to the small number of judges who hear any given case (usually panels of two, three or, more infrequently, five). The Chief Justice of India retains absolute discretion in determining the 'listing' of cases (ie when cases will be heard) and in the selection of panels for hearing cases. This ensures that even though the Indian Supreme Court is a 'polyvocal Court', the ex officio Chief Justice wields significant power in setting the agenda. While this chapter will not focus on the role of the Supreme Court's Chief Justices, these prefatory remarks are important to keep in mind as the argument progresses. In particular, critiques involving the Supreme Court's functioning cannot be adequately contextualised without cognisance of the fact that its functioning is largely under the control of the Chief Justice.[2]

In recent years, the role of the Indian judiciary – and, in particular, that of the Supreme Court of India – has come under increasing critical scrutiny, as part of a larger story of the relationship between the political executive and independent institutions.[3]

[1] The author was formally involved in some of the cases discussed in this piece: the first *NCT of Delhi v Union of India* case, the Aadhaar challenge and the Kashmir challenges.

[2] N Robinson, 'Structure Matters: The Impact of Court Structure on the Indian and US Supreme Courts' (2013) 61 *American Journal of Comparative Law* 173.

[3] See, eg A Dev, 'In Sua Causa: What the Judiciary Has Done to Itself' *The Caravan* (1 July 2019) https://caravanmagazine.in/law/what-judiciary-done-itself; T Khaitan, 'Killing a Constitution with a Thousand Cuts: Executive Aggrandizement and Party-State Fusion in India' (2020) 14 *Law and Ethics of Human Rights* 49;

An important feature of this critique is that a straightforward study of Supreme Court judgments is insufficient for understanding the true relationship between the Court and the executive. Indeed, a bird's-eye view of recent court judgments reveals a mixed – though rather familiar – judicial record. To take a few high-profile cases, the Supreme Court has decriminalised same-sex relations and struck down an anti-adultery law, whilst green-lighting (with some caveats) the government's national biometric identification programme and upholding criminal defamation laws. A study of High Court judgments would reveal a similarly mixed picture across the country.

However, as I have indicated above, this is precisely why it is particularly crucial, in the Indian context, to scrutinise judicial action beyond judgments. In this chapter, I will study a significant – and ongoing – constitutional dispute in India, between the government of the national capital territory of Delhi and the Union government. Through its career in the Delhi High Court, and then in two rounds of adjudication before the Supreme Court, the case raised – and continues to raise – crucial issues pertaining to federal structure, representative democracy, and the various checks and balances that the Indian Constitution places upon a strong central executive.

In this study, I will highlight how the Supreme Court's approach has resulted in significant empowerment of the central executive (the Union government) and has considerably weakened the constitutional system of checks and balances – but without adequate reasons to justify its findings. In particular, I will highlight three features of the Court's behaviour that have contributed to this outcome. The first is *judicial evasion*: through lengthy delays in hearing and adjudicating cases – where time is of the essence, and there is the risk of a fait accompli making the final adjudication infructuous – the Court implicitly endorses a status quo that has been created by the Union government and operates to the benefit of the Union government ('deciding by not deciding'). The second is *judicial vagueness*: the Court lays down abstract statements of constitutional principle that would seem to limit the powers of the Union government, endorse a strong system of checks and balances, and vindicate the claims of its challengers (whether based on the federal structure or individual rights). However, these statements are worded so vaguely that they do not place any genuine constraints upon constitutional functionaries of the Union government, or, when it comes to applying them to a concrete dispute, the Supreme Court either forgets or refuses to apply them altogether (an option partially enabled by the vague formulation to start with). The third feature is *judicial revisionism*: smaller benches of the Court actively depart from the judgments of larger benches, a situation at least partially enabled by the vague formulations set out by those larger benches.

A combination of judicial evasion, judicial vagueness and judicial revisionism, in sum, create a situation where the Court's judgments fail to correct executive overreach and implicitly endorse the weakening of checks and balances – but through stealth. In section IV of this chapter, I will point out that while the dispute between the Delhi government and the Union government is an illustrative example of the phenomena that I have outlined, these are by no means isolated 'bad apple' judgments. Rather, multiple

G Bhatia, 'ICLP Turns 7: A Constitutionalism without the Court' (*Indian Constitutional Law and Philosophy Blog*, 1 August 2020) https://indconlawphil.wordpress.com/2020/08/01/iclp-turns-7-a-constitutionalism-without-the-court/.

examples abound. Judicial evasion, judicial vagueness and judicial revisionism have, in recent years, become embedded in the Indian constitutional landscape, and have undermined constitutional resilience.

A final caveat, before I begin: the arguments in this chapter are distinct from the scholarship that focuses on the judicial inconsistency that flows from certain structural issues around the Supreme Court's expanded jurisdiction and vast case docket.[4] For example, scholars have focused on how the Court might be compelled to 'triage' precedent because of its workload (leading to problems of selective or under-citation).[5] The issues discussed in this chapter, however, are not structural: they refer to specific judicial conduct in dispute(s) involving the Union executive, which prima facie may appear neutral, but has had the effect of weakening constitutional oversight, or control, of executive action.

II. Laying Down the Principles: The Five Judge Bench

Federalism is a basic feature of the Indian Constitution. Its concrete manifestation is found in Article 245, which grants the Union Parliament the power to make laws for the Union of India, and grants the same to state legislatures in several states.[6] Schedule VII sets out three 'Lists': List I is the Union List, which contains the fields within which the Union Parliament has the power to legislate; List II is an equivalent list for the states; and List III is the 'Concurrent List', which sets out the fields in which both legislatures have jurisdiction.[7] Indian federalism is also commonly described as 'centralised':[8] residual powers lie with the centre, fiscal powers are tilted towards the centre and state law-making power can be overridden in certain circumstances.[9]

The federal relationship between the centre and the states has always been fraught. A significant chunk of the Supreme Court and the High Courts' energies, over the years, have gone into adjudicating disputes over legislative competence between the two levels of federal governance. For all that, however, it has never been doubted that under Schedule VII, the states have certain core powers of governance and administration, which the centre/Union cannot ordinarily take away (including, for example, the power to recruit and transfer civil servants, powers over land and police, and so on).

Even within the federal structure, however, there have always existed differences between different federal units, a historical legacy of the uneven and patchy political trajectories of different parts of the Indian Union under colonial British rule. From 1919,

[4] T Khaitan, 'The Indian Supreme Court's Identity Crisis: A Constitutional Court or a Court of Appeals?' (2020) 4 *Indian Law Review* 1; see also A Green and AH Yoon, 'Triaging the Law: Developing the Common Law on the Supreme' (2017) 14 *Journal of Empirical Legal Studies* 683.

[5] Green and Yoon (n 4).

[6] Constitution of India 1949, Art 245.

[7] Constitution of India 1949, sch VII. For the purposes of this chapter, 'Union' and 'centre', and their cognates, are used interchangeably.

[8] See, eg L Tillin, 'Building a National Economy: Origins of Centralised Federalism in India' (2021) 51 *Publius: The Journal of Federalism* 161.

[9] For a detailed examination of India's federal structure – and competing interpretations on the implications for Indian constitutionalism – see the majority and dissenting opinions in *State of West Bengal v Union of India* AIR 1963 SC 1241.

through a slow and evolutionary process, 'provinces' within British India began to develop institutions of self-governance, constituting a proto-federation. There were, however, special territorial units (for example, Chief Commissioner's Provinces) that were ruled directly from the centre. This asymmetric federal arrangement was carried forward into independent India. Citing both historical reasons as well as the uneven development of different parts of the country, even as the framers of the Constitution proclaimed a commitment to federalism, they divided states into different 'classes' (Part A, B, C and D states, albeit substantially reorganised in the first decade of the Constitution). Some of these states did not have representative institutions until as late as the 1970s, while other territorial units were granted a hybrid or *sui generis* status.

This second set of territorial units came to be called 'Union territories', and like the British-era Chief Commissioner's Provinces, were ruled directly by the central government.[10] One example was that of the national capital territory of Delhi) NCT of Delhi). As the former imperial capital, Delhi has always had a special status, which carried on into independence, when a part of it – New Delhi – was made the capital of free India. As the seat of national governance – much like Washington, DC, for example – Delhi was not clothed with the attributes of a 'state' under the Constitution, but was instead administered by a Lieutenant-Governor (LG) appointed by the central government.

As Delhi grew and expanded over the years, however, demands for self-governance grew as well. In 1991, the Constitution was amended to provide Delhi with an elected legislative assembly, and a cabinet that would be responsible to the assembly.[11] The assembly was empowered to legislate for Delhi with respect to all items in the state list (List II) except for land, the police and public order.[12] However, while, in these respects, Delhi was vested with 'state-like' powers, in other respects, it remained something less than a state. The Union Parliament retained all its powers under the Constitution to legislate for Union territories. And the LG – as the representative of the central government – remained in office and had the power to 'disagree' with the decisions of the elected assembly (following which, the 'disagreement' could be referred to the President of India for adjudication).

In essence, therefore, Article 239AA of the Constitution, which introduced this scheme of governance, set up two parallel governing authorities in Delhi: one directly elected to legislate and govern Delhi (the assembly and the executive), and one unelected (the LG), but installed by the nationally elected Union government. The powers and functions of these authorities intersected through ambiguously drafted provisions such as the proviso to Article 239AA(4):

> Provided that in the case of difference of opinion between the Lieutenant Governor and his Ministers on any matter, the Lieutenant Governor shall refer it to the President for decision and act according to the decision given thereon by the President and pending such decision it shall be competent for the Lieutenant Governor in any case where the matter, in his opinion, is so urgent that it is necessary for him to take immediate action, to take such action or to give such direction in the matter as he deems necessary.[13]

[10] Constitution of India 1949, Art 239.
[11] The Constitution (Sixty-Ninth Amendment) Act, 1991.
[12] Constitution of India 1949, Art 239AA.
[13] ibid Art 239AA(4), proviso.

For a couple of decades, this remained a workable arrangement. Matters came to a head in 2015, however, when two sharply antagonistic parties (at the time) – the National Democratic Alliance and the Aam Aadmi Party (AAP) – were in power in the centre and in Delhi, respectively. The central government issued notifications that, inter alia, removed control over the anti-corruption bureau, as well as over the state civil service, from the Delhi government. Arguing that its entire functioning had been stymied by this notification, the Delhi government went to court. After a judgment of the Delhi High Court that ruled in favour of the central government on almost all the issues, the matter reached the Supreme Court, where, after some delay (to be discussed below), it was referred to a five-judge Constitution Bench to hear and lay down the constitutional principles that would govern the relationship between the two governments.

At the heart of the dispute were two core issues. Article 239AA(4) of the Constitution made a provision for an elected Council of Ministers and a Chief Minister, who would 'aid and advise' the LG in the exercise of his functions.[14] The phrase 'aid and advise' is familiar to students of parliamentary democracy, and its default meaning is that the titular executive head will be bound to act upon the aid and advice offered to her by the Council of Ministers and the head of the government. Indeed, the Indian Constitution itself uses the phrase in the context of other federal units: at the Union level, the President acts upon the 'aid and advice' of the Union cabinet, while at the state level, that function is performed by the Governor.[15] The government of Delhi, therefore, made a simple argument. As Article 239AA granted it legislative power to enact laws in the fields in the state and concurrent lists, and as executive power was co-extensive with legislative power,[16] it followed that, just like in the case of the centre and the states, the phrase 'aid and advice' would have to be construed in a manner such that executive acts performed by the Delhi government would be binding upon the LG. On the other hand, the central government argued that Delhi was not a 'state', and was never meant to be one. As a Union territory, it was *meant* to be ruled from the centre, and therefore the Council of Ministers could, at best, play an 'advisory' role (an interpretation that would take the meaning of 'aid and advice' literally).

The second bone of contention was the interpretation of the proviso, which I have extracted above. The proviso empowered the LG to refer 'any matter' upon which there was a disagreement with the Council of Ministers to the President of India – also, at the time, a nominee of the ruling party at the centre, and at any rate obliged to act on the advice of the central government – for a decision. The central government argued, once again, that the proviso had to be read literally: 'any matter' meant, quite simply, 'any matter', and the phrase was not constrained in any way. The government of Delhi argued, on the other hand, that if *this* was the interpretation the Court gave to the provision, it would effectively install the LG – and, over him, the President, and the Union cabinet – as the ruling authority in Delhi. The role of the elected government would be reduced to a cipher.

The Supreme Court was faced with the following situation: there existed a set of ambiguous constitutional provisions, which were capable of being read in multiple ways.

[14] ibid Art 239AA(4).

[15] ibid Arts 73 and 161.

[16] See, eg *Ram Jawaya Kapur v State of Punjab*, 1955 2 SCR 225; *Shamsher Singh v State of Punjab*, 1975 SCR (1) 814.

Which way the Court chose to read it would have significant ramifications upon the division of powers between two state organs – in this case, the central government and the government of a federal unit. And, importantly, the case only came to Court because the central government had decided to test the outer limits of its powers under the constitutional scheme, to see how far they could go.

The Constitution Bench delivered three separate judgments, which deserve close study. Let us begin with a summary. All three judgments held that the Constitution intended to progressively democratise the Indian polity, and this background principle had to be kept in mind while interpreting ambiguous constitutional provisions.[17] Consequently, where a provision was open to more than one interpretation, the Court would favour the interpretation that supported the principles of democracy, political accountability and representation. Concretely, therefore, the Court held that the executive power of the Delhi government was co-extensive with its legislative power and that the role of the LG was not that of a superior administrative authority, but only that of a central government representative who, in certain cases where issues potentially stemming from Delhi's status as the national capital were at stake, could refer matters to the President.

The devil – as always – is in the detail. Let us, therefore, begin with the judgment authored by Chief Justice Dipak Misra, who wrote for himself and two other judges (Justice Khanwilkar and Justice Sikri). The Chief Justice structured his judgment by setting out, first, the interpretive principles that would guide the Court in determining the meaning of a provision such as Article 239AA(4). For example:

> Representative Governance in a Republican form of democracy is a kind of democratic setup wherein the people of a nation elect and choose their law-making representatives ... Another ideal for representative governance is accessibility and approachability. Since responsiveness to the needs and demands of the people is the basic parameter for evaluating the effectiveness of representative governance, it is necessary that elected representatives develop a sense of belonging with their constituents.[18]

Other constitutional principles articulated by the Chief Justice included 'checks and balances',[19] 'collective responsibility',[20] federalism as 'interdependence'[21] and 'democracy'.[22] On this basis, the Chief Justice concluded that:

> Drawing an analogy while interpreting the provisions of Article 239AA(3)(a) and Article 239AA(4) would reveal that the executive power of the government of NCT of Delhi is conterminous with the legislative power of the Delhi Legislative Assembly which is envisaged in Article 239AA(3) and which extends over all but three subjects in the State List and all subjects in the Concurrent List and, thus, Article 239AA(4) confers executive power on the Council of Ministers over all those subjects for which the Delhi Legislative Assembly has legislative power.[23]

[17] *NCT of Delhi v Union of India* (2018) 8 SCC 501 (SCI).
[18] ibid paras 49 and 55.
[19] ibid para 62.
[20] ibid para 83.
[21] ibid para 84.
[22] ibid para 106.
[23] ibid para 199.

Because:

> The exercise of establishing a democratic and representative form of government for NCT of Delhi by insertion of Articles 239AA and 239AB would turn futile if the government of Delhi that enjoys the confidence of the people of Delhi is not able to usher in policies and laws over which the Delhi Legislative Assembly has power to legislate for the NCT of Delhi.[24]

This reasoning was repeated by the Chief Justice, in different words, in the succeeding paragraphs, especially in the context of the fact that Article 239AA set out the representative structure of Delhi *within the Constitution itself* (unlike, for example, the Union Territory of Puducherry, where this was delegated to statute).[25] Effectively, therefore, the background principle of the Constitution's commitment to representative government, and to democratisation more generally, was invoked as an interpretive guide for answering the question of who held the reins of executive power in the national capital. As the Chief Justice made clear:

> Thus, it can be very well said that the executive power of the Union in respect of NCT of Delhi *is confined to the three matters in the State List for which the legislative power of the Delhi Legislative Assembly has been excluded under Article 239 AA (3) (a)*. Such an interpretation would thwart any attempt on the part of the Union Government to seize all control and allow the concepts of pragmatic federalism and federal balance to prevail by giving the NCT of Delhi some degree of required independence in its functioning subject to the limitations imposed by the Constitution. (emphasis added)[26]

What of the second issue before the Court, the interpretation of the proviso? Here again, the Court applied the background principles that it had set out previously. The Chief Justice correctly observed that if, indeed, the word 'any' was read literally, it would effectively allow the central government – acting through the LG – to 'obstruct … the stream of governance'.[27] At the same time, the Chief Justice rejected the Delhi government's suggestion to limit the scope of the proviso to the three excepted matters in the state list, noting that the text did not support a reading that would expressly exclude topics from the purview of disagreement.

What, then, was the answer? It was here that the judgment, regrettably, devolved from being a legal adjudication of a dispute between two parties to a series of platitudes. The Chief Justice began by noting that 'the words "any matter" occurring in the proviso to Article 239AA(4) does not necessarily need to be construed to mean "every matter"'.[28] But then, what did they mean? Some evasion followed. The Chief Justice noted:

> The power given to the Lieutenant Governor under the proviso to Article 239AA(4) contains *the rule of exception* and should not be treated as a general norm. The Lieutenant Governor is to act with constitutional objectivity keeping in view the high degree of constitutional trust reposed in him while exercising the special power ordained upon him unlike the Governor and the President who are bound by the aid and advice of their Ministers. The Lieutenant Governor need not, in a mechanical manner, refer every decision of his Ministers to the President. He has to be guided by the concept of constitutional morality. There has to

[24] ibid para 204.
[25] Constitution of India 1949, Art 239A.
[26] *NCT of Delhi v Union of India (I)* (n 17) para 221.
[27] ibid para 223.
[28] ibid para 232.

> be *some valid grounds* for the Lieutenant Governor to refer the decision of the Council of Ministers to the President in order to *protect the interest of the NCT of Delhi* and the principle of constitutionalism. (emphasis added)[29]

And:

> But it cannot be difference for the sake of difference. It cannot be mechanical or in a routine matter. The power has been conferred to guide, discuss and see that the administration runs for the welfare of the people and also NCT of Delhi that has been given a special status. Therefore, the word 'any' has to be understood treating as a guidance meant for the constitutional authority. He must bear in mind the constitutional objectivity, the needed advice and the realities.[30]

It is evident that little substance is to be found in these lengthy paragraphs. The Chief Justice clarified that (i) disagreement was not the norm, but an exception (ii) that it would have to be based on 'valid grounds' and (iii) that it would have to be connected in some way with the welfare of the National Capital Territory. At its highest, this would, in my view, impose a thin procedural obligation of providing written reasons in case of a disagreement; however, on the substantive grounds, these observations provided little clarity to either of the two actors – the Union government and the government of the NCT – about the specific instances where the LG could (or could not) disagree with the Delhi government.

There were two separate judgments in the case, authored by Chandrachud J and Bhushan J. The former's judgment provided marginally more clarity on the question of disagreement. While agreeing with the judgment of the majority with respect to the background interpretive principles that would govern the Court's understanding of Article 239AA, Chandrachud J laid out, in addition, a further interpretive principle specifically for the proviso: a balance between the democratic imperative and the status of Delhi as the 'national capital':

> The nature of the differences which may warrant a reference to the President cannot be exhaustively catalogued. But it would be appropriate to construe the proviso as a protector of national concerns in regard to governance of the NCT. The Lieutenant Governor is a watchdog to protect them. The Lieutenant Governor may, for instance, be justified in seeking recourse to the proviso where the executive act of the government of the NCT is likely to impede or prejudice the exercise of the executive power of the Union government. The Lieutenant Governor may similarly consider it necessary to invoke the proviso to ensure compliance with the provisions of the Constitution or a law enacted by Parliament. There may well be significant issues of policy which have a bearing on the position of the National Capital Territory as a national capital. Financial concerns of the Union government may be implicated in such a manner that it becomes necessary for the Lieutenant Governor to invoke the proviso where a difference of opinion remains unresolved.[31]

Thus, while Chandrachud J agreed with the majority that a categorical set of circumstances that warranted a 'difference' of opinion between the LG and the Council of Ministers could not be enumerated, he did, at least, provide an interpretive framework and a set of illustrations to determine when the proviso could – or could not – legitimately be used. In this, however, Chandrachud J was the only judge out of

[29] ibid para 233.
[30] ibid para 233.
[31] ibid para 141 (separate opinion of Chandrachud J).

the five: Justice Bhushan, in his judgment, muddied the waters even more by holding *both* that the word 'any' meant the 'entire extent of legislation'[32] *and* the proposition that proviso Article 239AA(4) 'envisages an extreme and unusual situation … is substantially correct'.[33] One notices here the unfortunate persistence of loose language: how correct, precisely, is 'substantially correct' when it comes to an *actual* tangible situation involving a difference of opinion between the two constitutional authorities? Justice Bhushan could not – or would not – say.

Before we explore the application of the judgment of the Constitution Bench to the specific dispute(s) between the government of Delhi and the Union of India, it is worthwhile taking a step back and considering the following point. All three judgments repeatedly emphasised the need for 'constitutional statesmanship', and 'cooperation' between the Council of Ministers and the office of the Lieutenant-Governor. This ideal of cooperation – as expressed in the judgment and as extracted in the opinion of the Chief Justice above – played a central role in the Court replacing a clear answer on the interpretation of the proviso with a set of platitudes. More importantly, however, what this seemed to ignore entirely was that the very reason why the matter came to court was because of conflict, not cooperation. The impugned notifications issued by the central government involved the first move in what was very self-evidently a power struggle; the case before the High Court and the Supreme Court was a case seeking judicial resolution of that struggle. For the Supreme Court then to answer the question before it in the language of cooperation was, effectively, to turn a blind eye to why it had been approached in the first place, effectively allowing the more powerful party to the dispute to prevail.

It is particularly important to note that the Court's finding – or non-finding – on the scope of the proviso did not have a symmetrical effect on both parties. Formally, the text of the Constitution continued to vest in the LG the power to disagree and escalate a disagreement to the President for decision. This position remained substantially the same after the Court's judgment because no actual constraint had been placed upon the LG's powers. The absence of clarity, in other words, created a grey zone, where the ambiguity of the constitutional provision was replaced by the ambiguity of the Supreme Court decision – which, in turn, could be exploited by only one of the two parties (the LG), leaving the other with the continuing – and repeated – burden (financial, political and otherwise) of challenging it in the Courts.

III. Applying the Principles: The Two-Judge Bench

As I have indicated, the Constitution Bench's task was to set out the constitutional principles underlying the interpretation of Article 239AA and delineate the scope of

[32] ibid para 95 (opinion of Bhushan J) The headnote of the SCC Reporter lists Bhushan J's judgment as a 'concurrence', and Chandrachud J himself noted in his opinion that all three judgments came to broadly similar conclusions. However, given that Bhushan disagreed on critical points, including his interpretation of the word 'any', the question of which subjects in List II were within the jurisdiction of the government of Delhi, and whether the central government had co-extensive executive power (on each of the issues, Bhushan J favoured the Union government), his opinion is better characterised as a partial dissent.

[33] ibid para 98 (opinion of Bhushan J).

legislative and executive power enjoyed by the government of Delhi and the Union government, respectively. In the previous section, I highlighted that on one of the core issues that were in dispute before the Constitution Bench – the scope of the proviso in Article 239AA(4) – the Constitution Bench did not return a finding with sufficient clarity, and that this lack of clarity was not neutral, but directly benefited the LG and through him, the Union government.

In this section, I want to shift focus. As I have noted above, the Constitution Bench had laid down certain overarching interpretive principles that – in its view – would form the framework for resolving concrete disputes between the LG and Delhi's Council of Ministers in any specific case. For the adjudication of those specific disputes, however, the case returned to the two-judge bench that had originally referred it to the Constitution Bench). This bench was comprised of Justices Sikri and Bhushan, who had been parties to the judgment of the Constitution Bench: Justice Sikri had joined the majority opinion of the Chief Justice and Justice Bhushan had written a separate opinion.

The proceedings before the two-judge bench – which concerned the resolution of six different disputes between the two governments – revealed the limitations of the Constitution Bench verdict. As the Court recorded,[34] both parties were at odds not only about the application of the judgment of the Constitution Bench, but even about what it said – down to a question as basic as whether the Union government retained executive power that was co-extensive with the power of the Delhi government or whether it was excluded from executive power except in the three entries in the state list which expressly accorded it that power. Coming a mere few months after the Constitution Bench's judgment, there was no reason for such a dispute to exist, but for the Bench's inability (or unwillingness) to lay down the law with sufficient clarity (note that the task of the Constitution Bench was, specifically, to spell out the legal position, which would then be applied to the facts of the specific dispute by the two-judge bench).

The two judges wrote separate opinions. Discussing the dispute between the parties on the interpretation of the Constitution Bench's judgment, Justice Sikri clarified that the Constitution Bench had indeed held that the executive power of the Delhi government, concerning matters in the state list, operated to the exclusion of the executive power of the Union government, save for the three excepted matters.[35] He then proceeded to consider the specific disputes. In this chapter, I examine his findings on the first three disputes, which were resolved in favour of the Union government.

The most significant dispute – and, indeed, the dispute that had caused the greatest amount of political controversy – involved control over 'services', ie which government had control over the internal transfers and postings of civil servants, once they had been assigned to Delhi. The context of the dispute arose out of the fact that in one of the impugned notifications, the central government had excluded Entry 41 of List II – 'state public services and state public service commissions' – from the purview of the Delhi government.[36]

[34] *NCT of Delhi v Union of India (II)*, CA No 2357/2017 (judgment dated 14 February 2019) (SCI).
[35] ibid para 61.
[36] ibid para 64.

The holding of the Constitution Bench – to which Justice Sikri had been party, and then reaffirmed in his separate opinion – appeared to gesture towards an answer to the question: once it had been held that the executive power of the Delhi government extended to all the entries under List II of the Seventh Schedule of the Constitution other than the three entries specifically excluded by the Constitution itself, it would follow that it could not be excluded from Entry 41 simply by a government notification. This was especially so because the justification set out in the impugned notification – that Entry 41 was inapplicable to Delhi because, like other Union territories, it did not have a public service of its own – had been at least implicitly rejected by the majority judgment of the Constitution Bench when it noted that the executive power of the Delhi government did in fact extend to all entries in List II apart from the three specifically excluded.[37]

Justice Sikri, however, now appeared to disagree with the implications of the judgment that he had signed. He repeated the Union government's submissions that there did not exist a 'State public service commission' in Delhi and went on to note that 'it is also doubtful to mention it as State public service';[38] no reasons were given to substantiate the cause of doubt. At the same time, as the Delhi government had argued, for the purposes of the Indian Administrative Service (Cadre) Rules, state governments oversaw service postings from joint cadres, and the Supreme Court had held that for this purpose, 'states' included 'Union territories'. Justice Sikri then came to the following strange conclusion, which deserves to be quoted in full:

> The aforesaid discussion leads to a very peculiar situation. The appellant has endeavoured to assume the executive power in respect of 'services' by relying upon Entry 41 of List II, which may be doubtful. That situation may give discretionary powers to the L.G. On the other hand, it also cannot be said that once the manpower is allocated to Union Territory of Delhi, the GNCTD should not have any power to deal with such employees, in view of C.B. Judgment. In such a scenario, and to avoid any conflict of exercise of powers between the LG on the one hand (as representative of the Central Government) and the Council of Ministers with Chief Minister as Head on the other hand, we are of the opinion that *for the smooth functioning of the system, it is necessary to carve out a just and fair mechanism*. Therefore, we are inclined to accept the suggestion of Mr. Sundaram in this behalf as recorded above. In this behalf, we reiterate the position as under:
>
> The transfers and postings of Secretaries, HODs and other officers in the scale of Joint Secretary to the government of India and above can be done by the Lieutenant Governor and the file submitted to him directly. For other levels, including DANICS officers, the files can be routed through the Chief Minister to Lieutenant Governor. In case of difference of opinion between the Lieutenant Governor and the Chief Minister, the view of the Lieutenant Governor should prevail and the Ministry of Home Affairs can issue a suitable notification in this regard. However, for Grade IV, III, II and I DASS officials, there is an existing delegation of powers where for Grades IV and III, all transfers and postings are done by the Secretary (Services); for Grades II and I, the transfers and postings are done by the Chief Secretary. (emphasis added)[39]

[37] ibid para 74.
[38] ibid para 86.
[39] ibid paras 89 and 90.

It is worthwhile to pause here and consider quite how extraordinary this 'finding' was. First, as pointed out above, Justice Sikri noted that it would be 'doubtful' to consider services in Delhi as 'state public services', but provided no reasons at all for his doubt; indeed, given the fact that Union Territories did not exist at the time of the framing of the Constitution, Entry 41 could not possibly have used any word other than 'state'. Furthermore, if there was ambiguity about the scope of Entry 41, the Constitution Bench verdict – to which Justice Sikri had signed on – had, in its articulation of the principles applicable to the dispute, held that interpretive doubt was to be resolved in favour of the more directly representative authority – in this case, the elected Delhi government.

Secondly, having noted that the application of Entry 41 was doubtful, Justice Sikri went on to set up an interpretive conflict that he then refused to resolve one way or another. Once again, the Constitution Bench had indicated the interpretive framework to be applied in case there was ambiguity in the distribution of powers – but those observations were sidestepped when it came to applying them to a concrete dispute. And thirdly, Justice Sikri's chosen resolution of 'carving out' a workable mechanism amounted to a complete acceptance of the 'solution' suggested by the Union government's counsel, Mr Sundaram (the 'Sundaram solution')! And not only this, the answer was no legal answer at all: it was the answer of a Solomon ordering the dismemberment of the child instead of settling the dispute over who the mother was.[40]

Furthermore, the 'Sundaram solution' was one-sided. Effectively, it granted to the LG either exclusive power (over high-level transfers) or veto power (over most other transfers). This was unsurprising, as the suggestion had emerged from the government counsel; but what was surprising – and unacceptable – was Justice Sikri's seizing upon it to resolve what was a legal question about the distribution of federal power. So, perhaps fittingly, Justice Sikri ended his analysis with the same platitudes that had plagued the majority judgment of the Constitution Bench: 'In the interest of good governance and smooth Governmental function, we expect that efforts will be made by both the Chief Minister as well as the LG for a harmonious working relation.'[41]

Issues of a similar kind were rife throughout the rest of Justice Sikri's judgment. In each dispute, there were important interpretive ambiguities in legal provisions. Following the principles laid out by the Constitution Bench would have meant that these ambiguities ought to have been resolved in favour of the government that – as pointed out above – was more directly representative (in this case, the government of the NCT, which enjoyed the confidence of the legislature that had been voted in by the people to govern Delhi, as opposed to the LG, an unelected official installed by Union government). Those principles, however, were conspicuous by their absence in the Bench's reasoning.

For example, a question that arose before the two-judge bench was whether the central government could have validly excluded the jurisdiction of Delhi's Anti-Corruption Bureau to investigate corruption offences committed by central government officials. This dispute turned upon whether the central government's impugned notification fell within the definition of 'police' (which was a List II entry that, for Delhi, was excepted from the legislative assembly's purview) or 'criminal procedure' (that remained within

[40] I am indebted to Prateek Chadha for this vivid imagery.

[41] *NCT of Delhi v Union of India (II)* (n 34) para 92.

the concurrent list). Justice Sikri decided the issue by holding that, according to the general rule of interpretation, entries in the lists had to be considered 'liberally'. On this basis, he held that the word 'police' had to be construed widely, to include the Anti-Corruption Bureau – which, thereby, took it out of the purview of the Delhi government.[42] This, however, was disingenuous at best: the rule of liberal interpretation of entries in the legislative lists had evolved from challenges to legislative competence and was premised on the general constitutional principle that a court should be slow to strike down laws enacted by representative bodies or to hold that representative bodies acted without jurisdiction. Construing the entries in the legislative lists broadly thus flowed from the principle that a court should lean towards preserving legislative power rather than invalidating it.

However, this was not a case where there was an isolated challenge to legislative competence, and where a court would be justified in saving a law by reading an entry in the Seventh Schedule broadly; this was a dispute between two federal units, where a broad reading of the powers of one would necessarily encroach upon the powers of the other. Once again, however, the interpretive principle discussed above to resolve this conflict was ignored in the application.

The third dispute involved jurisdiction over Commissions of Inquiry. The key dispute turned upon the fact that in the Commissions of Inquiry Act, the appropriate government for matters under Lists II and III was the 'State government'; the question, therefore, was whether the government of Delhi counted as a 'State government' within the meaning of the Commissions of Inquiry Act. Justice Sikri noted that under the General Clauses Act – India's umbrella interpretive legislation dating from a highly centralised colonial period – the phrase 'State government' had been specifically defined to mean 'central government' in the case of a Union Territory. He then relied upon a 1985 judgment of the Supreme Court, *Goa Sampling Employees' Association v General Superintendence Co of India*,[43] to hold that in the case of Union territories, there was no concept of a 'State government'. Interestingly, however, *Goa Sampling Employees' Association* – which was delivered before the constitutional amendment that inserted Article 239AA into the Constitution and created Delhi's *sui generis* status (a status categorically accepted by the Constitution Bench majority) – based its judgment on the specific understanding, as spelt out in Article 239(1), that 'every Union Territory is to be *administered* by the President' – an understanding that had not only been displaced textually by Article 239AA but interpretively by the Constitution Bench's judgment. In other words, therefore, Justice Sikri's interpretation of the General Clauses Act was sustained by a legal premise – that the President, and therefore the central government, 'administers' a Union Territory – that had been undermined by a judgment that he himself had signed on to a few months before.

Now, it is not my case here that Justice Sikri could not, through any interpretive manoeuvres, have come to the conclusions that he did. The point, however, is that – as the above analysis demonstrates – each of the disputes turned upon ambiguous legal and constitutional provisions where two plausible interpretations at the very least were available. To belabour the argument made above, the entire reason why the Constitution

[42] ibid.
[43] (1985) 1 SCC 206 (SCI).

Bench had been set up – and why it had delivered a verdict – had been precisely to resolve this constitutional question: what principles were to govern the distribution of power between the two federal units, especially where the legal provisions in question were ambiguous? But those principles vanished utterly in the resolution of the actual dispute (apart from a token nod on the issue of services).

Before concluding, brief mention deserves to be made of Justice Bhushan's judgment. Incredibly, on the issue of services, Justice Bhushan went even further than Justice Sikri: he directly contradicted the holding of the majority, and sought to resurrect a point that he had dissented on:

> There is no opinion of Constitution Bench as to whether Entry 41 of List II is available to Legislative Assembly of Delhi or not except a general statement that Legislative Assembly of Delhi shall have power to make laws with respect to any of the matters enumerated in List I and List II except Entries 1, 2 and 18 of State List.[44]

It is unclear what the phrase 'general statement' means. Either the Constitution Bench returned a finding on a point or it did not; at the very least, if Justice Bhushan wanted to discount something said by the Constitution Bench, it was incumbent upon him to show that it was not part of the questions referred to the Constitution Bench and, consequently, not binding upon him sitting as a two-judge bench. In the context of adjudication, however, 'general statement' means nothing at all, because the binding character of judgments is not decided by whether they are 'general' or 'specific' on a given point. In any event, having dismissed this 'general statement', Justice Bhushan went on to quote his own judgment on the point, cited his own test (that had not carried the support of any other judge), and noted that:

> In the above paragraphs [ie of his own separate judgment] the opinion is expressed that all matters including those relatable to the State List and Concurrent List are available to Legislative Assembly of Delhi except where an entry indicates that its applicability to the Union Territory is excluded by implication or by any express constitutional provision. The conclusion is, thus, that all entries of List II and List III are available to Legislative Assembly for exercising Legislative power except when an entry is excluded by implication or by any express provision.[45]

In what can only be described as continuing judicial indiscipline, Justice Bhushan went on to rely exclusively on a 1989 Report of the Ministry of Home Affairs' Committee on the Reorganisation of Delhi (the Balakrishnan Report) – which had been discounted by the majority judgment – to hold that services were entirely excluded from the Delhi government's jurisdiction. On this point, therefore, he disagreed with Justice Sikri, resulting in a split verdict on the first issue and thus, by default, the notification by the central government remained valid.[46]

At the time of writing this chapter, the split judgment has not yet been decided in a reference, and a review petition against the two-judge bench decision remains pending.

[44] *NCT of Delhi v Union of India (II)* (n 34) para 16 (separate opinion of Bhushan J).

[45] ibid para 24 (separate opinion of Bhushan J).

[46] While this author was not present in court for the pronouncement of the judgment, those who were informed him that the two judges seemed unaware that they had dissented on the issue of services until it was pointed out by counsel.

IV. Judicial Evasion, Judicial Vagueness and Judicial Revisionism

A. Judicial Evasion

On 10 February 2015, the AAP won a landslide victory in the New Delhi legislative assembly elections. The central government's notifications and directions, which constituted the heart of its legal conflict with the Delhi government, were issued (primarily) between May and December 2015. The judgment of the High Court – which decided almost all issues in favour of the central government – was delivered on 4 August 2016.

The Delhi government's appeal against the High Court's judgment came before the Supreme Court on 5 September 2016. Notice was issued to the central government on 9 September 2016, and eight weeks was granted for the pleadings to be completed. After a set of adjournments through November and December 2016 and January 2017, a two-judge bench of the Supreme Court began to hear the matter in the first half of February. On 15 February, in a brief order, the two-judge bench (of which Justice Sikri was a part) noted that:

> During the hearing of these appeals our attention is drawn to the provisions of Article 145(3) of the Constitution of India. Having gone through the matters and the aforesaid provisions, we are of the opinion that these appeals need to be heard by a Constitution Bench as these matters involve substantial questions of law as to the interpretation of Article 239AA of the Constitution.[47]

In short, therefore, it took the Supreme Court almost half a year – and six days of substantive hearings – to decide a preliminary issue that to an external observer would seem self-evident: a dispute between two federal units, involving the interpretation of a constitutional provision (a large part of which had not yet been considered by the Court before), deserved a hearing by a Constitution Bench.

But it took even longer – almost nine more months – and repeated oral 'mentionings' before the Chief Justice for the substantive hearing to commence.[48] Arguments began on 2 November 2017 and concluded on 6 December. It then took the Constitution Bench another seven months (with an intervening month-and-a-half long summer vacation) to deliver its judgment (4 July 2018).

The two-judge bench of Justices Sikri and Bhushan held various hearings from August to November 2018, before finally reserving judgment on 1 November. Their final judgment – which we have discussed above – was delivered on 14 February 2019. After that, to resolve the split verdict on the issue of services, a three-judge bench assembled on multiple occasions – but without a substantive hearing.

The term of the AAP government expired on 22 February 2020. In the just-concluded assembly elections, the party had been returned to power in another landslide victory. Immediately after its triumph, the AAP government was promptly embroiled in another

[47] *NCT of Delhi v Union of India*, Civil Appeal No 2357/2017, order dated 15 February 2017.

[48] A 'mentioning' is a process by which counsel orally request the Chief Justice to 'list' a matter for hearing because of its urgency.

legal dispute with the Union government (which had also been returned to power in a landslide, in the 2019 General Election): this time about the appointment of public prosecutors to oversee the handling of cases arising out of a communal pogrom/riot that had racked North-East Delhi that same month and had claimed (at least) 53 lives.

This chronology is important, as it demonstrates that a legal dispute about the constitutional powers of an elected government – that arose at the beginning of that government's term – outlived a full election cycle and continues to persist into that government's second term. This is not the simple – and ubiquitous – lament about the notoriously slow Indian judicial system. This is not even about the fact that one of the Supreme Court's primary tasks – along with resolving constitutional disputes and harmonising jurisprudence across the High Courts – is to settle litigation between federal units, on the scope of the federal scheme. What it *is* about is the Supreme Court's refusal to hear – for long periods – cases involving the ostensible pushing of constitutional boundaries by the Union government, a refusal which directly benefited the Union government as the status quo remained in place pending a judgment. Elsewhere, I have referred to this as 'judicial evasion': through its very failure to decide, the Court effectively does decide in favour of the party that benefits from the status quo, which is invariably the Union government.[49]

Judicial evasion has become a standard feature of the Supreme Court's conduct in cases involving constitutional challenges against the Union government. For example, for more than five years, the Union government carried on an aggressive expansion of a national biometric identification system (the Aadhaar) without any validating legislation. Constitutional challenges to the Aadhaar programme were first filed in 2012, but the case was not heard until 2018 – by which time, Aadhaar had become an effective fait accompli.[50] Interim orders of the Court prohibiting the government from making Aadhaar mandatory were flouted with impunity, but contempt petitions before the Supreme Court were not heard either. In its final judgment (authored, as it turned out, by Justice Sikri), the Supreme Court upheld Aadhaar in part and struck it down in part – but excused the government's illegal data collection (until the passage of the 2016 Aadhaar Act) with another 'Sundaram solution': giving people the option to 'opt-out' of the programme, while being fully aware that, having upheld mandatory Aadhaar for subsidies and taxpayers, nobody would be in a genuine position to 'opt-out'.

Similarly, in 2018, electoral law was amended to allow for unlimited, anonymous corporate donations to political parties ('electoral bonds'). The constitutionality of the law was challenged immediately after its passage. To date, multiple election cycles (including one general election and many state elections) have come and gone – with extensive documentation of massive amounts of anonymous election funding through electoral bonds, primarily to the benefit of the ruling party – but the challenge remains unheard. In 2019, during the general election, the then Chief Justice Ranjan Gogoi remarked, with astonishing chutzpah, that there 'was too little time' to decide a case

[49] See G Bhatia, 'O Brave New World: The Supreme Court's Evolving Doctrine of Constitutional Evasion' (*The Indian Constitutional Law and Philosophy Blog*, 6 January 2017) https://indconlawphil.wordpress.com/2017/01/06/o-brave-new-world-the-supreme-courts-evolving-doctrine-of-constitutional-evasion/. Needless to say, the position would be reversed if the Court had granted a stay of the Union government's notifications pending adjudication of the case.

[50] See *Justice KS Puttaswamy v Union of India* (2018) 5 SCC 1.

as complex as this with the ongoing general election, blithely ignoring the fact that at the time he spoke the case had already been pending before the Supreme Court for more than a year.[51] Other significant examples include the constitutional alteration to the erstwhile state of Jammu and Kashmir that – at the time of writing – is more than three years old.

It may be asked how the phenomenon of judicial evasion as outlined here differs from, or is particularly worse than, the phenomenon of strategic adjudication, which constitutional courts often resort to for the preservation of their institutional independence, especially in the teeth of an assertive political executive.[52] This kind of strategic adjudication may occur, for example, when heavily politicised issues (often pertaining to questions of policy or governance) are brought to the Supreme Court (often by one or the other party seeking to use the judicial forum to achieve goals that are unattainable through the political process) and when adjudication of such issues is likely to further entrench political polarisation (by creating winners and losers) and, in the process, threaten the Court's legitimacy as well as risking non-compliance.

There are three responses to this argument. First, it is the Indian Supreme Court itself that has, over the last four decades, carved out for itself a prominent and highly visible role as a constitutional 'watchdog', frequently intervening in matters that other jurisdictions would consider squarely within the domains of policy, and engaging in supervisory and implementational roles that go far beyond straightforward adjudication. A sudden, unexplained – and inconsistent – retreat from this role in a squarely legal, rather than policy, matter, therefore, calls for explanation. Secondly, while there may be merit in the idea of strategic adjudication in cases where there is a good argument for letting a contentious matter be resolved by the political process, the examples cited above are not of that kind. The dispute between Delhi and the Union was a classic dispute about the federal distribution of powers between two political units that were both claiming popular legitimacy, and fell well within the domain of disputes a federal judicial body was meant to arbitrate in the first place. The dispute over the constitutional status of Jammu and Kashmir is of the same character. The constitutional challenge to the electoral bond scheme involves the ground rules of the democratic process – party-political funding – which, in turn, affects the legitimacy of electoral outcomes. Thus, there can be no question of 'strategic adjudication' in cases of this kind. And finally, as pointed out above, the result of judicial evasion in such cases is to cause permanent – and irreversible – damage to core constitutional principles (such as the federal structure or transparent voting processes) by creating a fait accompli. This is, therefore, a far cry from the vision of a canny judiciary avoiding potential political minefields by kicking partisan controversies into the tall grass.[53]

[51] V Sachdev, 'Why the SC'S Electoral Bonds Order Leaves a Lot to be Desired' *The Quint* (12 April 2019) www.thequint.com/voices/opinion/why-supreme-court-electoral-bonds-interim-order-ineffective.

[52] See, eg E McWhinney, 'Judicial Restraint and the West German Constitutional Court' (1961) 75 *Harvard Law Review* 5.

[53] It may be noted, however, that when the Supreme Court does wish to act with alacrity, it is perfectly capable of doing so. In June 2022, amidst an ongoing political crisis in Maharashtra, a vacation bench of the Supreme Court passed an interim order preventing the Deputy Speaker of the Assembly from proceeding to disqualify certain 'rebel MLAs' in accordance with the Xth Schedule of the Constitution. While the Xth Schedule effectively stood suspended, the Court then ordered a 'floor test' in the Assembly. As a result of

B. Judicial Vagueness and Judicial Revisionism

The two *Delhi Government* cases discussed above are notable for another feature of recent judgments of the Supreme Court. In constitutional cases against the Union government, on more than one occasion, the Court has made grand declarations of constitutional values, committed itself to a set of interpretive principles, and, in its rhetoric, marked out its role as the supreme constitutional interpreter. However, when it comes to the operative parts of judgments or the application of these principles, two things happen. First, the outcome is framed in such vague language that it does not, in effect, place any genuine constraints upon the Union government (even though, on rhetoric, it appears to have 'lost' the case, or a part of it). Secondly, in the alternative, those principles set out by the court are simply ignored.

In the *Delhi Government* cases, both were in evidence. As I have discussed above, the Court refused to go beyond platitudes in determining the scope of 'disagreement' between the LG and the Council of Ministers. The Court's invocations of 'constitutional statesmanship' were, however, little more than paper pronouncements: without clarity on constraints, it remained entirely open to the LG to continue to interpret what 'any matter' might mean, with the burden of challenging abuse still upon the Delhi government. Furthermore, given that specific disputes between the two governments remained unresolved in the Supreme Court even after one full term of the government, the costs of litigating abuse were, evidently, prohibitively high. This has had a clear, and ongoing, political outcome. For example, in the dispute over the appointment of Special Public Prosecutors in the Delhi riots case – an issue that would materially affect the investigation of the riots and their prosecution in the courts – the Delhi government eventually gave in to the central government's insistence on appointing its own law officers as public prosecutors.[54] Similarly, during the ongoing coronavirus pandemic, despite 'health' being a List II subject, the LG passed a series of overriding orders, some of which – such as compulsory institutional quarantine – led to substantial chaos, before being reversed.[55] In effect, the Supreme Court's lack of clarity on the scope of the proviso amounted to an endorsement of the existing state of power relations in the national capital, and its record of evasion makes further litigation fruitless for the weaker party.

Furthermore, judicial vagueness directly enables judicial revisionism. In the *Delhi Government* cases, this took a particularly stark form: on the one hand, Justice Bhushan pretended that the majority had made a 'general statement' on a position of law that he was at liberty to ignore, and instead reiterated his own (dissenting) view as the position

the floor test, following from one Court order – where the MLAs under threat of disqualification could freely vote against the government, having been immunised by another Court order – the government fell, and another government (supported by the ruling party at the centre the BJP) replaced it. All this took place within 48 hours. At the time of writing, two months have passed since those two 'interim orders', and despite multiple requests, the Supreme Court has not taken up the case again.

[54] 'Only Recommended Special Public Prosecutors to Delhi Govt: Police' *The Indian Express* (13 January 2021) https://indianexpress.com/article/cities/delhi/only-recommended-special-public-prosecutors-to-delhi-govt-police-7143945/.

[55] 'Liueutenant Governor Anil Baijal Mandates 5-Day Institutional Quarantine for Covid Patients, AAP Calls Decision "Arbitrary"' *The Economic Times* (20 June 2020) https://economictimes.indiatimes.com/news/politics-and-nation/lieutenant-governor-anil-baijal-mandates-5-day-institutional-quarantine-for-covid-patients-aap-calls-decision-arbitrary/articleshow/76473366.cms.

of law while sitting on a smaller bench. On the other hand, Justice Sikri departed from the majority judgment that *he himself had signed on to*, a ruling that was at least in part enabled by the loopholes that the Constitution Bench had left through the vague wording that it had used. What we had, therefore, was a two-judge bench that – on the yardstick of common sense and constitutional principle – went squarely against the binding judgment of a five-judge bench, yet the absence of sufficient clarity in the latter enabled such an outcome and made the prospect of an immediate review or reversal more difficult.

Again, judicial vagueness is not a one-off incident. In the Aadhaar judgment, Justice Sikri struck down section 59 of the Aadhaar Act, which allowed private parties access to the Aadhaar database. However, the rationale for striking down section 59 was left entirely vague. In one part of its judgment, the Court suggested that it was striking down section 59 because it allowed private parties access even without a legal framework. At another point, however, the Court held that section 59 was struck down because it enabled commercial surveillance, and was therefore unconstitutional. Naturally, this lack of clarity was immediately exploited by the Union government: soon after the judgment, it issued an ordinance that substantially restored section 59, on the interpretation that the Supreme Court had not found it *unconstitutional*, but only legally deficient. In other words, despite a categorical holding that struck down the section, the central government simply revived it and nullified the judgment – something it could not have done had the finding been placed firmly on clear constitutional grounds.[56]

Challenges to the restoration of section 59 remain pending and unheard before the Court at the time of writing.

Similarly, in *Anuradha Bhasin v Union of India*, the communications blackout imposed upon Jammu and Kashmir after the alteration of its constitutional status on 5 August 2019 was challenged before the Supreme Court. This case also falls within the domain of judicial evasion, as the internet connection was cut off on 5 August, and the case was finally decided by the Supreme Court on 10 January 2020. Furthermore, in its judgment, the Court spelt out the contours of the proportionality standard for adjudicating restrictions upon constitutional rights, while also noting that the government's failure to produce the orders constituting the legal bases of the internet shutdown (and restrictions upon movement) was unacceptable. However, the Court neither struck down the orders on the ground of non-production nor did it apply the proportionality test to an actual adjudication of whether the internet shutdown was constitutionally valid or not. Instead, it stipulated periodic executive review of internet restrictions.[57] Further litigation led to a judgment that created a separate and extra-legal executive committee to review a restriction upon 4G internet, yet still no adjudication on merits.[58]

[56] See The Aadhaar and other Laws (Amendment) Act, 2019.

[57] *Anuradha Bhasin v Union of India*, Writ Petition (Civil) No 1031 of 2019, judgment dated 10 January 2020.

[58] *Foundation for Media Professionals v Union Territory of Jammu and Kashmir*, Diary No 10817 of 2020, judgment dated 11 May 2020. For a critique, see C Chandrachud, 'An Executive Court and a Judicial Committee: The Supreme Court's Decisions on the Internet Restrictions on Kashmir' (*The Indian Constitutional Law and Philosophy Blog*, 23 May 2020) https://indconlawphil.wordpress.com/2020/05/23/an-executive-court-and-a-judicial-committee-the-supreme-courts-decisions-on-the-internet-restrictions-in-kashmir/.

V. Conclusion

The purpose of this chapter has been to provide a conceptual vocabulary for understanding various ongoing issues involving the relationship between the political executive and the judiciary in India. This conceptual vocabulary will help to situate the Indian situation within the broader context of constitutional resilience, democratic decline and the role of the courts. As I have argued above, the Indian situation cannot be readily assimilated with other contexts, such as that of the USA, where anti-democratic tendencies are writ large in the judgments themselves,[59] or that of Poland,[60] where formal institutional capture has taken place. Judicial vagueness, judicial evasion and judicial revisionism are phenomena specific to the contemporary relationship between the Indian political executive and the judiciary, and in particular the Supreme Court.

With that in mind, I will briefly summarise. To a casual observer, the majority judgment of the Constitution Bench of the Supreme Court in *NCT of Delhi v Union of India* would seem an admirable – and balanced – articulation of constitutional principles, sensitive to federal concerns and concerned with crafting a solution that would respect the constitutional text and the place of the Union government in the federal scheme, while maintaining the system of checks and balances to prevent the concentration of power. A closer look at the entire litigation (which continues to this day), however, reveals a darker story: through judicial evasion, judicial vagueness and, ultimately, judicial revisionism, when it came to the actual balance of power between federal units, very little by way of tangible constraint was placed upon the Union government. Indeed, the ongoing controversy over the appointment of public prosecutors for the Delhi riots cases – on which even Justices Sikri and Bhushan, in the two-judge bench judgment, agreed belongs within the jurisdiction of the Delhi government – reveals how effectively helpless the Supreme Court finally left the Delhi government, an outcome with serious political ramifications. And as these concluding remarks have pointed towards, the *Delhi Government* cases are but one example of many of this phenomenon. Judicial evasion, judicial vagueness and judicial revisionism constitute a hollowing out of effective checks and balances on the concentration of power in the Union government, and as such damage the constitutional scheme. But worst of all, they do so by stealth: just like an 'Emergency' can be formally declared or undeclared, judicial abdication to the executive can be explicit (as in the notorious habeas corpus case)[61] or implicit. The latter is harder to identify and challenge, but for precisely that reason, it is an urgent and imperative task to do so.

[59] MJ Klarman, 'Foreword: The Degradation of American Democracy – and the Court' (2020) 134 *Harvard Law Review* 1.

[60] W Sadurski, 'Polish Constitutional Tribunal under PiS: From an Activist Court, to a Paralysed Tribunal, to a Government Enabler' [2019] *Hague Journal of the Rule of Law* 63.

[61] *ADM Jabalpur v Shivakanth Shukla* 1976 SCR 172.

PART VI

Fourth Branch (Guarantor) Institutions

12

Sri Lanka's Guarantor Branch: Constitutional Resilience by Stealth?

DINESHA SAMARARATNE[1]

I. Introduction

The Constitutional Council, the focal point of Sri Lanka's Guarantor branch, was described by an academic and public intellectual as an attempt by the people to 'conceptualise the limits to political power' and 'a reaction to an autocratic presidency'.[2] For this and related reasons, I argue in this chapter that in the face of failures in Sri Lanka's constitutional reform on the big-ticket items such as power-sharing and the executive presidency, modest steps are being taken towards constitutional resilience, through its Guarantor branch. These constitutional developments are an example of home-grown constitutional design and reform. I have chosen to study constitutional resilience in Sri Lanka through a study of its Guarantor branch due to the frequency of its reforms. While it demonstrates resilience through its adaptability, it is nevertheless an innovation that has not yet consolidated. Dominant political parties have undermined its independence and the judiciary is yet to recognise the Guarantor branch as a branch. However, early signs are that, unnoticed by many constitutional actors, Sri Lanka's Guarantor branch is an innovation that is developing resilience 'by stealth'.

I build this argument in four parts. I begin in section II with an assessment of the concept of constitutional resilience and of the broader global debate on the Guarantor

[1] Drafts of this chapter were presented at the workshop on the Fourth Branch in South Asia, convened by the Niti Foundation of Nepal, and at the reading group on Constitutionalism and the Global South at the Faculty of Law, University of New South Wales, Australia. Thanks to Ayesha Wijeyalath and Swati Jhaveri for their substantive feedback on drafts and to the interviewees for their engagement and time. 'Constitutional resilience by stealth' is an adaptation from a comment made by Theunis Roux on a draft of this chapter. At the time of preparing this chapter for publication, Sri Lanka enacted the Twenty First Amendment (2022), which yet again replaced the Parliamentary Council with a revised Constitutional Council. This chapter does not analyse the Twenty First Amendment, but I wish to note that this amendment affirms, to some extent, the claims I make about constitutional ping-pong and resilience by stealth.

[2] 'The People', meaning constituent power, is a contentious term that is the subject of ongoing scholarly debate. In the Sri Lankan context, this term has been contested throughout its state formation project. I use it here only to reproduce the observation of my interviewee.

branch. I then offer an account of the 'constitutional ping-pong' on Sri Lanka's Guarantor branch.[3] In section IV, I explain why I think Sri Lanka's Guarantor branch is gaining resilience by stealth even if it is still consolidating. In making these arguments, I focus on the Guarantor branch as presented in the 2000 Draft Constitution as well as four constitutional amendments, the Seventeenth (2001), Eighteenth (2010), Nineteenth (2015) and Twentieth Amendments (2020).[4] In section V, I illustrate the ways in which Sri Lanka has achieved constitutional resilience, by stealth, through its Guarantor branch.

The Guarantor branch in Sri Lanka has the following features:[5] (i) direct or indirect constitutionalisation;[6] and (ii) it limits the President's discretion to make appointments to high office or commissions.[7] In Sri Lanka, the judiciary, the Public Service Commission and the Attorney-General are included in the offices and institutions that come under this process. Therefore, I consider it to be a hybrid – a branch that includes older and established public institutions and new institutions such as the Election Commission. I note that, in relation to regulatory powers of public institutions, the Court has developed robust jurisprudence through judicial review of the exercise of administrative discretion, quasi-judicial power and on regulatory powers more broadly.[8] This jurisprudence has been the subject of scholarship as well.[9] Commonalities between this jurisprudence, and scholarship and the design and study of a Guarantor branch are emerging.[10] In this chapter, however, I limit myself to a constitutional perspective: I consider how constitutional reform and implementation has impacted the guarantor function of these institutions.

[3] The term 'constitutional ping-pong' was used by Justice Kate O'Regan, former judge of the Constitutional Court of South Africa, at an academic conference on Constitutional Resilience in South Asia at the Melbourne Law School, December 2019, to describe Sri Lanka's constitutional amendments. 'Ping-pong' is also used in the UK to refer to the passing of amendments to Bills to and fro between the House of Commons and the House of Lords.

[4] See the tabulated summary of the Guarantor branch-related reforms by each of these amendments annexed to this chapter.

[5] In addition to the Guarantor branch, the Committee on High Posts of Parliament examines the suitability of persons appointed/nominated to serve as secretary to cabinet ministries, Heads of Sri Lanka missions or as chairpersons of boards, corporations and other state institutions.

[6] An example of direct constitutionalisation is the Elections Commission, which is established by the Constitution. An example of indirect constitutionalisation is the Human Rights Commission, which is mentioned in the Constitution but established by legislation.

[7] Examples would include the Right to Information Commission. I note here the amendments made to add the concurrence of the Constitutional Council to the appointments to the Monetary Board, where the President makes appointments on the recommendation of the Minister of Finance, and the appointments made by the Minister to the Public Utilities Commission with the concurrence of the Council and to the Welfare Benefits Board in consultation with the Council (Amendments 24, 32 and 35 of 2002). The appointment of Governor of the Central Bank is an example of appointments that continue to be made at the discretion of the President. Under the Twenty First Amendment the appointment has to be approved by the Constitutional Council.

[8] See, eg S Rose-Ackerman, 'Administrative Law and Democracy' in P Cane et al (eds), *The Oxford Handbook of Comparative Administrative Law* (Oxford, Oxford University Press, 2020) 1076; T Ginsburg, 'Written Constitutions and the Administrative State: On the Constitutional Character of Administrative Law' in S Rose-Ackerman et al (eds), *Comparative Administrative Law* (Cheltenham, Edward Elgar, 2017) 60.

[9] M Gomez, 'The Modern Benchmarks of Sri Lankan Public Law' (2001) 118 *South African Law Journal* 581; M Gomez, 'Blending Rights with Writs: Sri Lankan Public Law's New Brew' [2006] (Suppl) *Acta Juridica* 451.

[10] Rose-Ackerman (n 8).

There are several limitations to focusing on the constitutional dimension of the Guarantor branch.[11] It occludes the administrative law dimensions to the regulatory function of the state and its judicial review. A related dimension is the empirical. How does the Guarantor branch actually function? What insights can we gain by studying the day-to-day functioning of the Human Rights Commission or that of Office of the Attorney-General? How does budgeting and financial allocations affect the Guarantor branch and what are the different perceptions about the significance, value, impact etc of this branch of those working in the branch and of others? These are questions that I do not consider in this chapter.

This chapter builds on my previous work on Sri Lanka's Guarantor branch. Previously, I have considered the process of 'depoliticisation' of Presidential appointments through the Constitutional Council[12] and argued that the Eighteenth and Twentieth Amendments are instances of constitutional vulnerability, in contrast with the Seventeenth and Nineteenth, which, I argue, are instances of 'simple' constitutional resilience.[13] Recently, I have borrowed the idea of 'constitutional ping-pong' to point to the partisan and opportunistic political intentions that underpin these amendments[14] and have argued that Sri Lanka's Constitution has been chameleon-like in the way in which it has taken colour from its political context.[15] More recently, I have engaged in a close study of Sri Lanka's first Election Commission, where I found that personal dispositions were central to its work.[16] In this present chapter, I build on this body of work to consider the evolution of Sri Lanka's Guarantor branch over the last three decades through the lens of constitutional resilience.

In developing my argument in this chapter, in addition to the relevant constitutional material, I draw upon six interviews that I conducted with senior practitioners and academics. They had made high level contributions to the different constitutional reform efforts, been members of the Constitutional Council or litigated the constitutionality of these amendments. They were selected for interviews based on their expert experience and availability, but I ensured that diverse views were included. Here, in studying constitutional resilience of the Guarantor branch, I use their anonymised insights on the substance and impact of these amendments on constitutional governance.

[11] Thanks to Melissa Crouch and Ben Schonthal for suggesting these perspectives to me.

[12] D Samararatne, 'The Constitutional Council and The Independent Commissions: The New Framework for Depoliticising Governance' in A Welikala (ed), *Nineteenth Amendment to the Sri Lankan Constitution* (Colombo, Centre for Policy Alternatives, 2016) 147–74.

[13] See section II for a discussion of these terms. See also D Samararatne, 'Resilience through Synergy? The Legal Complex in Sri Lanka's Constitutional Crisis' (2022) 9 *Asian Journal of Law and Society* 1.

[14] D Samararatne, 'Sri Lanka's Constitutional Ping-Pong' *Himal South Asian* (25 September 2020). As was pointed out by Ayesha Wijayalath, it is fair now to say that reform of Sri Lanka's regime type, with emphasis on reform of the Executive President, is also amounting to constitutional ping-pong, starting from the failed attempts at regime-type reforms in 2001 to the 19th Amendment and 20th Amendments.

[15] D Samararatne, 'Chameleon Constitutions and Sri Lanka's 20th Amendment' (*Law and Other Things Blog*, 11 January 2021) https://lawandotherthings.com/2021/01/chameleon-constitutions-and-sri-lankas-20th-amendment/.

[16] D Samararatne, 'Sri Lanka's First Election Commission: Strengthening Electoral Management or Advancing Electoral Integrity?' (2021) 16(Suppl S1) *Asian Journal of Comparative Law* S156.

II. The Guarantor Branch, Constitutional Resilience and Vulnerability

What do I mean by the terms 'Guarantor branch', 'constitutional resilience' and 'constitutional vulnerability? The labels may be relatively new but, as I suggest here, the substantive aspects of this inquiry are well established. The 'Guarantor branch' is more commonly described as the 'fourth branch', while discussion on constitutional resilience is a more recent companion to debates on democratic resilience. The difference, if any, between these terms is not yet clear. Moreover, the terms of academic debate on both these ideas are not very clear or stable. Nevertheless, as I illustrate in this chapter, they are useful in describing and interpreting constitutional practice.

A. The Guarantor Branch

There is a significant body of literature, discussed below, examining and theorising on the establishment of a fourth branch in constitutional design. However, in terms of theorisation, it is an area of inquiry that is still in the early stages and a broad consensus is yet to emerge, including on the question of terminology. There is agreement, however, that the institutions of the fourth branch represent an evolution in the separation of powers doctrine, though scholars have differing views on how exactly that works out. There is even disagreement on whether these institutions can, even broadly, be categorised as a 'branch'.

Ackerman named these institutions as the 'democracy branch', one which protects a governing ideal that is drawn from the conception of democracy in a given system.[17] He described it as 'a mechanism to ensure the continuing force of its ideal of democracy'. The South African Constitution labels them as 'Institutions Protecting Constitutional Democracy' and Tushnet uses the same term.[18] Tushnet offers a tentative account of 'a congeries of institutions that have something to do with the preservation of constitutional democracy' but are, for all intents and purposes, very diverse in terms of their institutional characteristics (constitutionalised/statutory, permanent/ad hoc).[19] As Bilchitz and Landau note, there is 'no unifying theory' of this branch except that 'the impulse' that created these institutions shares common ground with the separation of powers doctrine.[20] However, there is some consensus that these institutions, taken together, have the capacity to promote and protect values that underpin a constitutional democracy. For instance, Tushnet notes that these institutions bear 'a family resemblance' in that they seek to prevent a conflict of interest in governance and seek

[17] B Ackerman, 'The New Separation of Powers' (2000) 113 *Harvard Law Review* 634, 714.

[18] M Tushnet, 'Institutions Protecting Constitutional Democracy: Some Conceptual and Methodological Preliminaries' (2020) 70(2) *University of Toronto Law Journal* 95. See also ch 9 of the Constitution of South Africa 1996.

[19] Tushnet (n 18) 105.

[20] D Bilchitz and D Landau (eds), *The Evolution of the Separation of Powers: Between the Global North and the Global South* (Cheltenham, Edward Elgar, 2018) 12.

to protect democratic interests over time.[21] The common feature of these institutions is that their 'primary function is to investigate and hold government accountable for its actions or inactions'.[22]

Scholars have been critical of the stability of the resemblance among the institutions that are broadly construed as the 'fourth branch' and about their capacity to perform the tasks assigned. Tushnet, for instance, raises questions about the jurisdictional threshold of such institutions and even the actual ability of these institutions to protect democracy.[23] Charles Fombad too raises similar concerns in his analysis of what he describes as 'Hybrid Institutions of Accountability' in the African continent.[24] He argues that while these institutions have the potential to confront the challenges to constitutional democracy, they are nevertheless at risk of becoming a 'mirage' or 'smokescreen'.[25] For Fombad, the greatest concern is 'the failure of the other branches to recognize' the entry of hybrid institutions into the constitutional scheme, 'and reorientate and adjust their policies and functions in order to accommodate them'.[26] Fombad notes that an appointment process that can ensure independence of and clarity on the role of these institutions are important. The 'four guiding principles' of the South African Constitution are instructive in this regard.[27] On appointments to these bodies, Fombad makes several proposals, including a proposal for 'an appointment system which places the ruling party and opposition parties on a par'.[28] He notes that it would allow expertise and independence to be the relevant criteria rather than political loyalty. He also notes the 'incredible diversity of institutions' that come under this umbrella, including institutions that are independent from the three branches and ones that are not.[29]

It seems to me that concerns regarding consistency, threshold and clarity of purpose are misplaced. As I have argued elsewhere with William Partlett, constitutional principles have a universal character to them whereas constitutional practice is unique to each context.[30] Following from Vickie Jackson's work, it is useful to recall that constitutionalism is not a project of convergence but rather one of engagement.[31] Therefore, the more useful approach here would be one in which the evolution of the 'fourth branch' is examined in each context to better understand its scope and relevance. My view is that

[21] Tushnet (n 18) 105.

[22] CM Fombad, 'The Role of Emerging Hybrid Institutions of Accountability in the Separation of Powers Scheme in Africa' in CM Fombad (ed), *The Separation of Powers in African Constitutionalism* (Oxford, Oxford University Press, 2016) 325, 327. See further F Mahomed, 'The Fourth Branch: Challenges and Opportunities for a Robust and Meaningful Role for South Africa's State Institutions Supporting Democracy' in Bilchitz and Landau (n 20) 177; RE Kapindu, 'Separation of Powers and the Accountability Role of NHRIs: The Malawi Human Rights Commission through the Courts' in Bilchitz and Landau (n 20) 206.

[23] Tushnet (n 19) 106.

[24] Fombad (n 22).

[25] ibid 326 and 330.

[26] ibid 343.

[27] Constitution of South Africa, s191.

[28] Fombad (n 22) 337.

[29] ibid 326.

[30] W Partlett and D Samararatne, 'Redeeming the National in Constitutional Argument' (2021) 54 *World Comparative Law Journal* 461.

[31] V Jackson, *Constitutional Engagement in a Transnational Era* (Oxford, Oxford University Press, 2013).

each fourth branch is a unique formulation that maps onto the constitutional disharmonies and identity of that constitutional system. Because of the relatively new nature of academic inquiry into the fourth branch, we can see this clearly. However, this insight should also prompt us to recall that the same is applicable to the study of constitutionalism, separation of powers, etc. To the extent that studies of the fourth branch are a study of constitutional developments in the Global South, its implications instantiate Dann et al's point about a Southern Turn being a Double Turn.[32] Insights from studying developments in the Global South enriches and could even alter the terms of the global debate on the topic.

Here, I use Khaitan's terminology 'Guarantor branch' and his recent analytic work on the Guarantor branch because it offers a useful starting point – an ideal type. I look at Sri Lanka's experience and practice against this ideal type in (i) describing and explaining the nature of its Guarantor branch and (ii) assessing the branch's contribution to 'constitutional resilience by stealth'. Khaitan offers an internally coherent assessment of the distinct characteristics of the Guarantor branch.[33] He notes that 'the function is to provide a credible and enduring guarantee to a specific non-self-enforcing constitutional norm (or any aspect thereof)'.[34] He notes here that they are guarantor institutions to the extent that their existence is a sufficient guarantee that the norm in question will be respected over time.[35] As described by Khaitan, in order to best perform their function, Guarantor branches must be constitutionally entrenched, serve as specialist institutions with considerable indeterminacy in scope, ought to be mandated to protect a single value and are interest-protecting trustee institutions. His granular description of its internal account is useful in studying Sri Lanka's experience of the evolution of the Constitutional Council under the Seventeenth and Nineteenth Amendments and to explain its failure under the Eighteenth and Twentieth Amendments.

B. Constitutional Resilience and Vulnerability

In my previous work, I described constitutional resilience as comprising: (i) the ability to absorb deliberate attempts at undermining fundamental values of a constitutional democracy or other shocks, while retaining the same basic structure and ways of functioning; (ii) the capacity to limit the actions of those deriving power from it; and (iii) the capacity to adapt and innovate in response to deliberate attempts by those undermining the fundamental values of a constitutional democracy or other shocks. In offering this description of the concept, I adapt the definition of resilience provided by the Intergovernmental Panel on Climate Change. I suggested further that whereas 'simple' resilience is about responding to, coping with and recovering from an immediate crisis/disaster, 'reflexive' resilience is 'a power of resistance, which does not fear change

[32] P Dann et al (eds), *Global South in Comparative Constitutional Law* (Oxford, Oxford University Press, 2020) 3.

[33] T Khaitan, 'Guarantor Institutions' (2021) 16(Suppl) *Asian Journal of Comparative Law* S40.

[34] ibid S42.

[35] ibid S43.

and offers reflexive justifiable innovations'.[36] Reflexive resilience is key to consolidating constitutional governance in the Sri Lankan context. Sri Lanka's experience of governance under 'constitutions without constitutionalism' reveals that unless institutions (in particular) innovate and adapt, unconstitutional governance is likely to continue and advance.[37]

The concept of resilience is used in political science literature to consider the capacity of constitutional democracies to withstand different types of pressures, both internal and external. *Constitutional* resilience is a relatively new point of reference or analysis which accompanies this line of inquiry. While the term is used in academic debate and discussion, more theoretical work has to be undertaken to clarify its meaning, scope and implications. Even in the absence of such theorisation, however, there seem to be several advantages to using this approach to explain and interpret constitutional developments and processes. It complements the analysis of Sri Lanka's constitutional developments from a design perspective by allowing for consideration of constitutional practice (institutions and actors) in context (culture, political and constitutional, broadly understood). For instance, it provides a helpful framework for examining intra-institutional as well as inter-institutional constitutional practices while drawing upon the influence of constitutional culture.

In using and appreciating the concept of constitutional resilience, it is necessary to also consider the concept of 'constitutional vulnerability'. I take constitutional vulnerability to mean the 'structural features or specific provisions of a constitution which enable processes, bearers of office, or other actors to undermine the fundamental values of a constitutional democracy'. Using these working definitions, I claim here that Sri Lanka's Guarantor branch reflects simple resilience at the most and remains vulnerable (in the constitutional sense) due to several factors.

I place Khaitan's work on his ideal type description of the Guarantor branch in conversation with the emerging idea of constitutional resilience. I do this in an effort to develop an account of the resilience of the guarantor function in the Sri Lankan context. I extend the idea of 'guarantee' developed by Khaitan to other constitutional institutions and actors, and identify and assess the external conditions that enable the Guarantor branch to function. I argue that in Sri Lanka extra-constitutional actors such as political parties, constitutional actors such as courts and independent institutions such as the Attorney-General are a threat to the guarantor function of this branch. The structural features that lead to constitutional vulnerability in the Sri Lankan context include the lack of regulation of political parties and the concentration of power in the office of the Executive President, with minimal accountability. Sri Lanka's constitutional culture is a related dimension. However, I illustrate that the Guarantor branch is emerging as a resilient aspect of Sri Lanka's constitutional system. The branch itself is still in a state of consolidation, but early signs are that the branch is maturing slowly but surely.

[36] D Samararatne, 'Resilience through Synergy? The Legal Complex in Sri Lanka's Constitutional Crisis' (2022) 9 *Asian Journal of Law and Society* 1.

[37] R Edrisinha, 'Sri Lanka: Constitutions Without Constitutionalism: A Tale of Three and Half Constitutions' in R Edrisinha and A Welikala (eds), *Essays on Federalism in Sri Lanka* (Colombo, Centre for Policy Alternatives, 2008) 7.

III. Sri Lanka's Guarantor Branch: Constitutional Innovation

In Sri Lanka, the Guarantor branch is an innovative and resilient idea in constitutional discourse, but the actual establishment of the branch poses challenges and is under threat. I establish this claim in this section and the next. Here, I trace the milestones in the development of the idea of a Guarantor branch in Sri Lanka, assess the reforms introduced by the four amendments and consider civil society engagement with these reforms.

A. Birth and Evolution of an Idea

The idea of independent offices (such as the Attorney General and the Commissioner of Elections) and constitutional or statutory commissions (such as the public service commission and the judicial service commission) were part of Sri Lanka's constitutional system from pre-colonial times.[38] Branch-like thinking about these institutions emerged in Sri Lanka's constitutional discourse in the wake of the second youth insurrection (1989–90) led by the Janatha Vimukthi Peramuna (JVP), a Marxist party in Sri Lanka. As noted by an interviewee, this was a time in Sri Lanka where 'young people (both Sinhala and Tamil) had chosen the path of violence instead of democracy'. Another interviewee mentioned that the idea of a mechanism for depoliticising appointments was initially discussed at the All Party Conference convened in response to this insurrection in 1989 by the then President Premadasa.[39] Soon thereafter, a recommendation was made by the Youth Commission for the establishment of a Nominations Commission to address what they perceived to be the politicisation of public office and institutions and as a measure that would 'command the complete confidence of the public'.[40] An interviewee described two of the Commissioners as liberal constitutionalists who were 'attuned to global conversations on the third wave of democracy and of the idea of limited government'.[41] This dispensation, according to the interviewee, strongly influenced them in recommending the Nominations Council. Another interviewee attributed the idea to Chanaka Amaratunga of the Liberal Party and noted that the idea was originally proposed at the All Party Conference and debated further during the reform debate from 1995 to 2000.[42]

[38] Under Sri Lanka's independence Constitution, the judiciary and the public service were independent. An independent judiciary was established in Ceylon (as Sri Lanka was then known) under the Charter of Justice of 1801. The office of the Attorney General has existed in Sri Lanka since 1884.

[39] WA Wisa Warnapala, 'The All Party Conference in Sri Lanka' (1991) 47(4) *India Quarterly* 39, 44.

[40] This Commission was appointed by the President to, among other things, report on the causes for 'disquiet, unrest and discontent' which manifested 'in the rejection of existing institutions and acts of violence' and 'any inadequacy in the policies and administration of any governmental agency or other public body'. Report of the Presidential Commission on Youth, Sessional Paper No 1 – 1990 (March 1990) 5.

[41] Dr Radhika Coomaraswamy thereafter served as a chairperson of Sri Lanka's Human Rights Commission and Special Rapporteur on Violence against Women for the UN, and Prof GL Pieris went on to serve as the Minister for Constitutional Affairs at the time when the 2000 Draft Constitution was developed. However, he has since gone on record as having supported the 17th, 18th, 19th and 20th Amendments.

[42] See also R Coomaraswamy, 'Priorities for the Next President' 3, www.ices.lk/wp-content/uploads/2015/01/PRIORITIES-FOR-THE-NEXT-PRESIDENT.pdf.

An interviewee noted that the depoliticisation of public office and institutions is an older idea in Sri Lanka's constitutional discourse and can be traced back to the establishment of an independent public service and judiciary under the Independence Constitution (1948). He noted that the 'idea that public institutions ought to be depoliticised, has lingered'. This insight points to an older tradition in Sri Lanka's constitutional imagination and consciousness, which valued and presumed the independence of public institutions. The First Republican Constitution was a turning point in which centralisation and political control were constitutionalised.[43] The constitutional ping-pong of Sri Lanka's Guarantor branch reflects the ongoing contestation between these two approaches. Interestingly, the idea of centralisation and political control of state institutions was advocated and introduced by Sri Lanka's political left. The political demand for depoliticisation was made by the JVP in the late 1980s and was supported by civil society in the 1990s, and its constitutionalisation was advocated by the JVP in 2001 and thereafter. The political left in Sri Lanka has played a curious role in the evolution of the country's Guarantor branch, which deserves further study.

B. The Four Amendments

Since 2001, Sri Lanka has witnessed constitutional ping-pong over the very idea of an independent Guarantor branch. This ping-pong has been in effect through the 2000 Draft Constitution and the Seventeenth, Eighteenth, Nineteenth and Twentieth Amendments. Each of these constitutional developments was influenced by political developments unique to that time. It was noted by the interviewees that the idea of a Constitutional Council was inspired by the 1990 Constitution of Nepal.[44] In a rare instance of South-to-South transfer of constitutional design, this model was introduced to Sri Lanka through the Youth Commission and since then has taken a life of its own.

The 2000 Draft Constitution emerged at a high point in Sri Lanka's constitutional reform history. The election of President Chandrika Bandaranaike in 1994 had heralded an era in which many expected the consolidation of Sri Lanka's constitutional democracy. The Human Rights Commission was established as an independent commission along with the Commission to Investigate Allegations of Bribery and Corruption.[45] Peace talks and other efforts at addressing the root causes of the ethnic conflict culminated in the Draft Constitution of 2000, in which proposals for a Constitutional Council and the Guarantor branch were included for the first time.[46] The Minister for Constitutional Affairs, who had also been a member of the Youth Commission, described this Council as an 'all-party mechanism'[47] that is 'probably the most interesting single feature' of the

[43] The Public Service Commission and the Judicial Services Advisory Board were brought under the cabinet under the First Republican Constitution of 1972.

[44] The Constitutional Council and independent commissions have been provided in Nepal's current Constitution (2015) as well.

[45] Human Rights Commission of Sri Lanka Act No 21 of 1996 and Commission to Investigate Allegations of Bribery or Corruption Act No 19 of 1994.

[46] Draft Constitution of 2000, Art 122.

[47] GL Peiris, *Towards Equity* (self-published, 2000) 45.

Draft Constitution.[48] However, the Draft Constitution was not passed by Parliament due to disputes over the transitional provisions of the Bill.

In fact, the Constitutional Council and the Guarantor branch were the only aspects of reform that survived the initiatives of the 1990s. In the wake of the failed attempts at adopting a new Constitution, the People's Alliance was compelled to enter into a coalition with the JVP to maintain its majority in Parliament.[49] The JVP offered its support on the condition that a Constitutional Council should be introduced by way of constitutional amendment. This led to the adoption of the Seventeenth Amendment with the unanimous support of Parliament barring one abstention.[50] The inclusion of the judges of the appellate court and the Judicial Service Commission under the Constitutional Council for the first time expanded its purpose. This was no longer a body established to ensure the independence of the Guarantor branch but also of a traditional branch of the state – the judiciary.

The Eighteenth Amendment was enacted in 2010 in the aftermath of the military victory over the Liberation Tigers of Tamil Ealam (LTTE). The government was riding on a strong wave of popularity for having ended the war. Even though the President had given an undertaking to the international community that the government would seek to resolve the conflict and seek reconciliation, its first and only post-war constitutional amendment was one which undid the reforms introduced by the Seventeenth Amendment and removed the term limit to the Executive Presidency.[51] The same commissions and high offices that were held accountable by the Constitutional Council were brought under the Parliamentary Council. However, this Council had no binding powers, and the President was required to only seek the observations of the Council. Under the Eighteenth Amendment, therefore, the President acted in his sole discretion in making these appointments.

In 2015, Sri Lanka's trajectory in terms of constitutional governance experienced a significant shift. President Rajapakse declared an early presidential election. A common candidate (fielded by all the political parties in the Opposition), a minister from the Rajapakse government and secretary of his own political party supported by a broad coalition, defeated President Rajapakse.[52] Constitutional reform was central

[48] ibid 421.

[49] The People's Alliance was led by the Sri Lanka Freedom Party (1951), one of the two major political parties in Sri Lanka formed as a breakaway from the United National Party (1946). The JVP (1970) is a Marxist political party which was part of the People's Alliance in 2001. For a study on Sri Lanka's political parties, see A Shashtri and J Uyangoda (ed), *Political Parties in Sri Lanka: Change and Continuity* (Oxford, Oxford University Press, 2018); N DeVotta, 'Parties, Political Decay, and Democratic Regression in Sri Lanka' (2014) 52(1) *Commonwealth & Comparative Politics* 139.

[50] Samararatne, 'The Constitutional Council' (n 12) 154. J Wickramaratne, *Towards Democratic Governance in Sri Lanka: A Constitutional Miscellany* (Colombo, Institute for Constitutional Studies, 2014) 123. MP Champika Ranawaka abstained from voting. Fifteen MPs were absent on the day. *In re the Seventeenth Amendment to the Constitution* Parliamentary Debates (Hansard) 138(1) (24 September 2001) 3.

[51] Joint Statement by the UN Secretary-General and President Mahinda Rajapakse, May 2009. See also R Edrisinha and A Jayakody (eds), *The Eighteenth Amendment to the Constitution: Substance and Process* (Colombo, Centre for Policy Alternatives, 2011).

[52] K David, 'Revisiting the "Single-Issue Common-Candidate" Strategy: Successes and Failures' in A Welikala (ed), *Constitutional Reform and Crisis in Sri Lanka* (Centre for Policy Alternatives 2019) 89.

to the election campaign of the common candidate. President Sirisena proposed the Nineteenth Amendment to the Constitution within the first few months of his election with the promise of subsequently adopting a new Constitution. Two changes brought about by the Amendment were the reintroduction of a modified version of the Constitutional Council and reform of the regime type to a premier-presidential one.[53] In 2017, the Right to Information Act was enacted and the Right to Information Commission was also added to the Guarantor branch through legislation.[54] However, attempts at adopting a new Constitution were subsequently derailed and eventually collapsed.

Failure on the part of the coalition government to govern effectively ultimately led to its defeat at the presidential (2019) and parliamentary elections (2020). The Easter Sunday attacks (21 April 2019) and the allegations that negligence of the executive resulted in those attacks was another factor that contributed to this outcome.[55] Constitutional reform to repeal the Nineteenth Amendment and to restore powers to the Executive Presidency were highlights of the election campaign of the Sri Lanka Podujana Peramuna, the political party that was elected to power.[56] The campaign against the Nineteenth Amendment sought to attribute the dysfunction of the government to the increased powers of the Prime Minister. A wholesale repeal was promised and, accordingly, the Twentieth Amendment repealed the provisions on the Constitutional Council and restored the Parliamentary Council.[57] This Amendment also repealed several provisions which had changed Sri Lanka's regime type[58] to a premier-presidential system and repealed the Audit Commission and the National Procurement Commission. The government proposed the reintroduction of presidential immunity from suit during office, but the Supreme Court held that that proposal had to be approved in a referendum.[59] The two reforms from the Nineteenth Amendment that survived the Twentieth Amendment are the right to freedom of information and the judicial remedy for any violation or imminent violation of a fundamental right by the acts/omissions of the President.[60]

[53] See Samararatne, 'Sri Lanka's Constitutional Ping-Pong' (n 14); Welikala, *Nineteenth Amendment* (n 12).

[54] The Right to Information Act of 2016.

[55] On 19 April 2019, six incidents of suicide bombing took place in churches and hotels in Sri Lanka (five in Colombo and one in Battiacaloa) which killed over 270 individuals and injured many more by an alleged ISIS-inspired extremist group.

[56] The Sri Lanka Podu Jana Peramuna was formed in 2016 and its prominent leaders include the current Prime Minister and former President Mahinda Rajapakse and the current President Gotabaya Rajapakse.

[57] Twentieth Amendment of the Constitution, Art 41A.

[58] Sedelius and Linde describe a premier-parliamentary system as one in which the government can only be dismissed by Parliament. T Sedelius and J Linde, 'Unravelling Semi-presidentialism: Democracy and Government Performance in Four Distinct Regime Types' (2018) 25(1) *Democratization* 136, 138.

[59] As per Art 83 of the Sri Lankan Constitution, certain articles are entrenched and require approval by a two-thirds majority in Parliament as well as approval in a referendum. Only one referendum has been conducted in Sri Lanka (for a controversial extension of the life of the First Parliament under the 1978 Constitution). A Supreme Court determination that a Bill or a clause requires approval in a referendum therefore, in practice, results in the withdrawal of the Bill or clause.

[60] Constitution, Arts 14(A) and 35, respectively.

C. Civil Society

It was noted during the interviews that, in Sri Lanka, the demand for a Guarantor branch emerged from pro-constitutionalism groups in civil society. An interviewee noted that in the early 1990s those who came before the Youth Commission were concerned about addressing අසාධාරණය (injustice) and called for depoliticisation of public institutions, including justice institutions. In 2015, another movement led by Rev Sobhitha Thero focused on limiting and/or abolishing the Executive Presidency.[61] As was noted by an interviewee, 'when civil society was at its most influential, they pushed for depoliticisation but later it was converted to a parliamentary executive'. The Guarantor branch was constitutionalised and supported when political coalitions required civil society support and/or the support of minority political parties. Therefore, major political parties have subjected the Guarantor branch to vulnerability while minor political parties have acted as a source of support for resilience.[62] Moreover, a Guarantor branch is an aspiration that has emerged organically from civil society. As noted by several interviewees, the draft proposed by the Organization of Professional Associations in 2001 was a step towards the Seventeenth Amendment.[63]

For a long time, pro-constitutionalist civil society groups have also mobilised in support of constitutional reform for power-sharing and for abolishing the executive presidency. In comparison to the little or no progress made on these fronts, reforms on the Guarantor branch were enacted, although subjected to constitutional ping-pong. The only constitutional reform for power-sharing was the Thirteenth Amendment, enacted under pressure from the Indian government and not implemented effectively.[64]

Civil society groups that support a unitary state in Sri Lanka have argued against the Guarantor branch. In the main, they have raised questions about how the Guarantor branch, and particularly the Constitutional Council, undermines representative democracy.[65] An interviewee pointed out that the Seventeenth Amendment provided that three of the members were to be nominated in consultation with Members of Parliament 'who belong to the respective minority communities' and were nominated to 'represent minority interests'.[66] In contrast, it was pointed out that no similar provision ensured that the interests of the majority of the community were to be represented. For this interviewee, therefore, the motive behind the establishment of a Guarantor branch was suspected of deliberately ignoring the interests of the

[61] See, eg 'Sobitha Thero and team present constitutional reform proposal' *Daily FT* (5 April 2013); A Welikala, 'Constitutional and Governance Reforms in Sri Lanka: The Road to the Promised Land' (*ConstitutionNet*, 30 November 2015). Sobitha Thero was part of the National Movement for Social Justice.

[62] Thanks to Pritam Dey for drawing this distinction between major and minor political parties.

[63] 'Seventeenth Amendment to the Constitution' proposal by the Organization of the Professional Associations of Sri Lanka (2001).

[64] The 13th Amendment was enacted pursuant to the Indo-Lanka Accord of 1987. This agreement required Sri Lanka to enact reforms to introduce devolution. Sri Lanka entered into this agreement under the threat of military intervention by India.

[65] මනෝහර ආර් ද සිල්වා 'බෙදුම් වාදීන් ගේ උපායමාර්ග හා ව්‍යවස්ථා සංශෝධන' (විසිදුන 2017) Translation: MR de Silva, Tactics of Separatists and Constitutional Amendments' (Visiduni, 2017).

[66] Seventeenth Amendment of the Constitution, Art 41A(3).

ethnic majority. Counter-arguments were made by two other interviewees. They noted that given Sri Lanka's issues with discrimination against minority ethnic communities, it is necessary to ensure the ethnic representation of minorities.[67] An interviewee noted that for the people to have confidence in public institutions, 'they must see their faces in state institutions'. In other words, public institutions must be seen to represent them. He noted that 'the reality is that all our institutions are dominated by the Sinhala majority'. Another interviewee noted that while a nomination can be made on the basis of ethnic identity, they are certainly not expected to function merely in that representative capacity, but rather as independent experts.

The Nineteenth Amendment provided that five members of the Constitutional Council were to reflect 'the pluralistic character of Sri Lankan society, including professional and social diversity'.[68] Under this Amendment, in making recommendations for appointments to Commissions, the Council was to 'endeavour to ensure' that recommendations 'reflect the pluralistic character of Sri Lankan society'.[69] From the perspective of an interviewee, the reference to pluralism revealed that these amendments were concerned with the advancement of representation of ethnic interest (particularly of ethnic minorities) and not independence or merit. In fact, this interviewee went so far as to state that the Seventeenth and Nineteenth Amendments were 'strongly influenced by NGOs and various people with foreign connections' and that it allowed 'the NGOs to infiltrate the public service'. To him, 'religion and ethnicity should not matter' in the Constitutional Council and in the performance of their functions. The difference of opinion on representation at the Constitutional Council points to ethnic cleavages in Sri Lanka and its significance in any constitutional development.

It was further noted by the same interviewee that Parliament had failed to enact legislation to ensure that the Constitutional Council followed a transparent procedure. To him, the Constitutional Council was an institution that undermined constitutional democracy. This interviewee argued that instead of a Constitutional Council, it was the constitutional role of Parliament to check the excesses of the Executive President, including with regard to the power to make appointments to high offices and independent commissions.

IV. Threats and Constitutional Vulnerabilities

Thus far, I have argued that the Guarantor branch amounts to constitutional innovation and is a resilient constitutional idea that strengthens Sri Lanka's constitutional orientation towards constitutionalism. This resilience arises from an older idea about independence of institutions in Sri Lanka's constitutional imagination and

[67] N Wigneswaran, 'Minority Representation in the 17th Amendment: Nicety, Nepotism or Necessity' (2001) 5 *Moot Point: Legal Review* 62.

[68] Nineteenth Amendment of the Constitution, Art 41A(4).

[69] ibid Art 41B(3).

consciousness, demands by sections of civil society and support by minority political parties.[70] However, the Guarantor branch is vulnerable in the face of dominant political parties (in relation to reform and implementation), an ambivalent judiciary and an Attorney-General's office that has supported the constitutional ping-pong on the Guarantor branch.

A. Political Office and Implementation

Reform for establishing and strengthening the Guarantor branch and its implementation have been vulnerable to the political choices of dominant political parties and coalitions. Implementation of the constitutional reforms for the Guarantor branch have been undermined since the adoption of the Seventeenth Amendment. The Seventeenth Amendment was implemented approximately 2001–06. Even during that period, the Election Commission was not constituted. As discussed below, efforts at seeking a judicial remedy for the failure to implement this Amendment were unsuccessful. After the election of a new President in 2006, the Constitutional Council was no longer convened. Lack of political will to implement the Amendment and disagreements between political parties about the term 'minority party' were two reasons (again pointing to the tensions regarding the ethnic conflict) for non-implementation.[71] In the absence of a Constitutional Council, the President made direct appointments to high office and to commissions in violation of the Constitution. Attempts to hold the President accountable for violating the Constitution by way of judicial review failed due to the immunity from suit that was guaranteed to the President under the Constitution.[72]

Under the Eighteenth Amendment (2010), the only check against the President was impeachment, which for all practical purposes was ineffective as the government could easily secure the necessary two-thirds majority, which the government managed to secure not only for the adoption of the constitutional amendment but also thereafter. In the period that followed, the government increasingly came under the scrutiny of the Human Rights Council for failing to ensure accountability for allegations of violations of human rights, particularly in the last stages of the armed conflict.[73] If the Guarantor branch had functioned independently and on the basis of expertise (here I particularly have in mind the Human Rights Commission and the Commission against Bribery and Corruption), the government may have not come under such scrutiny.[74]

[70] Here I have in mind the Janatha Vimukthi Peramuna and the Tamil National Alliance in particular.

[71] 'The Forgotten Constitutional Council: An Analysis of Consequences of the Non-implementation of the Seventeenth Amendment' Position Paper (Transparency International, 28 August 2008) 2–3.

[72] Constitution, Art 35 before its amendment by the 19th Amendment. *Liyanage v Rajapakse* SC (FR) 297, 578/2008, SC Minutes 18 March 2021. Two other failed attempts to seek judicial review of the failure to implement the 17th Amendment are discussed in 'The Forgotten Constitutional Council' (ibid) 3.

[73] For concerns expressed about the 20th Amendment by the Special Rapporteur on the independence of judges and lawyers and the Special Rapporteur on the promotion of truth, justice, reparation and guarantees of non-recurrence to the President of Sri Lanka, 10 December 2020, see, eg the 'Promoting Reconciliation and Accountability in Sri Lanka' resolution adopted at the Human Rights Council (3 April 2012, A/HRC/RES/19/2) and the Report of the Secretary-General's Panel of Experts on Accountability in Sri Lanka (31 March 2011).

[74] In fact, during this time, the Sri Lanka Human Rights Commission was downgraded to B status in 2009 under the Paris Principles relating to the Status of National Institutions and upgraded to A status in 2018.

According to one of the interviewees, the push-back to the Guarantor branch is at least also in part explained by the emergence of a corrupt 'new elite' comprising, among others, businesspersons. According to this interviewee, this new elite not only seek political patronage but also state power, and therefore actively mobilise in support of the 'accumulation of political power in one individual or in one institution of government'.

The independence restored to the Guarantor branch under the Nineteenth Amendment (2015) advanced constitutional democracy in tangible ways. In terms of design, the Nineteenth Amendment dealt with some of the gaps in the Seventeenth Amendment that undermined its implementation. It provided that if the President fails to appoint the nominees to the Constitutional Council or the individuals recommended by the Council to commissions within 14 days, such appointments would be deemed to have been made.[75] This 'deemed clause' was aimed at avoiding possible deadlocks. The work of the Human Rights Commission, the Election Commission and the Right to Information Commission are three examples of the way in which commissions could function independently and effectively under the Nineteenth Amendment.[76] Nevertheless, the failure to adopt legislation that clarified the constitutional mandate of the Constitutional Council was a notable omission. However, the overall progressive impact of the Nineteenth Amendment was apparent in the way in which the Constitutional Crisis of 2018 was resolved. The independence of the judiciary, complemented by the independence of the Speaker of Parliament and of the Election Commission, effectively prevented an unconstitutional attempt at regime change in 2018.[77]

B. Judicial Ambivalence

The Supreme Court too has contributed to Sri Lanka's constitutional ping-pong on the Guarantor branch. This is evident in two types of determinations by the Court – Special Determinations on pre-enactment review of the four amendments and judicial review of the failures to implement the Seventeenth Amendment.

The Court's reasoning has been similar in all four of its Special Determinations, although the impact of the decisions advanced constitutionalism in the case of the Seventeenth and Nineteenth Amendments and were anti-constitutionalist in the Eighteenth and Twentieth Amendments. The reasoning is similar to the extent that in its review the Court only concerned itself with whether the President remains the final appointing authority regardless of whether the appointments by the President were subject to mandatory powers of the Constitutional Council or consultation with the Parliamentary Council. Using this approach, the Court has upheld the introduction of the Constitutional Council (Seventeenth and Nineteenth Amendments), as well as the repeal of the Constitutional Council and its replacement with a Parliamentary Council.

When the Seventeenth Amendment Bill was challenged before the Supreme Court, the Court noted that the Bill 'taken in its entirety' had the effect of 'altering the legal

[75] Constitution, Arts 41A(6) and 41B(4) as amended by the 19th Amendment.

[76] K Pinto-Jayawardena, 'The Right to Information in Sri Lanka: Fruits of Long and Hard Labour' (2018) 107 *The Round Table* 241; Samararatne, 'Sri Lanka's First Election Commission' (n 16).

[77] Welikala, *Constitutional Reform* (n 52).

regime' on appointments to high office and commissions, and that it 'places restriction on the discretion' vested in the President and the Cabinet. However, in light of the President's power to nominate a person to the Constitutional Council and that the appointment itself is made by the President, the Supreme Court concluded that the 'restriction per se' is not inconsistent with the sovereignty of the people.[78] It is noteworthy that the Court makes no further observations on how the proposed Constitutional Council would impact constitutional governance. In the case of the Seventeenth and Nineteenth Amendments, the Parliament approved the Bills with near unanimity, and in the case of the Eighteenth and Twentieth Amendments, with minimal opposition.

The Nineteenth Amendment had a significant impact in terms of restoring the Constitutional Council, in strengthening the institutions under the Guarantor branch and in reforms to the regime type (not discussed in this chapter).[79] The reintroduction of the Constitutional Council was upheld on the basis that the resulting restriction 'per se would not be an erosion of the Executive power by the President'. The Supreme Court further noted that

> [t]he purpose and object of the Constitutional Council is to impose safeguards in respect of the exercising of the President's discretion, and to ensure the propriety of appointments made by him to important offices in the Executive, the Judiciary and the to the Independent Commissions.[80]

Curiously, the Court has also upheld the repeal of the Council and its replacement by the Parliamentary Council (Eighteenth and Twentieth Amendments). In its review of the Eighteenth Amendment Bill, the Court upheld the constitutionality of the Parliamentary Council despite its effect of concentrating power on the Executive Presidency.[81] On the replacement of the Constitutional Council with the Parliamentary Council, the Court noted that it was 'abundantly clear … that the proposed amendment is only a process of redefining the restrictions that was placed on the President by the Constitutional Council' regarding the exercise of executive power, 'which is inalienable'.[82] The Court's view seems to be that as long as the President remains the final appointing authority, whether the President is subject to mandatory recommendations or not does not affect the constitutionality of the process or the outcome. Similarly, the Court upheld the replacement of the Constitutional Council with the Parliamentary Council under the Twentieth Amendment.[83]

Efforts by civil society organisations and individuals to seek judicial remedies against the non-implementation of the Seventeenth Amendment were turned down by the judiciary. The Court relied on the immunity of the President from suit in refusing to

[78] SC Determination (6/2001) Parliamentary Debates (Hansard) 138(1) (24 September 2001) 3, 4–6.
[79] See A Welikala, 'Constitutional Reforms in Sri Lanka – More Drift?' 108(2019) *The Round Table* 605.
[80] In re the Nineteenth Amendment Bill, S.C. (Special Determination) 4-19/2015 S.C. Minutes 6 April 2015.
[81] In re the Eighteenth Amendment Bill, S.C. (Special Determination) No 01/2010, 31 August 2010.
[82] ibid.
[83] *In re Twentieth Amendment to the Constitution* 278 (9) Parliamentary Debates (Hansard) 20 October 2020 1083.

hold with petitioners.[84] On previous occasions, however, the Court had held that even if the President is immune from suit, other actions that rely on unconstitutional actions of the President can be subject to judicial review.[85] In these cases, however, the Court did not follow that approach. An attempt at invoking the writ jurisdiction of the Court of Appeal to compel Parliament to constitute the Constitutional Council or to prohibit members of the National Police Commission and the Public Service Commission from assuming office failed as the Court took the view that judicial review cannot lie against Parliamentary affairs.[86]

It is worth noting here that the Court did hold that certain other proposals that were made for constitutional reform required approval in a referendum. Alongside the Seventeenth Amendment, the government further proposed the Eighteenth and Nineteenth Amendments in 2001. Among other things, the Eighteenth Amendment sought to vest the Constitutional Council with immunity from judicial review and from litigation, and provided that interference with the Council would be a punishable offence. The Nineteenth Amendment, among other things, sought to limit the powers of the President to dissolve Parliament and allow the Prime Minister to be appointed by resolution adopted in Parliament. The Supreme Court held that both amendments were inconsistent with the recognition of the sovereignty of the people and the allocation of that sovereignty amongst the executive, the legislature and the judiciary.[87] Since one of those articles is entrenched, the Court held that the proposed Eighteenth Amendment (2001) required approval by the people in a referendum.[88]

C. Attorney General

The Attorney-General has also engaged in constitutional ping-pong regarding Sri Lanka's Guarantor branch. The Attorney-General advocated for all four amendments, making arguments in support of the proposed Bills when they were challenged for their constitutionality. My view is that the Attorney-General is required to act independently, as an expert, and to assist the Supreme Court in constitutional adjudication, rather than defend the political choices of the government of the day.

The office of the Attorney-General in Sri Lanka has evolved since its introduction in 1884. It was depoliticised with the adoption of Sri Lanka's first written Constitution. There have been instances when the independence of this office has been undermined. However, the Sri Lankan judiciary has recognised an obligation on the Attorney-General to act independently in performing his numerous constitutional roles.[89] This view has

[84] *Public Interest Law Foundation v Attorney General* (CA 1396/2003) CA Minutes 17 December 2003; *Sumanasiri Liyanage v Rajapakse* SC(FR) 297/2008, SC Minutes 18 March 2011.

[85] *Karunathilake v Dissanayake* [1999] 1 Sri LR 157, N Anketell, 'The Executive Presidency and Immunity from Suit: Article 35 as Outlier' in A Welikala (ed), *Reforming Sri Lankan Presidentialism: Provenance, Problems and Prospects* (Colombo, Centre for Policy Alternatives, 2015) 262.

[86] *Visvalingam v Attorney General* (CA 668/2006) CA Minutes 2 June 2006.

[87] Constitution, Arts 3 and 4.

[88] *In re the Eighteenth Amendment to the Constitution* [2002] 3 Sri LR 71; *In re the Nineteenth Amendment to the Constitution* [2002] 3 Sri LR 85.

[89] *Land Reform Commission v Grand Central Limited* [1981] 2 Sri LR 147; *Victor Ivan v the Attorney-General* [1998] 1 Sri LR 340.

been affirmed in academic and professional opinions as well.[90] The Attorney-General, therefore, is a part of the Guarantor branch and is required to guarantee the constitutionality of the actions of the government. This has not been the case, however, in the constitutional ping-pong on the Guarantor branches. The Attorney-General has defended and advocated for all four amendments, despite the substantive differences in these amendments.

V. Resilience by Stealth?

My examination of the evolution of the Guarantor branch reveals that this aspect of Sri Lanka's constitutional system has been the most significant feature in terms of prospects for advancing Sri Lanka's constitutional democracy. Much political effort, negotiation, activism and intellectual heavy lifting has focused on the need to reform Sri Lanka's Executive Presidency and the need to introduce arrangements for power-sharing, as a means of resolving Sri Lanka's ethnic conflict. In retrospect, however, it seems that the idea of a Guarantor branch is taking root in Sri Lanka over time and has yielded a significant result in becoming the only restriction to the Executive Presidency developed thus far in its constitutional system. The Guarantor branch has been the most successful method of push-back to the abuse of power under the Executive Presidency, however limited and modest that success has been. Hence, the claim that it is a case of resilience by stealth.

A. Constitutional Innovation

Sri Lanka's Guarantor branch is constitutional innovation that took place over three decades but draws inspiration from older constitutional discourse on independence of the judiciary and state agencies. In 1990, it was envisaged as a branch comprising constitutional and statutory commissions to which appointments would be 'depoliticised' through the establishment of a Nominations Commission. From 2001 onwards, this idea was revised to include appointments to the Judicial Service Commission and to the higher judiciary. Sri Lanka's model therefore takes a hybrid form. Several interviewees noted that in the case of Sri Lanka, ensuring independence of the judicial branch was central to the proposal and establishment of a Constitutional Council. An interviewee went further to suggest that it was not that the judiciary was later brought under the purview of the Constitutional Council, but rather that the other independent

[90] KMMB Kulatunga, 'Attorney-General of Sri Lanka as Adviser to Government and as Guardian of the Public Interest' (1984) 10 *Commonwealth Law Bulletin* 1881; S Goonesekere, 'The Constitution and the Attorney-General' Fourth Kanchana Abahayapala Memorial Lecture (1994); K Pin-Jayawardena, 'Public Accountability of the Attorney General – To What Extent Should the Exercise of His Statutory Powers Be Reviewed by Court?' (2005) 15(211) *LST Review* 42; 'Rethinking the Attorney-General's Department in Sri Lanka: Ideas for Reform' (Colombo, Centre for Policy Alternatives, 2020); P Fernando, 'The Role of the Attorney General of Sri Lanka and the Rule of Law with Special Reference to the Criminal Justice System' oration delivered at the 3rd death anniversary of late Mr CR de Silva, Attorney General and Chairman LLRC (7 November 2016).

commissions were brought under the Council that was meant to depoliticise appointments to the judiciary.

Moreover, Sri Lanka's model is driven by three related political and constitutional goals: (i) to establish a Guarantor branch; (ii) to increase the accountability of the Executive President for the exercise of his power; and (iii) to improve inclusion and representation. Implicit within all these goals but perhaps more so in the second is the broader goal of bringing about reforms to Sri Lanka's regime type too. All attempts at the pro-constitutionalist reform of the Guarantor branch have been coupled with reform of the Executive Presidency and therefore also of its regime type. The Seventeenth and Nineteenth Amendments sought to relocate executive power in the Prime Minister and the cabinet, while the Eighteenth and Twentieth Amendments sought to further strengthen the Executive Presidency. In light of the repeated collapse of attempts to abolish or reform the Executive Presidency in Sri Lanka since the 1990s, Guarantor branch-related reform has been the primary means by which this reform agenda has been advanced. It is noteworthy that the Draft Constitution of 2000 and each of the subsequent constitutional amendments introduced reforms to the Guarantor branch alongside reforms to the office of the Executive President and to Sri Lanka's regime type. The attempts via the Nineteenth Amendment (2015) were successful to some extent, but were short lived. Inclusivity and minority representation were required specifically by the Seventeenth and Nineteenth Amendments, but were subject to criticism. In a context where political negotiations, peace talks and attempts at constitutional reforms to provide a solution to the ethnic conflict have hitherto failed, the Seventeenth and Nineteenth Amendments were successful in constitutionalising inclusion and representation of minority interests and diversity respectively, albeit in modest terms.

B. An Idea with Resilience

Even though Sri Lanka's Guarantor branch has in fact been unstable and subject to constitutional ping-pong, it is now part of Sri Lanka's constitutional discourse and imagination. Sri Lanka's constitutional discourse has been dominated by the power-sharing debate since its pre-colonial days.[91] With the adoption of the Constitution of 1978, abolishing or reforming the Executive Presidency has been added to this agenda. Unlike the constitutional reforms of the Guarantor branch, these ideas have been the subject of a back-and-forth movement primarily in the realm of political debate.

The concept of a Guarantor branch therefore demonstrates constitutional resilience in Sri Lanka. This is reflected in its adaptation as well as in its cyclical re-emergence. First, Guarantor branch-like thinking underwent a normative shift. It initially had depoliticisation as its goal but is now driven by an all-party consensus approach. Second, from a branch that was focused on guarantor institutions, from 2001, the Constitutional Council/Parliamentary Council has had the judiciary under its fold. However, the

[91] R Edrisinha et al (eds), *Power-Sharing in Sri Lanka: Constitutional and Political Documents 1926–2008* (Colombo, Centre for Policy Alternatives, 2008).

central and most contested feature of Sri Lanka's Guarantor branch, the Constitutional Council, has remained vulnerable. Over the last three decades in which this idea has evolved, in effect the Constitutional Council functioned for less than a total of 10 years, ie from 2001 to approximately 2006 and from 2015 to 2019. Between 2006 and 2010, the Seventeenth Amendment was ignored in a manner similar to the approach to the Thirteenth Amendment. This vulnerability of the Guarantor branch is discussed further below.

The political support for the Constitutional Council among loosely formed constellations of civil society actors, coming from the arts, voluntary social organisations, religious institutions, universities and the professions, is another factor that explains the resilience of the Guarantor branch.[92] These groups mobilised public opinion each time Sri Lanka's Guarantor branch was subjected to constitutional ping-pong. The Youth Commission and the Nineteenth Amendment are examples of outcomes of this type of mobilisation. It is worth noting that the mobilisation of public opinion in the build up to the Twentieth Amendment was different. Unlike in the previous instances, when mobilisation of opinion was largely in support of a particular approach (in 2015, largely in support of the Nineteenth Amendment; in 2001, largely in support of the Seventeenth Amendment), in the lead up to the Twentieth Amendment, contesting opinions were mobilised. These contestations were effective to the extent that certain proposals that were included in the originally gazetted Bill were revised at the second stage of the Bill in Parliament.[93] Furthermore, despite enjoying a near two-thirds majority, the government faced criticism even by Buddhist clergy with regard to its intention to roll back on the features of the Guarantor branch as revised under the Nineteenth Amendment.

C. Vulnerability

Four factors place the Guarantor branch in a place of vulnerability. This chapter only studies the first three. First, political parties that enjoy dominance in Parliament coupled with a charismatic Executive President have made Sri Lanka's Guarantor branch vulnerable. Second, the ambivalence of the judiciary and the Attorney-General towards the Guarantor branch has compounded this vulnerability. Third, the failure of the Constitutional Council, on the few occasions that it was functional, to self-regulate in a transparent manner has added to this vulnerability. The fourth factor is an ideological vulnerability which requires more substantial analysis, perhaps on a future occasion. As was noted by an interviewee, until recently, political power 'was numbers in Parliament but now it is also about the military'. Relatedly, a counter-ideology has re-emerged which is also influenced by the approach to governance of China, a transnational actor with strong economic influence in Sri Lanka. This counter-ideology prioritises economic activities of a particular type (such as large infrastructure projects), attaches a high political value to 'discipline' and is dismissive of core ideas of constitutional

[92] Examples include the Sudu Nelum movement (1995–2000), the Organization of Professional Associations, the Sri Lanka Bar Association and the National Movement for Social Justice.

[93] For instance, the government had proposed the reintroduction of the provision for the adoption of 'urgent Bills'. Subsequently, this provision was qualified as Bills that are urgent in the interest of national security or disaster management.

government, such as respect for fundamental rights, accountability and transparency of public institutions.

The relative political strength of the political parties in power has determined the effectiveness of the Guarantor branch in Sri Lanka. This is the point about constitutional ping-pong that I have made elsewhere in writing about both the Nineteenth and Twentieth Amendments. Whenever the political party/coalition in power required the support of other political parties to remain in power, advancements in the consolidation of the Guarantor branch were achieved. In contrast, when the political party in power comprised almost two-thirds of Parliament, the independence of the Guarantor branch was rolled back in significant ways. Where political parties have not had a strong majority or where their coalitions were weak, pro-constitutionalist civil society actors, well supported by minority political parties, have been effective in bringing about pressure to improve the constitutional design of the Guarantor branch.[94]

In Sri Lanka, political or constitutional accountability of political parties or elected representatives is weak. The lack of accountability of a political party can have, and has had, a correlation with the independence guaranteed to the Guarantor branch. This is a pathology in Sri Lanka's party system which allows a political party that gains dominance to 'control all levers of power and reduce the effectiveness of checks and balances in the system'.[95] With the adoption of the Constitution of 1978, measures to control election campaign financing were effectively repealed and never replaced. Elected representatives are required to file declarations of their assets, but those declarations cannot be made public. The Constitution provides that expulsion by a political party is subject to judicial review.[96] Because the Supreme Court has insisted on compliance with rules of natural justice, in effect, attempts by political parties to use this power to ensure party discipline has not been effective. As a result, in the enactment of the Eighteenth and Twentieth Amendments, cross-overs enabled the government to secure a two-thirds majority, and those Members of Parliament who crossed over have continued to remain in Parliament and have even been entrusted with ministerial portfolios.

The traditional constitutional institutions, the judiciary and the office of the Attorney-General have been ambivalent about the constitutional ping-pong on Sri Lanka's Guarantor branch. Each of these Amendments were defended before Court by the Attorney General on behalf of the government of the day. With the exception of certain amendments that were proposed to the office of the Executive President, each time the judiciary was required to engage in pre-enactment judicial review of these proposed amendments, the Court held that the proposed amendments did not violate the entrenched clauses of the Constitution or any other constitutional provision. As a result, despite the substantive contrasts between the successive amendments, each of them were more or less deemed constitutional at the pre-enactment review stage. It is worth noting that this was not for the want of parties challenging the constitutionality of the proposed Bills.[97]

[94] I have in mind here in particular the role of the Janatha Vimukthi Peramuna and the Tamil National Alliance (regarding the adoption of the 19th Amendment, 2015).

[95] Bilchitz and Landau (n 20) 13.

[96] See, eg *Dissanayake v Kaleel* [1994] 1 Sri LR 319.

[97] For instance, a record number of 39 petitions were filed before the Supreme Court when the Twentieth Amendment Bill was subject to pre-enactment review.

The Constitutional Council is the centrepiece of Sri Lanka's model of a Guarantor branch. Over the last three decades, the focus has been on who constitutes the Council. The need to develop and adopt procedures for the selection of members and the procedures to be followed in the exercise of the powers, particularly of the Constitutional Council, have been voiced occasionally. This is a significant omission, even though an interviewee did note that the Council, by way of convention, took all decisions unanimously.[98] The requirement of unanimity, however, runs the risk of a deadlock. An interviewee recalled that a member of the first Council had in fact drafted rules of procedure in 2015 and had preferred a process whereby the Council self-regulated itself by adopting its own rules, rather than Parliament adopting such rules.[99] The absence of transparent and publicly enacted rules of procedure casts an opaque character on the work of the Council, thereby contributing to the perception that the Council is unaccountable and that it engages in an arbitrary exercise of its powers. An interviewee noted that the 'the mechanism for selecting independently itself must be independent. When it is not transparent, you cannot expect them to function independently.'

No legislation, policy or even standard operating procedure has been adopted to guide the work of the Council under any of the amendments. A noteworthy exception is the first report of the Constitutional Council under the Nineteenth Amendment.[100] In this report, the Council notes that, in addition to any stipulated criteria, 'The most important criteria were integrity, independence and non-partisanship', followed by relevant professional experience, leadership, 'maturity', diversity and the ability to 'enjoy the confidence' of 'constituencies and the public in general'.[101] It is worth recalling here that in the run-up to the last parliamentary election, the conduct of a member of the Constitutional Council and a member of the Election Commission was subject to criticism. The member of the Election Commission was quoted as asking people not to vote for the Sri Lanka Podujana Peramuna and a member of the Constitutional Council was reported to have spoken at a public forum cautioning the public not to provide the alliance with a two-thirds majority.[102]

VI. Conclusion

The Guarantor branch is a case of resilience by stealth for several reasons. The demand for the Constitutional Council has come from civil society and has gradually become a part of Sri Lanka's constitutional imaginary and discourse. Though rejected twice by strong governments, the idea remains alive. The Commissions, particularly the Human Rights Commission and now the Right to Information Commission, continue to be viewed as institutions that offer redress for rights and governance-related grievances.

[98] See also First Report of the Constitutional Council from July 2015 to November 2015 (Parliament of Sri Lanka) 5.

[99] See also 'Editorial: Hands off the Constitutional Council' *The Sunday Times* (24 February 2019). On judicial appointments, the editorial notes that the Council received as many as 300 applications.

[100] First Report of the Constitutional Council from July 2015 to November 2015 (Parliament of Sri Lanka).

[101] ibid 5.

[102] 'Strong Executive Presidency Needed for Rapid Development – GL' *Daily Mirror* (22 September 2020).

Where long-standing attempts at regime-type reform have failed, the Constitutional Council has succeeded twice. Where a constitutional resolution to the ethnic conflict has failed, the Constitutional Council has been able to make some modest progress with regard to inclusion and representation. Even though the Guarantor branch has not been supported by strong governments or by the judiciary, it has been central to the state formation project as a means of advancing constitutionalism.

My analysis suggests that over the last three decades, the following aspects of the Guarantor branch have consolidated. First, the recognition of a hybrid Guarantor branch that includes high offices and Commissions from the executive and the judiciary, along with the bodies that are more commonly considered part of the fourth branch. Second, that the President's power of appointments to these bodies should be vetted or at least be subject to some consultation. The long-term view of Sri Lanka's experience with its Guarantor branch reveals the way in which incremental change can achieve, at least to some extent, what may not be possible through a constitutional moment. It does appear that the idea of amenability of the President's actions to the fundamental rights jurisdiction has established itself, at the very least, as a principle. Its enforcement would depend on the independence of the judiciary and of the office of the Attorney-General, as well as on the judicial approach to the interpretation of fundamental rights. However, the Supreme Court's decision, when reviewing the Twentieth Amendment, that returning to full immunity for the office of the President is inconsistent with the Constitution, is evidence of the shift that has been achieved in the orientation of the 1978 Constitution.

The same cannot be said of the Constitutional Council and its mandate in guaranteeing the independence of the Guarantor institutions. There is little evidence to suggest that the ideas of independence and expertise of these institutions have consolidated, although their independent, expert contribution has been documented and recognised by pro-constitutional civil society in Sri Lanka. My analysis of the successive amendments and the role played by extra-constitutional actors (political parties, civil society actors) and constitutional actors (the judiciary and the Attorney-General) establish that a Guarantor branch is not yet consolidated as a constitutional norm in Sri Lanka. Constitutional actors such as the judiciary, the Attorney-General and Parliament have, by and large, been non-committal. They have not defended it, but nor have they resisted it. It is primarily political parties that are playing constitutional ping-pong with it, with the constitutional actors conceding to them the opportunity and the political legitimacy to do so. Constitutional actors have been led by extra-constitutional actors.

Therefore, while the Guarantor branch itself is designed to guarantee norms essential for the functioning of a constitutional democracy, Sri Lanka's experience suggests that the very existence of a Guarantor branch itself is vulnerable to the actions of extra-constitutional actors such as political parties. This vulnerability is compounded by the failure of traditional branches of the state and traditional fourth branch institutions such as the Attorney-General to guarantee the existence of the Guarantor branch. This insight suggests, therefore, that the guarantee of Guarantor branches is, in and of itself, a dimension that requires consideration and study in the debates on the emergence and function of the Guarantor branch. This is the threat to the consolidation of the Guarantor branch. While that threat remains, the Guarantor branch remains vulnerable, but may continue to strengthen its resilience by stealth.

Table 12.1 Overview of Sri Lanka's Guarantor branch under the 17th, 18th, 19th and 20th Amendments

	Appointments to High Office and Commissions	**Inclusivity/Minority Representation**	**High Offices**	**Commissions**
Constitution of 1978	By the President, who enjoys immunity from suit during office		Chief Justice; Judges of the Supreme Court; President and Judges of the Court of Appeal; Judicial Service Commission; Attorney General; Inspector-General of Police; Ombudsman; Secretary-General of Parliament	Public Service Commission; Finance Commission; Delimitation Commission; Human Rights Commission; Commission to Investigate Allegations into Bribery or Corruption
17th Amend (2001)	Nominations by the President to High Office to be approved by the Constitutional Council Appointments to Commissions to be recommended by the Constitutional Council Constitutional Council: Prime Minister, Speaker, Leader of the Opposition, 1 appointed by the President, 5 nominated by the Prime Minister and Leader of the Opposition, 1 appointed by the President and nominated by the other political parties in Parliament	3 of the 5 persons must be nominated to represent minority interests Council has the duty to ensure that their recommendations (for chair, commissions) reflect the different ethnic groups	Chief Justice; Judges of the Supreme Court; President and Judges of the Court of Appeal; Judicial Service Commission; Attorney General; Auditor General; Inspector-General of Police; Ombudsman; Secretary-General of Parliament	Election Commission; Public Service Commission; National Police Commission; Human Rights Commission; Commission to Investigate Allegations into Bribery or Corruption; Finance Commission; Delimitation Commission

18th Amend (2010)	By the President, who enjoys immunity from suit during office. Term limit removed President 'shall' seek observations of the Parliamentary Council in making these appointments Parliamentary Council: Prime Minister, Speaker, Leader of the Opposition, an MP nominated by Prime Minister, an MP nominated by Leader of the Opposition		Chief Justice; Judges of the Supreme Court; President and Judges of the Court of Appeal; Judicial Service Commission; Attorney General; Auditor General; Ombudsman; Secretary-General of Parliament	Election Commission; Public Service Commission; National Police Commission; Human Rights Commission; Commission to Investigate Allegations into Bribery or Corruption; Finance Commission; Delimitation Commission
19th Amend (2015)	Nominations by the President to High Office to be approved by the Constitutional Council Appointments to Commissions to be recommended by the Constitutional Council Term limit reintroduced. Immunity from suit excluded in relation to fundamental rights petitions Constitutional Council: Prime Minister, Speaker, Leader of the Opposition, MP appointed by President, 5 appointed by the President and nominated by the Prime Minister and Leader of the Opposition, 1 MP nominated by other political parties in Parliament	In making the five nominations, the pluralistic character of Sri Lankan society, including professional and social diversity must be ensured The Council must endeavour to ensure that its recommendations reflect the pluralistic character of Sri Lankan society including gender	Chief Justice; Judges of the Supreme Court; President and Judges of the Court of Appeal; Judicial Service Commission; Attorney General; Auditor General; Inspector-General of Police; Ombudsman; Secretary-General of Parliament	Election Commission; Public Service Commission; National Police Commission; Human Rights Commission; Commission to Investigate Allegations into Bribery or Corruption; Finance Commission; Delimitation Commission; Audit Service Commission; National Procurement Commission

(continued)

Table 12.1 *(Continued)*

	Appointments to High Office and Commissions	Inclusivity/Minority Representation	High Offices	Commissions
20th Amend (2020)	By the President The President 'shall' seek observations of the Parliamentary Council in making these appointments Term limit and exclusion of immunity for fundamental rights petitions continued Parliamentary Council: Prime Minister, Speaker, Leader of the Opposition, an MP nominated by the Prime Minister, an MP nominated by Leader of the Opposition (to represent communities not represented by other members)		Chief Justice; Judges of the Supreme Court; President and Judges of the Court of Appeal; Judicial Service Commission; Attorney General; Auditor General; Inspector-General of Police; Ombudsman; Secretary-General of Parliament	Election Commission; Public Service Commission; National Police Commission; Human Rights Commission; Commission to Investigate Allegations into Bribery or Corruption; Finance Commission; Delimitation Commission

13

The South Asian Fourth Branch: Designing Election Commissions for Constitutional Resilience

MICHAEL PAL[1]

I. Introduction

This chapter analyses the constitutional dynamics underpinning the work of the election commissions of South Asia. Narrowly viewed, election commissions or 'Electoral Management Bodies'[2] are the institutions now tasked in most countries with interpreting and applying election laws. This grant of authority breaks from the traditional approach of permitting the executive or the legislature to administer or manage elections, with the accompanying risks to the integrity of the process.

More broadly understood, however, election commissions have assumed a heightened constitutional status in many countries, due to new approaches to the separation of powers.[3] The standard, tripartite separation of powers divides power into legislative, executive and judicial branches. Where the existence and powers of independent administrative institutions are defined in or protected by the constitution, questions arise as to whether to categorise one or more of these entities as a 'fourth branch'.[4] To the extent that we can say that a constitutionalised 'fourth branch' exists in some

[1] Thanks to Tarun Khaitan, Mark Tushnet, Aileen Kavanaugh, Ros Dixon, Mohsin Alam Bhat, Richard Albert, David Schneiderman, Dinesha Samararatne, Swati Jhaveri and Iain Payne for helpful comments on earlier versions of this chapter. I would also like to thank the election administrators who have shared their insights with me, including Jean-Pierre Kingsley, former Chief Electoral Officer of Canada, Babar Yaqoob, Secretary to the Election Commission of Pakistan, Tan Sri Rashid, Chairman of the Electoral Reform Committee of Malaysia and former Chairman of the Election Commission, and Halima Ismail Ibrahim, Chairperson of the National Independent Electoral Commission of Somalia.

[2] A Wall, S Staino, J Rukambe, A Ellis, A Ayoub and C Dundas, *Electoral Management Design: The International IDEA Handbook* (Stockholm, International IDEA, 2006); R Lopez-Pintor, *Electoral Management Bodies as Institutions of Governance* (New York, United Nations Development Programme, 2000); TS James, *Comparative Electoral Management: Performance, Networks, and Instruments* (London, Routledge, 2020).

[3] B Ackerman, 'The New Separation of Powers' (2000) 113(3) *Harvard Law Review* 633.

[4] See ibid; M Tushnet, *The New Fourth Branch* (Cambridge, Cambridge University Press, 2021); T Khaitan, 'Guarantor Institutions' (2022) 16(S1) *Asian Journal of Comparative Law* S40.

democracies, election commissions have arguably the strongest claim for inclusion in the category globally.[5]

The constitutions of South Asia generally reflect the deliberate design of election commissions as not only the guardians of the electoral process, but as central constitutional actors.[6] This chapter claims that despite cross-national variation within the region with regard to the separation of powers and institutional design, there is an identifiable South Asian model for election commissions. The chapter analyses the strengths and weaknesses of the South Asian model for ensuring electoral integrity, which is of paramount importance for democracy in the region.

This chapter also seeks to contribute to three ongoing scholarly debates in comparative constitutional law. First, through the focus on South Asia, it engages with the comparative study of what I will call 'fourth branch constitutionalism', meaning the constitutional practice and dynamics that stem from deviating from a three-branch vision of the separation of powers. Bruce Ackerman famously described global constitutional practice around the separation of powers as going beyond the traditional three branches to include multiple, newer branches.[7] Ackerman provided the constitutionally entrenched Election Commission of India (ECI)[8] as an example of a 'democracy branch'.[9]

Despite this insight, the constitutional politics of election commissions and the fourth branch has remained under-theorised and under-described in comparative constitutional law. Whether we should recognise four or perhaps many more branches is a matter of ongoing debate,[10] as is the relationship of election commissions to other constitutionally created, independent entities, such as central banks or human rights commissions. While the South African Constitution has been one of the key global case studies,[11] the ECI is another important example, as Ackerman highlighted early on.

[5] M Pal, 'Election Commissions as a Fourth Branch of Government' (2016) 21(1) *Review of Constitutional Studies* 87; S Chernykh, Z Elkins, T Melton and T Ginsburg, 'Constitutions and Election Management' in P Norris, R Frank and F Martinez i Coma (eds), *Advancing Electoral Integrity* (Oxford, Oxford University Press, 2014).

[6] A McMillan, 'The Election Commission' in NG Jayal and PB Mehta (eds), *The Oxford Companion to Politics in India* (Oxford, Oxford University Press, 2010); A McMillan, 'The Election Commission of India and the Regulation and Administration of Electoral Politics' (2012) 11(2) *Election Law Journal* 187; SH Rudolph and LI Rudolph, 'New Dimensions of Indian Democracy' (2002) 13(1) *Journal of Democracy* 52, 59; SH Rudolph and LI Rudolph, 'Redoing the Constitutional Design: From an Interventionist to a Regulatory State' in A Kohli (ed), *The Success of India's Democracy* (Cambridge, Cambridge University Press, 2001); R Saxena, 'The Election Commission and Indian Federalism' (2012) 15(1) *Think India Quarterly* 194.

[7] Ackerman (n 3).

[8] See Art 324 of the Constitution of India.

[9] Ackerman (n 3) 716–22.

[10] M Tushnet, 'Institutions Protecting Constitutional Democracy: Some Conceptual and Methodological Preliminaries' (2020) 70 *University of Toronto Law Journal* 95, 95 and fn 6.

[11] On the influence of the 1996 South African Constitution, see C Fombad, 'The Diffusion of South African-Style Institutions? A Study in Comparative Constitutionalism' in R Dixon and T Roux (eds), *Constitutional Triumphs, Constitutional Disappointments: A Critical Assessment of the 1996 South African Constitution's Local and International Influence* (Cape Town, Cambridge University Press, 2018) 359–87; C Fombad, 'Role of Emerging Hybrid Institutions of Accountability in the Separation of Powers Scheme in Africa' in C Fombad (ed), *Separation of Powers in African Constitutionalism* (Oxford, Oxford University Press, 2016) 325–44.

The evolution of Sri Lanka's election commission and other independent institutions[12] will be an important marker for how the fourth branch operates outside of the paradigmatic South African and Indian contexts.

Second, fourth branch constitutionalism feeds into concerns about how to stem constitutional decline and, instead, foster resilience in democratic systems. The threat of constitutional decline has been credibly raised in South Asia.[13] Influential definitions of democratic decline tend to agree that healthy political institutions are a necessary, if perhaps not sufficient, factor in the degree of resilience exhibited by a constitutional order.[14] In two of the important case studies of this current era of democratic backsliding, Poland and Hungary, partisan-minded changes to election administration were among the core strategies of the governments seeking to erode electoral and democratic accountability.[15] This chapter argues in line with the institutional emphasis in these theories that independent, non-partisan and constitutionally protected election commissions must be regarded as a key component of resilience in the face of potential decline. The South Asian constitutions generally reflect attempts, with varying degrees of success, to insulate election administration from interference by the executive, the legislature or a political party.

Third, the chapter seeks to contribute to the growing literature on South Asian constitutionalism.[16] In using the term 'South Asia' here, I include India, Pakistan, Sri Lanka, Bangladesh, Nepal, Bhutan, the Maldives and Afghanistan within the country case studies.[17] Much recent literature in comparative constitutional law has adopted a regional focus with regard to South Asia that seeks to facilitate fruitful comparisons within the group, as well as across regions. The potential drawbacks of a regional focus in South Asia are relatively obvious. There is tremendous diversity within the region, both at the societal level and between states, and in their degrees of democratic entrenchment. The countries face different dynamics in the battle against constitutional decline.

[12] See A Welikala, 'Sri Lanka – The Nineteenth Amendment to the Constitution from Start to Finish' (2015) http://constitutionnet.org/news/sri-lanka-nineteenth-amendment-constitution-start-finish. See also A Welikala (ed), *The Nineteenth Amendment to the Constitution: Content and Context* (Colombo, Centre for Policy Alternatives, 2016), including ch 7, D Samararatne, 'The Constitutional Council and the Independent Commissions: The New Framework for Depoliticising Governance'.

[13] S Ganguly, 'India under Modi: Threats to Pluralism' (2019) 30(1) *Journal of Democracy* 83; M Mate, 'Constitutional Erosion and the Challenge to Secular Democracy in India' in M Graber, S Levinson and M Tushnet (eds), *Constitutional Democracy in Crisis*? (New York, Oxford University Press, 2018) 377; T Khaitan, 'Executive Aggrandizement in Established Democracies: A Crisis of Liberal Democratic Constitutionalism' (2019) 17(1) *International Journal of Constitutional Law* 342, 350 and 352.

[14] See, eg N Bermeo, 'On Democratic Backsliding' (2016) 27 *Journal of Democracy* 5; A Huq and T Ginsburg, 'How to Lose a Constitutional Democracy' (2017) 65 *UCLA Law Review* 78; A Huq and T Ginsburg, *How to Save a Constitutional Democracy* (Chicago, University of Chicago Press, 2019).

[15] W Sadurski, *Poland's Constitutional Break*down (Oxford, Oxford University Press, 2019) 140–43, detailing the Polish case and comparing it to Hungary; S Levitsky and L Way, 'Competitive Authoritarianism' (2020) 31(1) *Journal of Democracy* 51, 61–62.

[16] M Tushnet and M Khosla (eds), *Unstable Constitutionalism: Law and Politics in South Asia* (Cambridge, Cambridge University Press, 2015); S Khilnani, V Raghavan and AK Thiruvengadam (eds), *Comparative Constitutionalism in South Asia* (Oxford, Oxford University Press, 2013); J Greene and M Khosla, 'Constitutional Rights in South Asia' (2018) 16 *International Journal of Constitutional Law* 470.

[17] This chapter focuses more on the jurisdictions of India, Pakistan, Sri Lanka and Bangladesh than those of Afghanistan, the Maldives, Nepal or Bhutan.

Further, the very term 'South Asia' is itself a colonial one[18] that may not be the most apt or relevant grouping, given this diversity and the varying post-colonial trajectories. While acknowledging that this chapter only analyses one aspect of how constitutional democracies function in South Asia, it concludes that, despite the drawbacks, there is merit in the regional focus, as it reveals important commonalities among the countries that fall within the definition. A regional lens also facilitates the investigation of trends that have already been identified, such as the influence of India in the migration of constitutional ideas throughout South Asia.[19]

This chapter will proceed as follows. Section II situates election commissions within the ongoing debates around democratic decline. It considers how election commissions are designed to function and how these functions play into decline or resilience. Section III details the election commissions in South Asia and draws out the particularities of the regional model. It considers constitutional design in relation to institutional independence, composition, the relationship with other branches and 'duty to assist' provisions that seek to shape the separation of powers. Section IV considers the emerging challenges facing the South Asian model, by focusing on recent allegations of partisanship in Indian election administration. Section V concludes the chapter by considering the implications raised by the South Asian commissions for comparative constitutional law more generally, particularly regarding constitutional design, the separation of powers and election administration.

II. Constitutional Resilience and Election Commissions

Constitutional decline is a complex phenomenon. The variations alone among the countries that have at times been identified as experiencing decline are enough to stymie analysis. The conceptual disagreements extend to which term best describes the phenomenon.[20] Recent accounts of decline have put forward a multitude of potential causes and factors, including political culture, history, individual bad actors, demographics and economic polarisation.

One common feature of several leading versions of the decline argument, however, is a focus on institutions. Nancy Bermeo, for example, defines in her influential formulation democratic backsliding as 'state-led debilitation or elimination of any of the political institutions that sustain an existing democracy'.[21] Aziz Huq and Tom Ginsburg advance a theory explaining decline that focuses to a great extent, though not exclusively, on institutions.[22] The accounts of Sam Issacharoff[23] and

[18] U Baxi, 'Modeling Optimal Constitutional Design for Government Structures' in Khilnani et al (n 16) 24–25.

[19] Greene and Khosla (n 16) 476: 'The third feature of constitutionalism in South Asia that we notice is the centrality of India to the South Asian region.'

[20] Various terms in use include 'decline', 'degradation', 'backsliding' and 'breakdown'. For an overview, see R Albert and M Pal, 'The Democratic Resilience of the Canadian Constitution' in Graber et al (n 13) 117.

[21] Bermeo (n 14).

[22] ibid.

[23] S Issacharoff, 'The Democratic Risk to Democratic Transitions' (2013) 5 *Constitutional Court Review*; S Issacharoff, *Fragile Democracies: Contested Power in the Era of Constitutional Courts* (Cambridge, Cambridge University Press, 2015).

Kim Lane Scheppele[24] also take the health of institutions and deliberate attempts to interfere with them as central to the issues at stake. Tarun Khaitan argues that the common link across different examples of clear decline, namely Poland, Hungary and Turkey, and more controversial or borderline cases, such as Israel, India, South Africa and the USA, is aggrandisement of the political executive at the expense of other branches or independent institutions.[25]

As I have argued elsewhere with Richard Albert,[26] constitutional resilience should be seen as the flip side of constitutional decline. If decline relates to the degradation of institutions, then resilience should be understood as its mirror image. Constitutional resilience is at least partly a question of how to foster health and resilience among the institutions that are necessary for a flourishing democracy.

If institutions are to be a focus of the resilience debate, then election commissions should be seen as central, in South Asia and globally, given their particular role in sustaining the quality of democracy. Election commissions are increasingly being recognised by constitutional orders as having a legal status different from other administrative bodies.[27] Election commissions interpret election laws, usually around voter registration, delimitation of electoral boundaries, campaign finance, candidate eligibility, political party funding, election advertising, and so on. They often investigate breaches and enforce the law as well. Election commissions are generally established as permanent entities, rather than being reconstituted simply at election time, with a Chief Electoral Officer or Commissioner and other Commissioners.[28] Appointments are generally made by the head of state or some intermediate body. The authority of commissions varies, but at times includes not only national but also sub-national elections as well. These discrete functions can be summarised as adding up to a remit to foster what Pippa Norris calls 'electoral integrity',[29] namely the application of the generally accepted minimum norms and standards that facilitate electoral competition.

As a best practice, election commissions are designed to be independent of government or any political party. The reasons are relatively straightforward. Allowing elected representatives in a legislature or the executive, or the civil servants who report directly to them, to administer elections would invite partisan manipulation and harm actual or perceived electoral integrity. Political actors with partisan interests have incentives to try to shape the rules of electoral competition in their favour. This risk might take the form of interpreting an election law to favour a particular candidate or party. Independent, non-partisan election administration is the global gold standard because it takes election administration out of the hands of the political branches and reduces opportunities for that kind of electoral malfeasance. Even where independent election commissions

[24] KL Scheppele, 'Autocratic Legalism' (2018) 85 *University of Chicago Law Review* 545.

[25] Khaitan, 'Executive Aggrandizement' (n 13) 342–44.

[26] Albert and Pal (n 20).

[27] RA Pastor, 'The Role of Electoral Administration in Democratic Transitions: Implications for Policy and Research' (1999) 6(4) *Democratization* 1; Chernykh et al (n 5).

[28] Wall et al (n 2).

[29] P Norris, 'The New Research Agenda Studying Electoral Integrity' (2013) 32 *Electoral Studies* 563; P Norris, *Why Electoral Integrity Matters* (New York, Cambridge University Press, 2014).

are in place, however, political actors may attempt to capture them, either by appointing partisans, curtailing the scope of their independent authority or starving them of funds.

The response in many democracies to this set of problems has been to constitutionalise the election commission as constituting or as part of a fourth branch of government. This response recognises that election administration as a function does not sit easily within the traditional three branches of government. The executive and legislature are hopelessly beset by conflicts of interest regarding election administration, in that they are composed of partisan political actors who have vested interests in how elections are run or are civil servants accountable to partisans. The courts generally lack the expertise or capacity to administer elections. As a result, constitutional designers have often opted to guarantee the existence of an independent election commission in the text and to attempt to insulate it from partisan interference or, indeed, capture.[30]

The fourth branch is an emerging reality in many countries, including in South Asia. Wherever independence is required to carry out a function essential to the state, such as fair elections, non-partisan prosecutions or anti-corruption activities, there is a logic in ensuring that regular political majorities cannot impede or capture their functions. Central banks, human rights commissions, prosecutorial services and others are all part of the fourth branch in some democracies. South Africa's Chapter 9 institutions are often seen as emblematic of this trend.[31] Election commissions are nearly invariably a central component of the set of institutions given constitutional protection in democracies that have opted for fourth branch constitutionalism in response to the failures of the political branches. By removing power from the political branches over most of the election administration,[32] constitutional designers thereby constrain temporary political majorities falling short of the supermajorities generally necessary to amend the text. The fourth branch model seeks to entrench independent and non-partisan election administration.

In the language of constitutional decline, election commissions as part of a fourth branch of government constrain the capacity of would-be autocrats to restrict free and fair electoral competition. Would-be autocrats rarely today seek to eliminate elections in their entirety.[33] They fear the domestic and international repercussions of being conclusively labelled as true autocrats beyond popular accountability or democratic control. By maintaining the superficial veneer of electoral democracy but hollowing out its actual substance so that the outcome is largely, even if not definitively, known in advance, they seek to maintain themselves in office. Constitutional protection for the existence, legal authority and composition of election commissions makes it more

[30] Pal (n 5); Chernykh et al (n 5). UK Singh and A Roy, *Election Commission of India: Institutionalising Democratic Uncertainties* (Delhi, Oxford University Press, 2019) 19–34 discuss in detail the evolution of the Indian constitutional provisions with regard to the ECI.

[31] Fombad, 'Diffusion' (n 11).

[32] Legislatures still generally write election laws, though they are often constrained by detailed constitutional rules on political participation as set out in constitutions.

[33] Scheppele (n 24). See Levitsky and Way (n 15) 55–59.

difficult for would-be autocrats to stifle meaningful electoral competition. The fourth branch checks potential abuses by the legislature and/or executive that are aimed at weakening the institutions of electoral democracy.

The fourth branch is not a panacea. Large, durable political majorities usually get what they want in the long run. Rules on constitutional amendment may not be much more onerous for parties with large legislative majorities than changing regular statutes. The Hungarian example is a cautionary tale here.[34] Judicial review of the decisions of election commissions may also hinder independence if the courts themselves have been captured or are partisan in orientation.[35]

Whatever their formal legal status, election commissions that contribute to electoral integrity will nearly always be central targets for would-be authoritarians in the dynamics of democratic decline, alongside the judiciary and the independent media. A closer look at Khaitan's executive aggrandisement argument helps bring out the underlying constitutional logic for why would-be authoritarians frequently seek to tame independent election commissions. Khaitan highlights three different kinds of executive accountability: (1) 'electoral or vertical accountability' to the people, primarily through popular elections; (2) 'horizontal or institutional accountability', including to the courts, opposition and the fourth branch; and (3) 'diagonal or discursive accountability' to the media, civil society and academia.[36] Democratic decline through executive aggrandisement occurs when these forms of accountability are curtailed.

Election commissions exist at the intersection of both type 1 electoral/vertical and type 2 horizontal/institutional accountability. By harming the efficient functioning of commissions, electoral integrity and hence vertical accountability are hindered. Starving a commission of funding, or reducing its legal authority or jurisdiction, harms the vertical accountability of the executive to the people, as it is the commission that is the main intermediary body ensuring that the primary accountability mechanism of the election operates fairly. If the independence of the commission or its willingness to take decisions contrary to the interests of the governing party are undermined, say through partisan appointments or pressure on incumbent commissioners, then horizontal or institutional accountability suffer.

Whether fourth branch constitutionalism can adapt to the current pressures of democratic decline and, if so, how emerge as important questions at this particular juncture in the life of constitutional democracy. These questions are especially pertinent in South Asia, where fourth branch constitutionalism has been a prominent aspect of constitutional theory and practice in the region. The ECI's hard-won reputation for independence has fallen during the years of the Modi government, with multiple, credible allegations that it has exercised its discretion in a manner that favours the incumbents at the centre. With this background in mind, I turn in the next section to setting out how the fourth branch model has been adopted in South Asia.

[34] See the sources above in n 33.
[35] Pal (n 5).
[36] Khaitan, 'Executive Aggrandizement' (n 13) 350.

III. The South Asian 'Fourth Branch'

This section delineates the contours of the South Asian model of election commissions. Despite meaningful variation across countries, the model has common traits and some shared weaknesses. The main, defining feature is that South Asian constitutions generally envision election commissions as part of a fourth branch of government. They reflect a particular vision of the separation of powers that includes a fourth branch as integral to sustaining and protecting democracy. Whether the election commission is *the* fourth branch or merely part of it as one among a host of independent institutions created by the constitution is a key point of divergence. This section analyses how constitutional designers have attempted to protect the independence of election commissions, the vision of the separation of powers underlying their approach to election administration and the relationship between the branches set out in the text, including the duty to assist other branches and their composition.

A. Election Commission Independence

Constitutional designers in South Asia appear largely to have intended the fourth branch to be independent of the other branches of government, though reality has diverged from formal legal status at times in particular countries. The 2013 International IDEA report on electoral management bodies or election commissions is the most comprehensive, global summary of these institutions.[37] It adopts a three-part classification system. It characterises election commissions as either 'independent', 'governmental' or 'mixed'. Independent commissions operate at arms-length from government and political parties. Governmental bodies are housed within departments of the civil service, such as a Ministry of the Interior or Justice, or within a central body, such as a Privy Council Office. Mixed institutions are some combination of the other types.

In the 2013 study, six of South Asia's eighth election commissions are defined as 'independent'. Sri Lanka and the Maldives are the exceptions. Sri Lanka's Nineteenth Amendment to the Constitution in 2015, which was passed after the study, meant its commission could be briefly classified as 'independent' as well, on the definition used by International IDEA. The Twentieth Amendment in 2020 undid the move towards independent institutions in Sri Lanka,[38] particularly by putting control over appointments once again in the hands of the President. The Maldives is the only other country in the region to deviate from the orthodoxy that election commissions should be formally and legally independent. The Election Commission in the Maldives has been the site of intense political contestation; recently all the country's election commissioners were arrested due to conflict with the government and courts.[39]

[37] Wall et al (n 2).

[38] See D Samararatne, ch 12 in this volume.

[39] 'Entire Maldives Election Commission Sentenced' *BBC News* (9 March 2014) www.bbc.com/news/world-asia-26508259. See A Nazeer, ch 10 in this volume.

It is worth noting that the International IDEA study is incomplete from the point of view of comparative constitutional law. It is agnostic as to whether independence is set out in the constitution, in statute or otherwise, and largely ignores the particular mechanisms, beyond appointment, that guarantee it.[40] It is, therefore, an important source, but misses the broader constitutional picture, including the vision of election commissions as part of a fourth branch.

It must also be pointed out that South Asian election commissions have at times been captured by partisan interests or actors. Where democracy has failed, so have the commissions failed, even if they have continued to exist as formally independent and, even, constitutionally protected entities. For example, Former General and then President Pervez Musharaff of Pakistan made partisan appointments to the Election Commission of Pakistan (ECP) and the institution served largely as a facilitator rather than a block against election-rigging during his time in office.[41] Post-Musharaff, the Eighteenth Amendment to the Constitution changed the appointment process to require input from the opposition.[42]

B. Election Commissions as (Part of) a Fourth Branch

The South Asian approach to election administration clearly emphasises the role of constitutional design. The election commissions of South Asia are creations brought into being by the constitutional text,[43] rather than being left to ordinary statutes shaped by political majorities in the legislature. Framed in Upendra Baxi's terms, the approach to constitutional design of election administration in the South Asian constitutions stands as an example of rupture from, rather than continuity with, the colonial past.[44]

The British model of political constitutionalism, going back to Dicey, traditionally viewed untrammelled parliamentary sovereignty as its defining feature. Parliament was sovereign even on matters such as the design of the electoral system and election administration. Political constitutionalism largely fails to provide an answer to the problem of why politicians were permitted to set the very rules by which they were supposed to compete for elected office, and what would happen if the rules tilted the electoral

[40] Wall et al (n 2) 46–48.

[41] See the detailed allegations of election-rigging and the role of the ECP in 'Reforming Pakistan's Electoral System' (International Crisis Group, 3 March 2011) www.crisisgroup.org/asia/south-asia/pakistan/reforming-pakistan-s-electoral-system. See also KA Khan, '2002 Elections in Pakistan: A Reappraisal' (2011) 18(1) *Journal of Political Studies* 93; L Goodson, 'Pakistan after Musharraf: The 2008 Elections' (2008) 19(4) *Journal of Democracy* 5; HN Mirbahar, 'Flawed Laws, Flawed Elections: Local Elections in Pakistan' (2019) 18(1) *Election Law Journal* 1.

[42] Constitution (18th Amendment) Act, 2010: www.pakistani.org/pakistan/Constitution/amendments/18amendment.html.

[43] See Constitution of India, Art 324; Constitution of the Islamic Republic of Pakistan, Part VIII, Arts 213–26; Constitution of the People's Republic of Bangladesh, Part VII, Arts 118–26; Constitution of the Islamic Republic of Afghanistan, Art 156; Constitution of Nepal, Part 24, Arts 245–47; Constitution of the Kingdom of Bhutan, Art 24; Constitution of the Republic of Maldives, Arts 167–78; Constitution of the Democratic Socialist Republic of Sri Lanka, Ch XIV(A), Arts 103–04J.

[44] Baxi (n 18).

playing field or, indeed, made democracy a sham.[45] Independent institutions taking power away from and overseeing Parliament are anathema to a pure vision of parliamentary sovereignty.

This intuition was reflected to some degree by the reluctance in the UK to create an independent election commission until relatively recently. The UK only created a statutory election commission in 2000,[46] and its actual independence has been chipped away already by changes to its composition and partisan appointments. The South Asian model clearly departs from this colonial baggage. The Indian Constitution granted the Election Commission status as an independent constitutional institution, for example, from the inception of the country.

While uniform in rejecting political constitutionalism for election administration, there is significant variation within South Asia on how to constitute the fourth branch. In some cases, the institution is positioned in the constitution as the main or only fourth branch institution. Take the original Indian Constitution, for example. The existence, powers and status of the traditional three branches of government are set out in detail. In addition to the detailed discussion of the three usual suspects, the Indian Constitution can be seen as treating the Election Commission of India as part of a fourth branch.[47] The same could be said of the current Pakistani Constitution. Bangladesh envisions a small number of other independent, constitutional entities, but the Election Commission is the main body within the category.[48] The thesis that the Indian model is influential in South Asian constitutionalism is at least partly evidenced by the widespread adoption of election commissions as part of a fourth branch or as the paramount institution within it.[49]

The alternative approach is reflected in the vision for the Sri Lankan Constitution provided by the Nineteenth Amendment.[50] The various versions of the Sri Lankan

[45] For a recent powerful criticism from within the tradition of political constitutionalism, see J Murkens, 'Democracy as the Legitimating Condition in the UK Constitution' (2018) 38 *Legal Studies* 42.

[46] NS Ghaleigh, 'A Model for Party Finance Supervision? The First Decade of the UK's Election Commission' in KD Ewing, J-C Tham and J Rowbottom (eds), *The Funding of Political Parties* (Oxford, Hart Publishing, 2011). The UK has an unwritten constitution and this statute arguably rises to the level of quasi-constitutional status. On Australia, as influenced by the British tradition, see N Kelly, *Directions in Australian Electoral Reform: Professionalism and Partisanship in Electoral Management* (Canberra, Australian National University Press, 2012); C Hughes, 'The Independence of the Commissions: The Legislative Framework and the Bureaucratic Reality' in G Orr, B Mercurio and G Williams (eds), *Realising Democracy: Electoral Law in Australia* (Sydney, The Federation Press, 2003).

[47] In addition to the Election Commission, Art 280(2) refers to the Finance Commission. Tarun Khaitan sets out a list of institutions that could potentially be included within the fourth branch in India. These institutions are of varying formal constitutional status. See T Khaitan, 'The Importance of Fourth Branch Institutions to Constitutional Democracy' (*Indian Constitutional Law and Philosophy Blog*, 7 April 2019) https://indconlawphil.wordpress.com/2019/04/07/the-importance-of-fourth-branch-institutions-to-constitutional-democracy-guest-post/. His complete list is the 'Election Commission, Lokpal, Central Bureau of Investigation, Reserve Bank, National Statistics Commission, National Human Rights Commission, Information Commission, commissions for various marginalised groups, Central Vigilance Commission, Comptroller & Auditor General, Attorney General, Public Service Commission, University Grants Commission, Finance Commission, Niti Aayog, media regulators and many others'.

[48] Part IV, Arts 127–32. It also establishes administrative tribunals as constitutional entities, but views them as part of the judicial system. See Part VI, 'The Judiciary', which creates in Ch I the 'Supreme Court', in Ch II the 'Subordinate Courts' and in Ch III the 'Administrative Tribunals'.

[49] Greene and Khosla (n 16).

[50] Constitution of the Democratic Socialist Republic of Sri Lanka.

Constitution have been amended multiple times and often on matters related to elections.[51] The Nineteenth Amendment of 2015 provided a major revision of the separation of powers following the end of the civil war in 2009 and the decade-long Rajapaksa presidency from 2005 to 2015. While provided for in earlier amendments, the Election Commission was only established for the first time in 2015. Part XIVA of the Constitution (Articles 103–104J) establishes the Election Commission, including its powers and structure. While certainly not conferring any additional legal status, it is perhaps indicative that the Election Commission comes prior to the judiciary in the text, which is created in Part XV. The Election Commission is created and empowered by the Constitution, but it is one among a swathe of entities forming a robust fourth branch. The Nineteenth Amendment established a bevy of other fourth branch institutions designed to act independently and to take over functions that were traditionally within the purview of the political branches.[52] These include a Constitutional Council that is supposed to recommend and approve appointments and institutions with authority over the public service, police, human rights, bribery and corruption, audit and procurement. In this sense, it is a clear reaction to the over-reaches and constitutional crises of the Rajapaksa era.[53]

If constitutional decline is partly driven by the abuse of executive authority, then the Nineteenth Amendment stood as one reform-minded reaction. As Dinesha Samararatne has written, 'The call for independence of public institutions and the depoliticisation of the selection and appointment of individuals to these institutions are premised on the idea that representative democracy, in the Sri Lankan context, has failed in this regard'.[54] As part of the practice of fourth branch constitutionalism, it envisions a host of functions that should be fulfilled by independent entities wherever concentrated executive power can be predictably anticipated to lead to perverse outcomes. Election administration is one key part of this mix of functions requiring independent, constitutionally mandated institutions to carry them out, but far from the only one.

The on-the-ground realisation of the formal constitutional text of the Nineteenth Amendment was a mixed bag and, with the passage of the Twentieth Amendment, the future of the independent bodies is in doubt. President Sirisena called for the repeal of

[51] The list includes: terminated the Delimitation Commission and increased the number of members in the House (1954); appointed a new Delimitation Commission to draw electoral boundaries (1959); created the post of Election Judge (1961); placed the post of Commissioner of Elections in the Constitution, as well as setting which public officers can run in elections (1964). See generally D Samararatne, 'Sri Lanka's First Election Commission: Strengthening Electoral Management or Advancing Electoral Integrity?' (2021) 16(Suppl S1) *Asian Journal of Comparative Law* 156.

[52] Welikala, *The Nineteenth Amendment* (n 12): 'Perhaps the strongest feature of the Nineteenth Amendment is the depoliticisation framework that is established with the Constitutional Council and the independent commissions.' Samararatne, 'The Constitutional Council' (n 12) 148–49 argues that '"de-politicisation" is a skin-deep solution to a more fundamental problem'.

[53] The Supreme Court ruled on the compliance of the 19th Amendment with a variety of constitutional and procedural rules, including a requirement to have a referendum in order to approve certain provisions, in 'A Bill Entitled, "Nineteenth Amendment to the Constitution" in the Matter of Applications under Article 121(1) of the Constitution' (2015) SD No 04/2015–SD No 19/2015, www.colombotelegraph.com/wp-content/uploads/2015/04/SC-SD-4-to-19-of-2015.pdf.

[54] Samararatne, 'The Constitutional Council' (n 12) 169.

the Nineteenth Amendment entirely and accused it of frustrating the harmonious functioning of government by creating competing power centres without obvious methods of dispute resolution.[55] His successor, President Gotabaya Rajapaksa, eventually carried this vision to fruition. The Twentieth Amendment of October 2020 re-tilts the field yet again in favour of the President over the Prime Minister, modifies the composition of the Constitutional Council and essentially grants unfettered discretion in making appointments to the President. Formally independent institutions remain but, in this context, their actual independence has been compromised.

C. Relationship with the Other Branches

Another significant marker of the fourth branch status of election commissions is their formal, legal relationship with the other branches of the state. Recent constitutions adopting a fourth branch model generally set out in detail the relationship between election commissions and the legislature, executive and judiciary. The reasoning behind doing so is an expansion of the practice in constitutional design to empower the branches of government and then delineate the terms of their engagement with one another. If they are the central institutions of the state, leaving aside the complications of federalism for the moment, then their respective functions should be clarified in the text. One of the markers that election commissions are taken as a true fourth branch in South Asia is the degree to which constitutions in the region are occupied with detailing the functions, powers, membership and structure of these institutions. The number of commissioners, their relationship with the Chief Commissioner or head of the commission, funding, hiring processes for staff and other relatively granular details are at times included.

Of particular note is the multifaceted relationship between election commissions and the judiciary. The constitutional text often tries to build on the model of judicial independence to ensure that the fourth branch has similar status and protections. Where this feature is most evident is in provisions regarding the removal of election commissioners. The Bangladeshi Constitution, for example, creates the Election Commission, the post of Chief Election Commissioner and up to four other Commissioners, and sets the terms of office.[56] Procedures for removal are tightly circumscribed. Election Commissioners can only be removed from office prior to the expiration of their constitutionally mandated five-year term,[57] 'except in like manner and on the like grounds as a Judge of the [Supreme Court]'.[58]

The link to the judiciary is directly relevant for the removal of commissioners because it establishes a higher standard for interference by the political branches with the fourth branch than for regular administrative bodies. The logic is similar to that of judicial

[55] 'Sirisena Demands Repealing of 19th Amendment, Blames it for Political Instability' *The Times of India* (23 June 2019) https://timesofindia.indiatimes.com/world/south-asia/sirisena-demands-repealing-of-19th-amendment-blames-it-for-political-instability/articleshow/69914507.cms.

[56] Constitution of the People's Republic of Bangladesh, Art 118.

[57] ibid Art 118(3).

[58] ibid Art 118(5).

independence. If judges are directly appointed or easily removed by politicians, or the political branches have a say over their remuneration, promotion and other aspects of judicial functioning, then there is a predictable risk that courts will be influenced to make decisions favourable to elected representatives. Constitutional systems to lesser or greater degrees, therefore, attempt to insulate courts from political interference, in order to foster actual and perceived judicial independence and impartiality.

By ensuring that removal of an Election Commissioner in Bangladesh must meet the higher standard for removal of judges, rather than that for civil servants or administrative staffers, the constitutional text uses judicial independence as a way to level up election commission independence. Similar provisions in other constitutions, such as Article 215(2) of the Pakistani Constitution, follow the same logic. While a full-scale analysis of judicial independence in South Asia is beyond the scope of this chapter, it should be relatively uncontroversial to say that the region only imperfectly protects judicial independence. Despite the potential failings of tying the independence of election administration to that of the courts, it has been a frequent strategy in South Asian constitutionalism, for relatively persuasive reasons. Even while imperfect, the standard for judicial independence is generally higher than for other comparable institutional templates.

When it comes to judicial review of decisions made by election commissions, constitutions at times presume that the direct relationship between courts and election commissions is more hostile or conflict-ridden. Even if independent, the choices made by the fourth branch are consequential to electoral outcomes, the interests of political parties and broad swathes of society.[59] They are therefore often challenged in court. How courts view the role of election commissions in the separation of powers and in facilitating democracy are key factors in jurisprudence on election administration and political rights.[60]

Courts have sometimes seen their authority to hear cases involving election administration and commissions taken away by the constitution and/or statutes, and granted to special electoral courts or administrative tribunals. Afghanistan had adopted this approach,[61] prior to the takeover by the Taliban in 2021. It could be that carving out these types of cases from the regular courts or the apex court helps to preserve their independence, as it keeps them out of the political fray that inevitably accompanies decisions made by commissions around elections. It could also reflect a sense that courts are actually partisan actors, where judges are aligned with the party that appointed them, or perhaps that the judiciary as a whole is hostile to a current government. Who can engage in judicial review of the decisions of the fourth branch around elections is a context-specific decision for constitutional designers that involves trade-offs specific to a particular time and political history.

[59] M Katju, 'Mass Politics and Institutional Restraint: Political Parties and the Election Commission of India' (2016) 4(1) *Studies in Indian Politics* 77.

[60] MA Bhat, ch 14 in this volume.

[61] The Constitution of Afghanistan, Arts 56 and 86, as well the relevant electoral statutes, set up a system of dispute resolution. See also the Pakistani Constitution, which in Art 225 sets up the Majlis-e-Shoora (Parliament) with the authority to determine who shall hear electoral petitions.

D. Composition

One of the defining design questions for election commissions is whether they should be composed of experts, civil servants or representatives of political parties.[62] The membership of election commissions is of great significance due to the scope and importance of the discretionary decision-making that falls within their authority. The South Asian democracies have uniformly opted for the expert model, though partisan appointments have often been alleged.[63]

The obvious advantage of opting for the expert model is that there is likely to be greater perceived and actual independence if election commissioners are selected for their knowledge and professional backgrounds rather than their partisan affiliations. There is symmetry between the constitutional status of the commissions as independent entities, and the appointments made to them. Appointing experts can also be said to be likely to foster impartiality in comparison to the appointment of explicitly partisan representatives, though independence and impartiality do not necessarily coexist in all instances.

A contrast can be made with other fourth branch commissions, particularly those in Latin America, that adopt a 'partisan balance'[64] approach. In that model, the main political parties must be represented in the election commission. They are designed to be accountable to political parties and to have appointees behave in a manner that protects partisan interests. The approach, however, tries to balance out the interests of political parties, usually by having an equal number of appointees from each major party. The goal is not to suppress partisanship and put the commissions at arm's length from the other branches, but to provide a bridge between them. The partisan balance approach has often been adopted in the move away from armed conflict so that all major political parties feel that their interests will be respected and no one faction will be able to capture the mechanisms of election administration.[65] Partisan balance has also been adopted outside of the context of actual or feared armed conflict, including in situations where there are two, long-established, dominant parties competing with one another, as in the USA.[66]

One explanation for the emphasis on expertise and independence in South Asia is perhaps because of recognition of the need for election integrity in a post-colonial context. The South Asian fourth branch has often imposed national standards on sub-national elections, for example, where a local authority might be more likely to be captured by political interests.[67] There is a nation-building or capacity-building

[62] Wall et al (n 2) raises the 'expert' classification.

[63] Pal (n 5).

[64] F Estévez, E Magar and G Rosas, 'Partisanship in Non-Partisan Electoral Agencies and Democratic Compliance: Evidence from Mexico's Federal Electoral Institute' (2008) 27 *Electoral Studies* 257; J Hartlyn, J McCoy and TM Mustillo, 'Explaining the Quality of Elections in Contemporary Latin America' (2008) 41(1) *Comparative Political Studies* 73; F Lehoucq, 'Can Parties Police Themselves? Electoral Governance and Democratization' (2002) 23(1) *International Political Science Review* 29.

[65] Estévez et al (n 64).

[66] B Jackson, *Broken Promise: Why the Federal Election Commission Failed* (Ann Arbor, Priority Press Publications, 1990).

[67] Pakistan, for example, grants control over national but also other elections to the central Election Commission.

function assigned to some central election commissions in South Asia, especially in federations. It also represents an attempt to minimise the likelihood of corruption or clientelism finding a foothold within the election commission.[68]

Such an approach is at times counter to the interests of dominant parties, of which there have been several in South Asia, especially in the period immediately following national independence. Dominant parties likely have an interest in directing all institutions of the state, particularly in the early post-colonial years. This tension between independent institutions, on the one hand, and dominant parties, on the other, has arguably explained some of the conflicts between the fourth branch and governments of the day in South Asia.[69] The emphasis on independence and impartiality also recognises a need to constrain the state, even in a post-colonial context, where capacity-building is a priority. Despite these tensions in the context of dominant parties, South Asia constitutional designers have prioritised independence and expertise in the composition of election commissions.

E. The Duty to Assist: Inter-branch Politics

Another notable, though perhaps unrealised, feature of fourth branch constitutional practice is how it attempts to shape the relationships between the branches themselves. Among the most notable features is the direction in constitutions that the other branches must assist the election commission. Article 126 of the Bangladeshi Constitution states, 'It shall be the duty of all executive authorities to assist the Election Commission in the discharge of its functions'. Article 220 of Pakistan's Constitution uses similar language, though it extends the duty to assist to the executive 'in the Federation and in the Provinces'. The language in Article 220 reflects Pakistan's federal nature and the fact that the Election Commission has jurisdiction over both national and provincial elections.

Such constitutional language is not limited to South Asian constitutions. The South African Constitution establishes in Chapter 9 'State Institutions Supporting Constitutional Democracy', including the Electoral Commission along with five others.[70] These institutions are 'independent' according to Article 181(2), with individuals and 'organs of the state' barred from 'interfer[ing] with their functions' according to Article 181(4). Other 'organs of state', however, also have an affirmative duty to 'assist and protect these institutions to ensure [their] independence, impartiality, dignity, and effectiveness' according to Article 181(3).

The presence of a duty to assist the other branches assumes to some extent that there will be inter-branch conflict. It reflects the view that there will be competition between

[68] On anti-corruption, see AJ Brown, 'The Integrity Branch: A System, an Industry, or a Sensible emerging Fourth Arm of government?' in N Groves (ed), *Modern Administrative Law in Australia* (Port Melbourne, Cambridge University Press, 2014) 301–25.

[69] See, eg S Deva, 'Democracy and Elections in India: Reviewing the Role of the Election Commission and the Courts' in P-J Yap (ed), *Judicial Review of Elections in Asia* (Routledge, 2016) 38. See also Katju (n 59) 80 and 83.

[70] Fombad, 'Diffusion' (n 11).

the branches and seeks to manage it by directing one side to lay down its arms. Whether this goal is realisable is another matter. It might be that inter-branch competition and conflict are healthy, including with the fourth branch. Attempts to capture the fourth branch, however, go counter to the intention reflected in the text that election commissions must be independent.

It is unclear how much importance should be attributed to 'duty to assist' clauses, given that there is no obvious enforcement mechanism for breaches. There is only modest evidence that these types of provisions have been taken seriously as aids in constitutional interpretation by courts in dealing with cases involving election commissions, whether in South Asia[71] or South Africa.[72] They remain an innovation in constitutional design that has found purchase in South Asia.

IV. The Challenges to the South Asian Model

Neither South Asia generally nor its fourth branch institutions have been immune from incomplete democratic consolidation or the pressures of democratic decline. This section considers recent controversies besetting election administration in India, which remains the most influential country in the region. India has been identified in the literature on decline as a key case study, where democratic norms and the actual or perceived independence of important institutions have eroded.[73] The independence of the ECI, or lack thereof, has been the defining story in this downturn.

Democratic decline involves a number of features, which vary based on the account,[74] but the erosion of both norms and institutions that sustain healthy political and electoral competition are inevitably two elements. Independent electoral institutions are prime targets globally, and they have been attacked in some of the recognised cases of decline, such as Hungary, Poland and Turkey. 'Decline' is perhaps an imperfect term to use, including for some countries in South Asia, where democratic consolidation was incomplete in the first place. Pakistan, with its frequent periods of military rule, and Sri Lanka, with its civil war, autocratic Rajapaksa presidency and recent parliamentary controversies, are two examples of arguably incomplete consolidation.

To date, the South Asian election commissions have mostly evaded the most ham-fisted attempts at full capture that have marred other jurisdictions, with the Maldives being the notable exception. The fourth branch has been far from unscathed, however, and remains embroiled in conflict and controversy. The independence of the central institution of election administration appears fragile. The decision of the ECI on 3 May 2019 that Prime Minister Modi and one of his long-term and closest allies,

[71] Deva (n 69) 66.

[72] Though see how the Constitutional Court used the concept of constitutional duty in another context in relation to the President and prosecutorial forces in *Economic Freedom Fighters v Speaker of the National Assembly* [2016] ZACC 1.

[73] Mate (n 13); Khaitan, 'Executive Aggrandizement' (n 13).

[74] Bermeo (n 14).

Amit Shah, had *not* violated the Model Code of Conduct regulating political behaviour was controversial to say the least.[75]

In India, the Modi-led BJP government won majorities in the national elections in 2014 and again, overwhelmingly, in 2019. Prime Minister Modi has been credibly accused of disregarding independent checks on his power of all sorts, from the free press to the judiciary. The Election Commission of India appears to have bent to some extent to protect the interests of his government. The ECI was held in high esteem, at least since the move away from a dominant party democracy helmed by the Congress Party towards more truly multi-party competition.[76] Fali Nariman wrote that the ECI 'has now become one of the most significant constitutional institutions in [Indian] democracy. It is greatly respected because it acts independently and not in accordance with the wishes of the government for the time being.'[77]

Overall, the ECI has been respected for its expertise and non-partisanship for at least two decades. That period appears to be over. Senior former civil servants wrote a scathing letter to the President about the ECI's 'crisis of credibility' in 2021, and Opposition leader Rahul Gandhi accused it of 'capitulation' to Prime Minister Modi.[78] Sumit Ganguly, in assessing the ECI's actions during the Modi years, concludes that 'The ECI now stands compromised in the eyes of voters. Given how long this crucial watchdog institution was revered for neutrality and independence, this represents a fall from grace that is real and serious.'[79]

The appointment process has always been a weak link in the design of the Indian commission and conflicts around it have been prominent.[80] The President formally has the power to make the appointments to the Commission according to Article 324(2). The potential for partisan appointments has been ever-present and arguably occurred under previous governments.[81] Commissioners are also potentially subject to pressure from powerful political actors. The exuberant defence of the ECI's independence by then-Commissioner TN Seshan from 1990 to 1996 attracted the ire of the government of the day. The conflict eventually led to a statute implementing a multi member ECI, which was contemplated by Articles 324(2) and (3) of the Constitution. Article 324 foresees and enables legislation by Parliament as a constraint on the President's discretion around appointments to the ECI. Whatever the merits of a multi-member commission, it seems likely that the change was motivated at least partly by the Congress government's wish to dilute Seshan's influence.[82]

The Commission is currently led by a Chief Commissioner and has two other Commissioners. The current Chief, Sunil Arora, was appointed by the Modi government

[75] SK Ramachandran, 'Election Commissioner Ashok Lavasa Opts Out of Meetings on EC Code Till Dissent Is Recorded' *Hindustan Times* (18 May 2019) www.hindustantimes.com/lok-sabha-elections/ashok-lavasa-opts-out-of-meetings-on-ec-code-till-dissent-is-recorded/story-W2iKVSRGP39bmHUhEZLiGI.html.

[76] Katju (n 59); A Ahuja and SL Ostermann, 'From Quiescent Bureaucracy to "Undocumented Wonder": Explaining the Indian Election Commission's Expanding Mandate' (2018) 31 *Governance* 759.

[77] Deva (n 69) 43.

[78] S Ganguly, 'An Illiberal India?' (2020) 31(1) *Journal of Democracy* 193, 197.

[79] ibid.

[80] Pal (n 5); Singh and Roy (n 30) 28–34.

[81] Bhat (n 60).

[82] Deva (n 69) 44; *Seshan v Union of India* (1995) (SC).

as a Commissioner in 2017 and then elevated to Chief in 2018. Commissioner Ashok Lavasa was appointed by the BJP in 2018, after a long career as a civil servant. Another former senior civil servant, Sushil Chandra, was appointed as a Commissioner in 2019. Commissioner Lavasa has reportedly dissented from some recent decisions of the ECI that favoured Prime Minister Modi and/or the BJP.[83]

The Election Commission appears to have exercised its authority to aid the BJP in the important state of Gujarat, of which Prime Minister Modi was once Chief Minister. One of the distinguishing features of the extensive authority of the ECI is its power to announce the dates of elections. For state elections, the practice of the Commission was typically to declare the dates for all upcoming votes simultaneously. For state elections in 2018, the Commission deviated from this practice by announcing the state election dates for Himachal Pradesh earlier than for Gujarat. The BJP looked at the time to be liable to lose the state election in its long-time stronghold of Gujarat, which could have been devastating politically, given that it was Prime Minister Modi's backyard.

The delay provided a strategic advantage to the incumbent BJP. The Commission's Code of Conduct prevents certain expenditures by a government once an election has been announced. The goal is to prevent profligate spending sprees in the immediate pre-election period to win the favour of voters. By calling the election in Gujarat 13 days later than in Himachal Pradesh, the window was opened for expansive spending by the BJP government, which took full advantage of the additional time. The decision of the Commission was widely criticised in the press as being partisan-motivated or at least the result of pressure brought to bear by the BJP, including by former Commissioners.[84]

A second controversy, the 'office-of-profit' scandal,[85] related to actions by the Commission that aided the political interests of the BJP. It further raised questions about the ECI's independence. It involved the Commission's disqualification of 20 members of the Delhi Legislative Assembly. The 20 members all belonged to the Aam Aadmi Party. The BJP seemed likely to benefit from the disqualification as they were the odds-on favourites in the by-elections that would result. The Delhi High Court overturned the decision of the Commission in no uncertain terms.[86] It held that the Commission had not complied with natural justice and it vitiated the decision. The reasoning of the High Court did not explicitly call out the Commission for partisanship in its decision-making. The absence of credible reasons on the record for reaching the decision and the deficiencies in the ECI's process, however, suggests either partisan sympathies or political pressure from the BJP placed upon the Commission.

A question emerging from these incidents is whether improved constitutional design could have encouraged better resilience in the face of pressure from the central government. The independence of the ECI from the government appears to have

[83] Ramachandran (n 75).

[84] 'Delay in Gujarat Poll Date Announcement Creates "Grounds of Suspicion", Says Former Chief Election Commissioner' (*Huffington Post*, 13 October 2017).

[85] A Ghosal, 'Office-of-Profit Case: Delhi HC Strikes Down Disqualification of 20 AAP MLAs, Says EC Order is Bad in Law' *Indian Express* (23 March 2018).

[86] *Kailash Gahlot v Election Commission of India*, Delhi High Court (23 March 2018) https://indiankanoon.org/doc/20117949/.

been compromised, which is the very risk that fourth branch constitutional design is intended to minimise. Authorising appointments made in essence by the Prime Minister despite legal authority formally resting with the President is a recipe for perceived partisan interference. The recent controversies involving the ECI suggest actual partisanship. If the fourth branch is to be independent and impartial, then an alternative appointment process to that originally envisioned in India in 1950 is required.

V. Conclusion

The constitutionalisation of election administration is an established global trend. The democracies of South Asia have nearly uniformly adopted the fourth branch model with regard to election administration, though with important variations in how that model is implemented. The fourth branch continues to evolve, as evidenced by Sri Lanka's Nineteenth and Twentieth Amendments. The South Asian commissions reflect a particular view of the separation of powers as requiring a redistribution of some of the legal authority typically found in the legislative or executive branches to newer, democracy-enhancing institutions. Constitutional designers have attempted to enshrine formal independence and non-partisanship, though those institutional commitments are being challenged in the current climate of democratic decline. Whether fourth branch constitutionalism of this type can rise to the challenge is likely to be an important component of constitutional resilience to such threats, in South Asia and beyond.

14

Between Trust and Democracy: The Election Commission of India and the Question of Constitutional Accountability

M MOHSIN ALAM BHAT

I. Introduction

Scholars of political processes have increasingly come to recognise the role of professional electoral management bodies in sustaining the health and resilience of democracies.[1] One such well-documented body is the Election Commission of India (ECI). The architects of India's Constitution, who wanted the democratic process to provide the basis for unifying 'a highly disparate and divided population',[2] were aware of the complexities of introducing a universal adult franchise in India.[3] They appreciated the need for an independent electoral body to maintain the integrity of elections. The ECI was expected to introduce professionalism, competence, neutrality and legitimacy in the country's demanding electoral process. While the Indian Constitution (1950) authorised the legislature to prescribe the electoral procedure, it is the ECI that has become the most significant fulcrum of regulatory activity. It is a paradigm example of Bruce Ackerman's proposal that a 'new separation of powers' – with a gamut of independent institutions operating the liberal democratic process – favours the creation of a 'democracy branch' for conducting elections in an apolitical manner.[4] Beyond the constitutionally delegated power to prepare election rolls,[5] the ECI is expected to sanitise the larger electoral

[1] M Tushnet, 'Institutions Protecting Democracy: A Preliminary Inquiry' (2018) 12 *Law & Ethics of Human Rights* 181; M Pal, 'Electoral Management Bodies as a Fourth Branch of Government' (2016) 21(1) *Review of Constitutional Studies* 85; T Khaitan, 'Guarantor Institutions' [2021] *Asian Journal of Comparative Law, First View* 1.

[2] D Gilmartin and R Moog, 'Introduction to "Election law in India"' (2012) 11 *Election Law Journal* 136, 137. See also G Austin, *The Indian Constitution: Cornerstone of a Nation* (Oxford, Clarendon Press, 1966) 144.

[3] For an engaging discussion of these early debates, see O Shani, *How India Became Democratic: Citizenship and the Making of the Universal Franchise* (Cambridge, Cambridge University Press, 2017). See also AK Thiruvengadam, *The Constitution of India: A Contextual Analysis* (London, Bloomsbury Publishing, 2017) 148–51.

[4] B Ackerman, 'The New Separation of Powers' (2000) 113 *Harvard Law Review* 633.

[5] Constitution of India, Art 324.

process, which is the basis of democratic accountability and the only meaningful popular check on political governance.[6]

A large body of scholarship has extensively dealt with numerous aspects of the institution, especially its functioning, its dynamic role in the country's political landscape and the often-vexed question of its structural reform.[7] But it has remained silent on its legal accountability. The issue of legal accountability is crucial for at least three interrelated reasons. First, particularly since the 1990s, the ECI's power and range of functions have perceptibly grown. This has simultaneously raised concerns about the institution's overreach. Writing in the early 2000s, Susanne and Lloyd Rudolph argued that the ECI, along with India's Supreme Court and the President, had become the central feature of the country's 'new regulatory state'.[8] According to them, the traditionally powerful Parliament and the Council of Ministers had 'ceded pride of place' to these institutions as 'enforcers of rules that safeguard the democratic legitimacy of the political system'.[9] In light of this, as political scientist Sanjay Kumar has noted, there has been a rising 'discomfort' with the widening of the ECI's functions, and a concern that it may be 'exceeding its jurisdiction'.[10] The ECI has been rightly credited with the country's record of free and fair elections,[11] and has traditionally enjoyed a high degree of public trust.[12] But the concerns of institutional overreach do not bode well for public trust in the Commission. Transparency and accountability are crucial to mitigate the negative fallouts of the ECI's growing powers.

Second, the political landscape in which the ECI operates has dramatically changed since the 1990s, raising credible concerns about its objective and bipartisan functioning. During the 1990s and the first decade of the 2000s, the Indian electoral field was relatively fragmented, with considerably large and politically powerful opposition parties. This contentious balancing of political power among various electoral players provided the ECI with plenty of room for manoeuvre and arguably preserved its authority and autonomy. As India moves into a phase of single-party domination – due to the rise of the ruling Bhartiya Janata Party (BJP) and an extremely fragmented and

[6] Y Yadav, 'Representation' in NG Jayal and PB Mehta (eds), *The Oxford Companion to Politics in India* (Oxford, Oxford University Press, 2010) 347.

[7] There is a vast scholarship on the ECI. An important genre includes books written by former ECI officials. See SY Quraishi, *An Undocumented Wonder: The Great Indian Election* (New Delhi, Rupa Publications 2014); JM Lyngdoh, *Chronicle of an Impossible Election: The Election Commission and the 2002 Jammu and Kashmir Assembly Elections* (Delhi, Penguin Books India 2004). For other scholarship, see UK Singh and A Roy, *Election Commission of India* (Oxford, Oxford University Press, 2019); M Katju, 'Election Commission and Functioning of Democracy' (2006) 41 *Economic and Political Weekly* 1635; A McMillan, 'The Election Commission of India and the Regulation and Administration of Electoral Politics' (2012) 11 *Election Law Journal: Rules, Politics, and Policy* 187; E Sridharan and M Vaishnav, 'Election Commission of India' in D Kapur, PB Mehta and M Vaishnav (eds), *Rethinking Public Institutions in India* (Oxford, Oxford University Press, 2018) 417.

[8] SH Rudolph and LI Rudolph, 'South Asia Faces the Future: New Dimensions of Indian Democracy' (2002) 13 *Journal of Democracy* 52.

[9] ibid 59.

[10] S Kumar, 'Reforming Indian Electoral Process' (2002) 37 *Economic and Political Weekly* 3489, 3490.

[11] A Ahuja and SL Ostermann, 'From Quiescent Bureaucracy to "Undocumented Wonder": Explaining the Indian Election Commission's Expanding Mandate' (2018) 31 *Governance* 759.

[12] See McMillan (n 7) 190; SK Mitra and VB Singh, *When Rebels Become Stakeholders: Democracy, Agency and Social Change in India* (London, Sage Publications 2009) 37, 208–09 (empirically noting that ECI enjoys the highest degree of trust compared to other institutions).

weak opposition – the ECI must remain neutral. Democratic legitimacy, in times of single-party domination, will remain significantly contingent on the visibility of the institution's bipartisan functioning. The ECI's transparency, and hence its legal accountability, are key factors in this.

Third, there have been an increasing number of political controversies that have shrouded the ECI's decisions. For instance, in the previous round of national general elections (April–May 2019), the role of the ECI has been criticised in an unprecedentedly sharp fashion. Opposition parties have suggested that the institution has taken a soft gloves approach to the BJP's electoral behaviour. Three issues, which I introduce in greater detail later in this chapter, have particularly had an impact on the perceived credibility of the institution. The first is the persistent questioning of the ECI's support of electronic voting machines (EVMs). On 14 April 2019, almost all opposition parties rallied publicly against the ECI and questioned the institution on the EVM issue.[13] The opposition not only argued that the technology was opaque, but also questioned some election results favourable to the ruling party. The second issue has been the consistent controversy over election schedules. Numerous critics, especially in the opposition, have argued that the ECI's arrangement of voting dates has placed the ruling party at an advantage. The third issue has been the ECI's arguably lackadaisical approach towards campaign finance. The opposition has specifically targeted the government's electoral bonds scheme that, among other things, relaxes disclosure requirements for corporate political donations. The ECI, which otherwise has historically been an advocate of exacting disclosure standards, has not taken a critical stance on the policy.[14] These controversies have raised concerns about institutional capture among critical observers of the ECI. Some recent events have heightened these fears. During the 2019 national elections, the ECI was perceptibly lenient towards Prime Minister Narendra Modi in the enforcement of election campaign norms.[15] In December 2021, officials of the ECI held a meeting with the Prime Minister's Office after having been 'summoned' according to newspaper reports.[16] The proliferation of these concerns may threaten India's democratic credentials in the long term. Therefore, irrespective of views on individual policies, it is essential to take the ECI's legal accountability seriously.

This chapter focuses on one facet of the ECI's legal accountability: its operational accountability. Operational accountability may be contrasted with structural accountability. Structural accountability, which has historically dominated the literature on the ECI, relates to the design of the institution, its composition and personnel, and the appointment and conditions of service of its officials. An institution's structure has an obvious relationship with its accountability, especially with the independence of its officials. Operational accountability, on the other hand, relates to the ongoing legal inter-institutional relationships of oversight, transparency and reason-giving. Thus, operational accountability relies on legal tools that seek to maintain standards of behaviour and assessment of performance. While structural reform usually relies on

[13] See nn 121–23 and the accompanying text.

[14] See nn 131–36 and the accompanying text.

[15] See MA Bhat, 'ECI Is Not Up To the Task of Sanitising a Chaotic Electoral Process' (*The Wire*, 4 June 2019) https://thewire.in/politics/election-commission-model-code-hate-speech-religion.

[16] SY Quraishi, 'Summoning CEC, EC to PMO Is Outrageous' *The Indian Express* (18 December 2021) https://indianexpress.com/article/opinion/columns/summoning-cec-ec-to-pmo-is-outrageous-7678391.

legislation, operational accountability also relies on evolving institutional practices and juristic norms.[17]

This chapter argues that India's constitutional jurisprudence suffers from crucial blind spots in relation to the institution's operational accountability. The political stakes for India's democratic resilience make the ECI's accountability a matter of urgent juristic attention. While scholars have noted the ECI's historically expanding powers, what is often overlooked is that this expansion has been supported by the Indian Supreme Court's attitude of deference towards the institution. As this chapter will show, the Court has historically demanded greater transparency and accountability from political actors in the electoral field, by adopting what I call the 'framework of democracy'. Under this framework, the Court has endorsed a specific view of Indian democracy that I characterise as 'discursive democracy', which places public opinion formation – entailing free speech, freedom of information and public awareness – at its core. In applying this framework, the Court extended these discursive values of democracy to politically partisan actors and elected institutions. Throughout these celebrated election law judgments, the Court relied on the ECI as an ally in electoral reform, facilitating the latter's expanding powers. In contrast to political actors, the Court has adopted what I call the 'framework of trust' in the case of the ECI. This framework entails deference towards institutions that can maintain credible commitments towards the polity's long-term goals. While it is justifiably deferential towards the ECI in many respects, I argue that the framework of trust as currently applied by the Indian courts has assumed that there is no need to secure the ECI's accountability. The Supreme Court's jurisprudence, I argue, has been inattentive to how and when the ECI should be held accountable in the discharge of its functions. Consequently, the framework has failed to generate transparency and uphold the ideals of operational accountability. This chapter does not aim to propose a comprehensive legal framework for addressing this lacuna. Rather, it invites serious attention to the question of the ECI's operational accountability and suggests the directions that such a framework should take.

Section II of this chapter provides an overview of the ECI's constitutional status and functions, and situates the institution's historically expanding powers in the country's changing political and electoral context. The section argues that the Indian Supreme Court's deferential jurisprudence towards the ECI has supported this expansion. The subsequent sections explore the Court's role in greater detail. Section III focuses on how the Court developed the framework of democracy in a series of electoral reform cases, to mandate heightened standards of transparency and accountability for political actors. The ECI became an ally of the Court in implementing these reforms. In light of these cases, section IV seeks to theorise the ECI's institutional relationship with the Supreme Court. It argues that this relationship is mediated by the framework of trust, which is based on the ability of competent and autonomous institutions to maintain credible commitments to a polity's long-term goals. The frameworks of trust and democracy offer distinct approaches to the problem of accountability. While the framework of democracy is based on publicity and discourse, the framework of

[17] Polities can also ensure operational accountability through the participation of political institutions like legislatures. This mode of political accountability can complement operational accountability through legal or judicial means. This chapter focuses only on legal accountability, not this form of political accountability.

trust secures conditions of credible commitment. Section V illustrates this contrast between the two frameworks, taking the controversy around EVMs as a reference point. The section also argues that the framework of trust is inadequate in addressing the concerns of the ECI's transparency and operational accountability. Section VI concludes by proposing potential directions that judicial review of the ECI can take to better integrate these concerns of operational accountability.

II. Jurisprudence of Deference

The Indian Constitution grants the ECI the power of 'superintendence, direction and control' of the preparation of the electoral rolls and the conduct of all elections in the country.[18] The institution consists of the Chief Election Commissioner (CEC), and any additional election commissioners (ECs) who the President, as the nominal head of the executive bound by the advice of the Council of Ministers, may appoint. The Constitution secures the independence of the CEC by mandating their parity with Supreme Court judges in terms of removal. Parliament can legislate on the appointment and removal of the additional commissioners of the ECI, and provide for their conditions of service. Under these powers, Parliament has legislated the procedures for the appointment of ECs, the salaries and conditions of service for all election commissioners, and has given the ECI the power to determine its internal procedures.[19]

Since its inception, the ECI has come to perform three sets of functions. First, under the Constitution, it operates the electoral process by preparing electoral rolls, conducting elections and counting the votes.[20] Second, the ECI has acquired more powers and responsibilities through the Representation of People Acts 1950 and 1951, which serve as the principal parliamentary enactments governing the electoral process. The enactments provide the legal umbrella under which the ECI regulates various issues related to the electoral process, including corrupt electoral practices and the registration of political parties. Third, the ECI has also increasingly come to play an important role in issues related to elections which are not strictly part of the voting process. These include enforcing transparency of the credentials and finances of election candidates. An interesting example of the extended functions of the institution is the Model Code of Conduct.[21] The Code was first issued by the ECI in 1960 to provide extensive guidelines for political parties during elections. At present, it has many ambitious features, like regulating election manifestos and the behaviour of parties in power. While the Code is not strictly legal, all political parties have accepted being bound by it in practice.

The wide powers of the ECI, many of which are evidently beyond the text of the Constitution and the strict confines of parliamentary legislation, are a result of several

[18] Constitution of India, Art 324.

[19] Election Commission (Conditions of Service of Election Commissioners and Transaction of Business) Act, 1991.

[20] In addition to the operationalisation of the electoral process, the Constitution also provides that the ECI may be asked by the president or provincial governors to give their opinion on the disqualification of sitting members of the parliament and state legislatures. Constitution of India, Arts 103 and 192.

[21] See UK Singh, 'Between Moral Force and Supplementary Legality: A Model Code of Conduct and the Election Commission of India' (2012) 11 *Election Law Journal: Rules, Politics, and Policy* 149.

historical contingencies. The institution's powers expanded significantly during the 1990s, when, under the stewardship of its activist Chief Commissioner TN Seshan, the ECI increasingly adopted an interventionist role by regulating election campaigns and the participation of parties, voters and candidates.[22] Political scientists studying the institution's behaviour have not always been convinced of the desirability of this expansion. For example, Alistair McMillan has argued that the expanded role of the ECI may eventually come to undermine its credibility. As he notes,

> The lack of specificity regarding the scope of the Election Commission's role has resulted in a widening of its range of functions and control of executive authority during election campaigns. It has taken a quasi-judicial role in the regulation of nominations and candidacy; intervening in the appointment and posting of civil servants and the police; and targeting individuals who are believed to be involved in disrupting elections. The Commission has increasingly been involved in the regulation and control of political parties, from a situation where the main role was to allocate electoral symbols (and originally colored ballot boxes), to one where party constitutions have to be authorized.[23]

McMillan expresses a common scholarly concern when he states: 'the Commission's actions raise questions about whether it has exceeded the scope of its constitutional authority'.[24]

The existing accounts suggest a combination of various factors in the expansion of the ECI's powers. First, the ECI's powers have expanded alongside a considerably expanded electoral process. There are more voters in the electorate, more political parties and larger budgets, and consequently more claims invoking its jurisdictional authority. Second, the institution has continued to enjoy public legitimacy. Available evidence of public opinion suggests that, at least until very recently, there was a comparatively high degree of public confidence in the ECI's competence and neutrality.[25] Third, it may be the case that with the weakening of the dominant party system under the Congress Party domination and the emergence of a highly competitive political field in the 1990s, the ECI was expected to play the role of a 'facilitator of electoral competition',[26] further expanding its responsibilities. Fourth, some scholars have argued that this expanded remit may also reflect the weakness of other branches of government. As Rudolph and Rudolph note, the powers of the ECI – and other institutions such as India's Supreme Court – have expanded because the institution became 'more visible and effective in the 1990s as the reputations and authority of ministers, cabinets, and legislatures suffered'.[27]

Among these factors, the important role of the country's Supreme Court has not been adequately highlighted. The relationship between the Court and the ECI is characterised by a close association, marked by deference and collaboration. It is important to highlight some of the jurisprudential coordinates of this relationship. First, the courts

[22] For the role of Seshan in expanding the powers of the ECI, see D Gilmartin, 'One Day's Sultan: TN Seshan and Indian Democracy' (2009) 43 *Contributions to Indian Sociology* 247; C Jaffrelot, 'TN Seshan and the Election Commission' in SY Quraishi (ed), *The Great March of Democracy: Seven Decades of India's Elections* (Harmondsworth, Penguin Books, 2019) 104.

[23] McMillan (n 7) 189.

[24] ibid 198.

[25] Katju, 'Election Commission and Functioning of Democracy' (n 7).

[26] M Katju, 'Election Commission and Changing Contours of Politics' (2009) 44(16) *Economic and Political Weekly* 8, 9.

[27] Rudolph and Rudolph (n 8) 60. See also McMillan (n 7) 199.

have emphasised what they call the ECI's 'plenary' powers regarding election regulation. The courts have relied on this interpretation of the ECI's constitutional function to permit the latter to step into the shoes of other branches of government, including the legislature. Take the 1978 case of *Mohinder Singh Gill*.[28] The Supreme Court had to decide if state high courts had the power to decide the legality of the ECI ordering a re-poll in a constituency. The case involved the allegation that the ECI had violated norms of natural justice. Despite high courts having a wide jurisdiction in deciding matters of legality, Iyer J said that this would not extend to the ECI's decisions in matters of elections. The Supreme Court noted that the Constitution had left the judiciary out from any determination on elections, leaving such questions to be decided by the ECI through an election petition after the election had concluded.[29] According to him, the Constitution had provided the ECI with 'plenary' powers concerning the election process, and vested 'the whole responsibility for national and State elections and, therefore, the necessary powers to discharge that function'.[30] The Constitution had also provided that Parliament may step in to regulate elections.[31] But 'in areas left unoccupied by legislation' or 'surprise situations', the ECI continued to have the power to regulate.[32] The Court held that the phrases 'superintendence, direction and control' and 'conduct of all elections' in the Constitution 'are the broadest terms'.[33]

Iyer J appreciated the petitioner's concern that such an expansive interpretation of the ECI's powers may create 'a constitutional despot beyond the pale of accountability', a 'Frankenstein's monster who may manipulate the system into elected despotism'.[34] But responding to this concern, he only noted that if the ECI misused its powers, the Court would 'call the bluff, quash the action and bring order into the process'.[35] The Court, rather than articulating and resolving the problem of accountability, postponed it.

The Supreme Court was soon facing the problem of accountability again in the 1985 case of *Kanhiya Lal Omar*.[36] The Court had to determine if the ECI was competent to pass the Symbols Order that, in the absence of legislation, specified, reserved and allotted symbols to candidates standing for elections. Following Iyer J in *Mohinder Singh Gill*, Venkataramiah J interpreted the ECI's powers in relation to the electoral process to include 'all powers necessary for the smooth conduct of elections'.[37] According to him, the word 'election' under Article 324

> is used in a wide sense so as to include the entire process of election which consists of several stages and it embraces many steps, some of which may have an important bearing on the

[28] *Mohinder Singh Gill v Chief Election Commissioner* [1978] 1 SCC 405.

[29] See Constitution of India, Art 329(b). The provision states that 'no election to either House of Parliament or to the House or either House of the Legislature of a State shall be called in question except by an election petition presented to such authority and in such manner as may be provided for by or under any law made by the appropriate Legislature'.

[30] *Mohinder Singh Gill* (n 28) para 38. The Court referred to Art 324, whose clause (1) states, 'The superintendence, direction and control of the preparation of the electoral rolls for, and the conduct of, all elections to Parliament and to the Legislature of every State and of elections to the offices of President and Vice-President held under this Constitution shall be vested in a Commission'.

[31] Constitution of India, Art 327.

[32] *Mohinder Singh Gill* (n 28) para 39.

[33] ibid.

[34] ibid.

[35] ibid.

[36] *Kanhiya Lal Omar v RK Trivedi* [1985] 4 SCC 628.

[37] ibid para 9.

> result of the process. India is a country which consists of millions of voters. Although they are quite conscious of their duties politically, unfortunately, a large percentage of them are still illiterate. Hence there is need for using symbols to denote the candidates who contest elections so that the illiterate voter may cast his vote in secrecy in favour of the candidate of his choice by identifying him with the help of the symbol printed on the ballot paper against his name.[38]

Reiterating *Mohinder Singh Gill*, Venkataramiah J held that the 'plenary' power of the ECI permitted it to freely regulate 'in areas left unoccupied by legislation'.[39] He held that

> any part of the Symbols Order which cannot be traced to [the rules] can easily be traced in this case to the reservoir of power under Article 324(1) which empowers ECI to issue *all directions necessary* for the purpose of conducting smooth, free and fair elections. (emphasis added)[40]

These two elements – an expansive reading of the electoral process and the ECI's 'plenary' powers in unlegislated areas – have become definitive of India's election jurisprudence. In the 1996 case of *Common Cause*,[41] petitioners in a public interest litigation (PIL) argued that the Supreme Court must take steps against the political parties that were violating financial transparency requirements under income tax and companies' laws. The Court eventually passed strictures against the defaulting political parties, which included directing government departments to conduct inquiries. But the Court went beyond this and empowered the ECI to operate this process. Singh J directed the political parties to submit financial records to the ECI. The Court agreed with the argument raised by the ECI that 'the entire gamut of election is under the supervision and control of the Election Commission. ECI can issue suitable directions to maintain the purity of election and in particular to bring transparency in the process of election.'[42] Relying on this expansive interpretation of the electoral process, Singh J held that

> the expression 'conduct of election' is wide enough to include in its sweep, the power to issue directions – in the process of the conduct of an election – to the effect that the political parties shall submit to the Election Commission, for its scrutiny, the details of the expenditure incurred or authorised by the parties in connection with the election of their respective candidates.[43]

This became the basis for the Court to extend the powers of the ECI to get these documents, despite the existence of statutory authorities authorised to receive them, during the elections.[44] According to the Court, the ECI was 'justified in asking a political party to file before it the account of expenditure insured or authorised by a political party in connection with the election of its candidates during the course of general election/election'.[45]

[38] ibid.
[39] ibid para 16.
[40] ibid para 17.
[41] *Common Cause v Union of India* [1996] 2 SCC 753.
[42] ibid para 25.
[43] ibid para 26.
[44] ibid para 25.
[45] ibid para 27.

Thus, the election jurisprudence had granted a high degree of discretion and power to the ECI, primarily through interpreting electoral process broadly and the ECI as the plenary institution regulating it. Furthermore, the question of standards and processes of accountability had been left unclear.

III. Democracy and Distrust

The interpretation of the ECI's constitutional status, based on the Supreme Court's jurisprudence of deference, is just one source of the ECI's capacious powers in India's electoral process. I argue that the institution's powers have also expanded because they are tied with the Supreme Court's electoral reform ambitions. The Court has carried out its reforms through the ECI, endorsed the broadening of its activities and, as I will indicate towards the end of the chapter, inadequately developed the inter-institutional mechanisms of constitutional accountability. This has happened simultaneously with the Court's increasingly imposing higher standards of accountability on political actors. I will show that the Court has applied divergent frameworks to political actors and the ECI. Although the Court has applied frameworks mandating exacting standards of transparency and accountability with respect to the former, it has been more willing to defer in the case of the ECI.

A. The Framework of Democracy

In the 1990s, the Supreme Court started activating its jurisprudence of deference towards the ECI in a series of ambitious electoral reform cases. In these celebrated judgments,[46] it adopted a very specific view of Indian democracy, as a discursive democracy, based on the need for open-ended and well-informed public opinion formation. Discursive democracy is distinct from the standard representative models in its emphasis on the legitimation of political action through consistent public engagement with the reasons and purposes of state action.[47] Under this conception, elections are not the only process that legitimates democratic politics. Rather, they serve the larger process of democratic dialogue. Elections are a culmination of a broader discursive exchange among citizens that constitutes democratic self-government.

These values animate the court-led reform cases. In these cases, the Supreme Court did not approach the electoral process as a way of ensuring equal access to political power or entailing authenticity of representation. These cases are best interpreted as based on the ideals of discursive democracy – reflected in the freedom of speech and expression – as their governing logic. While the Court did not explicitly invoke this paradigm of democracy, its reliance on discursive democratic values makes clear its understanding of democracy in India. The Court interpreted the act of voting as a species

[46] For an overview, see M Mate, 'High Courts and Election Law Reform in the United States and India' (2014) 32 Boston University International Law Journal 267.

[47] See *below* note 60.

of freedom of speech and expression. Take the prominent example of the *NOTA* case.[48] The Supreme Court considered the constitutionality of election rules that provided for a publicly available record of voters who had not voted for any candidate during elections. Relying on precedent, Sathasivam CJ held that participating in the voting process was a facet of freedom of expression,[49] suggesting that the Court considered the values of discursive democracy to govern the logic of elections. According to the Court, deciding not to vote is as much a form of expression as voting, and hence should receive the protection of secrecy, just as voters do.[50] According to the Court, secrecy is crucial to the integrity of the electoral process, ensuring that voters are under no compulsion. At the root of the Court's decision was the need to preserve voting as discourse-generative. Secrecy of all voting choices including 'none of the above' (NOTA) was crucial because it would permit voters to express themselves 'without fear of reprisal, duress or coercion', facilitate wider participation in the electoral process[51] and encourage political parties to reform in light of citizen disapproval.

The *NOTA* case followed other seminal cases where the Supreme Court had built this framework in the context of the voters' right to an informed opinion. The Court had already started evolving a robust constitutional right to information drawn from the freedom of speech and expression. In most of these cases, the Court had reasoned that the right to know was entailed by the need to have an informed citizenry in a democracy.[52] Even though these cases often involved commercial speech, the Court relied on the democracy-enhancing and democracy-preserving qualities of the freedom of information, to link it with free speech. The citizens had a right to information to generate well-educated public opinion necessary for democratic life. This jurisprudence fit neatly with the evolving framework of discursive democracy in the electoral reform cases. The same ideals of free speech, democracy and the freedom of information extended to the electoral process. The Court emphasised that the public should be fully aware of the functioning of the government, the credentials of the representatives, and their ambitions and motivations. Thus, the discursive democracy framework mandated the transparency of relevant political facts.

The two cases that represent the evolution of this framework are *Association of Democratic Reforms* (*ADR*) in 2002 and *Public Union of Civil Liberties* (*PUCL*) in 2003.[53] The Court had to decide whether – first in the absence of parliamentary legislation (*ADR*) and later in contravention of it (*PUCL*) – candidates standing for elections could be obliged to reveal their educational qualifications, assets and criminal antecedents, if any. In both cases, the Court's answer was yes. It ruled that the voters' right to know – flowing from the discursive democratic ideal of free speech – mandated these disclosures.

In *ADR*, the Court had to determine if the Delhi High Court was right in directing the ECI, in response to a PIL, to collect and publicise information related to the candidates,

[48] *People's Union of Civil Liberties v Union of India* [2013] 10 SCC 1.
[49] ibid para 28.
[50] ibid para 39.
[51] ibid para 55.
[52] See Mate (n 46) 399–404.
[53] *Union of India v Association for Democratic Reforms* [2002] 5 SCC 294 (hereinafter *ADR*); *People's Union for Civil Liberties v Union of India* [2003] 4 SCC 399 (hereinafter *PUCL*).

in particular, any existing criminal cases and financial assets. The argument against the high court judgment was straightforward – that the existing parliamentary statute did not lay down any of these requirements and Parliament was the most appropriate forum for determining these policies. In *ADR*, the Supreme Court set itself to interpret the content and implications of the republican and democratic forms of government, for the need to have transparency of candidates' credentials. According to the Court, it was completely up to the voters to decide – based on their own 'relevant criteria' – who they wished to elect, even if it meant electing persons with a criminal record.[54] Following *Mohinder Singh Gill*, it noted that in the Indian participative democracy, periodic elections allowed the citizenry to conduct a 'social audit' on the government, which made it necessary that it was 'well informed' about the candidates.[55] This view of democracy fit with the right of information of citizens, based on the constitutional right of free speech. Relying on the larger jurisprudence of the right to know as part of free speech, the Court held that

> The people of the country have a right to know every public act, everything that is done in a public way by the public functionaries. MPs or MLAs are undoubtedly public functionaries. Public education is essential for functioning of the process of popular government and to assist the discovery of truth and strengthening the capacity of an individual in participating in decision-making process. The decision making process of a voter would include his right to know about public functionaries who are required to be elected by him.[56]

The Court was offering a very specific framework for upholding the need for expansive electoral disclosure. It interpreted Indian democracy as a discursive democracy that entailed the citizens' expansive right to know about the credentials of candidates. The integrity of this democratic choice had to be protected. And to do so, the Court had to ensure that relevant facts were not 'suppressed' from the voters.[57]

The Court's judgment in *ADR* had immediate political ramifications. Despite legislating for some disclosure, Parliament watered down key requirements laid down by the Court. The constitutionality of this parliamentary law was the subject of *PUCL*. In this case, the Supreme Court re-emphasised the discursive democracy reading of elections by highlighting the connection between freedom of speech, the right of voters to know the antecedents of the candidates, and free and fair elections. Shah J's opinion made the theoretical framework very clear. Every citizen has the right to freedom of speech, which includes the right to information. This right is necessary for a 'healthy democracy'.[58] Transparency in information – or well-informed public opinion – is constitutive of democracy itself.[59] One implication of this right was its application in periodic elections and the need for transparency. Specifically, in the context of elections, the right to know was crucial to have a well-informed citizenry that makes well-informed electoral choices. The Court found the legislation wanting with respect to these values and held it to be unconstitutional.

[54] *ADR* (n 53) para 22.
[55] ibid para 23.
[56] ibid para 30.
[57] ibid para 46.
[58] *PUCL* (n 53) paras 17–18.
[59] ibid paras 25–26 (per Shah J).

This discussion has some important implications for this chapter's argument. First, this is significant for our understanding of how the Supreme Court has developed the relationship between democracy and the adjudication of electoral reforms. Similar to the theorists often associated with different versions of communicative, discursive or deliberative democracy,[60] the Supreme Court in these cases has not treated the electoral process as the central process of the Indian constitutional democracy requiring *sui generis* governing ideals. Rather, the Court has read the electoral process, while an important one, as one among many other communicative processes linking the public sphere to the channels of political decision-making.[61] Thus, the ideals of discursive democracy, which were articulated in the larger social field, are *ipso facto* applicable in the electoral domain, though with added sharpness required by the context.[62]

Second, the application of this framework has been both implicitly and explicitly based on a distrust of politicians, in their individual capacity as well as their institutional capacity in the form of the legislature. From *Common Cause* onwards, and very much in *ADR* and *PUCL*, the Court adopted a dramatic vocabulary of *purity* of elections posed against the *pollution* caused by monetary and other forms of corruption by the political class. For example, in *Common Cause*, the Supreme Court raised the concern about unaccounted funds – or 'black money' – during the election, its entrenchment and perpetuation in the electoral system, leading to further corruption by the electorally successful candidates.

[60] See JS Dryzek, *Deliberative Democracy and Beyond: Liberals, Critics, Contestations* (Oxford, Oxford University Press, 2002) 54 ('Participation in the communicative action of the public sphere is very different from voting as a form of interest aggregation. This does not mean that voting should be banished, because election campaigns do provide one opportunity (among many others) for discursive transmission, and elections themselves constitute a reason for state actors to listen to the public sphere. There is a major ontological shift entailed in terms of thinking of democracy in terms of intersubjective communication within the public sphere, as opposed to voting within the state.'). Similarly, Young argues that from the perspective of 'liberal democratic politics', voting 'is the primary political act' that 'consists in various groups putting out their interests and competing for those votes'. In contrast, she supports the deliberative model where there is an 'open discussion and the exchange of views leading to agreed-upon policies. In parliamentary discussions participants often claim that theirs is the most just and reasonable proposal. Most democracies contain other institutions and practices of political discussion and criticism in which participants aim to persuade one another of the rightness of their positions'. IM Young, *Inclusion and Democracy* (Oxford, Oxford University Press, 2002) 22. Deliberative democrats do not dismiss elections but treat elections not as the primary mode of democratic process but one among others. For example, Amy Gutmann and Dennis Thompson argue that, 'Deliberative democrats recognize of course that decisions must be made – even when the reason-giving process is incomplete. On any conception of democracy, elections must be held, and in elections citizens express their will without giving reasons. But deliberative democrats tend to emphasize the provisionality of political outcomes more than their finality'. A Gutmann and DF Thompson, *Why Deliberative Democracy?* (Princeton University Press, 2009) 15–16. They also note that, "[i]n deliberative democracy an important way these agents take part is by presenting and responding to reasons, or by demanding that their representatives do so, with the aim of justifying the laws under which they must live together. The reasons are meant both to produce a justifiable decision and to express the value of mutual respect. It is not enough that citizens assert their power through interest-group bargaining, or by voting in elections'. ibid 4.

[61] For a discussion of how the Indian Supreme Court's decisions in relation to electoral transparency and the right to information fit into a larger history of activism, see Mate (n 46) 119–24.

[62] Mate has characterised this oeuvre of the Indian Supreme Court as the Indian 'positive rights' participatory model, which focuses 'specifically on the rights of listeners to information and centers on individuals' ability to actually vote and effectively participate in the political system'. According to Mate, this model recognises the accountability function of free speech, by mandating that political actors and institutions have an 'affirmative obligation' to provide voters with information 'to promote better decision making and governance'. ibid 137–38.

Third, it should come as no surprise that the Court explicitly rejected the argument consistently made by the central government that the appropriate avenue for mandating these legal obligations is Parliament. One may be tempted to draw links with scholars like John Ely, who ground judicial review within anxieties over political trust.[63] But the text of these judgments gives us a reason to pause. While the distrust in political branches formed the background – even created the urgency – for the Court's intervention, it did not directly constitute the jurisprudential framing. Instead, the Court's justifications borrowed from the values of discursive democracy as the jurisgenerative framework for enhancing electoral transparency and mandating disclosure of politically relevant facts.

B. The ECI as an Ally

What is the role of the ECI in these court-led electoral reforms? This question came up in *ADR* and *PUCL*, and the Supreme Court followed the coordinates laid down in the previous cases. In both cases, political parties and the government argued that the governing legislation did not provide the ECI with any powers to regulate these facets of the electoral process. After having laid down the transparency requirements mandated by the ideals of discursive democracy, Shah J in *ADR* held that the ECI was well within its powers to actualise the voters' right to information. According to him, the institution's powers were plenary in all matters related to the electoral process. The Indian Constitution permitted the ECI to regulate areas that were 'left unoccupied by legislation',[64] since Parliament could not address every eventuality. The 'silence of statute' would, Shah J held, have 'no exclusionary effect except where it flows from necessary implication'.[65] By extension, the Court had the power to direct the ECI 'to fill the void' to facilitate voters to be well informed.[66] The 'judiciary must step in', noted Shah J, 'to provide a solution till such time the legislature acts to perform its role by enacting proper legislation to cover the field'.[67] This was an odd formulation simply because the non-inclusion of statutory requirements is arguably as good as their intended exclusion. The Court did not engage with the question of whether this was a case of legislative policy rather than legislative silence.

The absence of law was soon revealed to be a red herring. After the Court's ruling in *ADR*, Parliament amended the Representation of People Act 1951 to introduce a selection of disclosure requirements for candidates, many of which diluted the requirements laid down in the judgment. The amendments also introduced a provision that limited disclosure only to the requirements under legislation or executive rules, irrespective of any court order or ECI regulation. Parliament wanted to categorically rebut the argument that disclosure requirements were covered by legislative silence. In *PUCL*, the Court held that the dilution of requirements in *ADR* violated the voters' right to

[63] JH Ely, *Democracy and Distrust: A Theory of Judicial Review* (Cambridge, MA, Harvard University Press, 1980).
[64] *ADR* (n 53) para 23.
[65] ibid para 25.
[66] ibid para 45.
[67] ibid para 45.

information, and hence the constitutional right to freedom of speech and expression. But Shah J's majority opinion did not address the obvious institutional problem the amendment had created. Now that Parliament had explicitly removed what *ADR* interpreted to be legislative silence, on what basis could the ECI exercise its power to enforce the disclosure requirements? Reddi J was more forthcoming in his concurring opinion. He noted that in *ADR*, while the Court had recognised that the ECI could exercise 'residuary powers' in areas left unoccupied by legislation to regulate the electoral process, the Court had decided to lay down the guidelines itself, in order 'to give quietus to the possible controversies that might arise', and they would be enforced by the ECI.[68] The ECI was expected to be the mediating institution that would enforce transparency norms based on the Court's interpretation of democratic values. Thus, these expansive powers of the ECI – interpreted by courts as 'plenary' in the constitutional scheme – were tied to the Court's ambitions of sanitising the electoral process.

Between *ADR* and *PUCL*, a very specific picture of the ECI's constitutional authority emerges. In principle, the ECI's powers are bound by parliamentary legislation. But it no longer remained constrained by those boundaries when the Court decided to enforce its democratic norms through the ECI as its ally in electoral reforms. The ECI's expanding powers are entwined with those of the Court: specifically, the Court's expansive interpretation of the electoral process, its extensive interventions in the governance of this process and its endorsement of the ECI as an institution it can trust to enforce politically risky reforms. I propose that we should take precisely this curious aspect – the inter-institutional relationship of trust between the Supreme Court and the ECI – as a significant ingredient of the latter's constitutional status.

IV. Trust and Accountability

A. Theorising the Framework of Trust

Trust is not alien to constitutional theorising. Going back to the historical origins of liberal constitutionalism, when John Locke described the government as the trustee of the community, the notion has offered a significant background to constitutional relations.[69] This also applies to the constitutional theorising of the separation of powers.[70] Most famously, Ely's theory – based on a representation reinforcement theory

[68] *PUCL* (n 53) para 107 (per Reddi J).

[69] M Loughlin, *The Idea of Public Law* (Oxford, Oxford University Press, 2003) 100. Recently, Evan Fox-Decent has argued that the state should be understood as a fiduciary of people, which in turn should be understood as the basis of the rule of law. See E Fox-Decent, *Sovereignty's Promise: The State as Fiduciary* (Oxford, Oxford University Press, 2011).

[70] For some recent examples, see JL Neo, 'Autonomy, Deference and Control: Judicial Doctrine of Separation of Powers in Singapore' (2018) 5 *Journal International & Comparative Law* 461 (arguing that the ongoing discussions over the separation of powers in Singapore are intricately linked with the 'culture of trust' among institutions); C Möllers, *The Three Branches: A Comparative Model of Separation of Powers* (Oxford, Oxford University Press, 2013) 36; J Fowkes, *Building the Constitution: The Practice of Constitutional Interpretation in Post-Apartheid South Africa* (Cambridge, Cambridge University Press, 2016) 50–94 (using the notion of trust as a way of interpreting South Africa's voting rights jurisprudence).

of the judicial review – invokes the limits of trust we can have in democratically elected governments.[71] More recently, Rosalind Dixon has argued the relevance of trust in constitutional design and the ordering of judicial power.[72] But beyond constitutionally locating the judicial branch, constitutional conversations have not systematically taken the notion of trust as seriously in inter-institutional relations. For example, trust is only implicit in Ackerman's field-opening *The New Separation of Powers*,[73] which argues for constitutional scholarship to take non-judicial and non-political constitutional institutions seriously.

The political science literature has taken trust – in particular, institutional trust – as an important factor of institutional design and performance. For example, in his seminal work on the European Union institutions that I will draw from, Giandomenico Majone has argued that the delegation of powers to non-majoritarian institutions can be based on such institutions being conceived as either agents or trustees.[74] Delegation to agents is often done to reduce decision-making costs. Agents are expected to implement the policy choices of their principals. In contrast, delegation to trustees is often done to enhance credible commitments to long-term policy goals. Such institutions are not agents of the principal in an ordinary sense, but are trustees in a fiduciary relationship with an obligation towards the larger policy goals. Some institutions, like most independent central banks across the world, are trustee institutions, which are created to maintain economic credibility and direct their activities not to the enforcement of the government's policy choices, but rather to the long-term objective of economic well-being. Institutions can behave in both the modes of agency and trusteeship. Majone gives the example of the European Commission, which fluctuates between agency and trusteeship depending on its field of activity.

Some relevant features of trust are worth highlighting here. First, trust, in the words of Russell Hardin, is a 'three-part relation',[75] where the trustor is optimistic about the trustee performing certain things. Thus, a relationship of trust exists in the context of the trustee having relevant skills with respect to expected activities.[76] A person's trustworthiness is connected to her competence in the specified task. Second, in addition to competence, trustworthiness also includes the trustee's commitment to fulfil her obligations. Hardin and other scholars of trust describe this as the requirement of credible commitment.[77] In order to exhibit credible commitments, institutions must have an 'encapsulated interest' in fulfilling their trust obligations, which would make trust

[71] See Ely (n 63) 181–83.

[72] See R Dixon, 'Constitutional Drafting and Distrust' (2015) 4 *International Journal of Constitutional Law* 819.

[73] Above n 4.

[74] G Majone, 'Two Logics of Delegation: Agency and Fiduciary Relations in EU Governance' (2001) 2(1) *European Union Politics* 103.

[75] R Hardin, *Trust and Trustworthiness* (New York, Russell Sage Foundation, 2002).

[76] C McLeod, 'Trust' in EN Zalta (ed), *The Stanford Encyclopedia of Philosophy* (Fall 2015 edn) https://plato.stanford.edu/archives/fall2015/entries/trust/.

[77] See DC North and BR Weingast, 'Constitutions and Credible Commitments: The Evolution of Public Choice in 17th Century' (1989) 49 *English Journal Economic History* 803; M Levi, 'A State of Trust' in V Braithwaite and M Levi (eds), *Trust and Governance* (New York, Russell Sage Foundation 1998) 77, 86; M Levi and R Sherman, 'Rationalized Bureaucracies and Rational Compliance' in Cr Clague (ed), *Institutions and Economic Development* (Baltimore, Johns Hopkins University Press, 1997).

obligations self-enforcing.[78] There must be reputational and other costs to behaviour that deviates from trust obligations. Institutional incentives and disincentives should be structured in line with these obligations. Finally, trust is directly proportional to the extent of discretion held by institutional actors.[79] A polity delegates to trustees who exhibit credible commitment to fulfil its long-term goals without the pressures of the ordinary political calculus. Trustees consequently enjoy a domain of autonomous action insulated from interference.

Bureaucratic and expert bodies are central examples of entities that are expected to perform their respective functions as trustee institutions. Jurisdictions across the world have legally incorporated their independence by securing the appointment and removal of their members, autonomous functioning and the provision of competent staff.[80] Election management bodies like the ECI serve precisely as such trustees by precluding partisan capture of the democratic process. This model recognises that a bill of rights and regular elections are insufficient, and independent institutions are required to maintain electoral integrity in the polity.

Trust is relevant not only at the moment of the initial delegation, but also as part of the adjudication of institutional boundaries. Scott Shapiro argues that the conceptually central feature of the law is the 'economy of trust', where 'legal systems are not simply distributions of authority and responsibility, but of trust and distrust as well'.[81] Shapiro notes that legal systems are planning systems that arrange, on an ongoing basis, powers and responsibilities among the diversity of political actors and institutions, depending on the extent to which they can be trusted to accomplish the objectives of the plan. According to him, these attitudes of trust and distrust are central to judicial interpretive methodology because they determine the boundaries of discretion of the various actors in a polity.[82] Courts are involved in enforcing and distributing functions, powers and limitations. In doing so, they engage in the constitutional interpretation of trust.

The conceptualisation of trust illuminates how relationships of institutions like the ECI with other public institutions have evolved. In the case of the ECI, there are three different, yet overlapping, types of trust. The first is trust in the ECI based on its competence, which I call professional trust. Throughout India's election law jurisprudence, courts have seen the electoral process to be a logistically challenging exercise demanding administrative and technological expertise. These include the creation of electoral rolls, the registration of parties and candidates, and the conduct of elections through ballots or machines, among other responsibilities. The ECI, as a bureaucratic entity, has historically succeeded in fulfilling this need, and consequently created a ground for professional trust. The second is trust based on the independence of the ECI, since it is understood to be insulated from political interference. Political trust in the ECI is based on the notion that the institution will be constituted and operated in a non-partisan

[78] Hardin (n 75) 1–10.

[79] P Dasgupta, 'Trust as a Commodity' in D Gambetta (ed), *Trust: Making and Breaking Cooperative Relations* (Oxford, Blackwell, 1988) 49.

[80] See P Tucker, *Unelected Power: The Quest for Legitimacy in Central Banking and the Regulatory State* (Princeton, Princeton University Press, 2018).

[81] SJ Shapiro, *Legality* (Cambridge, MA, Harvard University Press, 2011) 313.

[82] ibid 331–52. For an application of the framework of trust to constitutional interpretation, see JM Balkin, *Living Originalism* (Cambridge, MA, Harvard University Press, 2011) 46–47.

fashion, that the ruling dispensation will not house it with partisans, and consequently its officials will not be beholden to any political party.[83] The third is trust based on the neutrality of the ECI in terms of their substantive beliefs. Ideological trust perceives the ECI to be an ideologically disinterested party, with the sole aim of professionally enforcing common rules of engagement in an objective manner. As scholars of ECI have noted, 'the long-term credibility of a referee institution', like the ECI, 'turns on its perceived neutrality' by political actors and the electorate.[84] The success of the ECI is the result of it having 'put in place a set of policies to ensure neutrality with respect to' voters, politicians and political parties.[85]

As would be evident, these types of institutional trust do not operate in isolation but are overlapping and interconnected. For example, ideological trust is compellingly dependent on the perception of the ECI as a professional entity – where professionalism is widely perceived to be substantively neutral and constitutional rules of engagement are accepted as objective. Note that each of these types of trust, by their very existence, also creates a corresponding mistrust in other entities – hence, there is an economy of trust and distrust. Professional trust in the ECI corresponds with courts' assessment of their own professional competence, or lack thereof, to deal with what they perceive to be a technocratic or material administrative exercise.[86] Political trust and ideological trust reflect mistrust in politically partisan actors or representative branches since there is a perceived assumption of their potential for bias.

This economy of trust is essential to fully appreciating the expanding contours of the ECI's powers through legal and judicial channels. Courts have shown reluctance to interfere in a range of the ECI's activities owing to trust in the institution's competencies and policy judgments. In many cases involving the ECI, courts have been inclined to not write detailed judgments, but to defer to the ECI through the instrument of unreasoned orders relying only on facts. For example, when the ECI decided to prohibit exit and opinion polls without legislative authority, the Supreme Court did not decide the matter on merits. Rather, it adjourned the case to await a decision by Parliament and left the issue at the 'liberty' of the ECI in the meantime.[87] This economy of trust thus explains the jurisprudence of deference and the Supreme Court's approach to the ECI as an ally in its electoral reform agenda.

B. Accountability Bounded by Trust

The frameworks of discursive democracy and trust offer different approaches to inter-institutional relationships. The framework of discursive democracy arrives at the

[83] These premises of political trust substantially depend on whether the appointment, tenure and service conditions of the ECI's officials, especially the CEC and other ECs, maintain their independence from the political executive. India has had a mixed record on this front. See MMA Bhat, 'Governing Democracy Outside the Law: India's Election Commission and the Challenge of Accountability' [2021] *Asian Journal of Comparative Law, First View* 1.

[84] Ahuja and Ostermann (n 11) 13.

[85] ibid.

[86] For a discussion on how 'material' competencies are central to how institutions like the ECI should be understood in the constitutional scheme, see Khaitan (n 1) 1, 6–11.

[87] Order quoted in McMillan (n 7) 197.

question of inter-institutional relationships from the perspective of distrust. It emphasises the role of public discourse to legitimise political practices and hence pushes for transparency of purposes, justifications and reasons for behaviour. In India's electoral reform cases, the Supreme Court applied the framework of discursive democracy to mandate higher disclosure requirements from electoral actors. The Court was far from deferential to the authority of politicians, and even held Parliament's attempt to narrow down these requirements as unconstitutional. In contrast, the framework of trust is designed precisely for respecting the decision of the authority based on expert – not public – reason. As such, the latter is based on the notion that there is good reason to believe that the authority is committed and competent in the exercise of its functions. As I have shown above, the framework of trust best captures the approach of the Indian Supreme Court towards the ECI. The Court has deferred to the ECI's discretion – based on professional, political and ideological trust in the ECI – even when the ECI's reasons are insulated from public view.

This orientation towards insulation and discretion in the framework of trust creates a certain tension with accountability. As Margaret Levi has noted, trust is risky because it is based on – and measured in – low investment in 'information, monitoring, and sanctioning'.[88] In larger-scale contexts, scholars of trust – whether interpersonal, political or institutional – have noted the importance of systems of accountability, shared values and sanctions in strengthening trust. But trust becomes relevant precisely when monitoring is either not feasible or is costly.[89] There is an inverse relationship between trustworthiness and the need to monitor.[90] As Levi notes, 'the more trusting an individual is the lower the personal investment she will make in learning about the trustworthiness of the trusted and in monitoring and enforcing his compliance in a cooperative venture'.[91] It should not be surprising that trustee institutions often encounter crises of legitimacy and accountability. As Majone notes, 'While agency costs result from a less than complete control of the agent's behaviour, fiduciary costs arise from a poorly defined accountability framework'.[92]

Despite this tension, the framework of trust has its own attendant model of accountability. The notion of accountability bounded by trust requires other institutions to secure the conditions of credible commitment. The judiciary would maintain the institutional structures and boundaries that ensure the independence, competence and neutrality of trustee institutions. Since these conditions can often be threatened by political interference, judicial review would be a key instrument for disciplining political action that threatens to undermine institutional design and arrangements. This is

[88] M Levi, 'A State of Trust' (unpublished manuscript, University of Washington, Department of Political Science, 1996), quoted in C Offe, 'How Can We Trust Our Fellow Citizens?' ME Warren (ed), *Democracy and Trust* (Cambridge, Cambridge University Press, 1999) 42, 46.

[89] See Offe (n 88) 47.

[90] For example, McLeod (n 76) notes that, 'The truster might try to reduce this risk by monitoring or imposing certain constraints on the behaviour of the trustee; yet after a certain threshold perhaps, the more monitoring and constraining s/he does, the less s/he trusts that person. Trust is relevant "before one can monitor the actions of … others" or when out of respect for others one refuses to monitor them. One must be content with them having some discretionary power or freedom. Hence, one cannot reject being vulnerable.'

[91] M Levi, 'A State of Trust' in Braithwaite and Levi (n 77) 77, 78.

[92] G Majone, *Dilemmas of European Integration: The Ambiguities and Pitfalls of Integration by Stealth* (Oxford, Oxford University Press, 2005) 75.

precisely what is at stake in the conversations around the institutional reforms of the ECI. Numerous reports have suggested changes in the institution's design – the removal of election commissioners, a transparent and consultative appointment process, the creation of a separate ECI secretariat – to secure its independence and competence.[93] Accountability within the framework of trust is also at stake in the constitutional evaluation of political decisions regarding these questions of design.[94] A comprehensive evaluation of the Indian Supreme Court's decisions from the perspective of accountability within the framework of trust is outside the purview of this chapter.[95] Instead, I will focus on whether this model is adequate to create transparency in all areas of the ECI's functioning.

V. Trust Over Democracy

I have argued that the framework of trust, despite the conceptual tensions, offers a model of accountability oriented towards securing the structural conditions of credible commitment of the ECI. But this notion of accountability bounded by trust does not have adequate resources to generate accountability of a different character: accountability of the ECI's ongoing performance, particularly the transparency and publicity of the reasons for its policy. This genre of accountability – what I will call operational accountability – is crucial to ensuring that the ECI is functioning optimally and there is ongoing democratic confidence in the institution.

This lacuna is most clearly visible in the high-pitched debate in India over electronic voting machines, or EVMs. The ECI introduced EVMs in earnest in the 2004 elections, after having tested them in a phased manner since 1998. This mode of voting in elections had been a subject of legal controversy for years, inviting courts to first decide upon the jurisdiction of the ECI to introduce the new technology and to subsequently find ways to make the process more politically acceptable. In 2013, the Supreme Court in *Subramanium Swamy* upheld the conduct of elections through EVMs but ordered the institution of VVPAT (voter verifiable paper audit trail) for authentication.[96] The controversy, though, emerged again during the 2019 general election cycle. Opposition parties and civil society organisations raised concerns about machine malfunction, with many claims of EVM tampering. The ECI consistently denied these allegations and

[93] See Core Committee on Electoral Reforms, 'Background Paper on Electoral Reforms' (December 2010) https://lawmin.gov.in/background-paper-electoral-reforms; Ministry of Law and Justice of India, 'Report of the Committee on Electoral Reforms' (May 1990) https://adrindia.org/sites/default/files/Dinesh%20Goswami%20Report%20on%20Electoral%20Reforms.pdf; Law Commission of India, 'Report No 255: Electoral Reforms' (March 2015) 69–79, https://lawcommissionofindia.nic.in/reports/report255.pdf.

[94] This question has most prominently come before the court in cases involving the appointment of additional election commissioners. The concern has been that such appointments are intended to compromise the independence of the institution, particularly by diluting the control of the chief election commissioner. See *SS Dhanoa v Union of India* [1991] 3 SCC 567; *TN Seshan v Union of India* [1995] 4 SCC 611.

[95] For a discussion of these questions of structural reform and a critique of the Indian Supreme Court's approach, see Bhat, 'Governing Democracy Outside the Law' (n 83); RR Iyer, 'The Election Commission and the Judgment' (1996) 31 *Economic and Political Weekly* 37.

[96] *Subramanian Swamy v Election Commission of India* [2013] 10 SCC 500 (hereinafter *Subramanian Swamy*).

insisted that EVMs were fully effective and secure. Despite these assurances, numerous opposition parties approached the Supreme Court, claiming to represent 75 per cent of the electorate that voted for them cumulatively in the previous national election in 2014. The petitioners argued that the ECI must conduct verification of at least 50 per cent of EVM VVPATs. In 2019, Gogoi CJ in *Chandrababu Naidu* denied the request.[97]

Before evaluating the Indian Supreme Court's approach based on the framework of trust in the EVM cases, it is useful to discuss how the framework of democracy may apply to the controversy. This is what the German Constitutional Court did in 2009.[98] The petitioners challenging the introduction of computer-controlled voting machines in Germany argued that the policy violated the rule of law, democracy and the principle of the public nature of elections. Of these, the most important ground for the German Court's decision was the public nature of elections. The petitioners argued that since the votes were stored and counted electronically, the public did not have any means of effectively monitoring the electoral process. The government accepted the existence of the constitutional principle of public elections, but argued that the German Constitution did not demand 'each individual act [be] subject to an individual check'.[99] The Court disagreed. It inferred the constitutional requirement of publicity from 'the fundamental constitutional options for democracy, the republic and the rule of law',[100] and held that

> [t]he public nature of elections is a fundamental precondition for democratic political will-formation. It ensures the correctness and verifiability of the election events, and hence creates a major precondition for the well-founded trust of the citizen in the correct operation of the elections. The state form of parliamentary democracy, in which the rule of the people is mediated by elections, in other words is not directly exercised, demands that the act of transferring state responsibility to parliamentarians is subject to special public monitoring.[101]

The maintenance of public trust was central in the German Court's conceptualisation of publicity. Note that the value of public trust here was different from what I have called the 'framework of trust' in the Indian cases. This framework of trust views institutions as possessing fiduciary duties towards the long-term policy goals of the polity. These institutions enjoy a high degree of discretion and deference. On the other hand, public trust – as invoked by the German Court in its EVM case – tethered its purpose, terms and boundaries to democracy. Publicity was required because citizens monitoring the electoral process was the very basis of democratic legitimacy. The Court was not operating with a discursive conception of democracy, and hence democratic discourse was not the centrepiece of its reasoning. It was operating with a more classical republican conception of democracy, where shared political discourse is seen to constitute the

[97] *N Chandrababu Naidu v Union of India*, [2019] SCC Online SC 686.

[98] See BVerfG, Judgment of the Second Senate of 3 March 2009 – 2 BvC 3/07, www.bverfg.de/e/cs20090303_2bvc000307en.html (hereinafter *German Voting* case). For a detailed discussion on the transnational policy and judicial discourse on electronic voting, see AD Maurer and J Barrat, *E-Voting Case Law: A Comparative Analysis* (London, Routledge, 2016).

[99] *German Voting* case (n 98) para 58.

[100] ibid para 108.

[101] ibid para 107.

public will over the meaning of the common good. This shared discourse was the 'basis of political integration'.[102] As the Court noted:

> The democratic legitimacy of the elections demands that the election events be controllable so that manipulation can be ruled out or corrected and unjustified suspicion can be refuted. This is the only way to facilitate the well-founded trust of the sovereign in the correct formation of the representative body. The obligation incumbent on the legislature and on the executive to ensure that the election procedure is designed constitutionally and is implemented properly is not sufficient by itself to impart the necessary legitimacy. Only if the electorate can reliably convince itself of the lawfulness of the transfer act, if the elections are therefore implemented 'before the eyes of the public' … is it possible to guarantee the trust of the sovereign in Parliament being composed in a manner corresponding to the will of the voters that is necessary for the functioning of democracy and the democratic legitimacy of state decisions …[103]

The German court held that the transparency of the electoral process – on the condition of 'public examinability' – was the rule, while any deviations in 'constitutional interests' were exceptions.[104] The tying in of democracy to this reasoning helps in identifying the elements in the governance process that are important enough to require publicity. Since democracy was a common concern of all citizens, each citizen should be able to comprehend its 'central steps' without requiring any expertise.[105] In short, the framework of democracy channelled the concerns of accountability, transparency and public-ness of the electoral process. In relying on this approach, the German Court proffered democracy as entailing an open process based on shared discourses and reasons that would engender public scrutiny, and thus the trust of the public. Implicit in the Court's decision was the view that a technocratic approach to elections would not be able to achieve this. Only publicly shared and comprehensible discourse could ground democratic legitimacy of this kind.

This is in contrast with the approach of the Indian Supreme Court. In the first constitutional case on EVMs, the 1984 case of *AC Jose*,[106] the Supreme Court was much more guarded about the ECI's powers. Before an amendment formally introduced the EVM system in India's legislative scheme in 1989, the ECI had already started using EVMs in some states. The ECI's introduction of electronic voting through a notification had not received the government's approval. In *AC Jose*, the petitioner had filed an election petition against the result, challenging electronic voting. The ECI argued that since it was the plenary constitutional authority for the conduct of elections, it did not require primary legislation to create new election processes. But the Supreme Court held that the ECI could not exercise legislative powers that overrode Parliament's authority. According to the Court, the Constitution vested in the ECI 'merely all the executive powers and not the legislative powers'.[107]

[102] ibid para 109.
[103] ibid para 109.
[104] ibid para 112.
[105] ibid para 153.
[106] *AC Jose v Sivan Pillai*, [1984] AIR 921.
[107] ibid para 22. The Supreme Court held that this 'would convert the Commission into an absolute despot in the field of election so as to give directions regarding the mode and manner of elections by passing the

Parliament endorsed and incorporated electronic voting in 1989. But there were continuing concerns about the security of EVMs. The constitutional challenge finally came in 2012, first in the Delhi High Court and later, on appeal, in the Supreme Court. During the challenge in the Delhi High Court, the main argument of the petitioners was that there was a lack of transparency in elections conducted purely through EVMs. They asserted that there was no 'convincing proof that the EVM has rightly registered the vote cast by a voter in favour of a particular candidate'.[108] Moreover, since there had been no comprehensive trials – something that ECI and the High Court accepted – and the technology was not completely confidential, there was 'a possibility of [a] machine being skewed or … vulnerable to fraud'.[109] The petitioners demanded the paper trail of EVM votes, failing which, they argued, 'the system cannot be treated as amounting to conducting free and fair elections'.[110] The Delhi High Court accepted that the 'trust and confidence in the electoral process is an essential prerequisite'.[111] But it constructed a dichotomy between transparency of the electoral process and secrecy of the ballot, noting rather mysteriously that with the introduction of a paper trail, 'the confidentiality in the system would be lost'.[112] This was an odd conclusion, considering that this reasoning would apply equally to traditional ballot voting. What appears to have been at stake for the High Court was the ECI's concern regarding the costs of the paper trail and the additional polling personnel. Between transparency and logistics, the High Court chose to favour the latter, by simply deferring to the ECI's assessment without any independent and clear reasons.

The Delhi High Court's deferential approach was doubtlessly a product of the framework of trust, specifically the reliance on the competence of the ECI in determining the logistical procedures and costs. The problem was that it reduced the complexity of the accountability question to a zero-sum game. On the question of accountability, the High Court held that the only 'appropriate course of action' was for the 'politicos … to make suitable provisions in the law by appropriate amendments'.[113] The High Court did accept towards the end of its order that some concerns regarding the vulnerability of the machines may be well-founded, and that wider consultation and further research may be required. But, for the Court, 'it would be for the Legislature or the Election Commission to consider the aforesaid or other related aspects'.[114] The Court did not explore the possibilities of introducing transparency, avenues of inclusive democratic oversight or justifications of the ECI's policy outside the assertions of expertise.

provisions of the Act … under cover of Art, 324. If the Commission is armed with such unlimited and arbitrary powers and if it ever happens that the persons manning the commission shares or is wedded to a particular ideology, he could by giving odd directions cause a political havoc or bring about a constitutional crisis, setting at naught the integrity and independence of electoral process, so important and indispensable to the democratic system': ibid para 21. Evidently, this approach to the ECI's powers is in tension with the position laid down in *Mohinder Singh Gill* (n 28).

[108] *Subramanian Swamy v Election Commission of India*, Writ Petition (Civil) No 11879 of 2009, 17 January 2012, para 11.

[109] ibid para 11.

[110] ibid para 11.

[111] ibid para 16.

[112] ibid para 17.

[113] ibid para 25.

[114] ibid para 26.

On appeal, the Supreme Court was more receptive to the petitioner's arguments. Early during the hearing, while the ECI was – in the language of the Supreme Court – 'reluctant' to introduce a paper trail,[115] the Court issued directions to the ECI to conduct consultations and tests. Pursuant to the Court's instructions, the ECI held meetings with political parties, which included demonstrations of the technology, and conducted – again, in the language of the Court – 'a thorough examination and full discussion'.[116] All this, in the view of the Court, indicated that the VVPAT system was successful. The Supreme Court in *Subramanian Swamy* ultimately mandated the ECI to introduce a paper trail through the VVPAT system. The Court noted that,

> [f]rom the materials placed by both the sides, we are satisfied that the 'paper trail' is an indispensable requirement of free and fair elections. The confidence of the voters in the EVMs can be achieved only with the introduction of the 'paper trail'. EVMs with VVPAT system ensure the accuracy of the voting system. With an intent to have fullest transparency in the system and to restore the confidence of the voters, it is necessary to set up EVMs with VVPAT system ...[117]

The Supreme Court was inclined to develop tools for transparency outside the framework of trust by directing the ECI to adopt a paper trail. But there continued to be serious limitations in the Supreme Court's approach. The Court did not adequately articulate its justifications, especially regarding why the paper trail – and nothing less, more or different – was indispensable for free and fair elections.[118] The judgment was unclear about why EVMs were consonant with voter confidence, though only when accompanied by VVPATs. The Court also did not develop a doctrinal structure for its decision. Nor did it elaborate upon the framework of democracy, including the normative foundations of transparency in the electoral process and the legal tools to ensure it, which it seemed to be alluding to in its judgment. Transparency, publicity and accountability were at best the subtexts of the judgment. Finally, the Court left the implementation of its order completely at the discretion of the ECI.[119] The Court noted that since the ECI 'has to handle one million' polling booths, it must be permitted to 'introduce VVPAT in gradual stages'.[120] But the Court did not mandate any specific scale or timeline for VVPATs. The extent of the electoral enterprise somehow justified a high degree of deference. The Court did not consider adopting remedial tools, including interim and supervisory orders, to ensure a transparent implementation on an ongoing basis.

The longer trajectory of the Supreme Court's engagement with the EVM issue reveals that these problems have persisted, and even heightened. After the Court's mandate on VVPATs, the immediate question that arose was whether additional steps were needed to secure voter confidence in the EVM system. For example, in *Prakash Joshi*,[121] the

[115] *Subramanian Swamy* (n 96) para 27.

[116] ibid para 27.

[117] ibid para 28.

[118] The Court referred to 'materials' on the basis of which it made up its mind, but did not reveal the substance of these materials, which continue to not be in the public domain.

[119] Sathasivam CJ 'permitted' ECI to introduce a paper trail 'in gradual stages or geographical-wise in the ensuing general elections. The area, State or actual booth(s) are to be decided by the ECI and the ECI is free to implement the same in a phased manner': *Subramanian Swamy* (n 96) para 29.

[120] ibid para 29.

[121] *Prakash Joshi v Election Commission of India*, Writ Petition (Civil) No 983 of 2017, 30 October 2017.

petitioners demanded verification and matching of VVPATs from at least 10 per cent of randomly selected polling stations. This, according to the petitioners, was key for the electorate to be confident that their votes were being properly recorded. After all, if public confidence in the EVM system was at stake, there was no reason to stop at recording VVPATs and not conduct subsequent verifications based on them. The underdeveloped understanding of transparency and voter confidence in *Subramanian Swamy* could not be of any assistance in deciding the controversy. In cases like *Prakash Joshi*, the Supreme Court refused to decide this question, while only noting that it had left the matter to the discretion of the ECI.[122] Despite judicial disinterest, 21 opposition leaders approached the Court again in *Chandrababu Naidu* (2019), demanding at least 50 per cent VVPAT verification. The petitioners argued that the practice of the ECI that verified only one polling station of each assembly segment in a parliamentary constituency, which amounts to only 0.44 per cent of the EVMs, was too little to inspire confidence. They argued that the enhanced extent of verification was of utmost importance to 'ensure a regular and statistically significant scrutiny process' to 'remove any doubt from the minds of the public that the EVM had been hacked or tampered with'.[123] The petitioners only implicitly and ambiguously relied on notions of the trust of the electorate, democratic legitimacy and transparency. This ambiguity – or, at any rate, imprecision – filtered into the Court's decision. Gogoi CJ noted that the ECI had not 'responded very favourably to the prayers' – a fact that may have eventually determined the Court's decision.[124] The ECI argued that increasing the verification would cause 'infrastructure difficulties', leading to a delay of five or six days.[125] It also argued that the Court should not accept the petitioner's argument because the ECI, 'a constitutional body, is satisfied on the integrity of the EVMs'.[126] Gogoi CJ accepted the ECI's claims.[127] While he endorsed the ECI's position, he noted that some 'reasonable' accommodation of the petitioner's concerns would 'lead to greater satisfaction amongst not only the political parties but the entire electorate of the country'.[128] He held that taking into account 'the totality of the facts of the case and need to generate the greatest degree of satisfaction in all', the verification should be increased to five polling stations in every assembly constituency.[129] The Court's order did not provide any clear reasons for this determination, a detailed description of the policy calculation of the ECI that may justify its reluctance or a description of what was normatively at stake in the 'greater satisfaction' of the political actors.

There is a clear line connecting *Subramaniam Swamy*, *Chandrababu Naidu* and the cases in between. There is a reluctance of the Supreme Court to evolve a jurisprudence

[122] See also *Kamal Nath v Election Commission of India*, Writ Petition (Civil) No 935 of 2018, 12 October 2018 (quoting *Prakash Joshi*).

[123] *N Chandrababu Naidu v Union of India*, Writ Petition (Civil) No 273 of 2019, Written Statement on behalf of the Petitioners, 27 February 2019, para 18 (on file with author).

[124] ibid para 4.

[125] ibid para 6.

[126] ibid para 7.

[127] ibid para 9 ('At the very outset the Court would like to observe that neither the satisfaction of the Election Commission nor the system in vogue today, as stated above, is being doubted by the Court insofar as fairness and integrity is concerned. It is possible and we are certain that the system ensures accurate electoral results').

[128] ibid para 9.

[129] ibid para 10.

of accountability for the ECI. Rather, the Court has approached the controversies before it either by adopting a deferential attitude towards the ECI or in an ad hoc manner.[130] The accommodation of the ECI's concerns was not backed by justification and principle, or an adequate account of its reasons that would facilitate transparency, publicity and accountability.

The most recent expression of the limitations of the Supreme Court's approach – where the framework of trust is untethered from a concern for constitutional accountability – is the as yet undecided *Electoral Bonds* case.[131] The case involves the constitutionality of the electoral bonds scheme introduced by Parliament in 2018. The scheme, among other things, allegedly undermines transparency in campaign finance by providing for anonymous political donations and the removal of limits for corporate donations. A recent study has revealed that until 2021, more than 870 million US dollars had been donated through the scheme, 92 per cent of which were corporate donations.[132] A sizeable majority of these funds was received by the ruling BJP. These findings have further raised concerns among the critics that the scheme undermines the integrity of the democratic process.

During the initial hearings for interim orders, the ECI had taken the position that the scheme would have 'serious repercussions [and] impact on the transparency aspect of political finance [and] funding of political parties'.[133] Despite this, Gogoi CJ, rather than demanding electoral transparency, issued an unseemly order that required that all political parties that had received donations through electoral bonds submit the details of the donors and the amounts to the ECI in a sealed envelope. This, according to him, would ensure that the interim arrangement did 'not tilt the balance in favour of either of the parties but … [ensured] adequate safeguards against the competing claims of the parties which are yet to be adjudicated'.[134] Since the Court continued to delay hearing the matter on merits, the petitioners approached the Court for an interim stay again. This time, the ECI, rather surprisingly, took the opposite view and told the Court that staying the scheme would undermine the efforts of reducing unaccounted money in the election system. On the other hand, the petitioners argued that an interim stay and an urgent hearing on merits were crucial for preserving democracy. Invoking the familiar framework of democracy in India's election jurisprudence, the petitioners argued that 'the electors have the right to know the source and background' of election finance.[135] The Supreme Court rejected this argument and denied the application

[130] The ad hoc nature of the Indian Supreme Court's adjudication may reflect the larger pattern of the institution's behaviour that Chintan Chandrachud called '*panchayati* eclecticism'. See C Chandrachud, 'Constitutional Interpretation' in S Choudhry, M Khosla and PB Mehta (eds), *The Oxford Handbook of the Indian Constitution* (Oxford, Oxford University Press, 2016) 73.

[131] *Association of Democratic Reforms v Union of India*, Writ Petition (Civil) No 333 of 2015 (hereinafter *Electoral Bonds*). For a detailed discussion of the case, see G Bhatia, ch 11 in this volume.

[132] Association for Democratic Reform, 'Electoral Bonds and Opacity in Political Funding' (10 August 2021) https://adrindia.org/sites/default/files/ElectoralBondsNote_March_July2021_updated.pdf.

[133] *Electoral Bonds* (n 131), Interim Order, 12 April 2019, para 5.

[134] ibid para 12.

[135] 'Supreme Court Reserves Orders on Plea to Stay Electoral Bonds; Election Commission Opposes Stay' (*Live Law*, 24 March 2021) www.livelaw.in/top-stories/supreme-court-reserves-orders-on-plea-to-stay-electoral-bonds-171639.

for an interim stay.[136] Bobde CJ noted that the ECI had received sealed covers from political parties, suggesting that this process – despite being completely opaque to the electorate – would meet democratic standards.

From the point of view of the Supreme Court's jurisprudence applying the framework of democracy to India's election process, its orders in the electoral bonds matter are both uncharacteristic and counterintuitive. But at the same time, these orders reflect that the Court's approach towards ECI is coming full circle. The Court has deferred to the ECI by making it the authority for assessing whether political parties are meeting the standards of electoral ethics. The Court has also deferred to the ECI's (somewhat alternating) assessments about the desirability of the scheme. This attitude towards the ECI has come at the expense of the values of transparency and accountability, which have been the hallmark of the Court's jurisprudence on democracy. As the framework of democracy slips out of the Court's reasoning, the only paradigm that remains is the framework of trust towards the ECI.

VI. Conclusion: The Challenge of Operational Accountability

This chapter has sought to highlight the entrenched blind spots in India's constitutional jurisprudence in relation to the ECI's operational accountability. First, it gave an account of the Indian Supreme Court's jurisprudence of deference towards the ECI. The Court also viewed the ECI as an ally in its election reform cases. Both these facets – deference and institutional alliance – have facilitated and supported the expansion of the ECI's powers over time. Second, the chapter showed how the Court's approach to the ECI is best understood within the framework of trust. This framework is based on deference to institutions like the ECI on the grounds of their neutrality, competence and objectivity. But the framework of trust, in contrast with the presumed framework of democracy that the Indian Supreme Court has applied in the case of politically partisan actors, does not ensure the ECI's operational accountability. Third, the chapter sought to illustrate this through the EVM and electoral bonds controversies, where trust in the ECI may have reached counter-productive proportions.

The need for greater operational accountability for the ECI is further substantiated by the fact that there have been serious questions about the institution's performance even in areas where it has functional competence. For instance, the ECI's performance in terms of voter registration appears to have violated legal norms on some notable occasions. In the 1995 case of *Lal Babu Hussein*,[137] the ECI removed persons from electoral rolls en masse on the grounds that some localities were predominantly concentrated with 'foreigners'. Ahmadi CJ struck down these orders, laying down that any exclusion from the electoral rolls required an individual assessment. Despite this, just two years later, the ECI passed orders to exclude more than 350,000 electors from the voting lists

[136] See *Electoral Bonds* (n 131), Interlocutory Application No 183625 of 2019, 26 March 2021.
[137] *Lal Babu Hussein v Electoral Registration Officer*, [1995] 3 SCC 100.

in the state of Assam, on the grounds that they were 'doubtful' citizens. In none of these cases has the ECI been fully transparent about the grounds of its orders.[138]

Another set of instances has involved the implementation of the Model Code of Conduct. During the previous national elections, critics argued that the ECI was favourable to the ruling BJP while enforcing the Code. The Code does not permit any candidate to appeal to religion or caste to garner votes. During the election cycle, there were complaints against at least 21 candidates. While the ECI found merit in 15 of these complaints, the only complaints it dismissed without citing any reasons were the ones against the Prime Minister and the party president of the BJP. To make matters worse, there was not much to separate their speeches from those who were found to have violated the Code.[139] When one of the commissioners wished to make his dissenting opinion public, the CEC rejected his request.[140]

These instances reveal the importance of operational accountability, especially in service of the credibility of India's election process. They also reveal that the ECI's neutrality, professionalism and objectivity must be interrogated based on evidence, rather than automatically presumed. But, as this chapter has shown, the present approach of courts, based on the framework of trust, does not adequately address this concern. The legislature can introduce legislation that secures operational accountability, but currently, there is no mandated system ensuring the ECI's operational accountability to Parliament. In this absence, there is a greater need for courts to address this lacuna. Courts are well suited for this role. First, as this chapter has shown, courts have been the major driver for extending the powers of the ECI. If courts have performed this role, the judicial space must also simultaneously generate democratic accountability to deepen the legitimacy of the ECI's widening powers. Second, courts are well positioned to use the tools of judicial review to enhance transparency, and demand public reasons without introducing partisan politics in the functioning of the ECI.

[138] For a recent study raising questions about voter deregistration, see K Saifullah, A Shariff and MA Bhat, 'Up to 15% of voters left out of rolls, without even a fair hearing' *The Times of India* (4 November 2018) https://timesofindia.indiatimes.com/blogs/toi-edit-page/up-to-15-of-voters-left-out-of-rolls-without-even-a-fair-hearing.

[139] See Bhat, 'ECI Is Not Up To the Task' (n 15).

[140] 'CIC Upholds Refusal of EC to Share a Note of Dissent by Ashok Lavasa over MCC Violation Complaints against PM during 2019 Lok Sabha Polls' (*The Leaflet*, 20 April 2020) https://theleaflet.in/cic-upholds-refusal-of-ec-to-share-a-note-of-dissent-by-ashok-lavasa-over-mcc-violation-complaints-against-pm-during-2019-lok-sabha-polls.

15

The Turbulent Journey and Overlooked Opportunities of Electoral Democracy in Bangladesh

MUHAMMAD OMAR FARUQUE

I. Introduction

Bangladesh is a parliamentary democracy with a system of periodic direct elections based on the universal adult franchise. Democracy is one of the four basic principles of the Bangladesh Constitution.[1] The operationalisation of electoral democracy in Bangladesh is delegated to the Election Commission (EC).[2] This constitutional delegation seemingly gives a strong mandate to the Commission, requiring the other branches of the government to assist it in its functions.[3] However, in the absence of strong democratic and guarantor institutions, the implementation of electoral democracy in Bangladesh has always been fraught. The country has experienced different degrees of consolidation, backsliding, decay and resilience in its 51-year-long constitutional journey since Independence. Despite its strong mandate, the lack of constitutional consolidation has prevented the EC from adequately performing its role in preserving and strengthening the culture of electoral democracy. Where there has been some progress in consolidation, it has not come from the operationalisation of some existing aspect of constitutional design. Rather, electoral democracy began to be consolidated under an allegedly 'undemocratic' caretaker government (CTG) system. The CTG is a consensus-based addition to the Constitution by way of the Thirteenth Amendment in 1996. However, the Appellate Division (AD) of the Supreme Court of Bangladesh[4] scrapped the CTG system on the grounds of it being 'undemocratic' and thus was ultra vires in accordance with the basic structure of the Bangladesh Constitution. In so doing, the AD ironically caused the de-consolidation of electoral democracy. The AD struck down the CTG system in order to ensure the continuation

[1] Constitution of the People's Republic of Bangladesh 1972, Arts 8 and 11.
[2] ibid Art 119.
[3] ibid Art 126.
[4] Bangladesh Supreme Court consists of two divisions namely Appellate Division and High Court Division under Art 94(1) of the Bangladesh Constitution.

of Bangladesh's democracy. While this was a compelling justification for striking down the Amendment, the Court's decision failed to appreciate the consolidation that had already been achieved by the CTG.

This chapter will first analyse the EC-centric design of electoral democracy, followed by an inquiry into the general history of the misuse of the EC that had resulted in the introduction of the CTG system. The chapter will then comparatively analyse how elections have worked under military, incumbent civilian and caretaker governments to explore and evaluate how democracy has been shaped by these three types of elections. Following this, through a critical analysis of the understanding of uninterrupted representative democracy in the majority judgment of the AD, it will be argued that the majority judgment has failed to take a consolidation-friendly approach to democracy. This is because the AD had failed to fully appreciate the way in which Bangladeshi democracy improved under the CTG system.

The chapter concludes with a consideration of the factors that could shape the future development and consolidation of a resilient electoral democracy. Overall, this chapter advocates for taking into account the history of constitutional struggles, including the use of martial law, the use of constitutionalism as a doctrine of political legitimacy,[5] the lack of institutional comity and the inherent potential of resilience in the polity.

II. Mandate of the Election Commission: A Toothless Tiger?

The initial constitutional design of the Constitution of Bangladesh positioned the EC at the centre of electoral democracy. The first constitutional document of Bangladesh, ie the Proclamation of Independence, 1971, laid down the foundation for its democracy.[6] For the first time, the 1972 Constitution conferred primary responsibility on the EC for holding free, fair, just and honest elections.[7] The Representation of the People Order, 1972 (RPO) detailed the necessary rules and procedures for all elections, including the election of Members of Parliament, the President and local government representatives.

The EC has been conferred plenary, supervisory and discretionary powers for such free, fair, just and honest elections, including the power to prepare the electoral roll and delineate the geographical boundaries of constituencies.[8] Furthermore, the law granted the EC broad powers to regulate and control the activities of any officials, staff and members of law enforcement agencies who are involved in the election process.[9] The EC has the power to transfer government officials, including high-ranking officials, such as Divisional Commissioners, Metropolitan Police Commissioners, Deputy Commissioners (the administrative chief of a district) and the Superintendents of Police (the Chief Police Officer at the district level).[10] This provision seeks to neutralise the risk

[5] MJA Chowdhury, 'Elections in 'Democratic' Bangladesh' in M Tushnet and M Khosla (eds), *Unstable Constitutionalism: Law and Politics in South Asia* (Cambridge, Cambridge University Press, 2015) 193.

[6] Tajuddin Ahmed's Radio Speech on 10 April 1972; MH Khan, 'Genesis of Bangladesh's Constitution' *The Daily Star* (17 April 2016) www.thedailystar.net/op-ed/genesis-bangladeshs-constitution-1209718.

[7] Bangladesh Constitution, Arts 118–26; see especially Art 119(2).

[8] ibid Art 119; *AFM Shah Alam v Mujibul Haque* [1989] 41 DLR (AD) 68.

[9] See generally Election Officers (Special Provisions) Act, 1991.

[10] The Representation of the People Order 1972 (RPO), Art 44E.

of incumbent governments attempting to create a partisan set-up through the placement of government employees.

The EC has the power to halt polling at any stage if it observes that fair and impartial elections are not possible due to political pressure, threats or other subversive activities.[11] The EC also has the power to suspend or cancel the candidacy of any party if the candidates or their agents engage in illegal activities.[12] In investigating any irregularities, the EC can form Electoral Inquiry Committees, comprising judicial officers.[13] Upon receiving complaints, those committees are given the power to hold investigations and inquiries, and can compel the presence of any person involved as they deem fit.[14] In doing so, Electoral Inquiry Committees can summon and enforce attendance, require the discovery and production of any document and material object, or, like civil courts, order the requisition of any public record under the Code of Civil Procedure, 1908.[15]

In addition to these 'semi-formal adjudicatory' committees, 'vigilance and observation' teams conduct in situ visits and submit reports to the EC every three days during elections.[16] Significantly, the EC also has the power to regulate its own procedures[17] to conduct its activities and fulfil its mandate. In doing so, the EC can exercise its inherent power to fill any gaps in the law,[18] and can order re-polling where irregularities are found anywhere in the entire electoral process.[19]

To discharge these responsibilities meaningfully, the EC has been granted significant powers and has been provided with the necessary financial and human resources. Under the Election Commission Secretariat Act, 2009, the government is required to allocate money to the EC. To ensure the financial independence of the EC, the current legal framework does not give the executive any veto powers over the EC's budget and expenditure.[20] As an independent body, the EC's officials are immune from legal action for the bona fide exercise of their powers.[21]

The discussion above shows how, on paper, the EC is an independent institution with a wide range of powers. However, as the discussion below will show, this independence has not been realised on the ground through the independent exercise of such powers.[22] The EC has been vulnerable to political capture, which has undermined its efficacy and reputation. Apart from the elections under the CTG, the activities of the EC demonstrate that it has been used to ensure and sustain favourable political arrangements for particular political actors. The EC operates in the broader context of a corrupt

[11] ibid Art 91.

[12] ibid Art 91e.

[13] ibid Art 91A.

[14] Bangladesh Election Commission, National Election Management Manual (Dhaka, 2018) 100.

[15] RPO (n 10) Art 91D(1).

[16] National Election Management Manual (n 14) 102.

[17] RPO (n 10) Art 91D (4).

[18] *Altaf Hussen v Abul Kashem* [1993] 45 DLR (AD) 53 [11].

[19] *Ataur Rahman v EC* [2010] 15 BLC (HCD) 506. [The HCD validated the order of re-polling by the EC when it was challenged on the ground that the allegations were not brought on election hours.] See particularly para 24.

[20] The Election Commission Secretariat Act 2009, ss 7(2) and 16.

[21] National Election Management Manual (n 14) 99.

[22] SM Akram and SK Das, 'Bangladesh Election Commission: A Diagnostic Study' (Transparency International Bangladesh, 2006) www.ti-bangladesh.org/research/ES_ElectionCommission.pdf.

political culture. It is a context in which constitutional actors have failed to develop and promote a democratic ethos or establish strong institutions.

For instance, although the electoral laws provide a degree of financial independence to the EC, it has been reported that this has been hindered. The salary of the Chief of the EC (CEC) was denied on technical grounds when he did not show support for the ruling political party.[23] The Court condemned such activities as being contrary to the EC's independence.[24]

Moreover, there is evidence to suggest that appointments to the EC have been politically motivated. For example, in 2006 it appeared that the CEC had urged the government to appoint additional commissioners to the EC in order to secure a majority vote for a fresh electoral roll favouring the incumbent government.[25] Under the existing provision, the number of commissioners was not specified. The move was widely criticised, and to thwart the risk of volatility as to the formation of the EC, the Fifteenth Amendment restricted the number of election commissioners to four.[26] But the problem had not been solved with that amendment either, as Bangladesh did not have any guiding law, rules or procedures for the appointments of election commissioners. Bangladesh's Constitution bestows on the President the power to appoint election commissioners within the ambit of a guiding law as required under Article 118(1). Ironically, the law was only enacted in 2022, after 50 long years of the adoption of the Constitution. In the absence of clear legal rules, in 2012, President Zillur Rahman formed a 'Search Committee' to obtain recommendations of possible candidates.[27] This system was revised in 2017 with a difference in the Committee's composition. Whereas the former Committee consisted of four members, the latter had six. Major political parties criticised the formation of these committees, although they both included a Supreme Court judge and several other ex officio members. They were the chairman of the public service commission, the Comptroller and the Auditor General. The 2017 version of the Search Committee had two civil society members as well.[28] The reason behind the criticism was the absence of a legal framework that could check the partisan composition of the Search Committee. Evidence suggests that the ECs formed under these two Search Committees could not conduct elections in a free and fair manner and without political manipulation.[29] However, The Appointment of the Chief Election Commissioner and other Election Commissioners Act, 2022 has now been passed in the Parliament, fulfilling a long-neglected constitutional requirement. This new law gives the President the power to constitute a Search Committee which is a slightly modified

[23] *CEC and Three Others v Comptroller and Auditor General* [2005] 57 DLR 113.

[24] ibid [31].

[25] Staff Correspondent, '2 Commissioners Appointed to Give CEC Majority: EC Secretary, Retired Judge Get Posts in Clever Govt Move' *The Daily Star* (17 January 2006) www.archive.thedailystar.net/2007/2006/01/17/d6011701011.htm.

[26] Bangladesh Constitution (Fifteenth Amendment) Act 2011, s 35.

[27] S Rukhsana, 'Search Committee Gothito (Search Committee Formed)' *BBC Bangla* (22 January 2012) www.bbc.com/bengali/news/2012/01/120122_mrk_search_committee.

[28] Bangabhaban and Secretariat Correspondents, 'President Puts Six in Search Committee to Find New Election Commissioners' (*Bdnews24.com*, 25 January 2017) www.bdnews24.com/bangladesh/2017/01/25/president-puts-six-in-search-committee-to-find-new-election-commissioners.

[29] B Irani, 'Jatiya Oikya Front Submits Memorandum to EC, Demands Fresh Polls' *Dhaka Tribune* (3 January 2019) www.dhakatribune.com/bangladesh/politics/2019/01/03/demanding-fresh-polls-jatiya-oikya-front-submits-memorandum-to-ec.

version of the earlier, informal ones. Regrettably, the recommendations made by civil society members concerning the content of the law were largely ignored.[30]

Under the 2022 Act, the Search Committee will be headed by a judge of the AD, nominated by the Chief Justice. The other five members would be a judge of the High Court Division, nominated by the Chief Justice, the Comptroller and Auditor General, the Chairman of Bangladesh Public Service Commission and two other eminent personages, including one woman nominated by the President.[31] This Committee is empowered to recommend two candidates for each of the posts in the EC, based on the qualifications and criteria set out in the 2022 Act. From these recommended candidates, the President will appoint the election commissioners. But the new system has also been criticised by political parties and civil society, as the existing constitutional framework allows for political interference in the appointment procedure. Under the Bangladesh Constitution, the President acts under the advice of the Prime Minister except for in two cases. The power to constitute the Search Committee does not fall under these two exceptions, thus the President does not have exclusive power in the process of appointment. Unfortunately, the Search Committee formed under the 2022 Act has also been criticised for the apparent importance given to the suggestions of political parties allied with the incumbent government.[32]

This section has shown that while the EC is given broad powers by different electoral laws, it is the formation and membership of the EC – especially appointments by the President, upon the advice of the Prime Minister – that carries the risk of political capture under the existing constitutional design.[33] Following on from this brief outline of the journey of electoral democracy, the next section analyses the activities of the EC further to show when it has the potential for capture and when it can positively contribute to democracy.

III. Dereliction of the Election Commission and the Emergence of the Non-party Caretaker Government

A. Elections under the Election Commission in Independent Bangladesh: Consolidation, Resilience and Decay

The EC has been entrusted with the arrangement of different kinds of elections as mentioned above, but the discussion in this chapter will be confined to general elections to the unicameral Parliament (the Jatiya Sangshad) of Bangladesh. Due to their central importance in the transfer of political power, the general elections attract more attention than other election processes. As of 2022, Bangladesh has held 11 general elections.[34]

[30] Staff Correspondent, 'Shujon Submits Draft Law on EC Formation' *The New Age* (18 November 2021) www.newagebd.net/article/155074/shujon-submits-draft-law-on-ec-formation.

[31] The Appointment of the Chief Election Commissioner and other Election Commissioners Act 2022, s 3.

[32] BA Majumder, 'Onushondhan Committee Ke Ja Bole Ashalm' *The Daily Prothom Alo* (13 February 2022) Opinion.

[33] Bangladesh Constitution, Art 48(3).

[34] In 1973, 1979, 1986, 1988, 1991, 1996 (two elections), 2001, 2008, 2014 and 2018.

These elections can be grouped into at least three categories: elections by an incumbent civilian government (1973, 1996 (first one), 2014, 2018); military-era elections by incumbent military rulers (1979, 1986, 1988); and elections by the non-partisan CTG (1991, 1996 (second one), 2001, 2008). Although the EC was constitutionally engaged in organising all of these elections, there is a notable pattern in their outcome. In the elections grouped under the first two categories (incumbent civilian government and military-era elections), the incumbent government won all the elections, whereas in the elections run by the non-partisan CTG, the incumbents failed to win any.[35]

In the context of the Indian subcontinent, where anti-incumbency is quite a familiar feature in general elections,[36] the stark difference in outcome under non-party CTGs raises the question of whether effective electoral competition is less likely under the incumbent civilian and military rule. The credibility of elections under incumbent governments is brought into question by this pattern.

Tied to the question of the credibility of the elections is the question of the independence and efficiency of the EC during these elections. Notably, a closer look into the timeline of the general elections makes it possible to identify a cycle of continuous struggle, recovery, resilience and then decay in the electoral process over time. As an institution, the EC did not find a favourable political climate for consolidation under the prevailing conditions of political and constitutional instability prior to 1991. The process of consolidation began in 1991, when the democratic environment was restored after the end of successive military-backed governments. With a non-partisan set-up during the election period, the EC generally produced fairer and more credible elections from 1991 to 2008. However, there has been backsliding of this progress at the end of this period, when irregularities were widely reported and the elections were boycotted by major parties. This chapter turns to consider this next.

B. The Emergence of the Caretaker Government

Before evaluating the performance of the EC in Bangladesh's journey of electoral democracy, it is important to understand the context in which the CTG system emerged. Democracy was restored in Bangladesh after the fall of successive de facto military regimes in 1991, due to a democratic political consensus and a growing demand for free and fair elections. Massive political demonstrations and protests marked the introduction of a consensus-driven CTG prior to the election of 1991. This new system created a favourable environment for holding a free, fair and credible election. Ironically, this early support for electoral democracy lost momentum in a considerable way when the newly elected government followed in the footsteps of its military predecessors by allegedly

[35] See www.ecs.gov.bd; *Abdul Mannan Khan v Government of Bangladesh, represented by the Secretary, Ministry of Law, Justice and Parliamentary Affairs and others* [2012] 64 DLR (AD) 169 [170].

[36] For India, see A Lee, 'Incumbency, Parties and Legislatures: Theory and Evidence from India' (2019) 52(2) *Comparative Politics* 1 (by analysing data from 1977 election, Lee shows why India does not have incumbency advantage like most of the developed country); N Ravishankar, 'The Cost of Ruling: Anti-Incumbency in Elections' (2009) 44(10) *Economic and Political Weekly* 92. In Pakistan, incumbents lost in most of the general elections, www.ecp.gov.pk.

engineering a by-election with reports of massive vote-rigging.[37] This by-election in Magura has been termed a crticial moment in Bangladesh's electoral history, eventually becoming a synonym for vote rigging. After losing two mayoral elections in the Dhaka and Chittagong city corporations, the incumbent Bangladesh Nationalist Party (BNP) became desperate to win the Magura-2 constituency by any means and used the EC to orchestrate a colossal rigging.[38]

Such irregularities fuelled distrust among the opposition parties, which had hoped that the coming of a properly elected government would lead to further consolidation of electoral democracy.

A robust political movement pressured the incumbent government to amend the Constitution and adopt the 1991 CTG system. When the government refused to do this, major political parties boycotted the first election of 1996. This boycott gave more momentum to the anti-government movement. The incumbent government remained adamant in its position, organising the election and forming a new government. However, this obstinacy could not continue in the face of violent political protest and overwhelming disapproval of bureaucrats and civil society.

Consequently, the CTG was introduced through the Thirteenth Amendment to the Constitution in 1996. It was, in essence, a system by which an interim election-time government facilitated the transfer of power by ensuring a level playing field. The small-size interim government was headed by the last former Chief Justice as its Chief Adviser, with some notable eminent national figures as other Advisers. The CTG was responsible to the President for its functions, and it was not empowered to pursue any policy decisions unless necessary.[39]

The non-partisan political climate under the CTG enabled the EC to continue its consolidation as an impartial institution. The EC organised three general elections, in 1996 (the second of that year), 2001 and 2008, increasing the perceived credibility of the electoral process until deliberate attempts were made by outgoing governments to manipulate the system. This attempted interference will be analysed hereafter.

C. How the EC Performed in the Journey of Electoral Democracy

Under incumbent governments, the EC arranged four general elections, the incumbents winning them all. The first general election, in 1973, was an exceptional one where the Awami League (AL) won a sweeping majority on the back of their historical leadership

[37] MS Islam, 'Memories of Magura 1994' *The New Age* (11 February 2020) www.newagebd.net/article/99198/memories-of-magura-1994.

[38] ibid.

[39] Articles 58(B), (C), (D) and (E) were included in the Constitution and keep the following major provisions regarding caretaker government: (i) after the dissolution of the Sangsad there will be an 11-member non-party caretaker government headed by the Chief Adviser; (ii) the caretaker government will be collectively responsible to the President; (iii) the Chief Adviser will be appointed by the head of the state while 10 other advisers will be selected as per the advice of the Chief Adviser; (iv) the Chief Adviser will hold the status of Prime Minister while an adviser will enjoy the status of a minister; (v) the non-party caretaker government will discharge its functions as an interim government and will carry on routine jobs; except in the case of necessity, it will not make any policy decisions; (vi) the caretaker government will assist the Election Commission to hold general polls impartially, fairly and peacefully; (vii) this caretaker government will be dissolved on the date a new Prime Minister assumes his office.

in the war of independence and the absence of a strong opposition party in newly independent Bangladesh. However, the other three elections saw the incumbents capture the EC, winning almost all of the seats without any contestation by abusing the incumbency advantage. For example, the most recent general election, in 2018, has been criticised for the alleged co-option and capture of the EC through governmental agencies. The EC's dereliction of its constitutional duties in this election has led to it being widely considered as the most inefficient and partisan Commission since the country's founding.[40] The statistics bear witness to this: in 1177 polling centres, the major opposition party (BNP) did not receive a single vote; in 590 centres, all votes were cast for a single party (AL); and in 213 polling centres, 100 per cent of votes of the respective electoral rolls were cast, which was not realistic at all.[41] The ruling party secured more than 80 per cent of the seats in Parliament.[42] The major opposition parties were speculating about this type of capture when they boycotted the 2014 election based on their demand for the restoration of the CTG system, leaving 153 out of 300 seats uncontested. However, in 2018, the opposition parties contested the elections against the incumbents, having faced widespread criticism for their 2014 boycott. After the 2018 election, the opposition alliance claimed that the result confirmed their speculation and validated their stand of not contesting the previous election.[43]

It is apparent that the current electoral system is suffering from an integrity crisis since it lacks the trust of the political parties and the people at large. As a result, Bangladesh has slipped down in several global democracy indices and is failing to ensure respect for pluralism, civil liberties and political inclusivity.[44] The process of institutionalising democracy is in dire straits and elections have become a matter of 'winner takes all' while the losers are forced into a 'Darwinian test of survival'.[45]

The EC organised three general elections, in 1979, 1986 and 1988, under the de facto military-backed governments. In those three elections the incumbent party, either the BNP or the Jatiya Party, won outright. Each of those elections has been criticised vehemently for being rigged and controlled. For instance, in 1986, the then Army Chief Hussein Muhammad Ershad was compelled to organise a general election, after his failure to fulfil his promise to arrange one in 1983. Ershad formed his own political party, the Jatiya Party, following in the footsteps of Ziaur Rahman, who had formed the BNP in 1978.[46] The EC organised the general election on 7 May 1986, with the military-backed Jatiya Party winning 153 seats. The BNP and their allies boycotted the election because their demand to lift martial law went unheeded. One study of the Bangladesh

[40] Majumder (n 32).

[41] ibid.

[42] Staff and Agencies, 'Bangladesh Elections: Sheikh Hasina's Party Wins Large Majority Amid Accusations of Vote-Rigging' *The Independent* (31 December 2018) www.independent.co.uk/news/world/asia/bangladesh-election-latest-sheikh-hasina-awami-league-won-parliament-vote-rigging-violence-a8704791.html.

[43] Irani (n 29).

[44] 'Economist Intelligence Unit Democracy Index: Bangladesh Slips to 92th Position' *The Daily Star* (1 February 2018); see also www.eiu.com/topic/democracy-index.

[45] Chowdhury (n 5) 193.

[46] BNP was founded on 1 September 1978 by Ziaur Rahman after the presidential election of 1978. Ziaur Rahman was in de facto power from 1975 and assumed the presidency from 1977; the Jatiya Party was established by former Chief of Army Staff, Hussain Mohammad Ershad, on 1 January 1986. He had seized power through a coup d'état on 24 March 1982.

Institute of Parliamentary Studies quoted a team of British observers (consisting of a former Labour minister, a Conservative lawmaker and a BBC journalist), who termed the election a 'tragedy for democracy' and a 'cynically frustrated exercise'. The other election in this era of military-backed rule took place in 1988, with the incumbents winning 251 seats out of 300. This clearly shows the inability of the EC to ensure a free and fair election under this set-up.

In sharp contrast, the elections organised by the EC under the CTG system have been more fair, participatory and credible, based on statistical evidence, assessments of election observation teams and the number of allegations of irregularities, including corruption and vote rigging. None of these elections were boycotted by the major political parties and no incumbent managed to win, thus demonstrating the existence of a relatively impartial and inclusive environment. Indeed, the percentage distribution of votes reveals a tight contest. In 1991, the BNP won 140 seats with 30.81 per cent of the votes, while the AL received 30.08 per cent. In the 1996 (second) election, the AL won 146 seats with 37.44 per cent voting share, while the BNP secured 116 seats and 33.61 per cent. In 2001, the BNP (along with its alliance) won the election with 193 seats and 40.97 per cent voting share. The AL was a close second, with 40.13 per cent. The last election under the CTG was in 2008, when the Grand Alliance led by the AL won 263 seats and 56.45 per cent of the votes, and the BNP-led Four Party Alliance received 33 seats and 37.61 per cent. The anti-incumbent outcomes under the CTG system signal that the EC has better fulfilled its constitutional duties as a guarantor institution.

However, successive incumbent governments have tried to manipulate the otherwise efficient system by using advantages made available to them by their incumbency. In 2006, the CTG system was tested when the incumbent BNP sought to increase the retirement age of Supreme Court judges, allegedly in an attempt to ensure the position of Justice KM Hasan (perceived as a pro-government member of the judiciary) as chief adviser of the CTG.[47] This unsuccessful attempt triggered a violent movement to suspend the ensuing election. It was also alleged that the incumbent government had sought to control the EC and manipulate the electoral roll.[48] While the CTG system had seen the consolidation of electoral democracy in the post-military era, it was the incumbent government's attempted manipulation which caused considerable damage to this progress. Unfortunately, these actions resulted in a crisis of trust among the major political parties – the Grand Alliance led by the AL and the Four Party Alliance led by the BNP – and paved the way for a military-backed emergency situation during which the 22 January 2007 election was postponed for almost two years. The CTG was supposed to organise the election within three months; however, it failed miserably, given the rigged voter roll and the alleged partisan appointment attempt of its Chief Adviser.

[47] J Acharjee, 'KM Hasan Not Willing to Become Chief Adviser to the Next Caretaker Govt' (*Bdnews24.com*, 15 October 2005) bdnews24.com/politics/2005/10/15/km-hasan-not-willing-to-become-chief-adviser-to-the-next-caretaker-govt; Reporter, 'Political Parties in Bangladesh Urges Justice Hassan Not to Become the Caretaker Chief' *Voice of America, Bangla* (2 April 2005) www.voabangla.com/a/a-16-2005-04-02-voa4-94387779/1390361.html.

[48] Staff Reporter, 'Bangladesh Voters List Has 12 mln False Names – Report' *One India* (2 December 2006) www.oneindia.com/2006/12/02/bangladesh-voters-list-has-12-mln-false-names-report-1165061245.html.

Unfortunately, the democratic political parties had to rely on the army to help organise the general election. The army responded to popular demand and got involved in the time-consuming preparation of the electoral rolls. The unelected CTG remained in office for another two years to ensure a valid electoral roll and proper election environment. During this unusual stay, the CTG not only confined itself to discharging election-related activities, but also engaged in many policy decisions beyond its constitutional mandate. Its prolonged stay and some military-backed activities, which were not directly linked to the preparation of the election but which impacted the political and economic elites, were opposed by the political parties. Its activities were widely criticised from all political fronts, and sometimes harshly compared to their achievement in the consolidation of electoral democracy. Ironically, the desperation for power among the political parties seriously damaged the 'work-in-progress' consolidation of electoral democracy achieved by the unelected CTG.

It is apparent from the aforementioned history that both the systems of EC and CTG have repeatedly been manipulated by the political parties. However, it is undeniable that the elections organised under the auspices of the CTG were fairer and more participatory. Although in stronger democracies elections under incumbent governments are conducted routinely, this is so because institutions that support the function of democracy – such as the EC – are robust in their independence, accountability and capacity to check any potential manipulation by the incumbent.

It is pertinent to mention here that the CTG system might be an unusual guardian of democratic legitimacy, given that it is constituted by unelected civil society members. However, the system creates an impartial political environment – even within an ill-designed framework – that is conducive to the discharge of the constitutional and statutory mandates of the EC. This chapter now turns to look at how the AD of the Supreme Court trivialised the positive role of the CTG in the broader project of consolidating democracy.

IV. The Thirteenth Amendment Judgment: An Assessment from the Perspective of Consolidation of Electoral Democracy

As outlined above, the CTG system came into existence in 1996 through the Thirteenth Amendment and has been responsible for three more elections since then. Its members, including the Chief Adviser, were not elected. This Amendment was challenged for its constitutionality and the first petitioner was substituted twice during the litigation. Advocate M Salem Ullah filed writ petition 4112 of 1999 challenging the Thirteenth Amendment, arguing that it violated the basic structure of the Bangladesh Constitution. After the demise of the petitioner, Advocate Ruhul Quddus was substituted till his elevation as a justice to the High Court Division (HCD). Following this, Abdul Mannan Khan assumed the role and appealed in the AD. In its subsequent decision in *Abdul Mannan Khan*, the Supreme Court struck down the Thirteenth Amendment and as a result this adversely impacted the consolidation of electoral democracy in Bangladesh. The majority in *Abdul Mannan Khan* invalidated the CTG system on the basis that it infringed the basic structure of the Bangladesh Constitution – namely, the system of electoral democracy that forms part of the basic structure.[49] This decision has itself undermined democracy. It has also been argued that the Court's judgment precipitated the start of a 'controlled democracy',[50] with two successive less credible, less participatory national elections. This chapter argues that the majority judgment in *Abdul Mannan Khan* has failed to adopt a consolidation-friendly approach and highlights those aspects of its reasoning that inhibited the Court's understanding of its need and the constitutional means to do so.

A. High Court's Upholding of CTG: Appreciating the Collective Wisdom of the Legislators

Prior to the Appellate Division Judgment, the issue of the Thirteenth Amendment came before the HCD in *Syed Muhammad Mashiur Rahman v President of Bangladesh*.[51] The HCD dismissed the application for judicial review on the ground that the CTG was only a temporary arrangement. The second challenge came in the case of *M Saleem Ullah v Bangladesh*,[52] where the HCD held that the CTG was introduced to consolidate democracy, one of the four basic principles of the Constitution, and accordingly it was not unconstitutional.

In *M Saleem Ullah*, it was also argued that appointing a Supreme Court judge as a chief adviser to the CTG is a violation of the separation of powers and therefore undermined judicial independence. However, again, the HCD dismissed this argument on the basis that it was non-justiciable – it was a question for the legislature to determine. In both *Syed Muhammad* and *M Saleem Ullah*, the HCD was mindful of the underlying consolidation and institutionalisation of electoral democracy achieved by the CTG.[53] Mirza Hossain Haider J of the HCD held in *M Saleem Ullah* that the system of a temporary unelected government – such as the CTG – was not problematic or novel, since the Constitution allowed officials in several elected posts to continue beyond their tenure while waiting for the election of their successor.[54]

B. The Appellate Division's Decision: Issues, Contradictions and Missed Opportunities

While the HCD restrained itself from delving into the political wisdom of the CTG, the AD did not similarly ignore this issue. Compared to the HCD, the majority judgment was less sympathetic to the broad democratic impact of the CTG. Rather, the majority judgment emphasised the importance of 'continued representation' as an element of democracy. It was clear, therefore, that there were two different aspects of electoral democracy at play in the HCD and the AD of the Supreme Court. The former focused

[49] *Anwar Hossain Chowdhury v Bangladesh* [1989] BLD (spcl) 1.

[50] 'Controlled Democracy: Bangladesh' *The Economist: Espresso* (15 February 2017) https://espresso.economist.com/581b41df0cd50ace849e061ef74827fc.

[51] *Syed Muhammad Mashiur Rahman v President of Bangladesh* [1997]17 BLD (HCD) 55.

[52] *M Saleem Ullah v Bangladesh* [20005] 57 DLR (HCD)171.

[53] ibid [90] (Haider J).

[54] ibid [82].

on the values of fair and impartial election of government, whereas the latter focused on the continuous democratic and representative credentials of government.

The AD invited eight amici curiae on the issue. Six of them made submissions on the need for a restrained approach, including the suggestion that deference should be given to Parliament.[55] However, the majority judgment harshly criticised this approach.[56] The Court initially issued a short order declaring the Constitution (Thirteenth Amendment) Act, 1996 as prospectively void and ultra vires in accordance with the Constitution.

It ordered, in rather ambiguous terms, that the next two elections may be held under the provisions of the Thirteenth Amendment. It did so on the grounds of three principles: *quod alias non est licitum, necessitas licitum facit* (that which otherwise is not lawful, necessity makes lawful), *salus populi suprema lex* (safety of the people is the supreme law) and *salus republicae est suprema lex* (safety of the state is the supreme law). The short order further stated: 'Parliament, however, in the meantime, is at liberty to bring necessary amendments excluding the provisions of making the former Chief Justices of Bangladesh or the Judges of the Appellate Division as the head of the Non-Party Care-taker Government.'

The full written judgment came almost a year after this short order. However, in the meantime, the government introduced the Fifteenth Amendment, which repealed the provisions for the CTG immediately, without waiting for the next two elections. The full written judgment, therefore, had to be amended in light of the new Amendment.

While the Court's judgment in Abdul Mannan Khan was rendered obsolete by the Fifteenth Amendment, it set the tone for the constitutional meaning of 'democracy', and set a benchmark for understanding electoral democracy in Bangladesh. Therefore, it merits close attention despite the Fifteenth Amendment.

When the majority judgment proposed (using the word 'may') to continue an unconstitutional arrangement for the next two elections, it showed the Court's awareness of the political climate, the ongoing democratic consolidation and the risk of backsliding. Apparently, that propelled the majority judges to invoke 'state necessity' to allow the CTG to further consolidate the system by providing a conducive environment for the EC. Although the majority judgment did not elaborate on what a strengthened EC would look like, it has put the EC at the centre of its analysis of democracy in Bangladesh. However, in their respective dissenting judgments, Justice Abdul Wahhab Miah, Justice Md Imman Ali and Justice SK Sinha shed light on what can strengthen the EC and the dissenting judges found the CTG to be a prerequisite for a strong EC in the context of Bangladesh.

C. A Narrow View Overlooking Historical and Cultural Experience

In a 4:3 split, the majority of the AD declared the Thirteenth Amendment prospectively invalid.[57] The majority emphasised the necessity of a strong EC under incumbent

[55] *Abdul Mannan Khan* (n 35) [93].
[56] eg ibid [1240].
[57] ibid [1121].

governments, rather than a CTG, for holding free and fair elections and to ensure the functioning of electoral democracy.[58] It criticised the CTG system for undermining the party system and for questioning the capacity of incumbent governments to hold free and fair elections.[59] Further, the AD urged 'all knowledgeable and talented people' to find a way out from the crisis earnestly and authentically, although it did not clarify who they are and why the opinions of those 'knowledgeable and talented' will supersede the collective wisdom of the Parliament.[60] In reaching its decision, the AD did not consider the collective political wisdom that underpinned the CTG system in the years 1991 and 1996 and the way the CTG was designed to ensure that a select group of individuals were to be trusted with helping the EC to ensure the integrity of elections. While the majority commended the calibre and talent of the advisers of the CTG system, it held that the fact that they were unelected undermined their overall credentials.[61]

The majority disregarded various historical and politico-cultural factors related to the CTG and electoral democracy in Bangladesh. First, the judgment is premised on certain very limited conceptions of democracy. It perceives democracy in the sense of the 1972 Constitution instead of the post-autocratic democratic model of 1991.[62] The 1972 Constitution had allowed unelected ministers to serve for six months, and was formed on the basis of a few assumptions and experiments, whereas the 1991 constitutional reform had been based on the experience of two decades where the country exerpeinced successive *coups d'état* and military usurpation in the democratic space. The consensus that led to the Thirteenth Amendment was the result of the collective political movement of most political parties, if not all of them. This consensus came about as a result of the failure of the newly independent country to successfully organise fair elections reflecting the will of the people.

Secondly, the judgment only axed the CTG-related provisions for being 'undemocratic'; it did not comment on a handful of similar provisions.[63] For example, the existing Constitution allows for one-tenth of the total ministers to be unelected technocrats.[64] Similarly, in pursuit of gender equality, there is a provision for 50 Members of Parliament to be women, selected by political parties based on their proportion of seats, rather than directly elected.

Thirdly, the CTG system was introduced to meet the demand of all political parties, reflecting a shared consensus. Misunderstanding this ground-level sentiment, the majority judgment labelled it an 'insult' to political parties.[65] In response to this, Dr Kamal replied in his amicus submission that the CTG system has not insulted any political party. Dr Kamal is a politician and led the grand alliance including one of the two major political parties, BNP, in the 2018 election. His response was based on his own experience. Contrary to the majority's assertion, he claimed (although without evidence or reference) that the CTG system has acquired a global reputation.

[58] ibid [1123].
[59] ibid [1124] and [1250].
[60] ibid [1128].
[61] ibid [872].
[62] ibid [1362]–[1422].
[63] Bangladesh Constitution, Arts 56(2) and 65(3). See *Abdul Mannan Khan* (n 35) [1531] (Imman Ali J).
[64] Bangladesh Constitution, Art 56(2).
[65] *Abdul Mannan Khan* (n 35) [1496 (43)].

Finally, the application of the Basic Structure Doctrine disregarded the historical particularities of Bangladesh's political context – in particular, as discussed in section III above, the history of defective elections held by incumbent non-CTG governments.[66] The Supreme Court did not fully articulate the basis for its recognition of 'representative democracy' as part of the basic structure of the Constitution. Nor was it clear that having unelected governance in any form necessarily undermines democracy. As shown above, the Constitution allows unelected individuals to hold constitutional positions in other contexts.

D. An Elegy to Democracy

While the majority judgment in *Abdul Mannan Khan* rested on the notion of 'representative democracy' as part of the basic structure of the Constitution, it failed to provide a basis for this concept and its genesis in Bangladesh in its discussion on different theories of democracy – including those which are prevalent in autocratic regimes.[67]

The majority in *Abdul Mannan Khan* did not sufficiently articulate the precise nature of Bangladesh's own constitutional vision of 'electoral' democracy, but nonetheless based its decision on the CTG on such a deficient view of democracy. The majority placed an emphasis on 'representation' in Parliament – in the form of elected representatives – without considering the need for those representatives to be returned via free and fair elections and a credible, consolidated and institutionalised electoral system. Justice Abdul Wahhab Mia in his dissent rightly argued: 'we should not also have any special fascination and love for the Parliament if its members are not elected by the people in a free and fair election and thus, do not have a true representation to the people'.[68]

E. The Achilles Heel, the Misunderstood Concept of 'Representation' and Myopic Reasoning

The constitutionally determined three-month interim period between two elected governments has been crucial in securing a democratically elected representative government. This interim period can be described as an Achilles heel. It is a period during which the democratic process is vulnerable to capture. The CTG system had been incorporated at this crucial juncture of electoral democracy in Bangladesh.

However, even after arranging four credible elections – in the sense of participation and overall statistics, as shown above – the CTG was considered unconstitutional by the AD on the ground that it discontinued representation by the people[69] and on the basis that a strengthened EC with the guidance of the president would be able to hold a free and fair election. But the reality of the situation shows that the view of the AD

[66] R Hoque, 'The Judicialization of Politics in Bangladesh Pragmatism, Legitimacy, and Consequences' in Tushnet and Khosla (n 5) 281.

[67] *Abdul Mannan Khan* (n 35) [290].

[68] ibid [1423].

[69] ibid [204].

was rather myopic. In the absence of a non-partisan election-time government during this interim period, the elections were losing their 'representative' character. In 2014, 153 out of 300 seats went uncontested due to a boycott. Thus, subsequent developments suggest that the AD's trust in a strengthened EC, with the direction of the President, did not bear fruit. The elections failed miserably in solving the 'representation' problem. Striking down the CTG only addressed the problem of the discontinuation of an elected government, but that too for the short interim period.

F. Unsubstantiating the Idea of 'Free and Fair Elections'

While it ascribed insufficient weight to it, there was some recognition by the majority of judges of the importance of elections as a precondition of democracy.[70] The majority held that the basis of popular sovereignty set out in Article 7 of the Constitution rests on free and fair elections.[71] The thread of this can be seen in earlier decisions of the HCD. For example, in *Abdul Momen Chowdhury v Bangladesh* (WP No 2561 of 2005), the HCD held that even in the absence of an explicit reference in the law, it was implicit in Article 119 of the Bangladesh Constitution that the EC has the responsibility of supervising and controlling the conduct of elections. The powers of the EC are all aimed at holding free and fair elections.[72]

While recognising the importance of free and fair elections, the courts have not yet articulated how fairness will be ensured under a partisan set-up with a long history of abuse of power. For example, the majority underscored the importance of holding the election within 90 days of the dissolution of the preceding parliament.[73] However, the Court did not consider the fact that this time frame has been used in the past to manipulate the electoral roll. It is not the time frame per se that has been problematic, but the way in which those responsible for the organisation of elections have used that time. In the earlier decision of *Sultana Kamal v Bangladesh*,[74] the Court held that even if an election is not held within 90 days of the dissolution of Parliament, it is nonetheless valid since the preparation of a fault-free electoral roll was a precondition of a fair election. How the AD declared the extension of the interim period for a fresh electoral roll to be unconstitutional in *Abdul Mannan Khan* is not clear.

G. The Fear of Abuse

A further foundation for the majority judgment is the fear that it is open to abuse. This fear was compounded by the fact that the 'temporary' CTG had been in place indefinitely under a so-called state of emergency. The Court's concern appears to be

[70] ibid [88].

[71] ibid [1362]–[1422].

[72] *Abdul Momen Chowdhury v Bangladesh* [2005] WP No 2561 (Unreported); M Islam, *Constitutional Law of Bangladesh*, 3rd edn (Dhaka, Mullick Brothers, 2011) 960.

[73] eg *Abdul Mannan Khan* (n 35) [1027], [1029].

[74] *Sultana Kamal v Bangladesh* [2009] 14 BLC 141.

founded on certain actions by the CTG in 2007 and 2008. This includes, for example, the perceived interference of the CTG in the transfer of officials[75] and delays in preparing the necessary electoral rolls by two years, which was arguably ultra vires the CTG's power. Although, theoretically, these activities were beyond their power, the majority judgment could have considered the background of the actions that appear to have been done in pursuit of the overarching motive of strengthening and consolidating the electoral process. For example, the delaying of elections in January 2007 was done to correct the allegedly rigged electoral roll stuffed with 14 million fake names,[76] which was clearly an important step in strengthening the electoral process and its fairness.

There was a further concern that the CTG system manipulated the judicial appointment system. The applicant argued that after the introduction of the CTG, the fifteenth, sixteenth, and eighteenth Chief Justices were promoted to the AD ahead of their 'seniors', who, from the perspective of years of service, were ahead of them in line for elevation to the position of Chief Justice.[77] However, there is no explicit constitutional requirement that the appointment of a Chief Justice should be determined solely on the basis of the number of years of service in the AD. The majority, however, seem to have been of the view that the Chief Justice – who would be the Chief Adviser to the CTG – would be appointed on the basis that they would be somehow aligned to the CTG. But even in the absence of a CTG system, the position of Chief Justice can still be subject to a political check. It would be more convincing to rely on the immediate ex-Chief Justice, with the proven qualities of honesty, integrity and acumen to conduct the general election rather than to rely on the incumbent Prime Minister, who has a clear conflict of interest.

H. On the Reform of the EC

The reasoning in the majority and dissenting judgments and the submissions of the amici curiae in *Abdul Mannan Khan* dealt with the question of reform of the EC, the nucleus of electoral democracy in Bangladesh. The majority judgment was of the view that the EC needs significant reform in order to be powerful, autonomous and self-governing.[78] The judgment underscored the importance of financial independence and enhanced administrative powers, including control over the recruitment of its staff.[79] It held the view that it is the EC that is constitutionally charged with the responsibility for holding free and fair elections, not the CTG.[80]

What was absent from the majority judgment was precise guidance on how to reform the EC. There was a general call by one of the judges – Justice SK Sinha – to Parliament to formulate laws to strengthen the EC.[81] However, as discussed in section II, the EC is already given significant formal powers. The real issue, therefore, is how to ensure that those formal powers can be freely exercised.

[75] *Abdul Mannan Khan* (n 35) [1022].

[76] S Sengupta, 'In Bangladesh, State of Emergency and Election Delay' *New York Times* (12 January 2007) www.nytimes.com/2007/01/12/world/asia/12bangladesh.html.

[77] See generally Chowdhury (n 5) 224.

[78] *Abdul Mannan Khan* (n 35) [1123].

[79] ibid [1129].

[80] ibid.

[81] ibid [1308] (Sinha J).

There are two larger changes needed for this guarantor institution – one formal and one outside the formal law. First, the political environment is what really hinders the proper functioning of the system. Secondly, the problem is rooted in the appointment procedure of the election commissioners. Under the current law as adopted in 2022, commissioners are being appointed by the President from proposals made by the Search Committee. But the President is under a constitutional obligation to follow the advice of the Prime Minister as to who will be on the Search Committee and the EC. This scope of influence by the partisan actors in the institutional, personal or operational feature of the EC should be curtailed and replaced by a system of political accountability premised on cross-party involvement in the system that could thwart any kind of partisan capture of this guarantor institution.[82]

V. Conclusion

Although the majority struck down the Thirteenth Amendment for being undemocratic and therefore unconstitutional, this decision has not led to an improvement in the overall health of democracy in Bangladesh. This chapter has outlined how notions of democracy require more complex articulation, focusing not just on formal representation, but also on how to ensure it in practice. One prerequisite for representation is free and fair elections – a specific challenge in the Bangladesh context. The institution responsible for facilitating this key facet of Bangladesh's democracy, the EC, must be strengthened. If the election process cannot be made fairer, the ultimate goal of a resilient, consolidated and sustainable democracy will remain illusory. The majority decision in *Abdul Mannan Khan* enables the abuse of the Bangladeshi constitutional framework for the purposes of interfering with, and damaging, electoral democracy. This decision is premised on the Court's failure to recognise the unique challenges to free and fair elections arising from the political culture of Bangladesh – namely, a compromised EC. The Supreme Court should have recognised the CTG not merely as a form of government lacking 'formal' representative credentials, but as an institutional arrangement devised in response to Bangladesh's troubled history of electoral democracy.

[82] See T Khaitan, 'Guarantor (or "Fourth Branch") Institutions' in J King and R Bellamy (eds), *Cambridge Handbook of Constitutional Theory* (Cambridge, Cambridge University Press, forthcoming).

PART VII

The Military

16

Rescuing the Agency and Resilience of Civilian Political Actors: Civil–Military Relations in Pakistan, 2008–20[1]

FARHAN HANIF SIDDIQI

I. Introduction

In 1999, when the Pakistani military overthrew the democratically elected government of Prime Minister Nawaz Sharif owing to civil–military conflict over the Kargil war with India,[2] Larry Diamond – one of the world's foremost democracy experts – was quick to brand the military coup as the 'single most serious reversal of democracy during the third wave of democratisation'.[3] In contrast, assessing the state of global democracy in 2014, Diamond identified a disturbing 'democratic recession' in the USA and the world at large, as evidenced by indicators such as bad governance, low rates of political participation and declining political and civil liberties.[4] However, Diamond identified Singapore and Pakistan as two countries outside the West as more free today – even if only modestly – compared to Egypt, Bangladesh, Turkey, South Africa, Taiwan, Mexico and Thailand, among others.[5] Diamond's analysis of Pakistan provides an intriguing conundrum: its 1999 military coup indicated a gross reversal in an otherwise global third democratic wave,[6] while the state of its democracy in the second decade of the 2000s presents a mildly optimistic case study in a world looking down the barrel of democratic recession, backsliding and a third wave of autocratisation.[7]

[1] This chapter analyses civil–military relations in Pakistan up to 2020. Hence, the dismissal of former Prime Minister Imran Khan's government through a vote of no-confidence in April 2022 does not come under its purview. Readers, however, are encouraged to think about and analyse whether this government's dismissal and subsequent events are relevant to the conclusions on civil–military relations reached in this chapter.

[2] N Zehra, *From Kargil to the Coup: Events That Shook Pakistan* (Lahore, Sang-e-Meel Publications, 2018).

[3] L Diamond, 'Is Pakistan the (Reverse) Wave of the Future?' (2000) 11 *Journal of Democracy* 91.

[4] L Diamond, 'Facing up to the Democratic Recession' (2015) 26 *Journal of Democracy* 141.

[5] ibid 150–51.

[6] SP Huntington, *The Third Wave: Democratization in the Late Twentieth Century* (Oklahoma, University of Oklahoma Press, 1991).

[7] RS Foa and Y Mounk, 'The Democratic Disconnect' (2016) 27 *Journal of Democracy* 5; N Bermeo, 'On Democratic Backsliding' (2016) 27 *Journal of Democracy* 5; A Luhrmann and SI Lindberg, 'A Third Wave of Autocratization Is Here: What Is New about It?' (2019) 26 *Democratization* 1095.

The present chapter seeks to understand the state of Pakistan's democracy from 2008 to 2020, particularly with respect to civil–military relations and the prospects for democratic consolidation. The stated period is marked by Pakistan's return to democracy in 2008 as General Pervez Musharraf's 'controlled democracy' experiment came to an end,[8] and the political parties driven out by Musharraf's military regime returned as participatory actors. However, existing political commentaries do not see the post-2008 phase as a return to democracy, but rather one of assertive reinforcement of the military's control and influence over the political system. For example, Siddiqa argues that the military has honed the art of 'hybrid democracy' by using its sanctioning power to keep civilian governments unstable and utilising subtle tactics to prevent two Prime Ministers – Yusuf Raza Gillani and Nawaz Sharif – from completing their terms in office.[9] In a similar vein, David O Smith contends that the Pakistan army has achieved a 'coup-less coup', as the army now controls the country's nuclear and missile programmes, key foreign relationships, the military budget and national security decision-making.[10] Katharine Adeney argues that Pakistan's hybrid regime is characterised by a confluence of three features: (i) political competitiveness, which is offset by (ii) the suboptimal protection of civil liberties, and (iii) the presence of reserved domains for the military. This leads Adeney to conclude that 'Pakistan is likely to remain a hybrid regime for the foreseeable future'.[11] These analyses offer a pessimistic assessment of the consolidation of democracy, on the grounds that political elites remain dispensable and disempowered, with little authority to challenge military dominance. In short, arguments flowing from such accounts lead to the conclusion that Pakistan is unlikely to make the much-needed transition to a more coup-proof, democratic political system.

This chapter makes a radical departure from the above-stated analyses, and argues that despite recent estimations of Pakistan's political system as a 'hybrid regime' with both democratic and authoritarian features,[12] Pakistan's political trajectory since 2008

[8] I adapt and modify the idea of control from Ian Lustick's formulation relative to deeply divided societies where the majority group controls and censures minority groups from the exercise of political functions. I Lustick, 'Stability in Deeply Divided Societies: Consociationalism versus Control' (1979) 31 *World Politics* 325. Applying the idea of control to a democracy, I utilise the term 'controlled democracy' where a ruling elite (usually the military) frames exclusionary laws that debar key members of the political opposition from electoral participation or imposing legal constraints that allow incumbent political leaders and governments to be dismissed from office.

[9] A Siddiqa, 'Of Kings, Queens and Pawns: Civil–Military Relations in Pakistan' in B Zahoor and R Rumi (eds), *Rethinking Pakistan: A 21st Century Perspective* (Lahore, Folio Books, 2019) 170.

[10] DO Smith, 'Civil–Military Relations in Pakistan: Positive Evolution or More of the Same?' [2020] *Georgetown Journal of International Affairs* https://gjia.georgetown.edu/2020/01/24/civil-military-relations-in-pakistan/.

[11] K Adeney, 'How to Understand Pakistan's Hybrid Regime: The Importance of a Multidimensional Continuum' (2017) 24 *Democratization* 119, 131.

[12] The Economist Intelligence Unit (EIU) Democracy Index 2020 lists Pakistan as a hybrid democracy, which is defined as a political system embodying both democratic and authoritarian features, including 'election irregularities, government pressure on opposition parties, corruption, weak rule of law and civil society, non-independent judiciary, and harassment of and pressure on journalists'. The EIU's definition of the hybrid regime does not include military intervention. The Economist Intelligence Unit, 'Democracy Index 2020: In Sickness and Health?' (London, EIU, 2020). Larry Diamond provides a more succinct conceptualisation of hybrid regimes, including electoral authoritarianism and military generals legitimising their rule by running as presidents and/or carving out autonomous spheres of political influence and economic domination. L Diamond, 'Thinking About Hybrid Regimes' (2002) 13 *Journal of Democracy* 21.

offers a story of optimism for the consolidation of democracy.[13] Moreover, the chapter contends that the hybrid democracy/regime lens of understanding Pakistan's civil–military relations suffers from a fundamental flaw, as it inflates the role of the military and in the process undermines the resilience and challenge of civilian political elites. Civilian resilience in civil–military relations is best captured by directing attention to the dynamics of contestation between civilian and military elites, as opposed to an outcome-oriented analysis fixated on who wins or who gets what. In the outcome-oriented analysis, military domination and control assume prominence, as a *coup d'état* is an easily identifiable and documentable event. In contrast, civilian strategies are more of a set of relationships lacking sharpness, which makes them harder to observe and analyse.[14] The broader literature on civil–military relations in Pakistan is based on an outcome-oriented analysis that takes the military's ascendant position for granted and denigrates the role of political elites. Hoffman, for example, argues that Pakistan's democratic interlude in the 1990s was a 'temporary democracy' resulting from the military's calculated self-extrication from politics, a decision informed by its confidence that it could regain power whenever it wished to do so.[15] This, it will be argued, was not the case, and a better explanation of the military's role in the 1990s was rooted in the military's 'fear' as opposed to 'confidence'. As Feaver persuasively shows, coups not only indicate military strength, but also reveal weaknesses in their capacity to influence, control and 'get what it wants through the normal political process'.[16] In light of these shortcomings in the existing literature, the chapter brings into sharper focus the resilience of political elites in the analysis of civil–military relations.

Civilian resilience is best captured in a concept that I identify as *military embeddedness*, which is juxtaposed against the more conventional 'causal-deterministic' explanation. The latter framework borders on wholly attributing the military's hegemony to anaemic political processes, dynastic political parties, and inefficient and corrupt political leaders. Hence, if democracy is to be consolidated, political parties and leaders will have to make the transformative leap from weak/corrupt/inefficient to robust/honest/efficient governance. The causal determinism at the argumentative level is expressed in the frailty of one institution – civilian leadership – adding to the power of another – the military. This, I argue, is an archaic analysis as it reinforces the hegemony of the military without attending to civilian resistance. The framework of military embeddedness employed here is not causal-deterministic, but rather directs attention to the dynamic nature of civil–military interactions, and in doing so shows that the military is incentivised to embed itself in politics. The military has a number of tangible material interests: exploitation of societal resources, including manpower for both war-fighting and security-maintaining purposes, as well as financial investments to support its

[13] The post-2008 period is consequential for the fact that two elected governments completed their five-year tenures, with the 2013 general elections marking only the first time in Pakistan's history where a democratic, peaceful transfer of power from an incumbent government to another took place. A Malik, 'Pakistan in 2013: A Milestone in Democratic Transition' (2014) 54 *Asian Survey* 177.

[14] CE Welch Jr, 'Civilian Control of the Military: Myth and Reality' in CE Welch Jr *Civilian Control of the Military: Theory and Cases from Developing Countries* (Albany, State University of New York Press, 1976) 1.

[15] M Hoffman, 'Military Extrication and Temporary Democracy: The Case of Pakistan' (2011) 18 *Democratization* 75.

[16] PD Feaver, 'Civil–Military Relations' (1999) 2 *Annual Review of Political Science* 211, 218.

economic base. However, the resourcefulness of the military as a political, coercive and financial power is weighted against the intangibility of public support, which it seeks for its continued legitimacy. Public support is intangible at the ideational level, given there are times when the public expresses support for military regimes but then also engages in collective protests against military rule. The intangibility of public support and the need for widespread legitimacy make the military a vulnerable institution, much like democratically elected governments. This vulnerability is left unexamined in 'military as a dominant actor' accounts of civil–military relations.

Civilian and military elites compete horizontally against each other for power and influence, and also vertically for support amongst the public. On the horizontal axis of competition, the military retains the coercive power to overthrow elected governments, a measure that is not available to civilian political elites. However, civilian political elites do not uncritically accept the coercive power of the military; instead, military interventionism gives rise to civilian disapproval and resentment. On the vertical axis of competition, military elites are sensitive to political context, public appeal, legitimacy deficit and their self-image. In fact, when in power, the military must provide justification not only for its security and military roles, but also for governance indicators such as economic growth, development and institutional reforms in order to satisfy the basic needs of the citizenry. This embeddedness puts the role of the military in an entirely new light. This more complex conceptualisation of the military's position is necessary for a succinct understanding of Pakistan's constitutional health and democratic consolidation. The next section critically analyses the literature on civil–military relations in Pakistan, setting the context for why civilian resilience must be seriously considered. The following section provides a descriptive and explanatory analysis of political elites in the 1990s and the post-2008 period, asserting that civilian resilience is manifest and will remain a constant feature of Pakistani politics.

II. The Existing Narrative on Military Dominance in Pakistan

The existing literature on civil–military relations in Pakistan includes political, sociological, external/internal threat-oriented and economic standpoints that provide varying explanations for why the military has assumed dominance in Pakistan's political system. This section examines these analyses with a view to demonstrating their shared assumption of military dominance – seeing that dominance as a given and focusing on how to explain it.

Ali,[17] Cheema,[18] Schiff[19] and Tudor[20] argue that the incompetence and defective decision-making of political elites, combined with an underdeveloped system

[17] Z Ali, 'Contradiction of Concordance Theory: Failure to Understand Military Intervention in Pakistan' (2014) 40 *Armed Forces and Society* 544.

[18] PI Cheema, *The Armed Forces of Pakistan* (New South Wales, Allen & Unwin, 2001).

[19] RL Schiff, *The Military and Domestic Politics: A Concordance Theory of Civil–Military Relations* (London, Routledge, 2009).

[20] M Tudor, *The Promise of Power: The Origins of Democracy in India and Autocracy in Pakistan* (Cambridge, Cambridge University Press, 2013).

of political parties, paves the way for military intervention in politics.[21] The causal-deterministic analysis is important in these accounts, for one agency can only be understood in the context of the other. In this analysis, if a successful democratic experiment is to endure in Pakistan, an emaciated civilian leadership provides little room for optimism. However, the problem with the causal-deterministic analysis is that it puts the onus of democratic deficit in Pakistan solely on political elites. Only if political elites could institute good governance and practice democratic values in the sense of providing robust, exemplary leadership would it then be harder for the military to intervene. The military, in this sense, assumes the position of a disinterested and reluctant actor that is forced into politics by dubious and frivolous civilian political actors. This is certainly not the case in Pakistan, where the military's political role has been geared towards upscaling its support base amongst the population in contradistinction to the political class. This attention to its political ambitions and interests determines the military's incessant political interference and constitutional engineering for the purpose of undermining political elites, and ensuring its own vitality and continuance as the primary national political actor. Aziz,[22] Rizvi[23] and Shafqat[24] undertake a historical analysis looking at how and when the military emerged as a dominant actor exercising unrestrained control and authority. Included in their analyses is a path-dependent formulation that historicises the military's ascendancy since 1947. As with causal-deterministic accounts, Aziz, Rizvi and Shafqat elevate the military's professional and political interests as primary, while political elites function as mere subjugated subjects at the behest of the military. This subjugation persists when the military regime is in power, but also in the post-withdrawal phase where the military manipulates the system to its relative advantage. Cohen,[25] Hussain[26] and Shah[27] offer a dispositional analysis emphasising the military's subjective beliefs, attitudes and preferences in exerting its control and power over the state and society. In contrast to the causal-deterministic argument, Cohen, Hussain and Shah present the military's dominance in Pakistan from a constitutive socio-psychological perspective based on the military's self-definition of Pakistani nationalism and identity. This is intimately linked to a saviour complex, whereby the military assumes the role of the protector of Pakistan's ideological and physical frontiers not only against external enemies, but also against rapacious civilian leaders. Though this framework employs a non-causal logic of analysis, its conclusions are myopically tinged towards the overbearing military actor, while condemning the agency of civilian actors as puny or inconsequential. Siddiqa brings forth a political economy perspective positing the military's entrenched

[21] See M Salman and M Raza, ch 17 in this volume, who make a similar argument about deficiencies in Pakistan's political parties, including the failure to devolve power at the grassroots, reliance on locally influential politicians, corruption and willingness to strike deals with the military as detrimental to Pakistan's democratic outlook. Although the authors are critical of the military's role in politics and the political engineering that it undertakes, the analysis puts the onus on weak political institutionalisation facilitating the intervention of the military as imperative in accounting for the democratic deficit in Pakistan.

[22] M Aziz, *Military Control in Pakistan: The Parallel State* (London, Routledge, 2008).

[23] HA Rizvi, *Military, State and Society in Pakistan* (London, Macmillan, 2000).

[24] S Shafqat, *Civil–Military Relations in Pakistan: From Zulfikar Ali Bhutto to Benazir Bhutto* (Boulder, CO, Westview Press, 1997).

[25] SP Cohen, *The Pakistan Army*, 1998 edn (Karachi, Oxford University Press, 1998).

[26] E Hussain, *Military Agency, Politics and the State in Pakistan* (New Delhi, Samskriti, 2013).

[27] A Shah, *The Army and Democracy: Military Politics in Pakistan* (Cambridge, MA, Harvard University Press, 2014).

economic interests as the bedrock of its political power.[28] The economic interests that Siddiqa labels as *Milbus* (military-business) are a routinised form of military spending that is unaccounted for in the defence budget and which the military jealously guards against its civilian counterparts. This preservation of its core economic interests facilitates the military's complete autonomy from civilian political elites and augments its status as an independent class. Staniland addresses the 'threat argument' in civil–military relations, arguing that while external threats preoccupy the military and ought to inhibit military involvement in politics,[29] this has not been true in Pakistan. Despite the high level of external threat and the state's strategic and military competition with India, the military overthrew elected governments and assumed power in 1958, 1977 and 1999. The reasons for military takeover, according to Staniland, are rooted in weak political processes and low civilian legitimacy.

As evident, most commentaries on the military in Pakistan assume a dominant military that seemingly has the power to determine socio-political outcomes in its favour, with political elites having little to no agency or legitimacy. They are instead characterised as mere pawns whose hold on power is dependent on the decisions and choices of the all-powerful military.[30] Moreover, the military continues to assume dominance both when it formally rules the country after a military coup and when it does not, as when elected governments are at the helm of political affairs. This framework makes the exercise of conceptualising civil–military relations ahistorical, tautological and a closed totality characterised by a circular logic that constantly reinforces the military's hegemony. It is ahistorical because it does not allow for changing circumstances and contexts. All three military regimes, for example, contended with popular protests that were instrumental in their downfall. Unlike General Zia-ul-Haq, who was killed when his airplane crashed, Ayub Khan and Pervez Musharraf both abdicated power due to popular protests and the public's yearning for democratic space. General Zia's time in power was also marked by popular protests when political parties organised themselves under the umbrella framework of the Movement for the Restoration of Democracy in 1981.[31] It is tautological because the inquiry into civil–military relations begins and ends with military domination. It is a closed totality because it fails to appreciate civilian strategies of reclaiming and recovering their own space against the military as irrelevant or largely ineffective.

In contradistinction to these theories of an all-powerful military, a far more fruitful inquiry entails an analysis of civil–military interactions with a view to rescuing the agency of civilian political elites. Political elites have been wrongly characterised as weak, inactive agents whose role in the political system is determined by what the military compels them to do. In the section that follows, the dynamic agency of political elites is brought out by detailing how they contend with the military for the establishment

[28] A Siddiqa, *Military, Inc: Inside Pakistan's Military Economy* (London, Pluto Press, 2007).

[29] P Staniland, 'Explaining Civil–Military Relations in Complex Political Environments: India and Pakistan in Comparative Perspective' (2008) 17 *Security Studies* 322.

[30] GA Heeger, 'Politics in the Post-Military State: Some Reflections on the Pakistani Experience' (1977) 29 *World Politics* 242. An important work focused on how the military in Pakistan creates constraints and limitations on the successor civilian regimes is, Shafqat, *Civil–Military Relations in Pakistan* (n 24).

[31] T Ali, 'Movement for the Restoration of Democracy in Pakistan' (1984) 11 *India International Centre Quarterly* 57.

of their own autonomous space. Comparing the politics of civilian actors in the 1990s and in the post-2008 period, this section will demonstrate that their preference for the continuation of democracy is manifest, that Pakistan's evolving political space is increasingly and explicitly critical of military intervention, and that these developments are potentially positive for the consolidation of democracy over the long term.

III. Mainstreaming the Agency of Political Elites

Political elites in the civil–military equation are confronted with dual tendencies: first, the urgency to display collective unity despite political differences in the face of the military, which I term 'cohesiveness'; and second, competing with each other electorally and also in the process pursuing tactical alliances with the military. This is the 'divisiveness' variable. The cohesiveness variable implies a consensus, on the part of political parties of whichever ideological persuasion, to agree to keep the military out of politics through constitutional safeguards. The divisiveness variable implies a situation in which such a consensus is missing, and political elites are eager to make self-serving tactical alliances with the military with the objective of bringing themselves into power or destabilising their political competitors. Comparing the practice of cohesiveness and divisiveness variables, the foremost objective for political elites in the 1990s was to devise self-serving strategies that installed them into power at the expense of their political competitors even if it required making compromises and backdoor deals with the military. This was how political contestation ensued between Benazir Bhutto and Nawaz Sharif, with their short-sighted politics inclined less towards long-term democratic consolidation and more towards sustaining themselves in power. However, the irony is that despite tactical alliances, once in power, the incumbent political parties and governments found themselves in an inescapable conflict with the military. It was precisely this conflict with the military, as opposed to voter preference in elections, that determined the short lifespans of the two Benazir Bhutto and two Nawaz Sharif governments in the 1990s.

Benazir Bhutto was elected as the Prime Minister of Pakistan in November 1988 after President Zia-ul-Haq's death in a mysterious plane crash in August of the same year. The military feared the gruesome prospect of the Pakistan People's Party (PPP) coming to power and settling scores for the execution of Zulfikar Ali Bhutto. Therefore, it cobbled together a coalition of right-wing political parties called the Islami Jamhoori Ittehad (IJI).[32] Initially, Prime Minister Benazir Bhutto was sensitive to the military's political position. For example, she retained Ghulam Ishaq Khan, a Zia loyalist, as the President of Pakistan,[33] and appointed Lieutenant General Sahibzada Yaqub Khan

[32] Shah (n 27) 166.

[33] According to the Constitution of Pakistan, the Chairman of the Senate assumes the position of the President if the seat becomes vacant. Ghulam Ishaq Khan, the then Chairman of the Senate, was elevated as the President of Pakistan after General Zia-ul-Haq's death in August 1988. He was an influential member of General Zia's inner cabinet. O Siddique, 'The Jurisprudence of Dissolutions: Presidential Power to Dissolve Assemblies under the Pakistani Constitution and Its Discontents' (2005) 23 *Arizona Journal of International and Comparative Law* 616, 659.

(Zia's foreign minister) in her cabinet. However, elite competition and differences between the civilian government and military became manifest soon after.[34] In a daring decision defying the advice of the Chief of Army Staff (COAS), Bhutto sacked the powerful Chief of the Pakistani Inter-Services Intelligence (ISI), General Hamid Gul, a key strategist in Pakistan's support to the Afghan Mujahideen.[35] Bhutto was wary of General Hamid Gul and the ISI's destabilising influence in domestic politics especially in setting up a collective opposition against her party in the form of the right-wing conservative party, the IJI.[36] Similarly, the military distrusted Bhutto for her cultivation of independent foreign relations with India, accusing her of providing India with sensitive information on Sikh militants that had developed connections with the ISI.[37] Bhutto also tried to influence the army selection board by seeking to extend the tenure of the Corps Commander Lahore. The board refused this extension and, contrary to the wishes of the Prime Minister, appointed Lieutenant General Ashraf Janjua to the post.[38] The army conveyed its displeasure with the PPP government to President Ghulam Ishaq Khan after a Corps Commander meeting in July 1990, where the decision to remove Bhutto's government from power was ostensibly agreed upon.[39] Only a few weeks later, on 6 August 1990, the President dismissed the Benazir Bhutto government and dissolved the National Assembly by exercising his powers under Article 58(2)(b) of the Constitution.[40]

The dismissal and ensuing elections brought the IJI to power and with it Zia's protégé, Nawaz Sharif, as Prime Minister. Nawaz Sharif was Punjab's Chief Minister during the PPP government's tenure and a bitter rival of Benazir Bhutto. Sharif courted the military's support in his desire to gain power, resulting in tense relations between the Punjab and PPP government over the transfer of federal civil servants and delays in the allocation of funds.[41] Sharif also appealed to ethnic sentiments and interests, arguing that Punjabis were under threat from the Sindhi Prime Minister-led federal government.[42] Despite the military's preference for Nawaz Sharif and the latter's drive to secure the former's support, ensuing developments did not result in cordial civil-military relations. The Nawaz Sharif government and the military disagreed initially

[34] Rizvi (n 23) 205.

[35] S Shafqat, 'Pakistan under Benazir Bhutto' (1996) 36 *Asian Survey* 655, 661.

[36] 'Hamid Gul accepts Responsibility for Creating IJI' *Dawn* (30 October 2012) www.dawn.com/news/760219/hamidgul-accepts-responsibilty-for-creating-igi.

[37] Rizvi (n 23) 207.

[38] Shafqat, 'Pakistan under Benazir Bhutto' (n 35) 663.

[39] The Corps Commanders are elite level officers who, along with the head of the military – the Chief of Army Staff – are responsible for administering the military establishment and also decision-making. P Staniland, A Naseemullah and A Butt, 'Pakistan's Military Elite' (2018) 43 *Journal of Strategic Studies* 74.

[40] The arbitrary presidential power to dismiss the Prime Minster and dissolve the National Assembly was the result of constitutional engineering by the Zia-ul-Haq military regime, which in 1985 inserted the 8th Amendment to the 1973 Constitution. The Amendment, specifically Art 58(2)(b), ordained the President to dismiss the National Assembly if, in his opinion, a 'situation has arisen in which Government of the Federation cannot be carried on in accordance with the provisions of the Constitution and an appeal to the electorate is necessary'. Quoted in F Mohammed, 'Exploring Power Politics and Constitutional Subversions in Pakistan: A Political and Constitutional Assessment of Instability in Pakistan' (2010) 7 *Loyola University Chicago International Law Review* 229, 231.

[41] Rizvi (n 23) 208.

[42] ibid 208.

on foreign policy as the COAS, General Mirza Aslam Beg, pursued an aggressive tone against the USA for its increased collective security efforts to support Kuwait against the Iraqi invasion. The COAS favoured supporting Saddam Hussein and presented his case for 'strategic defiance', which Saddam Hussain had displayed against the USA. On one occasion, the COAS maintained that after Iraq's invasion, Iran would be next and then Pakistan could also face the American wrath.[43] While the military chief toed an anti-American, pro-Saddam stance, the Nawaz Sharif government disagreed and made 5000 troops available to Saudi Arabia in support of the collective security forces led by the USA.[44] The government also differed from the military over the Karachi Operation in 1992 targeting the Mohajir Qaumi Movement (MQM), which at the time was an ally of Nawaz Sharif's government at the federal level.[45] Furthermore, the military accused the Nawaz Sharif government of buying off 'generals' through material rewards and sowing the seeds of divisions and corruption in the army.[46] Sharif also set aside the military chief's preferred candidate for Director-General of the ISI and instead appointed Lt General Javed Nasir, yet another example of his push for civilian autonomy.[47]

As Nawaz Sharif, once the military's preferred political ally, asserted independence, the military once again moved the President to exercise his powers under the Eighth Amendment and dismiss the government in April 1993. The dismissal was sparked in part by deteriorating relations between the President and Prime Minister over the appointment of the new Chief of Army Staff, after the incumbent General Asif Nawaz Janjua passed away in office. Exercising his presidential powers over and above the Prime Minister, President Ghulam Ishaq Khan appointed General Abdul Waheed Kakar as the new army chief instead of Nawaz Sharif's preferred choice, Lt General Muhammad Ashraf.[48] President Ghulam Ishaq Khan, in his dismissal of the Sharif's government, levelled allegations of corruption, economic mismanagement and 'subversion of the authority of the armed forces'.[49] Nawaz Sharif challenged his government's dismissal in the Supreme Court, which, in a landmark decision, restored the government on the basis that the President's actions were 'not within the ambit of powers conferred' on the President by the Constitution.[50] In its detailed judgment, the Supreme Court reasoned that

> [the] Prime Minister in administering the affairs of the government, is neither answerable to the President nor is in any way subordinate to him. He is answerable only to the National Assembly. It is the President who is bound by the advice of the Prime Minister or the Cabinet

[43] ibid 211.

[44] ibid 201–11.

[45] The Karachi Operation was launched by the military on account of increasing lawlessness in Karachi and Hyderabad in which the primary target was the MQM, an ethnopolitical party, which was accused of intimidating, harassing and killing ethnopolitical opponents and indulging in organised crime and violence. N Khan, *Mohajir Militancy in Pakistan: Violence and Transformation in the Karachi Conflict* (New York, Routledge, 2010).

[46] Rizvi (n 23) 212.

[47] Shah (n 27) 172.

[48] Rizvi (n 23) 214.

[49] Shah (n 27) 173.

[50] S Yasmeen, 'Democracy in Pakistan: The Third Dismissal' (1994) 34 *Asian Survey* 572, 579–80.

> in all matters concerning the formulation of policies and the administration of affairs of the government, and not the other way about.[51]

The Court added that

> no man, howsoever high, can destroy an organ consisting of chosen representatives of the people unless cogent, proper, and sufficient cause exists for taking such a grave action, and that no such situation had arisen or could be said to have arisen on account of the Prime Minister.[52]

Moreover, the Court held that

> the allegations of corruption, maladministration and incorrect policies being pursued in financial, administrative and international matters were held to be neither independently decisive nor within the domain of the President for action under Article 58 (2) (b) and thus wholly extraneous.[53]

Despite this landmark decision in support of democracy, the opposition, led by Benazir Bhutto, denounced the Court's decision, calling for new elections and also threatening a public protest (the Long March) against the government.[54] The military stepped in to avert the political impasse between the now-restored Prime Minister and President Khan, by calling on both of them to quit and hold new elections.[55] As a result, Nawaz Sharif submitted his advice for the dissolution of the National Assembly to the President, along with his resignation.[56] After dissolving the National Assembly, President Ghulam Ishaq Khan tendered his own resignation and brought to an end his long and ignominious tenure as President of Pakistan.[57] The ensuing elections brought the PPP into power for a second time, with Prime Minister Benazir Bhutto this time treading a more careful line with the military. Bhutto offered public support to the military's backing of the Taliban, although she herself was inclined to the establishment of a national unity government in Afghanistan.[58] Moreover, unlike in her first term, Bhutto avoided interfering in military appointments so as to avoid the military's displeasure. However, the military continued to keep a check on the government by monitoring its political and economic performance. In 1996, senior commanders conveyed their disapproval of the Bhutto government to President Farooq Leghari, who obliged by dismissing the government on charges of corruption, nepotism and economic mismanagement.[59] According to Rizvi:

> [The dismissal was] carried out in coup style. The Army took control of the Prime Minister's house and secretariat, and Benazir Bhutto was not allowed communication with her colleagues

[51] *Muhammad Nawaz Sharif v Federation of Pakistan*, PLD 1993 SC 473. Quoted in H Khan, *A History of the Judiciary in Pakistan* (Karachi, Oxford University Press, 2016) 293–95.

[52] *Muhammad Nawaz Sharif* (n 51).

[53] ibid.

[54] A Iqbal, 'Supreme Court Restores Pakistani Government', *United Press of India* (26 May 1993) www.upi.com/Archives/1993/05/26/Supreme-Court-restores-Pakistani-government/3276738388800/.

[55] Rizvi (n 23) 218.

[56] ibid 219.

[57] ibid 219.

[58] H Mir, 'My Personal Account of Dealing with Two Generations of Taliban' *India Today* (20 August 2021) www.indiatoday.in/opinion-columns/story/my-personal-account-of-dealing-with-two-generations-of-taliban-1843357-2021-08-20.

[59] Shah (n 27) 174.

for several hours. The Army also took over the headquarters of the Intelligence Bureau (IB) and other important government installations. For the first time, all airports were closed and mobile phones were shut off.[60]

Benazir Bhutto's dismissal saw Nawaz Sharif return as Prime Minister for a second term, and one of his first measures was to institute changes in the Constitution to offset military intervention. With a resounding two-thirds majority in the national legislature,[61] the Nawaz Sharif government passed the Thirteenth Amendment to the Constitution, which repealed Article 58(2)(b) and with it the power of the President to dismiss an elected government and National Assembly.[62] In passing this amendment, the government displayed resolve and paved the way for parliamentary supremacy, by removing the military's ability to engage in mala fide constitutional engineering. Moreover, the Bill was unanimously passed in both Houses, indicating that both the PPP and the Pakistan Muslim League-Nawaz (PML-N) had realised that Article 58(2)(b) served no purpose other than to allow for their own arbitrary removal from government.

This assertion of civilian supremacy did not sit well with the military, and two further events irreparably soured civil–military relations, ultimately leading to the military takeover of October 1999. The first related to the COAS Jehangir Karamat's suggestion to establish a National Security Council in order to formalise the military's role in policymaking. The second was the military's ill-planned military adventure in Kargil, in the wake of the government's pursuit of peaceful relations with India.[63] In October 1998, Jehangir Karamat ruffled the government's feathers by blaming 'politicians for carrying out vendettas and insecurity and expedient policies while Pakistan capsized and called for the creation of a three-tiered national security council that would include the military, credible advisers and a think tank of experts'.[64]

Taken aback by the provocative demand for formalising the military's role in decision-making, Prime Minister Nawaz Sharif forced the COAS to resign, marking the first time that a sitting Chief had resigned in office. This was no small feat, given that it is usually the Prime Minister who is sent packing as a result of civil–military dissonance. This dissonance widened further after Nawaz Sharif appointed General Pervez Musharraf as the new Chief of Army Staff in October 1998. General Musharraf was eventually instrumental in forging and executing Operation Koh-i-Paima in the Kargil sector of disputed Kashmir, disregarding the Prime Minister's pursuit of peaceful diplomatic relations with India. In Sharif's view, a reset of Pakistan's foreign policy with India was necessary, particularly after both countries' nuclear tests in May 1998.[65] In light of this, Sharif argued that Pakistan should gradually move towards discontinuing its armed support for Kashmiri militants.[66] As General Musharraf and the military generals approved Operation Koh-i-Paima in Kargil, the Prime Minister was kept in

[60] Rizvi (n 23) 224–25.

[61] AH Syed, 'Pakistan in 1997: Nawaz Sharif's Second Chance to Govern' (1998) 38 *Asian Survey* 116.

[62] The Constitution (Thirteenth Amendment) Act, 1997, www.senate.gov.pk/en/essence.php?id=1053&catid=3&subcatid=182&leftcatid=148&cattitle=Legislative%20Documents.

[63] Zehra (n 2).

[64] T McGirk, 'The General Speaks Out' *Time* (19 October 1998) http://content.time.com/time/world/article/0,8599,2054276,00.html.

[65] Zehra (n 2) 86.

[66] ibid 102.

the dark.[67] The resultant operation proved an international embarrassment for Pakistan, and resulted in the deterioration of civil–military relations. Nawaz Sharif criticised the military brass for not factoring in the strategic consequences of the Kargil operation, and took the decision to withdraw troops from the Kargil sector.[68] In the ensuing months, the civil–military equation deteriorated further, leading eventually to General Musharraf's military takeover in October 1999.

The discussion above demonstrates two important facets in Pakistan's civil–military equation: first, civilian political elites in this period were not disempowered political actors in the face of military dominance, but instead took actions to undermine military authority and influence in the political system; and second, despite their dominance, the military was forced to prevent civilian supremacy, as the strengthening of political processes and democracy negatively affected the military's ability to affect outcomes in their own favour. In this sense, the vulnerability and anxiety of being superseded by civilian leadership is a necessary factor in understanding military machinations, as opposed to simplistic presumptions of military dominance and hegemony.

The disjointed approach of political elites in the 1990s transformed into a cohesive stance in 2006, when the formerly bitter rivals, Benazir Bhutto and Nawaz Sharif, signed the Charter of Democracy. Going beyond their short-sighted politics of the previous years, the two committed themselves not to 'join a military regime or any military sponsored government', and agreed that they would not 'solicit the support of the military to come into power or to dislodge a democratic government'.[69] This explicit commitment to democratic politics demonstrated cohesiveness on the part of the previously divided civilian elite on the issue of pushing the military out of politics. In doing so, the political elites were expressing not only a value preference for democracy, but also a simple self-serving consideration: democracy in Pakistan ensures they have a shot at power against the military.[70] The Charter conveyed the political elites' expectations of what a democratic system in Pakistan should look like – most importantly, the confinement of the military to the barracks and its authority subject to civilian government. On civil–military relations, the Charter of Democracy offered the following recommendations:

(a) 'The ISI, MI and other security agencies shall be accountable to the elected government through the Prime Minister Secretariat, Ministry of Defence, and Cabinet Division respectively … the political wings of all intelligence agencies will be disbanded';
(b) 'the defence budget shall be placed before Parliament for debate and approval';
(c) 'all senior postings in the security agencies shall be made with the approval of the government'; and

[67] ibid 120.

[68] ibid 279.

[69] 'Text of the Charter of Democracy' *Dawn* (16 May 2006) www.dawn.com/news/192460.

[70] Siddiqa terms the Charter of Democracy inconsequential and a mere protest against Musharraf rather than a solution to push the military back permanently. Siddiqa, *Military Inc* (n 28) 291–92. I disagree with Siddiqa's analysis on account of it not differentiating between the symbolic and substantive value of the Charter of Democracy. The Charter exhibited a symbolic value on the part of political elites and in this sense can be termed a success. The substantive value as understood with respect to concrete achievements was not inherently possible because the Charter was not a legal document. The substantive shape was provided via the 18th Amendment to the Constitution, which embodied the civilian spirit of the Charter of Democracy.

(d) 'military land allotment and cantonment jurisdictions will come under the purview of defence ministry'.[71]

The Charter was an outcome of Pakistani politics after the October 1999 coup, in which General Pervez Musharraf engaged in constitutional engineering with the motive of offsetting resistance from dissident political leaders. Having organised sham elections in October 2002, Musharraf reinstated the power of the President to dismiss a sitting government and the National Assembly through the Seventeenth Amendment to the Constitution.[72] With the dreaded Article 58(2)(b) restored, President Musharraf gave himself the power to sabotage political processes to the military's advantage. However, despite his power and authority, President Musharraf's regime was rocked by the lawyers' protest movement. This movement arose in response to his attempts to control the judiciary by unconstitutionally dismissing the sitting Supreme Court Chief Justice, Iftikhar Choudhary.[73] The Lawyers' Movement, the return of both Nawaz Sharif and Benazir Bhutto to Pakistan and wider calls for democratisation on the part of the civil society ultimately led to the military dictator's downfall. In early 2008, President Musharraf conceded to general elections which brought the PPP into power. Both the PPP and the PML-N committed to the Charter of Democracy, and provided it legal standing in the form of the Eighteenth Amendment to the Constitution.[74] Despite being in the opposition, Nawaz Sharif assented to the amendment as it privileged the parliamentary form of government and strengthened Article 6 of the Constitution, which prevents the military and the judiciary from toppling the democratic government and usurping power arbitrarily.[75]

This push-back against the military on the part of the political elites subsequently led to significant episodes of civil–military discord under the ruling governments of the PPP (2008–13) and the PML-N (2013–18). During the PPP's rule, President Asif Ali Zardari's announcement that Pakistan was ready to commit to a policy of no first use of nuclear weapons set civil–military relations off to a poor start.[76] This was a radical departure from Pakistan's existing position of maintaining ambiguity and retaining the

[71] 'Text of the Charter of Democracy' (n 69).

[72] R Asghar, 'NA Okays 17th Amendment: ARD, Allies Boycott Vote' *Dawn* (30 December 2003) www.dawn.com/news/131650/na-okays-17th-amendment-ard-allies-boycott-vote.

[73] S Shafqat, 'Civil Society and the Lawyers' Movement of Pakistan' (2018) 43 *Law and Social Inquiry* 889.

[74] The PPP and PML-N were coalition partners in the Parliament after the 2008 elections, but differences over the reinstatement of sacked judges and the choice of a neutral candidate as Pakistan's President dented the alliance as Nawaz Sharif opted out: 'Nawaz Sharif Pulls Out of Coalition' *France24* (25 August 2008) www.france24.com/en/20080825-nawaz-sharif-pulls-out-coalition-pakistan-politics. Despite the disagreement and the PML-N on opposition benches, the PML-N voted for the 18th Amendment, with the ball passing unanimously in the National Assembly and Senate: 'Senate Approves 18th Amendment Bill' *Dawn* (16 April 2010) www.dawn.com/news/852442/senate-approves-18th-amendment-Bill.

[75] High treason is dealt with in Art 6 of the Constitution. According to clause (1), any person who abrogates, subverts, suspends or holds in abeyance, or attempts or conspires to abrogate, subvert, suspend or hold in abeyance, the Constitution by use of force, show of force or any other constitutional means shall be guilty of high treason. The 18th Amendment introduced the words 'suspend or hold in abeyance', which were not part of the original Article. Moreover, a new clause (2A) was appended to Art 6 stating that the act of high treason mentioned in clause (1) shall not be validated by any court, including the Supreme Court or a High Court. MR Rabbani, *A Biography of Pakistani Federalism: Unity in Diversity* (Islamabad, Leo Books, 2012) 271.

[76] M MacDonald, 'Zardari Says Ready to Commit to No First Use of Nuclear Weapons' *Reuters* (22 November 2018) http://blogs.reuters.com/pakistan/2008/11/22/zardari-says-ready-to-commit-to-no-first-use-of-nuclear-weapons/.

option of using nuclear weapons in the event of a war.[77] President Zardari also argued that he was against nuclear warfare and suggested a South Asian pact to prevent the use of nuclear weapons.[78] Zardari's announcement was made without prior consultation of the military, and was met with strong disapproval from the army chief, General Ashfaq Pervez Kiyani, who denounced such a policy, according to a Wikileaks cable.[79]

This initial civil–military dispute was followed by a more intense conflict over what came to be known as the 'memogate scandal'. The memogate scandal emanated from an article in the *Financial Times* in October 2011 where a Pakistani-American businessman, Mansoor Ijaz, alleged that he had delivered a memo to the US military chief, Admiral Mike Mullen, in which President Zardari sought American security guarantees in order to rein in the country's military and intelligence agencies, and provide support for democratic processes in Pakistan.[80] A high-level judicial investigation was initiated against Pakistan's Ambassador to the USA, Hussain Haqqani, the alleged author of the memo. In his response to the Supreme Court, the Chief of Army Staff rebuked the memo for compromising Pakistan's national security and asked the Court to set up an independent commission to investigate the incident.[81] As the memogate scandal gathered steam, civil–military relations hit a low after Prime Minister Yusuf Raza Gilani questioned the role of the military on the floor of the National Assembly and scornfully lamented, 'if the Army considers itself a state within a state, then it is unacceptable'.[82] This was followed by Prime Minster Gilani firing his Defence Secretary, a retired Lieutenant General, on the basis of 'gross misconduct and illegal action' and for 'creating misunderstanding between the state institutions'.[83] Almost eight years later, in 2019, the Chief Justice dismissed the petition against Hussain Haqqani, questioning whether the foundations of the Pakistani state were so weak as to be shaken by a mere memo.[84] The memogate scandal episode reveals an incessant dissonance between civilian and military elites. This dissonance emerged out of a civilian worldview opposed to the policy of supporting non-state actors and the military's proclivity to co-opt such actors in the pursuit of strategic geopolitical advantages. In his article, Mansoor Ijaz also alluded to the government's desire to set up a new security team within Pakistani intelligence to replace the unit which was charged with maintaining relations with the Taliban and the Haqqani network.[85] Moreover, the episode also exposed the limitations

[77] S Tasleem, 'Pakistan's Nuclear Use Doctrine' *Regional Insight: Carnegie Endowment for International Peace* (30 June 2016) https://carnegieendowment.org/2016/06/30/pakistan-s-nuclear-use-doctrine-pub-63913.

[78] 'Pakistan Ready for Nuclear No First Use: Zardari' *Dawn* (22 November 2008) www.dawn.com/news/956201/pakistan-ready-for-nuclear-no-first-use-offer-zardari.

[79] 'Kayani, Zardari Differ on "No-First-Use" Nuclear Policy' *Business Recorder* (7 May 2011) www.brecorder.com/news/3871592/kayani-zardari-differ-on-no-first-use-nuclear-policy-201105071185875.

[80] 'Resurrection of "Memogate": Key Developments So Far' *Dawn* (29 March 2018) www.dawn.com/news/1398063.

[81] 'COAS Affirms Faith in Democracy, Resolves to Pursue Memo Case' *Dawn* (24 December 2011) www.dawn.com/news/682849/coas-affirms-faith-in-democracy-resolves-to-pursue-memo-case.

[82] Z Khan and S Khan, 'You're Subservient, or You're Mistaken – PM Tells Military' *The Express Tribune* (23 December 2011) https://tribune.com.pk/story/310422/pm-gilani-fears-ouster.

[83] K Brulliard, 'Army–Government Rift Deepens in Pakistan' *The Washington Post* (12 January 2012) www.washingtonpost.com/world/asia_pacific/army-government-duel-escalates-in-pakistan/2012/01/11/gIQAerfrqP_story.html.

[84] 'Eight Years on, SC Disposes of Memogate Case' *Dawn* (15 February 2019) www.dawn.com/news/1463939.

[85] 'Pakistan US Ambassador Offers to Resign over "Memogate"' *BBC News* (17 November 2011) www.bbc.com/news/world-asia-15782297.

of the military's power to topple governments which had emerged since the 1990s. The changes documented above, particularly the Eighteenth Amendment, have led to a strengthened environment for civilian supremacy, whereby the Constitution can not be so easily subverted.

The next elected government, formed by the PML-N in 2013, was drawn into a conflict with the military on two counts: first, the question of control over projects under the China–Pakistan Economic Corridor (CPEC) agreement; and second, the PML-N government's fervent criticism of the military over its support to non-state actors in what became known as the Dawn Leaks scandal. The PML-N government hosted the Chinese President, Xi Jinping, in April 2015, which led to Pakistan and China formally inaugurating CPEC projects worth $46 billion.[86] As the project commenced, Prime Minister Nawaz Sharif expressed his reluctance to share project contracts with the military's powerful business empire.[87] This challenge to the military's *Milbus* was a colossal decision by the incumbent political elite.[88] The fracas over the CPEC between the government and the military was exacerbated further when reports of a meeting between the government and the Director-General of the ISI were leaked to the media. In this meeting, the military was held responsible for Pakistan's diplomatic isolation as a result of its support for banned militant outfits.[89] During the meeting, Prime Minister Nawaz Sharif insisted on the timely conclusion of the Pathankot investigation, and demanded a restart of the stalled antiterrorism trial relating to the 2008 Mumbai attacks. The resulting news report carried out in Pakistan's leading English newspaper, *Dawn*, led to a bitter public dispute between the government and the military, and ultimately to the resignation of the government's Minister of Information and Broadcasting.[90] Though the civil–military tension led to the resignation of the government's information minister, the conflict over CPEC and the Dawn Leaks revealed that in the new post-Eighteenth Amendment environment, the political elite feels relatively empowered to undertake policy actions and discussions which contradict the military's political and economic interests. Given the changed environment, the only route for military intervention is through the direct route, which means an outright coup and is a distant possibility. It can be argued that, considering the history of the post-2008 period, a decisive shift is visible in the military's strategy after the Eighteenth Amendment that revolves around undermining political leaders and not removing political governments.

[86] K Houreld, 'China and Pakistan Launch Economic Corridor Plan Worth $46 Billion' *Reuters* (20 April 2015) www.reuters.com/article/us-pakistan-china-idUSKBN0NA12T20150420.

[87] K Ghumman, 'PML-N Unwilling to Share CPEC Control?' *Dawn* (18 July 2016) www.dawn.com/news/1271483.

[88] In order to overcome civil–military tensions, the Chinese proposed the establishment of a new institution for effective participation of all stakeholders, the CPEC Authority. The PML-N resisted the proposal during its tenure, signalling its resolve to resist the military's business empire. The CPEC Authority was finally established through a government ordinance in October 2019, with Lt General (Retd) Asim Saleem Bajwa appointed its chairman. A Yasin, 'Asim Bajwa Made Chairman of Newly Created CPEC Authority' *Dawn* (27 November, 2019) www.dawn.com/news/1519047.

[89] C Almeida, 'Exclusive: Act against Militants or Face International Isolation, Civilians Tell Military' *Dawn* (6 October 2016) www.dawn.com/news/1288350.

[90] 'Information Minister Pervaiz Rasheed Asked to Step Down amid *Dawn* Story Probe' *Dawn* (29 October 2016) www.dawn.com/news/1293026.

As evidence of this strategy, the Panama Papers leaks in 2016 provided a perfect opportunity to the military in its conflict with the Nawaz Sharif government. In these leaked documents, eight offshore companies were reported to have links with the family of the Prime Minister and his brother, Shahbaz Sharif, the Chief Minister of Punjab.[91] Tensions mounted as the opposition political parties put pressure on the government to form an inquiry commission to probe the Prime Minister's family assets and offshore companies, with the then COAS, General Raheel Sharif, impressing on the Prime Minister the need to swiftly resolve the issue.[92] Imran Khan[93] filed a petition with the Supreme Court to review the Prime Minister's alleged money laundering, tax evasion and foreign property holdings, and further seeking the Prime Minister's disqualification.[94] The Supreme Court's verdict in a split decision decided on the formation of a Joint Investigation Team (JIT), comprising the ISI as well as the Military Intelligence, to investigate whether the Prime Minister and his family members had acquired wealth beyond their stated sources of income.[95] In its findings submitted to the Supreme Court, the JIT found an anomaly in Nawaz Sharif's nomination papers for the 2013 election where he had failed to disclose his holding in a Dubai-based company. Relying on these findings, the Court disqualified Nawaz Sharif from holding public office on the basis of dishonesty to Parliament and the courts.[96] Even though the Prime Minister was ultimately removed from power, it was clear that the military needed to utilise more indirect means to exert influence on politics. The Eighth Amendment was no longer an option.

Subsequent general elections in 2018 brought the Pakistan Tehreek-i-Insaf (PTI) into power on the basis of its anti-corruption and pro-accountability manifesto. The military had an instrumental role to play in ensuring the PTI's electoral success. After Nawaz Sharif's dismissal, the military attempted to muzzle independent voices from the media that perceived the dismissal not as an outcome of the Prime Minister's or the government's corruption, but as a consequence of civil–military conflict. Two media outlets, *Geo News* and the *Dawn* newspaper, were taken off air and their circulation blocked, respectively, after they provided coverage of Nawaz Sharif's views.[97] In addition, an unprecedented 371,000 soldiers were mobilised in order to ensure 'free and fair elections'.[98] That the elections were anything but free and fair is evidenced

[91] H Cheema, 'How Pakistan's Panama Papers Probe Unfolded' *Dawn* (3 April 2016) www.dawn.com/news/1316531.

[92] 'Raheel Urges PM to Resolve Panama Issue' *Dawn* (11 May 2016) www.dawn.com/news/1257602.

[93] Imran Khan and his political party, the Pakistan Tehreek-i-Insaf, served as the major opposition to Nawaz Sharif. In August 2014, Khan mobilised his supporters and organised a sit-in in Islamabad for almost four months, castigating the recently elected Sharif government for engaging in electoral fraud and corruption. As the Panama Papers scandal made its way in the national media, Khan once again mobilised his supporters against the government and was the net gainer as Sharif was removed as Prime Minister.

[94] Cheema, 'How Pakistan's Panama Papers Probe Unfolded' (n 91).

[95] N Iqbal, 'Supreme Court Gives Reprieve to Sharif, but No Clean Chit' *Dawn* (21 April 2017) www.dawn.com/news/1328323.

[96] H Bhatti, 'Nawaz Sharif Steps Down as PM after SC's Disqualification Verdict' *Dawn* (28 July 2017) www.dawn.com/news/1348191.

[97] The Interior Minister of the PML-N, Ahsan Iqbal, asserted that neither the Pakistan Electronic Media Regulatory Authority (PEMRA) nor the Ministry of Information had issued any directions for Geo News's suspension, which pointed figures directly at the military. 'Geo News Blackout' *The Nation* (3 April 2018) https://nation.com.pk/03-Apr-2018/geo-news-blackout.

[98] A Shahzad, 'Pakistan's Army Denies Meddling, to Deploy 371,000 Troops to Guard Vote' *Reuters* (10 July 2018) www.reuters.com/article/us-pakistan-politics-military-idUSKBN1K01S7.

by widespread reports of irregularity, opposition parties claiming their polling agents were expelled from polling stations and military officials directing that vote counting was to take place behind closed doors.[99] This institutional overreach on the basis of fairness and impartiality was in fact a strategy to prevent the unlikely scenario of the PML-N emerging as the majority party in Parliament. After assuming power, Prime Minister Imran Khan visited the General Headquarters (GHQ) of the Pakistan army for a security briefing in his very first month, in which he assured the military that the government would provide all required resources to maintain the capability and capacity of the army.[100] Some media outlets claimed that this was the first instance in which a Prime Minister had chaired a meeting at the GHQ disregarding previous practice, such meetings previously being co-chaired by the Prime Minister and the Chief of Army Staff.[101] During the meeting, the COAS was reported to have dispelled the common impression that the military interferes in civilian matters, with the Federal Information Minister claiming that 'this time both the civil and military leadership are on one page and the same book'.[102] This emphasis on 'one page' was repeated many times by both the Prime Minister and the COAS in subsequent months to dispel the rising tide of criticism against the military's interventionist role in politics. The opposition political parties, the PML-N and the PPP, publicly denounced the PTI government and Imran Khan as 'selected',[103] that is, brought to power at the behest of the military rather than legitimately elected. In response, Imran Khan accused Nawaz Sharif himself of being nurtured by the military, arguing that the PTI's rise was the outcome of a 20-year struggle against the status quo.[104] What this suggests is that association with the military carries overt political risks for civilian leaders in a transformed Pakistani civil society and electorate less supportive of military interference.

IV. Conclusion

Writing in 2010, Oldenburg asserted that the Pakistan of today has never experienced the 'supremacy of the elected' over its state apparatus.[105] Siddiqa likewise argues that '*Milbus* in Pakistan is not easy to root out without concerted efforts by political actors to strengthen democratic institutions'[106] and that the 'civilian governments during the 1990s were equally responsible for strengthening the economic power of the armed forces and bolstering the organization's capacity'.[107] This is archaic reasoning for it fails

[99] H Javid and M Mufti, 'Electoral Manipulation or Astute Electoral Strategy? Explaining the Results of Pakistan's 2018 Election' [2020] *Asian Affairs: An American Review* 1.
[100] 'Monitor: Civil–Military Relations in Pakistan' (Pakistan Institute of Legislative Development and Transparency, 2018) 3.
[101] ibid 3.
[102] ibid 4.
[103] A Yasin, 'Bilawal Takes a Dig by Calling Imran Prime Minister-Select' *The News International* (18 August 2018) www.thenews.com.pk/print/356586-bilawal-takes-a-dig-by-calling-imran-prime-minister-select.
[104] 'I'm the Only Politician Who Wasn't Nurtured at GHQ: PM Imran Khan' *The News International* (16 January 2021) www.thenews.com.pk/print/774994-i-m-the-only-politician-who-wasn-t-nurtured-at-ghq-pm.
[105] PK Oldenburg, *India, Pakistan and Democracy: Solving the Puzzle of Divergent Paths* (New York, Routledge, 2010) 9.
[106] Siddiqa, *Military Inc* (n 28) 201.
[107] ibid 201.

to take into account the challenges posed by civilian actors and correlates the military's augmented power with the failure of politicians and political elites. The present argument makes the case for 'process' as opposed to 'outcome', with the former focused on how civilian elites pit themselves against the military while the outcome-oriented analysis is fixated on winners and losers. Of course, civilian leaders have played second fiddle in a military-dominated system, but equally valid is the assertion that the military's embeddedness in politics and society is the result not only of its 'power', but also, most crucially, its fear. This fear emanates from the relative strengthening of civilian agency specially since 2008, with political parties opposed to the idea of a military takeover, instead expressing staunch support for long-term democratic consolidation. This chapter has reasoned that, despite civilian setbacks witnessed in the dismissal of governments via Article 58(2)(b) or the disqualification of elected Prime Ministers in the post-Eighteenth Amendment state of affairs, the space for military interventionism is shrinking in Pakistan. The military stands exposed today for its political meddling as it strives to reclaim its political space against emboldened political leaders. After his removal as Prime Minister, Nawaz Sharif organised huge public rallies in the military's heartland, Punjab, and criticised it for his alleged dismissal. Not only did his slogan, '*mujhe kyun nikala?*' (why was I removed from office?),[108] reverberated through his support base, but other political parties also joined in to express their collective resentment. The result was the creation of an alliance of opposition parties, the Pakistan Democratic Movement (PDM), which stands opposed to both the PTI government and the military.[109]

Looking into the future, the civil–military duel in Pakistan will continue to be a see-saw affair between an embedded military reluctant to give up its hold on political processes and an empowered civilian elite that seeks opportunities to establish its constitutional supremacy through the consolidation of both democracy and federalism. To this can also be added a vibrant media and activist judiciary that is supportive of democracy as opposed to dictatorship. In short, Pakistan's political system today provides little incentive for the military's direct and indirect intervention.

[108] C Almeida, 'For Nawaz, Its Not Over Till Its Over' *Dawn* (12 May 2018) www.dawn.com/news/1407192.
[109] 'PDM to Work on Fresh "Charter of Democracy"' *Dawn* (9 November 2020) www.dawn.com/news/1589406/pdm-to-work-on-fresh-charter-of-democracy.

17

A Frozen Democratic Transition: Pakistan's Hybrid Regime and Weak Party System

MUHAMMAD SALMAN AND MARZIA RAZA

I. Introduction

Multiple factors stand in the way of constitutional and democratic consolidation in Pakistan. The focus of this chapter is on the country's weak system of party politics, a fact that compromises electoral competition. Pakistan is a federal parliamentary republic. Since 2008, three different political parties – the Pakistan People's Party (PPP), the Pakistan Muslim League-Nawaz (PML-N), the Pakistan Tehreek-e-Insaf (PTI) – and, most recently, the multi-party coalition Pakistan Democratic Movement (PDM) have alternated control of the central government through multi-party elections and a no confidence motion (in the PDM's case). The entry of the PTI as a ruling party in the centre transformed Pakistan's erstwhile two-party system, dominated by the PPP and factions of the PML, into a three party system. However, allegations of the PTI's collusion with Pakistan's powerful military establishment during the 2018 election period tainted the party's rise into the national mainstream. The Pakistan military has directly ruled the country for 33 non-consecutive years since the country's independence in 1947. This long history of military rule has hampered the consolidation and institutionalisation of Pakistan's political parties, and military rulers have often tampered with elections to disintegrate certain parties. The starkest examples in this regard were the non-party-based elections conducted by the government of Zia ul-Haq in 1985,[1] as well as the Martial Law Order 65 of 1985,[2] in which the military government of Zia appropriated the right to disqualify any candidate it deemed 'political' and thus undesirable. Post-2007, the Supreme Court and election tribunals have further undermined political parties by expansively interpreting and applying Articles 61 and 62 of

[1] In July 1985, international and domestic pressure for political reform forced the military government of Zia ul-Haq to call general elections that he had been promising but putting off since taking power in 1979. However, these elections were held on a non-partisan basis, ie without political parties and with independent candidates.

[2] S Aziz, 'Elections Held on Non-party Basis' *Daily Dawn* (9 August 2015) www.dawn.com/news/1199038.

Pakistan's Constitution, which require legislators to be 'honest' and 'truthful'.[3] On a variety of grounds – including contempt of court, concealment of facts and concealment of assets – the apex court and election tribunals have disqualified former Prime Ministers Yusuf Raza Gillani, Shahid Khaqan Abbasi and Nawaz Sharif from elected office. Other methods of controlling political parties have included sending party leadership into exile while pressuring the second-tier leadership – who represent their parties in the media and are mostly members of national and provincial assemblies, but do not necessarily occupy cabinet positions – to switch sides through constant harassment or the offering of material incentives. This tactic proved successful in bifurcating the PML into two factions following General Musharraf's military coup in 1999, where not only the second tier but also former cabinet members joined the political coalition formed by the military. Similarly, in collusion with former President Ghulam Ishaq Khan, the military establishment undermined Benazir Bhutto's electoral prospects in the 1990 elections by doling out hefty bribes to her political rivals.[4] More recently, the military establishment has faced allegations of pre-poll rigging or 'election management' by manipulating polling outcomes, tilting electoral competition in favour of one party (in this case, the PTI) through the control of the media.[5] In the days leading up to the 2018 general election, there were strong indications that the military establishment was backing the PTI. These perceptions triggered the mass defection of 'electables'[6] from the PPP and PML-N to the PTI and thus severely limited the chances of the former two. Furthermore, between 2008 and 2013, political parties faced pre-election and election day violence by militant Islamist groups, such as the Tehreek-e-Taliban Pakistan. The worst hit was the Awami National Party (ANP), which lost nearly 500 of its members, from party leaders to workers, in terrorist attacks. Smaller ethnic parties, such as the Muttahida Qaumi Movement (MQM), have suffered enormous disintegration in state-led violent action spearheaded by the military. Pakistan's political parties thus operate in a radically insecure environment.

Recent years have seen issues such as service delivery[7] and, to a small extent, intra-party democratisation become central to voting preferences, which has further accentuated these insecurities. Urban working- and middle-class voters have taken issue with the dynastic leadership structure, centralised decision-making and corruption

[3] M Guruswamy, 'Adjudicating "Honesty": Prime Minister(s) and the Supreme Court of Pakistan' (*International Journal of Constitutional Law Blog*, 5 December 2017) www.iconnectblog.com/2017/12/adjudicating-honesty-prime-ministers-and-the-supreme-court-of-pakistan-i-connect-column/.

[4] Prominent names include Nawaz Sharif, Abida Hussain, Javed Hashmi and Ghulam Mustafa Khar, all of whom later denied the allegation.

[5] Pakistani press and media associations claim that the military uses various tactics, including violence and broadcast/circulation disruptions, to gag the media and force self-censorship in the news industry. See 'Pakistan Military "Quietly" Stifling Press through Intimidation' *Al Jazeera* (12 September 2018) www.aljazeera.com/news/2018/9/12/pakistan-military-quietly-stifling-press-with-intimidation.

[6] Locally influential candidates with fixed constituency support, who play a major role in determining electoral outcomes by switching from one party to another during election time.

[7] According to Gallup Pakistan, 'Pakistan's General Election 2018: Exit Poll Survey Report – Who Voted for Whom, Why, and What Does It Mean for Pakistan's Future?' (26 July 2018) http://gallup.com.pk/wp/wp-content/uploads/2019/03/Gallup-Pakistan-Exit-Poll-Survey-2018-Report-1.pdf, most of the surveyed voters (30%) in GE-2018 voted for parties and candidates they trusted to deliver on development commitments. In contrast, party loyalists, patronage seekers, legislation-focused, morality-bound and biraderi-bound voters comprised 11%, 23%, 14%, 12%, and 6% of the sample respectively.

within the PPP and PML-N.[8] It is within this context that many saw the PTI as a viable alternative to these parties. Moreover, the failure of political parties to devolve power and conduct elections of local bodies has hampered good governance and consequently affected voters' perceptions of parties' willingness or capacity to entrench democracy. This has also increased the dependency of political parties on 'electables'. Additionally, allegations of corruption and willingness to strike backdoor deals with the military establishment have further dented the credibility of political parties. These issues – centralisation and dynasticisation of party structure, inconsistency between political rhetoric and action, corruption and failure to devolve power – are all symptoms of a weak party system. These deficiencies of Pakistan's political parties exist in a symbiotic relationship with the political interference of the military. Taken together, both contribute to the weakening of democratic rule in Pakistan.

Several regimes like Pakistan, which adopted electoral politics in the post-third wave of democratisation, are often referred to as 'hybrid regimes', where the elements of both liberal democracy and authoritarianism coexist.[9] After the restoration of democracy in 1988, Pakistan's weak yet competitive multi-party system became overshadowed by the predominance of the military in certain areas of statecraft, particularly foreign and security policies. Poorly organised political parties and a weakly institutionalised party system enable military interference in politics.[10] On the one hand, constitutional changes enacted by military regimes continue to determine inter-party interaction both within and outside Parliament. On the other hand, legislation sanctioning military involvement in politics has been enacted by recent democratic governments with full support from opposition parties. In the July 2018 elections, Pakistan marked its third consecutive transition of power from one elected government to another since the end of the last military rule in 2008. Nonetheless, Pakistan's transition to consolidated democracy is far from complete. The scholarly literature on Pakistan has linked its democracy deficit to the 'tutelary interference' by the military. Despite having more than one form, tutelary interference is often strictly understood as military intervention in studies on Pakistan. Not only has interference by other tutelary actors received scant attention, but a host of other factors influencing democratic consolidation remain under-studied. These include judicial interference, party system institutionalisation, level of cohesion in the organisation of the political elite and lack of elite consensus on democratic norms.

In this study, we focus on weaknesses in the institutionalisation of the party system. We employ a framework that combines the concept of party system institutionalisation[11]

[8] Based on informal interviews conducted in-person and online between 2016 and 2020 with a mixed group of over 100 voters based in Karachi, Lahore and Islamabad.

[9] K Adeney, 'How to Understand Pakistan's Hybrid Regime: The Importance of a Multidimensional Continuum' (2017) 24 *Democratization* 119.

[10] For a contrarian argument, see FH Siddiqi, ch 16 in this volume. He contends that political parties in Pakistan are more averse to military intervention now than ever before. According to him, it is the 'fear' of the growing agency of civilian politicians which leads to tutelary interference instead of the perceived preponderance of tutelary actors.

[11] S Mainwaring and TR Scully, 'Introduction: Party Systems in Latin America' in S Mainwaring and TR Scully (eds), *Building Democratic Institutions: Party Systems in Latin America* (Stanford, Stanford University Press, 1995).

with the two-dimensional typology of hybrid regimes[12] to explain weak democratisation in Pakistan.

Party system institutionalisation broadly refers to the degree of predictability regarding the behaviour of political parties as well as the political outcomes they seek to achieve. In full democracies, party systems normally reflect greater levels of predictability, and thus institutionalisation, compared to weak democracies. Research on democratisation in Pakistan has only recently begun to focus on political parties.[13] This is a welcome change because political parties are key institutions of democracy. Pakistan's political history is marred by repeated military interventions, legalised by the courts. Among other factors, periods of military rule have contributed to a weak party system in Pakistan. For the political elite to reject military intervention and reclaim domains of governance traditionally appropriated by the military – for example, foreign and security policy – it is important to reconsider the institutional set-up of political parties.

II. Pakistan as a 'Hybrid' Regime

The third wave of democratisation significantly altered the world order by increasing the number of electoral regimes. This change was received with much optimism. Francis Fukuyama announced the triumph of Western values of freedom and the free market over its ideological rival, communism. However, it quickly became evident that many of the new electoral regimes were far from democratic consolidation and instead stuck in transition. A plethora of terminology has been coined to describe these regimes, including illiberal democracy, democracy with reserved domains, tutelary democracies and delegative democracies.[14] These regimes are understood as diminished sub-types of democracy. Some scholars argue that, due to the high level of democratic deficit in certain regimes, they must be classified as diminished sub-types of authoritarianism. Semi-authoritarianism, competitive authoritarianism and liberalised autocracy are examples of the labels used to describe these regimes.[15] However, this classificatory approach engenders more conceptual confusion than it resolves. For instance, one single regime is classified as a variant of democracy by some scholars and as a variant of authoritarianism by others.[16] This approach also fails to capture the inherent stability of these regimes, as many fail to show signs of transition to either stable democratic rule or full-scale authoritarianism. As a result, a new strand of scholarship has emerged which

[12] M Wigell, 'Mapping Hybrid Regimes: Regime Types and Concepts in Comparative Politics' (2008) 2 *Democratization* 230.

[13] See M Mufti et al, *Pakistan's Political Parties. Surviving between Dictatorship and Democracy* (Washington DC, Georgetown University Press, 2020).

[14] See D Collier and S Levitsky, 'Democracy with Adjective: Conceptual Innovation in Comparative Research' (1997) 3 *World Politics*, 430; L Diamond, 'Elections without Democracy: Thinking about Hybrid Regimes' (2002) 2 *Journal of Democracy*, 21.

[15] M Bogaards, 'How to Classify Hybrid Regimes? Defective Democracy and Electoral Authoritarianism' (2009) 16 *Democratization*, 399.

[16] ibid 410.

prefers the term 'hybrid' for such regimes, and proposes that hybrid regimes must be considered and analysed as a separate regime type.[17]

To position hybrid regimes as a distinct category, it is essential to clarify what is meant by 'regime'.[18] A regime comprises institutions that must project a certain degree of stability in terms of intra-institutional functioning and inter-institutional dynamics.[19] Polities lacking minimal stabilisation can be considered to be in a transition phase.[20] As far as the term 'hybrid' is concerned, a regime cannot be considered democratic if it fails to fulfil any of the criteria of minimal democracy, which include free and fair political competition, universal electoral participation, free and vibrant media, no tutelary interference and guarantee of civil rights.[21] Meanwhile, the existence of a significantly competitive electoral environment distinguishes hybrid regimes from authoritarian regimes. Though some scholars prefer the term 'competitive authoritarianism' for such regimes,[22] the lack of scholarly agreement over whether to classify these regimes as diminished sub-types of democracy or authoritarianism leads us to consider 'hybrid regime' a more appropriate term for exploring the ambiguities found within these regimes.[23]

A hybrid regime is one that follows a period of minimal democracy – characterised by tolerance, liberalisation and relatively unrestricted political pluralism – after the end of authoritarian or traditional rule but is still 'subjected to the intervention of non-elected bodies – the military, above all – that place restrictions on competitive pluralism without creating a more or less stable authoritarian regime'.[24]

In competitive electoral regimes such as Pakistan, where the parliamentary process has been repeatedly disrupted by multiple military interventions, institutions exhibit a degree of ambiguity pertaining to their character, orientation and goals – an element specific to hybrid regimes. For instance, in stable democracies, the elected civilian leadership enjoys autonomy in policymaking while other institutions, such as the military, pursue those civilian-set policies after giving their input when required. In addition, the judiciary is expected to perform its duties in a non partisan manner. However, in hybrid regimes, institutions do not necessarily operate within their constitutionally defined domains. Regular elections or the restoration of formal civilian rule do not guarantee the transition to a stable – or stabilising – democracy. Legal institutions, such as apex courts, may not necessarily oppose military rule out of a commitment to democracy or a concern for advancing constitutionalism, but may support its control over

[17] See TL Karl, 'The Hybrid Regimes of Central America' (1995) 6 *Journal of Democracy*, 72; L Morlino, 'Are There Hybrid Regimes? Or Are They Just and Optical Illusion?' (2009) 1 *European Political Science Review*, 273; Diamond (n 14); L Gilbert and P Mohseni, 'Beyond Authoritarianism: The Conceptualization of Hybrid Regimes' (2011) 46 *Studies in Comparative International Development*, 270; M Mufti, 'What Do We Know about Hybrid Regimes after Two Decades of Scholarship?' (2018) 6 *Politics and Governance*, 112.

[18] Morlino (n 17).

[19] ibid.

[20] ibid 277.

[21] ibid.

[22] S Levitsky and LS Way, *Competitive Authoritarianism: Hybrid Regimes after the Cold War* (Cambridge, Cambridge University Press, 2010).

[23] Diamond (n 14).

[24] Morlino (n 17).

elected governments.[25] Some courts interfere in executive functions under the pretext of their self-assumed role as 'guardians of the regime', but in fact they may be doing so to assert and expand their own institutional power.

Gilbert and Mohseni[26] propose a configurative approach to analyse and compare different hybrid regimes. In their conceptualisation, the nature and level of competitiveness, the extent of tutelary interference and the state of civil liberties are three important indicators relating to democratic deficits of different hybrid regimes. Their approach is suitable for comparative studies involving many cases, where analytical precision takes precedence over thick descriptions of individual cases. For single case studies such as the present one, conceptual intension is preferable to conceptual extension. In other words, we limit the scope of this chapter to Pakistan and examine this case using a denser, as opposed to minimal, conception of 'hybrid regime'. For this objective, we employ Wigell's two-dimensional approach to map political regimes.[27]

A. Hybrid Constitutionalism and Democratic Deconsolidation

Wigell[28] outlines two key dimensions of liberal democracy: electoralism, which provides popular endorsement to the power enjoyed by the ruling elite, and constitutionalism, which limits the exercise of that power through the entrenchment of the rule of law. Electoral regimes, however, do not follow a linear path when it comes to the manifestation of these two dimensions. Some regimes can be widely popular but do not necessarily fare well on constitutionalism indicators. Here, constitutionalism is not just narrowly concerned with limited government or respect for civil liberties, but has a broad definition focusing on the balance and separation of powers between different organs of the state. Certain cases demonstrate that political parties or leaders, riding high on popularity, alter the rules of business to benefit their parties at the expense of political rivals. Hindutva-inspired policies of the Narendra Modi-led Bharatiya Janata Party (BJP) government in India, and the emerging possibility of single-party rule in Turkey due to Erdogan's proclivity towards centralisation, are two examples of 'abusive constitutionalism'.[29] Wigell[30] outlines several features of electoralism and constitutionalism that are not found in many electoral regimes. Under this schema, inadequate levels of either (or both) electoralism and constitutionalism render certain regimes as not fulfilling the minimum criteria of democracy.

The conditions of electoral empowerment, sovereignty, integrity and irreversibility[31] are essential to ensuring that those who succeed in elections enjoy freedom from

[25] Y Kureshi, 'Judicial Politics in a Hybrid Democracy. Pakistan's Judiciary and Political Parties' in Mufti et al (n 13).

[26] Gilbert and Mohseni (n 17) 270.

[27] Wigell (n 11) 234–42.

[28] ibid 234.

[29] D Landau, 'Abusive Constitutionalism' (2013) 47 *UC Davis Law Review* 189.

[30] Wigell (n 11) 234–42.

[31] Following Wigell (n 11), we refer to electoral irreversibility as the general democratic concept that election outcomes should be accepted by all institutional and political players and elections should be the only legitimate means to assume government office. According to Wigell (240), 'the winners of elections must be able to assume office, exercise power, and conclude their term in accordance with constitutional rules.

intervention by non-elected entities in their subsequent governance of a polity. On the other hand, the constitutional features of executive accountability and bureaucratic integrity impose necessary limits on the powers of elected officials, in order to keep them from abusing state machinery for the sake of their personal or party interests. Landau[32] uses the term 'abusive constitutionalism' to explain a prevalent phenomenon among various hybrid regimes: that of mobilising constitutional changes to derail democracy. Furthermore, in hybrid regimes, arbitrariness in the exercise of executive authority persists due to the protracted weaknesses of institutions otherwise responsible for the consolidation of constitutionalism. Other accountability institutions may reduce their checks on the executive branch due to the material and non-material costs associated with holding the government accountable. In Pakistan's case, the systematic weakening of constitutionalism, or refusal by incumbent and opposition parties to submit to its tenets, has engendered restricted electoral sovereignty. Parties' quest for power is weakly confined by constitutionalism as party leaders often enable tutelary interference to secure a competitive advantage over their rivals. This is the condition of hybrid constitutionalism wherein rule of law is not upheld in an even, patterned and predictable manner, thus leading to a persisting condition of uncertainty in the electoral realm. This problem is indicative of poorly institutionalised political parties and weak party system institutionalisation more generally.

B. The Spoilers in Democratic Consolidation: Weak Political Parties and the Insufficient Institutionalisation of a Party System

The health of electoral democracy is significantly affected by the extent to which the population is politically empowered and organised, and the capacity of political parties to resolve disputes emanating from societal cleavages. Political parties play a central role in mobilising different interest groups and incorporating their demands in policy-making upon securing power via elections. Interactions between political parties create patterns of behaviour that impact the overall health of the party system.

A party system refers to:

> systems of interaction resulting from inter-party competition. That is, the system in question bears on the relatedness of parties to each other, on how each party is a function of the other parties and reacts, competitively or otherwise, to the other parties.[33]

The interaction among parties is affected by path dependencies relating to their emergence and internal organisation. In many post-colonial states, parties that had been instrumental in the freedom movement continued to enjoy a dominant position for a long period after independence. The same advantage is enjoyed by parties that played a central role in toppling an authoritarian regime. A feature also common to many parties

Losers must accept that the winners have the legitimate right to wield power on behalf of all citizens … for the electoral method to function as expected by democratic theory, elections need indeed be seen as the only means of filling elected offices, and electoral outcomes as irreversible'.

[32] Landau (n 29).

[33] G Sartori, *Parties and Party Systems: A Framework for Analysis* (Cambridge, Cambridge University Press, 1976) 144.

in post-third-wave democracies is a lack of programmatic linkage with people – ie the pursuit of universalistic policy programmes that share benefits and costs with all citizens, including non-voters.[34] Most parties in Pakistan are poorly organised and highly personalistic in their orientation.

Personalistic parties can be categorised into two sub-categories: charismatic and non-charismatic.[35] In charismatic personalistic parties, the leader makes transformational promises. The intention is to inspire people to engage in coordinated action for social change instead of simply offering them another option in an existing electoral pool. In the non-charismatic category, the relationship is transactional and largely based upon promises of post-election patronage.[36] Intra-party organisation of personalistic parties can be analysed in terms of two key features. First, a dominant leader and weak organisational capacity as its consequence. The leader of the party enjoys permanent leadership authority, and his retirement or death creates an existential crisis for the party. The question of succession is central to understanding the prominence of another category of personalistic political organisations: dynastic parties.[37] In the cases of some leading parties in Pakistan, India and Bangladesh, the next of kin succeed deceased party leaders and continue to mobilise constituent support by inspiring feelings of reverence for themselves by emphasising familial links with their predecessors. Chhibber[38] argues that in the absence of independent party organisation or broader civil society associations, it is likely that dynastic succession determines party leadership. The size of the party is irrelevant as both large and small parties can be dynastic and non-dynastic. As in the case of India, the leadership structure of the Congress Party is dynastic, whereas this is not, arguably, the case for the Modi-led BJP. Similarly, also in India, the Shiv Sena party, a small party, is dynastic but other, smaller parties are not. In Pakistan, with few exceptions, most parties are dynastic, whether ethnically rooted or national parties. Where decision-making is centralised and unilateral, the organisational capacity of the party remains weak. This is due to a lack of intra-party democracy, with loyalty to the leader taking precedence over programmatic commitments.[39] Recruitment of party office holders or members is determined by the leader, and formal rules, if there are any, are no more than a smokescreen.[40]

This takes us to the final broad category of 'movement parties'.[41] Such parties are less concerned about the internal organisation of their party.[42] They seek their institutional share by means of electoral participation and combine it with the mobilisation of their

[34] H Kitschelt, 'Linkages between Citizens and Politicians in Democratic Polities' (2000) 33 *Comparative Political Studies* 846.

[35] T Kostadinova and B Levitt, 'Towards a Theory of Personalist Parties: Concept Formation and Theory Building' (2014) 4 *Politics and Policy* 490.

[36] ibid 494.

[37] See P Chhibber, 'Dynastic Parties: Organization, Finance and Impact' (2011) 19 *Party Politics* 277; K Chandra, 'Democratic Dynasties: State, Party and Family in Contemporary Indian Politics' in K Chandra (ed), *Democratic Dynasties: State, Party and Family in Contemporary Indian Politics* (New York, Cambridge University Press, 2016) 12–55.

[38] ibid.

[39] Kostadinova and Levitt (n 35) 500–01.

[40] ibid 502.

[41] R Gunther and L Diamond, 'Species of Political Parties: A New Typology' (2003) 9 *Party Politics* 167.

[42] Kitschelt (n 34) 845.

followers beyond Parliament. Green parties or anti-immigrant right-wing parties in Europe are key examples of movement parties. Mossige[43] also proposes the category of 'personalistic-movement parties', which he places under the broader category of 'catch-all parties'. This type of party differs from traditional personalistic parties in terms of mobilisation during the inter-election period. These parties emphasise the mobilisation of their members and periodically engage in anti-institutional activities such as calling for strikes or taking control of public buildings to register their protest.[44] They tend to avoid a clear programmatic orientation and instead rely on populist slogans, such as eradicating corruption, massive job creation or rapid economic growth. Their main purpose remains to further the agenda propounded by their leader, who usually happens to be the founder of the party.[45] In Pakistan, the PTI is one such party. The leader of the PTI, Imran Khan, founded the party on the singular agenda of accountability. He believes that lack of accountability is a root cause of poor governance and pervasive corruption in Pakistan. After facing successive electoral defeats through three national elections, Khan struck alliances with many of Pakistan's traditional politicians, representing the same politics of patronage he stood up against, for the 2018 election.[46] This strategy attracted a lot of criticism and commentators were quick to identify how it contradicted Khan's political rhetoric of accountability.[47] In his defence, Khan stated that a fish rots from the head down – as long as he was not corrupt, he could keep his legislators and political allies in check.[48] Although the PTI has taken several traditional politicians into its fold, it nonetheless qualifies as a movement party because it has kept its populist agenda intact. Khan's repeated emphasis on the scrupulousness of political leadership indicates his belief that committed ideological leaders can constrain transactional behaviour by party members and allies within the framework of party ideology. Furthermore, the PTI's heavy and active social media presence indicates that the party does not view voter mobilisation as a one-off event taking place near election cycles, but as a consistent, discursive exercise to consolidate its control over the political narrative between elections.

In both full-scale democracies and hybrid regimes, one or both types of these political parties exist. The set of rules or norms determining their interaction with each other, with potential voters and how they respond to the interventions by different tutelary actors constitute the party system of a given regime.

A prominent feature which distinguishes advanced democracies from most of the post-third wave electoral regimes is the rootedness of political parties in society, or 'party system institutionalisation', which exists on a continuum, and where institutionalisation

[43] DD Mossige, 'The Personalistic Movement-Party and the Dangers of Duality' (PhD thesis, Ohio State University, 2009).

[44] ibid 18.

[45] ibid 22.

[46] We understand 'traditional politicians' as those politicians who are chiefly motivated by transactionalism, instead of ideology or programmatic commitments, in the conduct of their politics.

[47] See M Jumma, 'The "Electables" in Imran Khan's PTI' (*Global Village Space*, 14 April 2021) www.globalvillagespace.com/the-electables-in-imran-khans-pti/; D Jorgic, 'Political "Turncoats" Boost Imran Khan's Prospects in Pakistan Poll' *Reuters* (11 July 2018) www.reuters.com/article/us-pakistan-politics-electables-idUSKBN1K120Y.

[48] A Rehman, 'You Can't Win without Electables and Money: Imran' *Daily Dawn* (5 July 2018) www.dawn.com/news/1418060.

occurs to varying degrees.[49] Party system institutionalisation is the 'process through which practices and organisations become well-established and widely known, if not universally accepted'.[50] In an institutionalised party system, it is clear who the main parties are, and a high level of predictability exists about their expected course of action in the wake of an election or impending legislation.

Mainwaring and Torcal[51] propose four indicators of an institutionalised party system. First, the patterns of competition should be stable. They consider it the most obvious element as stability and institutionalisation are interlinked. Second, party systems are rooted in society by means of strong party identification and close linkage with certain interest groups, such as labour or trade unions, political action committees, bar associations and so on. In advanced democracies, for example, political parties spearheaded the expansion of the electoral franchise by appealing to specific gender and race interests, while parties in new democratic regimes have not played such a role, which is critical to party rootedness and overall stabilisation of the party system.[52] In the case of the latter, universal franchise was a given. Third, parties should be understood as the only legitimate source of representation. Fourth, parties should work as organisations composed of interdependent members, instead of being instruments to further the personal interest of a few leaders or individuals.

The volatility of new electoral regimes suggests that party systems in these countries are fluid, unlike the 'frozen' party systems of Western democracies.[53] Multiple factors determine this volatility, and improvement in human development indicators is known to reduce it.[54] At the same time and contrary to the assumption that volatility declines as the regularity of elections increases,[55] it remains high in developing countries despite the conduct of successive elections.[56]

Drawing upon the literature on party-voter linkages informed by ideological proximity[57] and sociological positions,[58] Mainwaring and Torcal[59] contend that in post-third-wave regimes such voter linkages do not necessarily exist and thus voting can be personalistic. Voters choose a party or a candidate for a variety of different reasons, including expected clientelist favours, personal or kinship linkages, or the leader's charisma. A voter can also choose a candidate to advance his material interests

[49] S Mainwaring and M Torcal, 'Party System Institutionalization and Party System Theory after the Third Wave of Democratization' in RS Katz and W Crotty (eds), *Handbook of Party Politics* (London, SAGE Publications, 2006).

[50] ibid 206.

[51] ibid 205–07.

[52] ibid.

[53] M Shamir, 'Are Western Party Systems "Frozen"? A Comparative Dynamic Analysis' (1984) 17 *Comparative Political Studies* 35.

[54] Mainwaring and Torcal (n 49) 207.

[55] PE Converse, 'Of Time and Partisan Stability' (1969) 2 *Comparative Political Studies* 139.

[56] S Mainwaring and E Zoco, 'Political Sequences and the Stabilization of Interparty Competition: Electoral Volatility in Old and New Democracies' (2007) 13 *Party Politics* 155.

[57] G Rabinowitz and SE Macdonald, 'A Directional Theory of Issue Voting' (1989) 83 *American Political Science Review* 93.

[58] SM Lipset and S Rokkan, 'Cleavage Structures, Party Systems, and Voter Alignments: An Introduction' in SM Lipset and S Rokkan (eds), *Party Systems and Voter Alignments: Cross-National Perspectives* (Toronto, The Free Press, 1967).

[59] Mainwaring and Torcal (n 49) 216.

irrespective of the candidate's professed programmatic or ideological platform.[60] Thus, in fluid party systems,[61] individual candidates and their links with the voters becomes more important than political parties. The ability of individual candidates to win elections does not depend on their association with any specific party, but rather parties hunt for potentially winning candidates to increase leverage over rivals and guarantee electoral success. Additionally, the dismal service delivery of governing parties in post-third-wave regimes has discredited political parties altogether.[62] This paves the way for non-party politicians to secure constituencies and sometimes the presidential office as well, as happened in Peru in 1990 and Colombia and Ecuador in 2002.[63]

The impetus for party system institutionalisation also flows from partisanship.[64] Firstly, politics in new democracies or regimes that have experienced periodic disruptions in electoral politics due to military coups are not partisan enough. This is due to the short history of elections, which has prevented the development of clear political identities, and thus partisanship, among voters. Therefore, newer generations of voters do not get the 'partisan push' through their families and regions of residence.[65] Secondly, periodic disruption of the electoral process means that political partisanship that was developed earlier loses its impact on the next generation of voters. The problem of low partisanship among voters in new electoral regimes can be solved by a consensus among elites regarding the necessity for regular and sustainable elections.[66] The periodic participation of citizens in elections would inculcate the element of party identification among voters. In the absence of a consensus among the elite about democracy and periodic elections, tutelary interference emerges as a stubborn feature of hybrid regimes.[67]

Tutelary intervention is a persisting pathology in Pakistan's political history, including its more recent democratic experience. It is understood as '[the ability of] unelected bodies, such as the military, religious authorities, or a monarch, [to] unduly constrain the agency of elected leaders or veto national legislation'.[68] The coexistence of authoritarian and democratic features of governance is a quintessential marker of hybrid regimes. Scholarly attempts to understand tutelary interference in Pakistan have produced divergent and contradictory approaches and have focused extensively on causes and forms of military intervention. A recent body of literature has explored tutelary interference by the judiciary.[69] Scant attention has been given to the role of

[60] ibid.

[61] The fluidity of the party system can be measured by the number of anti-party or independent candidates contesting and winning elections. ibid.

[62] M Tavits, 'Party System in the Making: The Emergence and Success of New Parties in New Democracies' (2007) 38 *British Journal of Political Science* 113.

[63] Mainwaring and Torcal (n 49) 216.

[64] RJ Dalton and S Weldon, 'Partisanship and Party System Institutionalization' (2007) 13 *Party Politics* 179.

[65] ibid 184.

[66] ibid.

[67] GMD Dore, 'Democracy Is Not the Only Game in Town! Democratic and Authoritarian Attitudes in Indonesia, Korea, and Thailand' in GMD Dore, JH Ku and KD Jackson (eds), *Incomplete Democracies in the Asia-Pacific*, Critical Studies of the Asia-Pacific Series (London, Palgrave Macmillan, 2014).

[68] Gilbert and Mohseni (n 17).

[69] See, eg I Niaz, 'Judicial Activism and the Evolution of Pakistan's Culture of Power' (2020) 109 *The Commonwealth Journal of International Affairs* 23; P Oldenburg, 'The Judiciary as a Political Actor' in C Jaffrelot (ed), *Pakistan at the Crossroads: Domestic Dynamics and External Pressures* (Haryana, Random House India, 2016); Y Kureshi, 'When Judges Defy Dictators: An Audience-Based Framework to Explain the Emergence of Judicial Assertiveness against Authoritarian Regimes' (2020) 53 *Comparative Politics* 233.

party system institutionalisation in entrenching tutelary interference and consequently regime hybridity in Pakistan. This is not to suggest that political parties are primarily responsible for tutelary intervention, but that deficiencies in their structure and behaviour fail to create substantial buffers against such interventions.

In Pakistan, mobilisation by opposition parties against incumbent parties has been a constant phenomenon. The inability of the opposition and governing parties to reach a consensus over election results has facilitated tutelary interference in politics. In the pre-2008 period, such tensions, among other factors, created political instability subsequently exploited by the military to launch coups. In the post-2008 period, bitter wrangling between political parties and their refusal to accept their rivals' mandates has enabled the military to retain some of its prerogative powers in terms of policymaking by exploiting the contested legitimacy of the ruling party.[70] It can be observed from these examples that the Pakistani military often assumes the role of an arbitrator, which only serves to strengthen its position as an institution that has historically remained above parliamentary and judicial scrutiny. This results in the compromised protection of civil liberties and erodes the quality of democracy as military agencies continuously engage in authoritarian practices with full impunity.[71] Due to their weak societal rootedness and poor organisation, political parties in Pakistan have always remained vulnerable to the strategies of the military establishment. The weak organisation makes opposition parties seek the military's patronage to pressurise the incumbent party to settle politically explosive issues a certain way or against structural reforms. As a result, the military's self-assumed role as a guardian institution is further consolidated at the expense of political parties.

Situating Pakistan's case in a party system institutionalisation framework allows us to capture structural flaws within Pakistan's political parties that contribute to – but do not fully explain – regime hybridity in Pakistan.

III. Pakistan's Political Parties: Flaws and Struggles

The post-2008 period of electoral democracy in Pakistan has been substantively different from the country's democratic moment in the 1990s, when consolidation of the older political parties, like the MQM, PPP and PML-N, suffered due to the self-serving nature of the party leadership. Party system institutionalisation was prevented due to party splitting, party switching and tutelary interference in the realm of electoral politics. Between 1996 and 2002, new parties – the Pakistan Muslim League-Quaid-e-Azam (PML-Q, a splinter group of the PML-N formed by the military ruler Pervez Musharraf) and the PTI (comprised of both new political faces and defectors from older parties) – emerged on the electoral scene. However, after the reinstatement of democratic rule in 2008, military interference in politics has become more subtle. Allegations of defections and the coercive undermining of political parties engineered by the military establishment are still prevalent. Nonetheless, the failure of political parties to ensure

[70] Z Hussain, 'Dynastic Politics' *Daily Dawn* (2 June 2013).

[71] A Shah, 'How Pakistan's Politicians Help the Military' *New York Times* (23 January 2020).

the accountability of central leadership, to democratise intra-party decision-making, to engage in consistent inter-party interaction[72] and to live up to their political rhetoric has also contributed to weak party system institutionalisation in Pakistan in the post-2008 period. Additionally, in the same period, openly partnering with the military establishment to ensure electoral success, such as in the case of the PTI, has also emerged as a novel example of weak party system institutionalisation. The PTI's electoral success in 2018 was due to the tacit support of certain sections of the military establishment, even though the party enjoys a support base in the urban middle class and among the Pakistani youth. Huge crowds attracted to rallies by its leader Imran Khan are a testament to the substantial voter base he relies upon. Although his electoral success cannot be reduced to the support he gathered from the military establishment, it was evident that the playing field was tilted against his political opponents in the lead-up to the 2018 elections. The PPP and PML-N, on the other hand, struggled to keep their act together as a united political front against the military-backed PTI. Both parties suffered from party switching, but somehow managed to retain their strongholds in Sindh (PPP) and northern and central Punjab (PML-N).

An analysis of the major political events beginning from the leak of the Panama Papers in 2016 – which implicated Nawaz Sharif (leader of the PML-N) – to Yusuf Raza Gillani's election in the Senate in 2021 demonstrates that a lack of accountability, political expediency and high levels of centralisation combine to undermine political parties by highlighting the inconsistency of their actions and their publicly made claims. These weaknesses expose and exacerbate the vulnerability of political parties, erode the institutionalisation of the party system and make it difficult to scale back the prerogative powers of tutelary actors.

IV. Inconsistency, Centralised Decision-Making and Weak Accountability in Political Parties

A. The Panama Papers Case and its Aftermath

One sociological reason for the army's dominance in Pakistan is the fact that its major recruitment base is the Punjab region. Due to its large population size and the rich tradition of army recruitment in the provincial hinterland dating back to the colonial era, Punjab sends more recruits to the army than any other province. Nearly 53 per cent of Pakistan's population resides in the Punjab province. Therefore, it is generally only if a party secures a majority in Punjab that it can comfortably form a national government. Hence, in the 2013 general election, the PML-N formed the central government by securing an overwhelming majority in Punjab. Punjabi politicians – mainly the landed elite – are often accused of enabling the sustained tutelary role of the military.

[72] For example, Pakistani political parties frequently employ extremely polarising narratives against one another, but they sometimes form alliances when it may be politically expedient to do so. At the same time, being in a political alliance offers no guarantee of political cooperation or protection against violent contestation.

Therefore, when Nawaz Sharif launched his movement against the '*khalai makhlooq*'[73] following his dismissal by the Supreme Court in 2017, he was received with much optimism and fanfare in sections of the intelligentsia.[74] This was because, for the first time, a sitting government dominated by Punjabis (mainly from central and northern Punjab) was mobilising its supporters by raising slogans of civilian and parliamentary supremacy. Nawaz's political tirade against the military establishment centred on two reasons. First, in the Panama Papers case, military officials became party to the joint investigation team (JIT) formed by the Supreme Court to investigate his family's offshore assets. Second, it was alleged that the PTI's 2014 sit-ins against the PML-N government in Islamabad were orchestrated with support from the Inter-Service Intelligence agency. During the Panama Papers trials, Nawaz constantly blamed the military establishment for keeping him from pursuing independent foreign and security policies. Nonetheless, when the Supreme Court attempted to block the extension of the army chief in 2019, Nawaz and his party thronged to support the military establishment ostensibly to secure relief in the corruption cases pursued then by the PTI government.

The political crisis triggered by the leak of the Panama Papers provides an understanding of inter- and intra-party dynamics and the state of the party system in Pakistan. In April 2016, the Panama Papers revealed details of offshore companies and undeclared properties of wealthy individuals around the world. Among others, the leaked documents named individuals from Pakistan, including the children of then Prime Minister Nawaz Sharif. Offshore companies and properties belonging to the Sharifs included a number of apartments in Avenfield House in London, which they have been accused of possessing since the early 1990s. The Sharif family denied ownership of the Avenfield apartments for nearly two decades; however, shortly before the Panama Papers were released in April 2016, Nawaz Sharif's youngest son, Hussain, appeared on different news channels and accepted ownership of the properties.[75] Meanwhile, Imran Khan, then opposition party leader of the PTI, launched a campaign for a judicial investigation to probe whether the Sharif family acquired their London properties by lawful means.[76] The PTI also demanded Nawaz Sharif's resignation. The PML-N continued to claim that the London properties of its leadership were rightfully owned and legally purchased. In his address to the national assembly on 16 May 2016, Nawaz Sharif confidently presented the financial trail detailing the purchase of the properties.[77] However, Imran Khan persisted with his demand for a judicial inquiry and filed a petition with

[73] *Khalai makhlooq* (aliens) is one of many euphemisms used for Pakistan's military and its intelligence agencies.

[74] This includes prominent journalists, op-ed writers and academics, such as Najam Sethi, Murtaza Solangi, Ayesha Siddiqa and Raza Rumi.

[75] Hussain Nawaz accepted ownership of the Avenfield apartments in a talk show with journalist Javed Chaudhary on 7 March 2016, nearly a month before the Panama Papers were released. The Sharif family gained knowledge of the impending Panama leaks through Pakistani journalist Umar Cheema, who represented Pakistan in the ICIJ investigative consortium that spearheaded the Panama leaks. In his statement to the Joint Investigation Team recorded on 17 May 2017, Cheema stated that he disclosed this information to the Sharif family to get their response/clarification before publication of the Panama Papers. The Panama JIT report with Cheema's statement is available at www.dawn.com/news/1344640. Hussain Nawaz's interview with Javed Chaudhary can be seen at www.youtube.com/watch?v=akk0_fkVgWc.

[76] H Cheema, 'How Pakistan's Panama Papers Probe Unfolded' *Daily Dawn* (6 July 2018) www.dawn.com/news/1316531.

[77] ibid.

the Supreme Court.[78] Initially reluctant to take up the case, the Court had to eventually admit Khan's petition due to simmering political tensions between the PTI and the PML-N and the pressures of the court's self-identification as a harbinger of justice in Pakistan. This self-image is at the root of much of the Pakistani judiciary's activism.[79] The PPP, another major opposition party, maintained that the institutions of Pakistan were incapable of holding Punjabi politicians – especially the Sharif family – accountable.[80]

Political temperatures soared as the judicial inquiry progressed. Day-to-day press conferences by political parties following each court proceeding became commonplace. While mainstream media contributed to creating highly charged narratives around this case, social media degenerated into an arena of harsh exchanges between PML-N and PTI supporters. In November 2016, Bilawal Bhutto jumped on the anti-Sharif bandwagon, terming the Panama Papers 'the world's biggest corruption scandal',[81] whilst assuring Imran Khan of the PPP's commitment to 'fighting for accountability' if the PTI were to give up its anti-corruption legal mobilisation against the Sharifs.[82] Senior PPP leaders perceived the Panama Papers investigation as a moment of poetic justice for the Sharif family and dispelled the PML-N's claims of being subject to 'revenge', insisting that the investigation was instead an instance of accountability.[83] For its part, the PML-N targeted the court through charged polemics, with some of its parliamentarians threatening members of the JIT and Supreme Court judges investigating the Panama Papers case.[84] This was not the first time that the PML-N had been at loggerheads with the Supreme Court. In 1997, supporters of the party stormed the Supreme Court premises shortly after Nawaz Sharif – Prime Minister at the time – appeared in court proceedings on contempt of court charges. President Farooq Leghari wrote a letter to the Prime Minister asking him to summon the army under Article 190 of the Constitution, to protect the Supreme Court premises and Chief Justice Sajjad Ali Shah; Nawaz Sharif rejected his appeal. There was a repeat of such pressure tactics to influence the JIT and related court proceedings as well, though they remained limited to verbal threats or disparaging remarks about the court in political rallies. In one such political gathering, the Minister of Railways, Khawaja Saad Rafique, from the PML-N, warned the judiciary against making humiliating remarks against the PML-N leadership.[85]

[78] ibid.

[79] Kureshi, 'When Judges Defy Dictators' (n 69).

[80] The PPP leader, Aitzaz Ahsan, expressed this opinion in a television talk show with journalist Saadia Afzal, www.youtube.com/watch?v=6gKWF5dNIF4&feature=youtu.be.

[81] 'Imran May Surrender on Panama Leaks but PPP Will Fight for Accountability' *Daily Dawn* (3 November 2016) www.dawn.com/news/1294045.

[82] ibid.

[83] A Mahmood, 'PPP Leaders Say Sharif Deserves What JIT Is Putting Him Through' *Daily Dawn* (4 July 2017) www.dawn.com/news/1343030.

[84] Fiery statements against SC judges and members of the JIT were issued by the PML-N Senator Nehal Hashmi and the Minister for Railways Khawaja Saad Rafique. In a political rally, Hashmi discredited the accountability process and threatened the judges involved in these words: 'We will make this land (Pakistan) narrow for you and your children. You are now in service, but will retire one day. We will not leave you then.' The PML-N spokeswoman, Maryam Aurangzaib, distanced her party from Hashmi's remarks and clarified that they did not reflect official party policy. See 'PML-N Senator Threatens JIT Members, SC Judges of "Dire Consequences"' *Pakistan Today* (31 May 2017) www.pakistantoday.com.pk/2017/05/31/pml-n-senator-threatens-jit-sc-judges-of-dire-consequences/.

[85] See Khawaja Saad Rafique's statement in a talk show with journalist Arshad Sharif, www.youtu.be/g_cxtWL-5IA.

In the court's split 3:2 verdict, two judges found sufficient grounds to disqualify Nawaz Sharif as Prime Minister; however, three judges ruled in favour of forming a JIT.[86] The JIT comprised six members of different civil and military investigation agencies and was tasked with finding and authenticating the money trail of the Sharif family's London properties.[87] The JIT's mandate included interrogating the Sharif family and their associates. PML-N leaders and supporters erupted in celebrations as the party welcomed the court's decision with much enthusiasm.[88] Following the decision, the prevalent view among most commentators was that the JIT will fail to achieve any results.

After a two-month-long probe, the JIT recommended filing corruption charges against Nawaz and his children as they failed to satisfy the investigative body concerning financial transactions conducted during the purchase of the Avenfield apartments.[89] The JIT also found that Nawaz Sharif was the chairman of a Dubai-based offshore company and he was drawing a monthly salary amounting to 10,000 AED in this position.[90] He failed to declare his chairmanship in his nomination papers for the 2013 elections.[91] The investigation also revealed that a trust deed dated 2006 submitted by Maryam Nawaz – Nawaz Sharif's daughter – as evidence of her ownership of the London properties was forged.[92] A letter from Qatar's prince, submitted as evidence of Nawaz Sharif's financial transactions, was declared unverifiable and a 'fictional myth' by the chief investigator of the JIT, Wajid Zia.[93] Zia further stated that 'the Qatari prince tried to use delaying tactics when the JIT asked him to record a formal statement about his letter. Later he asked for assurances that he would not be ordered to appear in any Pakistani court.'[94] After hearing the arguments of both sides for two weeks, the court ordered the National Accountability Bureau (NAB) to prosecute charges against the Sharif family and disqualified Nawaz Sharif from partaking in electoral politics and holding public office for life.[95] Sharif was replaced by Shahid Khaqan Abbasi, a prominent PML-N minister. However, Abbasi continued to maintain that his Prime Minister was Nawaz Sharif.[96] In fact, according to party sources, Abbasi was a placeholder for Nawaz Sharif's brother Shehbaz Sharif.[97] The PML-N rejected the verdict as another setback for democracy

[86] Cheema, 'Pakistan's Panama Papers' (n 76).

[87] ibid.

[88] 'Dance, Dhol and Sweets as PML-N Supporters Celebrate Supreme Court's Verdict' *Daily Dawn* (20 April 2017) www.dawn.com/news/1328169.

[89] Cheema, 'Pakistan's Panama Papers' (n 76).

[90] ibid.

[91] ibid.

[92] '#Fontgate: Maryam Nawaz Accused of Document Forgery' *Al Jazeera* (13 July 2017) www.aljazeera.com/news/2017/07/fontgate-maryam-nawaz-accused-document-forgery-170713084436017.html.

[93] See 'Qatari Letter Seems to Be a "Fictional Myth", Court Told' *Daily Times* (19 October 2018) dailytimes.com.pk/311908/qatari-letter-seems-to-be-a-fictional-myth-court-told/. The report quotes Zia's explanation on how he arrived at the conclusion that the Qatari letter was fake: 'Hussain Nawaz had told the JIT that he had showed the documents of the settlement with the Qataris to his brother Hassan Nawaz. Hassan Nawaz, however, denied ever seeing these documents. The JIT came to the conclusion that these documents are fake and have been created just to fill a gap in the money trail.'

[94] ibid.

[95] Cheema, 'Pakistan's Panama Papers' (n 76).

[96] See Shahid Khaqan Abbasi's statement in a political rally at www.youtube.com/watch?v=-KltQHlhj00.

[97] B Singh, 'Shahid Khaqan Abbasi Replaces Nawaz Sharif as Pakistan's Prime Minister' *NDTV India* (1 August 2017) www.ndtv.com/world-news/shahid-khaqan-abbasi-replaces-nawaz-sharif-as-pakistan-prime-minister-1732069.

and accused non-elected institutions of meddling with the will of the people.[98] Nawaz turned his disqualification into a political campaign and raised the slogan *vote ko izzat do* (respect voters' mandate). Nawaz Sharif and his daughter Maryam claimed that they were reprimanded for their unflinching commitment to civilian supremacy.[99]

Meanwhile, the PTI gained popularity at the expense of the PML-N in Punjab. Several 'electables' switched to the PTI from the PML-N and Imran Khan was elected Prime Minister in the July 2018 general election. The PPP and PML-N declared the elections rigged in favour of the PTI but agreed to be part of the newly elected Parliament. The government set up following the election has been referred to as 'Project Imran',[100] 'Imran Experiment'[101] and pejoratively as just 'selected',[102] as opposed to elected. Weeks before the 2018 elections, Nawaz and Maryam were sentenced to ten and seven years imprisonment respectively by the accountability court.[103] The opposition parties continued to criticise the 'selectors' for installing an incompetent government. Chairman Jamiat Ulema-e-Islam (Fazal) and Maulana Fazal-ur-Rehman staged a sit-in in Islamabad demanding the Prime Minister's resignation and a fresh election. Initially, the PML-N and PPP supported the sit-in, but they did not actively participate. In their speeches, opposition leaders urged the 'backers' of the government to withdraw their support.[104] In this tense political environment, the Lahore High Court permitted Nawaz Sharif to travel abroad for medical treatment.[105] The media speculated that there was a 'deal' between the opposition and the 'establishment' as such relief for a convicted politician was unprecedented. Shehbaz Sharif, the younger brother of Nawaz, was largely perceived as the dealmaker, while Nawaz himself was portrayed by his supporters in the media and civil society as the figure standing up against the diktats of the military. However, to the surprise of many, it was Nawaz Sharif who wrote the letter to his parliamentary party to vote in favour of the amendments in the Army Act, enabling army chief General Qamar Javed Bajwa's extension for another tenure.[106] The PPP also fell in line as its leaders were granted bail in cases of money laundering. As a result, the PTI

[98] 'PML-N Rejects SC's Verdict, Terms It "Awful Example of Prejudice, Bigotry"' *Pakistan Today* (8 November 2017) www.pakistantoday.com.pk/2017/11/08/pml-n-senior-leaders-reject-scs-review-petition-verdict/.

[99] Maryam Nawaz made these remarks in a television talk show with journalist Iram Abbasi, www.youtube.com/watch?v=Ewy8h4k3OjI.

[100] A Zehra, '4 Years of Authoritarianism: Can Pakistan's Wounded Democracy Recover from Project Imran?' *The Friday Times* (11 April 2022) www.thefridaytimes.com/2022/04/11/4-years-of-authoritarianism-can-pakistans-wounded-democracy-recover-from-project-imran/.

[101] A Siddiqa, 'Imran Was an Experiment That Went Wrong. Now, Bajwa Has to Face Challenge from Within Army' *ThePrint India* (28 April 2022) https://theprint.in/the-fineprint/imran-was-an-experiment-that-went-wrong-now-bajwa-has-to-face-challenge-from-within-army/933254/.

[102] '"No More Selection": Bilawal Says Won't Accept Rigging in No-Trust Vote' *Daily Dawn* (23 March 2022) www.dawn.com/news/1681444.

[103] FK Pasha, 'Nawaz, Maryam Convicted' *The News International* (7 July 2018) www.thenews.com.pk/print/338538-nawaz-maryam-convicted. An accountability court is a specific type of Pakistani courts mandated to hear cases of corruption and abuse of office.

[104] Z Ali, 'Fazl Asks State Institutions to Stop Backing Govt' *Daily Dawn* (6 October 2019) www.dawn.com/news/1509290.

[105] R Bilal, 'LHC Allows Nawaz to Travel Abroad for 4 Weeks; Orders Govt to Remove Name from ECL sans Conditions' *Daily Dawn* (16 November 2019) www.dawn.com/news/1517068.

[106] 'Nawaz Sharif Writes Letter to Khawaja Asif over Army Act Amendment' *ARY News* (3 January 2020) https://arynews.tv/nawaz-sharif-letter-khawaja-asif-army-act-amendment/.

gained legitimacy for its 'selected' government when major opposition parties unconditionally came to rescue the 'selector' from criticisms that the PTI and Imran Khan lacked political legitimacy.

Political events during and after court trials in the Panama Papers case demonstrated the organisational weakness of political parties in Pakistan. Centralisation gives little room for parties to retain their political base in the wake of any crisis pertaining to their central leadership. If the main leader dies or faces disqualification, it paves the way for massive party switching due to a low degree of party identification not only among voters, but also among electoral candidates. The lack of programmatic linkage and the clientelist nature of politics provides space for the tutelary forces to manoeuvre to engineer electoral outcomes. The results of the 2018 elections are a testament to this weak party system institutionalisation, which is marred by personalistic political parties. The following section will further demonstrate how inconsistent political rhetoric further damages the already weak political parties and leaves their voters with uncertainty as to what course their leadership will take when it comes to tough political choices.

B. Rescuing the 'Selector' and Consolidating Military Presence

A constitutional crisis ensued for the PTI-led incumbent coalition government in November 2019, when the Supreme Court of Pakistan suspended the extension of the tenure of the Chief of Army Staff, General Qamar Javed Bajwa. The PTI, which had articulated an anti-extension position when it was voted out of Parliament in 2013,[107] was now bending over backwards to justify General Bajwa's extension due to 'geopolitical exigencies'.[108] It was not the first time that the military chief's tenure was extended, the PTI citing the need for 'continuation of leadership' in the wake of a geopolitical crisis. Ayub Khan, Pakistan's first military ruler, appointed General Musa Khan as his successor after relinquishing the post of Chief of Army Staff and assuming the role of Field Marshal and later President. Khan gave Musa two extensions to maintain his grip over the military through his handpicked general, who, as a Pashtun, shared the same ethnic background as him. Similarly, after imposing martial law in 1977, General Zia ul-Haq held dual offices of President and military chief. Pervez Musharraf followed suit and did not give up army command until November 2007, and only then due to the unprecedented resistance against his regime by the higher judiciary and bar associations. Musharraf's successor, General Ashfaq Pervez Kayani, was also given a three-year extension by the PPP government. The judiciary has generally not questioned the legitimacy of such extensions, instead providing legal cover to the excesses of military rulers.

[107] When the PPP government decided to extend the tenure of COAS General Ashfaq Pervez Kayani, Imran Khan had said that 'in order to curtail crime, national institutions needed to be strengthened, as opposed to individuals and therefore General Kayani's tenure should not be extended'. See 'Kayani's Term as COAS Should Not Be Extended: Imran Khan' *The Express Tribune* (12 September 2013) www.tribune.com.pk/story/603439/kayanis-term-as-coas-should-not-be-extended-imran-khan.

[108] M Afzal, 'The Curious Case of the Pakistani Army Chief's Extension' (*The Brookings Institution Blog*, 4 December 2019) www.brookings.edu/blog/order-from-chaos/2019/12/04/the-curious-case-of-the-pakistani-army-chiefs-extension/.

In the most recent episode of the military chief's extension of tenure, however, the judiciary set aside the precedence of being a silent observer by taking up the petition of a serial petitioner, Riaz Hanif Rahi. It is pertinent to note that Rahi had twice been fined by high courts for filing frivolous public interest litigation (PIL) petitions.[109] In 2005, Rahi was sentenced to imprisonment for one month for misbehaving with a judge.[110] In 2010, he was temporarily banned from the premises of the Supreme Court for challenging the reinstatement of Supreme Court judges.[111] He also attempted to withdraw his petition against the extension of the military chief; however, the Supreme Court denied his right of withdrawal and seized the matter *suo moto* under Article 184(3) of the Constitution.[112] While Rahi filed this petition immediately after the government issued General Bajwa's extension notification in August 2019, the Supreme Court took it up only days before the general's retirement, provoking rumours of collusion between the higher judiciary and the general's presumed successor. In print and electronic media, this instance of judicial intervention generated a mixed response. One section of the media termed it a step forward on the path of civilian supremacy, while other commentators perceived this move as an instance of judicial overreach.[113]

In its detailed judgment, the Supreme Court highlighted several deficiencies in the Army Act 1952 relating to the tenure, age of retirement and extension of tenure of a general, and directed the government to amend the Army Act to include provisions regulating the tenure of the army chief.[114] Given government assurances during multiple case hearings, the court set a six-month deadline to pass the necessary amendments and indicated that failure to do so would result in the end of General Bajwa's tenure as army chief.[115] General Bajwa, whose extension notification was suspended by the apex court in November 2019, was now temporarily reinstated as army chief by the same court. The unprecedented decision of the Supreme Court raised questions about the capacity of the government to implement the court's order as the ruling party lacked the necessary majority in the Upper House of Parliament and had a razor-thin majority in the Lower House. The impression of weak parliamentary capacity was further reinforced by the dysfunctional conduct of legislative business in Parliament at the time, as was made apparent by the highly contentious environment in the Lower House. Several opposition leaders, including party heads, were either under arrest or facing corruption inquiries. Much to the surprise of political commentators and party members, both leading opposition parties, the PPP and PML-N, readily agreed to unconditionally

[109] M Asad, Petitioner in Justice Isa Case Fined Twice for Filing Frivolous Petitions' *Daily Dawn* (25 March 2018) www.dawn.com/news/1397311.

[110] Z Gishkori, 'Frivolous Litigation Overburdens SC' *The New International* (5 April 2018) www.thenews.com.pk/print/300879-frivolous-litigation-overburdens-sc.

[111] ibid.

[112] M Sarfraz, 'Pakistan Army Chief Extension Suspended by Supreme Court' *The Hindu* (26 November 2019) www.thehindu.com/news/international/pakistan-army-chief-extension-suspended-by-supreme-court/article30085645.ece.

[113] For instance, prominent lawyer and former senator, Aitzaz Ahsan, repeatedly criticised the SC for encroaching upon the domain of the executive in his media appearances, www.youtube.com/watch?v=uQ3KKW-Ftz8.

[114] 'Army Chief's Extension: SC Issues Detailed Verdict' *The News International* (16 December 2019) www.thenews.com.pk/latest/584318-army-chiefs-extension-sc-issues-detailed-verdict.

[115] N Siddiqui and H Bhatti, 'Gen Bajwa to Stay On as COAS for 6 More Months: SC' *Daily Dawn* (28 November 2019) www.dawn.com/news/1519326.

support the legislative Bills legalising the extension of services chiefs' tenures, contradicting their earlier stance on the issue. When some PML-N legislators dissented against their party leadership's volte-face, they were reminded of their obligation to vote along party lines.[116] The PPP intended to propose amendments to the Bills, but did not do so as a 'show of cooperation' towards the government.[117] As a result, General Bajwa received another term of office with the near-unanimously passed amendments to the Army Act. This show of co-operation on the part of opposition parties was intriguing as they had relentlessly criticised General Bajwa for his role in the 2018 general elections, accusing him of pre-poll engineering to facilitate the PTI's victory. Long before the elections in July 2018, the PML-N had built a narrative accusing the PTI of receiving the military establishment's support at the expense of other parties. In the post-election period, opposition parties pejoratively referred to the PTI government as 'selected' and insinuated that the selectors were the military establishment, in collusion with the judiciary. This narrative was the mainstay of the opposition during the PTI's entire term in office until the proposed amendments to the Army Act were presented. Amid heavy criticism from its supporters in the media and civil society, the PML-N voted in favour of amendments as per the directions of their ailing leader, Nawaz Sharif, who sent a letter from London instructing PML-N parliamentarians to play their part and to play it quickly – a 10-day deadline was given – in the passage of the respective legislation.[118]

Khawaja Asif, a prominent PML-N leader, held party supporters responsible for the leadership's surrender after three long years of 'resistance' against the establishment. He stated that PML-N supporters wanted party leaders to stand up for civilian supremacy, but they are not willing to agitate on the streets to demonstrate their support.[119] On the other hand, the PPP showed some 'resistance' by requesting the government to follow parliamentary procedures by first presenting the Bill to the parliamentary committees before voting could commence. That the PPP had upheld the 'democratic legislative process' was hailed as a 'victory' by the party chairman, Bilawal Zardari.[120] Both Houses of Parliament approved the amendments with an overwhelming majority of votes from three major parties, the PTI, PML-N and PPP.[121] Lawmakers from the erstwhile FATA (Federally Administered Tribal Areas) and those belonging to religious parties with a smaller parliamentary presence boycotted the vote on account of political differences with the PTI government as well as the military.

General Bajwa's extension indicated a consolidation of regime hybridity in Pakistan where, despite two successive civilian transfers of power, the army continued to retain

[116] Former defence minister and senior PML-N leader Khawaja Asif had reminded the dissenters that all were bound to follow party policy. See 'Senate Committee, NA Approve Services Acts Amendment Bills' *Geo News* (7 January 2020) www.geo.tv/latest/265990-Bills-formalising-tenures-of-services-chiefs-sail-through-national-assembly.

[117] ibid.

[118] 'Nawaz Sharif Writes Letter to Kh Asif over Amendment to Army Act' *Daily Times* (4 January 2020) www.dailytimes.com.pk/532254/nawaz-sharif-writes-letter-to-kh-asif-over-amendment-to-army-act/.

[119] Khawaja Asif made these remarks in a talk show with Pakistani journalist Kashif Abbasi, www.youtube.com/watch?v=bNIy9BYdpyg&ab_channel=ARYNews.

[120] A Yasin, 'Amendment to Army Act: Following Parliamentary Procedure Victory for Democracy: Bilawal' *The News International* (5 January 2020) www.thenews.com.pk/print/593830-amendment-to-army-act-following-parliamentary-procedure-victory-for-democracy-bilawal.

[121] A Saeed, 'Army Act Approved by Pakistan National Assembly' *Arab News* (7 January 2020) www.arabnews.com/node/1609526/world.

its influence over the political leadership. Further, dissent within and among political parties on matters pertaining to the armed forces was not reflected in parliamentary voting. As much as this may be due to arm twisting by the army, other factors – including dynastic and personalistic party structures, and a politics characterised by cut-throat transactional interests instead of programmatic commitments – also play a role in sustaining tutelary interference in Pakistan. For example, dysfunctional parliamentary practices in the form of floor-crossing during crucial parliamentary votes remained a key feature following the 2018 general election. Such practices point to the lack of discipline within political parties and the propensity of legislators to sacrifice publicly stated party claims at the altar of political expediency. In this sense, party members are not entirely different from party leadership, as the discussion of the army chief's extension case shows. There is no evidence of accountability within political parties against compromised legislators or pliable party leadership for betraying their stated ideological claims and goals and instead voting to entrench military power.

C. Floor-Crossing: Indictment of Weakly Organised Parties

Floor-crossing is a form of party switching where certain members of a parliamentary party choose not to vote in accordance with their party's directives during a parliamentary session in which they are required by law to vote in accordance with party policy.[122] Party switching is an under-studied phenomenon as most of the literature pertaining to democratisation and party systems focuses on established democracies, where party switching is rare, potentially due to entrenched ideological bonds between candidates and their parties. However, after the emergence of new electoral regimes in the non-Western world, scholars have started to study the phenomenon and advocated for anti-defection laws to discourage the practice to strengthen the institution of political parties.[123] Party switching may take place for several reasons, major ones being ideological alienation, dwindling chances of the party in elections and prospective personal gains.[124] In nascent electoral regimes, where party systems tend to be fragile, ideological resonance is not the main factor guiding legislators' behaviour.

The practice of floor-crossing is undemocratic.[125] In a democracy, if a candidate wins a seat on a ticket of a particular party but later develops differences with the party, he has the option to resign and seek a fresh mandate.[126] This is necessary because defecting while holding the seat that belonged to the party is a breach of faith.[127] Janda[128] highlights the positive influence of anti-defection laws on democratic health. Firstly, it

[122] Under Pakistani law, parliamentarians must follow party policy during voting on money Bills, election of the Leader of the House, votes of confidence and votes on constitutional amendments.

[123] See GR Montinola, 'Parties and Accountability in the Philippines' (1999) 10 *Journal of Democracy* 126; SW Desposato, 'Parties for Rent? Ambition, Ideology, and Party Switching in Brazil's Chamber of Deputies' (2006) 50 *American Journal of Political Science* 62.

[124] K Janda, 'Laws against Party Switching, Defecting, or Floor-Crossing in National Parliaments' (World Congress of the International Political Science Association, 2009) 6.

[125] PM Kamath, 'Politics of Defection in India in the 1980s' (1985) 25 *Asian Survey*, 1039, 1051.

[126] ibid.

[127] ibid.

[128] Janda (n 124) 16.

prevents larger parties from luring members of smaller parties and therefore hampers the formation of hegemonic party systems. It is observed that party defections mostly serve the interests of the party holding the executive office because they have more resources at their disposal to attract defectors from the opposition. This leads to the second impact, which is prevention of corrupt practices among parliamentary parties – as material incentives often play a key role in encouraging defections in electoral regimes where accountability remains weak. Thirdly, it promotes ideological coherence within parties which is essential for a strong party system, as parties should represent all sections of the society. However, this positive impact comes with a caveat that it might discourage dissent within the party.[129] Like all fragile electoral regimes, Pakistan also grapples with large-scale party switching and floor-crossing. In comparison to the 1990s and early 2000s, party loyalty among elected representatives has grown stronger, but some recent developments demonstrate there are still issues.

After the 2018 elections, opposition parties were looking for opportunities to embarrass the elected PTI and its coalition partners. They decided to introduce a motion of no confidence against the Chairman of the Upper House (the Senate) – Sadiq Sanjrani. The alliance of opposition parties, the PDM, had a collective majority in the Senate and were confident of replacing Sanjrani with an opposition-backed candidate. Sanjrani's election to the position of Chairman of the Senate in March 2018 was supported by the PPP in return for the position of Deputy Chairman. Before the Senate elections in March 2018, the PML-N was set to secure a majority in the Upper House but the defection of party members from Balochistan, and the consequent change of government in the province, reduced its chances of victory. According to some members of the PML-N, the military establishment allegedly orchestrated in-house change in Balochistan,[130] while the PPP's co-chairman Asif Ali Zardari was accused of political manipulation in that province to secure more seats for his party in the Senate.[131] The PTI suggested Sanjrani's name for the position of Senate chairman. The PPP agreed only reluctantly, as it was also aspiring for the coveted position. After the PTI's rise to power in the 2018 elections, the PPP joined the PML-N and other parties to ally against the new government.

In their first attempt to pressurise the government coalition, opposition parties came up with a plan of de-seating the Senate chairman, who is also considered an establishment-backed appointee. On the day of the vote of no confidence, the opposition alliance had a clear majority of 64 seats out of 103, which was evident when the resolution to move the no-confidence vote was passed. Voting took place through a secret ballot and, to the surprise of many, the opposition alliance only received 50 votes in favour of the motion, falling three votes short of the required number of 53 votes.[132] This was seen as a repeat of the politics of the 1990s, when floor-crossing was prevalent. However, the executive has not always been the beneficiary of floor-crossing in Pakistan.

[129] ibid.

[130] See MA Notezai, 'Analysis: PML-N Humbled in Balochistan' *Daily Dawn* (14 January 2018) www.dawn.com/news/1382777; 'Senate Elections: Zardari's Overtures in Balochistan "Amount to Horse-Trading"' *The Express Tribune* (26 January 2018) tribune.com.pk/story/1618956/1-senate-elections-zardaris-overtures-balochistan-amount-horse-trading.

[131] ibid.

[132] N Guramani, 'Sadiq Sanjrani Survives No-Confidence Vote in Shock Victory: Opposition Falls 3 Short' *Daily Dawn* (1 August 2019) www.dawn.com/news/1497466.

The opposition parties have also manipulated elections and utilised floor-crossing for their benefit.

The 1973 Constitution – the first to be framed by elected representatives – did not introduce anti-defection laws in Pakistan. Till the late 1990s, floor-crossing and party switching remained prevalent. It was during Nawaz Sharif's second tenure as Prime Minister that anti-defection laws were introduced through the Fourteenth Amendment in 1997. The Fourteenth Amendment gave the parliamentary leader of the party enormous disciplinary powers. Parliamentarians could be deprived of party membership if they voted against party policy. After the coup in1999, General Pervez Musharraf introduced several ad hoc changes to the Constitution, including anti-defection laws to dilute sweeping powers of party leaders. For instance, termination of parliamentary membership was only permitted if a member voted against party directions on electing the Leader of the House, financial Bills or motions of no-confidence, and the head of the parliamentary party, instead of the head of the party, was given powers to initiate disqualification proceedings against party members. Furthermore, the Election Commission of Pakistan (ECP) could reject the parliamentary party head's appeal, which was not the case in the original Fourteenth Amendment passed by Nawaz Sharif. In the Eighteenth Amendment, passed in 2010, the powers to initiate disqualification proceedings were given back to the party chief.[133]

Despite express legal prohibition, floor-crossing continues to be a problem. For instance, former Prime Minister Yusuf Raza Gilani was elected as Senator from the electoral college of the National Assembly in 2021 despite lacking the required votes. It was evident that some members of the government coalition either voted for him or deliberately wasted their votes to enable his election. Due to the use of secret ballots for elections to the Upper House, floor crossing becomes easier for the compromised members of a party. Nevertheless, in the past, legislators have defected from their parties openly and no action was taken against them. Mufti[134] argues that the lack of legal action against defectors is due to the complicity of every party in promoting this malpractice. For instance, the PML-N also encouraged the defection of a majority of the PML-Q's parliamentary members after the 2008 elections to secure the office of Chief Minister of Punjab.[135]

Floor-crossing is particularly entrenched in Senate elections in Pakistan. The Electoral College for the Senate is comprised of the members of provincial and national assemblies, and certain candidates manage to secure their seats without having the required number of votes from their party members. Parties do not usually punish the indiscipline of parliamentary members. One potential reason is the secrecy and non-traceability of votes. PTI leader Imran Khan was the first party head to expel provincial assembly legislators (he who expelled 14) from his party for taking bribes to vote in

[133] S Memon, 'Striking a Balance between Right to Vote and Discouraging Floor-Crossing' *The Friday Times* (23 March 2022) www.thefridaytimes.com/2022/03/23/striking-a-balance-between-right-to-vote-and-discouraging-floor-crossing/.

[134] M Mufti, 'Factionalism and Indiscipline in Pakistan's Political Party System' in RD Long, G Singh, Y Samad and I Talbot (eds), *State and Nation-Building in Pakistan: Beyond Islam and Security* (London, Routledge, 2015) 232.

[135] ibid.

favour of a PPP candidate in the Senate elections of 2018.[136] Imran Khan claimed that the PTI leadership possessed video evidence to substantiate its allegations against compromised party members. However, the ECP did not initiate any action against the expelled members. Before the Senate elections of March 2021, the PTI suggested that votes be made traceable to ensure transparency, but opposition parties, including the PPP and PML-N, opposed this recommendation. This was despite these two parties agreeing in the Charter of Democracy, signed between Benazir Bhutto and Nawaz Sharif in 2006, to ensure open ballots in Senate elections.[137] At the same time, the PTI itself benefited from floor-crossing when its candidate, Chaudhary Sarwar, secured a seat in the Senate from the provincial assembly of Punjab in March 2018 with a total of 44 votes, far more than his party's 30 members.

In March 2021, Yusuf Raza Gilani's election to the Senate was crucial on several accounts. First, he returned to the political scene after his disqualification for five years by the Supreme Court in 2012. Secondly, the PTI was struggling to keep its coalition intact due to differences within the party and with its coalition partners, the PML-Q and MQM. One of the PTI's candidates, Abdul Hafeez Sheikh, needed to be elected to keep his position as the Federal Minister of Finance as the law requires that a non-elected cabinet member (which Hafeez was) must be elected in either of the Houses within six months of their ministerial appointment. Hafeez, formerly an advisor to the Prime Minister, was appointed a federal minister after the Islamabad High Court issued directives that advisors could not exercise executive and administrative powers. The verdict stated that only elected Members of Parliament could exercise such authority.[138] Opposition parties characterised the Gilani–Sheikh contest as a vote of no-confidence against Prime Minister Imran Khan. Sheikh managed to secure 164 votes while Gilani got 169, with seven votes rejected. Prior to the Senate election, some videos emerged on social media in which Gilani's son, Ali Haider Gilani, could be seen giving a tutorial to a few PTI members on wasting their votes.[139] The ECP took notice, but no concrete action was taken against Gilani, his son or the PPP, who ostensibly undermined the integrity of the election. To dispel the narrative of the opposition parties, Imran Khan decided to introduce a fresh vote of confidence in Parliament, which he secured.

Gilani then stood for the position of Chairman of the Senate as the opposition parties had a majority in the Senate. History repeated itself and Sanjrani again managed to retain Senate chairmanship by securing 48 votes while Gilani secured 42 votes, with seven votes rejected.[140] The opposition parties protested, while the PTI and its coalition partners celebrated their 'success'. It is thus evident that all parties have been complicit

[136] F Shinwari, 'PTI Terminates Membership of 14 MPAs: Shaukat' *The Frontier Post* (9 May 2018) thefrontierpost.com/pti-terminates-membership-of-14-mpas-shaukat/.

[137] The Charter of Democracy was signed between Nawaz Sharif and Benazir Bhutto in 2006 while both were in exile. Both parties pledged in the agreement not to seek the support of military for political gains.

[138] M Asad, 'IHC Says Unelected Aides to PM Can't Run Ministries' *Daily Dawn* (27 August 2020) www.dawn.com/news/1576640.

[139] 'Ali Haider Gilani Video Where He Allegedly Tells Lawmaker to Waste Senate Vote Surfaces' *The News International* (2 March 2021) www.thenews.com.pk/latest/798056-ali-haider-gilanis-video-where-he-allegedly-tells-lawmaker-to-waste-senate-vote-surfaces.

[140] A Shabbir, W Kamran and U Khan, 'PTI-Backed Sadiq Sanjrani Becomes Senate Chairman for the Second Time' *SAMAA English* (12 March 2021) www.samaaenglish.tv/news/2021/03/pakistan-senate-chairman-and-deputy-chairman-elections/.

in manipulating elections and promoting the culture of floor-crossing. The opposition's campaign about the sanctity of the vote became meaningless when they facilitated electoral malpractice and could not ensure party discipline during crucial votes. The reluctance of parties to take disciplinary action against defectors exposes their fraught commitment to democracy, and the rule of law more generally. Indifference on the part of the ECP also raises questions about bureaucratic integrity – an essential component of democratic and transparent governance.

V. Conclusion: Political Expediency, Weak Party System Institutionalisation and Regime Hybridity

When the PML-N came to power in 2013, the party had to grapple with an enormous energy crisis left behind by the PPP government. A significant debt of PKR 450 billion accumulated in the power sector and the government was a defaulter to different power companies. Then the PML-N Finance Minister, Ishaq Dar, paid back the government's debt to power companies with the assistance of the Governor of the State Bank. The Auditor General of Pakistan, Akhtar Buland Rana, objected to these payments and initiated an inquiry. Ishaq Dar halted the auditing process and got Rana sacked through the Public Accounts Committee of the National Assembly on charges of abusing his office for self-aggrandisement.[141] This action by the PML-N Finance Minister ties into the largely weak financial regulation landscape in Pakistan.

In December 2018, a Supreme Court-sanctioned JIT submitted its report about mysterious fake bank accounts created on the basis of stolen identity cards for depositing laundered money whose beneficiaries included Zardari and his sister, Faryal Talpur.[142] The JIT investigation revealed that a new banking group by the name of Summit Bank was specially created to launder money for Asif Ali Zardari, his sister and his business partners in the Omni Group. Not only that: the PPP government in Sindh arbitrarily changed or disregarded privatisation rules to transfer the ownership of government-owned industrial units, including a cement factory and three sugar mills, for low sale prices to benefit Zardari and his cronies.[143] Furthermore, revelations about dubious banking transactions have surfaced about Shehbaz Sharif – the former Chief Minister of Punjab – and his sons.[144]

Such brazen disregard for the rule of law by civilian politicians makes them vulnerable to the pressures of tutelary forces. In the face of political scandal and impropriety,

[141] 'Program *Muqabil*' (*92 News*, 19 July 2018) www.youtube.com/watch?v=qtRXVBHn9bM&t=215s&ab_channel=92NewsHD.

[142] See WA Sheikh, '29 Fake Accounts Used to Launder Rs42bn, JIT Tells Apex Court' *Daily Dawn* (25 December 2018) www.dawn.com/news/1453414; 'Zardari, Omni Group Responsible in Fake Accounts Scam: JIT' *The News International* (24 December 2018) www.thenews.com.pk/latest/410276-zardari-omni-group-responsible-in-fake-accounts-scam-jit; '29 Fake Accounts Used for Laundering Rs35 Billion: JIT Report' *Dunya News* (31 December 2018) dunyanews.tv/en/Pakistan/472204-29-fake-accounts-used-for-transaction-of-Rs35bn-JIT-report.

[143] 'The Zardari System?' *Daily Times* (28 December 2018) dailytimes.com.pk/337660/the-zardari-system/amp/.

[144] SI Raza, 'Shahbaz's 10 Front Firms Found: PM's Aide' *Daily Dawn* (14 May 2020) www.dawn.com/news/1556947.

they tend to resort to extra-parliamentary manoeuvring to sustain their power, which includes striking deals with the military establishment to secure relief from corruption charges and inquiries. This also means that accountability is eventually used as a stick to discipline civilian politicians in Pakistan. Military regimes in Pakistan have promulgated different ordinances to establish institutions, such as the EBDO (Elective Bodies Disqualification Order) in 1959 and the NAB in 1999. These institutions seem to co-opt politicians into joining the ranks of military-backed parties by means of selective accountability. Although civilian governments remained critical of these accountability institutions while in opposition, once in power, they have instrumentalised them to pursue discriminatory accountability against political opponents.[145]

Further, the politics of clientelism inhibits party system institutionalisation in hybrid regimes. In a culture of clientelist politics, it becomes imperative for political parties to remain in power because their political survival becomes directly linked with their control of state resources. Thus, party–voter linkages become transactional and end up providing an undue advantage to the ruling party. In such a scenario, opposition parties seek alliances with non-political forces or tutelary actors to dislodge incumbents and level the electoral playing field. At the same time, clientelism is not only used to lure voters, but also to attract candidates who have better chances of winning elections.[146] Such candidates can be offered lucrative ministries, development funds or favourable policies for their businesses in return for their support of political parties. This kind of political culture negatively impacts the efficiency of bureaucracy and eventually the quality of democracy. Wigell[147] emphasises bureaucratic integrity as one of the key features of constitutionalism. He explains that in a liberal democracy, the bureaucracy should operate independently of partisan competition and interests. It should become neither a tool nor a part of clientelist politics. However, in hybrid regimes, bureaucratic integrity is not valued by the ruling elite. Bureaucracy becomes part of the politics of patronage, resulting in a dismal state of governance due to politically motivated allocation of state resources. Powerful interest groups, such as traders, and business or landed elite provide funds to political parties in return for favourable economic policies. Zulfikar Ali Bhutto, being the first elected Prime Minister, purged the bureaucracy and appointed party loyalists to ensure the bureaucracy's obedience. The culture of preferring loyal instead of efficient bureaucracy subsequently prevailed in both civil and military regimes. Undoubtedly, this has resulted in a corrupt state structure that is largely responsible for suboptimal governance as well as rent-seeking in politics, which makes parties less dependent on mass membership to raise funds for their electoral campaigns. Such lack of grassroots organisation and penetration costs them heavily during political crises.

This was evident during the Panama Papers case proceedings. Instead of distancing themselves from Nawaz Sharif and letting the legal process take its course, the top brass of the PML-N chose to defend him because their political fortunes were tied to him. The same was apparent when fake accounts associated with the PPP leadership emerged.

[145] A Naveed, 'The Dark Side of Authority: A Critical Analysis of Anti-corruption Frameworks in Pakistan' (2013) 15 *Law, Social Justice & Global Development Journal* 1.

[146] O Protsyk and ML Matichescu, 'Clientelism and Political Recruitment in Democratic Transition: Evidence from Romania' (2011) 43 *Comparative Politics* 207.

[147] Wigell (n 11) 234–42.

The party accused the NAB of being a tool of political manipulation. Some leaders demanded the dismantling of the NAB as a remnant of the military rule of Pervez Musharraf. Ironically, during their respective tenures, neither the PML-N nor the PPP introduced the necessary amendments to the NAB legislation, a fact which exposes their demands as politically opportunistic.

After facing a few tough years of corruption inquiries between 2016 and 2019 and mobilising extremely polarising rhetoric against the military establishment as well as the PTI, in a complete volte-face, both the PML-N and the PPP decided to extend unconditional support to the PTI government regarding the extension of the army chief's tenure. This matter had been a thorn in the flesh for the PTI government in November 2019, when the Supreme Court struck down army chief Qamar Javed Bajwa's extension as illegal. It ultimately culminated in early January 2020, when amendments to the Army Act to institutionalise tenure extension for the army chief were passed by full support from the PTI, PPP and PML-N. These events coincided with Nawaz Sharif being allowed to go abroad for medical treatment in November 2019 despite being convicted. Zardari also got bail in the fake accounts case in September 2020. In this instance, PTI leader Imran Khan also made a political compromise to secure and consolidate power. When General Ashfaq Pervez Kayani was granted an extension of tenure by the PPP-led government, he stated that such extensions weakened the institutional integrity of the army and that if he ever came to power, he would end this practice.[148] However, over time, he has learned to prioritise his survival in the government over institutional integrity. As a result, the military continues to enjoy its role of guardian institution, thus diminishing electoral sovereignty and the consolidation of constitutionalism.

Weak institutionalisation of the party system and political parties is essential to understanding the persistence of hybrid regimes. Political parties are the basic institution of any democracy.[149] Weakly institutionalised political parties result in a democratic deficit and facilitate the intervention of non-political forces into the political mainstream. In hybrid regimes like Pakistan, where tutelary actors hold a firm grip over the system due to their better-developed institutional capacity, a powerful institution can only challenge their intrusive behaviour. For this purpose, political parties will have to reach an agreement on the value of elections and democracy and honour it. While in power, they must move beyond the pork-barrel sort of spending and divert state resources towards human development. The benefit of such spending will be twofold. First, it will increase the trust of the masses in political parties, and second, party–voter linkages will grow beyond the client–patron relationship. Political parties should co-operate to transform the legislature into a meaningful institution legislating for greater social good rather than instrumentalising it for myopic political gains. The lack of internal democracy within political parties continues to weaken them and the overall party system. The Panama Papers verdict against Nawaz Sharif is telling about the culture of Pakistan's political parties. In this case, the entire party, instead of submitting to the notion of accountability, tried its best to keep Nawaz in the position of party leader. Despite multiple stints in power, political parties succumbed to the pressure of

[148] 'Kayani's Term as COAS Should Not Be Extended' (n 107).

[149] For a deeper analytical engagement with the role of political parties in arresting democratic consolidation by attenuating mechanisms and institutions for executive accountability, see T Khaitan, ch 7 in this volume.

the military. This exemplifies the weak roots of political parties in Pakistan. Instead of relying on their voter base, they must depend on the favours they grant to the military time and again. As long as politics remains a means to secure the end of personal gains by means of corrupt practices, the party system in Pakistan will remain weakly institutionalised and entrench a hybrid regime. Party loyalties will remain fragile, and turncoats will remain available to be manipulated by tutelary actors.

PART VIII

The People

18

Rethinking Constitutional Resilience from Below: Dalit Rights and Land Reform

FAIZAN JAWED SIDDIQI[1]

I. Introduction

The Indian Constitution has attracted significant interest from scholars in recent years. Comparative constitutionalism,[2] constitutional performance,[3] transformative constitutionalism[4] and the 'everyday life' of the Indian Constitution[5] are just some of the topics that have been explored. This recent scholarship on the Indian Constitution and its performance follows some general themes. First, the analysis is predominantly historical, focusing on the social and political histories that birthed the Constitution. Second, the analysis is almost exclusively focused on analysing the jurisprudence and politics of apex courts and the Constituent Assembly. Third, scholars have tried to explain constitutional performance by focusing on socio-political trends and aggregate socio-economic indicators collected from surveys and opinion polls. In my view, macro-analyses focusing only on top-level institutions of the state – such as the apex judiciary, Parliament and large political parties – and aggregate nation-level socio-economic indicators provide a severely limited view of constitutional performance. This is because the law also has a semi-autonomous social life in spaces adjacent to, or beyond, the formal bounds of the state. As such, this semi-autonomous life plays out in the shadow of the Constitution.

[1] I would like to thank the editors of this volume, Tarun Khaitan, S Jhaveri and D Samararatne, for being intellectually engaging, encouraging and considerate leaders of this project. I also want to thank the Karthik Rao Cavale, Anand Verma and the anonymous reviewer for their input. Importantly, I want to thank the activists and Dalit brothers and sisters who shared their life stories with me.

[2] OV Vieira, U Baxi and F Viljoen, *Transformative Constitutionalism: Comparing the Apex Courts of Brazil, India and South Africa* (Pretoria, Pretoria University Law Press, 2013); M Tushnet and M Khosla (eds), *Unstable Constitutionalism: Law and Politics in South Asia* (Cambridge, Cambridge University Press, 2015).

[3] T Ginsburg and A Huq (eds), *Assessing Constitutional Performance* (Cambridge, Cambridge University Press, 2016).

[4] G Bhatia, *The Transformative Constitution: A Radical Biography in Nine Acts* (Delhi, HarperCollins India, 2019).

[5] R De, *A People's Constitution: The Everyday Life of Law in the Indian Republic*, vol 7 (Princeton, Princeton University Press, 2018).

Ordinary citizens – the subjects of constitutional law – have ingenious methods of understanding and using the law – thus mediating their unique relationship with it – in ways that remain invisible if we focus solely on state-centric analyses of constitutional performance. As such, these ordinary sites of constitutional interpretation and practice have a key bearing on the question of constitutional performance. Scholars of law and social mobilisation, for instance, have shown that law – including constitutional law – can support struggles for social justice in a variety of ways and on different scales. For instance, the law can be a source of 'politics by other means' for social movements,[6] it can lend symbolic support to movements of marginalised people[7] and it can allow for bargaining in the shadow of the law.[8] As I will show with evidence from my field research in Gujarat, the Constitution's role as an authoritative text with a moral message (of equality) can help give a renewed sense of political agency and self-esteem to individuals and groups that have historically faced marginalisation in the social and economic spheres. These multiple valences of the law have not been fully appreciated by constitutional performance scholarship in India. I believe that by taking an expanded view of the ways and scales in which law influences society, we can enrich our understanding of how the Constitution performs.

One could argue that, over the last decade, a new trend has begun to emerge in legal scholarship in India. Some anthropologists and political sociologists have provided grounded insights into how the law is used by social movements to deepen the citizenship claims of marginalised populations.[9] Some legal scholars have begun to make similar connections.[10] But these studies remain few and far between, and, as such, have not been recognised in the constitutional performance scholarship literature. Besides, when it comes to the law and the Constitution, Indian social scientists have predominantly considered such ground-level uses of the Constitution and the law to be epiphenomenal, ie a by-product of politics and practically irrelevant in determining what goes on in the name of the law.[11] Worse yet, some scholars have argued that the law is merely a tool in the hands of the elite to befool the poor into believing that the

[6] R Abel, *Politics by Other Means: Law in the Struggle against Apartheid, 1980–1994* (Routledge 1995). See also B Rajagopal, 'The Role of Law in Counter-Hegemonic Globalization and Global Legal Pluralism: Lessons from the Narmada Valley Struggle in India' (2005) 18 *Leiden Journal of International Law* 345.

[7] M McCann, *Rights at Work: Pay Equity Reform and the Politics of Legal Mobilization* (Chicago, University of Chicago Press, 1994).

[8] M Galanter, 'Justice in Many Rooms: Courts, Private Ordering, and Indigenous Law' (1981) 13 *Journal of Legal Pluralism and Unofficial Law* 1; RH Mnookin and L Kornhauser, 'Bargaining in the Shadow of the Law: The Case of Divorce' (1978) 88 *Yale Law Journal* 950.

[9] eg AG Nilsen, 'Adivasis in and against the State: Subaltern Politics and State Power in Contemporary India' (2012) 44 *Critical Asian Studies* 251; KB Nielsen and AG Nilsen, 'Law Struggles and Hegemonic Processes in Neoliberal India: Gramscian Reflections on Land Acquisition Legislation' (2015) 12 *Globalizations* 203; AG Nilsen, *Adivasis and the State: Subalternity and Citizenship in India's Bhil Heartland* (Cambridge, Cambridge University Press, 2018); A Singh, 'Many Faces of the Pathalgadi Movement in Jharkhand' (2019) 54 *Economic and Political Weekly* 28; C Correndo, 'The Counter-Hegemonic Potential of Law: From the Wilkinson's Rules to the Pathalgadi Movement in India' (2021) 46 *DPCE Online*.

[10] GN Rosenberg, S Krishnaswamy and S Bail (eds), *A Qualified Hope: The Indian Supreme Court and Progressive Social Change* (Cambridge, Cambridge University Press, 2019); Bhatia (n 4); KR Cavale, 'The Art of Buying Time' in Rosenberg et al (ibid) 151–83.

[11] R Bhargava, 'Introduction: Outline of a Political Theory of the Indian Constitution' in R Bhargava (ed), *Politics and Ethics of the Indian Constitution* (Oxford, Oxford University Press, 2009) 1–42.

constitutional guarantees of the right to life, freedom and equality can be realised in practice.[12]

Such a conceptual foreclosure is limiting, especially for progressive politics, because however 'inherently unstable, contingent, and manipulable' they may be,[13] constitutionally sanctioned rights and entitlements are a powerful weapon that marginalised groups possess to amass legitimacy for their claims. Recent events in India, for instance, lend support to this line of reasoning. The Constitution featured prominently in the recent protests in India against the Constitutional Amendment Act (CAA).[14] Thousands of ordinary Indians assembled in peaceful protest across the country and read the Constitution out aloud to remind their fellow citizens – and, importantly, the federal government in power at the centre – of the secular liberal egalitarian values that the founding fathers had promised to the nation. Some scholars believe that these protests may have had a role in stopping the central government from rapidly implementing the CAA and the National Register of Citizens.[15]

These insights notwithstanding, largely, the scholarship on constitutional performance in India – irrespective of the authors' intellectual pedigree or ideological leanings – seems to have overlooked a basic point made by Marc Galanter four decades ago: that the law is more 'capacious as a system of cultural and symbolic meaning than as a set of operative controls'.[16] Seen from this perspective, constitutional performance research should analytically and empirically engage with how the normative vision of the Constitution is received and mobilised by ordinary citizens in their social and political life. Research focusing on individuals or groups claiming basic constitutional rights they have been historically deprived of would be of particular interest. Given the Indian Constitution's normative vision of social inclusion, and the persistence of social and economic inequities along the vectors of caste, gender, religion, etc, such cases would represent a case of constitutional success and resilience. This investigation would have to be rigorous, empirical and engaged with the real lived experience of poor and marginalised groups.

'Looking to the bottom' to understand how 'standard texts' such as constitutions are appropriated by the most marginalised citizens to realise justice has been a part of the agenda for critical legal scholarship for over three decades.[17] In that spirit, I will focus

[12] O Sircar, 'Spectacles of Emancipation: Reading Rights Differently in India's Legal Discourse' (2011) 49 *Osgoode Hall Law Journal* 527.

[13] M Tushnet, 'Social Welfare Rights and the Forms of Judicial Review' (2004) 82 *Texas Law Review* 1895.

[14] The Citizenship (Amendment) Act was passed in the Lower House of the Indian Parliament on 10 December 2019. The law allowed select non-Muslim individuals from Muslim-majority Afghanistan, Pakistan and Bangladesh to apply through a 'fast track' process to gain refugee status and eventually citizenship. While, on the one hand, the law created a process for fast-tracking citizenship for non-Muslims, on the other hand, it reserved the category of 'illegal migrant' to Muslims alone. The passage of the law in the Lower House gave rise to protests around the country. See H Akins, 'The Citizenship (Amendment) Act in India' (United States Commission on International Religious Freedom, 2020) www.uscirf.gov/sites/default/files/2020%20Legislation%20Factsheet%20-%20India_0_0.pdf; 'India's Citizenship Protests' *Reuters Graphics* (30 March 2020) https://graphics.reuters.com/INDIA-CITIZENSHIP/PROTESTS/jxlbpgqlpqd/index.html.

[15] AK Thiruvengadam, 'Constitutional Idolatry, Literacy, and Identity' (*IACL-AIDC Blog*, 26 January 2021) https://blog-iacl-aidc.org/cili/2021/1/28/constitutional-faith-or-constitutional-idolatry-insights-from-recent-mass-protests-in-india.

[16] Galanter, 'Justice in Many Rooms' (n 8).

[17] MJ Matsuda, 'Looking to the Bottom: Critical Legal Studies and Reparations' (1987) 22 *Harvard Civil Rights – Civil Liberties Law Review* 323.

on and draw from the example of socio-legal mobilisation by Dalits[18] in Gujarat for the implementation of land reform laws. Through this process, Dalits made progress in realising key expressive norms enshrined in the Indian Constitution – equality and dignity – which had largely eluded them in everyday life despite India becoming an independent nation and constitutionally guaranteeing these to its citizens over a half-century ago! The key organiser of Dalits in Gujarat was a non-governmental organisation (NGO) called Navsarjan Trust. Navsarjan mobilised the law by two key routes: entrenching rights-consciousness in the Dalit community by focusing their narrative on constitutional expressive norms (equality before the law and between citizens) and strategically using statutes meant to safeguard Dalits, thus demonstrating Navsarjan's efficacy to mount a real challenge to upper-caste dominance. I will argue that this is a clear example of constitutional resilience from below.

The rest of this chapter is divided into four sections. First, I will draw from recent constitutional performance scholarship to sketch out the assessment criterion. Then, by comparing and contrasting the engagement of Indian constitutional performance scholarship with key insights from my field research, I will argue that we need to pay attention to the ways constitutional law shapes these processes that do not make themselves visible if we rely solely on case law, political economy, public opinion surveys and other proxy indicators when assessing a constitution's performance. We must look in spaces adjacent to, or even far removed from, the conventional loci of legal performance – the courts and the legislature. Second, I will draw on my research on Dalit mobilisations for eradicating caste-based untouchability and implementing long-standing land redistribution laws in Gujarat, India to show how the social expressive function of law, coupled with legal mobilisation from below, helped entrench a rights-conscious and rights-based political praxis. Such a political programme, I will argue, is consistent with BR Ambedkar's normative vision of social ordering and functioning in India. In the final two sections, I will reflect on the study of constitutional performance in India.

II. Constitutional Performance Reconsidered

A. The Criteria Question

I understand constitutional resilience to be closely related to, if not a subset of, constitutional performance. Therefore, a key question to answer before any evaluation is: what criteria should be used for assessing a constitution's performance? In *Assessing Constitutional Performance*, Tom Ginzburg and Aziz Huq grapple with this specific question in the context of comparative constitutional scholarship.[19] They distinguish between 'internal' and 'external' criteria that an evaluator must choose to evaluate a

[18] 'Dalit', which literally means 'broken', is a term used by members belonging to the lowest castes in the Hindu caste system. Officially, the Indian Constitution recognises Dalit castes as 'scheduled castes'. Prior to the eradication of untouchability, these castes were referred to as 'untouchable' castes.

[19] Ginsburg and Huq (n 3).

constitution's performance. 'Internal' criteria refer to the objectives a constitution sets for itself while 'external' criteria refer to some other normative benchmark that an evaluator might choose. Ginzburg and Huq recognise that properly identifying a constitution's internal criteria is not an easy task. It involves discerning the relevant goals in the constitutional text, which would have to be derived 'from the circumstances of the constitution' or deduced from the writings of constitutional framers. To complicate matters further, in the case of a constitution with multiple framers – which is usually the case with constitutions – one would be hard pressed to coherently identify the precise internal criteria.

'External' criteria, on the other hand, would be chosen on the basis of normative arguments. Legal and political philosopher Martha Nussbaum, who is also a contributor to the *Assessing Constitutional Performance* project, echoes Ginsburg and Huq's concern that properly interpreting the meaning and aims of a constitutional text (ie the 'internal' criteria) is an important but difficult and time-consuming task.[20] It requires in-depth historical research, and even then, the conclusions may remain ambiguous. As a pragmatic workaround to not having to wait until the 'originalist' constitutional meaning has been found before one can assess a constitution, Nussbaum chooses to consider instead the extent to which the Indian Constitution's principal framer – Bhimrao Ramji Ambedkar, a Dalit – was able to achieve his own goals 'through the means available to him'.[21] This seems like a reasonable criterion to adopt to assess the Indian Constitution's performance. Nussbaum describes Ambedkar's normative vision as one promoting inclusion and opposing the tyranny of the majority.[22] These ideas were arguably informed by Ambedkar's philosophical commitment to the idea of the equal moral worth of all humans, which was both informed by his own life experience and intellectually influenced by the American pragmatist John Dewey, and later Gautam Buddha.[23]

The next step in the evaluation is to determine the empirical indicators we consider relevant for determining progress towards the normative goals. Nussbaum refers to case law and draws on aggregate socio economic indicators and public opinion survey data on caste, gender rights and minority rights. Based on these aggregate data, she concludes that constitutional performance has been less than satisfactory and Ambedkar's main political objective of 'annihilation of caste' remains unfulfilled. The provisions he made to achieve this aim, including caste-based reservations in political offices, have backfired as they have facilitated the persistence of caste rather than its annihilation. Quotas in government jobs and educational institutions have been implemented half-heartedly and have therefore failed to make socio-economic mobility for Dalits a reality.[24]

[20] MC Nussbaum, 'Ambedkar's Constitution: Promoting Inclusion, Opposing Majority Tyranny' in Ginsburg and Huq (n 3) 295–336.

[21] ibid 301–02. An important assumption here is that Ambedkar's normative vision can be surmised reasonably well through dependable primary and secondary historical sources.

[22] ibid 295.

[23] For Ambedkar's political philosophy, see V Rodrigues, 'Ambedkar as a Political Philosopher' (2017) 52 *Economic and Political Weekly* 101; L Cabrera, 'Ambedkar on the Haughty Face of Dignity' (2021) 14 *Politics and Religion* 83. On John Dewey's influence on Ambedkar's thought and praxis, see SR Stroud, 'What Did Bhimrao Ambedkar Learn from John Dewey's Democracy and Education?' (2017) 12 *The Pluralist* 78.

[24] Evaluation of affirmative action (commonly referred to as 'reservations') policies has been an area of lively debate. For pre- and post-Mandal Commission and economic liberalisation-era evaluations, see M Galanter, *Competing Equalities: Law and the Backward Classes in India* (Chicago, University of Chicago

An honest assessment will present both the good and the bad sides of the story. To that extent, aggregate data tell us that Dalits are still behind on economic indicators and face hurtful forms of social exclusion, especially in rural areas. But is this the end of the story of constitutional performance? I believe not. To get a fuller (and richer) picture of constitutional performance, the high-level view should be complemented with both qualitative and quantitative insights into the ways in which the Constitution affects the social position of its vulnerable subjects. To learn about those details, we must leave the world of survey indicators and jurisprudence for a moment and step into the social world to observe the workings of the law. Let me illustrate with key findings from field research in Gujarat.

B. Law's Expression and Bargaining in the Shadow

In my observation of Dalit activism in Gujarat and individual interviews with Navsarjan caseworkers and local Dalits, I consistently noticed overwhelming evidence of what would be called the *social expressive value* of the Constitution. Speakers consistently referred to – implicitly and explicitly – the moral norms they considered evident in the Constitution: that everyone is equal; that the rules are the same for everyone; and that what they were asking for is 'constitutionally guaranteed'. Second, I found that strategic mobilisation of laws meant to protect Dalits from caste-based harms in many cases helped provide an upper hand to proactive Dalits in bargaining with upper-caste members in the 'shadow of law'.[25]

Elizabeth Anderson and Richard Pildes define 'expression' as the 'way that an action or a statement (or any other vehicle of expression) manifests a state of mind' and expressive norms as 'rules that regulate actions by regulating the acceptable justifications for doing them'.[26] By definition, then, understanding the 'expression' is an interpretive act

Press, 1984); M Galanter, 'The Long Half-Life of Reservations' in Z Hasan, E Sridharan and R Sudarshan (eds), *India's Living Constitution. Ideas, Practices, Controversies* (Ranikhet, Permanent Black, 2004) 306–18; NG Jayal, 'Affirmative Action in India: Before and After the Neo-liberal Turn' (2015) 27 *Cultural Dynamics* 117. On the logic of affirmative action in India, see generally M Galanter, 'Pursuing Equality in the Land of Hierarchy' in DK Basu and R Sisson (eds), *Social and Economic Development in India: A Reassessment* (New Delhi, SAGE Publications India, 1986) 185–207; F De Zwart, 'The Logic of Affirmative Action: Caste, Class and Quotas in India' (2000) 43 *Acta Sociologica* 235. Some critics of affirmative action have argued that the institutional structure of Indian affirmative action policies have enabled certain sub-groups from the intended beneficiary population to corner the benefits. Such claims have been acknowledged by some while refuted by others. See C Jaffrelot, 'Reservations and the Dalits at the Crossroads' (*India in Transition*, 7 May 2007) https://casi.sas.upenn.edu/iit/cjaffrelot; S Ma, 'Impact of Reservation Policies: India's Quota Politics during the Post-Independence Period, 1950–2011' (PhD Dissertation, Johns Hopkins University, 2011); S Dasgupta, 'SC-ST Creamy Layer Is Insignificant, Inequalities Still Glaring: Dalit Chamber of Commerce' *The Print* (14 April 2021) https://theprint.in/india/sc-st-creamy-layer-is-insignificant-inequalities-still-glaring-Dalit-chamber-of-commerce/639027/; A Lee, 'Does Affirmative Action Work? Evaluating India's Quota System' (2021) 54 *Comparative Political Studies* 1534.

[25] Marc Galanter has argued that 'bargaining in the shadow' is an important phenomenon enabled by law that conventional legal research that focuses on the courtroom only fails to capture. See Galanter, 'Justice in Many Rooms' (n 8). Galanter develops his argument drawing on examples from American case law and American legal studies literature. To my knowledge, the relevance of this idea in legal research has not been considered in the scholarship on the Constitution and law in India.

[26] ES Anderson and RH Pildes, 'Expressive Theories of Law: A General Restatement' (2000) 148 *University of Pennsylvania Law Review* 1503, 1511.

with adjudicative potential.[27] Expressive theories of law help evaluate state action by subjecting it to the regulative principles that flow from expressive norms. Sociologically speaking, if the legal system has at least some semblance of legitimacy in society and if members of the public understand it as being sufficiently coercive, then it can be speculated that the expressive norms supposed to regulate state action should also have at least some moral and/or political valence for members of the public. So when the Constitution says that every citizen is equal before the law and a judge interprets it as such, this could be read as the law not only fixing the responsibility of the state to protect citizens' rights, but also 'expressing' an attitude (or preference, if you will) on behalf of the Republic that establishes the equal moral worth of all citizens not only in front of the state, but also – by implication – between all citizens. As such, in its expressive role, the law has the potential to create and shift social norms and meaning.[28]

More recently, Tarunabh Khaitan has argued that the ideal of dignity is best realised in law as an expressive norm.[29] Reading constitutional court judgments from the USA, Khaitan shows that judges have defended dignity by interpreting it as an expressive norm. Evaluation of state action by judges, on the basis of expressive norms, which are informed by moral attitudes, signal to the members of the public a set of moral values.[30] In common law systems, the authoritative interpretation of constitutional law is primarily the domain of courts and judges, but not exclusively so. In Surendranagar, it was Navsarjan activists – non-state actors – who popularised their interpretation of the Constitution's expressive value. Navsarjan caseworkers popularised their interpretation of the 'expression' in the Constitution as one of the equal moral worth of all citizens and equality before the law. This served to legitimise their campaign, which was a major advantage for a small civil society organisation and social movement trying to oppose historical upper-caste hegemonic control of agricultural land!

Relatedly, while leveraging the social expressive value of the Constitution, working in the 'shadow' of law was also crucial to Navsarjan's success: using its punitive potential to pressurise individuals from socially dominant upper castes who harassed local Dalits to come to them and apologise. The psychological and symbolic value of these outcomes was positive and substantial for local Dalits; they helped them claim moral equality vis-à-vis upper-caste social groups that have long enjoyed social dominance and refused to accept Dalits' humanity. In the process, Dalits also expanded their capabilities to exercise rights by not only becoming conversant in rights language, but also learning to mobilise rights in courts, in police stations, in the local government office and so on. In other words, Navsarjan leveraged the Constitution and constitutional law to create a confident Dalit citizenry in Surendranagar.

In my view, Navsarjan's unusual success in Surendranagar in helping create a confident Dalit citizenry 'from below' cannot be explained without referring to the role that the Constitution's expressive function and 'bargaining in the shadow of law' played in the campaign. Given this, it is perplexing to me that the literature on constitutional

[27] 'To interpret what an action means, we try to identify what the agent is doing': ibid 1507.

[28] CR Sunstein, 'On the Expressive Function of Law' (1996) 144 *University of Pennsylvania Law Review* 2021.

[29] T Khaitan, 'Dignity as an Expressive Norm: Neither Vacuous nor a Panacea' (2011) 32 *OJLS* 1.

[30] Judges interpret the 'moral attitude' based on the Constitution.

performance has largely failed to engage with this 'behind the scenes' role that the Indian Constitution and constitutional law play in struggles for social justice. Questions of constitutional performance and resilience cannot be answered without looking at this key aspect of the law's social and political life. Nussbaum acknowledges the expressive function of the Constitution, noting that 'specific normative commitments of the Constitution, *as subsequently understood*, had some legal value and a broader *social expressive value* in connection with Ambedkar's announced goals' (emphasis added).[31] However, she is quick to dismiss it as a relevant locus of constitutional performance because for her, in the absence of broad-based social and economic measures, these normative commitments have 'proven insufficient to counteract the social tyranny of the majority'.[32] To me, this is an insufficient reason for not considering this phenomenon, which on first glance appears to be merely symbolic and non-material influences of the law, as valid empirical loci of constitutional performance. While such effects of the law are hard to measure in neat indicators, understanding them through case studies would expand our knowledge of how the Constitution is performing against our chosen criterion. Further, such analyses over time will help us build a nuanced understanding of not just constitutional performance as it exists, but also the transformative potential of the Constitution for progressive social change.

C. Constitutional Performance Scholarship: Limitations and a New Trend

To recap, thus far, I have drawn from the scholarship on constitutional performance and settled on a criterion for evaluation. I have claimed that there are a variety of ways in which the Constitution and the law can promote or impede movement towards Ambedkar's normative commitments (ie our criterion) of eradicating caste-based social and economic disparities. Further, I have argued that existing studies on constitutional performance in India have contained little empirical and theoretical engagement with the way expressive norms, and the social life of law outside the courtroom and legislative arenas, influence policy and social outcomes. Instead, the predominant thrust of constitutional performance scholarship has been on case law, aggregate indicators and the politics of elite actors (the executive, the legislature and the judiciary). This focus is understandable because, after all, groups such as political parties and militaries are embodiments of the concentration of power, and one of the functions of democratic constitutions is to regulate the use of power in society by fixing rights and duties, and providing checks and balances on the use of power by laying down 'due process'. Constitutional law scholarship has investigated how these rules are influenced by the politics of institutional actors.

In a publication contemporaneous to *Assessing Constitutional Performance*, Mark Tushnet and Madhav Khosla develop the idea of *Unstable Constitutionalism* to capture and analyse the divergence between law on the books and socio-political realities that

[31] ibid.
[32] ibid.

disrupt the stability that constitutions are supposed to ensure.[33] For these scholars, the central concern is not interpretative debates about a constitution's text; rather, 'it is questions of constitutional design and negotiation that can address and resolve pressures on the overall system and the domestic risks to which it is exposed'.[34] The actors that the contributors in this volume focus on and analyse are political parties (at the national and state level), apex courts and judges, and the military. Sujit Choudhry suggests that our understanding of constitutional law and politics is limited because of disciplinary silos. On the one hand, the political scientists and historians studying the process of constitutional development have presented 'highly truncated' analyses of constitutional jurisprudence. On the other hand, the analysis of constitutional jurisprudence in South Asia by legal scholars, he argues, is formalistic and doctrinal.[35] In a similar vein, I believe that constitutional performance and constitutional law scholarship that has limited its empirical scope to the traditional actors and institutions will productively gain from engaging with a broader, multi-sited approach to research.

For Choudhry, though, this gap in South Asian constitutional scholarship can be bridged by close readings of apex court judgments in relation to politics. He argues that close examination of 'leading judgments' will shed light on how 'the broader constitutional politics was presented in terms cognizable under formal legal categories to the court'. Read in this context, judgments become key political acts and judges become important political actors.[36] I think that while Choudhry's observation about the truncated and siloed nature of analyses is highly relevant for the community of scholars involved in researching the performance of constitutions, his solution should be read as one of the several (much-needed) ways of doing constitutional law and politics in South Asia.[37] We have good empirical and rational grounds to open the study of constitutional law and performance by engaging with a multiplicity of sites, agents, actors and institutions, and on different scales – from the personal to the institutional.

To take a slightly older example, the *Politics and Ethics of the Indian Constitution*, edited by the political theorist Rajeev Bhargava, opens with a critical observation. He notes that 'current academic fashions' treat the law as 'epiphenomenal', which results in the Constitution not being read as a moral text, 'to be understood and interpreted in terms of values and ideals'.[38] *Politics and Ethics* sought to correct that. Chapters in the book cover a wide range of topics, including 'Citizenship and the Indian Constitution', 'Democracy and Constitutionalism, 'Constitutional Justice', 'Religion and the Indian Constitution' and 'Affirmative Action for Disadvantaged Groups'. Constitutional performance and resilience are not explicitly the focus here, but evaluative statements

[33] Tushnet and Khosla, *Unstable Constitutionalism* (n 2).

[34] M Tushnet and M Khosla, 'Unstable Constitutionalism' in ibid 5.

[35] S Choudhry, 'How to Do Constitutional Law and Politics in South Asia' in Tushnet and Khosla, *Unstable Constitutionalism* (n 2) 18–42.

[36] Choudhry uses two case law vignettes: the basic structure doctrine formulated by the Supreme Court of India and constitutional jurisprudence on affirmative action policies.

[37] The title of Choudhry's chapter is 'How to Do Constitutional Law and Politics in South Asia'.

[38] Bhargava, 'Introduction' (n 11) 4. Bhargava cites the works of Shibani Chaube and Shobhanlal Datta Gupta as examples of scholarship that sees law as epiphenomenal. See SK Chaube, *Constituent Assembly of India: Springboard of Revolution* (New Delhi, People's Publishing House, 1973); SK Chaube, *The Making and Working of the Indian Constitution* (Delhi, National Book Trust, India, 2009); SD Gupta, *Justice and the Political Order in India: An Inquiry into the Institutions and Ideologies, 1950–1972* (K Bagchi, 1979).

regarding the Constitution are present throughout the book. The analysis of constitutional performance – implicit as it is in the current volume – is best described in Sujit Choudhry's words: 'highly truncated'.[39] The explanations and arguments presented are historical and draw on reading jurisprudence in relation to national-level politics, animated by political parties and the politics of founding fathers. As a result, even though the book starts on a promising note by recognising that attention needs to be paid to understanding the Constitution in terms of 'ideals and values', the analysis is limited to judges and founding fathers.

In this volume, Upendra Baxi's attempt at outlining a 'Theory of Practice' of the Indian Constitution is pregnant with theoretical arguments, yet engagement with the details of actual practice is ironically missing.[40] Such omissions are particularly concerning because if constitutionalism 'provides contested sites for ideas and practices concerning justice, rights, development, and individual associational autonomy',[41] then surely the analysis of constitutional performance and constitutional resilience must go beyond theoretical musings about courts, judges, jurisprudence and political parties. In this view, the study of constitutionalism – including constitutional performance and resilience – must also understand and analyse how people receive, understand and use constitutional principles in their everyday lives. Of course, the elite cast of actors will feature in such accounts, but those must not be the only actors. The other side of the constitutional performance coin – the people – must be an integral part of the research agenda.

On this count, even Marc Galanter's magisterial *Competing Equalities* on the law and caste inequality in India – which has taught us a lot about the interaction of constitutional law and socio-political systems in the context of India's preferential treatment policies for backward classes – offers an aggregated, high-level view. Surprisingly, there is not a single mention of the mechanism of bargaining in the shadow of law in India, despite the fact that Galanter published an influential paper making the case for pluralism in legal research in which he draws specifically on this idea, even mentioning in passing that Indian villagers have been able to use courts 'directly to secure outcomes in line with indigenous norms, even when these are not officially recognized by the Anglo-Indian law'.[42] The lack of a single mention of the concept, which we have reason to believe Galanter was aware of at the time, suggests that the genre of legal research has bound scholars to primarily focus on particular voices, institutions and actors in research on constitutional performance.

To clarify, I am not suggesting that Galanter should have included the bargaining in the shadow of law or other such 'non-traditional' perspectives in this piece of scholarship on preferential treatment and law. I understand that constitutional performance scholarship is a wide area of research and enquiry and not every volume published on the Constitution's direct and indirect influence on society will – or must – engage with the multi-sited, multi-scalar, pluralistic approach to law that I am arguing for here.

[39] Choudhry (n 35) 20.

[40] U Baxi, 'Outline of a "Theory of Practice" of Indian Constitutionalism' in Bhargava, *Politics and Ethics* (n 11).

[41] U Baxi, 'Postcolonial Legality: A Postscript from India' [2012] *Verfassung und Recht in Übersee/Law and Politics in Africa, Asia and Latin America* 178, 180.

[42] Galanter (n 8) 25.

Nevertheless, the bias in constitutional scholarship in India of sticking to a narrow view of the working of law in society, featuring primarily a state institution-centric view, needs to be acknowledged and corrected because it limits our understanding of constitutional performance. To sum up, the scholarship on Indian constitutional performance and its political and moral import,[43] while hoping for better outcomes for marginalised groups,[44] has focused exclusively on what judges and politicians do rather than what ordinary people and marginalised groups do.

Over the last few years, an encouraging new trend in constitutional performance scholarship focused on South Asia has emerged. This body of work has begun to expand the understanding of the Indian Constitution and constitutional law by bringing in new actors, conducting multi-sited research and studying new ways in which law, society and politics interact through institutional and political spaces enabled by the Constitution.[45] *A Qualified Hope* – a book project led by Gerald Rosenberg and colleagues on the performance of the Indian Supreme Court includes research that shows the symbolic and strategic value of the courts and law for social movements.[46] Anuj Bhuwania's work on public interest litigation, judicial politics and urban development has shown the linkages between law and urban displacement.[47] Rohit De has provided a historical understanding of how ordinary Indians exercised their fundamental rights by seeking justice in the Supreme Court during the early independent period.[48] Drawing from the (fictional) story of a poor and hardworking rickshaw puller whose day-to-day life is made torturously hard at every turn by an anti-poor state, Oishik Sircar has provided a scathing critique of Indian constitutionalism.[49]

Some scholars of development studies too have analysed the relationship between citizenship, law and contentious political mobilisation from below, and their findings are pertinent for understanding constitutional resilience in the country.[50] For instance, drawing on the study of social movements in minerally rich but socio-economically backward regions of central India, Nandini Sundar has argued that the law is not only a key institution that movements rely on to galvanise new and old constituencies around rights claims, but also the site at which definitions of equality and citizenship take substantive shape.[51] Studying resistance by Adivasis (tribals) in Central India to members of the Indian Forest Service in central-western India, Alf Gunvald Nilsen

[43] U Baxi, 'Taking Suffering Seriously: Social Action Litigation in the Supreme Court of India' [1985] *Third World Legal Studies* 107; U Baxi, *The Future of Human Rights* (Oxford, Oxford University Press, 2007); U Baxi, 'Voices of Suffering, Fragmented Universality, and the Future of Human Rights' in BH Weston and SP Marks (eds), *The Future of International Human Rights* (Ardsley, NY, Transnational Publishers, 1999) 101–56.

[44] Some critical commentators do not share this hopefulness. See, eg Sircar (n 12).

[45] This chapter and the volume are examples of this new trend.

[46] For strategic use of law by social movements, see Cavale (n 10). For view of the court as a symbolic resource for social movements, see MA Bhat, 'Court as a Symbolic Resource' in Rosenberg et al (n 10). See generally Rosenberg et al (n 10).

[47] A Bhuwania, *Courting the People: Public Interest Litigation in Post-Emergency India* (Cambridge, Cambridge University Press, 2017).

[48] De (n 5).

[49] Sircar (n 12).

[50] See, eg Nilsen, 'Adivasis in and against the State' (n 9); Nielsen and Nilsen (n 9); Nilsen, *Adivasis and the State* (n 9); Singh (n 9); Correndo (n 9).

[51] N Sundar, 'The Rule of Law and Citizenship in Central India: Post-Colonial Dilemmas' (2011) 15 *Citizenship Studies* 419; Nilsen, 'Adivasis in and against the State' (n 9); Nilsen, *Adivasis and the State* (n 9).

has shown how the law changed 'local rationalities' that governed social relations: the social movement of Adivasis framed their right to the forest in the language of constitutional rights and mobilised statutes in the courts to push back against excesses; in the process, local Adivasis went from being perennially colonial subjects that were deferential to abusive forest guards to confident citizens.[52] The takeaways in this ground-informed work, however, are not all rosy. Much like the story of the rickshaw puller in Sircar's critique of the Constitution, the law – and especially colonial-era laws that have not been reformed – has been used by successive governments to forcibly displace poor peasants off their traditionally held lands. At the same time, on the hopeful side, these studies show that many social movements – especially the ones that have been successful at organising their constituents – have been able to mount a serious challenge to the state's development projects by mobilising constitutional politics and law.

Together, this new research has helped expand our knowledge of the role and reach of the Constitution and constitutional law in promoting, and hindering, progressive change in modern India. But it is still early days and much needs to be discovered. This chapter is an attempt to contribute to this emerging multi-sited sociological research on the 'performance' of the Indian Constitution. I focus on the experiences of ordinary Dalits and the Navsarjan Trust – an NGO whose local caseworkers provided leadership to a multi-year campaign – in Surendranagar, Gujarat in their attempts to secure possession of the land that they had become owners of through land reform laws. Drawing from this fieldwork in Gujarat in 2016–17 and in 2020, I will show that constitutional expressive norms of equality and dignity were central to Navsarjan's philosophical-political positioning and mobilisation strategy. The caseworkers presented the Constitution as an important legacy of Bhimrao Ambedkar. Coupled with the fact that BR Ambedkar – a Dalit – was a key framer of the Constitution, Navsarjan strategically positioned the Constitution as a moral and political document that promised emancipation for Dalits through its commitment to equality and dignity for all. This helped solidify an emotional bond between the Constitution and Dalits. Along with teaching Dalits a new language in which to articulate their demand for recognition and redistribution (dignity and self-esteem), Navsarjan's legal mobilisation strategy also opened the terrain for politics in the 'shadow of law'.[53] This case, I believe, is an example of good constitutional performance and resilience.

III. Dalit Mobilisation and Land Reform in Surendranagar

A. Looking to the Bottom

Gopal Guru has argued that the idea of democracy has provided the meaning and context for two different sets of languages: the language of 'self-rule and national pride' that was used by nationalist elites, and the language of 'self-esteem and self-respect'

[52] Nilsen, *Adivasis and the State* (n 9) esp chs 5 and 6.
[53] Mnookin and Kornhauser (n 8).

that is used by marginalised groups to articulate their normative aspirations.[54] The equal moral worth of humans, equality before the law, and equal civil and political rights – cornerstones of the liberal conception of justice – have also been central to the Dalit struggle for emancipation.[55] Gopal argues that assessing the efficacy of liberal democracy in India solely from the perspective of changes in material inequality would be incomplete. The more important question for Guru is, 'to what extent has liberal democracy, through institutional intervention at various levels, created opportunities for Dalits to enhance their self-esteem and gain self-respect?'[56] Guru argues that the actual realisation of the idea of equal moral worth for Dalits has been an uphill battle because the upper castes have not been forthcoming in recognising Dalits as equals.[57] Despite this call by a leading Dalit thinker and social scientist, it is surprising that the role of law (and in particular, the everyday life of law) remains underexplored in the scholarship on Dalit social movements and politics.

Bhimrao Ambedkar, a Dalit who defied the norm of his day and earned a doctorate from Columbia University in New York City, was the principal framer of the Constitution of India. He was also an iconic leader of the Dalits in India, who idolise and revere him as an emancipatory hero. For many, Ambedkar and the Constitution are synonymous; there are thousands of statues of Ambedkar in India that show him in a blue suit clutching the Constitution in his hand.[58] It is common knowledge that Dalits celebrate Ambedkar's birthday, 14 April, treating it similarly to a holy festival. Is it not possible that the veneration Dalits and many non-Dalits in India bestow on Ambedkar also extends to the Constitution? Would not 'Ambedkar's Constitution' create an affinity for it in the mind of the Dalit? I think it would. Therefore, it is surprising that there are very few examples of ground-informed sociological research that analyse the role of constitutional law as a source of normativity and as a terrain for advancing political demands in Dalits' mobilisation.[59] There could be two reasons for this: either the law is epiphenomenal to social outcomes or we need to study the law's working and social influences purposively. I support the latter view.

Everyday constitutionalism anchored in interpretations of expressive norms of the Indian Constitution, as I will try to show in the case study that follows, played a central role in providing legitimacy and momentum to Dalit politics in Surendranagar. Dalits who had traditionally lived under upper-caste hegemony and experienced blows to their self-esteem have made progress in realising dignity and self-esteem, in addition to

[54] G Guru, 'Twentieth Century Discourse on Social Justice: A View from Quarantine India' in S Bhattacharya (ed), *Development of Modern Indian Thought and Social Sciences* (Oxford, Oxford University Press, 2007) cited in Gopal Guru, 'Liberal Democracy in India and the Dalit Critique' (2011) 78 Social Research 99.

[55] Guru, 'Liberal Democracy in India and the Dalit Critique' (n 54) 100.

[56] ibid 102.

[57] G Guru, 'Constitutional Justice: Positional and Cultural' in Bhargava, *Politics and Ethics* (n 11) 230–48.

[58] K Kaushik, 'Travelling with Ambedkar' (*Outlook Traveller*, 26 January 2021) www.outlookindia.com/outlooktraveller/explore/story/71117/br-ambedkar-statues-across-india.

[59] On moral outrage and constitutional values, see N Jaoul, 'The "Righteous Anger" of the Powerless: Investigating Dalit Outrage over Caste Violence' [2008] *South Asia Multidisciplinary Academic Journal*. For an ethnographic account of Dalit activism and the law at the local level, see N Jaoul, 'A Strong Law for the Weak: Dalit Activism in a District Court of Uttar Pradesh' in D Berti and D Bordia (eds), *Regimes of Legality: Ethnography of Criminal Cases in South Asia* (Oxford, Oxford University Press, 2015) 171–201. On the Dalit Movement in Maharashtra, see also S Waghmore, *Civility against Caste: Dalit Politics and Citizenship in Western India* (New Delhi, SAGE Publications India, 2013).

many of them becoming landowners for the first time. Constitutional expressive norms not only served to morally legitimate Dalit demands for land reform and equality in Surendranagar, but also, crucially, served to reverse the old 'local rationality',[60] which made Dalits live in constant deference to often-misbehaving upper castes. Let us take a closer look at how this happened.

B. Land Reform in India and the Navsarjan Trust

The post-independence state in India took up land redistribution as one of its first major agrarian developmental projects. Dalits, formerly referred to as 'untouchables' in the prevalent Hindu caste hierarchy, constitute one of the poorest, historically landless and socially marginalised groups in India. In the spirit of uplifting the poor and marginalised, the land redistribution laws in newly independent India gave Dalits high priority in the allocation of land. However, barring the example of a few states where communist parties were elected to power, land redistribution laws failed to be implemented in any significant way.[61] In Gujarat, in 1960, the state government enacted the Gujarat Agricultural Land Ceiling Act 1960 (ALCA). This law was aimed at land redistribution by putting a ceiling on the amount of land a family could own (irrespective of family size) and redistributing the 'excess lands' acquired by the government to landless peasants. Dalits, or Scheduled Castes (as the Constitution classifies them), were given high priority in receiving the land awards. Later, through the Government Lands Program, which was officially added to the ALCA, the government also brought 'wastelands' into the land redistribution legal system.[62] Through these laws, a large number of Dalits in the state have become landowners.

Data from the seventieth round of the Land and Livestock Holdings Survey of the National Sample Survey Office indicates that more than half of all Dalit households in the country do not own any land other than homestead land. In Gujarat, landlessness among Dalit households is 1.7 times the total landlessness across all social groups.[63] Scholars and activists estimate that Dalits have received possession of only between 10 and 40 per cent of the land awarded to them under land ceiling laws in Gujarat.[64]

[60] Nilsen, *Adivasis and the State* (n 9).

[61] A Kohli, *The State and Poverty in India: The Politics of Reform* (Cambridge, Cambridge University Press, 1987).

[62] On land reform and governance in Gujarat, see G Iyer, 'Caste and Land Reforms in Gujarat' in G Shah and DC Shah (eds), *Land Reforms in India: Performance and Challenges in Gujarat and Maharashtra*, vol 8 (New Delhi, SAGE Publications India, 2002) 147–85; N Sud, 'From Land to the Tiller to Land Liberalisation: The Political Economy of Gujarat's Shifting Land Policy' (2007) 41 *Modern Asian Studies* 603; FJ Siddiqi, 'Realizing Dignity: Dalits Rights, Land Reform, and the Learning of Democratic Citizenship' (PhD Thesis, Massachusetts Institute of Technology, 2020). On land reform, see generally RJ Herring, *Land to the Tiller: The Political Economy of Agrarian Reform in South Asia* (New Haven, Yale University Press, 1983); D Bandyopadhyay, 'Land Reforms in India: An Analysis' [1986] *Economic and Political Weekly* A50; T Besley and R Burgess, 'Land Reform, Poverty Reduction, and Growth: Evidence from India' (2000) 115 *Quarterly Journal of Economics* 389; BB Mohanty, 'Land Distribution among Scheduled Castes and Tribes' [2001] *Economic and Political Weekly* 3857.

[63] I Anand, 'Dalit Emancipation and the Land Question' (2016) 51 *Economic and Political Weekly* 12.

[64] M Pathak, 'Land Reforms May Have Played a Role in Patel, Dalit Protests' (*Livemint*, 18 September 2016) https://bit.ly/2sffs3p; D Dhar, 'What Brought the Dalits' Fight for Land to the Streets' (*The Wire*, 1 October 2016)

In many cases, possession is still with the original owners, who belong to dominant castes. In other cases, government agencies have not completed surveying and mapping the lands, which is a necessary step before possession of land can be given to the beneficiaries.[65] Against this backdrop of failed implementation, I examine a case of success in land reform implementation in rural Surendranagar, Gujarat, which was the result of legal and social mobilisation spearheaded by the Navsarjan Trust.[66] Navsarjan started working in the Surendranagar area in 1995, with land reform implementation as its focus. Through social and legal mobilisation spanning several years, more than 750 families (out of a total of 2300) in Surendranagar that had received land under the redistribution laws were able to take possession of their lands.

Navsarjan was founded in the late 1980s with the objective of eliminating untouchability, campaigning for 'equality of status and opportunities to all, regardless of caste, class or gender, and [ensuring] prevalence of the rule of law'.[67] At its peak, the organisation was active in more than 3000 villages and most major cities in Gujarat. Its founder, Martin Macwan, was born into a poor Dalit family.[68] He was educated at Christian educational institutions in Gujarat and landed his first job at the Behavioural Science Centre (BSC) – a Jesuit-run organisation affiliated with St Xavier's College in Ahmedabad. As a BSC employee, Macwan spent time in rural Gujarat raising social consciousness among Dalits and helping build resistance to upper-caste oppression.

Macwan's boss at BSC was a Spanish priest transplanted into Gujarat named José Heredero, who was deeply influenced by Mohandas Gandhi and Paulo Freire's philosophy and David McCelland's research on behaviour change.[69] While working in the

https://thewire.in/rights/why-Dalits-have-taken-their fight-for-land-to-the-streets; M Laxman, *Land Reforms and Dalits in Gujarat* (Ahmedabad, Unique Book House, 2019).

[65] Laxman (n 64).

[66] This chapter is based on a larger PhD research project on land reform and Dalit mobilisation in Surendranagar, Gujarat. Siddiqi (n 62). Here, I primarily draw from my research on the early phase of Navsarjan's work in Surendranagar from the mid-1990s until the mid-2000s. It is pertinent to note that in late 2016, the Government of India cancelled Navsarjan Trust's permission to accept funds from foreign donors, which caused major upheaval in the organisation. Most caseworkers were relieved of their duties. This has caused consternation and dissatisfaction among sections of the caseworker community. These facts notwithstanding, the effects of decades of Navsarjan Trust's work to eradicate untouchability and entrench the democratic rights of Dalits has had a lasting influence, as evidenced from the interviews and my participant observation of Dalit politics. See SK Ahmed, 'FCRA Licence Cancelled, NGO Navsarjan Lays Off All Staffers' *Indian Express* (27 December 2016) https://indianexpress.com/article/cities/ahmedabad/fcra-licence-cancelled-ngo-navsarjan-lays-off-all-staffers-4440969/; A Mirror, 'Trust Sitting on Funds of Rs 22 Cr: Navsarjan Ex-Staff' *Ahmedabad Mirror* (20 February 2017) https://ahmedabadmirror.indiatimes.com/ahmedabad/crime/trust-sitting-on-funds-of-rs-22-cr-navsarjan-ex-staff/articleshow/57239673.cms; 'Gujarat Dalit Rally in Surendranagar Takes Strong Exception to Calling Human Rights NGO Navsarjan Anti-National' (*Counterview*, 25 January 2017) www.counterview.net/2017/01/gujarat-Dalit-rally-in-surendranagar.html.

[67] Navsarjan Trust, https://navsarjantrust.org.

[68] This account is based on published accounts as well as several interviews the author had with Macwan between 2016 and 2020. Published sources include F Franco, J Macwan and S Ramanathan, *Journeys to Freedom: Dalit Narratives* (Kolkata, Samya, 2004); M Macwan, 'Tales from an Autography: The Violent Cost of Struggle for Equality' (2014) 1 *Journal of Social Inclusion Studies* 183; M Macwan, '(Un)Touchable in Durban' (2001) 508 *Seminar*, www.india-seminar.com/2001/508/508%20martin%20macwan.htm; M Macwan, 'Prof Pheroz Tehmurasp Contractor: Silent, Unnoticed Warrior against Casteism' (*Counterview*, 1 February 2021) https://counterview.org/2021/02/01/prof-pheroz-tehmurasp-contractor-silent-unnoticed-warrior-against-casteism-at-st-xaviers/.

[69] JM Heredero, PT Contractor and BB Siddiqui, *Rural Development and Social Change: An Experiment in Non-Formal Education* (New Delhi, Manohar, 1977) 171–75.

Kheda district of Gujarat, Macwan and his associates started using the law to help create better economic opportunities for Dalits. Their actions included petitioning the local administration to allocate vacant land to Dalit agricultural co-operatives so that Dalits were not dependent on upper castes for employment. The upper castes in the village became angry seeing Dalits raise such demands. Things took a dark turn in 1986, when his close associates in a village named Golana (in Kheda) were massacred by an upper-caste mob. The victims were local Dalit leaders affiliated with the BSC who were leading the campaign for Dalit rights.

Golana victims received overwhelming support both from the Dalits and the state government. The perpetrators were sentenced to life in prison.[70] Macwan described this as a very emotional period for him – initially filled with sadness and anger, and later with passion and hope. He decided to meet caste discrimination head-on by founding Navsarjan in the late 1980s. Lessons that Macwan had learned throughout his life – the reality of caste-based subjugation, pathways to social change through behavioural change, the importance of meticulous implementation and the potential of law – came together in the programmatic strategy of Navsarjan. Its three foundational precepts were: legal mobilisation as a key strategy to challenge caste-based oppression; the leadership of the campaign for Dalit rights should remain with Dalits because only they can understand the lived reality of caste-based oppression; and the organisation would centre on creating hope by focusing on successes rather than failures in Dalit mobilisation.

(i) Methodology

I conducted fieldwork in Gujarat for nine months between 2016 and 2019. Most of my time was spent in Surendranagar, with some time spent in Ahmedabad, Rajkot, Botad and Gandhinagar. Following an inductive and exploratory research framework, I conducted detailed interviews with two types of informants: (i) Navsarjan workers ($n = 10$) who have been active in the area since the organisation started working there. These individuals were the main mobilisers during the movement for implementation of land reform; and (ii) Dalits ($n = 60$) who participated in the land reform movement and took possession of land that was formerly theirs only on paper. In addition, I conducted interviews with Land Revenue officials ($n = 8$) who oversee the land bureaucracy in the area, including two District Collectors, two Deputy District Collectors and four lower-level bureaucrats.[71] The interviews were semi-structured, and typically one to two hours long. Interviews took place in a variety of settings: Dalit homes, caseworker homes, Navsarjan offices, government offices, chai shops, public spaces, etc. While interviewing, I followed a diachronous approach: obtaining an oral history of how things unfolded during the mobilisation by Dalits a decade and a half ago as well as details of the current social relationships between Dalits and other caste groups in the villages. The descriptions of the actions and positions taken by the informants over time, as narrated by them, offer a window to construct the locus of how Dalit subjectivity has changed in this area, ostensibly as a result of participation in the mobilisation for the implementation of land reform. In addition to the interviews, I participated in numerous Dalit community

[70] Macwan, 'Tales from an Autography' (n 68) 198.

[71] All informants, except Macwan, have been given pseudonyms.

meetings and group actions in Surendranagar and Ahmedabad; on some days, I would accompany the caseworkers on their daily social and work visits. I also attended public and private events organised by the Navsarjan Trust and its sister organisation, the Dalit Shakti Foundation, in Ahmedabad and Surendranagar. To ensure breadth and depth, I conducted interviews with several different types of informants (young and old; men and women; caseworkers and ordinary Dalits, etc). Where necessary, I conducted several rounds of interviews with key informants. Additionally, I cross-checked time-lines and sequences of events in different informants' accounts.

(ii) 'Social Expressive Value' in Action

Navsarjan built its cadre by recruiting young adult Dalits to serve as field-based case-workers in select districts. A typical caseworker recruited during that time was in their early twenties, had a high-school education and lived in a joint family, which meant that the recurring living costs were relatively low. Navsarjan leadership sought spirited individuals who were passionate about social justice but did not necessarily have formal knowledge of the law, public administration or organisational management. These topics would be covered during their training period, which spanned over one year. A caseworker recruited during this period recounted the training as follows:

> We were trained in law, society and individual development. What are our rights [as citizens]? What are the injustices that are done to us [Dalits]? We received detailed knowledge of funda-mental rights, public administration and different sections of the Indian Penal Code. We were also taught about leadership through discussion of various topics, including: What are the salient characteristics of good leaders? How does a [good] leader view things? Gradually, little by little by little, we developed … we learned the language … we learned to speak. Later, we conducted workshops in villages and we taught the material we had learned during our train-ing to rural Dalits.[72]

As is evident here, the training programme was centred around Ambedkar's famous dictum: 'Educate, Agitate, Organize!' Navsarjan not only trained its cadre of casework-ers in the procedural aspects of law, but also gave them working knowledge of the moral norms and political philosophy of the Constitution. 'Individual development' meant creating confident and capable Dalit leaders who could influence the rural Dalit constit-uency in their fieldwork. In the late 1990s and early 2000s, Navsarjan in Surendranagar decided to start working on the unimplemented land reform laws from which hundreds of local Dalit families potentially stood to benefit. In a village in Surendranagar, I visited Kanjibhai, a middle-aged Dalit who received land under the Gujarat Agricultural Land Ceiling Act 1960, which he now farms commercially. Speaking of the changes that becoming a landowner has brought to his status as a citizen, he said the following:

> We always wanted to be independent but our wish was not accomplished until we got posses-sion of this land. Back in the day, when we saw other people's farms, we used to dream of having our own farm with its own irrigation. We did not desire to snatch someone else's land. With the help of Navsarjan, we were able to realise our dream. In the village, people respect

[72] Interview with Navsarjan caseworker in Surendranagar, May 2017.

> me now. They cannot take me lightly. They consider me a man of knowledge, law, and legal rights.[73]

As a result of becoming an owner of agricultural land, he is now an owner-producer instead of a wage labourer. Since coming into possession of the land, his household income has increased considerably. Kanjibhai's home, where we met before travelling to his field, is located in the middle of a group of houses owned by his relatives. He showed me the house he currently lives in – a spacious two-bedroom house made of bricks, mortar and concrete. It stands next to an old house with mud walls and a thatch roof, which is smaller in size than the new building. Kanjibhai pointed to the old house, saying that his parents and siblings used to live there two decades ago. With increased income, he could afford to build a better house for his family. Neither Kanjibhai nor anyone else in his family is forced to migrate for work. As a result, his children can now attend school regularly. Overall, his household is doing better on all socio-economic indicators of development. The changes in Kanjibhai's life are not just material. He feels more effective as a political actor. His perception of how others in the village perceive him has changed too. He believes that he is not a man that others, especially majority caste groups, can take lightly. This was not the case 10 years ago, when he first became associated with Navsarjan and campaigned to take possession of his land.

Since he is now a landowner and raises two crops a year, he does not have to look for agricultural wage work on other people's farms. Previously, he had had to ask for work from other landowners in the village, most of who belonged to majority caste groups. They often treated him with disrespect, but he had no choice but to tolerate it. Today, people belonging to upper-caste groups approach him for employment. Over the last few years, even non-Dalits from his village have partnered with him to work on his land as contract farmers. All of this makes him feel a more confident person.

Importantly, he has become conversant in the language of human rights and law. He has learned what Ludwig Wittgenstein called a 'language game':[74] in this case, the language game of law and rights. Kanjibhai has also become a local Dalit leader. If a Dalit in his village has a problem, it is likely that Kanjibhai is the first person that will be approached for help. As a result of his affiliation with Navsarjan, he has not just learned about the constitutional promise of equality, but has also developed familiarity with various statutes. Furthermore, as a result of his frequent visits to local land and revenue administration offices during his petitioning for the land award, he has also developed familiarity with the working of the local bureaucracy; local officials recognise him.

Kanjibhai's life has changed in pertinent economic and political ways over the last two decades. In the Surendranagar district of Gujarat, where Kanjibhai is from, I met and interviewed many other Dalits whose lives have experienced change similar to his. These changes appear to have staying power because of two kinds of entrenchments: first, the consolidation of property rights of Dalits such as Kanjibhai over land; second, the deep psychological internalisation of the constitutional ideal of equality and rights. These two entrenchments are supported by the development of the capacity to assert these equality claims in the public and legal spheres.

[73] Interview with Kanjibhai (pseudonym) near Sayla, Gujarat, June 2017.
[74] L Wittgenstein, *Philosophical Investigations* (New York, John Wiley & Sons, 2009).

My original objective in going to Surendranagar was to investigate how Dalits were able to come into possession of land in rural areas that legally belonged to them but had remained under the control of socially dominant upper-caste groups. Soon after beginning field research, I was struck by the remarkable consistency in how the speakers legitimised their claims to land and equal citizenship based on the constitutional norm of equality. It was as if the speakers themselves had become legal adjudicators. Consider Kanjibhai again, who is talking about his personal transformation:

> You know, I was a landless labourer as a teenager. I also lacked confidence regarding my rights. I was hesitant to ask for my rights even if they were legitimate demands. In the process of taking possession of this land, I have become much more courageous and confident. I realised that the other person who was holding my land illegally was in the wrong. I had received this land through the *right process*. I questioned myself why I was so afraid of taking what was mine *when I was in the right and the other person in the wrong*. (emphasis added)[75]

While adjudication is an everyday occurrence in our lives (individuals make decisions considering questions of right and wrong every day), what made these Dalits' adjudicative arguments special was that they were based on the constitutional 'expression' that all citizens have equal moral worth and that due process has intrinsic value. Rather than justifying their demand for equality in terms of material interests (eg 'I need this land because it will improve my financial situation'), the individuals I interviewed, all made their claims by referring to the Constitution (eg 'This constitution, which Ambedkar drafted, has given us the right to equality and due process. The land redistribution is part of that promise, and therefore, should be transferred to me'). In other words, Navsarjan and its caseworkers have been able to raise rights consciousness among Dalits in the region. How did this change happen?

As part of its mobilisation strategy, Navsarjan prioritised the organisation of legal education workshops with the aim of building a community of legally conscious Dalits. The workshops were led by caseworkers, who saw this as a chance to raise the rights-consciousness of the Dalits, just as their own rights-consciousness had developed during the training period. Since the caseworkers were Dalits from nearby areas, it was relatively easy for them to build rapport with local Dalits. The workshops were often held in villages instead of the town centre to minimise travel time and cost for participants. As a consequence, the workshops saw participation not only from men but also from women, and often children. In the workshops, Navsarjan caseworkers spoke of Ambedkar's normative emphasis on the fundamental equality of humans, the reflection of this philosophical idea in the Constitution and the provisions in the Indian legal system to safeguard Dalits from *atyachaar* (hate crimes/atrocities) at the hands of the upper castes. Summarising the messaging in the legal awareness workshops, another Navsarjan caseworker told me:

> [During the workshops and generally in conversation] We told our Dalit brothers and sisters that the constitution, rights, and legal provisions such as Scheduled Caste and Scheduled Tribe (Prevention of Atrocities) Act, 1989[76] were Babasaheb's [Bhimrao Ambedkar's] gift to us.

[75] Interview with Kanjibhai near Sayla, Gujarat, June 2017.

[76] Caseworkers colloquially refer to the Scheduled Caste and Tribes (Prevention of Atrocities) Act, 1989 as 'anti-atrocity law'.

> Ambedkar also said that living like a slave is not a good thing … We spoke of realizing the rights that are given to us by Babasaheb in the Constitution. We were not trying to fight with swords. We wanted to stay within the legality of the Constitution because that is our method. However, we know that these rights cannot be realised without struggle and persistence, so we have to keep trying. This is the first thing we put forth in every village we went to. We told people [Dalits] that if they respected Babasaheb, they had to fight for what he gave them [rights, land].[77]

Navsarjan's efforts to raise legal awareness and rights consciousness did not end with the workshops. The caseworkers developed ongoing relationships of trust with local Dalit families. I visited the home of Kodabhai (pseudonym), a Dalit man in rural Botad (neighbouring Surendranagar) who has been petitioning the local administration to grant him title to a piece of land he currently works on (informally). The administration was inclined to evict him. In the back and forth with the local administration, his key ally is the local Navsarjan worker, who has provided guidance and help. The relationship between Kodabhai and the local Navsarjan worker is informal yet respectful. Whenever Kodabhai is in town, he visits the local Navsarjan office (about five to six times a month). At the office, over a cup of chai, he usually reads the newspaper and discusses politics of the day with whoever is present (usually, one or two Navsarjan caseworkers and whoever else might be there).

When I asked Kodabhai how he finds the fortitude to persist with his demand for land against the government's push-back, he answered, 'by attending their programs where they introduced me to Babasaheb's [BR Ambedkar's] philosophy, the constitution, and the laws meant to protect us … I understood the importance of fighting for my rights from Navsarjan'. I followed up with Kodabhai asking how his relationship with upper castes has changed as a result of his association with Navsarjan and developing a rights consciousness. His immediate response, which echoes answers I received to similar questions posed to other interviewees, was: 'the relationship has changed; I don't feel subservient to them any longer'.[78]

Kanjibhai, referenced earlier, corroborated the importance of learning from Navsarjan, saying: 'I used to go to the meetings regularly. We used to discuss issues. They taught me about the law … they asked me why I was so afraid of them [the upper castes] … they said we are all human beings and deserved equal respect'.[79] It took Kanjibhai a few years to completely get over his fear and reticence to raise his voice against upper castes. After some prodding by me, he put a date on when he thinks he lost this fear: the year 2001. He said, 'by that year, I had come to realise that there was no reason to be afraid of them. We are all equals. That is what the constitution says'.[80] Interestingly, this was the year he also received possession of the land that belonged to him but was illegally occupied by an upper-caste person.

There are many ways in which individuals like Kanjibhai could have explained their efforts to gain possession of the land. He could have used the language of economic improvement to explain his actions. He could have spoken of exacting revenge on the

[77] Interview with Navsarjan caseworker in Limdi, Surendranagar, May 2017.
[78] Interview with Kodabhai near Botad, Gujarat, February 2017.
[79] Interview with Kanjibhai near Sayla, Gujarat, June 2017.
[80] ibid.

former dominant caste landowner for caste-based exploitation and stigmatisation. Yet, Kanjibhai and the other Dalits I interviewed argued their actions were not just about material gain or revenge: it was a matter of self-respect; they were trying to realise their constitutional rights to equality and a dignified life.

Theorists of egalitarian democracy have long argued that democratic polities require a public culture in which individuals see themselves as moral equals of others.[81] Seen from that view, the transformation in the perception of rightful self-worth of these Dalits is a movement towards the deepening of democratic culture. What makes it special in this case is the central importance of the Constitution and constitutional norms. Navsarjan caseworkers strategically built their narrative around constitutional norms, democratic rights and appeals to equality before the rule of law. To help create a sense of ownership and loyalty to the Constitution, Navsarjan activists made sure to attribute the principal authorship of the Constitution to Ambedkar.

The deepening of rights consciousness among Dalits was also crucially predicated on them experiencing the law's potential in practice. For this, it was crucial to develop capacity among rural Dalits for navigating various levels of state bureaucracy and judiciary. The caseworker in Botad elaborated:

> In addition to introducing them to the laws, we also train them in how to use them. How to write applications, who to talk to, etc. They learn which issues to highlight and include in the paperwork. [When we first started work in the area,] Dalits were afraid to engage with the state machinery and use the laws meant to protect them and improve their lives. They feared state agencies [eg the Police]. After the training [and hand holding,] Dalits in the area are significantly less afraid of using the legal provisions to fight for justice. For example, the police would not easily lodge FIRs [First Information Report] from Dalits. We would have to accompany them to the station. Now, after years of practice and hand holding, Dalits are more confident and, in many cases, they can go file FIRs on their own.[82]

The next case I present shows what navigating the courts and legal bureaucracy looked like for a Dalit family that managed to gain control of land through litigation, and the consequent emergence of rightful self-confidence. In this example, the Dalit family received title to 11 acres of land in 1992 under section 9 of the Gujarat Agricultural Land Ceiling Act, 1960.[83] Like most other landless Dalits in the area, agricultural wage labour was the primary means of livelihood until the land award. The path to ownership and the consequent economic independence was not straightforward: it involved years of legal battle with the former landowner's family. The outcome of this difficult experience was not just becoming landowners: members of this family also developed unusual confidence in citizenship and rights due to the struggle they had undergone.

The land awarded to the Dalit originally belonged to a large landowning family from an OBC (Other Backward Class) caste. This family, while not a member of the

[81] J Rawls, *A Theory of Justice* (Cambridge, MA, Belknap Press, 1971); J Rawls, *Political Liberalism* (New York, Columbia University Press, 2005); MC Nussbaum, *Political Emotions* (Cambridge, MA, Harvard University Press, 2013); R Bernstein, 'Dewey's Vision of Radical Democracy' in M Cochran (ed), *The Cambridge Companion to Dewey* (Cambridge, Cambridge University Press, 2010).

[82] Interview with Navsarjan caseworker in Botad, February 2017.

[83] This account is based on an interview with the beneficiary family in the village of Doliya, Surendranagar, April 2017.

highest-ranking caste, was above Dalits in the caste order. Additionally, the original landowners' family was much stronger economically than the Dalit family (the family patriarch owned close to 100 acres of land in the village).[84] The Dalit beneficiary, along with his family members, tried taking possession of the land allotted to him in 1990. At that time, members of the original landowner's family warned them against taking possession; both sides claimed that the land belonged to them. In the meantime, the grandson of the original landowner challenged the expropriation of his grandfather's land before the Deputy Collector in Limdi (an administrative sub-division of Surendranagar).[85] The Deputy Collector, by his order dated 31 December 1992, dismissed the appeal. Next, in 1993, the grandson approached the Gujarat Revenue Tribunal and argued that due process had not been followed in the expropriation of his grandfather's land. The Tribunal issued an order in favour of the grandson in 1994, overturning the Deputy Collector's order. This put the Dalit family's ownership in jeopardy.

In response, in 1995, Laxmanbhai (pseudonym) – the head of the Dalit family allotted land – filed a petition in the Gujarat High Court challenging the Tribunal's order. It was around this time that the family met Navsarjan caseworkers, who had just started working in Surendranagar. Laxmanbhai explained his land dispute to the caseworkers. Over repeated meetings starting in late 1995, Navsarjan caseworkers built rapport and trust with the family. Once they had developed a rapport, the family became active in the mobilisation for Dalit rights and land reform. Members of the family started participating in meetings, rallies and demonstrations. Even though Laxmanbhai filed the petition in the Gujarat High Court before coming into contact with the Navsarjan caseworkers, he started discussing it with them and soliciting advice right from the early days of interaction. In 1997, the Gujarat High Court issued an interim order granting status quo: the possession of the land was to remain with the petitioner.[86] In 2002, Laxmanbhai – the main petitioner in the High Court – passed away. His wife and son replaced him in the petition. Navsarjan caseworkers continued to provide advice and counsel to the family, making several trips to the High Court. In 2007, in its final order, the Gujarat High Court overturned the Tribunal's order.[87]

The defeat in High Court did not go down well with the former landowner's grandson. The family told me that the grandson felt slighted at having lost to Dalits – people he considered inferior and less deserving of a good life than he did. In 2010, more than two years after the Gujarat High Court overturned the Tribunal's order, the grandson decided to file a Letter Patent Appeal (LPA) in the Gujarat High Court requesting a review of the single judge's 2007 order.[88] Typically, LPAs are filed within a few months after a judgment is passed – a considerably shorter period than in this case. The Dalit family claims that the original owner's grandson filed the LPA primarily to prolong the legal hardship of the Dalit family. The Gujarat High Court dismissed the LPA in 2012.[89]

[84] *Dalwadi Trikambhat Talsibhai v State of Gujarat & Others*, Ahmedabad, CA 4134 of 2017, HC Guj, 30 August 2017.

[85] Limdi is a sub-division of Surendranagar district.

[86] *Jagabhai Ghelabhai Harijan v State of Gujarat & Others*, Ahmedabad, SCA 6121 of 1995, HC Guj.

[87] *Maniben Wd/O Harijan Jagabhai Polabhai v State of Gujarat & Others*, Ahmedabad, SCA 6121 of 1995, HC Guj, 4 October 2007.

[88] *Dalwadi Trikambhai Talsibhai v State of Gujarat & Others*, Ahmedabad, LPA 562 of 2010, HC Guj, 15 June 2012.

[89] ibid.

Still not satisfied, in 2013 the grandson filed a Special Leave Petition in the Supreme Court of India challenging the Gujarat High Court's LPA judgment. This was a historically unprecedented situation. Until then, no one in this village had ever been involved in litigation in the Supreme Court of India, let alone litigation involving a Dalit. Initially, the Dalit family was worried about the legal escalation. In 2017, a Supreme Court order directed the Gujarat High Court to decide on merits, since the latter court had, in its 2012 judgment, wrongly assumed that procedure did not allow a review on merits.[90] The Gujarat High Court, reviewing the LPA again, overturned the Tribunal's order, thus cementing the Dalit family's claim to the land.[91]

In 2013, the Dalit family had been hesitant to take the battle further – going to the Supreme Court seemed too daunting. However, the Navsarjan caseworker, who by then was very close to the family, had convinced them to continue their fight. This step had made local news among Dalits as well as non-Dalits. For the locals, a 'Dalit had gone all the way to the Supreme court and litigated their claim', and the outcome was that their claim was cemented by force of law! This was a huge boost to the confidence of the family as well as the Dalit community. On several occasions, Navsarjan caseworkers in the Surendranagar area told me that this also encouraged other Dalits in the area, who had been afraid to demand their rights until then. Several of these newly enthused Dalits are reportedly now looking for ways to take possession of the land that they have title to on paper.

At the end of a long interview with the victorious Dalit family, my last question was, 'you must still run into this person in the village once in a while … how does this person behave towards you now, given the history of his transgression and your victory?' One member of the family, a man in his 60s, replied, 'he is afraid of us now. When he sees me approaching, he changes course [to avoid running into me].' As I left his house, the man came to see me to the door. He raised his fist and in an emotional-but-confident voice said: '*Uske paas danda hai … magar hamare paas Qaeda hai*' ('He [the former landowner] has the stick … but we [Dalits] have the Constitution and law').[92]

IV. Law and Navsarjan's Efficacy: Politics in the 'Shadow of Law'

Martin Macwan, while talking to me about social change, the law, and the Navsarjan experience, recounted another story of how legal knowledge helped the Navsarjan cadre raise their image in the village, which in turn contributed to their becoming effective activists. It is important here to quote Macwan at some length:

> You met our caseworker, Ramabhai (pseudonym), right? In this village, during the first training in 1992, I used to go and drop him back in his village every day after we were done with

[90] *Dalwadi Trikambhai Talsibhai v State of Gujarat & Others*, New Delhi, SLP 9171 of 2013, SC, 23 February 2017.

[91] *Dalwadi Trikambhai Talsibhai v State of Gujarat & Others*, Ahmedabad, LPA 562 of 2010, HC Guj Order dated 30 August 2017.

[92] *Qaeda* literally means law in Gujarati. However, universally in my interviewing, interactions and participant observation, I heard *qaeda* being used to mean both the law and the Constitution.

> work. The other workers who were at the training would take their own transport back but I decided to take Ramabhai personally to his village because *kshatriyas* [upper castes] were trying to take revenge on him for raising a lot of issues against them. He was not safe. I used to drop him at his village that was 20 kilometers from Nadiad, where I lived. The upper caste used to call him Rameya – a derogatory 'slang' version of his name invented by the upper castes. After six months into the training, an old man, a *Khsatriya* came to Ramabhai's house and said, 'is this Ramabhai's house?' His sister said yes. Rama came out and asked what the issue was. The old man said he had received some kind of letter from the government but he did not know what it was. He requested Rama to help him understand it. Rama agreed and asked the man to sit. He asked his sister to bring some water for the old man. Rama knew exactly what he was doing. The old man, since he was a visitor to Rama's house, and was there to seek help, could not afford to brush off Rama's hospitality. So he accepted the water. [For Kshatriyas] *Rama had become Ramabhai.* Word spread around the village that this is a man who knows the law and the procedure. He was instrumental in sending several people behind bars and fighting cases. Suddenly, he had become a well-respected and feared man. In this time, did he grow physically? No Does he carry a revolver? No His power came from the knowledge that he has. Power, in society as we understand it, does not come from caste. It comes from knowledge. With knowledge, you can break caste.[93]

Psychological-symbolic politics in the 'shadow of law' was an important tool in Navsarjan's day-to-day practice of fighting caste-based oppression and inequality. Navsarjan started using the Scheduled Castes and the Scheduled Tribes (Prevention of Atrocities) Act, 1989 (SCSTPA) to start criminal proceedings against majority castes who treated Dalits unfairly or did not accede to them their due land. A wide range of derogatory, humiliating and unfair treatments by upper castes towards Dalits were recounted by Navsarjan caseworkers. These infractions included deliberate dumping of trash outside Dalit homes in the villages, verbal humiliation of Dalits in public places and illegal possession of Dalit lands. The Dalits in the area reacted by bringing criminal cases against the perpetrators of the abuse. The news of an SCSTPA case being filed against them was a serious matter. There were stringent provisions against the accused in the SCSTPA (including the issue of non-bailable arrest warrants). This, coupled with Navsarjan's resources and ability to bring criminal cases to court, made the perpetrators of abuse 'tremble with fear', I was told.

Navsarjan caseworkers proudly recounted that they made even the strongest and most arrogant majority caste individuals afraid once they started legal proceedings against them. The caseworkers maintained that their intention was not to trouble or exact revenge on the upper castes. In their own words, their main purpose was to realise the constitutional ideal of equality. Having made the 'stronger party' vulnerable, Navsarjan workers would then ask the accused to come to their office to talk if they wanted. 'By now, they were really afraid of getting involved with the law', one caseworker told me. These were the same people who regularly treated Dalits as sub-human and not worthy of respect. They would inevitably agree to come to the Navsarjan office. This was a radical change: an upper-caste person was *summoned* to 'negotiate' with the Dalits. Just a few years before Navsarjan began mobilising, such a turn of events was beyond the imagination of either Dalits or the upper castes.

[93] Interview with Martin Macwan, Ahmedabad, June 2017.

With the 'show cause' summons, Navsarjan won an important psychological battle. Traditionally, as a mark of their lower status, Dalits were expected to make the journey to an upper caste's location and sit on the floor. Not so when the majority caste person visited the Navsarjan office to negotiate. Navsarjan offices typically have just one or two rooms, and the only furniture is cotton-filled mattresses on the floor. The only option was for Navsarjan caseworkers and their adversaries to sit on the floor together, on equal ground. They told me that initially this even startled Dalits, who were used to sitting on the ground while upper castes sat on a charpoy or chair.

With everyone seated at the same level, the caseworkers moved to step two in the psychological politics of symbolism: they would offer the visitors water and tea. Offering tea to visitors is customary in Gujarat, as it is in many other parts of India. With a laugh, a caseworker told me,

> [when we offered tea] sometimes, they would make excuses … saying that they did not want tea or water because they had just had it before leaving home. They were afraid of accepting food and water from the hands of a Dalit.[94]

In Gujarati culture, guests typically do not refuse tea. Hosts can pressure guests – in good faith – to accept. However, in this case, since upper castes consider Dalits impure, they were loath to accept food or water from their hosts. If the situation were reversed and a Dalit visited an upper-caste household, they would be given tea and water in a utensil reserved only for Dalits. Given the circumstances under which the upper castes were meeting with Dalits to negotiate a deal, they were afraid of offending the Dalits. Therefore, during these meetings at Navsarjan's offices, the upper-caste visitors had no choice but to accept what was offered. Referring to the moral-political aspect of this symbolic act, the Navsarjan workers observed, 'we knew exactly what we were doing. We were trying to destabilise the caste hierarchy.' Again, the reason Navsarjan and their Dalit constituents could be so daring with their intergroup demands on upper castes was that they had figured out how to work the law to their benefit: Dalits who allied with Navsarjan not only could speak the language of constitutional norms to justify their rights claims, but also were capable of bringing legal action against the abusive upper castes.

V. Rethinking Constitutional Resilience

Navsarjan's efforts to deepen rights consciousness among Dalits and push for implementation of land reform in Surendranagar have had lasting consequences. Over two decades later, all the individuals and families I interviewed credited their association with Navsarjan as a transformational experience during which they deepened their understanding of rights and developed legal capabilities. As such, the three examples that I have included in this chapter represent a broader transformation in the capabilities and political psychologies of the Dalits in Surendranagar who have come into contact with Navsarjan's campaign since the mid-1990s. Over time, the Navsarjan Trust has emerged as one of the most powerful Dalit rights organisations working in Gujarat.

[94] Interview with Navsarjan caseworker in Surendranagar, May 2017.

This was publicly evidenced a few years ago, when the organisation threw its weight behind the spontaneous Dalit mobilisation in Gujarat following the lynching of young Dalits in Una (in the Gir Somnath district in Gujarat).[95] The nationwide coverage of Navsarjan's critical stance irked the national ruling establishment so much that the government of India barred Navsarjan Trust from accepting funds from foreign donors, thus undermining the organisation.[96] Some caseworkers lost their jobs and a few have expressed dissatisfaction with the organisation as a result. However, the organisation continues to be politically significant in Gujarat. The Vice President of the Indian National Congress, Rahul Gandhi, visited Navsarjan Trust's campus in Ahmedabad as part of his party's electoral campaign for the Gujarat Assembly elections in 2017. Several caseworkers interviewed as part of this research were involved in campaigning for the Congress in the assembly elections, in which the Congress put up a tough fight against the ruling Bharatiya Janata Party (BJP).[97]

There is little doubt that Navsarjan's efficacy in Surendranagar was in large part the outcome of a dedicated corps of caseworkers. These men and women have performed the essential role of being the 'mappers in the middle',[98] making sure that constitutional norms do not remain a fiction but are understood and mobilised by ordinary Dalits to realise justice. But Navsarjan's power also comes from the loyalty of the Dalits it has influenced over time. The tone and tenor in the way Dalit interviewees spoke of Navsarjan conveyed a sense of pride in the association. As the testimonies and life stories included earlier show, these individuals reported feeling more confident, capable and 'rightful'. Admittedly, factors other than Navsarjan's intervention may have contributed to the changes in Dalits' sense of self. After all, the last two decades have seen important changes in the overall socio-economic condition in India. Education, per capita income and other key human development indicators have improved across the board.[99] Information and communication technologies have improved, and smartphone penetration is unprecedentedly high even in rural areas.[100] All of these changes have the

[95] 'Dalits Thrashed for Skinning Cow: Two Accused Arrested as Protests Continue in Una' *The Indian Express* (20 July 2016) https://indianexpress.com/article/india/india-news-india/dalits-thrashed-for-skinning-cow-two-accused-arrested-as-protests-continue-in-una-2912461/.

[96] Ahmed (n 66); *Counterview* (n 66).

[97] 'Congress Puts up a Tough Fight in Gujarat, Gives BJP The Jitters' (*India.com*, 18 December 2017) www.india.com/news/india/gujarat-assembly-election-results-2017-congress-puts-up-a-tough-fight-in-gujarat-gives-bjp-the-jitters-2766414/; 'Gujarat Election Result: We'll Analyse the "Tough Fight", Says BJP Leader' *Hindustan Times* (18 December 2017) www.hindustantimes.com/india-news/assembly-election-results-2017-we-will-analyse-the-tough-fight-in-gujarat-says-bjp-leader/story-lx2yYsFLA8823cTuyvn4rN.html.

[98] SE Merry, 'Transnational Human Rights and Local Activism: Mapping the Middle' (2006) 108 *American Anthropologist* 38.

[99] The Human Development Index for India went from 0.429 in 1990 to 0.645 in 2019. United Nations Development Programme, 'Human Development Reports' http://hdr.undp.org/en/indicators/137506.

[100] In May 2011, Telecom Regulatory Authority of India reported a total of 285.53 million rural wireless phone subscribers. In March 2021, the corresponding number of subscribers was 535.75. Overall teledensity in Gujarat is close to 100%, with rural teledensity at 60%. TRAI, 'Information Note to the Press' (Telecom Regulatory Authority of India, 2011) Press Release No 41/2011, www.trai.gov.in/sites/default/files/PR-TSD_may_07_07_11.pdf; TRAI (Telecom Regulatory Authority of India, 2021) Press Release No 33/2021. My observations and informal interactions with Dalits in rural Surendrangar also indicated that mobile phone penetration has created a new way of accessing information. At the time of my fieldwork in Gujarat, Reliance Industries Pvt Ltd had created history by offering the world's cheapest mobile data plans (under the trade name Reliance Jio). This service was very popular among consumers. K Anand, 'Reliance Jio 4G Unleashes War on Telcos; Top 10 Takeaways from RIL's 42nd AGM' *The Economic Times* (1 September 2016)

power to alter social relations and improve an individual's self-perception. However, these changes alone cannot fully explain the specific transformation in the sense of self of Dalits in Surendranagar.

Take, for instance, education, which is commonly considered a key prerequisite to upward mobility. Improvements in access to education can expand individuals' capabilities. Economically speaking, because of better reading and writing skills, individuals may be able to move up from low-skilled, low-paid to higher-skilled, higher-paid jobs. This could mean an increase in incomes and a better standard of living. That, in turn, could translate into the development of social prestige and respect. However, there is evidence that stigma does not leave Dalits even if they manage to climb the socio-economic ladder, often by securing admission to educational institutions or government jobs through India's affirmative action policies.[101] An infamous example from 2016 is the case of Rohith Chakravarti Vemula, a doctoral candidate at the University of Hyderabad, who was hounded by upper-caste faculty and students at his university for being a Dalit and securing admission through affirmative action policies instead of 'merit'. This ultimately led Vemula to commit suicide.[102] These disturbing facts notwithstanding, in theory, it is possible for education and technology to change social relations. But these changes alone do not determine what arguments a person would give to make claims in the political sphere. In the case of those I interviewed in Gujarat, the constitutional rights framework, with its underlying 'expression' of fundamental human equality, seemed to serve as one dominant moral framework for political argumentation.[103] If one were to take a bird's eye view of Surendranagar and look only at income and schooling data for Dalits and compare that to the national average, one might conclude that Dalits are poorer here than in other places. But that would say nothing about how fiercely confident in their constitutional rights hundreds of Dalits in this area have become and all the different democratically important ways they are putting them to use.

How do expressive norms like 'dignity of individuals' and 'equality of all before the law' enshrined in the Constitution matter in making this resilience possible? My answer is that they matter *constitutively* yet *contingently*. With its expressive norms of dignity and equality, the Constitution serves as a powerful meaning-making and justificatory framework that appeals to marginalised populations as the framework of choice on which to base their struggle for a dignified life. As I have explained earlier, this centring served to legitimise the struggle and challenge the traditional 'local rationality' of Dalit deference and reticence against upper-caste excesses. To substantiate, consider the

https://economictimes.indiatimes.com/markets/stocks/news/reliance-jio-unleashes-war-on-telcos-top-10-takeaways-from-rils-42nd-agm/articleshow/53957893.cms.

[101] K Hoff and P Pandey, 'Discrimination, Social Identity, and Durable Inequalities' (2006) 96 *American Economic Review* 206; A Deshpande, 'Social Justice through Affirmative Action in India: An Assessment' in J Wicks-Lim and R Pollin (eds), *Capitalism on Trial* (Cheltenham, Edward Elgar, 2013); A Deshpande, 'Double Jeopardy? Stigma of Identity and Affirmative Action' (2019) 46 *Review of Black Political Economy* 38.

[102] O Farooq, 'Rohith Vemula: The Student Who Died for Dalit Rights' *BBC News* (19 January 2016) www.bbc.com/news/world-asia-india-35349790.

[103] 'Dominant narrative' does not mean the only narrative. The Dalits I interviewed who came into contact with Navsarjan Trust caseworkers repeatedly and unequivocally emphasised the constitutionally mandated norm of equality (as a philosophical-moral idea) as the basis for their demand for fair treatment, dignity and self-esteem.

following elaboration of the approach followed by the Navsarjan team during the land reform campaign:

> We spoke the language of law. We told them that *tumhare baap ki zameen nahi hai* ('This is not your father's land'). We told them that the land was given to us Dalits by the government under the constitution. We told them that our fight was not with them. We were just trying to get what was *rightfully* ours. We also told them if they didn't comply with the law, they would go to prison. They understood this could indeed happen. A few people didn't listen to us but most of them did. The upper castes were psychologically afraid of us. We had been able to go to the top levels of the government and obtained orders to supersede the power of the local elites … they were helpless, for once. The local government officials, who might otherwise have let the illegal encroachment continue, were bound by the court order. They would tell the upper castes that they would go to prison if they didn't hand over possession to the Dalit landowners.[104] (emphasis added)

In particular, notice the stress on 'rightfulness' in the argument. These efforts to instil a new local rationality emphasising moral equality, due process and legal rights were not in vain. The Dalits who came into contact with Navsarjan, including the beneficiaries of land reform implementation, could not describe their claims without referring to the Constitution. In talking to me about why they felt confident taking on a powerful upper-caste local contractor, Rameshbhai and Savitribehen, a middle-aged Dalit couple in a village of Surendranagar called Thoriyali, remarked, 'the upper caste person has money and bulldozers and political influence … we don't have much but the way shown by Babasaheb [BR Ambedkar]. Using this pen that costs five rupees, I can invoke my legal rights against him.'[105]

The longer story is that an influential building contractor from the Surendranagar area sent bulldozers to illegally occupy government-owned common grazing land adjoining Rameshbhai and Savitribehen's (pseudonyms) house in Thoriyali. The husband and their teenage children were away when the bulldozers arrived. Savitribehen, who was home, was not afraid: she climbed on the roof and told the contractor's men to leave 'or she would go to Gandhinagar [the state capital] and get them behind bars'. According to her, this scared the men and they left. With their rightful confidence, Rameshbhai and Savitribehen are popularising what Martha Nussbaum calls the 'public myth of equality' in the public sphere.[106] They may not be wealthy or as well connected to politicians and bureaucrats as the contractor; they may be Dalits who have historically been oppressed by upper castes. However, they believe in their rightful moral equality and their capability to use the law to protect not only their rights, but also those of society as a whole (in this case, by defending the commons). This is the legacy of Navsarjan and an example of how it has created 'constitutional rights resilience' at the grassroots by empowering ordinary Dalits who draw inspiration from constitutional norms and are capable of exercising them in a different setting in day-to-day life. Critics who write the Constitution off merely as a 'spectacle of emancipation' or construe rights to be 'whatever people in

[104] Interview with Navsarjan caseworker in Limdi, Surendranagar, May 2017.

[105] Interview with Rameshbhai and Savitribehen (pseudonyms) in the village of Thoriyali, Surendranagar, January 2019.

[106] MC Nussbaum, *Hiding from Humanity: Disgust, Shame, and the Law* (Princeton, Princeton University Press, 2009) 17.

power say they are' also write off the generative meaning-making that it offers people at the margins on which they can build radical claims to equality and justice. Indeed, constitutional principles offered Navsarjan caseworkers and the Dalits associated with them an 'outline of a theory of practice'.[107]

Thus far, I have argued that constitutional norms matter in bringing rights resilience to marginalised populations fighting for justice. Now, I want to qualify this salubrious view of constitutional performance (the 'contingency' aspect). Under what conditions do the constitutional norms and ideals appeal to the marginalised populations and penetrate political psychologies? The answer includes understanding hopefulness and the role of effective translation. One of the three founding principles of Navsarjan was

> to be very positive in life because problems are galore. What one needs, especially for the poor, are hope and success. We have enough failures, enough bad things in life, enough problems – one doesn't want to hear about them, one wants to hear success stories.[108]

At the time of Navsarjan's founding, Macwan *hopefully* decided that caste oppression and untouchability would be challenged legally. To ensure success, Macwan raised a legally informed and effective cadre of caseworkers. The caseworkers spent several years training both in the classroom as well as in the field. The field experience gave them grounded knowledge of the situation in the villages; the classroom gave them a tour of moral philosophy and legal procedure so that they could become teachers of constitutional principles, in their own ways, to local Dalits they came into contact with. The reliance on constitutional norms for making political claims gave the caseworkers legitimacy in front of all parties: Dalits, non-Dalits and the government. The combination of legitimacy and procedural legal capacity was potent: Navsarjan leveraged it initially towards small wins, which led to bigger wins. In less than five years, Navsarjan had mounted enough pressure on the government to transfer possession of 6000 acres of land that legally belonged to Dalits but was under upper-caste occupation.[109] All of this transpired under the 'shadow' or directly under the auspices of the Constitution. But to understand how exactly the Indian Constitution 'performed' in this case, I had to change my lens. This story of constitutional resilience can only be properly grasped by taking into account how ordinary Dalits understand and practice constitutionalism. A judge's jurisprudence on the Constitution or income data on the population in Surendranagar (or Gujarat) would not be helpful without understanding the 'view from below' to appreciate the performance of the Constitution. Such a broadening of the constitutional research programme in India is bound to make our understanding of constitutional resilience more comprehensive and nuanced.

[107] Baxi, 'Outline of a "Theory of Practice" of Indian Constitutionalism' (n 40).
[108] Franco et al (n 68) 314.
[109] For details, see Siddiqi (n 62) ch 3.

19

Constitutional Patriotism in India: Appreciating the People as Constitutional Actors

JAHNAVI SINDHU AND VIKRAM ADITYA NARAYAN[1]

I. Introduction

In Indian legal scholarship, there has been limited analysis of the role of people as constitutional actors. There are, of course, vast bodies of work examining India's many social movements and the complex interactions between society, politics and law.[2] However, these bodies of scholarship rarely characterise these movements as being led by 'constitutional actors' – who we understand as actors seeking to preserve or enhance constitutionalism.[3] To a large extent, this may be attributed to the inherent limits of and blind spots in constitutional theory.[4] As Gavin Anderson argues, 'bringing social movements into proximity with constitutional theory calls into question assumptions that constitutionalism is inherently institutional, western in origin, and normatively positive'.[5] Liberal constitutionalists and constitutional lawyers appear to avoid engaging with instances of mass politics or popular resistance in order to sidestep this theoretical discomfort.[6]

[1] We are grateful to Swati Jhaveri, Tarunabh Khaitan and Mirza Rizwaan Ahmad for valuable editorial feedback, and to Gautam Bhatia, Anuj Bhuwania and Radhika Chitkara for comments and suggestions on an earlier draft of the chapter. All errors remain ours.

[2] Including, eg M Galanter, *Law and Society in Modern India* (Berkeley, University of California Press, 1989); G Omvedt, *Reinventing Revolution: New Social Movements and the Socialist Tradition in India* (London, Routledge, 1994); F Agnes, *Law, Justice and Gender: Family Laws and Constitutional Claims* (Oxford, Oxford University Press, 2011).

[3] L Lazarus, 'Constitutional Scholars as Constitutional Actors' (2020) 48 *Federal Law Review* 483.

[4] LB Solum, 'Constitutional Possibilities' (2008) 83 *Indiana Law Journal* 307; T Roux, 'Interdisciplinary Synergies in Comparative Research on Constitutional Judicial Decision-Making' (2019) 52 *Verfassung und Recht in Übersee/World Comparative Law* 413.

[5] GW Anderson, 'Societal Constitutionalism, Social Movements, and Constitutionalism from Below' (2013) 20 *Indiana Journal of Global Legal Studies* 881.

[6] B Rajagopal, 'Pro-human Rights but Anti-poor? A Critical Evaluation of the Indian Supreme Court from a Social Movement Perspective' (2007) 8 *Human Rights Review* 157.

This chapter argues that it is particularly important to study the people as constitutional actors at moments when ordinary institutional accountability mechanisms appear to break down. We argue that performing such a study enables us to view the people as a source of and tool for constitutional resilience, and that this is an important step in developing a 'forward-looking',[7] solution-oriented approach to the problem of 'constitutional decay'.[8] We seek here to develop the concept of 'constitutional patriotism' that emerged in German political discourse, and apply it to the Indian context to understand the current moment of popular resistance to Indian constitutional erosion.[9] By constitutional patriotism, we refer to an allegiance to constitutional principles and a particular allegiance to the principle of free and equal participation as the basis for political integration.[10] The chapter argues that applying constitutional patriotism to India produces insights in two directions, by providing a deeper understanding of how constitutional resilience is manifesting in India while also helping to refine the meaning of constitutional patriotism.

The chapter is structured as follows: section II discusses how the dominant method by which 'the people' are brought within frameworks of constitutional analysis in India focuses on institutions that represent the people, with a special focus on how the judiciary is seen to speak for the people in the Indian context. However, we argue that in the context of a judiciary that now regularly engages in strategic silence, deferral and deference, it is valuable to develop approaches to evaluate the role of the people independent of the manner in which their claims are adjudicated. Section III traces the history of the concept of constitutional patriotism, outlines its scope and explains its relevance as a framework for understanding the diffusion of constitutional values. In this section, we also distinguish the concept of constitutional patriotism as used in this chapter from the meaning given to it by the Indian Supreme Court, pointing out several flaws in the Supreme Court's conception. In section IV, we argue that India offers fertile ground for the application of the concept of constitutional patriotism, employing a historical and contextual analysis of the Indian Constitution to argue that it may well be viewed as a document seeking to manifest constitutional patriotism instead of ethnic or cultural nationalism. Section V discusses how the Indian experience with constitutional democracy can enrich our understanding of constitutional patriotism and constitutional resilience, and the relationship between the two. In particular, this section focuses on the role of recent popular movements in pushing back against the rise of Hindu nationalism, and in seeking to hold institutions accountable to constitutional values. Section VI concludes.

II. Beyond Institutions – People as Constitutional Actors

There is undoubtedly a strong link between the people and their constitution in that the creation of a constitution is commonly dependent on the exercise of constituent

[7] Introduction to this volume.

[8] TG Daly and W Sadurski, *Democracy 2020: Assessing Constitutional Decay, Breakdown and Renewal Worldwide* (IACL ebook, 2020).

[9] M Mate, 'Constitutional Erosion and the Challenge to Secular Democracy in India' in M Graber, S Levinson and M Tushnet (eds), *Constitutional Demcracy in Crisis?* (Oxford, Oxford University Press, 2018).

[10] See section III below.

power – so much so that constituent power is often said to be vested in the people.[11] However, following the creation of a constitution, it appears that the dominant method by which the people are brought within existing frameworks of constitutional analysis is by focusing on institutions that represent the people.[12] While this includes legislative bodies, which consist of elected representatives, in the Indian context, it would also include the judiciary, which has gradually and significantly expanded its power over the last five decades, often acting 'in the name of the people'.[13]

'The people' have often been studied based on a refraction of their claims through the judiciary. The works by Rohit De[14] and Anuj Bhuwania[15] are two recent and noteworthy – albeit differing – examples of this. De generates 'a social history of constitutional law' that focuses on 'the citizen litigant' as the central actor in several Supreme Court cases decided between 1950 and 1966.[16] Through this approach, De demonstrates that the Constitution was not merely an elite pact imposed on the Indian people,[17] but 'was produced and reproduced in everyday encounters' wherein even Indians belonging to marginalised sections of society played an important role in shaping constitutional meaning through their advancement of constitutional claims.[18] Bhuwania provides a revisionist account of the origin of public interest litigation in India, starting in the 1970s, and examines several cases to argue that public interest litigation (PIL) enabled a 'transformation in the nature of adjudication' that fundamentally reconstituted the relationship between the judiciary and the people.[19] His critique shows how the judiciary displaced vast sections of the people as potential actors by claiming to

[11] For analysis on this point, see M Forsyth, 'Thomas Hobbes and the Constituent Power of the People' (1981) 29 *Political Studies* 191; A Kalyvas, 'Popular Sovereignty, Democracy, and the Constituent Power' (2005) 12 *Constellations* 223. For a contextual approach to construing constituent power, see Z Oklopcic, 'Three Arenas of Struggle: A Contextual Approach to the Constituent Power of "the People"' (2014) 3 *Global Constitutionalism* 200.

[12] As Bui Ngoc Son notes, 'the participation of social movement actors in public constitutional reasoning has been largely under-considered', especially in Asia. BN Son, 'Social Movements and Constitutionalism in Japan, South Korea and Taiwan' [2019] *Asian Journal of Comparative Law* S51, S58. Notwithstanding the dominance of institution-centric analysis, some recent scholarship has sought to examine the people as constitutional actors more directly by examining the significance of social movements in pushing for constitutional change. See, eg BN Son and P Nicholson, 'Activism and Popular Constitutionalism in Contemporary Vietnam' (2017) 42 *Law & Social Inquiry* 677. Aside from this recent scholarship, the idea of 'the people' as constitutional actors occasionally appears in analyses of the nature of constitutional referenda and in debates about the nature and the scope of the power to amend a Constitution. On this, see, eg S Tierney, 'Constitutional Referendums: A Theoretical Inquiry' (2009) 72 *MLR* 360; J Colón-Ríos, 'The Legitimacy of the Juridical: Constituent Power, Democracy, and the Limits of Constitutional Reform' (2010) 48 *Osgoode Hall Law Journal* 199.

[13] U Ramanathan in M Suresh and S Narrain, *The Shifting Scales of Justice: The Supreme Court in Neo-liberal India* (Hyderabad, Orient Blackswan, 2014) 39; PN Bhagwati, 'Judicial Activism and Public Interest Litigation' (1985) 23 *Columbia Journal of Transnational Law* 561; U Baxi, *Courage, Craft and Contention: The Indian Supreme Court in the Eighties* (Mumbai, NM Tripathi, 1985).

[14] R De, *A People's Constitution: The Everyday Life of Law in the Indian Republic* (Princeton, Princeton University Press, 2019).

[15] A Bhuwania, *Courting the People: Public Interest Litigation in Post-Emergency India* (Cambridge, Cambridge University Press, 2017).

[16] De (n 14).

[17] S Dasgupta, 'A Language Which Is Foreign to Us: Continuities and Anxieties in the Making of the Indian Constitution' (2014) 34 *Comparative Studies of South Asia, Africa and the Middle East* 228.

[18] De (n 14).

[19] Bhuwania, *Courting the People* (n 15).

speak for 'the people' – as an undifferentiated class – without hearing those who would be disadvantaged by its decisions. In his words, he examines how the jurisdiction of PIL, 'which arose with the court speaking in the name of the people, became parasitical on the very same people'.[20]

In light of the expanded role of the judiciary in India,[21] it is perhaps unsurprising that the role of people as constitutional actors has largely been studied, critically and otherwise, based on how their claims have filtered through the process of adjudication. However, this chapter argues that the rise of ethnonationalism in India since the Bharatiya Janata Party (BJP)'s electoral victory in 2014, and the corresponding weakening of Indian institutions, including the judiciary,[22] necessitates an examination of the people's role as constitutional actors directly, and not merely on how their claims are mediated through institutions. Admittedly, there has always been a section of Hindu nationalists who consider India a 'Hindu nation', with religion seen to be the source of the nation's identity.[23] This vision of India was defeated in the Constituent Assembly,[24] though it has re-emerged from time to time with political support thereafter. Two of the most reprehensible examples of the resurgence of Hindu nationalism with political patronage are the destruction of Babri Masjid in 1992 and the Godhra riots of 2002. However, it is widely believed that the ongoing fusion of political power and Hindu nationalism at the national level since 2014 is deeper and more systematic, and poses a greater threat to Indian constitutionalism than ever before.[25]

Since the BJP's coming to power in 2014, the state apparatus has been deployed to further the Hindu nationalist agenda.[26] Many state-level governments have sought to revise history in textbooks and school curriculums to downplay the contributions of Muslims throughout Indian history and glorify 'Hindu civilisation', despite there being little evidence to back their specific claims.[27] Legislative enactments banning cow slaughter or imposing considerable procedural hurdles for religious conversion and inter-religious marriages in various BJP-ruled states have legitimised right-wing

[20] ibid.

[21] SP Sathe, *Judicial Activism in India: Transgressing Borders and Enforcing Rights* (Oxford, Oxford University Press, 2002); PB Mehta, 'India's Unlikely Democracy: The Rise of Judicial Sovereignty' (2007) 18(2) *Journal of Democracy* 70.

[22] Mate (n 9); T Khaitan, ch 7 in this volume.

[23] M Vaishnav, *Religious Nationalism and India's Future* (Washington, DC, Carnegie Endowment for International Peace, 2019); C Jaffrelot and C Schoch, *Modi's India: Hindu Nationalism and the Rise of Ethnic Democracy* (Princeton, Princeton University Press, 2021).

[24] As Amartya Sen noted, 'when India became independent nearly half a century ago, much emphasis was placed on its secularism, and there were few voices dissenting from that priority', A Sen, 'Secularism and Its Discontents' in R Bhargava (ed) *Secularism and its Critics* (Delhi, Oxford University Press, 1998) 454. See also section IV below.

[25] Jaffrelot and Schoch (n 23); A Narrain, *India's Undeclared Emergency: Constitutionalism and the Politics of Resistance* (Westland, 2022).

[26] ibid. See also T Khaitan, ch 7 in this volume.

[27] A Truschke, 'Hindutva's Dangerous Rewriting of History' (2020) 24/25 *South Asia Multidisciplinary Academic Journal* 1; P Dhoop and V Dhoop, 'Are Indian Students Losing Out on Past History as Textbooks Are Being Changed?' (*The Leaflet*, 10 April 2021) www.theleaflet.in/are-indian-students-losing-out-on-past-history-as-textbooks-are-being-changed/; 'Historians Write to Parliamentary Panel against Proposed Changes to NCERT History Textbooks' *The Hindu* (20 July 2021).

conspiracy theories depicting Muslims as 'cow smugglers' or engaging in 'love jihad'.[28] Against the backdrop of such laws, vigilante attacks on both Muslims – many of whom are employed in the cattle trade – and inter-faith couples have increased manifold. More recently, there has also been an increase in attacks on churches due to allegations of forced conversions. Vigilante groups often enjoy the tacit support of the police,[29] who then arrest victims of vigilante attacks on trumped-up charges. A recent example of the complicity of the police in the Hindu nationalist project can be seen in the Delhi Police's role in the communal pogrom against Muslims in Delhi in February 2020, with aggrieved Muslims arrested and the political leaders who had publicly incited violence going unpunished.[30]

At the national level, the ruling government has pushed through a slew of constitutional amendments and legislation that seek to cement the status of Muslims as second-class citizens. In August 2019, the government revoked the special autonomy granted to the state of Jammu and Kashmir, and downgraded and divided the state into two union territories. Through this move, the central government gained substantial control over the only Muslim majority state in India.[31] Notably, these measures were rushed through Parliament without deliberation by sidestepping the constitutional requirement for consultation with the Jammu and Kashmir Assembly. In the aftermath of this amendment, a communication blackout was imposed in the region which lasted for over a year.[32] In December 2019, Parliament passed the Citizenship Amendment Act (CAA), granting citizenship to only Hindu, Sikh, Buddhist, Jain, Parsi or Christian persons migrating to India without valid documents from Bangladesh, Pakistan and Afghanistan because of religious persecution. Constitutional scholars have demonstrated how the exclusion of Muslims in the Act infringes the principle of equality and secularism,[33] and can have a calamitous effect on the basic rights of Indian Muslims if the government proceeds with its plans to create a nationwide National Register

[28] A Dhonchak, 'Copycat "Love-Jihad" Laws in BJP States Shred Women's Autonomy' (*Article 14*, 12 January 2021) www.article-14.com/post/copycat-love-jihad-laws-in-bjp-states-shred-women-s-autonomy.

[29] A Dhillon, '"Free Pass for Mobs": India Urged to Stem Vigilante Violence against Minorities' *The Guardian* (19 February 2019) www.theguardian.com/world/2019/feb/19/a-free-pass-for-mobs-to-kill-india-urged-to-stem-cow-vigilante-violence.

[30] N Thapliyal, '"Sorry State of Affairs, Lackadaisical": 10 Times When Courts Slammed Delhi Police over Riots Probe in 2021' (*LiveLaw*, 31 December 2021) www.livelaw.in/top-stories/10-times-when-courts-slammed-police-over-delhi-riots-probe-2021–188556.

[31] H Regan, 'India Downgrades Kashmir's Status and Takes Greater Control over Contested Region' *CNN* (31 October 2019) www.edition.cnn.com/2019/10/31/asia/jammu-kashmir-union-territory-intl-hnk/index.html.

[32] J Sindhu and VA Narayan, 'Parliament Doesn't Have the Power to Downgrade J&K's Status to UT (*The Quint*, 8 August 2021) www.thequint.com/voices/opinion/kashmir-bifurcation-union-territory-unconstitutional-violation-federal-structure; The restrictions on communication carried on for more than a year, with them only being removed gradually. See N Maish et al, 'India's Internet Shutdown is now the Longest in the World' *Washington Post* (16 December 2019) www.washingtonpost.com/world/asia_pacific/indias-internet-shutdown-in-kashmir-is-now-the-longest-ever-in-a-democracy/2019/12/15/bb0693ea-1dfc-11ea-977a-15a6710ed6da_story.html. The Supreme Court, despite having heard a challenge to the communication shutdown, failed to give any remedies. See *Anuradha Bhasin v Union of India* (2020) 3 SCC 637.

[33] F Ahmed, 'Arbitrariness, Subordination and Unequal Citizenship' (2020) 4 *Indian Law Review* 121; A Chandrachud, 'Secularism and the Citizenship Amendment Act' (2020) 4 *Indian Law Review* 138.

of Citizens (NRC).[34] Under the NRC, citizens would have to prove their lineage and citizenship on the basis of documents such as their birth certificate or school leaving certificate and those of their ancestors, which many citizens do not possess.[35] It is in this context that India has been labelled an 'ethnocracy', under which a specific expression of nationalism 'where a dominant ethnos gains political control and uses the state apparatus to ethnicise the territory and society in question'.[36]

Scholars have documented how the Indian judiciary has withdrawn from its role of checking legislative and executive excesses.[37] The pathologies afflicting the Indian judiciary, and particularly the Indian Supreme Court, have been analysed in detail in other chapters of this volume,[38] and elsewhere.[39] Briefly, the Court has adopted a policy of judicial evasion, where it does not list cases of constitutional importance or political significance.[40] Cases challenging the validity of the downgrading and reorganisation of Jammu and Kashmir, the anti-conversion laws and the CAA are still pending.[41] In other cases, the Court has adopted an extremely deferential approach wherein it dilutes the standard of review applicable while evaluating rights claims, and has granted weak remedies even where strong remedies are constitutionally mandated and contextually warranted.[42] In some cases, the Court has even gone beyond the executive in pushing

[34] S Shankar, 'How Democratic Processes Damage Citizenship Rights: The Implications of CAA-NRC' (Centre for Policy Research, 16 December 2019) www.cprindia.org/news/8339#:~:text=The%20Citizenship%20Amendment%20Act%20%28CAA%29%202019%2C%20when%20viewed,and%20documentless%20could%20deprive%20one%20of%20citizenship%20rights.

[35] T Agarwala, 'Explained: Which Papers Really Work as Proof of Citizenship in Assam?' *The Indian Express* (29 February 2020).

[36] O Yiftachel, '"Ethnocracy" and Its Discontents: Minorities, Protests and the Israeli Polity' (2000) 26 *Critical Inquiry* 725; I Roy, 'Modi's India: Hindu nationalism and the rise of ethnic democracy' (*The India Forum* 3 September 2021) www.theindiaforum.in/article/india-world-s-largest-democracy-ethnocracy?utm_source=website&utm_medium=organic&utm_campaign=featured-articles&utm_content=Homepage.

[37] G Bhatia, 'Judicial Evasion and the Status Quo: On SC Judgments' *The Hindu* (10 January, 2019) www.thehindu.com/opinion/lead/judicial-evasion-and-the-status-quo/article25953052.ece; G Bhatia, 'A Tale of Evasion, Deference and Inconsistency' *Hindustan Times* (10 December 2020) www.hindustantimes.com/columns/a-tale-of-evasion-deference-and-inconsistency/story-uPCbRzn40SLooj6mVLbpOJhtml; A Bhuwania, 'The Indian SC in the Modi Era' (*IACL*, 23 November 2020): www.iacl-democracy-2020.org/blog/2016/3/23/blog-post-sample-9wntn-6ye75-hwawc-xx9lz-p6k2z-85m67-nkxzl-m76y3-gmmc6; Narrain (n 25).

[38] See the chapters by T Khaitan and G Bhatia, chs 7 and 11 respectively in this volume.

[39] Special issue on 'The Indian Supreme Court in Crisis' (2018) 51(3) *Verfassung und Recht in Übersee/World Comparative Law* 269, www.nomos-elibrary.de/10.5771/0506–7286–2018-3-269/titelei-inhaltsverzeichnis-jahrgang-51-2018-heft-3?page=1; IACL roundtable on 'Crisis at the Supreme Court India' (*IACL*, 2018) https://blog-iacl-aidc.org/crisis-at-the-supreme-court-of-india.

[40] Bhatia, 'Judicial Evasion and the Status Quo' (n 37); Bhatia, 'A Tale of Evasion' (n 37); G Bhatia, 'Evasion, Hypocrisy and Duplicity: The Legacy of Chief Justice Bobde' (*Indconlawphil*, 2021) https://indconlawphil.wordpress.com/2021/04/23/evasion-hypocrisy-and-duplicity-the-legacy-of-chief-justice-bobde/.

[41] Freedom House Report on India (2020) https://freedomhouse.org/country/india/freedom-world/2021; Also, Freedom House, 'Democracy under Siege' (2021) https://freedomhouse.org/sites/default/files/2021-02/FIW2021_World_02252021_FINAL-web-upload.pdf; G Bhatia, 'India's Growing Surveillance State' *Foreign Affairs* (19 February 2020) www.foreignaffairs.com/articles/india/2020-02-19/indias-growing-surveillance-state.

[42] S Hegde, 'Social Distancing from the Powerless' *The Hindu* (19 May 2020) www.thehindu.com/opinion/lead/social-distancing-from-the-powerless/article31617566.ece; G Bhatia (*Indconlawphil*, 11 May 2020) https://indconlawphil.wordpress.com/2020/05/11/the-supreme-courts-4g-internet-order-evasion-by-abnegation/; J Sindhu, 'Judicial Remedies for the Jammu and Kashmir Net Restrictions' *The Hindu* (18 August 2020) www.thehindu.com/opinion/op-ed/judicial-remedies-for-the-jk-net-restrictions/article32378877.ece.

for measures that undermine the value of secularism and disproportionately affect religious minorities.[43]

Finally, the structure of the Supreme Court, where judges sit on benches of two or three, also leads to inconsistencies across opinions and creates an unpredictability of outcomes. This constitutional jurisprudence marked by evasion and incoherence has played a crucial role in enabling the growth and consolidation of power in the hands of the political executive in the last few years.[44] Studying the people as constitutional actors based solely on how their claims are decided by the judiciary in such a context tends to prioritise and amplify the cases that the judiciary has chosen to decide, and in many ways reinforces and reproduces the limited image of the world painted by the executive – collapsing our otherwise broad *nomos* into the narrow narrative presented by the executive in Court.[45] Simply put, such an approach presents a partially distorted picture of the people and their understanding of the Constitution.

We do not mean to suggest here that the Indian project of constitutionalism has collapsed entirely, or that it is futile to critically examine the functioning of the Indian judiciary. The Indian Constitution has been 'relatively resilient',[46] especially when compared to some of the other constitutional democracies in the South Asian region.[47] Studying Indian constitutionalism through its institutions, particularly the judiciary, continues to be of value in understanding some significant dimensions of how the people use, shape and are shaped by constitutional law. However, the claim advanced in this part of this chapter is that there are other dimensions of peoples' understanding and engagement with the Constitution that are difficult to capture when we focus on institutions, particularly where the judiciary is at the centre of the discourse. It is argued that focusing on the people directly can help one to appreciate how they seek to hold institutions, including even the judiciary, accountable for their failure to uphold constitutional values.

In present-day India, where most institutions appear to be severely restrained in checking executive power, it is the people that have often led the protection of

[43] A John, 'The Fate of Those Excluded from NRC Will Haunt India: Senior Advocate Sanjay Hegde' *The Caravan* (30 July 2019) https://caravanmagazine.in/government/sanjay-hegde-nrc-supreme-court; G Bhatia, 'A Little Brief Authority: Chief Justice Ranjan Gogoi and the Rise of the Executive Court' (*Indconlawphil*, 17 November 2019) https://indconlawphil.wordpress.com/2019/11/17/a-little-brief-authority-chief-justice-ranjan-gogoi-and-the-rise-of-the-executive-court/; M Andra, 'Why the Nationwide NRC Is Unconstitutional' (*Bar and Bench*, 7 January 2020) www.barandbench.com/apprentice-lawyer/why-the-nationwide-nrc-is-unconstitutional.

[44] Bhuwania, 'The Indian SC' (n 37); R Ramachandran, 'Supreme Court's Inconsistent Stand on Civil Rights Gives State a Window to Defeat Them' (*The Print*, 23 September 2019) https://theprint.in/opinion/supreme-courts-inconsistent-stand-on-civil-rights-gives-state-a-window-to-defeat-them/295378/.

[45] R Cover, 'The Supreme Court, 1982 Term – Foreword: Nomos and Narrative' (1983) 97 *Harvard Law Review* 4. On the Indian Supreme Court's role in reifying narratives supplied by the central executive, see G Bhatia, ch 11 in this volume. Andras Jakab's argument that the study of judicial decisions in an authoritarian context using ordinary tools of constitutional analysis can 'legitimise the theater of legalism' is pertinent here. A Jakab, 'Bringing a Hammer to the Chess Board: Why Doctrinal Conceptual Legal Thinking is Futile in Dealing with Autocratizing Regimes' (*Verfassungsblog*, 23 June 2020) https://verfassungsblog.de/bringing-a-hammer-to-the-chess-board/.

[46] Mate (n 9).

[47] D Shah and M Gomez, ch 2 in this volume.

constitutional values. The country erupted into protests immediately after the passing of the CAA. One of the most remarkable features of the recent protests was their scale, in terms of both their absolute numbers and their reach across diverse parts of the country. While we analyse the CAA protests in detail in section V, it is worth noting at the outset that the push-back by the people was so powerful that the central government subsequently denied having plans for a nationwide NRC.[48] At the time of writing, the government has not framed the rules to implement the CAA, but has sought multiple extensions from Parliament for this purpose.[49]

It is against this backdrop that it becomes important to examine the people as constitutional actors and appreciate their resilience against constitutional erosion. Framing the people's actions in the language of constitutional theory recognises the depths from which dissent emerges, and is also necessary to repel the dehumanising and discrediting tactics of othering dissenters and protestors.[50] In the next section, we introduce and break down the concept of constitutional patriotism to emphasise its utility in examining people as constitutional actors.

III. Constitutional Patriotism

In this section, we trace the evolution of the idea of constitutional patriotism as a response to the view that having common ethnic identities is a necessity for political integration in nation-states. This view reached its ultimate expression through the Nazi regime in Germany. Years after the fall of the Nazi regime, an intense public debate took place in Germany over what form of attachment to the idea of a nation is appropriate, and constitutional patriotism was suggested as a form of political allegiance to the rule of law and common liberties.[51] In our view, the lessons learnt from the German experience are relevant for the current crisis in Indian constitutionalism, with constitutional patriotism serving as an appropriate model of political legitimacy to combat ethnic nationalism and to push back against moves aimed at undermining secularism and equality in a constitutional democracy. In this section, we seek to show how constitutional patriotism entails a reflexive relationship with history and identities, redefining and revisiting them in light of universal principles. We demonstrate that constitutional patriotism has the potential to foster a constitutional culture based on debate and deliberation, where dissent and conflict are considered legitimate. Sections IV and V will then employ this idea of constitutional patriotism to show how it can and is being used to challenge constitutional decay in India.

[48] 'No Plans for NRC Now, Will Talk to Everyone if We Approach It: Home Minister Amit Shah' *India Today* (30 May 2020) www.indiatoday.in/india/story/no-plans-for-nrc-now-will-talk-to-everyone-if-we-approach-it-home-minister-amit-shah-1683774–2020-05-30.

[49] V Singh, 'MHA Applies for Another Extension to Frame CAA Rules' *The Hindu* (10 January 2022) www.thehindu.com/news/national/mha-applies-for-another-extension-to-frame-caa-rules/article38221609.ece.

[50] M Ganguly, 'Dissent Is Anti-national in Modi's India – no Matter Where It Comes From' (*Scroll*, 31 December 2019) www.scroll.in/article/946488/dissent-is-anti-national-in-modis-india-no-matter-where-it-comes-from.

[51] JW Müller, *Constitutional Patriotism* (Princeton, Princeton University Press, 2007) 16.

A. Evolution of Constitutional Patriotism

Constitutional patriotism is understood as a means of conceptualising 'the beliefs and dispositions required for citizens to maintain a particular form of political rule'.[52] This disposition is expressed as a commitment of citizens to view each other as free and equal, and to find fair terms of cooperation through which they can justify and evaluate the application of collective decisions of the state and its institutions.[53] As mentioned above, the concept first found articulation in Germany following the Second World War in an effort to search for a basis for social integration in the Federal Republic of West Germany.[54] The experience of Nazism and the Third Reich laid bare the risk of exclusion and violence that follows when ethnonationalism takes over and a common ethnic identity becomes a condition for membership to a state and the enjoyment of fundamental rights.

In this context, Habermas argued that while historically the 'nation' and 'state' have gone together, with the 'nation' serving as a mode of legitimation for the 'state' to create 'nation-states' and with citizenship mapping onto common ethnic identities, the two are not conceptually related.[55] The 'state' is a legal term that refers

> to a state power that possesses both internal and external sovereignty, at the spatial level over a clearly delimited terrain (the state territory) and at the social level over the totality of members (the body of citizens or the people).[56]

The term 'nation' denotes 'a political community shaped by common descent, or at least by a common language, culture, and history'.[57] According to Habermas, the latter only played a functional or catalytic role in creating political consciousness and the emergence of liberal democratic states. However, political consciousness need not always be based on common ethnic descent,[58] and mature polities would outgrow the need for pre-political identities and learn to 'stand on [their] own two feet'.[59] A common ethnic

[52] JW Müller, 'A General Theory of Constitutional Patriotism' (2007) 6 *International Journal of Constitutional Law* 72, 77.

[53] Müller, *Constitutional Patriotism* (n 51) 53–55.

[54] Early attempts can be traced back to Karl Jaspers, writing in *The Question of German Guilt*, who argued that Germany's 'negative past could become a source of social cohesion' as long as 'the Germans shouldered collective responsibility'. For Jaspers, this responsibility entailed a constant engagement with the past through 'free public communication' among equals. In 1979, this idea was introduced in the language of constitutional patriotism (*Verfassungspatriotismus*) by the political scientist Dolf Sternberger, who viewed the concept as a form of allegiance to the rule of law and common liberties. In Sternberger's understanding, constitutional patriotism required a nation-state closely modelled on Karl Loewenstein's notion of 'militant democracy'. Habermas built on this idea in the 1980s in response to neo-conservative efforts to rehabilitate German nationalism, which, according to Habermas, amounted to 'laundering' the German past and resurrecting social integration on the basis of common identities and proposed an alternative mode of integration of citizens in the Federal Republic of Germany. See Müller, *Constitutional Patriotism* (n 51) 16–28.

[55] J Habermas, *Inclusion of the Other* (C Cronin and PD Greiff eds, Cambridge, MA MIT Press, 1998) 207–08.

[56] ibid.

[57] ibid.

[58] J Habermas, *Between Facts and Norms Contributions to a Discourse Theory of Law and Democracy* (W Rehg trans, Cambridge, MA, MIT Press, 1996) 495.

[59] See P Markell, 'Making Affect Safe for Democracy? On "Constitutional Patriotism"' (2000) 28 *Political Theory* 38, 43.

identity was also incompatible with the promise of equality and human dignity provided for under the German Constitution – the Basic Law.[60] Habermas argued that the place of common ethnic identity as the basis of integration in a nation state could be taken by identification with basic norms of rational discourse through which universal principles such as equality and dignity acquire effectiveness and can be a reality in society.[61] This form of identification[62] is referred to as constitutional patriotism, and identities which so emerge are referred to as 'post-national'.[63]

Constitutional patriotism thus provides a model for ensuring the legitimacy of political rule in a state as well as for developing solidarity between citizens in a pluralistic society.[64] The social bonds in such communities are legal, moral and political, as opposed to historical, cultural and geographical.[65] Democratic citizenship or political identity in such states is understood to be rooted not in a national ethnic identity, but in a status defined by basic rights implied by the practice of self-government.[66] By valorising a set of universal norms instead of a particular historical community, constitutional patriotism avoids the pitfalls of nationalism and does not invite hostility towards some people or groups as others.[67] These universal principles can serve as an in-built defence against the use of ethnic identities for anti-liberal and anti-democratic ends.[68] Crucially, as Jan Werner Müller argues, a collective identity which is grounded in such a shared political culture in which all members can participate equally as opposed to one group dominating over another can win the allegiance of people belonging to different diverse groups without subsuming their distinct identities into a homogeneous national narrative.[69]

B. Unpacking the Concept of Constitutional Patriotism

Constitutional patriotism has met with its share of objections, especially with respect to its transferability, its abstractness and its associated inability to generate affect. We address these objections below to help better explain the concept and construct a preliminary case for applying the concept to contexts outside Germany.

One objection against constitutional patriotism is that it is a specifically German phenomenon.[70] While other states' histories are not identical to that of Germany, most states have their own history of repression, violence and discrimination that need to be contended with.[71] Constitutional patriotism, as will be argued below, allows for a critical

[60] ibid.

[61] ibid 41.

[62] ibid.

[63] Habermas, *Inclusion of the Other* (n 55) 119.

[64] Müller, 'A General Theory of Constitutional Patriotism' (n 52).

[65] J Lacroix, 'For a European Constitution' (2002) 50 *Political Studies* 944, 946.

[66] C Cronin, 'Democracy and Collective Identity: In Defence of Constitutional Patriotism (2003) 11 *European Journal of Philosophy* 1, 3–4.

[67] Markell (n 59) 44.

[68] CR Hayward, 'Democracy's Identity Problem: Is Constitutional Patriotism the Answer?' (2007) 14 *Constellations* 182.

[69] Müller, 'A General Theory of Constitutional Patriotism' (n 52) 78.

[70] Lacroix, 'For a European Constitution' (n 65) 951.

[71] ibid.

relationship with one's history.[72] In this way, the concept is adaptable and can be applied to different national contexts.[73]

Constitutional patriotism is also discredited as a purely abstract and idealised concept that is 'too thin' to evoke affect.[74] Scholars have argued that constitutional patriotism requires allegiance to abstract principles and it is inconceivable that citizens of a polity will be able to come to an agreement on and then swear allegiance to abstract moral principles.[75] If true, this would also suggest that constitutional patriotism is of little use as a tool for constitutional resilience. However, as Habermas explains, constitutional patriotism does not rely on an attachment to abstract universal principles alone but to their particular interpretations in a state – these universal principles 'are given a specific interpretation and take on a concrete institutional shape in a constitution'.[76] Each society will develop a distinctive interpretation of these principles in light of its own history.[77] After all, there is no single voice representing the universal, and 'it can only appear through something particular; only a particular can make the universal known'.[78] In the Indian context, for example, even though the rights and values recognised in the Constitution are identifiable as being partly drawn from a global language of constitutional law, the struggles and stories that give them depth belong to the Indian people. As Raghu Kesavan argues,

> our constitutional rights and values may be universal, but the struggles through which they were won belong only to us. There is no German Ambedkar, nor is there a British Gandhi. People, places and songs become symbols for these values.[79]

In the same vein, constitutional patriotism is incorrectly labelled as contrary to national ties. Although constitutional patriotism is viewed as a 'post-national form of political identification and attachment for pluralistic societies', it does not entail a denial of

[72] J Lacroix, 'Does Europe Need Common Values? Habermas v Habermas' (2009) 8 *European Journal of Political Theory* 141, 152.

[73] We argue in section IV that the concept is of particular relevance for nations containing pluralistic societies like India. Notably, even Habermas argued that constitutional patriotism was an appropriate response to multiculturalism – 'Today, as the nation-state finds itself challenged from within by the explosive potential of multiculturalism and from without by the pressures of globalisation, the question arises of whether there exists a functional equivalent for the fusion of the nation of citizens with the ethnic nation': Habermas, *Inclusion of the Other* (n 55) 117.

[74] See K Tonkiss, 'Constitutional Patriotism and the Post-National Paradox: An Exploration of Migration, Identity and Loyalty at the Local Level' (thesis, University of Birmingham, February 2012) 92; Cronin (n 66) 5.

[75] AD Baumeister, 'Diversity and Unity: The Problem with Constitutional Patriotism' (2007) 6 *European Journal of Political Theory* 483, 496; M Canovan, 'Patriotism Is Not Enough' (2000) 30(3) *British Journal of Political Science* 41.

[76] M Kumm, 'Why Europeans Will Not Embrace Constitutional Patriotism' (2008) 6 *International Journal of Constitutional Law* 117, 123.

[77] Hayward (n 68) 186. For instance, in the Indian context, secularism does not imply a complete separation of church and state, but includes religious reform where state intervention is necessary to correct inequalities perpetuating in religion. See R Bhargava, 'Outline and Introduction of a Political Theory of the Indian Constitution' in R Bhargava (ed), *Politics and Ethics of the Indian Constitution* (Oxford, Oxford University Press, 2009) 1.

[78] M Koskenniemi, 'International Law in Europe: Between Tradition and Renewal' (2005) 16 *European Journal of International Law* 113.

[79] R Kesavan, 'When Bullets Are Aimed at the Constitution, Who's the Patriot and Who's the Traitor?' (*The Wire*, 31 January 2020) https://thewire.in/politics/anti-caa-protests-constitutional-patriotism.

regional, local or national identities, nor an expectation that people no longer feel an attachment to their pre-political identities.[80] Advocates of constitutional patriotism concede that national polities and pre-political membership continue to be the starting point of states as well as sites of constitutional patriotism. People continue to find inspiration in common historical struggles.[81] The freedom movement in India is a pertinent example in this regard, where drawing from this history can and does provide a method of deepening conceptions of equality, liberty, dignity and fraternity.[82]

However, this attachment to a shared history and tradition is not as exclusionary as it is in the context of nationalism. This is because constitutional patriotism entails a reflexive or critical attitude towards one's history and pre-political identities.[83] The content and meanings of these identities are not considered fixed, but are constantly reconsidered and reconfigured using universal principles as a deontological standard. Thus, universal principles and particular conceptions of these principles informed by history, traditions and values exist in a reflexive relationship where the latter are viewed critically and reinterpreted to accommodate cultural pluralism.[84] This reflexive attitude thus allows for previously oppressed minorities as well as members who do not share the same history, such as refugees and immigrants, to find allegiance with the constitutional project of a state.[85] In this sense, constitutional patriotism is better characterised as 'post-nationalist' as opposed to 'post-national', as it rejects the chauvinistic interpretations of national identity but preserves national character.[86]

Constitutional patriotism presupposes the existence of principles to which allegiance is required as provided for in the constitution, and the specific interpretation of those principles is arrived at when citizens employ terms of fair cooperation that constitutional patriotism entails. As Habermas notes, it is through the process of free and open deliberation that citizens arrive at the meanings of the constitution.[87] Democratic deliberation becomes the medium through which members belonging to diverse ethnic groups can identify with the shared constitutional project.[88] The constitution thus becomes the common language dissenters can use to contest the decisions of those in power, which in turn must be used by those holding political power to justify their decisions.[89] Müller argues that 'constitutional patriots in a minority will have a way of appealing to the majority's attachment to principles of fairness – in which case the majority cannot simply dismiss the minority as those whose self-interests have lost out with particular decisions'.[90] A political system rooted in constitutional patriotism

[80] Cronin (n 66) 3. See also Lacroix, 'For a European Constitution' (n 65).

[81] Habermas, *Inclusion of the Other* (n 55) 212.

[82] KG Kannabiran, *Wages of Impunity: Power, Justice and Human Rights* (Hyderabad, Orient Blackswan, 2004); G Bhatia, *The Transformative Constitution: A Radical Biography in Nine Acts* (New York, HarperCollins, 2019).

[83] Müller, *Constitutional Patriotism* (n 51) 61–67.

[84] ibid. Cronin (n 66) 7. We expand on how this may be done through the example of India in sections IV and V of this chapter.

[85] Tonkiss (n 74).

[86] Cronin (n 66) 16; Müller, 'A General Theory of Constitutional Patriotism' (n 52) 86.

[87] See generally Habermas, *Inclusion of the Other* (n 55).

[88] ibid.

[89] Müller, 'A General Theory of Constitutional Patriotism' (n 52) 80.

[90] ibid.

thus stands in sharp contrast to nationalism, where majorities and minorities have no common language to draw upon, and deliberation and debates by minorities are delegitimised as anti-national.

We demonstrate the suitability of applying this concept in the Indian context in section IV. We build on it in section V by showing how its application enables us to view constitutional patriotism as a form of constitutional resilience.

C. Indian Supreme Court's Flawed Understanding of Constitutional Patriotism

Before analysing how recent Indian social movements may be understood as manifestations of constitutional patriotism pushing back against constitutional erosion, it is worth briefly acknowledging that the Indian Supreme Court has sought to use the concept in a drastically different sense from that in which we develop the concept here. The Court's invocation of constitutional patriotism can be found in an order passed in January 2018, mandating all cinema halls to play the national anthem before screening films and correspondingly requiring all film-goers to show respect to the national anthem by standing silently while it is played. As part of the Court's directions, this order, passed in the case of *SN Chouksey v Union of India*,[91] declared that the:

> National Anthem or a part of it shall not be printed on any object and also never be displayed in such a manner at such places which may be disgraceful to its status and tantamount to disrespect. It is because when the National Anthem is sung, the concept of protocol associated with it has its inherent roots in National identity, National integrity and Constitutional Patriotism.[92]

The Court explained the basis of its order by further stating that:

> the directions are issued, for love and respect for the motherland is reflected when one shows respect to the National Anthem as well as to the National Flag. That apart, it would instill the feeling within one, a sense of committed patriotism and nationalism.[93]

This judgment has been criticised for multiple reasons, including on the ground that the writ petition as originally filed was not maintainable as no fundamental right infringement was claimed in seeking a direction to cinema halls to play the national anthem.[94] As Gautam Bhatia points out, even once the initial petition was amended, the contention that the Prevention of Insults to National Honour Act violated the right to equality of persons because it did not protect the national anthem as much as it protected the national flag is strikingly absurd. The absence of reasoning and the application of constitutional patriotism to command respect for national symbols and as a vehicle for

[91] (2017) 1 SCC 421.
[92] ibid para 9.3.
[93] ibid para 10.
[94] G Bhatia, 'The Illegality of the Supreme Court's National Anthem Order' (*Indconlawphil*, 30 November 2016) https://indconlawphil.wordpress.com/2016/11/30/the-illegality-of-the-supreme-courts-national-anthem-order/.

strengthening nationalism may be explained away as part of the Indian Supreme Court's demonstrated record of 'uninhibited theorising'.[95] As Kanad Bagchi argues, the reasoning of this judgment is based on 'tossing around concepts of profound significance without the slightest enquiry into its meaning or relevance',[96] with the Court ironically suggesting that this understanding of constitutional patriotism overrides individual rights.[97]

Based on this broader context, one might argue that the use of constitutional patriotism by the Indian Supreme Court says more about the institution than the concept, and that this may be resolved by continuing to critically examine the Court's decisions and bringing more nuance and theory to the discussion. One might also argue that this instance also speaks to a misconception that constitutional patriotism encounters owing to the use of the word 'patriotism' in the term,[98] that manifestations of constitutional patriotism may seem similar to those of patriotism, such as feelings of pride associated with national symbols such as the national anthem. However, as Cronin points out, constitutional patriotism finds expression in deeper and more complex forms, and encompasses a range of emotions beyond pride, such as expressions of shame, guilt and anger towards discriminatory acts and acts based on social prejudice.[99] We seek to capture some of the complex manifestations of constitutional patriotism in section V of this chapter when we discuss the CAA protests.

IV. India as a Site of Constitutional Patriotism

In the previous section, we examined the theoretical underpinnings of the concept of constitutional patriotism. In this section, we argue that constitutional patriotism is a useful conceptual tool to appreciate the present moment in India when the people exhibit constitutional patriotism in their push-back against constitutional decay and the rise of ethnocracy.

[95] P Baruah, '(De)Valuing Dignity: Three Risks of Dignity Inflation in the Indian Supreme Court's Reasoning' (2020) 55(31) *Economic and Political Weekly*. One might even point to the fact that the decision was authored by Justice Dipak Misra, who was known for writing unclear, 'unintelligible' judgments that play fast and loose with legal concepts. On this point, see G Bhatia, 'A Look Back at Chief Justice Dipak Misra's Errors of Commission and Omission' (*The Wire*, 3 October 2018) https://thewire.in/law/supreme-court-chief-justice-dipak-misra; A Shourie, *Anita Gets Bail – What Are Our Courts Doing?* (New York, HarperCollins, 2018); A Mandhani, 'SC Slams Bombay HC for "Unintelligible" Order, but Courts Are Full of Convoluted Rulings' (*The Print*, 7 November 2019) https://theprint.in/judiciary/sc-slams-bombay-hc-unintelligible-order-courts-full-of-convoluted-rulings/317171/.

[96] K Bagchi, 'The Supreme Court is Perpetuating the Myth of Constitutional Patriotism' (*The Wire*, 13 December 2016) https://thewire.in/law/constitutional-patriotism-national-anthem-sc.

[97] ibid para 11. Relying on the clause of the Constitution recognising 'Fundamental Duties' (Art 51A), the Court held that 'it is clear as crystal that it is the sacred obligation of every citizen to abide by the ideals engrafted in the Constitution. And one such ideal is to show respect for the National Anthem and the National Flag. Be it stated, a time has come, the citizens of the country must realise that they live in a nation and are duty-bound to show respect to National Anthem which is the symbol of the constitutional patriotism and inherent national quality. It does not allow any different notion or the perception of individual rights, that have individually thought of have no space. The idea is constitutionally impermissible.'

[98] Müller, *Constitutional Patriotism* (n 51) 78–80.

[99] Cronin (n 66) 14. See also Jaspers, cited in Müller, *Constitutional Patriotism* (n 51) 16. See Markell (n 59) 40 (arguing that constitutional patriotism is best understood as resisting particular identifications).

To build this argument, we first examine the degree to which constitutional patriotism is compatible with the Indian constitutional project.[100] We argue that India being a 'state-nation' as opposed to a 'nation-state' required a basis of integration other than a uniform ethnic identity.[101] Moreover, during the framing of the Indian Constitution, the universal principles were also seen as a vehicle for transformation to overcome historical oppression faced by social groups prior to independence, as well as to transcend differences based on religion. Constitutional patriotism can enable such transformation as it entails an allegiance to constitutional principles and a reflexive attitude to a state's historical past. Finally, we argue that the members of the Constituent Assembly, especially Ambedkar, underscored the need to foster such an allegiance to the Constitution. Since the enactment of the Constitution, there has been a consistent refrain that the members' fears were true and that the Indian people have not developed an allegiance to the Constitution. This section lays the foundation for the argument that constitutional patriotism can manifest as a response to the breakdown of constitutional checks and balances and allows the people to serve as a source of constitutional resilience.

A. India as a 'State-Nation'

Pre-Independence, Indians were often reminded that their claims to citizenship were unviable as India did not satisfy the definition of a nation.[102] However, as we noted in section III, this traditional understanding of nations as 'nation-states' goes back to nineteenth-century Europe,[103] where the territorial boundaries of a state always coincided with the cultural and ethnic boundaries of a nation.[104] Since the Second World War, the presumed conceptual link between states and nations has been questioned and 'nation-states' such as Germany have moved beyond ethnic identities being the basis of social integration.[105] The traditional conception of 'nation-states' cannot explain states like India, with deep diversity of religion, language and dialect.[106] Instead, the concept of 'state-nations' which respect multiple socio-cultural identities and seek their accommodation in a state, as opposed to privileging one social or pre-political identity, is more suitable to define India.[107]

[100] There has been little effort to relate the concept of constitutional patriotism to India. Two exceptions are: CR Prasad, 'Pluralism and Liberalism: Reading the Indian Constitution as a Philosophical Document for Constitutional Patriotism' (2012) 16 *Critical Review of International Social and Political Philosophy* 676; Kesavan (n 79). Chakravarthi advances a 'philosophical' interpretation of the text of the Indian Constitution and does not discuss the role played by the people. While partially building on Kesavan's work, this chapter seeks to go beyond it in demonstrating how constitutional patriotism can be viewed as a source of constitutional resilience.

[101] See nn 102–15 and accompanying text.

[102] NG Jayal, *Citizenship and its Discontents: An Indian History* (Cambridge, MA, Harvard University Press, 2013) 52.

[103] P Dann and AK Thiruvengadam, *Democratic Constitutionalism in India and the European Union: Comparing the Law of Democracy in Continental Polities* (Cheltenham, Edward Elgar, 2021) 2.

[104] Y Yadav et al, *Crafting State Nations: India and Other Multinational Democracies* (Baltimore, Johns Hopkins University Press, 2011) 1.

[105] Habermas, *Inclusion of the Other* (n 55); Habermas, *Between Facts and Norms* (n 58).

[106] Yadav et al (n 104).

[107] ibid 4.

The pre-political diversity of India was well established before the framing of the Constitution, so that members of a particular group were unlikely to accept a state where any one identity was given preference to enable the repression of others.[108] It is thus fair to state that the Indian constitutional project was an exercise in state-nation building where the framers were conscious of not imposing any one pre-political or social identity as dominant or homogenising identity.[109]

In this respect, it is important that citizenship in the text of the Indian Constitution was not rooted in an ethnic identity. Through Article 5, the Constitution adopted a *jus soli* framework, where citizenship was granted to all persons born on Indian territory, born to Indian parents or naturalised as Indian citizens.[110] A survey of the Constituent Assembly Debates shows that there was a clear awareness of the distinction between *jus soli* and *jus sanguinis* as the basis of citizenship. Many members appeared to argue in favour of a *jus sanguinis* framework, especially in respect of the grant of citizenship to Muslims seeking to return to India after having initially gone to Pakistan. Despite this strong push-back, the Constituent Assembly finally adopted clauses that were textually neutral in respect of religion.[111] Supporters of the *jus sanguinis* principle in the Constituent Assembly were cautioned about its incompatibility with a diverse polity like India.[112] For instance, KM Munshi noted that the 'world is divided between the idea of racial citizenship and democratic citizenship', and India wanted to align itself with the democratic principle.[113] Similarly, Sardar Patel remarked that it was wrong to want to introduce racial phraseology into the Constitution and that 'our general preface or the general right of citizenship under these fundamental rights should be so broad-based that anyone who reads our laws cannot take any other view than that we have taken an enlightened modern civilised view'.[114] Thus, as Jayal notes, *jus soli* remained the defining doctrine of the Indian Constitution.[115]

[108] ibid 5.

[109] ibid.

[110] Jayal (n 102) 57.

[111] See G Bhatia, 'Citizenship and the Constitution' in R Thapar et al, *On Citizenship* (New Delhi, Aleph, 2021). It is pertinent to note that Jayal also points out that the *jus soli* framework was eventually 'tempered by domicile and descent-based considerations arguably meant to complement, rather than to undermine or qualify, the primary form of citizenship based on birth': Jayal (n 102) 57. In this regard, see also Chandrachud (n 33) 3–10. Chandrachud points out that the origins of citizenship were 'somewhat unsecular' insofar as a permit system was introduced in respect of the second wave of immigration into India from Pakistan in 1948 under the permit system rules, which in effect applied to Muslims who had migrated to Pakistan in the first wave of immigration but sought to return to India. Chandrachud explains that, in practice, these permits were difficult to obtain and were dependent on executive discretion. Eventually, these provisions were encapsulated in Art 7 of the Constitution, which, despite great support in the Constituent Assembly for a *jus sanguinis* framework, were neutrally worded. Chandrachud's important intervention cautions us that the exercise of these textually neutral provisions was not always neutral. Indeed, this exercise began before the commencement of the Constitution under the Permit System Rules. It may be argued that the arbitrary or mala fide exercise of this power could be challenged as violative of fundamental rights after the commencement of the Constitution.

[112] Jayal (n 102); Bhatia, 'Citizenship and the Constitution' (n 111).

[113] Bhatia, 'Citizenship and the Constitution' (n 111); Constituent Assembly Debates, vol III (29 April 1947) (speech of KM Munshi).

[114] Bhatia, 'Citizenship and the Constitution' (n 111); India, Constituent Assembly Debates, vol III (29 April 1947) (speech of Sardar Vallabhbhai Patel).

[115] Jayal (n 102) 57.

B. The Particularity of Universal Fundamental Rights

Against the backdrop of a bloody partition on religious lines and historical oppression on the grounds of caste and gender, the framers of the Indian Constitution made universal ideas of equality and non-discrimination, secularism and fraternity the founding principles of the Constitution.[116] These universal principles find express mention in the Preamble and the chapter on fundamental rights of the Indian Constitution, much like other constitutions.[117] However, in the Indian constitutional project, they were understood as not only defences available to individuals against the state, but as a vehicle for the transformation of society.[118] Dr BR Ambedkar, the Chairman of the Constitution's Drafting Committee, stressed that the Constitution was aimed at achieving not only political democracy, but also social and economic democracy.[119] Ambedkar noted that casteism, a practice prevailing in India for generations, was 'anti-national' as it fostered jealousy and division, and it was necessary to overcome these difficulties to make fraternity in India a reality.[120]

Accordingly, in the Constitution, the right to equality is provided in universal terms in Article 14 but is also reiterated in subsequent Articles as a right against discrimination on grounds of religion, caste, place of birth, sex and race,[121] as a right against discrimination in public employment,[122] as a declaration of the abolition of untouchability[123] and forced labour,[124] as well as affirmative action provisions for women, children and backward classes.[125] The right to freedom of religion also includes exceptions allowing the state to undertake social-welfare reforms, including making provisions for temple entry by scheduled castes in response to the historical practice of excluding them from temples.[126]

The Constitution did not provide universal principles in an abstract sense. These principles were provided with a degree of particularity, whereby the Indian people could see India's particular historical and social context and their pre-political identities, but could also see the tools necessary to fight against the shackles of traditional social hierarchies.[127] The Constitution thus preserved India's historical and social traditions but also served as a benchmark to review and revise them.[128] Through the practice of

[116] Bhatia, *The Transformative Constitution* (n 82).

[117] The Preamble encapsulates an aspiration to secure to all Indians social, economic and political justice, liberty of thought, expression and belief, equality of status, and opportunity and fraternity to ensure the dignity of the individual and unity of the nation. The fundamental rights provisions lay out abstract guarantees of rights, such as the rights to equality, liberty, religion and culture, and freedoms, such as the freedoms of speech, association and movement. See Constitution of India.

[118] Bhatia, *The Transformative Constitution* (n 82) xxv.

[119] India, Constituent Assembly Debates, vol XI (25 November 1949).

[120] ibid.

[121] Constitution of India, Art 15.

[122] ibid Art 16.

[123] ibid Art 17.

[124] ibid Art 23.

[125] ibid Arts 15 and 16. These provisions have since been expanded by way of amendment.

[126] ibid Arts 17 and 25(2).

[127] Kannabiran (n 82).

[128] Yet, reflexivity must also not end with the Constitution. As Bhatia argues, 'any historically grounded interpretation must therefore acknowledge its own potential to exclude and marginalize voices from the past, and commit to remaining both open-ended and subject to revision': Bhatia, *The Transformative Constitution* (n 82) xliii.

reflexivity, the Constitution contains within it the potential to achieve its ideal of being transformative, and the onus to maintain this reflexivity lies on all constitutional actors. In this manner, the adoption of constitutional patriotism could further the transformative potential of the Constitution.[129]

C. Concerns Over the Absence of Constitutional Morality

Throughout the framing of the Indian Constitution, BR Ambedkar expressed, in more ways than one, the need to build allegiance to the Constitution. For instance, in his speech introducing the draft of the Constitution, he expressed his concern that democracy was only the topsoil in India, beneath which was an essentially undemocratic society.[130] In the same speech, he argued that the persons in charge of administration would lack 'constitutional morality' and subvert the Constitution, without having to make any changes to it, by undermining its administration.[131]

On 25 November 1949, Ambedkar delivered his famous final speech in the Constituent Assembly, which appears to have been directed more at the people of India than the framers of the Constitution. Among other things, Ambedkar stressed that the people of India must not be content with a 'political democracy', but must make 'political democracy a social democracy as well'.[132] He explained that 'political democracy cannot last unless there lies at the base of it social democracy', which meant '*a way of life* which recognizes liberty, equality and fraternity as the principles of life' (emphasis added).[133]

According to him, each of these principles was essential for constitutional democracy in India to remain meaningful. Of particular interest here is how Ambedkar employed the principle of fraternity in a way that appears to portend the concept of constitutional patriotism developed decades later. He explained that 'without fraternity, liberty and equality could not become a natural course of things' but 'would require a constable to enforce them'.[134] For him, both equality and fraternity were missing in Indian society, even as the Constitution elevates them to foundational principles. Regarding equality, he argued that it is necessary to remove the contradiction between the recognition of civic and political equality by law and the existence of social and economic inequality in society 'or else those who suffer from inequality will blow up the structure of political democracy' which the Constitution provides.[135] He defined fraternity as 'a sense of common brotherhood of all Indians' and as 'the principle which gives unity and solidarity to social life'.[136] While noting that it would be difficult to achieve this in the Indian

[129] Tonkiss (n 74) 96; Müller, *Constitutional Patriotism* (n 51) 56.
[130] India, Constituent Assembly Debates, vol VII (4 November 1948).
[131] ibid.
[132] India, Constituent Assembly Debates, vol XI (25 November 1949).
[133] ibid.
[134] ibid.
[135] ibid.
[136] ibid.

context, he argued that only if it was achieved could India become a nation in the true sense of the word. Ambedkar's speech, strikingly, underscores the point that only if the people of India internalise this 'way of life' based on the principles of liberty, equality and fraternity could the notion of India as a nation come into being.[137]

On 24 May 1950, in response to questions after a public address, Ambedkar reportedly stated that the success of the Constitution would be dependent on *all* persons committing to constitutional morality:

> There are moments when I think that the future of Democracy in India is very dark. But, I do not want to say that I have not other moments when I feel that if all of us put our shoulders together and pledge ourselves to 'constitutional morality' we should be able to build up a regular party system in which there could be liberty, equality and fraternity[138]

Thus, for Ambedkar, the success of the Constitution depended on how persons would approach one another under the constitutional system. He hoped citizens would view one another through the lens of fraternity and that officials in power would adopt an egalitarian approach in applying or implementing the Constitution. Ambedkar's focus on attitudes appears to be similar to the commitment that constitutional patriotism entails to viewing each other as free and equal, and finding fair terms of cooperation that they can justify to one another.[139]

It should be clarified here that we do not mean to suggest an equivalence between constitutional morality and constitutional patriotism. For Ambedkar, constitutional morality also had a specific substantive content that reflected his vision of the Indian Constitution, where liberty, equality and fraternity go together.[140] On the other hand, constitutional patriotism refers to an attachment by citizens to the norms and values of a constitution, such as, and in particular, fairness and mutual cooperation as means of interacting with one another.[141]

Nonetheless, Ambedkar's discussion on constitutional morality, social democracy as a way of life and fraternity point to the stress he laid on fostering allegiance to the principles of the Constitution and developing fair terms of cooperation that constitutional patriotism also stresses. In one sense, the concept of constitutional patriotism could provide the path to the allegiance to the Constitution that Ambedkar hoped could be achieved.

[137] ibid.

[138] *Dr Babasaheb Ambedkar Writing and Speeches*, vol 17, part II (H Narke et al eds, New Delhi, Dr Ambedkar Foundation, Ministry of Social Justice & Empowerment, Government of India, 2014) 378.

[139] Müller, *Constitutional Patriotism* (n 51) 55.

[140] In this context, see Ambedkar's comments in the debate on the Constitution Fourth Amendment Bill in V Moon (ed), *Babasaheb Ambedkar Writings and Speeches*, vol 15 (New Delhi, Ambedkar Foundation, Ministry of Social Justice & Empowerment, Government of India, 2019) 946–47: 'But as soon as Swaraj presented itself, everybody thought – at least many of the minorities thought – that there was the prospect of political authority passing into the hands of a majority, which did not possess what might constitutionally be called constitutional morality. Their official doctrine was inequality of classes. Though there is inequality in every community, or whatever be the word, that inequality is a matter of practice. It is not an official dogma. But with a majority in this country, inequality, as embodied in their Chaturvarana is an official doctrine.'

[141] Müller, 'A General Theory of Constitutional Patriotism' (n 52) 82. It is important to caution here that constitutional patriotism cannot manifest in systems that do not provide modes of fair cooperation such as in Apartheid South Africa. As Müller notes (at 79), 'Political situations look very recognizably different where such a mode is absent, where fair cooperation or even just somehow trying to share a political space have ceased to be common goals …'.

V. Indian Constitutional Patriotism as a Tool of Constitutional Resilience

The above discussion posits India as an important site to study constitutional patriotism, where the people's allegiance to universal principles and fair cooperation are necessary for the success of the Indian constitutional project. However, since the framing of the Constitution, many have expressed the view that democracy and constitutionalism have remained mere topsoil, as Ambedkar had feared.[142] Some have lamented how the Constitution has not had a 'trickle down' effect as it was intended to, and that the Indian people remain inherently communal, casteist and sexist.[143] Indeed, these critiques of Indian constitutional democracy have come more into focus after the Modi government was voted in for a second term with an even larger majority than its first term.

The Indian example is also relevant to address the most prominent criticism of constitutional patriotism – that it fails to generate affect among citizens.[144] This criticism is typically levelled against constitutional patriotism while comparing it to cultural or ethnic nationalism, with emphasis on how the latter concepts can, and have, easily mobilised individuals and groups through symbols such as the national flag, slogans, anthems and republic day parades, as well as stories of war and defence of national borders. The term 'constitutional patriotism' may even be viewed as an oxymoron.[145] As Lacroix notes, 'the word "constitutional" is often believed to have cold and juridical connotations whereas the word "patriotism" evokes a warm feeling coming from our hearts'.[146] Müller points out that the concept has been criticised as 'a pale thought born in a seminar room'.[147] One critic argued that it was 'a beautiful idea – but it doesn't work because people don't feel that way'.[148]

The conception of constitutional patriotism proffered can and sometimes does seem relatively dry. To a large extent, the debate over the potential of constitutional patriotism to function as an alternative to cultural nationalism has focused on the likelihood of polities based on constitutional patriotism succeeding in facilitating 'social integration' and creating a sense of solidarity where citizens are willing 'to make sacrifices for each other'.[149] As we have stressed in sections III and IV, one way in which constitutional patriotism manifests itself is by celebrating diversity and by giving dissenters a

[142] A Masoodi, 'Lessons for Freedom from the Emergency' (*Livemint*, 15 August 2019) www.livemint.com/news/india/lessons-for-freedom-from-the-emergency-1565877013901.html; D Dave, 'Ambedkar is Losing, Modi is Winning' (*The Wire*, 10 March 2017) https://thewire.in/government/under-modi-india-is-moving-from-constitutional-democracy-to-a-populist-one. K Jayakumar, 'Relevance of India in Today's India' *The New Indian Express* (18 April 2018) www.newindianexpress.com/opinions/2018/apr/18/relevance-of-ambedkar-in-todays-india-1802901.html.

[143] B Biswas and N Mandalaparthy, 'New Survey Shows Many Indians Preach Respect but Don't Practice It' *Foreign Policy* (14 July 2021) https://foreignpolicy.com/2021/07/14/india-religion-pew-survey-hindu-nationalism-bjp-modi-ambedkar/.

[144] Hayward (n 68).

[145] Müller, *Constitutional Patriotism* (n 51) 5.

[146] Lacroix, 'For a European Constitution' (n 65) 949.

[147] Müller, *Constitutional Patriotism* (n 51) 6.

[148] ibid.

[149] JW Müller and KL Scheppele, 'Constitutional Patriotism: An Introduction' (2008) 6(1) *International Journal of Constitutional Law* 67, 70.

legitimate language in which to express their views, so long as they do not contest the basic values, norms and even procedures recognised by the constitution. As a corollary to this, claims may be seen as more legitimate relative to other claims if they are seen to protect those basic values, norms and procedures.[150]

In this section, we argue that constitutional patriotism is manifesting in India in protests led by the people against the ruling government's authoritarian and communal policies. The Indian experience demonstrates that a polity infused with constitutional patriotism can serve as a counterforce to the rise of ethnonationalism and authoritarianism.

A recent notable example of the exhibition of constitutional patriotism is the eruption of protests after the passage of the Citizenship Amendment Act, referred to in section II. The Bill was passed with little advance notice, but within a day of its passing,[151] the country was engulfed in protests.[152] People gathered in designated areas of protest, such as Jantar Mantar, as well as iconic public sites, such as India Gate in Delhi, Gateway of India in Mumbai and Town Hall in Bangalore, and other central sites in smaller cities. Universities also became sites of protest. Protestors gathered daily at these sites and expressed their allegiance to constitutional principles in different ways. They held up pictures of Ambedkar as well as copies of the Preamble. Reciting the Preamble – which best distils the vision of the Constitution – became a ritual across protests in the country.[153] Several creative posters communicated the idea that no one government could topple the very idea of India. The Constitution became a symbol of protest. However, contrary to displays of ethnonationalism, the expression of constitutional patriotism was not limited to expressing pride through symbols but through allegiance to constitutional principles of fraternity, equality, secularism and deliberation by practising them.[154]

This can be seen through the manner in which protests intensified after incidents of police brutality against Muslim protestors. Three days after the passing of the Act and continuous protests, on 15 December 2019, the police entered Jamia Milia University in Delhi and Aligarh Muslim University in Uttar Pradesh and reportedly attacked unarmed students with tear gas shells.[155] Horrifying visuals of burnt hostel rooms and injured students came streaming out even as the government suspended the internet in these areas. The impunity with which the police attacked predominantly Muslim students joined a long list of injustices against Muslims since 2014, which had to date not met with significant outrage from the Indian people.

[150] Faizan Siddiqi's chapter in this volume (ch 18) demonstrates this point while explaining how Dalits in Gujarat have sought implementation of land reform laws. The use of constitutional vocabulary in this way may also be likened to what Son and Nicholson (n 12) refer to as a strategic form of 'popular constitutionalism'.

[151] An earlier version of the Bill had lapsed in 2016, when it was clear that the government would not have the numbers. See R Sabha, 'Explained: Why the Citizenship Amendment Bill Is Dead, for now, *Indian Express* (13 February 2019).

[152] 'Citizenship Acts and Protests: Three Dead and Thousands held in India' *BBC News* (19 December 2019) www.bbc.com/news/world-asia-india-50833361.

[153] S Biswas, 'Why Protesting Indians Have Been Channelling the Constitution' *BBC News* (14 January 2020) www.bbc.com/news/world-asia-india-51088907.

[154] See nn 171–78 below and accompanying text.

[155] 'Students, Activists Recount Brutal Attack on Jamia Students in 2019' (*Newsclick*, 15 December 2021) www.newsclick.in/Students-Activists-Recount-Brutal-Police-Attack-Jamia-Students-2019.

However, the passing of the CAA coupled with the visuals of bleeding students appeared to have a stirring effect. The next day, students from other universities broke out in protests in solidarity with the students and protestors, and continued for days on end, with people maintaining the practice of holding up pictures of Ambedkar and the Constitution itself, and reciting the Preamble. Protestors continued to gather across different cities despite the police in some cases using force and making detentions, and universities issuing circulars warning of disciplinary action.[156] Notably, a cross-section of groups joined the protests to show solidarity with the students and Muslims, to challenge the symbolic and consequential impact of the CAA and the NRC on them,[157] and to protest the attacks on the constitutional values of equality and secularism.[158]

Several leaders and activists were detained or arrested. Akhil Gogoi in Assam was charged under the draconian Unlawful Activities Prevention Act, and fought and won elections in jail.[159] Chandrashekar Azad, a Dalit leader, was jailed for over a month for reading out the Preamble before thousands of people who had gathered to protest against the Act. While surrendering to police custody, he emerged at Jama Masjid, holding up a picture of Ambedkar, and returned to the same spot to recite the Preamble upon being released on bail. Upon his release, he noted that 'It is a telling comment that reading the Constitution has become an act of protest today, even as the republic completes seven decades'.[160]

In terms of the scale and the cross-section of groups that demonstrated their commitment to the Constitution, the CAA protests were indeed unparalleled in history. As Arun Thiruvengadam argues, the CAA protests serve as a reminder 'that people do have emotive attachments to constitutional texts, which may lead them to act on these very real and tangible sentiments'.[161]

These protests came at a great cost to individuals, especially Muslims, as most public institutions have not only failed to check atrocities committed against them, but have also played a key role in 'othering' and villainising them. The government crackdown against protests was far greater in Muslim localities, with protests being crushed through brutality and illegal arrests. In Uttar Pradesh, 23 people lost their lives owing to

[156] 'Nationwide Protests against Citizenship Law Continue; Many Booked' *Hindustan Times* (21 December 2019) www.hindustantimes.com/india-news/nationwide-protests-continue-1000s-booked/story-rKTsjqpH7m2LJlILe3d9gP.html.

[157] On protests by Dalit groups and Adivasis against the CAA and NRC, see A Regi, 'At "Chalo Delhi" Rally, Stories of a Country-wide Ambedkarite Uprising against the CAA and NRC' *The Caravan* (6 March 2020). On the specific protests against the CAA-NRC in North-East India, see NC Dev, 'India Needs to Understand Why the Northeast Is Protesting against CAA' (*The Wire*, 5 January 2020) https://thewire.in/rights/caa-protest-northeast-indigenous.

[158] KVA Bharadwaj, 'How People Have Turned to the Constitution to Articulate Their Vision of India' *The Hindu* (1 February 2022) www.thehindu.com/society/how-people-have-turned-to-the-constitution-to-articulate-their-vision-of-india/article30702085.ece.

[159] 'Anti-CAA Activist Akhil Gogoi Becomes First MLA in Assam to Win Election from Jail' *CNN News 18* (3 May 2021) www.news18.com/news/politics/assam-assembly-election-2021-anti-caa-activist-akhil-gogoi-first-to-win-election-from-jail-3703676.html.

[160] Bharadwaj (n 158).

[161] AK Thiruvengadam, 'Constitutional Faith or Constitutional Idolatry: Insights from Recent Mass Protests in India' (*IACL*, 26 January 2021) https://blog-iacl-aidc.org/cili/2021/1/28/constitutional-faith-or-constitutional-idolatry-insights-from-recent-mass-protests-in-india.

police violence in Muslim-dominated areas.[162] The Uttar Pradesh government issued an ordinance to recover money from organisers of protestors for supposed damage caused to public property and even put up hoardings with their photographs and addresses.[163] The election campaign for the Delhi Legislative Assembly elections became highly charged with communalism, with both the BJP (the ruling party at the Central level in India) and the Aam Aadmi Party (the ruling party in Delhi) endorsing calls to clear the Muslim protestors through violence. The press painted the protestors as 'anti-national' and showed isolated acts of violence as representative of the protests and movement, and even sought to justify police brutality.[164] Following the horrific reports of police brutality against students in Jamia University and Aligarh Muslim University, activists filed petitions before the Supreme Court seeking action against the police. The Supreme Court refused to entertain the petition, with the then Chief Justice, SA Bobde, remarking to the lawyers that the 'rioting' by students should stop before their rights claims would be considered.[165]

Police brutality in Jamia carried on through the night of 15 December 2019. In a nearby, predominantly working-class Muslim locality, several worried parents were trying to obtain news about the well-being of their children at Jamia University.[166] As people scurried to get students to hospitals, several people assembled on the road connecting Delhi to Noida in Uttar Pradesh and decided to block it in protest. Aware that the police would not hesitate to clear the protest by force, the women in the locality took it upon themselves to fight for their children and the injustices of the system.[167] Thus began the Shaheen Bagh 'sit-in', where Muslim women sat in protest for days on end to protest the constitutional erosion caused and enabled by the ruling government, with the attack on Muslim students and children being the final straw Thousands of people came from all over the country to express solidarity with the protests and stayed for long durations.[168] These Muslim women chose to respond to the ruling government's violence with peaceful resistance. Ideas of constitutional resilience and resistance were expressed through art. The stage of Shaheen Bagh saw various artists perform in favour of India's unity. An 'India Gate' similar to the one in Central Delhi was constructed, bearing the names of all the persons who had lost their lives in anti-CAA protests. A map of India encapsulating the words 'We the People of India reject CAA and NRC' stood tall, reflecting the essence of the protest. Graffiti and banners adorned the walls and pedestrian bridges.

[162] AA Jafri, 'Who Were 23 People Killed in UP during Anti-CAA-NRC Protests?' (*Newsclick*, 18 January 2020) www.newsclick.in/who-were-23-people-killed-during-anti-caa-nrc-protests.

[163] J Sindhu and VA Narayan, 'Why UP Name & Shame Banners Were Brought Down – And Must Stay Down' (*The Quint*, 10 March 2022) www.thequint.com/news/india/why-up-name-and-shame-banners-were-brought-down-and-must-stay-down.

[164] K Goel, 'Republic Says Anti-CAA Protester Fired at Jamia, Facts Be Damned' (*The Quint*, 30 January 2022) www.thequint.com/news/webqoof/republic-tv-falsely-implicates-anti-caa-protesters-for-jamia-shooting.

[165] 'Let Rioting Stop, Says Chief Justice on Crackdown on Jamia, AMU Protesters' *Hindustan Times* (16 December 2019).

[166] S Pasha, 'Women Violence and Democracy' in S Mustafa (ed), *Shaheen Bagh and the Idea of India, Writings on a Movement for Justice Liberty and Equality* (New Delhi, Speaking Tiger, 2020).

[167] ZU Salam and U Ausuf, *Shaheen Bagh from Protest to a Movement* (New Delhi, Bloomsbury, 2020).

[168] In particular, Dalit and Ambedkarite organisations and farmers from Punjab came to express solidarity. Both groups would eventually go on to mount important protests against the ruling government's policies.

The protest sites welcomed people from all backgrounds, and they quickly became a microcosm of India's diversity. In this microcosm, there was a focus on fostering a culture based on deliberation. Various political leaders and intellectuals spoke on the values of secularism and unity, India's history, and the merits and demerits of the Bill. Dialogue became the spirit of the protest. Persons with doubts about opposition to the CAA were invited on stage to air their views and protestors were encouraged to listen.[169] A talking corner was set up for people with opposing views on CAA to engage with one another.[170] A bus stop was converted into the Fatima Sheikh–Savitribai Phule Library, where Ambedkar's famous words, 'Educate, Agitate, Organise', hung, and was where people gathered to organise reading groups or individually read texts about the history of India and the freedom struggle, and on issues of justice, freedom and equality.[171] This protest library, which was the first to arise on a pavement near Jamia University, was seen as an appropriate response to the police who had attacked students in Jamia's library.[172] It was meant to serve as a source of empowerment for people in their fight to win back the republic,[173] and emphasised the importance of the 'collective learning process'. The mothers and grandmothers of Shaheen Bagh even made an application to visit the country's Home Minister to present their demands. This became the inspiration for several other such sit-ins in other parts of the country.[174]

The blocking of the kilometre-long stretch was seen as a drastic step and became a polarising point, especially as the police blocked more roads and blamed it on the protestors.[175] The protest withstood hostility from sections of the media, the public and vigilante groups who had the backing of political leaders. However, those complaining on grounds of inconvenience lost sight of what the women were protesting: the near and total breakdown of the principle of fair and equal participation that ought to ground all law-making and actions of institutions, and help foster solidarity in India's constitutional system. They were protesting the absence of avenues or institutions for marginalised communities, and Muslims in particular, to articulate their grievances or appeal to the majorities that a political system entails for both legitimation and stability.[176]

[169] PK Datta, 'Shaheen Bagh: A New Kind of "Satyagraha" with a Fresh Grammar of Protest' (*Business Line*, 6 February 2020) www.business-standard.com/article/current-affairs/shaheen-bagh-a-new-kind-of-satyagraha-with-a-fresh-grammar-of-protest-120011601102_1.html.

[170] E Puranas, 'Why Shaheen Bagh Protests Are an Important Moment in India's History' *Al Jazeera* (3 February 2020) www.aljazeera.com/features/2020/2/3/why-shaheen-bagh-protests-are-an-important-moment-in-indias-history.

[171] S Bhura, 'The Story behind the Library at Shaheen Bagh' *The Week* (18 February 2020) www.theweek.in/news/india/2020/02/17/the-story-behind-the-library-at-shaheen-bagh.html#!%23:~:text=He%20has%20aptly%20named%20it,and%20their%20access%20to%20education.

[172] S Singh, 'Why the Libraries on Anti-CAA Protest Sites Are Essential to Their Democratic Politics' *Indian Express* (14 February 2020) https://indianexpress.com/article/express-sunday-eye/why-the-libraries-on-anti-caa-protest-sites-are-essential-to-their-democratic-politics-6268398/.

[173] ibid.

[174] Such protests came up in different parts of Delhi, Mumbai, Kolkata and Lucknow. N Dixit, 'The Women at the Front Lines of India's Citizenship Law Protests' *Al Jazeera* (23 December 2019) www.aljazeera.com/features/2019/12/23/the-women-at-the-front-lines-of-indias-citizenship-law-protests.

[175] ibid.

[176] As Seemi Pasha observes on the decision to block the road: 'Call it naivety, but it came from the conviction that as citizens of the world's largest and uniquely secular democracy they enjoyed certain privileges'. S Pasha, 'Women Violence and Democracy' in Mustafa (n 166).

The Indian Supreme Court appeared to ignore the values underlying the protest and held, albeit after the protest had been cleared by the police due to the onset of COVID, that the road could not be blocked indefinitely as the right to protest was subject to certain duties.[177] This is based on a misreading of the Indian Constitution, as it makes no such restrictions on the right to protest.[178]

Vigilante groups often came near the protest site, holding up the national flag as well as the BJP's saffron flag, and made calls to shoot the protestors. In turn, the women of Shaheen Bagh stood close to these men holding flowers, and in response to the chants of their shooting called for the showering of flowers on the men.[179] One day, one person eventually opened fire on the protestors while chanting '*Jai Shri Raam*'[180] and declaring that '*Hamare Desh mein aur kisi ki nahin chalegi, sirf Hindu ki chalegi*' ('Only Hindus shall have a say in our country, no one else').[181] The women of Shaheen Bagh in response called for calm and prevented a chaos-ridden stampede. One woman reportedly even desired to speak and reason with the shooter.[182]

In such moments, the contrast between the form of attachment rooted in ethnonationalism and constitutional patriotism becomes even sharper. The former, clothed with pride in symbols such as the national flag, supports the idea of a Hindu nation that is incompatible with India's Constitution. The latter is rooted in a commitment to the constitutional principles of equality and secularism which determine both participation in the political sphere and interaction among citizens. The efforts to delegitimise the protest were not successful – the government was unable to employ force to remove the protesters and was only able to clear it once a curfew due to COVID compelled the women to leave the site.[183]

It is interesting to note that allegiance to constitutional principles was finally displayed not in everyday acts like standing up for the national anthem, as was sought by the Supreme Court, nor in daily chants in favour of the nation, but in the form of protests against a statute which manifested a real threat to the Constitution. In this sense, the CAA protests confirm the claims of scholars like Cronin that constitutional patriotism

[177] *Amit Sahni v Commissioner of Police*, Delhi, Civil Appeal No 3283 of 2020.

[178] J Sindhu and VA Narayan, 'Why Shaheen Bagh Verdict Threatens Rights and Favours Restrictions' (*The Quint*, 13 February 2021) www.thequint.com/voices/opinion/shaheen-bagh-protest-supreme-court-verdict-fundamental-rights-indian-constitution-restrictions.

[179] Salam and Ausuf (n 167).

[180] A slogan that valorises the Hindu god, Rama, and is used by supporters of Hindu nationalism to represent pride in India as a Hindu state. In recent years, right-wing extremists have increasingly used the phrase before engaging in acts of violence against persons not identifying as Hindu and persons refusing to chant the slogan. S Poonam, 'The 3 Most Polarizing Words in India' *Foreign Policy* (13 February 2020) https://foreignpolicy.com/2020/02/13/jai-shri-ram-india-hindi/.

[181] S Misra, 'Taking a Close Look at Shaheen Bagh' (Observer Research Foundation, 4 February 2020) www.orfonline.org/expertspeak/taking-a-close-look-at-shaheen-bagh-61045/; Salam and Ausuf (n 167).

[182] ZM Khan, 'How Shaheen Bagh Became a Symbol of Dialogue and Solidarity' in Mustafa (n 166).

[183] V Venugopal, 'Delhi Lockdown: Anti-CAA Protesters Removed from Shaheen Bagh, Other Places' *The Economic Times* (25 March 2020) https://economictimes.indiatimes.com/news/politics-and-nation/coronavirus-lockdown-delhi-police-vacate-protesters-at-shaheen-bagh/articleshow/74785253.cms?from=mdr. The central government has since persecuted those seen as the main organisers of protests. Several activists have been arrested under the draconian anti-terror law, which makes it nearly impossible to get bail, so many activists remain in jail with their bail petitions still pending. See G Bhatia, 'How UAPA Is Wrecking Lives' *The Hindu* (7 April 2022) www.thehindu.com/opinion/op-ed/how-the-uapa-is-wrecking-lives/article65296638.ece.

expresses itself in complex forms, and may not be expressed unless the Constitution itself is threatened. The invisibility of the manifestation of constitutional patriotism at various points of time, however, does not imply an absence of allegiance to constitutional norms or solidarity based on these norms. Even the endurance of a constitution per se may be considered a manifestation of constitutional patriotism. Viewing the acts of the people from the lens of constitutional patriotism also shows that the people can be a source of push-back amid constitutional decay.

VI. Conclusion

In this chapter, we have sought to demonstrate the utility of constitutional patriotism in combating constitutional erosion driven by an ethnonational, exclusionary ideology. We have argued that constitutional patriotism is a compelling basis for social integration in a culturally pluralistic nation like India, whose Constitution is committed to secularism and equality. Crucially, constitutional patriotism affirms and reinforces the legitimacy of peaceful protest and dissent aimed at safeguarding constitutional principles, and, we argue, in doing so it can become a valuable source of constitutional resilience.

The Indian experience exemplifies how constitutional patriotism can contribute to constitutional resilience. Addressing concerns raised by several critics of constitutional patriotism, the Indian example shows that constitutions can generate affect, and that people are willing to fight for the preservation of constitutional values and a system of constitutional democracy. We argue that this role of people assumes great significance in contexts of constitutional erosion, where institutional accountability mechanisms break down.

Drawing on the anti-CAA protests across India and particularly the Shaheen Bagh sit-in, we have demonstrated how the people of India took it upon themselves to defend the constitutional guarantees of equality, dignity, fraternity and secularism. While it may be impossible to definitively evaluate the success of the protests against the CAA, it is noteworthy that to date the law has not been implemented. Given the speed at which the ruling government was taking steps to dismantle institutions and repurpose them to substitute Indian constitutional democracy with an ethnocracy,[184] it is difficult to imagine the government stalling these steps if not for the impassioned, but peaceful, expressions of constitutional patriotism by the people.

While this chapter has focused on the anti-CAA protests, it is worth noting that these protests represent only some of the ways in which constitutional patriotism has manifested in India in recent years. A wider range of examples can be found beyond protests, demonstrating, among other things, how constitutional patriotism can contribute to constitutional resilience in different ways. This includes latent manifestations of constitutional patriotism, such as the steady stream of efforts made by grassroots organisations and research organisations across India to further the diffusion of constitutional norms.[185] These efforts involve broadening the constitutional discourse by

[184] Jaffrelot and Schoch (n 23).
[185] Thiruvengadam (n 161).

translating constitutional analysis into regional languages[186] and other awareness creation programmes, such as organising quizzes on the Constitution, collaborating with schools[187] and simplifying the concepts in the Preamble to enable children to engage with them.[188] More recently, these efforts have embraced the tools of social media to disseminate constitutional ideals. Two Instagram accounts, Project Anti Caste Love and the India Love Project, document stories of couples with different castes and religions who have navigated the long-standing stigma attached to inter-caste and inter-religion marriage in India. These pages have assumed greater significance as a response to the recent anti-conversion laws passed in some states which are based on the myth of 'love jihad'. The stories help cut across the narrative of 'forceful conversions' for marriage by celebrating inter-religious marriage, and in the process affirm the ideas of equality, dignity and individual autonomy that the Indian Constitution is seen to represent.

The examples demonstrate a complex range of emotions, as opposed to mere pride in national symbols or overt chants in the name of India. They represent a deeper commitment to India and to the Indian people, and deserve further study. However, the general lesson that can be drawn from them is that the role of people as constitutional actors ought to be appreciated. Viewing the people's actions through the lens of constitutional patriotism is one way of appreciating their role as a source of constitutional resilience.

[186] See, eg the podcast in Hindi with constitutional scholar T Khaitan, https://sociolegalliterary.in/samvidhan-samvad-with-tarunabh-khaitan/.

[187] ibid.

[188] L Seith, *We, the Children of India* (Delhi, Penguin Books India, 2010); J Mazumdar, 'School Students Pledge to "Respect All Religions and Beliefs"' *Telegraph India* (23 January 2022) www.telegraphindia.com/my-kolkata/news/kolkata-students-pledge-to-respect-all-religions-and-beliefs/cid/1848820.

PART IX

Conclusion

20

Epilogue: Resilience and Political Constitutionalism in South Asia and Beyond

PHILIPP DANN

I. Foreword to the Epilogue

By its location and designation, this is an epilogue. And yet, I have to admit that I am not very familiar with the format of the epilogue in academic writing. In fact, it seems to be a curious and not very well reflected format of writing. What we know better perhaps is the epilogue in *fiction*. There, it is a means to provide a somewhat distant, reflective gaze on the prior text, often addressing the reader directly, sometimes from a much later time and an outsiders' perspective. But in *non-fiction*, academic writing? Any ideas? To some extent, it seems easier to describe what it is *not* than what it is. It is *not* an introduction, which would outline the research question, introduce central theoretical notions, frame the issues and preview some of the contents. It is also *not* a book review that critically comments on the chapters and the overall composition of a book.

So what is it then? From looking at other examples, I gather that the honour of being asked to write an epilogue comes with the expectation to reflect on the broader themes of a volume from a more personal and external perspective of the often older colleague (thanks for this!). If we cannot make up fiction writing's epilogue from the future, it seems that in academic writing the age and location of the 'epilogist' shall provide that temporal and spatial distance. And so, this is what I shall try to do here – reflect on some of the notions introduced and issues raised in the volume, triggered by my reading and thinking about the rich variety of chapters, using my external perspective as a non-South Asian, German legal scholar with some expertise in international, comparative and European law and much curiosity about theoretical matters.

II. Introduction

If the field of comparative constitutional studies is fast evolving, the South Asia chapter is an energetic driver of this evolution. The present volume, which brings together 19 chapters that were first presented at a conference in Melbourne in late 2019, pushes, invigorates or reformulates three current but also structural debates in comparative constitutional studies and raises questions that reverberate around the globe: on case selection (geographic rather than functional?), on modes of constitutionalism (resilience as opposed to everyday evolution?) and on political constitutionalism ('beyond courts' rather than legal constitutionalism focusing on rights and courts). In comparison to its sibling publication, the 2020 issue of the journal *World Comparative Law* on 'Constitutional Resilience and the Laws of Democracy in India', which contains four fine pieces originating from the same Melbourne conference on judicial review of legislation, social and participatory rights, as well as electoral speech,[1] this volume is broader in scope and larger in volume, but follows a number of trajectories set out there. The concern about lively and resilient constitutional democracy drives all contributions.

My contribution will be organised around the three core and framing ideas: South Asia, constitutional resilience and political constitutionalism. I will end with some thoughts on desiderata for future research.

III. South Asia and the Question of Case Selection

It is a rather recent phenomenon to use South Asia as a category for comparative constitutional law.[2] This echoes older traditions in Europe or Latin America and mirrors similar current movements in Africa and Asia.[3] Surely, the present volume is one of the most comprehensive in terms of assembling voices from around South Asia. Each South Asian jurisdiction (except for Myanmar) is represented. Even though India (six contributions) and Sri Lanka (four contributions) dominate, Pakistan, Afghanistan, Maldives, Bhutan, Bangladesh and Nepal are also studied in one or two chapters each.

This is impressive, but also makes one wonder whether South Asia is actually a useful lens for constitutional law scholarship.[4] It raises, to put it another, more general way, the question of case selection. Is a geographic rather than a functional selection useful? Most comparison is functional or infers functional commonality from regional proximity. Regional approaches often assume that geographical proximity translates into functional similarity, ie a similarity of approaches to law and politics, a similarity of challenges, a similarity of contexts. For example, all Latin American countries share

[1] (2020) 53 (special issue) *World Comparative Law* 357.

[2] S Khilnani, V Raghavan and AK Thiruvengadam (eds), *Comparative Constitutionalism in South Asia* (Oxford, Oxford University Press, 2013); M Tushnet and M Khosla (eds), *Unstable Constitutionalism: Law and Politics in South Asia* (Cambridge, Cambridge University Press, 2015); Springer South Asian Studies in Comparative and International Law (www.springer.com/series/13448), curated by the South Asian University in Delhi.

[3] See, eg CH Mendes, R Gargarella and S Guidi (eds), *The Oxford Handbook of Constitutional Law in Latin America* (Oxford, Oxford University Press, 2022); Stellenbosch Handbooks in African Constitutionalism (C Fombad ed, Oxford University Press); Bloomsbury series on Constitutionalism in Asia.

[4] For an earlier engagement with this question, see S Khilnani, V Raghavan and AK Thiruvengadam, 'Reviving South Asian Constitutionalism' in Khilnani et al (n 2) 1.

a history of Spanish colonisation, in particular a legacy of Catholicism and the Spanish (or the very similar Portuguese) language, of multi-nationalism or of a peripheral position in the world economy and domination by the big Northern neighbour.

This, however, might be different here. What characterises South Asia as a region seems to be its plurality. While it is, of course, united by geography and hence necessarily a certain shared history, its human and political activity is rather characterised by animosity or (to the outsider) a confusing sequence of shifting alliances and divorces. Countries and societies of South Asia are also much more diverse in terms of their size, their religions, their political regimes and their languages. Finally, the role of India might stand in the way of the emergence of a shared constitutional culture in that India is an outsized entity, which often triggers antagonism by others rather than equal collaboration (see Prussia in the former German Reich) – politically and culturally.

In this plurality, South Asia is markedly different from Europe, Africa or Latin America. While there was and still is a big country and potential hegemon in Europe too (France in earlier centuries; Germany since its unification in 1870), though not so much in Latin America and Africa, they never established a lasting hegemony. But it is not merely the contingency of size. There is also no overarching value system (such as a shared religion) in South Asia or a uniting (instead of dividing) common history, which could form the base of a shared culture of constitutionalism. It is not quite surprising, therefore, that there is no relevant regional legal and constitutional framework in South Asia (nothing comparable to the EU, the African Union or Mercosur, to the regional human rights courts in Europe, Africa and Latin America), no normative and institutionalised multi-level system to speak of.

The traditional lack of South Asian comparativism might also be explained by reasons of the political economy of knowledge – less funding, an orientation to the (supposedly more important) West instead of neighbours, etc. South Asia as a category seemed more the product of British imperialism than of bottom-up exchange and cooperation.

From this perspective, the choice of South Asia as an organising principle of case selection seems odd at first. Surely, this volume was not designed as a directly comparative book and was not meant to be a systematic, social-science exploration or comparison. The chapters are (with one exception[5]) not comparative; comparative insights come mainly by reading through the whole volume and the readers' own thoughts.[6]

But then again, the volume triggers the nonetheless thought-provoking question whether the regional perspective pays off here. Or would a rather functional approach have been more convincing, selecting countries from the region but on a more functional basis? How 'should' one do South Asian comparison? Surely, different answers and approaches are conceivable.

One way to think of this is to restrict oneself to India and to conceive of India not as a traditional state (or, if at all, a state-nation), but rather as a continental polity, and in fact as a region in itself. In a way, India itself is such a broad and diverse polity that

[5] See M Pal, ch 13 in this volume.

[6] Directly on this point, see S Jhaveri, T Khaitan and D Samararatne, ch 1 in this volume.

it can be seen as a region. This would lead, for example, to comparisons between India and the EU.[7] Another approach could be an inner South-Asian comparison that is less broad, more in-depth and more systematic in design. The present volume is not the product of a finely designed research project but of a conference. That makes a big difference.

But there are also merits in studying South Asia as a constitutional space: for one, there is value in plurality. We only slowly learn that constitutionalism has many varieties and that it faces not one threat but many. The global discussion about democratic backsliding is too much about authoritarian constitutionalism and not analysing enough the wide variety and complexity of challenges. Also, differences between constitutional systems do not matter that much. There is a variety of constitutionalism – and constitutionalism can exist in democratic and non-democratic contexts (*cf* nineteenth-century Germany, twentieth-century Taiwan, etc).

For the concrete theme of the volume (constitutional resilience in the face of democratic backsliding), the regional lens is also productive. Backsliding is a global phenomenon. Comparing the South Asian case studies with those in other places and wondering about their regional particularity is fruitful. We learn, for example, how unique and problematic the absence of a regional framework is. In Europe, the EU is an important, though surely imperfect, player and (potential) guarantor institution; in Latin America, regional courts and intra-continental academic communication play that role; last but not least, in Africa, the AU is playing an important role in safeguarding constitutionalism. Also and again, studying the plurality of scenarios and threats is a value in itself; not all scenarios and challenges are similar and take place at the same time.

And ultimately, the regional bracket can even trigger a search for more South Asian commonalities: there is, after all, a shared legacy of British colonialism that generated distinct regional experiences – of 'divide-and-rule legacies' and partition, of parliamentary democracy and first-past-the-post election regimes, of distrust (or incomprehension) of federalism, etc. Through this post-colonial lens, common phenomena might be better understood.[8]

IV. Constitutional Resilience and the Diversity of Challenges

Resilience has been a buzzword in many fields of research (especially in developmental studies and psychology), but it is fairly new in the context of constitutional studies.[9]

[7] P Dann and AK Thiruvengadam (eds), *Democratic Constitutionalism in India and the European Union* (Cheltenham, Edward Elgar, 2020).

[8] On the study of distinct constitutional experiences in the South, see P Dann, M Riegner and M Bönnemann, 'Southern Turn in Comparative Constitutional Law' in P Dann, M Riegner and M Bönnemann (eds), *Global South and Comparative Constitutional Law* (Oxford, Oxford University Press, 2020) 1.

[9] First seen on *Verfassungsblog* in 2018 (https://verfassungsblog.de/category/debates/constitutional-resilience-debates/).

It is convincingly understood by the authors of this volume in a rather simple way as the 'ability of institutions to react against and survive challenges against them'.[10]

The notion signals a double broadening of scope of constitutional scholarship. For one, it is a shift to study not the content and normal, day-to-day evolution of constitutional systems, but their crisis. In that regard, it is a contribution to the well-known and large debate on democratic backsliding/crisis of democratic constitutionalism, authoritarian constitutionalism, etc. But in that context, the notion of resilience also sets out an important new theme and perspective: it adds the question of ex ante preparation and of how to overcome the crisis. That way, the notion has the potential to trigger thoughts on strategies and responses. In a way, it is similar to the notion of 'constitutional restoration' that deals with how to clean up after constitutional vandalism.[11] In a way, the debate is moving from decline to preparation, restoration and resilience!

Resilience also signals that we seek not medication for a short-term ill and one-time accident but a longer-term, persistent problem. In that way, introducing the notion of resilience is a welcome invitation to extend the debate, to look ahead and strategise. But we also learn from resilience studies that even though the notion has been used for quite some time now, it is not easy to understand how resilience is actually achieved. The central aim, according to insights from other fields, is adaptation. It is how to develop abilities to adapt to an environment full of challenges, how to deal with a variety of ongoing and diverse challenges, to absorb and deflect them, to have a good 'immune system'. But then again, how to become resilient, how to devise instruments and strategies of adaption, has in many areas remained a puzzle. In fact, for psychology or developmental studies, finding the path to resilience has become the search for the holy grail.

Regarding a path to constitutional resilience, however, this volume makes a clear suggestion. It asks us to turn our attention to matters beyond courts. It proposes an actor-oriented perspective that foregrounds the role of non-judicial, political or technical actors, but also informal ones, such as movements or sections of society, and hence to some extent away from the courts.[12]

But before moving to this important part, it might be useful to spend a moment reflecting what is to be protected – and against what. What object should become resilient and against what type of challenges? To start with what is to be protected (what is the object that might be shocked and can hopefully adapt), here it is constitutionalism. Interestingly, the editors did not choose 'democratic constitutionalism'. They hence focus our attention on the particular value that resides in the concepts and practice of the rule of law, constitutionalism, and perhaps a constitutional morality. This makes sense, since South Asia also has countries that are on the way to become a democracy (Bhutan), and there is also a long tradition of non-democratic constitutional systems (Germany, China/East Asia, etc) that should be studied too. Constitutionalism seems to

[10] See D Shah and M Gomez, ch 2 in this volume; on the notion of resilience in Afghanistan, see also E Afsah, ch 9 in this volume; on the notion of resilience generally, see E Arban, ch 5 in this volume.

[11] See the larger US debate in the context of the Trump presidency.

[12] In a way, it is a parallel concept to that of militant democracy, which emerged in German constitutional thinking, when this was challenged by Nazism. See J-W Müller, Militant Democracy' in A Malkopoulou and AS Kirchner (eds), *Militant Democracy and Its Critics: Populism, Parties, Extremism* (Edinburgh, Edinburgh University Press, 2019) 13.

be a precondition for a liberal democracy, but one does not necessarily follow from the other. There is constitutionalism without (liberal) democracy – but liberal democracy without constitutionalism is hardly possible. In a way, the focus on constitutionalism could unburden the discussion a bit. It is 'only' about constitutionalism, not about democracy – even though in most chapters the two are not distinguished.

Even more important, however, is the analysis of the challenges. Against what and which challenges should constitutionalism be protected? It is here where the breadth of the case studies play out their full strength. It becomes clear that constitutional systems in South Asia have to contain a whole variety of challenges and deal with constant risks.

Surely, the unavoidable presence of ethnic, religious and linguistic cleavages mark the situation in different countries and is the reason for many political upheavals that translate into challenges for constitutionalism. There is ethnic pluralism in Sri Lanka; there is the nationalist-majoritarian/religious agenda in India; there are political clans that divide Bangladesh. Underlying many of the identity-based conflicts are economic struggles. Economic inequality and the struggles for economic justice often exacerbate cleavages.

Another categorisation of challenges that becomes apparent especially when reading about Afghanistan is the relevance of external challenges. Here, the almost cyclical foreign interventions enhance the anyway fragmented polity – and ferment the challenges to constitutionalism that always presupposes a certain institutional stability.

This latest thought triggers the question of resilience against whom: who is undermining constitutionalism, who is the challenger? This more actor-oriented lens provides rich outcomes in the different chapters. While the assault on constitutionalism in India is organised by the government, in Sri Lanka it is rather a kleptocratic clan that exploits ethnic divisions. In Pakistan, it is the military complex that has over the years undermined constitutional structures, though perhaps not as single-handedly as many have argued.[13] In contrast to these examples of internal challenges, Afghanistan stands out as an example of how an external shock (and internal confusion) undermines the possibility of constitutionalism ever taking hold.[14]

Especially with regard to India, a more granular picture of the problematic actors and challengers emerges through the chapters. Tarun Khaitan demonstrates that assaults take place on various levels, levelled by the executive (in its many shapes and forms) and not checked or sanctioned by the courts; Damle and Roy examine how Parliament in particular is made ineffective by boycotting the mundane but highly important exercise of scheduling; Bhat, in another fascinating chapter, outlines how too much trust of the Supreme Court in the Election Commission of India has undermined the latter's accountability. On a similar line, Bhatia describes the failures of the court.

All in all, constitutional resilience (and hence the question of how to adapt to persisting problems) turns out to be a productive framework of analysis. It can and

[13] See FH Siddiqi, ch 16 in this volume.

[14] For an ingenious perspective on the resilience not of constitutionalism but of its challenges, see E Afsah, ch 9 in this volume.

should trigger, I would argue, a deeper analysis of the particular challenges of constitutionalism. With regard to South Asia, we learn that many challenges do in fact reside in persistent structures, such as ethnic diversity or religious plurality. These could only be dissolved by tearing apart the fabric of many South Asian societies. Nobody in their right mind can want such partitions or separations. Adaption must come instead in the form of fair accommodations and proceduralisation. Even in India, where one might be led to believe all grief started with election of Modi's Bharatiya Janata Party, it is important to realise that Indian constitutionalism had consistent problems and blind spots before.[15]

But while some challenges are structural, others are human-made and in particular economic in nature. Economic inequality is the fire accelerant. But there are also ideological challenges that could be avoided if certain ideologies were outlawed (such as religious hatred) and these laws enforced. Interestingly, none of the contributions mention social media and media structures more generally as problems, which I would see as another explaining factor for and severe challenge to constitutionalism today.

This distinction between more structural, non-alterable and alterable challenges triggers the question of what vision of constitutionalism is underlying the concept of resilience. The aim, in my opinion, can only be in part to adapt the constitutional structure – it must also be to lay foundations for sustained change! It is not simply about containing problems and dealing with symptoms. The vision would be to have a transformation and a society that is at peace with living in its distinct constitutional framework.

V. 'Beyond Courts' – or Political Constitutionalism and the Paths to Resilience

The most important intellectual move of this volume is, in my opinion, the idea to look 'beyond courts'. This move is hardly taken voluntarily, but comes from bitter learning. Against the widely held belief that mainly courts protect rights and are actually the true guarantor institutions of the rule of law (and perhaps even liberal values), the past years of authoritarian assaults on constitutionalism have taught us that courts can be turned into enemies of the rule of law, that they can become useless. But then, who, in fact, guards the constitution? In the face of democratic backsliding and the undermining of constitutional structures, the volume aims to study other actors and other instruments than courts and rights.

In fact, the material that the chapters of this volume present about a broad variety of constitutional instruments and actors that might help to develop a resilience against challenges is rich and impressive. A number of actors and instruments come into view, which deserve all the attention.

[15] Just read A Bhuwania, *Courting the People* (Cambridge, Cambridge University Press, 2016).

One important focus that this new perspective opens up is on constitutional design, especially on federalism. Erika Arban argues that while federalism and devolution of power is an important element, in itself it is not enough unless they also help to strengthen the idea and dynamics of solidarity between individuals and institutions, such as the idea of *Bundestreue* (federal loyalty) or fiscal federalism. Equally important is a reflection on how the dispersion of power (federalism) can be institutionalised in a country and context (post-colonial and post-British South Asia) that sees federalism with suspicion.

Just beginning but surely flourishing in the years to come in constitutional studies is the attention to the military. All over the world (certainly in Latin America, Africa and Europe), there is a long tradition of the military not just overthrowing regimes, but deploying the constitution to safeguard its political and economic power. The hybridity of such regimes (military–political–economic–constitutional) has so far been woefully understudied.

Another, really innovative, promising and somewhat liberating move is giving attention to the people as constitutional actors. This provides new insights, not least by opening up new idioms and methodologies of constitutional research. This shines through as giving attention to civil society in several contributions. Vikram Narayan and Jahnavi Sindhu, using the idiom of constitutional theory, foreground the people as constitutional protagonists by exploring the concept of constitutional patriotism, hence pointing to a concept that could explain and guide social integration and constitutional commitment in a highly diverse polity and hence shore up constitutional resilience. And it takes centre stage where the impact of Dalit activism is studied through the means of constitutional anthropology (Siddiqi).

Surely the most prominent spot in this list of important actors in providing constitutional resilience in this volume goes to the so-called guarantor institutions. A quarter of all contributions deal with the fourth branch, and in particular election commissions – and hence with institutions that (supposedly) stand outside the traditional scheme of three separate, but functionally integrated, branches. The attention and especially the mostly positive perception of these institutions is remarkable, in particular the almost always positive spin on depoliticisation.

This contrasts sharply with a very different direction of discussion in European and international law. There, the talk of experts safeguarding supposedly technical or neutral values has encountered increasingly loud and substantiated doubts. One wonders whether guarantors are really that neutral – or have (perhaps necessarily) separate agendas. An important question to be asked, it seems to me, is what values do they guarantee. Electoral fairness (election commissions), non-corruption or price stability (central banks) are all considered values to be guaranteed by the fourth branch – but do we really consider them to be equally neutral or even apolitical? I think it is important to distinguish especially between institutions that guard the very existence of constitutional democracy from those that guard particular values, such as an economic model (central banks).[16] We have to acknowledge, I would say, that some of these institutions

[16] For an insight in these debates, see P Tucker, *Unelected Power: The Quest for Legitimacy in Central Banking and the Regulatory State* (Princeton, Princeton University Press, 2018); A Vauchez, 'The Genie of Independence and the European Bottle', iCourts Working Paper 266/2021.

are more political than might meet the eye. From my perspective, it is never quite clear what depoliticisation really means (and the demand for it produces) when we are at the same time realising that there is nothing really depolitical. Isn't every order built on values that we have to defend – and such defence is ultimately political?

So what about courts? Even in this volume, courts feature as important actors too. They perform different functions, but are surely implicated in undermining constitutionalism (or constitutional democracy) – by their failure to hold accountable other institutions, safeguarding institutional or constitutional structures, and hence actively or passively abdicating their responsibility. One wonders whether the talk of a fourth branch would be necessary if courts would actually do their jobs, ie hold all actors accountable to the spirit and the word of the laws …

One odd blind spot in this rich volume are parliaments. Except for one contribution, the heart of democratic constitutionalism draw hardly any attention. But to reflect more on this, another contribution would be necessary.[17]

VI. Conclusion and Some Desiderata for Future Research

I conclude with three observations regarding future research.

The first concerns the dynamics of academic exchange, the migration of ideas and ultimately the geopolitics of knowledge production. While resilience is a fairly new notion, the observation is old: constitutional systems are in constant danger of being undermined. This is in fact a very German experience. The shift from a constitutional monarchy to a constitutional democracy after World War I (1919) and then the overthrow of the constitutional order by Nazi fascism in 1933 triggered much thinking and writing about constitutional resilience. Your dear author and epilogist cannot therefore quite hide a bit of disappointment to see so little German literature being used.[18] The prominence of US literature, in contrast, is curious, as the US has hardly dealt with a foundational constitutional crisis (since the Civil War) and surely no external threat. This points, one more time, to the deep problem of language and language hegemony in constitutional studies.[19] Only English literature seems to exist – and we suffer from this dearth. But from another angle, it triggers the question of the regional or global migration of ideas. This volume showcases fascinating South Asian experiences and innovations (such as about the Election Commission in Indian constitutionalism or the Constitutional Council in Sri Lanka) that should receive more attention in comparative scholarship around the world.

[17] As a starting point see P Dann and AK Thiruvengadam, 'Federalism and Democracy' in Dann and Thiruvengadam, *Democratic Constitutionalism* (n 7) 252.

[18] The notable exceptions are E Arban, ch 5 in this volume; J Sindhu and VA Narayan, ch 19 in this volume. With regard to German authors and publications, a good starting point is the volume edited by AJ Jacobson and B Schlink (eds), *Weimar: A Jurisprudence of Crisis* (B Cooper trans, Berkeley, University of California Press, 2000); further authors to be discovered are Gerhard Leibholz and Franz Neumann, and later Hasso Hofmann. In terms of concepts, the easiest comparative starting point is the concept of militant democracy.

[19] M de Visser, 'Towards a More Inclusive Constitutional Discourse: Overcoming Linguistic Barriers' (*ICONnect*, 18 May 2022) www.iconnectblog.com/2022/05/towards-a-more-inclusive-constitutional-discourse-overcoming-linguistic-barriers/

The second observation is methodological: it is important to note that the challenges to constitutionalism are in almost all instances not legal but political, economic, cultural, etc – and can hence be studied only in an interdisciplinary way. It is not surprising that the notion of 'resilience' itself is borrowed from other disciplines. What we need is much more attention to political economy analysis, critical theory, etc – and actually more methodological rigour. If legal scholars use non-legal, empirical terms (such as resilience), they should be more careful and methodological in how they deploy and study them.

My final point is the study of political constitutionalism. That constitutionalism has a legal but also a political dimension seems a rather trite observation from a German perspective, but surely also from a South African or Argentinian perspective, and it is surprising how English authors (and others from the Commonwealth) seem to be discovering this now. But, finally, the global debate is shifting. By way of ending these thoughts, I would like to point to a few directions: first, in thinking about political constitutionalism, one has to acknowledge the political, not seek the neutral, depoliticised. It doesn't exist. Also, we should use a wide lens and study democratic constitutionalism beyond elections and formal institutions. There is a much broader, general law of democracy to be studied – with a fair and open democratic process at the heart of it all that goes beyond formal state organisations and should include political parties, social movements and different sections of society (women, religious groups, etc) in their respective formation and participation. Finally, the study should include the role of political mobilisation, legal education and scholarship.

But now, this epilogue is itself gliding into a (hopefully not too) distant far future and should end.

INDEX